BASIC CONVERSATIONAL FRENCH

Basic
Conversational
French

THIRD EDITION

Julian Harris
André Lévêque

UNIVERSITY OF WISCONSIN

HOLT, RINEHART AND WINSTON, NEW YORK

TABLE OF CONTENTS

v

CONTENTS

CONTENTS

REFERENCE MATERIALS

INTRODUCTION

This edition differs from the revised edition of our *Basic Conversational French* primarily in the form in which exercises are presented. In constructing teaching materials, we have always proceeded from the known to the unknown, one step at a time, for we regard this procedure as absolutely basic in language teaching and language learning. In the present edition, we have reviewed every exercise in the book, rewritten most of them, and tried to arrange them in such a way that students can see at once what is the new element in each item of each exercise. The dialogs have been revised only slightly — sometimes to introduce a new word or phrase, sometimes to avoid an infelicitous repetition, sometimes to improve the rhythm of a phrase. Prices of articles, meals, and so on have of course been expressed in terms of the new franc. The grammar units have been tightened up here and there. The section entitled "How to Get a Good French Accent" has been completely rewritten following the pattern of the section entitled "How to Improve Your French Accent" that we worked out for our *Intermediate Conversational French.*

In order to give the students a *feel* for the rhythm of French from the beginning, we have included exercises in which we indicate the number of syllables to be pronounced. We have found this kind of exercise extremely effective for teaching the pronunciation or omission of mute e's — among other things. There is no possible doubt that the easiest way to pronounce French vowels and consonants properly is to produce them in a phrase that is uttered with a French rhythm.

The basic philosophy of the book remains unchanged. We always take as our point of departure the following assumptions: that language is something you *do,* that the easiest and most natural way to learn a language is by using it, and that — at least for literate adults and adolescents — a systematic study of practical grammar is an invaluable aid. Dialogs and grammar units are so arranged that students learn concrete examples before being introduced to abstract principles of grammar. For example, before they come to the first grammar unit, they have four units with dialogs and exercises that give them practice in answering and asking questions in French, in thinking in French about a few very simple matters, and in "reacting" in French to a few everyday situations. From the very beginning, they are building up the habit of hearing, understanding, and saying simple things in French.

The exercises of the first dialogs are nothing more than a series of devices to get the students to use correctly, intelligently, and with confidence the phrases of the dialogs. The first grammar unit presents systematically what they have already more or less learned about the forms and use of definite and indefinite articles. It is based entirely on examples that have appeared in the preceding dialogs. The exercises of this and other grammar units, like those in the units devoted to dialogs, should be done orally of course, and with books closed. They are frankly intended to drive home the principles of French grammar. Although we try to avoid an over-emphasis upon grammar, we are convinced that such material should be presented fully and with the greatest possible clarity; because if students are not given comprehensible explanations, they will make rules for themselves — phony rules, of course, since they are certainly not in a position to make tenable generalizations about French usage. We have not attempted to explain all the fine points of French grammar; but we have tried to explain without over-simplification whatever we *do* present, and we have emphasized points of syntax in which French is different from English — points which have been stumbling blocks for generations and generations of young Americans. Each grammar unit throughout the book is preceded by dialogs in which a few new forms and constructions are worked on orally and aurally preparatory to being considered from the point of view of grammar. Thus, instead of trying to learn the subtleties, say, of the use of the partitive by poring over abstract explanations, the students first learn a few concrete examples in easily remembered contexts, and, a few days later, come fore-armed to the complicated matter of the use of *du, de la, des,* and *pas de.* With rare exceptions, new vocabulary items are also introduced in the dialogs so that the grammar lessons can be devoted exclusively to the business of understanding principles of grammar and learning how they work in practice. It is surprising to see how quickly a grammar unit can be assimilated when the students know, in advance, what the examples really mean: some of them even understand at once why you say "Nous n'avons *pas de* café", but "Nous n'aimons *pas le* café."

A word about timing. We recommend that all exercises be done at a fairly rapid tempo. In the first place, it is much easier to avoid diph-

thongization of vowels and over-emphasis on consonants if a phrase is
uttered quickly; (2) a class in which one student is allowed to ponder
endlessly over a response that is obvious to other students becomes very
tiresome; and (3) if students are given time to break each utterance up
into words, to translate each word into English, to decide the proper
response, and to translate this response into French, some of them will
do so! After all, students have the habit of analyzing whatever they do
not understand in English; but while it is appropriate to analyze difficult
passages, it is bad practice to go through a long rigmarole over things
that are perfectly obvious.

The exercises in which students merely repeat phrases present no difficulty in timing — since the instructor determines the rhythm. This exercise should set the pace for responses in subsequent exercises so that the
answer to questions (*Répondez en français*) should be almost in the same
rhythm. It should take only a *little more time* for students to respond
to a command (*Dites-moi* or *Demandez-moi*) than it does to repeat a
phrase. But this type of exercise calls for a little dramatization — at least
until the students get the hang of it. At first it is necessary to reiterate
the rubric for each question and to give a sample response. For example,
we say *"Demandez* (point to the student) *à Monsieur Hughes* (point to
an imaginary Mr. Hughes) *comment il va."* Then we ask (looking at the
imaginary Mr. Hughes) *"Comment allez-vous, monsieur?"* Then we
repeat the command *without gestures: Demandez à Monsieur Hughes comment il va.* By this time the students catch on and are ready to do the
exercise. This seems terribly roundabout at first because it is so much
easier just to have the students repeat phrases. But the idea is not to get
students to repeat phrases as many times as possible (the way they used
to copy verb forms 500 times), but to get them to understand and use
phrases intelligently, correctly, and with assurance. By understanding the
"new word" *il va* without having it explained, the students begin to
develop the ability to sense what words *must* mean. This kind of exercise calls their imagination into play, makes them swim beyond their depth
for a moment, and helps to wean them from a sort of literal-mindedness
that besets the path of beginning foreign language students.

Pattern Practice exercises also should be done with verve. The purpose
of these exercises is to give students further practice in using and varying
authentic patterns of the language. At first glance, some of them may
look absurdly simple and "much too easy for college students!" But by
doing good pattern practice exercises, students repeat over and over a

pattern that they understand while concentrating upon remembering and repeating a variation of one element of the pattern. We believe this helps to drive the pattern home far better than mere repetition; because we hold that learning a foreign language is not a matter of memorizing words, conjugations, rules, or even patterns of the language, but, rather, a matter of learning to understand and use them all intelligently and correctly. Listening and repeating until one can say phrases correctly and glibly looms large in this method at first. In fact, that is all a student can do at first. However, *at first* does not mean the first few days, weeks, or months, but *the first few minutes of the first class.* As soon as a student can understand and repeat a phrase correctly, he must move into the next stage of learning, and use the phrase correctly in response to a question or a statement. The third stage of mastery of a pattern is the point at which the student can recall and use it without outside stimulus. The fourth stage is the point at which the student can recall the basic pattern and use it with variations without outside stimulus.

We have constructed a great number of exercises that will give students practice in varying the subject of a sentence, or the verb, or the object, or the adjective modifiers, or the adverbial modifiers, and so on. At first they are so simple that beginners can do them quickly, correctly, and with confidence. The answers are implicit in the questions — and intentionally so. After a few weeks, the exercises become more subtle; but throughout the book, we have tried to construct exercises in such a way that students can scarcely avoid making correct responses. In reality, hearing and understanding in French what they are supposed to do is perhaps quite as instructive as giving the correct response. The experience of hearing a phrase and retaining it long enough to answer it is a necessary step towards remembering it for twenty-four hours or six weeks. In spite of the old saw, we find that instead of learning by making mistakes, beginning language students who can not do exercises correctly build up dreadful inhibitions against foreign language study!

Each dialog is accompanied by an English translation whose functions are (1) to provide a means by which students can understand precisely and immediately what a given sentence means, and (2) to serve as a prompt-script from which they can practice saying the French sentences of the dialog at home. With this arrangement, it is possible to proceed without having them begin by studying definitions and memorizing lists of words; in fact, they begin to work on the first day at the stage which many classes reach only after long and tedious manipulation of more or less artificial sentences, word-lists, and abstract definitions. And what is more important, from the first day students begin to acquire mastery of authentic French word patterns — patterns which they will always find useful in speaking, reading, or writing French.

We have also continued the discreet use of *Dites en français* exercises and of the *Thèmes d'imitation*. We find, and many colleagues in different institutions report the same experience, that for many students, the *Dites en français* exercise is absolutely indispensable: until they can bring out a French phrase in response to an English equivalent, they feel no confidence in their mastery or even their understanding of the French phrase. Moreover, when anyone is at a loss for a word or expression in speaking a foreign language, he inevitably finds himself thinking in English; it is surely useful, therefore, to have some practice in going from English to French. Be it said, moreover, that our *Dites en français* exercises merely serve as an additional way of getting students to remember and use the phrases they are learning. They have practically nothing in common with traditional translation exercises that invite students to concoct phony sentences in French. The *Thèmes d'imitation*, likewise, show students how to put known patterns of French together so as to make simple French prose. At first glance, they look frightfully difficult for first year French students; but on closer inspection, they turn out to be almost as easy as the oral practice exercises.

Written work. We recommend that students begin to write in the second or third week of their study of the language — on the day when they take up the fifth dialog (orally only, of course), writing only the phrases of the first dialog. By this time, every member of the class knows the first dialog so well that he can learn to write it correctly in ten or fifteen minutes. Thereafter, for each new dialog, the students are expected to learn to write the phrases of an old one which they have already studied. In this way, students are made to realize that the art of spelling is merely a means of recording a language (rather than the language itself).

Quizzes. We find that a short weekly or at least a fortnightly quiz is an invaluable teaching device. Throughout the week, students should be encouraged to use the language orally as much as possible, and without worrying too much about mistakes; but it is necessary to keep a very careful check on the progress each student makes, and to keep each student informed as to the result of his work. The first quiz will necessarily consist only of a *dictée,* a few questions asked orally in French which are to be answered in French and a series of sentences in French for which the students will be expected to give the English equivalent. All the items in the first quizzes will of course be taken from the dialogs. As the first semester progresses, and as the exercises become more and more varied, any of the types of questions found in the exercises can be used. For variety, true-false statements may be included, but it is practically impossible to avoid being trite in such questions. The *dictée* may occasionally be replaced by a simple anecdote which the students retell in their own words though, again, it is difficult to find anecdotes that are simple enough to be comprehensible and at the same time capable of interesting students. After a few grammar units have been studied, questions calling for a mastery of the grammar units can be included, and after a reader has been begun, passages can be included for translation into English or as a basis for questions in French to be answered in French.

Reading in French. We have included in the present edition eight very brief sketches which deal with the same subject matter as the dialogs and which make use of words and phrases with which the students are familiar. We have tried to combine text, subject matter, and illustrations in such a way that the students can have the salutary experience of reading in French something that they can actually understand *in French.*

In our classes, before we have students begin to read, we explain to them that reading is, essentially, understanding what is written or printed, and that reading the sketches in this book is little more than understanding the written form of a few phrases — slightly rearranged, of course — that they have been understanding and using orally for some time. The first step in learning to read in a foreign language is to realize that reading is a very different operation from translating, and that it is actually possible to read and understand a text in French without translating it into English. The second step is to learn to infer from the context the meaning of unfamiliar words. And the third step is to learn to consult the vocabulary — that is, to look up a word and select the meaning it has in the context. In all three steps, the emphasis, we think, should always be upon trying to understand the meaning of the text in French.

We try to give students the experience of reading in French with understanding and pleasure, in the hope that they will not form the habit of trying to find a supposed English equivalent of every word in a passage before they attempt to understand what it is all about. If they are left to their own devices, however, they will go to any amount of trouble to avoid thinking — underlining "new" words, looking up the same words time after time, writing them down, memorizing English equivalents, and "overlearning" them. Meanwhile, instead of learning to read in French, they are building the habit of not even trying to learn!

We recommend that after about three weeks, students be given short reading assignments once a week in a French reader, brief periods of practice in sight reading, and, eventually, a little outside reading. The readers best adapted to our method are, in our opinion, the Harris and Lévêque, *Basic French Readers* and the Harris, *French Reader for Colleges* (both published by Holt, Rinehart and Winston, Inc.). It goes without saying that students who ask and answer questions in French in connection with the dialogs and grammar units, can do the same in connection with easy texts of a French reader. Such exercises need not be used to the exclusion of brief translation exercises, but whenever one can be sure the students understand a passage in French, it is obviously good practice to ask them questions on it in French rather than to have them translate it into English.

We find that questionnaires such as those we have provided help students reach the point where they can understand the text in French without translating every word into English. When a student can not grasp the meaning of a question — and this will frequently happen, of course — there are several ways of helping him understand it: (1) Let him read the question. (2) Have him repeat the question in French before trying to answer it. (3) Answer the question in French and then ask the student to answer it. (4) Explain what the question means. (5) Tell him precisely where the answer may be found in the book. Only after a great deal of practice in listening to questions and finding the answer in the book can students be expected to prepare a reading lesson well enough to answer questions in French without referring to the book. It should be borne in mind that the purpose of this exercise is to help students learn to *read* intelligently.

This may seem like a lot of trouble. And it certainly takes more effort, at least at first, than it does to have students look up words, write them between the lines (or elsewhere) and "translate". But it is worth the trouble, because students learn to read a printed text more rapidly if the emphasis is always upon understanding *meaning* instead of on learning words. Translating a word or phrase here and there can frequently give a clue to the meaning of a passage in the foreign language, but it is all but impossible to make a decent translation of a paragraph if you do not really know precisely what it means.

How we go about it. We have been so often asked for a description of the way we teach the dialogs and grammar lessons, that although it may seem almost supererogatory, we have decided to explain here precisely how we proceed. We realize that there are many other ways of going about it and that some of them are undoubtedly better than ours. We also realize that excellent results can be had by strictly following the exercises as they are printed in the book. But here is the way we do it.

At the first meeting of the class, we give the students a mimeographed schedule of assignments and quizzes for the semester. (We give 30-minute quizzes every two weeks and we cover 38 units in the first semester — that is, not quite three units per week, on the average, for sixteen weeks.) We explain very briefly the basic assumptions of the course and the procedures that are to be used, insisting especially on the importance (1) of listening with all possible attention to the way the instructor and the voices on the tapes utter each phrase, (2) of trying to understand the meaning of each French phrase each time it is repeated, and (3) of trying to reproduce each phrase precisely as the instructor and the voices on the tapes utter it — with proper intonation and, when appropriate, gestures. We explain that the difficult part of French pronunciation is not *producing* the sounds but *hearing* them as they are! We point out also that a foreign language must be learned bit by bit and that trying to learn two weeks' work on the night before quizzes — as students do in certain courses — simply will not work.

After this brief introduction (five minutes at most) , we explain that the first dialog takes place between John Hughes, a young American chemical engineer who is living in Paris, and the concierge, or caretaker-superintendent, of the apartment house in which he lives. Then we say, "The concierge says to John, Good morning, Sir, *Bonjour, monsieur.* *Bonjour, monsieur. Bonjour, monsieur.* Please listen with all possible concentration. Notice that the greeting contains four short, equally-stressed syllables. *Bonjour, monsieur.* Now repeat after me: *Bon-jour mon-sieur.*" It takes a great many repetitions and much listening to get the students to utter this phrase correctly. In fact, this may be the most difficult and important step in their entire language-learning career! But the best time to give students a realistic idea of French pronunciation is before they build up bad habits of pronunciation and phony notions about French accent. If they start off saying something like: bong-zhoor', mon-shoor', instead of really learning how to say it, they will find it vastly more difficult to learn to say it correctly later on.

After they can say *Bonjour, monsieur* in four short, equally-stressed syllables and without adding an *r* to *monsieur,* we introduce John's answer *Bonjour, madame.* While it takes six or seven minutes to teach them to say *Bonjour, monsieur,* it then takes only a minute or two to get them to say *Bonjour, madame* correctly — again in four short, equally-stressed syllables. But the accent-less rhythm of French phrases must be carefully practiced day after day so that the students will not slip into the habit of uttering French phrases with American rhythms. Detailed suggestions for this sort of practice will be found in the special section on "How to Get a Good French Accent" (page 289 ff.) .

When the first two lines are more or less mastered, we say to the class: "*Dites-moi bonjour*" with an appropriate gesture at the word *moi.* Some of the students will understand at once and say "*Bonjour, monsieur.*" We then repeat "*Dites-moi bonjour*" and all the students respond. In teaching the first class, we say "Repeat after me" a few times in English, but thereafter we give the direction in French. Translation or explanation of *Répétez* or *Répétez après moi* at that juncture is quite unnecessary.

As soon as they can respond easily to *Dites-moi bonjour,* we point to an imaginary John Hughes and say "*Dites bonjour à Monsieur Hughes, Dites bonjour à la concierge,*" and so on. We do this at a fairly quick tempo so the students will develop the habit of grasping meaning immediately.

After the initial greeting is more or less mastered, the next two lines are taken up in the same way. We say "The concierge says, Are you Mr. Hughes, *Êtes-vous Monsieur Hughes?*" and so on. But instead of seven or eight minutes, the second two lines can be introduced in three or four. As soon as they can say *Êtes-vous Monsieur Hughes?* we say "*Demandez-moi si je suis Monsieur Hughes,*" as above, and then, "*Demandez à ce monsieur* (point to an imaginary person) *s'il est Monsieur Hughes.*"

Each pair of lines takes less time than the preceding pair. After each pair of lines, we return to the beginning of the dialog and have the students say as much of it as they can — prompting whenever it is necessary. We work through the entire dialog in this way, but at an increasing tempo. This takes about 25-30 minutes.

We then use ten to twelve minutes in a variety of ways. Sometimes we have the students repeat the phrases of the dialog while looking at the French text, or again we tell them to look only at the English — for the first two or three weeks. We are not sure that there is any difference in the result, but we rather think it is a good idea to have students see the French as soon as they have learned how it sounds so that they will begin to learn the relationship between spelling and pronunciation. We find, moreover, that even when we tell them not to look at the French, many of the students do so anyway; and if they have no copy of the material used, they will write down in a phony phonetic spelling what they think they hear. This is infinitely worse than French orthography! Besides, there are always a certain number of visual-minded students who find it very upsetting to be told not to look at the French text. In any case, if students are constantly working with the tapes — listening, responding, recording, comparing their pronunciation with that of French voices — conventional French spelling will not be such a handicap as it was in the days when students were supposed to figure out from a lot of rules about silent letters how each word *would be* pronounced. Sometimes (but not the first day) we have students run through a dialog while looking at the IPA transcription so that they will know how to consult a transcription whenever they wish to do so. Usually, we do as many of the exercises as we can; but whatever else we do on the first day, we always make it a point to work seriously on the French uvular **r** and the French **u** (see pp. 292-293) .

Finally, we devote the last ten minutes or so of the hour to running rapidly through the dialog in a variety of ways: the teacher says the lines of the concierge and the students, those of John. Then we reverse the rôles. Next, one half of the class says the lines of the concierge and the others those of John. Then two of the more dynamic students run through the dialog alone.

As we remarked above, we are not at all sure that this way of doing it produces any better results in the long run than following the lesson precisely as it stands in the book; but we feel that the class may possibly get off to a faster start if the students are constantly being told (forced) to listen, to repeat, to answer, to ask, and so on. This change of pace is one way of getting them to practice a great deal without lapsing at any time into the stultifying business of absent-minded parroting.

As for the grammar units, we run through the explanation of one paragraph, have the students repeat the examples carefully and do the exercises based on that paragraph at once. Then we take up the rest of the lesson paragraph by paragraph.

In addition to the work in class, we recommend that students work on the exercises three or four hours a week in small sections with skilled teaching assistants or with tapes under the guidance of an experienced laboratory assistant. We believe it is better to begin to work on a dialog in class than to have students study it ahead of time. When they study a dialog before the class, they are sure to make all sorts of mistakes in pronunciation; but after a dialog has been thoroughly worked over in class, serious study at home or in the laboratory will greatly strengthen the correct impressions that have been planted.

Acknowledgments. Although it would be impossible to mention by name all who have contributed to the improvement of successive versions of the Harris and Lévêque books, we would like to express again our deep indebtedness to Pierre Delattre and Madame Jeanne Varney Pleasants for help in planning the pronunciation exercises and to our colleagues in this University — including hundreds of young and knowledgeable teaching assistants. Many of them have given us invaluable suggestions for clarifying details of pronunciation, usage, or presentation. Others have passed on to us teaching devices that they have found effective. Still others have tried out new kinds of exercises for us. We take this opportunity also of thanking the teachers from all over the country who have generously sent us their observations and impressions as well as their desiderata for new editions. Without their ideas, their interest and their encouragement, we might never have undertaken the present edition. We hope they will give us their reaction to it and especially that they will call our attention to its weaknesses so that they may eventually be corrected.

J. H.   The University of Wisconsin
A. L.   Madison, Wisconsin
March, 1962

BASIC CONVERSATIONAL FRENCH

Getting Acquainted

As John Hughes, a young American chemist, leaves his apartment on the Avenue de l'Observatoire in Paris, he speaks to the concierge of the building. (A concierge is the doorkeeper, janitress, and general caretaker of an apartment house or hotel.)

LA CONCIERGE —¹Bonjour, monsieur.

JOHN HUGHES —²Bonjour, madame.

LA CONCIERGE —³Êtes-vous M. Hughes?

JOHN HUGHES —⁴Oui, madame. Je suis M. Hughes.

LA CONCIERGE —⁵Comment allez-vous, monsieur?

JOHN HUGHES —⁶Bien, merci. Et vous?

LA CONCIERGE —⁷Pas mal, merci.

JOHN HUGHES —⁸Parlez-vous anglais?

LA CONCIERGE —⁹Non, je ne parle pas anglais. ¹⁰Mais vous parlez français, n'est-ce pas?

JOHN HUGHES —¹¹Oui, madame, je parle un peu français.

LA CONCIERGE —¹²Voici une lettre pour vous.

JOHN HUGHES —¹³Merci beaucoup.

LA CONCIERGE —¹⁴De rien, monsieur.

JOHN HUGHES —¹⁵Au revoir, madame.

LA CONCIERGE —¹⁶Au revoir, monsieur.

THE CONCIERGE —¹Good morning, sir.

JOHN HUGHES —²Good morning, (Madame).

THE CONCIERGE —³Are you Mr. Hughes?

JOHN HUGHES —⁴Yes, (Madam) I am Mr. Hughes.

THE CONCIERGE —⁵How do you do, sir?

JOHN HUGHES —⁶Well, thank you. And you?

THE CONCIERGE —⁷Not bad (thank you).

JOHN HUGHES —⁸Do you speak English?

THE CONCIERGE —⁹No, I don't speak English. ¹⁰ But you speak French, don't you?

JOHN HUGHES —¹¹Yes, (Madam) I speak French a little.

THE CONCIERGE —¹²Here is a letter for you.

JOHN HUGHES —¹³Thank you very much.

THE CONCIERGE —¹⁴You are welcome, (sir).

JOHN HUGHES —¹⁵Good-bye, (Madam).

THE CONCIERGE —¹⁶Good-bye, sir.

I. EXERCICES DE RYTHME.*

A. QUATRE SYLLABES. Repeat in four short, equally stressed syllables:
1. Bonjour monsieur.
2. Bonjour madamє.
3. Merci monsieur.
4. Merci madamє.
5. De rien monsieur.
6. De rien madamє.
7. Au rєvoir monsieur.
8. Au rєvoir madamє.

B. CINQ SYLLABES. Repeat in five short, equally stressed syllables:

(1)

1. Bonjour madєmoisellє.
2. Merci madєmoisellє.
3. De rien madєmoisellє.
4. Au rєvoir madєmoisellє.

(2)

1. Êtes-vous Monsieur Hughes?
2. Comment allez-vous?
3. Parlez-vous français?
4. Je nє parlє pas français.
5. Parlez-vous anglais?
6. Je nє parlє pas anglais.
7. Jє parlє un peu français.
8. Jє parlє un peu anglais.

C. SIX SYLLABES. Repeat in six short, equally stressed syllables:
1. Merci beaucoup monsieur.
2. Merci beaucoup madamє.
3. Voici unє lettrє pour vous.
4. Mais vous parlez français.
5. Mais vous parlez anglais.

D. SEPT SYLLABES. Repeat in seven short, equally stressed syllables:
1. Vous parlez français n'est-cє pas?
2. Vous parlez anglais n'est-cє pas?
3. Jє parlє un peu français monsieur.
4. Jє parlє un peu français madamє.
5. Jє parlє un peu anglais monsicur.

---

* In order to make the rhythm exercises perfectly clear, silent e's are printed є and commas are omitted. For additional pronunciation exercises, see pp. 291-293.

6. Je parle un peu anglais madame.
7. Je ne parle pas français monsieur.
8. Je ne parle pas français madame.
9. Je ne parle pas anglais monsieur.
10. Je ne parle pas anglais madame.

II. *Donnez une réponse convenable à chacune des expressions suivantes*
(Give a suitable response to each of the following expressions):

1. Bonjour, monsieur. [Bonjour, monsieur. *or,* Bonjour, madame. *or,* Bonjour, mademoiselle.]
2. Êtes-vous Monsieur Hughes? [Oui, madame. Je suis Monsieur Hughes.]
3. Comment allez-vous? [Bien, merci. Et vous?]
4. Parlez-vous anglais? [Non, je ne parle pas anglais.]
5. Vous parlez français, n'est-ce pas? [Oui, je parle un peu français.]
6. Voici une lettre pour vous. [Merci beaucoup.]
7. Merci, madame. [De rien, monsieur.]
8. Au revoir, madame. [Au revoir, monsieur.]

III. *Dites en français* (Say in French):

1. Dites-moi bonjour. [Bonjour, monsieur. Bonjour, madame. Bonjour, mademoiselle.]
2. Dites bonjour à Monsieur Hughes. [Bonjour, monsieur.]
3. Dites bonjour à la concierge. [Bonjour, madame.]
4. Dites-moi au revoir. [Au revoir, monsieur. Au revoir, madame. Au revoir, mademoiselle.]
5. Dites au revoir à M. Hughes. [Au revoir, monsieur.]
6. Dites au revoir à la concierge. [Au revoir, madame.]
7. Dites-moi merci. [Merci, monsieur, madame, mademoiselle.]
8. Dites merci à M. Hughes. [Merci, monsieur.]
9. Dites merci à la concierge. [Merci, madame.]

IV. *Demandez en français* (Ask in French):

1. Demandez-moi si je suis M. Hughes. [Êtes-vous Monsieur Hughes?]
2. Demandez-moi si je parle français. [Parlez-vous français?]
3. Demandez à M. Hughes s'il parle français. [Parlez-vous français?]
4. Demandez à la concierge si elle parle anglais. [Parlez-vous anglais?]
5. Demandez-moi comment je vais. [Comment allez-vous, monsieur? *or,* Comment allez-vous, madame? *or,* Comment allez-vous, mademoiselle?]
6. Demandez à M. Hughes comment il va. [Comment allez-vous, monsieur?]
7. Demandez à la concierge comment elle va. [Comment allez-vous, madame?]

V. Dialogue.

Act out the scene between John Hughes and the concierge. Practice doing the scene until you are perfectly at home in both roles.

VI. *Dites en français* (Say in French) :

I. Good morning, sir.   2. Good morning (Madam).   3. Are you Mr. Hughes? 4. Yes (Madam), I am Mr. Hughes.   5. How do you do, sir? 6. Well, thank you. And you? 7. Not bad (thank you).   8. Do you speak English? 9. No, I do not speak English.   I0. But you speak French, don't you? II. Yes (Madam), I speak French a little. I2. Here is a letter for you. I3. Thank you very much. I4. You are welcome, sir. I5. Good-bye (Madam). I6. Good-bye, sir.

Asking for Directions

John Hughes is spending a few days visiting some of the interesting places in the Île-de-France (the region around Paris). He has just arrived at Chantilly where he plans to see the château, museum, racetrack, etc. He asks for information first in the railroad station and then on the street.

A la gare

JOHN —¹Où est le château, s'il vous plaît?

UN EMPLOYÉ —²Tout droit, monsieur.

JOHN —³Où est le musée?

L'EMPLOYÉ —⁴Le musée est dans le château.

JOHN —⁵Y a-t-il un restaurant près du château?

L'EMPLOYÉ —⁶Oui, monsieur. Il y a un restaurant près du château.

JOHN —⁷Merci beaucoup.

L'EMPLOYÉ —⁸De rien, monsieur.

Dans la rue

JOHN —⁹(*A un passant*) Pardon, monsieur. Où est le bureau de poste?

LE PASSANT —¹⁰Sur la place, là-bas, à gauche.

JOHN —¹¹Y a-t-il un bureau de tabac* près d'ici?

At the Station

JOHN —¹Please tell me where the château is.

AN EMPLOYEE —²Straight ahead, sir.

JOHN —³Where is the museum?

THE EMPLOYEE —⁴The museum is in the château.

JOHN —⁵Is there a restaurant near the château?

THE EMPLOYEE —⁶Yes, sir. There is a restaurant near the château.

JOHN —⁷Thank you very much.

THE EMPLOYEE —⁸You are welcome, sir.

In the Street

JOHN —⁹(*To a passer-by*) Pardon me, sir. Where is the post office?

THE PASSER-BY —¹⁰On the square, over there, to the left.

JOHN —¹¹Is there a tobacco shop near here?

---

* A **bureau de tabac** is a tobacco shop in which one can buy also stamps, stationery, newspapers, and in which there is usually a bar.

LE PASSANT —[12]Mais oui, monsieur. Il y a un bureau de tabac dans la rue de la Paix.

JOHN —[13]Où est la rue de la Paix?

LE PASSANT —[14]A droite, monsieur.

JOHN —[15]Merci beaucoup.

THE PASSER-BY —[12]Oh yes, sir. There is a tobacco shop on (in) the Rue de la Paix.

JOHN —[13]Where is the Rue de la Paix?

THE PASSER-BY —[14]To the right, sir.

JOHN —[15]Thank you very much.

I. EXERCICES DE RYTHME. *

  A. QUATRE SYLLABES:

  1. Où est le château?

  2. Où est le musée?

  B. CINQ SYLLABES:

  1. Où est le bureau de poste?

  2. Où est le restaurant?

  C. SIX SYLLABES:

  1. Où est le bureau de tabac?

  2. Où est la rue de la Paix?

  3. Y a-t-il un restaurant . . . ?

  4. Il y a un restaurant . . .

  D. SEPT SYLLABES:

  1. Où est le château, s'il vous plaît?

  2. Où est le musée, s'il vous plaît?

II. SUBSTITUTIONS. *Répétez les phrases suivantes, en substituant les mots indiqués* (Repeat the following with the suggested substitutions) :

  1. Où est [le château]?
    le musée/ le bureau de tabac/ le bureau de poste/ le restaurant

  2. [Le château] est près d'ici.
    Le musée/ Le bureau de tabac/ Le bureau de poste/ Le restaurant

  3. Le musée est [près d'ici].
    tout droit/ là-bas, à droite/ là-bas, à gauche

  4. Il y a un restaurant [près du château].
    près d'ici/ sur la place/ dans la rue de la Paix

  5. Y a-t-il un restaurant [près d'ici]?
    près du château/ dans le château/ sur la place/ dans la rue de la Paix

III. *Répondez en français, d'après le texte* (according to the dialog):

  1. Où est le château, s'il vous plaît? **2.** Où est le musée? **3.** Y a-t-il un

---

* For additional pronunciation exercises, see p. 294.

restaurant près du château? **4.** Où est le bureau de poste? **5.** Y a-t-il un bureau de tabac près d'ici? **6.** Où est la rue de la Paix? **7.** Comment allez-vous? **8.** Parlez-vous français? **9.** Parlez-vous anglais?

IV. *Demandez-moi:*

Ex.:—Demandez-moi où est le château.
    —**Où est le château, s'il vous plaît?**

1. où est la gare. **2.** où est le bureau de poste. **3.** s'il y a un restaurant près d'ici. **4.** s'il y a un bureau de tabac près d'ici. **5.** s'il y a un restaurant près du château. **6.** s'il y a un musée dans le château. **7.** s'il y a un restaurant dans la rue de la Paix. **8.** s'il y a un bureau de tabac dans la rue de la Paix.

V. *Comptez en français de un à dix* (Count in French from 1 to 10) :

1. un (1), deux (2), trois (3), quatre (4), cinq (5). **2.** six (6), sept (7), huit (8), neuf (9), dix (10). **3.** un franc, deux francs, trois francs. **4.** quatre francs, cinq francs, six francs. **5.** sept francs, huit francs, neuf francs, dix francs. **6.** un étudiant, deux étudiants, trois étudiants. **7.** quatre étudiants, cinq étudiants, six étudiants. **8.** sept étudiants, huit étudiants, neuf étudiants, dix étudiants.

VI. CONVERSATIONS:

(1)

"Good morning, sir *(Mlle), (Madame)*. Do you speak English?"
"No, sir, I do not speak English."
"Please tell me where the station is."
"Straight ahead, sir."
"Thank you very much."
"You are welcome."

(2)

You stop someone and ask for the location of a restaurant.

VII. *Dites en français:*

1. Please tell me where the château is. **2.** Straight ahead, sir. **3.** Where is the museum? **4.** The museum is in the château. **5.** Is there a restaurant near the château? **6.** Yes, sir. There is a restaurant near the château. **7.** Thank you very much. **8.** You are welcome, sir. **9.** Pardon me, sir. Where is the post office? **10.** On the square, over there, to the left. **11.** Is there a tobacco shop near here? **12.** Oh yes, sir. There is a tobacco shop on (in) the Rue de la Paix. **13.** Where is the Rue de la Paix? **14.** To the right, sir. **15.** Thank you very much. **16.** At the station. **17.** On the street. **18.** To a passer-by.

Getting a Hotel

Dans la rue

JOHN —[1]Pardon, où est l'hôtel du Cheval blanc?

UN AGENT DE POLICE —[2]Sur la place, monsieur.

JOHN —[3]Est-ce que c'est loin d'ici?

L'AGENT —[4]Non, ce n'est pas loin d'ici.

JOHN —[5]Est-ce que c'est un bon hôtel?

L'AGENT —[6]Oui, monsieur, c'est un très bon hôtel.

JOHN —[7]Est-ce que la cuisine est bonne?

L'AGENT —[8]Certainement, monsieur. La cuisine est excellente.

JOHN —[9]Y a-t-il un autre hôtel ici?

L'AGENT —[10]Oui, il y a un hôtel en face de l'église.

JOHN —[11]Merci beaucoup.

L'AGENT —[12]De rien, monsieur.

A l'hôtel du Cheval blanc

JOHN —[13]Quel est le prix de la pension?

L'HÔTELIER —[14]Vingt-cinq francs* par jour.

JOHN —[15]Quel est le prix des repas?

L'HÔTELIER —[16]Quatre francs pour le petit déjeuner, [17]huit francs pour le déjeuner, [18]et huit francs pour le dîner.

On the Street

JOHN —[1]Pardon me, where is the White Horse Inn?

A POLICEMAN —[2]On the square, sir.

JOHN —[3]Is it far from here?

THE POLICEMAN —[4]No, it isn't far (from here).

JOHN —[5]Is it a good hotel?

THE POLICEMAN —[6]Yes, sir, it is a very good hotel.

JOHN —[7]Is the food (cuisine) good?

THE POLICEMAN —[8]Certainly, sir. The food is excellent.

JOHN —[9]Is there another hotel here?

THE POLICEMAN —[10]Yes, there is a hotel opposite the church.

JOHN —[11]Thank you very much.

THE POLICEMAN —[12]You are welcome, sir.

At the White Horse Inn

JOHN —[13]What is the price of board and room?

THE INNKEEPER —[14]Twenty-five francs per day.

JOHN —[15]What is the price of meals?

THE INNKEEPER —[16]Four francs for breakfast, [17]eight francs for lunch, [18]and eight francs for dinner.

---

* 1 franc is currently worth about 20 cents.

8

I. SUBSTITUTIONS. *Répétez les phrases suivantes, en substituant les mots indiqués.**

   1. Est-ce que c'est [près d'ici]?
      près du château/ près de la gare/ loin de la gare/ loin d'ici

   2. Est-ce que [l'hôtel] est loin d'ici?
      l'hôtel du Cheval blanc/ l'autre hôtel/ la gare/ le musée

   3. [L'hôtel] n'est pas loin d'ici.
      Le musée/ La gare/ L'autre hôtel/ La rue de la Paix

   4. Y a-t-il un bon restaurant [près d'ici]?
      sur la place/ près de la gare/ près du musée/ en face du musée

   5. Il y a un hôtel [en face de l'église].
      en face de la gare/ près de la gare/ en face du château/ près du château

II. *Répondez en français:*

   1. Où est l'hôtel du Cheval blanc?   **2.** Est-ce que c'est loin d'ici?   **3.** Est-ce que c'est un bon hôtel?   **4.** Est-ce que la cuisine est bonne?   **5.** Y a-t-il un autre hôtel ici?   **6.** Quel est le prix de la pension?

III. *Demandez en français:*

   1. où est l'hôtel du Cheval blanc.   **2.** si c'est loin d'ici.   **3.** si c'est un bon hôtel.   **4.** si la cuisine est bonne.   **5.** s'il y a un autre hôtel ici.   **6.** le prix de la pension.   **7.** le prix des repas.

IV. *Mettez les phrases suivantes à la forme interrogative en plaçant* **est-ce qu(e) . . . ?** *devant chacune d'elles* (Put the following sentences in the interrogative form by placing **est-ce qu(e) . . . ?** in front of each of them) :

Ex.:—Il y a un bon hôtel près d'ici.
    —**Est-ce qu'il y a un bon hôtel près d'ici?**

1. L'hôtel du Cheval blanc est près d'ici.   **2.** L'hôtel du Cheval blanc est loin d'ici.   **3.** Il y a un bon restaurant près d'ici.   **4.** Il y a restaurant en face de l'église.   **5.** Il y a un bureau de tabac dans la rue de la Paix.   **6.** Il y a un bureau de tabac en face de la gare.   **7.** Il y a un restaurant dans la gare.   **8.** La cuisine de l'hôtel du Cheval blanc est bonne.   **9.** La cuisine de l'autre hôtel est bonne.

---

* For pronunciation exercises, see pp. 296-297.

V. *Comptez en français de onze à vingt:*

1. onze (11), douze (12), treize (13). **2.** quatorze (14), quinze (15), seize (16). **3.** dix-sept (17), dix-huit (18), dix-neuf (19), vingt (20). **4.** onze étudiants, douze étudiants, treize étudiants, quatorze étudiants, quinze étudiants, seize étudiants, dix-sept étudiants, dix-huit étudiants, dix-neuf étudiants, vingt étudiants. **5.** Donnez les nombres pairs de deux à vingt (Give the even numbers from 2 to 20). **6.** Donnez les nombres impairs (odd numbers) de un à dix-neuf. **7.** Dites en français: 1 franc, 11 francs; 2 francs, 12 francs; 3 francs, 13 francs; 4 francs, 14 francs; 5 francs, 15 francs; 6 francs, 16 francs; 7 francs, 17 francs; 8 francs, 18 francs; 9 francs, 19 francs; 10 francs, 20 francs.

VI. CONVERSATION.

"Is there another hotel here?"
"Yes, there is the Hotel Continental."
"Where is the Hotel Continental?"
"On the square, opposite the station."
"What is the price of board and room?"
"Twenty-five francs a day."

VII. *Dites en français:*

1. Pardon me, where is the White Horse Inn? **2.** On the square, sir. **3.** Is it far from here? **4.** No, it isn't far. **5.** Is it a good hotel? **6.** Yes, sir, it is a very good hotel. **7.** Is the food good? **8.** Certainly, sir. The food is excellent. **9.** Is there another hotel here? **10.** Yes, there is a hotel opposite the church. **11.** Thank you very much. **12.** You are welcome. **13.** What is the price of board and room? **14.** Twenty-five francs per day. **15.** What is the price of meals? **16.** Four francs for breakfast, eight francs for lunch, and eight francs for dinner.

Catching a Train

A l'hôtel	At the Hotel
JOHN —[1]Quelle heure est-il?	JOHN —[1]What time is it?
L'HÔTELIER —[2]Il est onze heures.	THE INNKEEPER —[2]It is eleven o'clock.
JOHN —[3]Est-ce que le déjeuner est prêt?	JOHN —[3]Is lunch ready?
L'HÔTELIER —[4]Non, monsieur, pas encore. [5]A quelle heure voulez-vous déjeuner?	THE INNKEEPER —[4]No, sir, not yet. [5]At what time do you want to have lunch?
JOHN —[6]A onze heures et quart, [7]ou à onze heures et demie.	JOHN —[6]At a quarter past eleven, [7]or at half past eleven.
L'HÔTELIER —[8]A quelle heure allez-vous à la gare?	THE INNKEEPER— [8]At what time are you going to the station?
JOHN —[9]Je vais à la gare à midi. [10]Le train pour Paris arrive à midi et quart, n'est-ce pas?	JOHN —[9]I am going to the station at noon. [10]The train for Paris arrives at a quarter past twelve, doesn't it?
L'HÔTELIER —[11]Non, monsieur. Il arrive à deux heures moins le quart.	THE INNKEEPER —[11]No, sir. It comes at a quarter of two.
JOHN —[12]Alors, je vais déjeuner à midi, comme d'habitude. [13]Est-ce que le bureau de poste est ouvert cet après-midi?	JOHN —[12]Then I am going to have lunch at noon, as usual. [13]Is the post office open this afternoon?
L'HÔTELIER —[14]Oui, monsieur. [15]Il est ouvert de huit heures du matin à sept heures du soir.	THE INNKEEPER —[14] Yes, sir. [15]It is open from eight o'clock in the morning to seven o'clock in the evening.

I. SUBSTITUTIONS. *Répétez les phrases suivantes, en substituant les mots indiqués:*

1. Il est [onze heures].
dix heures et demie/ neuf heures et quart/ huit heures moins le quart/ midi

2. A quelle heure allez-vous [à la gare]?
à l'hôtel/ au restaurant/ au musée

3. Je vais à la gare [à midi].
à six heures/ à dix heures et quart/ à cinq heures et demie

4. Le train pour Paris arrive [à midi et quart], n'est-ce pas?
à une heure et quart/ à deux heures et quart/ à deux heures moins le quart/ à cinq heures moins le quart

5. Est-ce que [le bureau de poste] est ouvert cet après-midi?
le musée/ le château/ le bureau de tabac

6. Il est ouvert de [huit heures] du matin à sept heures du soir.
neuf heures/ dix heures/ onze heures

7. Il est ouvert de neuf heures du matin [à six heures] du soir.
huit heures/ neuf heures/ dix heures/ sept heures

8. Je vais au musée [ce matin].
ce soir/ cet après-midi/ à midi et demi

II. EXERCICES D'APPLICATION.

A. *Mettez les phrases suivantes à la forme interrogative en plaçant* **Est-ce qu(e)** *... devant chacune d'elles:*

1. Le déjeuner est prêt. 2. Le bureau de poste est ouvert cet après-midi. 3. Le dîner est prêt. 4. Le musée est dans le château. 5. Il y a un restaurant près du château. 6. Il y a un bureau de tabac en face du château. 7. Il y a un train pour Paris cet après-midi. 8. Il y a un bon restaurant sur la place. 9. Le train pour Paris arrive à midi et quart. 10. Il y a un bureau de tabac dans la rue de la Paix.

B. *Mettez les phrases suivantes à la forme négative:*

Ex.:—Je parle français.
—**Je ne parle pas français.**

1. Je suis M. Hughes. 2. Je parle anglais. 3. Je vais à la gare. 4. Je vais déjeuner à onze heures et demie. 5. C'est loin d'ici. 6. C'est un bon hôtel. 7. Le déjeuner est prêt. 8. Le dîner est prêt. 9. Le bureau de poste est ouvert. 10. Il est ouvert à huit heures.

III. *Répondez en français, d'après le texte:*

1. Quelle heure est-il? **2.** Est-ce que le déjeuner est prêt? **3.** A quelle heure voulez-vous déjeuner? **4.** A quelle heure allez-vous à la gare? **5.** Le train pour Paris arrive à midi et quart, n'est-ce pas? **6.** Est-ce que le bureau de poste est ouvert cet après-midi? **7.** Est-il ouvert à midi? **8.** Est-ce qu'il est ouvert à six heures du soir? **9.** Est-ce que le train pour Paris arrive à midi et demi?

IV. *Demandez à quelqu'un* (Ask someone):

(1)

1. quelle heure il est. **2.** si le déjeuner est prêt. **3.** si le train pour Paris arrive à midi et quart. **4.** si le bureau de poste est ouvert cet après-midi. **5.** si le bureau de poste est ouvert à neuf heures du matin. **6.** si le bureau de poste est loin d'ici. **7.** s'il y a un bureau de tabac près d'ici. **8.** s'il y a un train pour Paris cet après-midi.

(2)

1. s'il parle français. **2.** s'il parle anglais. **3.** comment il va. **4.** à quelle heure il va à la gare. **5.** à quelle heure il va déjeuner. **6.** s'il va au musée cet après-midi. **7.** s'il va déjeuner à l'hôtel du Cheval blanc. **8.** s'il veut *(wants to)* déjeuner à midi. **9.** s'il veut déjeuner à midi et quart. **10.** à quelle heure il veut déjeuner.

V. Conversation.

"What time is it?"
"It is noon. Where are you going?"
"I am going to the station. Does the train for Paris arrive at 12:15?"
"Yes."
"Thank you very much."
"You are welcome."

VI. *Dites en français:*

1. What time is it? **2.** It is eleven o'clock. **3.** Is lunch ready? **4.** No, sir, not yet. **5.** At what time do you want to have lunch? **6.** At a quarter past eleven or at half past eleven. **7.** At what time are you going to the station? **8.** I am going to the station at noon. **9.** The train for Paris arrives at a quarter past twelve, doesn't it? **10.** No, sir. It comes at a quarter of two. **11.** Then I am going to have lunch at noon, as usual. **12.** Is the post office open this afternoon? **13.** Yes, sir. It is open from eight o'clock in the morning to seven o'clock in the evening.

Articles and Prepositions *de* and *à*

1. Masculine and feminine gender.

In French, nouns fall into two classes, or, as they are traditionally called, GENDERS: masculine and feminine. You have noticed that we say «Y a-t-il **un restaurant** près d'ici» but «Voici **une lettre** pour vous.» **Un restaurant** belongs to the masculine gender; **Une lettre** belongs to the feminine gender. While in English the question of gender is of little importance, it is very important in French because the form of articles and adjectives as well as pronouns must conform to the gender of the noun to which they refer. There is no dependable rule for finding the gender of nouns: it is true that the gender of nouns which denote persons normally corresponds to their sex, but the gender of those which denote animals, inanimate objects, ideas, etc., does not follow so simple a pattern.

The easiest and most effective way to learn the gender of a noun is to practice using the noun with its article in a phrase. Of course it would be a simple matter to learn each day a short list of detached words with their genders; but unfortunately words which are merely memorized are soon forgotten. On the other hand, it is relatively easy to remember words learned in context: the meaning of the sentence, its sounds, its rhythm—everything helps you recall all the parts of the sentence. Therefore, even in grammar exercises, we shall continue to work with complete phrases rather than with detached words.

2. Indefinite article (Eng. *a, an*).

The masculine form **un** is used with **masculine singular nouns**; the feminine form **une,** with feminine singular nouns:

un restaurant	*a* restaurant
un bureau de tabac	*a* tobacco shop
un hôtel	*a* hotel
un bon hôtel	*a* good hotel
un autre hôtel	*another* hotel

une lettre	*a* letter
une gare	*a* railroad station
une place	*a* public square
une rue	*a* street
une église	*a* church
une autre église	*an*other church

3. Definite article (Eng. *the*).

A. Form **le**:

The form **le** (masculine singular) is used before nouns or adjectives which are masculine and singular if they begin with a consonant other than a mute **h***:

le bureau de tabac	*the* tobacco shop
le déjeuner	lunch, or *the* lunch
le restaurant	*the* restaurant
le bon restaurant	*the* good restaurant
le bon hôtel	*the* good hotel
le petit hôtel	*the* little hotel

B. Form **la**:

The form **la** (feminine singular) is used before nouns or adjectives which are feminine and singular if they begin with a consonant other than a mute **h**:

la gare	*the* railroad station
la rue	*the* street
la pension	board and room
la bonne cuisine	good cooking

---

* Although all **h**'s in French are silent in everyday conversation, they fall into two groups traditionally known as mute **h**'s and aspirate **h**'s:

Before a word beginning with a mute **h**, linking and elision take place precisely as if the word began with a vowel. Ex.: **l'hôtel, les‿hôtels.**

Before a word beginning with an aspirate **h**, linking and elision do not take place. Ex.: **Le/héros** *(the hero),* **les/héros.**

In the vocabulary of this book, and in most dictionaries, words beginning with an aspirate **h** are marked with an asterisk.

For a discussion of linking, see pp. 294-296.

C. Form **l':**

The form **l'** (masculine or feminine singular) is used before nouns or adjectives of either gender if they begin with a vowel or mute **h:**

l'agent de police *(m.)*	*the* policeman
l'hôtel *(m.)*	*the* hotel
l'autre hôtel	*the* other hotel
l'église *(f.)*	*the* church
l'autre église	*the* other church
l'autre restaurant *(m.)*	*the* other restaurant
l'autre gare *(f.)*	*the* other station

In order to explain the form **l'**, it is usually said that the vowel of **le** or **la** is elided or that elision takes place. However, do not infer that this is an operation that *you* are supposed to perform: there is no point in imagining a vowel and then eliding it! Just say, think, and write **l'hôtel** and be done with it.

D. Form **les:**

The form **les** is used before any plural noun or adjective:

les restaurants	the restaurants
les autres restaurants	the other restaurants
les églises	the churches
les hôtels	the hotels
les bons restaurants	the good restaurants
les autres hôtels	the other hotels

(1) Note that the **s** of **les** is linked (and pronounced **z**) if the noun or adjective which follows begins with a vowel or mute **h.**

(2) In writing, the plural of French nouns is usually formed by adding "s" to the singular. This "s" is of course not pronounced.

In speaking, the plural of nouns is usually distinguished from the singular by the article used.

4. Preposition **de** *(of, from).*

A. **du, des:**

When the preposition **de** is used with a noun before which the definite article **le** or **les** would normally stand, you say **du** or **des**—never **de le** or **de les.**

le déjeuner	le prix **du** déjeuner	the price *of* lunch
les repas	le prix **des** repas	the price *of* meals
les hôtels	la cuisine **des** hôtels	the cooking *of the* hotels

Since you say **près de, loin de,** as in **près d'ici** *(near here)* and **loin d'ici** *(far from here),* you say:

le château	**près du** château	*near the* chateau
les églises	**près des** églises	*near the* churches

B. de la, de l':

When the preposition **de** is used with the noun before which the definite article **la** or **l'** would normally stand, you say **de la** or **de l'**— just as you would expect:

la pension	le prix **de la** pension	the price *of* board and room
la gare	près **de la** gare	*near the* station
l'hôtel	le cuisine **de l'**hôtel	*the* hotel's cooking
l'autre hôtel	la cuisine **de l'**autre hôtel	*the* other hotel's cooking

5. Preposition à *(to, in, at).*

A. au, aux:

When the preposition **à** is used with a noun before which the definite article **le** or **les** would normally stand, you say **au** or **aux**—never **à le** or **à les:**

le château	Il est **au** château	He is *in the* chateau
le bureau de tabac	Je vais **au** bureau de tabac	I am going *to the* tobacco shop
les bons restaurants	Je vais **aux** bons restaurants	I go *to the* good restaurants
les étudiants	Je parle **aux** étudiants	I am talking *to the* students

B. à la, à l':

When the preposition **à** is used with a noun before which the definite article **la** or **l'** would normally stand, you say **à la** or **à l',** as you would expect:

la gare	Je vais **à la** gare	I am going *to the* station
la concierge	Je parle **à la** concierge	I speak *to the* concierge
l'église	Je vais **à l'**église	I am going *to (the)* church
l'hôtel	Je vais **à l'**hôtel	I am going *to the* hotel
l'autre hôtel	Je vais **à l'**autre hôtel	I am going *to the* other hotel

6. Use of the definite article.

The definite article is used much more commonly in French than in English. Specific cases of its use or omission will be studied later. But meanwhile, note that in French you say:

Quel est le prix **des** repas?	What is the price *of* meals?
Huit francs **pour le** déjeuner et huit francs **pour le** dîner.	Eight francs *for* lunch and eight francs *for* dinner.
Je vais **à l'**église.	I am going *to* church.
Le déjeuner et **le** dîner.	Lunch and dinner.

I. EXERCICES D'APPLICATION.

A. *Répétez en remplaçant l'article défini* (**le, la, l'**) *par l'article indéfini* (**un, une**):

Ex.:—le restaurant.
 —**un restaurant**

1. le bureau de tabac, le musée, le déjeuner.
2. la gare, la place, la rue.
3. l'hôtel, l'agent de police, l'église.

B. *Répétez en remplaçant l'article défini* (**le, la, l'**) *par* **au, à la,** *ou* **à l'**:

Ex.:—le déjeuner.
 —**au déjeuner.**

1. le bureau de poste, le dîner, le passant.
2. la gare, la rue, la place.
3. l'hôtelier, l'employé, l'étudiant.

C. *Donnez le pluriel des mots suivants:*

1. le dîner, le repas, le train.
2. la gare, la rue, la place.
3. l'employé, l'hôtelier, l'église.
4. l'autre hôtel, l'autre église, l'autre train.
5. le bon dîner, le bon restaurant, le petit restaurant.

D. *Répétez et remplacez l'article défini* (**les**) *par* **aux:**

Ex.:—les employés.
 —**aux employés.**

1. les restaurants, les bons restaurants, les repas.
2. les étudiants, les étudiantes *(f.)*, les autres étudiants.

II. *Complétez les phrases suivantes, en employant les mots indiqués:*

1. Je vais (à) . . .

Ex.:—(le) restaurant.

   —**Je vais au restaurant.**

(le) musée/ (le) château/ (le) petit hôtel

2. Je parle (à) . . .

Ex.:—(les) passants.

   —**Je parle aux passants.**

(les) étudiants/ (les) agents de police/ (les) employés
(la) concierge/ l'étudiante/ l'hôtelier

3. L'autre hôtel est près (de) . . .

Ex.:—(le) château.

   —**L'autre hôtel est près du château.**

(le) musée/ (le) bureau de poste/ (le) bureau de tabac
(la) gare/ (la) place/ (la) rue de la Paix
l'église/ l'autre gare/ l'autre place.

III. *Répondez en français:*

1. A quelle heure allez-vous à la gare? **2.** A quelle heure allez-vous au théâtre? **3.** A quelle heure allez-vous à l'hôtel? **4.** A quelle heure allez-vous à l'église? **5.** A quelle heure allez-vous au restaurant? **6.** Y a-t-il une lettre pour moi? **7.** Est-ce que le déjeuner est prêt? **8.** Quel est le prix de la pension? **9.** Quel est le prix du dîner? **10.** Quel est le prix du déjeuner? **11.** Quel est le prix du petit déjeuner?

IV. *Demandez en français:*

1. s'il y a un restaurant près d'ici. **2.** si c'est un bon restaurant. **3.** si la cuisine est bonne. **4.** si l'hôtel du Cheval blanc est un bon hôtel. **5.** si c'est loin d'ici. **6.** le prix de la pension. **7.** le prix des repas. **8.** le prix du déjeuner. **9.** le prix du dîner. **10.** le prix du petit déjeuner.

V. *Dites en français:*

1. Where are you going to have lunch? **2.** At what time are you going to have lunch? **3.** At what time do you want to have lunch? **4.** Where do you want to have lunch? **5.** Is there a good restaurant on the square? **6.** Is there a good restaurant near the square? **7.** Is there a good restaurant on the Rue de la Paix? **8.** I am going to the restaurant. **9.** I am at the restaurant. **10.** I am going to have lunch at the restaurant. **11.** The cooking of the restaurant is excellent.

Special Note

The exercises of Conversation 5 will include a short dictation taken from Conversation 1. Before the next meeting of the class, you should learn to write all the sentences of the first dialog.

The easiest and most natural way to do this is to spell through a phrase while looking at it, then write it down without looking at it, and finally check what you have written against the original. When you can write the first phrase correctly, continue the same exercise until you can write all the sentences of the first dialog.

The purpose of this exercise is to help you learn to write correctly in French. A brief dictation will be included in the exercises of each new dialog hereafter, and you should learn to write the sentences of the dialog that is indicated in the lesson.

Getting Identification Papers

A la préfecture de police*

L'EMPLOYÉ —[1]Comment vous appelez-vous, monsieur?

JOHN —[2]Je m'appelle John Hughes.

L'EMPLOYÉ —[3]Quelle est votre nationalité?

JOHN —[4]Je suis Américain.

L'EMPLOYÉ —[5] Où êtes-vous né?

JOHN —[6]Je suis né à Philadelphie.

L'EMPLOYÉ —[7]Quel âge avez-vous?

JOHN —[8]J'ai vingt et un ans.

L'EMPLOYÉ —[9]Quelle est votre profession?

JOHN —[10]Je suis ingénieur-chimiste.

L'EMPLOYÉ —[11]Où demeurez-vous?

JOHN —[12]Je demeure à Paris.

L'EMPLOYÉ —[13]Quelle est votre adresse à Paris?

JOHN —[14]Quinze, avenue de l'Observatoire.

L'EMPLOYÉ —[15]Où habitent vos parents?

JOHN —[16]Mon père habite à Philadelphie. [17]Ma mère est morte.

L'EMPLOYÉ —[18]Avez-vous des parents en France?

At the Prefecture

THE EMPLOYEE —[1]What is your name, sir?

JOHN —[2]My name is John Hughes.

THE EMPLOYEE —[3]What is your nationality?

JOHN —[4]I am an American.

THE EMPLOYEE —[5]Where were you born?

JOHN —[6]I was born in Philadelphia.

THE EMPLOYEE —[7]How old are you?

JOHN —[8]I am twenty-one.

THE EMPLOYEE —[9]What is your profession?

JOHN —[10]I am a chemical engineer.

THE EMPLOYEE —[11]Where do you live?

JOHN —[12]I live in Paris.

THE EMPLOYEE —[13]What is your Paris address?

JOHN —[14]Fifteen Observatory Avenue.

THE EMPLOYEE —[15]Where do your parents live?

JOHN —[16]My father lives in Philadelphia. [17]My mother is dead.

THE EMPLOYEE —[18]Have you any relatives in France?

---

* Administrative offices of Prefect of Police (in Paris).

JOHN —[19]Non, je n'ai pas de parents en France.

JOHN —[19]No, I haven't any relatives in France.

L'EMPLOYÉ —[20]Voilà votre carte d'identité.

THE EMPLOYEE —[20]Here is your identification card.

JOHN —[21] Merci, monsieur.

JOHN —[21]Thank you, sir.

I. SUBSTITUTIONS. *Répétez les phrases suivantes, en substituant les mots indiqués:*

   1. Quelle est [votre nationalité]?
votre profession/ votre adresse/ la nationalité de
Roger/ la profession de Roger/ l'adresse de Roger

   2. Quel est le prix [des repas]?
du déjeuner/ du dîner/ du petit déjeuner/ de la pension

   3. J'ai [vingt et un] ans.
dix-huit/ dix-sept/ dix-neuf/ vingt-deux

   4. Je n'ai pas encore [vingt et un ans].
vingt/ dix-neuf/ vingt-deux/ vingt-cinq

   5. Où habite votre [père]?
mère/ sœur/ frère/ oncle

   6. [Mon père] habite à Philadelphie.
Mon frère/ Ma sœur/ Mon oncle/ Ma tante

II. *Répondez en français à chacune des questions suivantes, d'après le texte* (according to the text) :

   1. Comment vous appelez-vous? **2.** Quelle est votre nationalité? **3.** Où êtes-vous né? **4.** Quel âge avez-vous? **5.** Quelle est votre profession? **6.** Où demeurez-vous? **7.** Quelle est votre adresse? **8.** Où demeure votre père? **9.** Où demeure votre mère? **10.** Avez-vous des parents en France?

III. *Répondez en français à chacune des questions personnelles suivantes:*

   1. Comment vous appelez-vous? **2.** Quelle est votre nationalité? **3.** Où êtes-vous né(e)? **4.** Quel âge avez-vous? **5.** Quelle est votre profession? (étudiant, étudiante). **6.** Où demeurez-vous? **7.** Quelle est votre adresse? **8.** Où demeurent vos parents? **9.** Avez-vous des parents en France?

IV. *Demandez à un autre étudiant (à une autre étudiante):*

   1. comment il (elle) s'appelle. **2.** où il (elle) est né (née). **3.** quel âge il (elle) a. **4.** où il (elle) demeure. **5.** quelle est son (*his* or *her*) adresse.

6. quelle est sa (*his* or *her*) nationalité. **7.** quelle est sa profession. **8.** s'il (si elle) a des parents en France. **9.** s'il (si elle) a des frères. **10.** s'il (si elle) a des sœurs. **11.** s'il (si elle) a des oncles. **12.** s'il (si elle) a des tantes. **13.** où demeurent ses (*his* or *her*) parents. **14.** si ses parents demeurent près d'ici.

V. Nombres.

(1) *Répétez en français les nombres suivants:*
vingt et un (21), vingt-deux (22), vingt-trois (23), vingt-quatre (24), vingt-cinq (25), vingt-six (26), vingt-sept (27), vingt-huit (28), vingt-neuf (29), trente (30).

(2) *Comptez par cinq* (by fives) *de cinq à trente.*

(3) *Comptez par trois de trois à trente.*

(4) *Dites en français:* 1, 11, 21   2, 12, 22   3, 13, 23   4, 14, 24

VI. Dictée d'après le dialogue, p. 1.

VII. Conversation.

Inquiries about birthplace, age, family connections, etc. between students.

Première Lecture Illustrée, p. 1, *Arrivée à Paris.*

Having Lunch

JOHN —[1]J'ai faim.

ROGER —[2]Moi aussi.

JOHN —[3]Allons déjeuner.

ROGER —[4]Voici un restaurant. Entrons.

JOHN —[5]Voilà une table libre. Asseyez-vous.

ROGER —[6]Garçon, donnez-moi la carte, s'il vous plaît.

LE GARÇON —[7]Voici, monsieur. Voulez-vous des *hors-d'œuvre?

ROGER —[8]Oui, apportez-moi des hors-d'œuvre. [9](à John) Voulez-vous du vin blanc ou du vin rouge?

JOHN —[10]Du vin rouge, s'il vous plaît.

ROGER —[11]Qu'est-ce que vous voulez comme plat de viande?

JOHN —[12]Du rosbif et des pommes de terre frites.

LE GARÇON —[13]Qu'est-ce que vous voulez comme dessert?

ROGER —[14]Qu'est-ce que vous avez?

LE GARÇON —[15]Nous avons des pommes, des bananes, des poires et du raisin.

ROGER —[16]Apportez-moi une poire.

JOHN —[1]I am hungry.

ROGER —[2]So am I.

JOHN —[3]Let's go have lunch.

ROGER —[4]Here is a restaurant. Let's go in.

JOHN —[5]Here is a (free) table. Sit down.

ROGER —[6]Waiter, give me the menu, please.

THE WAITER —[7]Here (it) is, sir. Do you want hors d'œuvres?†

ROGER —[8]Yes, bring me some hors d'œuvres. [9](to John) Do you want white wine or red wine?

JOHN —[10]Red wine, please.

ROGER —[11]What do you want for your meat course?

JOHN —[12]Roast beef and French fried potatoes.

THE WAITER —[13]What do you want for dessert?

ROGER —[14]What have you?

THE WAITER —[15]We have apples, bananas, pears, and grapes.

ROGER —[16]Bring me a pear.

---

* The h in **hors-d'œuvre** is aspirate *(See note, p. 15).*

Hors d'œuvre, highly seasoned dishes (olives, radishes, anchovies, salami, etc.), usually served on a large tray at the beginning of a meal.

LE GARÇON —[17]Voulez-vous du café?

THE WAITER —[17]Do you want coffee?

ROGER —[18]Oui, donnez-moi du café noir.

ROGER —[18]Yes, give me some black coffee.

LE GARÇON (à John) —[19]Et vous, monsieur?

THE WAITER (to John) —[19]What about you, sir?

JOHN —[20]Merci, je n'aime pas le café.

JOHN —[20]No, thank you, I don't like coffee.

ROGER (au garçon) —[21] Garçon, l'addition, s'il vous plaît.

ROGER (to the waiter) —[21]Waiter, the bill, please.

LE GARÇON —[22]Tout de suite, monsieur.

THE WAITER —[22]Right away, sir.

I. SUBSTITUTIONS. *Répétez les phrases suivantes, en substituant les mots indiqués:*

1. Allons déjeuner [au restaurant].
   à l'hôtel/ à l'hôtel du Cheval blanc/ à l'autre hôtel/
   à l'autre restaurant

2. Voulez-vous [des hors-d'œuvre]?
   du vin blanc/ du rosbif/ des pommes de terre frites/ du café

3. Apportez-moi [des hors-d'œuvre].
   du vin rouge/ du rosbif/ des pommes de terre frites/ du café noir

4. Qu'est-ce que vous voulez [comme plat de viande]?
   comme dessert/ comme hors-d'œuvre/ comme vin

5. Est-ce que vous avez [des pommes]?
   des bananes/ des poires/ du raisin/ du rosbif

6. Nous avons [des pommes].
   des bananes/ des poires/ du raisin/ des pommes de terre frites

7. Je n'aime pas [le café].
   le café noir/ le vin rouge/ les pommes/ les poires/ le raisin

II. *Répondez en français à chacune des questions suivantes:*

1. Quelle heure est-il? 2. Avez-vous faim? 3. A quelle heure allez-vous déjeuner? 4. Y a-t-il un restaurant près d'ici? 5. Où est le restaurant? 6. Y a-t-il une table libre? 7. Voulez-vous des hors-d'œuvre? 8. Voulez-vous du vin blanc ou du vin rouge? 9. Qu'est-ce que vous voulez comme plat de viande? 10. Qu'est-ce que vous voulez comme dessert? 11. Qu'est-ce que vous avez comme dessert? 12. Voulez-vous du café noir? 13. Aimez-vous le café? 14. Aimez-vous les hors-d'œuvre?

III. *Dites à un autre étudiant (à une autre étudiante):*

1. qu'il est midi. 2. que vous avez faim. 3. qu'il y a un restaurant en face.
4. que c'est un bon restaurant. 5. d'entrer dans le restaurant. 6. qu'il y a
une table libre là-bas à droite. 7. de s'asseoir (*to sit down*). 8. de vous
donner la carte. 9. de vous apporter l'addition. 10. de vous donner son
adresse.

IV. *Demandez à quelqu'un* (someone):

1. s'il a faim. 2. à quelle heure il va déjeuner. 3. à quelle heure il va dîner.
4. où il va déjeuner. 5. où il va dîner. 6. s'il veut (*if he wants*) des hors-
d'œuvre. 7. s'il veut du café.

V. RÉVISION. *Dites en français:*

1. Right away. 2. Please. 3. Over there. 4. To the right. 5. To the left.
6. Straight ahead. 7. Not yet. 8. Me too (So do I). 9. Near the station.
10. Across from the station. 11. How old are you? 12. What's your name?
13. How are you? 14. Where were you born? 15. And (what about) you?
16. Sit down. 17. Let's go to lunch. 18. Let's go in. 19. What time is it?
20. It's 7:00 A.M. 21. It's 7:00 P.M. 22. As usual. 23. At 11:15. 24. At
2:30. 25. At a quarter of four.

VI. DICTÉE D'APRÈS LE DIALOGUE, p. 5.

VII. CONVERSATIONS.

(1)

"What time is it?"
"It's twelve o'clock noon."
"I'm hungry. Let's go have lunch."
"Is there a restaurant near here?"
"Yes, here is a restaurant. Let's go in."

(2)

"What time is it?"
"It's 6:15."
"I'm hungry. Let's go have dinner."
"Is there a good restaurant near here?"
"Yes. There is a good restaurant on the square."

(3)

"Waiter, give me the menu, please."

"Here it is, sir."

"Bring me some hors d'œuvres."

"Yes, sir. What do you want as a meat course?"

"Bring me some roast beef and French fried potatoes."

"What do you want for dessert?"

"What have you?"

"Pears, apples, bananas, and grapes."

"Bring me some grapes, please."

"Right away, sir."

Nouns Used in a Partitive Sense

7. Explanations of nouns used in a partitive sense.

—Voulez-vous **du café?**	Do you want *some coffee?*
—Voulez-vous **des pommes?**	Do you want *some apples?*
—Apportez-moi **des hors-d'œuvre.**	Bring me *some hors d'œuvres.*
—Avez-vous **des parents** en France?	Have you *any relatives* in France?

The nouns **café, pommes, hors-d'œuvre,** and **parents** are taken in a partitive sense; i.e., they refer to A PART OF the beverage, the fruit, the food, or the people in question.

In English the partitive sense is frequently expressed by the words *some* or *any,* but it is often implied rather than expressed. You can say: *Do you want some coffee? Do you want any coffee?* or *Do you want coffee?* In French, however, the only possible way to express the idea is: **Voulez-vous du café?**

8. The use of **du, de la, de l', des** in expressing the partitive.

When nouns are used in a partitive sense in affirmative statements, commands, and questions, they are preceded by one of the special partitive forms, **du, de la, de l',** or **des.**

A. The form **du** is used with a masculine singular noun before which **le** would normally stand:

le café	Voulez-vous **du café?**	Do you want *(some) coffee?*
le café noir	Voulez-vous **du café noir?**	Do you want *(some) black coffee?*

B. De la is used with a feminine singular noun before which **la** would normally stand:

la crème	Donnez-moi **de la crème.**	Give me *some cream.*
la monnaie	Avez-vous **de la monnaie?**	Have you *any change?*

28

C. De l' is used with a masculine or feminine singular noun before which l' would normally stand:

l'argent *(m.)*	Avez-vous **de l'argent?**	Have you *any money?*
l'eau *(f.)*	Donnez-moi **de l'eau.**	Give me *some water.*

D. Des is used with masculine or feminine plural nouns:

les fruits *(m.)*	Avez-vous **des fruits?**	Have you *any fruit?*
les pommes *(f.)*	Nous avons **des pommes.**	We have *apples.*
les poires *(f.)*	Voulez-vous **des poires?**	Do you want *pears?*

9. Use of **de** alone.

A. De is used instead of **du, de la, des,** when a noun in the partitive sense is the direct object of the negative form of a verb:

—Nous n'avons **pas de café.**	We have *no coffee.*
BUT: Avez-vous du café?	Have you *any coffee?*
—Nous n'avons **pas de crème.**	We have *no cream.*
BUT: Avez-vous de la crème?	Have you *any cream?*
—Je n'ai **pas de parents** en France.	I have *no relatives* in France.
BUT: Avez-vous des parents en France?	Have you *any relatives* in France?
—Il n'y a **pas d'eau** sur la table.	There is *no water* on the table.
BUT: Y a-t-il de l'eau sur la table?	Is there *any water* on the table?

B. De is used instead of **un, une,** when the noun is the direct object of the negative form of a verb:

—Je n'ai **pas de carte d'identité.**	I have *no identification card.*
BUT: J'ai une carte d'identité.	I have *an identification card.*
—Il n'y a **pas d'hôtel** près d'ici.	There is *no hotel* near here.
BUT: Y a-t-il un hôtel près d'ici?	Is there *a hotel* near here?

C. De is frequently used instead of **des,** when the noun is preceded by an adjective:

—Il y a **de bons restaurants** sur la place.	There are *good restaurants* on the square.
(BUT: Il y a **des restaurants** sur la place.)	There are *restaurants* on the square.
—Y a-t-il **d'autres hôtels** ici?	Are there *other hotels* here?
(BUT: Y a-t-il **des hôtels** ici?)	Are there *any hotels* here?

D. De alone is used after adverbs **beaucoup** *much*, **un peu** *a little*, and most expressions of quantity:

—Il y a **beaucoup de restaurants** sur la place.　　There are *many restaurants* on the square.

—Voulez-vous **un peu de café?**　　Do you want *a little coffee?*

10. Remarks about when to use the partitive forms.

(1) With verbs such as *want, have, eat, order, bring*, etc., you often use nouns in a partitive sense because you are likely to want, have, order, etc., only a part of the thing or things you are talking about.

(2) After **aimer** *(to like)*, however, nouns are taken in a general (not partitive) sense, and therefore you use the definite article **le, la, l', les.** You say:

—J'aime le café.　　I like coffee.

—J'aime le café noir.　　I like black coffee.

—Je n'aime pas le café.　　I don't like coffee.

If you say "I like *some* coffee", you are still not using the noun in a partitive sense because you like *all* the particular kind of coffee you are referring to. The partitive could not be used to express this phrase which means "I like certain kinds of coffee."

(3) Observe the sense in which the nouns are taken in the following sentences and try to see how the different shades of meaning are expressed:

(a)

—Aimez-vous les pommes?　　Do you like apples? (in general)

—Voulez-vous la pomme?　　Do you want the apple? (a whole object)

—Voulez-vous les pommes?　　Do you want the apples? (a whole group of objects)

—Voulez-vous des pommes?　　Do you want some apples? (a part of the whole group of objects)

(b)

I like *coffee* (**le café**). I want to buy *some coffee* (**du café**). I go to the grocery store where they sell *coffee* (**du café**). I go to the counter where *the coffee* (**le café**) [i.e., all the coffee they have for sale] is sold. I buy *some coffee* (**du café**) [i.e., some of the coffee that is for sale]. The salesman puts *the coffee* (**le café**) [i.e., all the coffee I bought] into a bag. I take *the coffee* (**le café**) home.

Now I want to make *some coffee* (**du café**) [i.e., some of the beverage that can be brewed with ground coffee beans]. I take *the coffee* (**le café**) from the table and put *some coffee* (**du café**) [i.e., some of the coffee that is in the bag] and some boiling water into a coffee maker and make *coffee* (**du café**). I pour *coffee* (**du café**) into a cup. I drink *the coffee* (**le café**) that is in the cup. I always drink *coffee* (**du café**) [i.e., some of the beverage which can be made from coffee beans] for breakfast because I don't like milk (**le lait**).

I. EXERCICES D'APPLICATION.

A. *Répétez en remplaçant l'article défini* (**le, la, l', les**) *par le partitif* (**du, de la, de l', des, de**):

I. le café. Donnez-moi [du café], s'il vous plaît.
le café noir/ le lait (milk) / le rosbif/ le raisin

2. la crème. Donnez-moi [de la crème].
la monnaie/ la viande/ la salade

3. l'eau. Donnez-moi [de l'eau].
l'argent/ l'omelette/ l'aspirine

4. les pommes. Donnez-moi [des pommes].
les bananes / les poires/ les hors-d'œuvre/ les fruits

5. les pommes. Nous n'avons [pas de pommes].
les bananes / les poires/ les hors-d'œuvre/ les fruits

B. *Dites au pluriel:*

Ex.:—Avez-vous un frère? Avez-vous [des frères]?
une sœur/ un oncle/ une pomme/ une poire

C. *Mettez à la forme négative:*

I. J'ai un frère. Je n'ai [pas de frère].
une sœur/ un oncle/ une pomme/ une poire

2. J'ai des frères. Je n'ai [pas de frères].
des sœurs/ des oncles/ des pommes/ des poires

3. Il y a un hôtel près d'ici. Il n'y a [pas d'hôtel] près d'ici.
un restaurant/ des restaurants/ un bureau de tabac/ des bureaux de tabac

D. *Mettez chacune des phrases suivantes à la forme négative:*

Ex.:—Il y a une table libre.
   —**Il n'y a pas de table libre.**

I. Il y a des tables libres.   **2.** Il y a une lettre pour vous.   **3.** Il y a des lettres pour vous.   **4.** Il y a de l'eau sur la table.   **5.** Il y a du vin rouge sur la table. **6.** Il y a de la crème.   **7.** Il y a des fruits.   **8.** Il y a des hors-d'œuvre.

E. *Employez* **beaucoup,** *puis* **un peu,** *avec chacun des mots suivants:*

Ex.:—le vin.

—**beaucoup de vin, un peu de vin.**
le rosbif/ le lait/ l'argent/ le sucre/ l'eau/ la monnaie/ la crème

F. *Répétez les deux phrases suivantes, en substituant les mots indiqués:*

Ex.:—le lait.

—**Avez-vous du lait?   —Aimez-vous le lait?**
le vin blanc/ la viande/ la crème/ le café noir

Ex.:—le lait.

—**Je n'ai pas de lait.   —Je n'aime pas le lait.**
le vin blanc/ la viande/ la crème/ le café noir

II. *Demandez en français:*

A. *Demandez à un autre étudiant (à une autre étudiante):*

1. s'il (si elle) a un frère.   2. s'il (si elle) a des sœurs.   3. s'il y a un hôtel ici.
4. s'il y a un autre hôtel ici.   5. s'il y a de bons hôtels ici.

B. *Imaginez que vous êtes dans un restaurant et demandez au garçon:*

1. s'il y a une table libre.   2. s'il y a d'autres tables libres.   3. s'il y a des poires.   4. s'il y a du raisin.   5. s'il y a du rosbif et des pommes de terre frites.

III. *Dites en français:*

1. (*a*) Do you like coffee? (*b*) Have you any coffee? (*c*) I have no coffee.
2. (*a*) Do you like grapes? (*b*) Have you any grapes? (*c*) I have no grapes.
3. (*a*) Do you like pears? (*b*) Do you want some pears? (*c*) I have no pears.
4. (*a*) Here are some apples. (*b*) Here are some good apples. (*c*) I like good apples. (*d*) Do you want some apples?   5. (*a*) Do you want some water? (*b*) Give me some water. (*c*) There is no water on the table.

Making Plans

JOHN —[1]Quelle est la date aujourd'hui?

ROGER —[2]C'est aujourd'hui le trente septembre. [3]Quand allez-vous à Marseille?

JOHN —[4]Au mois d'octobre. [5]Voici mon emploi du temps: [6]octobre et novembre à Marseille; [7]décembre, janvier et février à Paris; [8]mars et avril à Lyon; [9]mai, juin, juillet et août à Paris.

ROGER —[10]Est-ce que vous êtes libre la semaine prochaine?

JOHN —[11]Voyons . . . Quel jour sommes-nous aujourd'hui?

ROGER —[12]C'est aujourd'hui vendredi.

JOHN —[13]Je vais au laboratoire lundi, mardi, mercredi et jeudi. [14]Je suis libre vendredi, samedi et dimanche.

ROGER —[15]Voulez-vous venir à Rouen avec moi?

JOHN —[16]Volontiers. A quelle heure partez-vous?

ROGER —[17]Le train part à cinq heures.

JOHN —[18]C'est entendu. A jeudi après-midi.

JOHN —[1]What's the date today?

ROGER —[2]Today is September 30. [3]When are you going to Marseilles?

JOHN —[4]In (the month of) October. [5]Here is my schedule: [6]October and November in Marseilles; [7]December, January, and February in Paris; [8]March and April in Lyons; [9]May, June, July and August in Paris.

ROGER —[10]Are you free next week?

JOHN —[11]Let's see . . . What's today?

ROGER —[12]Today is Friday.

JOHN —[13]I go to the laboratory Monday, Tuesday, Wednesday and Thursday. [14]I am free Friday, Saturday and Sunday.

ROGER —[15]Do you want to go (come) with me to Rouen?

JOHN —[16]Gladly. What time are you leaving?

ROGER —[17]The train leaves at five o'clock.

JOHN —[18]Agreed. See you Thursday afternoon.

I. SUBSTITUTIONS. *Répétez les phrases suivantes, en substituant les mots indiqués:*

1. C'est aujourd'hui [le 30 septembre].

   le 30 octobre/ le 30 novembre/ le 30 décembre/
   le 11 avril/ le 11 mai/ le 11 juin/
   le premier juillet/ le premier août/ le premier septembre

2. Je vais à Marseille au mois [d'octobre].

   de janvier/ d'avril/ de juin/ d'août

3. Je vais à Lyon [le 15 mars].

   le 10 février/ le 16 juin/ le 13 juillet/ le 14 mai

4. Est-ce que vous êtes libre [la semaine prochaine]?

   lundi prochain/ mardi prochain/ mercredi prochain

5. C'est aujourd'hui [jeudi].

   vendredi/ samedi/ dimanche

6. Êtes-vous libre [ce matin]?

   ce matin à onze heures/ cet après-midi/ cet après-midi à quatre
   heures/ ce soir/ ce soir à dix heures

7. Je suis libre [aujourd'hui à midi].

   cet après-midi à trois heures/ ce soir à six heures/
   ce soir à neuf heures et demie

8. Le train part [à cinq heures].

   à quatre heures et quart/ à cinq heures et quart/ à midi/ à minuit

II. *Répondez en français à chacune des questions suivantes, d'après le texte:*

1. Quelle est la date aujourd'hui? **2.** Quand allez-vous à Marseille? **3.** Quels jours allez-vous au laboratoire? **4.** Quels jours êtes-vous libre? **5.** Quel jour sommes-nous? **6.** Voulez-vous venir à Rouen avec moi? **7.** A quelle heure le train part-il? **8.** A quelle heure allez-vous à la gare?

III. *Répétez en français après le professeur:*

1. Premier (*m.*), première (*f.*) (*first*). **2.** deuxième (*second*). **3.** troisième (*third*). **4.** quatrième (*fourth*). **5.** cinquième (*fifth*). **6.** sixième (*sixth*). **7.** septième (*seventh*). **8.** huitième (*eighth*). **9.** neuvième (*ninth*). **10.** dixième (*tenth*). **11.** onzième (*eleventh*). **12.** douzième (*twelfth*).

IV. *Répondez en français:*

Ex.:—Quel est le premier mois de l'année?
—**Janvier est le premier mois de l'année.**

1. Quel est le deuxième mois de l'année? **2.** Quel est le troisième mois de l'année? **3.** Quel est le quatrième mois de l'année? **4.** Quel est le cinquième mois de l'année? **5.** Quel est le sixième mois de l'année? **6.** Quel est le septième mois de l'année? **7.** Quel est le huitième mois de l'année? **8.** Quel est le neuvième mois de l'année? **9.** Quel est le dixième mois de l'année? **10.** Quel est le onzième mois de l'année? **11.** Quel est le douzième mois de l'année? **12.** Quel est le dernier mois de l'année?

V. *Dites en anglais ce que vous suggère chacune des dates suivantes* (Say in English what each of the following dates suggests to you) :

1. Le premier* avril. **2.** Le dernier jeudi de novembre. **3.** Le trente et un octobre. **4.** Le quatre juillet. **5.** le vingt-cinq décembre. **6.** Le vingt-deux février. **7.** Le vingt-neuf février.

VI. *Dites en français:*

1. Are you free this afternoon? **2.** Are you free Friday evening? **3.** What time are you leaving? **4.** What time are you free? **5.** I am free at five o'clock. **6.** At eight o'clock. **7.** At noon. **8.** Do you want to have lunch with me? **9.** See you Thursday afternoon. **10.** See you next Thursday. **11.** See you next week. **12.** See you this evening (See you tonight). **13.** See you tonight at 8:00. **14.** Agreed. **15.** Gladly.

VII. *Demandez à un autre étudiant (à une autre étudiante):*

1. quel jour nous sommes aujourd'hui. **2.** quelle heure il est. **3.** à quelle heure il (elle) déjeune. **4.** si le bureau de poste est ouvert à neuf heures. **5.** si le bureau de poste est ouvert cet après-midi. **6.** comment il (elle) s'appelle. **7.** quel âge il (elle) a. **8.** où il (elle) est né (née). **9.** où il (elle) habite. **10.** s'il (si elle) est libre dimanche. **11.** quand il (elle) va à Marseille. **12.** à quelle heure il (elle) part.

VIII. Dictée d'après le dialogue, p. 8.

IX. Conversation:

Vous invitez un de vos amis (une de vos amies) *(a friend of yours)* à dîner ce soir. Vous fixez un rendez-vous *(Decide upon a time and place to meet)*.

---

* Note that the ordinal number is used for the first of the month, but that the cardinal numbers are used for the other days of the month.

Present Indicative *être, avoir;*
Regular Verbs, First Conjugation

11. How to learn verb forms.

The best way to learn *anything* is to associate the thing to be learned with something which you already know. In studying the present indicative of the verb **être**, for example, you should bear in mind the forms which you have already mastered and relate the unfamiliar forms to them.

If you make it a point to think what each form means each time you say it or hear it, you will have little difficulty in learning verb forms.

12. Present indicative of **être, *to be:*** irregular.

—**Êtes-vous** Français?	*Are you* French ?
—Non, **je ne suis pas** Français.	No, *I am not* French.
Je suis Américain.	*I am* an American.
—Quelle heure **est-il?**	What time *is it?*
—**Il est** dix heures.	*It is* ten o'clock.
—Où **sont** Roger et John?	*Where are* Roger and John?
—**Ils sont** à Paris.	*They are* in Paris.

The forms of the present indicative of **être** are:

AFFIRMATIVE		NEGATIVE
je suis	*I am*	je ne suis pas *(I am not)*
tu es	*you are*	tu n'es pas
il est	*he is*	il n'est pas
elle est	*she is*	elle n'est pas
on est	*one is, they are*	on n'est pas
nous sommes	*we are*	nous ne sommes pas
vous êtes	*you are*	vous n'êtes pas
ils sont	*they are (m.)*	ils ne sont pas
elles sont	*they are (f.)*	elles ne sont pas

36

est-ce que je suis? *(am I?)*
es-tu?
est-il?
est-elle?
est-on?
sommes-nous?
êtes-vous?
sont-ils?
sont-elles?

(1) The **tu** form, the second person singular, is used only within families, in addressing children, and between very intimate friends. Young people are tending to use it more and more. It is not used in the oral practice exercises, but you will often find it in reading French books.

(2) **On** is always used with the third person singular of the verb, even when it corresponds to English "they" (as in *They say . . .*).

(3) The form given for the first person singular of the interrogative is **Est-ce que je suis?** This form is given because the inverted form **suis-je?** is hardly ever used except in literary style. **Est-ce que?** may of course be used with the other forms.

13. Present indicative of **avoir, to have:** irregular.

—**Avez-vous** des frères?	*Have you* any brothers?
—Non, **je n'ai pas** de frères.	No, *I have no* brothers.
—Qu'est-ce que **vous avez** comme dessert?	What *do you have* for dessert?
—**Nous avons** des pommes et des poires.	*We have* apples and pears.

The forms of the present indicative of **avoir** are:

AFFIRMATIVE		NEGATIVE
j'ai	*I have*	je n'ai pas *(I have not)*
tu as	*you have*	tu n'as pas
il a	*he has*	il n'a pas
elle a	*she has*	elle n'a pas
on a	*one has, they have*	on n'a pas
nous avons	*we have*	nous n'avons pas
vous avez	*you have*	vous n'avez pas
ils ont	*they have (m.)*	ils n'ont pas
elles ont	*they have (f.)*	elles n'ont pas

est-ce que j'ai? *(have I?)*
as-tu?
a-t-il?
a-t-elle?
a-t-on?
avons-nous?
avez-vous?
ont-ils?
ont-elles?

Note that in the inverted form of the third person singular, the subject pronoun (**il, elle, on**) is always preceded by the sound *t*. For verbs whose third person singular ends in a **t** (or **d**), it is simply a matter of linking the final consonant. Ex.: **Est-il?** For verbs whose third person does not end in a **t** (or **d**), a **t** is inserted between the verb and pronoun subject anyway.

14. Present indicative of **déjeuner, *to lunch*:** first conjugation, regular.

—A quelle heure **déjeunez-vous?**	At what time *do you have lunch?*
—**Je déjeune** à midi et quart.	*I have lunch* at a quarter past twelve.
—A quelle heure Roger **déjeune-t-il?**	At what time *does* Roger *have lunch?*
—**Il déjeune** à midi et demi.	*He lunches* at half past twelve.
—A quelle heure **déjeunent** vos parents?	At what time *do* your parents *have lunch?*
—**Ils déjeunent** à une heure.	*They lunch* at one o'clock.

The forms of the present indicative of **déjeuner** are:

AFFIRMATIVE	NEGATIVE	INTERROGATIVE
je déjeune	je ne déjeune pas	est-ce que je déjeune?
I have lunch	*I do not have lunch*	*Am I having lunch?*
I am having lunch	*I am not having lunch*	*Do I have lunch?*
tu déjeunes	tu ne déjeunes pas	déjeunes-tu?
il (elle) (on) déjeune	il (elle) (on) ne déjeune pas	déjeune-t-il (elle) (on)?
nous déjeunons	nous ne déjeunons pas	déjeunons-nous?
vous déjeunez	vous ne déjeunez pas	déjeunez-vous?
ils (elles) déjeunent	ils (elles) ne déjeunent pas	déjeunent-ils (elles) ?

(1) Note that the endings of the first, second, and third person singular and of the third person plural are all silent, and that the verb forms in

je déjeune, tu déjeunes, il déjeune, and **ils déjeunent** are all pronounced alike.

(2) The present indicative of regular verbs of the first conjugation consists of a stem and endings: the stem may be found* by dropping the **-er** of the infinitive; the endings are **-e, -es, -e, -ons, -ez, -ent.**

(3) The first conjugation has by far the largest number of verbs. You have already met the following verbs of this conjugation: **parler, apporter, donner, dîner, entrer, demeurer, habiter, arriver, fermer, s'appeler,** as well as **demander,** and **compter.**

I. Exercices d'application.

A. *Répétez les phrases suivantes, en substituant les formes indiquées:*

1. [Je suis] au restaurant.

 Il est/ Il n'est pas/ Êtes-vous?/ John et Roger sont/ Ils sont/ Nous sommes

2. [Il a] des parents en France.

 Elle a/ A-t-elle . . . ?/ Avez-vous . . . ?/ Nous avons/ A-t-il . . . ?/ Ont-ils . . . ?

B. *Mettez les phrases suivantes au pluriel:*

Ex.:—Je suis Américain.

 —**Nous sommes Américains.**

(*a*) **1.** Je suis étudiant. **2.** Je suis libre ce soir. **3.** Je ne suis pas libre ce soir. **4.** J'ai faim. **5.** Je n'ai pas faim. **6.** J'ai de la monnaie. **7.** Je n'ai pas de monnaie. **8.** J'ai une carte d'identité.

(*b*) **1.** Il est ingénieur-chimiste. **2.** Il n'est pas Américain. **3.** Où est-il? **4.** Il a faim. **5.** Elle a vingt et un ans. **6.** Il n'a pas de monnaie. **7.** Quel âge a-t-il? **8.** Elle est Américaine. **9.** Elle n'est pas Française.

(*c*) **1.** Je déjeune à midi. **2.** Je dîne à sept heures. **3.** Je demeure avenue de l'Observatoire. **4.** J'habite à Paris. **5.** J'arrive le 30 novembre. **6.** J'entre. **7.** Je parle un peu français. **8.** Je ne parle pas anglais.

---

*For a few verbs in which the final vowel of the stem is an **e** (e.g. acheter), it is necessary to note that this **e** is silent in forms in which the ending is pronounced (**nous achetons, vous achetez**), and that it is pronounced like the **è** in **père** in the persons whose endings are silent (**j'achète, tu achètes, il achète,** and **ils achètent**). For **acheter,** this difference in pronunciation is indicated by writing **è** instead of **e.**

In **appeler,** however, this difference in pronunciation of the final vowel of the stem is indicated by writing **ll** instead of **l** in the singular and in the third person plural: **appelle, appelles, appelle, appelons, appelez, appellent.**

(d) **I.** Il habite à Paris. **2.** Il arrive le 29 novembre. **3.** Il parle anglais. **4.** Elle entre. **5.** Elle déjeune à l'hôtel. **6.** A quelle heure arrive-t-il? **7.** Où demeure-t-elle? **8.** Parle-t-il français? **9.** Il n'habite pas à Paris. **10.** N'habite-t-il pas à Paris?

C. *Répondez affirmativement, puis négativement:*

Ex.:—Êtes-vous Américain?
— **Je suis Américain.** **Je ne suis pas Américain.**

I. Êtes-vous étudiant? **2.** Êtes-vous libre dimanche? **3.** Est-ce que le déjeuner est prêt? **4.** Le bureau de poste est-il ouvert cet après-midi? **5.** Avez-vous faim? **6.** Sommes-nous Américains? **7.** Êtes-vous étudiants? (*Réponse au pluriel.*)

II. *Répondez en français:*

I. A quelle heure dînez-vous? **2.** A quelle heure déjeunez-vous? **3.** Où demeurez-vous? **4.** Parlez-vous français? **5.** Comment vous appelez-vous? **6.** A quelle heure Roger déjeune-t-il? **7.** A quelle heure dîne-t-il? **8.** Où demeure-t-il? **9.** Parle-t-il français? **10.** A quelle heure déjeunez-vous? (*Réponse au pluriel*) **11.** A quelle heure dînez-vous? (*Rép. au pl.*) **12.** Parlez-vous français? (*Rép. au pl.*) **13.** Où demeurez-vous? (*Rép. au pl.*) **14.** Où John et Roger demeurent-ils? **15.** Où dînent-ils? **16.** Est-ce qu'ils parlent français? **17.** Le garçon apporte-t-il des hors-d'œuvre? **18.** Apporte-t-il du rosbif et des pommes de terre frites?

III. *Demandez à un autre étudiant (à une autre étudiante):*

I. s'il (si elle) est libre ce soir. **2.** s'il (si elle) est Français (Française)? **3.** s'il (si elle) est ingénieur-chimiste. **4.** où il (elle) est. **5.** quand il (elle) est libre. **6.** quelle est son adresse. **7.** quelle est sa nationalité. **8.** sa profession. **9.** la date. **10.** s'il (si elle) a faim. **11.** quel âge il (elle) a. **12.** s'il (si elle) a de la monnaie. **13.** s'il (si elle) a des frères. **14.** combien de frères il (elle) a. **15.** à quelle heure il (elle) déjeune aujourd'hui. **16.** à quelle heure il (elle) dîne d'habitude. **17.** où il (elle) demeure. **18.** à quelle heure il (elle) arrive.

IV. *Demandez à quelqu'un:*

I. si Roger a faim. **2.** si Marie a faim. **3.** si Marie et Roger ont faim. **4.** quel âge a Marie. **5.** quel âge a Roger. **6.** si John a des frères. **7.** si Marie a des sœurs. **8.** quels sont les jours de la semaine. **9.** quels sont les mois de l'année. **10.** à quelle heure dîne Roger. **11.** où demeure Marie. **12.** si Marie parle anglais. **13.** si Roger parle anglais. **14.** si Roger et Marie parlent anglais. **15.** si le garçon apporte des hors-d'œuvre. **16.** à quelle heure arrive le train.

Buying a Paper

Dans la rue

ROGER —¹Où allez-vous?

JOHN —²Je vais acheter un journal. ³Où vend-on des journaux? *

ROGER —⁴On vend des journaux au bureau de tabac.

Au bureau de tabac

JOHN —⁵Avez-vous des journaux, madame?

MME COCHET —⁶Oui, monsieur. Les voilà.†

JOHN —⁷Donnez-moi *Le Figaro*, s'il vous plaît.

MME COCHET —⁸Le voici, monsieur.

JOHN —⁹Combien est-ce?

MME. COCHET —¹⁰Vingt-cinq centimes.§

JOHN —¹¹Voilà un franc.

MME COCHET —¹² Voilà la monnaie: soixante-quinze centimes.

JOHN —¹³Avez-vous des cigarettes américaines?

On the Street

ROGER —¹Where are you going?

JOHN —²I am going to buy a paper. ³Where do they sell papers?

ROGER —⁴They sell papers at the tobacco shop.

At the tobacco shop

JOHN —⁵Have you any newspapers, madam?

MRS. COCHET —⁶Yes, sir. Here they are.

JOHN —⁷Give me *Le Figaro*, please.

MRS. COCHET —⁸Here it is, sir.

JOHN —⁹How much is it?

MRS. COCHET —¹⁰Twenty-five centimes.

JOHN —¹¹Here is one franc.

MRS. COCHET —¹²Here is the change: seventy-five centimes.

JOHN —¹³Have you any American cigarettes?

---

* Although the plural of French nouns (and adjectives) is usually found by adding an **s** to the singular, most nouns ending in **-al** have the plural ending **-aux: journal — journaux, cheval — chevaux.**

† In spoken French, **voici** and **voilà** are practically interchangeable. **Voilà** is more usual.

§ The French monetary unit is the franc. It is divided into 100 centimes. **Vingt-cinq centimes** is written 0,25 NF. **Deux francs cinquante (centimes)** is written 2,50 NF. NF means Nouveaux (New) Francs. 1 nouveau franc = 100 old francs. The change was made on Jan. 1, 1960. 1 franc is currently worth about 20 cents.

MME COCHET —[14]Je regrette, monsieur. [15]Nous n'avons pas de cigarettes américaines.

JOHN —[16]Je n'aime pas les cigarettes françaises.

MME COCHET —[17]Nous avons du tabac américain.

JOHN —[18]Combien coûte-t-il?

MME COCHET —[19]Il coûte deux francs cinquante le paquet.

JOHN —[20]Voilà un billet de cent francs. [21]Avez-vous la monnaie de cent francs?

MME COCHET —[22]Je crois que oui. La voilà. [23]Est- ce tout, monsieur?

JOHN —[24]Oui, c'est tout pour aujourd'hui.

MRS. COCHET —[14]I am sorry, sir. [15]We have no American cigarettes.

JOHN —[16] I don't like French cigarettes.

MRS. COCHET —[17]We have some American tobacco.

JOHN —[18]How much does it cost?

MRS. COCHET —[19]It costs 2 francs 50 per package.

JOHN —[20]Here's a 100 franc bill. [21]Have you change for 100 francs?

MRS. COCHET —[22]I think so. Here it is. [23]Is that all, sir?

JOHN —[24]Yes, that's all for today.

I. SUBSTITUTIONS. *Répétez les phrases suivantes en substituant les mots indiqués:*

1. Je vais acheter [un journal].
   des journaux/ des cigarettes/ un paquet de cigarettes/ du tabac/ un paquet de tabac

2. Je ne vais pas acheter [de journal] aujourd'hui.
   de journaux/ de fruits/ de tabac

3. Où vend-on [des journaux]?
   des cigarettes/ du lait/ du tabac

4. Où achète-t-on [des journaux]?
   de la crème/ du café/ du vin

5. Combien coûte [le tabac américain]?
   le journal/ le lait/ le paquet de tabac/ le paquet de cigarettes

II. *Répétez les phrases suivantes en remplaçant le nom par le pronom* **le, la** *ou* **les:**

Ex.:—Voilà *Le Figaro.*
   —**Le voilà.**

1. Voilà la carte. 2. Voilà l'addition. 3. Voilà les journaux. 4. Voilà les cigarettes. 5. Voilà votre carte d'identité. 6. Voilà les hors-d'œuvre. 7. Voilà mon adresse.

III. *Répondez en français:*

1. Où allez-vous? **2.** Où vend-on des journaux? **3.** Avez-vous des journaux?
4. Avez-vous *Le Figaro?* **5.** Combien est-ce? **6.** Avez-vous des cigarettes
américaines? **7.** Avez-vous du tabac américain? **8.** Combien coûte-t-il?
9. Avez-vous la monnaie de cent francs? **10.** Où John achète-t-il un journal?
11. Quel journal achète-t-il? **12.** Où achète-t-on des cigarettes en France?

IV. *Répondez (1) affirmativement et puis (2) négativement à chacune des
questions suivantes:*

1. Avez-vous des cigarettes américaines? **2.** Aimez-vous les cigarettes américaines? **3.** Aimez-vous le café? **4.** Avez-vous du café? **5.** Aimez-vous le
vin rouge? **6.** Avez-vous du vin rouge? **7.** Avez-vous des frères? **8.** Avez-
vous de la monnaie?

V. *Posez la question à laquelle répond chacune des phrases suivantes* (Ask
the question to which each of the following sentences is the answer):

Ex.:—C'est un franc le paquet.
    —**Combien est-ce?**

1. C'est loin d'ici. **2.** C'est un bon hôtel. **3.** C'est tout. **4.** C'est deux
francs le paquet. **5.** C'est à dix heures. **6.** Le train arrive à midi.

VI. *Demandez à un autre étudiant (à une autre étudiante):*

1. où il (elle) va. **2.** pourquoi (*why*) il va au bureau de tabac. **3.** si
l'on* vend des journaux au bureau de tabac. **4.** si l'on vend des cigarettes
au bureau de tabac. **5.** quel journal il (elle) va acheter. **6.** combien coûte
Le Figaro. **7.** s'il (si elle) a des cigarettes américaines. **8.** s'il (si elle) aime
les cigarettes américaines. **9.** s'il (si elle) a du tabac américain. **10.** s'il (si
elle) a la monnaie de cent francs. **11.** si c'est tout. **12.** où John achète le
journal. **13.** quel journal il achète. **14.** où l'on achète des cigarettes en
France.

VII. Dictée d'après le dialogue, p. 11.

VIII. Conversations:

(1)

"Do you have any pears?"
"I am sorry, sir. We have no pears. We have bananas and grapes."
"I don't like bananas. Bring me some grapes."

---

* The form **l'on** is often used instead of **on** when the word immediately preceding is **où** or **si**.

(2)

"Waiter, bring me the bill, please."
"Here it is, sir."
"How much is it?"
"Eight francs, sir."
"Have you the change for a hundred francs?"
"I think so. Here it is."

(3)

"What day of the week is today?"
"It's Tuesday."
"Is it the first Tuesday of the month?"
"No, it is the second. Today is November 8th."

Numbers

15. Cardinal numbers (one, two, three, etc.).*

1	un, une	22	vingt-deux	73	soixante-treize
2	deux	23	vingt-trois	80	quatre-vingts
3	trois	30	trente	81	quatre-vingt-un
4	quatre	31	trente et un	82	quatre-vingt-deux
5	cinq	32	trente-deux	83	quatre-vingt-trois
6	six	33	trente-trois	90	quatre-vingt-dix
7	sept	40	quarante	91	quatre-vingt-onze
8	huit	41	quarante et un	92	quatre-vingt-douze
9	neuf	42	quarante-deux	100	cent
10	dix	43	quarante-trois	101	cent un
11	onze	50	cinquante	102	cent deux
12	douze	51	cinquante et un	103	cent trois
13	treize	52	cinquante-deux	200	deux cents
14	quatorze	53	cinquante-trois	300	trois cents
15	quinze	60	soixante	1000	mille **
16	seize	61	soixante et un	1100	onze cents
17	dix-sept	62	soixante-deux	1200	douze cents
18	dix-huit	63	soixante-trois	1300	treize cents
19	dix-neuf	70	soixante-dix	1400	quatorze cents
20	vingt	71	soixante et onze	1900	dix-neuf cents
21	vingt et un	72	soixante-douze	2000	deux mille ***

2100	deux mille cent			
2110	deux mille cent dix		100.000	cent mille
20.000	vingt mille ****		1.000.000	un million

---

* For phonetic transcription of numbers, see pp. 305-306.

** From 1100 to 1900 you may also say: **mille cent, mille deux cents**, etc., though **onze cents, douze cents**, etc., are more commonly used.

*** Beginning with 2,000, you always count in thousands in French. In English you may say: *twenty-one hundred, twenty-two hundred,* etc., but in French you may say only: **deux mille cent, deux mille deux cents**, etc.

**** In French numbers, a period is used where we use a comma, and vice versa: ENGLISH: 12,000.85; FRENCH: 12.000,85.

(1)   The French count by tens from 1 to 60 but by twenties from 61 to 100. The Celts, whose language was spoken in Gaul before the Roman conquests, counted by twenties. The Romans counted by tens. The French system of numbers is a combination of the two.

(2)   **Et** is used only in the numbers 21, 31, 41, 51, 61, and 71.

(3)   Pronunciation of final consonant of numbers:
(*a*)   The final consonant of numbers is ordinarily silent when the word immediately following the number begins with a consonant. Ex.: **cinq francs; six pommes; huit lettres; dix poires; vingt francs,** etc.

(*b*)   The final consonant of numbers is pronounced when the word immediately following the number begins with a vowel or a mute **h.** Ex.: **trois ans; cinq ans; six étudiants; sept heures; huit étudiants; cent ans,** etc. Note, however, that in **cent un** (101) the **t** is not pronounced.

(*c*)   The final consonant of **cinq, six, sept, huit, neuf** and **dix** is pronounced when the numbers are used alone, in counting, or at the end of a phrase or sentence. Ex.: **Combien de frères avez-vous? —Cinq.**

16. Ordinal numbers (*first, second, third, etc.*).

—Lundi est **le premier** jour de la semaine.   Monday is *the first* day of the week.

—Quel est **le troisième** mois de l'année?   What is *the third* month of the year?

—C'est un étudiant de **deuxième** année.   He is a *second year* student.

premier, première	*first*	huitième	*eighth*
second, seconde; deuxième	*second*	neuvième	*ninth*
troisième	*third*	dixième	*tenth*
quatrième	*fourth*	onzième	*eleventh*
cinquième	*fifth*	douzième	*twelfth*
sixième	*sixth*	vingtième	*twentieth*
septième	*seventh*	vingt-et-unième	*twenty-first*

Note that the word **an** is used with cardinal numbers but that **année** is used with ordinals. Ex.: **trois ans** (*three years*)*;* **la troisième année** (*the third year*).

17. Dates.

C'est aujourd'hui le onze juin.   Today is *the eleventh of June.*

Je vais à Marseille le huit octobre.   I am going to Marseilles *on October 8th.*

Louis XIV est mort en 1715 (dix-   Louis XIV died *in 1715.*
sept cent quinze).

(1) You always use the cardinal numbers for the days of the month except for the first of the month. Ex.: le **deux** mai, le **trois** mai, etc., but **le premier mai.**

(2) In English, we say: seventeen fifteen, seventeen hundred fifteen, or seventeen hundred and fifteen. In French, 1715 can be read in only two ways: **dix-sept cent quinze** or **mille sept cent quinze.** Do not omit the word **cent.**

18. Time of day.

A. In conversation:

—Quelle heure est-il?   What time is it?

—Il est onze heures et quart.   It is quarter past eleven.

—Il est onze heures et demie.   It is half past eleven.

—Il est midi moins le quart.   It is a quarter to twelve.

—Il est midi. Il est minuit.   It is noon. It is midnight.

—Il est trois heures vingt-cinq.   It is twenty-five minutes past three.

—Il est quatre heures moins dix.   It is ten minutes to four.

(1) To express the quarter-hours, you say **et quart** *(quarter past),* **et demie** *(half past),* **moins le quart** *(quarter to).*

(2) To express minutes between the hour and the half hour following *(e.g., 4:00-4:30),* you say **quatre heures cinq** *(4:05);* **quatre heures dix** *(4:10);* **quatre heures vingt-cinq** *(4:25).*

But to express minutes between the half hour and the following hour *(e.g., 4:30-5:00)* you measure back from the next hour. Thus 4:35 is **cinq heures moins vingt-cinq;** 4:50 is **cinq heures moins dix.**

(3) To express A.M., you say **du matin;** for P.M., you say **de l'après-midi** *(in the afternoon)* or **du soir** *(in the evening).* Ex.: **Neuf heures du matin** *(9:00 A.M.);* **trois heures de l'après-midi** *(3:00 P.M.);* **onze heures du soir** *(11:00 P.M.).*

B. Official time (twenty-four hour system):

une heure trente (1 h. 30)	1:30 A.M.
treize heures trente (13 h. 30)	1:30 P.M.
six heures cinquante (6 h. 50)	6:50 A.M.
dix-huit heures cinquante (18 h. 50)	6:50 P.M.
zéro heure vingt (0 h. 20)	12:20 A.M.
douze heures vingt (12 h. 20)	12:20 P.M.

(1) The twenty-four hour system is used in all official announcements: railroads, banks, theatres, offices, army, navy, etc.

(2) In this system, fractions of an hour are always expressed in terms of minutes after the hour.

I. Exercice sur les nombres:

   1. Comptez par dix de dix à cent.

   2. Comptez par cinq de cinquante à cent.

   3. Dites en français: 21, 31, 41, 51, 61, 71, 81, 91, 101.

   4. Dites en français: 1, 11; 2, 12, 22; 3, 13, 30; 4, 14, 40, 44; 5, 15, 50, 55; 6, 16, 60, 66, 76; 7, 17, 77; 8, 18, 80, 88, 98; 9, 19, 90, 99; 20, 24, 80, 84, 40, 24.

II. Substitutions.

   A. *Répondez à chacune des questions suivantes en employant les nombres indiqués:*

   1. Quel âge a-t-il? Il a [dix ans].
   neuf ans/ huit ans/ sept ans/ six ans/ cinq ans

   2. Quel âge a-t-elle? Elle a [dix-sept ans].
   dix-huit ans/ dix-neuf ans/ vingt ans/ vingt et un ans

   3. Combien coûte ce livre? Il coûte [dix francs].
   neuf francs/ huit francs/ sept francs/ six francs/ cinq francs

   4. Quelle heure est-il? Il est [dix heures].
   neuf heures/ huit heures/ sept heures/ six heures/ cinq heures

   B. *Répétez la phrase suivante en substituant les mots indiqués:*

   [Lundi] est le [premier] jour de la semaine.
   mardi . . . deuxième/ mercredi . . . troisième/ jeudi . . . quatrième/ vendredi . . . cinquième/ samedi . . . sixième/ dimanche . . . dernier

III. *Répondez en français par une phrase complète à chacune des questions suivantes:*

1. Combien de jours y a-t-il en mars?   **2.** Combien de jours y a-t-il en févier?
3. Combien de jours y a-t-il en décembre?   **4.** Combien de jours y a-t-il dans
une année?   **5.** Quel âge avez-vous?   **6.** Quel âge a votre père? **7.** Quel
âge a votre mère?   **8.** Quel est le premier jour de la semaine?   **9.** Quel est
le troisième jour de la semaine?   **10.** Quel est le troisième mois de l'année?
11. Quel est le deuxième mois de l'année?   **12.** Êtes-vous un étudiant de
troisième année (une étudiante de troisième année)?

IV. *Lisez (Read) en français les heures suivantes d'après le système officiel
et donnez l'équivalent anglais de chaque heure indiquée:*

1. 1 h. 10, 2 h. 27, 4 h. 55.   **2.** 5 h. 33, 6 h. 05, 8 h. 31.   **3.** 9 h. 37, 10 h.
45, 12 h. 10.   **4.** 13 h. 08, 14 h. 22, 16 h. 50.   **5.** 17 h. 50, 18 h. 55, 20 h. 39.
6. 21 h. 39, 22 h. 13, 23 h. 14, 0 h. 45.

V. *Dites en français:*

1. May 10th, May 13th, May 21.   **2.** June 5, Aug. 5, July 5.   **3.** Dec. 31,
March 31, Jan. 31.   **4.** April 1, March 1, Aug. 1.   **5.** Feb. 1, Feb. 11, Feb. 21.

VI. Exercice sur les nombres:

1. *Comptez en français:* onze cents, douze cents, etc. jusqu'à dix-neuf cents.
2. *Lisez les dates suivantes en français:* (a) 1900, 1940, 1945, 1845, 1745.
(b) 1645, 1545, 1515, 1615, 1715. (c) 1815, 1915, 1940, 1950, 1960, 1962, 1972.

Taking a History Quiz

Roger's fiancée, Marie Bonnier, is checking up on John's knowledge of French history.

MARIE —[1]Connaissez-vous* l'histoire de France?

MARIE —[1]Do you know the history of France?

JOHN —[2]Certainement. Je connais Jeanne d'Arc et Napoléon.

JOHN —[2]Certainly. I know about Joan of Arc and Napoleon.

MARIE —[3]Qu'est-ce que vous savez de Jeanne d'Arc?

MARIE —[3]What do you know about Joan of Arc?

JOHN —[4]Je sais qu'elle est née à Domremy.

JOHN —[4]I know she was born in Domremy.

MARIE —[5]Savez-vous où est né Napoléon?

MARIE —[5]Do you know where Napoleon was born?

JOHN —[6]Il est né en Corse, au dix-huitième siècle.

JOHN —[6]He was born in Corsica in the 18th century.

MARIE —[7]Quelle est la date de la bataille de Waterloo?

MARIE —[7]What is the date of the battle of Waterloo?

JOHN —[8]Dix-huit cent quinze est la date de la bataille de Waterloo. [9]Napoléon est mort un peu plus tard.

JOHN —[8]1815 is the date of the battle of Waterloo. [9]Napoleon died a little later.

MARIE —[10]En quelle année Louis XIV (quatorze) est-il mort?

MARIE —[10]In what year did Louis XIV die?

JOHN —[11]Il est mort en dix-sept cent quinze.

JOHN —[11]He died in 1715.

MARIE —[12]Vous connaissez le quatorze juillet, n'est-ce pas?

MARIE —[12]You know about July 14, don't you?

---

* **Savoir** and **connaître** both mean "to know." **Savoir,** however, has a much broader use: it governs clauses introduced by **que, quand, quel, pourquoi, où, à quelle heure,** etc. When it has a noun or pronoun object, it is used to refer chiefly to dates, time, names, age, prices, etc.

Connaître always takes a noun or pronoun object and is used to refer to persons, places, books, fields of learning, works of art, etc.

JOHN —[13]Bien entendu. C'est le jour de la fête nationale en France.

MARIE —[14]Savez-vous pourquoi?

JOHN —[15]Parce que c'est le jour de la prise de la Bastille, [16]le quatorze juillet dix-sept cent quatre-vingt-neuf.

MARIE —[17]Je ne vais plus vous poser de questions. [18]Vous savez tout!

JOHN —[13]Certainly. It is the day of the French National Holiday.

MARIE —[14]Do you know why?

JOHN —[15]Because it is the day of the fall (taking) of the Bastille, [16]July 14th, 1789.

MARIE —[17]I am not going to ask you any more questions. [18]You know everything!

I. SUBSTITUTIONS. *Répétez les phrases suivantes en substituant les mots indiqués:*

1. Connaissez-vous [l'histoire de France]?
   la concierge/ l'hôtel du Cheval blanc/ le château de Chantilly/ le 14 juillet

2. Je connais [l'histoire de France].
   la concierge/ l'hôtel du Cheval blanc/ le château de Chantilly/ le 14 juillet

3. Savez-vous [où est née Jeanne d'Arc]?
   quand elle est née/ où est né Napoléon/ quand est né Napoléon/ quelle est la date de Waterloo/ la date de la prise de la Bastille

4. Je ne sais pas [la date de la prise de la Bastille].
   où est née Jeanne d'Arc/ en quelle année Louis XIV est mort/ l'adresse de John Hughes/ pourquoi il est à Paris

II. *Répondez en français, d'après le texte, aux questions suivantes:*

1. Connaissez-vous l'histoire de France? 2. Où Jeanne d'Arc est-elle née?
3. Savez-vous où elle est morte? 4. Savez-vous où est né Napoléon? 5. Quelle est la date de la bataille de Waterloo? 6. Quand Napoléon est-il mort?
7. Savez-vous quand Louis XIV est mort? 8. Connaissez-vous le 14 juillet?
9. Pourquoi est-ce la fête nationale? 10. Quelle est la date de la prise de la Bastille?

III. *Demandez à quelqu'un:*

1. s'il connaît l'histoire de France. 2. s'il connaît Jeanne d'Arc. 3. s'il sait où Jeanne d'Arc est morte. 4. s'il sait quand Napoléon est mort. 5. la date de la prise de la Bastille. 6. la date de la bataille de Waterloo.

IV. *Répondez en français à chacune des questions suivantes:*

1. En quelle année êtes-vous né (née)? **2.** Quelle est la date aujourd'hui?
3. Quel jour de la semaine est-ce aujourd'hui? **4.** Quel âge a votre père?
5. En quelle année est-il né? **6.** En quel mois êtes-vous né (née)? **7.** Quelle
est la date de votre anniversaire (*birthday*)?

V. *Dites en français:*

1. On (**le**) May 9th. On July 15th. On August 12. On December 20.
2. In (**en**) 1890. In 1850. In 1790. In 1789. In 1689.
3. In (**au**) the 20th century. In the 19th century. In the 18th century. In the
17th century.

VI. *Lisez les dates suivantes:*

1. Le 30 septembre 1965. **2.** Le 1er juin 1945. **3.** Le 27 avril 1889. **4.** Le
1er janvier 1837. **5.** Le 31 août 1698. **6.** Le 17 mars 1950. **7.** Le 29 juillet
1930. **8.** Le 12 octobre 1492.

VII. Dictée d'après le dialogue, p. 21.

VIII. Conversations.

(1)
"Do you know when George Washington was born?"
"Yes, he was born in 1732."
"Where was he born?"
"He was born in (at) Fredericksburg."
"When did he die?"
"He died in 1799."

(2)
"Do you know (the significance of) the 4th of July?"
"Yes, certainly. It is the day of the American National Holiday."
"Do you know why?"
"It is Independence Day (**le jour de la Déclaration de l'Indépendance
américaine**)."
"What is the date of the Declaration of Independence?"
"July 4, 1776."

A Friend Is Getting Married

ROGER —¹Connaissez-vous Louise Bedel?

JOHN —²Non, je ne la connais pas.

ROGER —³Mais si.* Vous avez fait sa connaissance chez Marie samedi dernier.

JOHN —⁴Est-ce† une petite jeune fille brune?

ROGER —⁵Mais non. C'est† une grande jeune fille blonde.

JOHN —⁶De quelle couleur sont ses yeux?

ROGER —⁷Elle a les yeux bleus, comme toutes les blondes.

JOHN —⁸Oh! vous parlez de la jeune fille habillée en bleu? ⁹Elle a les cheveux blonds, les joues roses et les lèvres rouges, n'est-ce pas?

ROGER —¹⁰Oui, c'est ça.

JOHN —¹¹Eh bien?

ROGER —¹²Elle va se marier jeudi prochain.

JOHN —¹³Avec qui?

ROGER —¹⁴Avec Charles Dupont.

JOHN —¹⁵Je connais très bien Charles.

ROGER —¹⁶Qu'est-ce qu'il fait?

JOHN —¹⁷Il est ingénieur.††

ROGER —¹Do you know Louise Bedel?

JOHN —²No, I don't know her.

ROGER —³Yes, you do. You met her (made her acquaintance) at Marie's last Saturday.

JOHN —⁴Is she a small brunette girl?

ROGER —⁵Oh, no. She's a tall blonde.

JOHN —⁶What color are her eyes?

ROGER —⁷She has blue eyes, like all blondes.

JOHN —⁸Oh! You are speaking of the girl dressed in blue? ⁹She has blond hair, rosy cheeks, and red lips, hasn't she?

ROGER —¹⁰Yes, that's right.

JOHN —¹¹Well?

ROGER —¹²She is going to be married next Thursday.

JOHN —¹³To whom?

ROGER —¹⁴To Charles Dupont.

JOHN —¹⁵I know Charles very well.

ROGER —¹⁶What does he do?

JOHN —¹⁷He is an engineer.

---

* **Si** meaning *yes* is used only to contradict a negative statement.

† Observe that *He is* or *She is* is expressed in French by **C'est** when **est** is directly followed by the articles **le, la, un,** or **une.**

†† Note that *He is, She is* is usually expressed in French by **Il est, Elle est** when **est** is directly followed by an adjective standing alone or by an unmodified noun.

ROGER —[18]Que pensez-vous de Charles?	ROGER —[18]What do you think of Charles?
JOHN —[19]Je pense qu'il a de la chance. [20] Sa fiancée est jolie et elle est très gentille.	JOHN —[19]I think he is lucky. [20]His fiancée is pretty and she is very nice.

I. SUBSTITUTIONS. *Répétez les phrases suivantes en substituant les mots indiqués:*

1. Vous avez fait sa connaissance [chez Marie] samedi dernier.
chez ma sœur/ chez Roger/ au laboratoire/ à Paris

2. C'est une [petite] jeune fille brune.
grande/ gentille/ jolie

3. Elle a [les yeux bleus].
les yeux noirs/ les yeux rouges (she's been crying) / les cheveux blonds/ les cheveux noirs/ les cheveux blancs/ les lèvres rouges/ les joues roses

4. Elle va se marier [jeudi prochain].
la semaine prochaine/ le mois prochain/ au mois d'août/ au mois de juin / le 16 avril/ le 15 mars/ le 29 février

5. Il est [ingénieur].
agent de police/ hôtelier/ Américain/ Français/ chimiste/ étudiant

6. C'est [un ingénieur].
un agent de police/ un hôtelier/ un Américain/ un Français/ un chimiste/ un étudiant

7. C'est [un jeune ingénieur].
un jeune Américain/ une jeune Américaine/ un jeune Français/ une jeune Française/ un jeune étudiant/ une jeune étudiante

8. Elle est habillée [en bleu].
en rouge/ en blanc/ en noir/ en rose

II. *Répondez en français à chacune des questions suivantes, d'après le texte:*

1. Connaissez-vous Louise Bedel? **2.** Où avez-vous fait sa connaissance? **3.** Quand avez-vous fait sa connaissance? **4.** Est-ce une grande jeune fille blonde? **5.** A-t-elle les yeux bleus? **6.** A-t-elle les joues roses? **7.** A-t-elle les lèvres rouges? **8.** Quand va-t-elle se marier? **9.** Avec qui va-t-elle se marier? **10.** Connaissez-vous Charles Dupont? **11.** Qu'est-ce qu'il fait? **12.** Que pensez-vous de Charles? **13.** Est-ce que sa fiancée est jolie? **14.** Est-elle gentille?

III. *Répondez en français à ces questions personnelles:*

1. Avez-vous les cheveux blonds? 2. Avez-vous les yeux bleus? 3. De quelle couleur sont vos yeux? 4. Comment êtes-vous habillé(e)? 5. Est-ce que votre voisine (neighbor) a les cheveux blonds? 6. A-t-elle les yeux bleus?

IV. *Dites en français:*

A. c'est un, c'est une

1. She's a tall blonde. 2. She's a small blonde. 3. It's a good hotel. 4. It's a good restaurant. 5. It's a good lunch. 6. She's a small brunette. 7. It's a good newspaper. 8. It's a good apple. 9. It's a good pear.

B. il est, elle est

1. He's an engineer. 2. He is a hotelkeeper. 3. He is a policeman. 4. He is tall. 5. She is tall. 6. She is nice. 7. She is a concierge. 8. She is beautiful. 9. He is French. 10. She is French. 11. She is an American. 12. He is an American. 13. She is blonde. 14. She is a brunette. 15. She is very nice.

C. c'est un, c'est une, il est, elle est

1. She is a small brunette. 2. She is very nice. 3. He is an engineer. 4. He is a good engineer. 5. It is a good paper. 6. She is young. 7. He is young. 8. He's a student. 9. He's a young student. 10. He's a good student. 11. She is an American. 12. She's a young American.

V. Dictée d'après le dialogue, p. 24.

VI. Conversations.

(1)

"Do you know Louise Bedel?"
"Yes, why?"
"She is going to get married next Wednesday."
"To whom?"
"To Charles Dupont."
"He is lucky."

(2)

"Do you know when Napoleon was born?"
"No, but I know the date of the battle of Waterloo."
"Well?"
"1815."

Deuxième Lecture Illustrée, p. 9, *La cuisine française.*

Word Order in Asking Questions

19. Questions by inversion and with **Est-ce que?**

A. When the subject of the verb is a personal pronoun:

—**Êtes-vous** libre dimanche?
—**Est-ce que vous êtes** libre dimanche? } *Are you* free Sunday?

—**Connaissez-vous** Louise Bedel?
—**Est-ce que vous connaissez** Louise Bedel? } *Do you know* Louise Bedel?

When the subject of the verb is a personal pronoun, you ask a question *either* by inverting the order of subject and verb *or* by using the expression **est-ce que** and normal order of subject and verb. Both patterns are commonly used in French.

If you use an interrogative word or expression such as **où?** *(where)*, **quand?** *(when)*, **combien?** *(how much)*, **à quelle heure?** *(at what time)*, etc., the interrogative word comes first and is followed *either* by inverted order of subject and verb *or* by the expression **est-ce que?** and normal order. Ex.:

—**Où allez-vous?**
—**Où est-ce que vous allez?** } Where *are you going?*

—A quelle heure **voulez-vous** déjeuner?
—A quelle heure **est-ce que vous voulez** déjeuner? } At what time *do you want* to have lunch?

B. When the subject of the verb is a noun:

—Le déjeuner **est-il** prêt?
—**Est-ce que** le déjeuner **est** prêt? } *Is* lunch ready?

—Le train **arrive-t-il** à cinq heures?
—**Est-ce que** le train **arrive** à cinq heures? } *Does* the train *arrive* at five o'clock?

56

When the subject of the verb is a noun, you *either* express the noun-subject, the corresponding pronoun-subject and the verb in the following order: noun-subject, verb, pronoun-subject, *or* use **est-ce que?** and normal word order.

If you use an interrogative word or expression, such as **où?, quand, combien?, à quelle heure?,** the interrogative word or expression comes first and is followed by either of the patterns described above. Ex.:

—**Où** vos parents **demeurent-ils?** } *Where do* your parents *live?*
—**Où est-ce que** vos parents **demeurent?**

—**A quelle heure** le train **arrive-t-il?** } *At what time does* the train
—**A quelle heure est-ce que** le train **arrive?** *arrive?*

Note also that in questions introduced by an interrogative word or expression, it is very common to ask a question simply by inverting the order of the noun-subject and the verb, *if the noun subject would be final in the question.* Ex.:

—**Où demeurent vos parents?**   Where *do your parents live?*
—**A quelle heure arrive l'avion?**   At what time *does the plane arrive?*

If the noun subject would not be final, only the two patterns described above are possible. Ex.:

—**Où votre père achète-t-il** son journal?   —**Quand votre père va-t-il** en France?

—**Où est-ce que votre père achète** son journal?   —**Quand est-ce que votre père va** en France?

20. Questions with **n'est-ce pas?**

—**Vous connaissez Louise Bedel, n'est-ce pas?**   You know Louise Bedel, *don't you?*

—Oui, je la connais.   Yes, I know her.

—**Vous ne connaissez pas sa sœur, n'est-ce pas?**   You don't know her sister, *do you?*

—Non, je ne la connais pas.   No. I don't know her.

You often ask a question by simply adding **n'est-ce pas?** to a declarative statement—especially if you expect an answer which agrees with what you have said. **N'est-ce pas?** corresponds to a number of expressions in English, such as: *don't you think so?, don't I?, don't you?, will you not?, wouldn't you?, didn't you?,* etc.

21. Negative questions.

—**N'avez-vous pas** faim?
—**Est-ce que vous n'avez pas** faim? } *Aren't you* hungry?

—**Ne voulez-vous pas** de café?
—**Est-ce que vous ne voulez pas** de café? } *Don't you want* any coffee?

You ask a negative question by putting **ne** before the inverted form and **pas** after it. Ex.: Avez-vous? —N'avez-vous **pas?** A-t-il? —N'a-t-il **pas?**

I. *Mettez chacune des phrases suivantes à la forme interrogative, par inversion, puis en employant* **est-ce que?**

Ex.:—Vous êtes étudiant.
  —**Êtes-vous étudiant?**
  —**Est-ce que vous êtes étudiant?**

1. Vous êtes en France. 2. Vous allez à la gare. 3. Ils sont à Paris. 4. Elles sont à Paris. 5. Elles ont des frères. 6. Il y a un restaurant près d'ici. 7. C'est une grande jeune fille blonde. 8. Elle va se marier. 9. Elle va au théâtre. 10. Le bureau de poste est sur la place. 11. Le théâtre est près d'ici. 12. Votre père dîne à sept heures. 13. Vos parents demeurent à Paris. 14. John achète des cigarettes au bureau de tabac.

II. *Demandez en français, en employant la forme interrogative par inversion:*

1. si l'hôtel Continental est sur la place. 2. si c'est loin d'ici. 3. si c'est un bon hôtel. 4. si c'est un grand hôtel. 5. s'il y a un autre hôtel près de la gare. 6. s'il y a d'autres hôtels sur la place. 7. si John est à Paris. 8. quelle est son adresse. 9. si son père est ici. 10. si John et Roger sont au laboratoire. 11. à quelle heure arrive le train pour Paris. 12. si Jeanne d'Arc est née au quinzième siècle. 13. où Napoléon est mort. 14. quand Louise Bedel va se marier. 15. en quelle année François Premier est mort.

III. *Posez en français la question à laquelle répond chacune des phrases suivantes en commençant par* **où?, quand?, combien?, quel?, comment?,** *etc.* (Ask in French the question to which each of the following sentences is the answer.)

Ex.:—Je demeure à Paris.
  —**Où demeurez-vous?**

1. Mes parents demeurent à Paris. 2. Napoléon est mort en 1821. 3. Les cigarettes coûtent deux francs le paquet. 4. Il est trois heures. 5. Le train arrive à six heures. 6. C'est aujourd'hui jeudi. 7. Mercredi est le troisième jour de la semaine. 8. Je vais très bien.

IV. *Mettez les questions suivantes à la forme négative.*

Ex.:—Voulez-vous du vin?
   —Ne voulez-vous pas de vin?

1. Voulez-vous du café? **2.** Voulez-vous des hors-d'œuvre? **3.** Avez-vous des cigarettes américaines? **4.** Aimez-vous les cigarettes françaises? **5.** Y a-t-il un hôtel dans la rue de la Paix? **6.** Y a-t-il des hôtels sur la place? **7.** Y a-t-il de bons restaurants près du château? **8.** Demeurez-vous à Paris? **9.** Roger demeure-t-il à Paris? **10.** Savez-vous quand Jeanne d'Arc est morte? **11.** Savez-vous quel jour nous sommes aujourd'hui? **12.** Savez-vous à quelle heure on dîne à Paris?

V. RÉVISION. *Dites en français:*

(*a*) **1.** What color are her eyes? **2.** What color is her hair? **3.** What time is it? **4.** What time does the train leave? **5.** What does he do? **6.** What is the price of *Le Figaro?* **7.** What do cigarettes cost? **8.** What's the weather like? **9.** What's the date? **10.** What's today? **11.** What year were you born (In what . . .)? **12.** How old is she?

(*b*) **1.** He is lucky. **2.** He is out of luck. **3.** You are lucky. **4.** You are out of luck. **5.** I am sorry. **6.** Agreed. **7.** A little later. **8.** An hour later. **9.** Two years later. **10.** Gladly. **11.** I think so (**Je crois que oui**). **12.** Where do they sell papers?

Taking a Walk

ROGER —[1]Voulez-vous faire* une promenade?

MARIE —[2]Je veux bien. Quel temps fait-il?

ROGER —[3]Il fait beau. [4]Mais il fait du vent.

MARIE —[5]Est-ce qu'il fait froid?

ROGER —[6]Non, pas du tout. [7]Il ne fait ni trop chaud ni trop froid. [8]C'est un beau temps pour une promenade.

MARIE —[9]Faut-il prendre un imperméable?

ROGER —[10]Ce n'est pas la peine. [11]Il ne va pas pleuvoir.

MARIE —[12]Êtes-vous sûr qu'il ne va pas pleuvoir?

ROGER —[13]Oui. Le ciel est bleu et il fait du soleil.

MARIE —[14]Je vous crois. [15]J'ai confiance en vous.

(Une heure plus tard)

MARIE —[16]Il pleut; il pleut à verse. [17]Je suis mouillée jusqu'aux os. [18]C'est votre faute.

ROGER —[19]Ma faute? Comment cela?

MARIE —[20]Vous savez bien. Je n'ai plus confiance en vous.

ROGER —[1]Do you want to take a walk?

MARIE —[2]Yes (I am quite willing). How is the weather?

ROGER —[3]The weather is fine. [4]But it is windy.

MARIE —[5]Is it cold?

ROGER —[6]No, not at all. [7]It is neither too hot nor too cold. [8]It is fine weather for a walk.

MARIE —[9]Must one (Is it necessary to) take a raincoat?

ROGER —[10]It is not worth the trouble. [11]It is not going to rain.

MARIE —[12]Are you sure it is not going to rain?

ROGER —[13]Yes. The sky is blue and the sun is shining.

MARIE —[14]I believe you. [15]I have confidence in you.

(One hour later)

MARIE —[16]It is raining; it is pouring. [17]I am wet to the skin (right to the bones). [18]It is your fault.

ROGER —[19]My fault? How (can you say) that?

MARIE —[20]You know (very well). I no longer have confidence in you.

---

* **Faire** (to do, to make) is used in a number of idiomatic expressions, such as **faire une promenade** (to take a walk) and in impersonal expressions describing the weather.

60

I. Substitutions. *Répétez les phrases suivantes en substituant les mots indiqués:*

   1. Il fait [beau].
     froid/ chaud/ du vent/ du soleil/ très beau/ très froid/ très chaud/ trop froid/
     trop chaud/ trop de vent

   2. Il ne fait [pas froid].
     pas très froid/ pas trop froid/ pas chaud/ pas très chaud/ pas trop chaud/ pas de vent/
     pas beaucoup de vent/ pas trop de vent

II. *Répondez en français, d'après le texte, à chacune des questions suivantes:*

   1. Voulez-vous faire une promenade? **2.** Quel temps fait-il? **3.** Est-ce qu'il fait froid? **4.** Fait-il chaud? **5.** Est-ce un beau temps pour une promenade? **6.** Faut-il prendre un imperméable? **7.** Est-ce la peine de prendre un imperméable? **8.** Ne va-t-il pas pleuvoir? **9.** De quelle couleur est le ciel? **10.** Fait-il du soleil? **11.** Êtes-vous sûr qu'il ne va pas pleuvoir? **12.** Avez-vous confiance en moi? **13.** [*Une heure plus tard*] Est-ce qu'il pleut maintenant (*now*)? **14.** Êtes-vous mouillé(e)? **15.** Est-ce ma faute?

III. *Répondez en français à chacune des questions suivantes:*

   1. Quel temps fait-il aujourd'hui? **2.** Est-ce qu'il fait du vent? **3.** Fait-il du soleil? **4.** Est-ce qu'il va pleuvoir? **5.** Quel temps fait-il au mois de juillet? **6.** Quel temps fait-il au mois de décembre? **7.** Fait-il du vent au mois de mars? **8.** Fait-il très froid ici au mois de janvier?

IV. *Demandez à quelqu'un:*

   1. s'il veut faire une promenade. **2.** quel temps il fait. **3.** s'il fait froid. **4.** s'il fait trop froid. **5.** s'il fait trop chaud. **6.** s'il fait du soleil. **7.** si c'est un beau temps pour une promenade. **8.** s'il faut prendre un imperméable. **9.** si c'est la peine de prendre un imperméable. **10.** s'il est sûr qu'il ne va pas pleuvoir.

V. *Mettez les phrases suivantes à la forme négative en employant* **ne . . . pas,** *puis* **ne . . . plus.**

   Ex.:—J'ai confiance en vous.
     —**Je n'ai pas confiance en vous.**
     —**Je n'ai plus confiance en vous.**

   1. J'ai faim. **2.** Nous avons des cigarettes. **3.** Il pleut. **4.** Il fait du vent. **5.** Il fait froid. **6.** Elle est étudiante. **7.** Elle a de la monnaie. **8.** C'est un bon hôtel. **9.** Il y a un restaurant dans le musée. **10.** Je déjeune au restaurant. **11.** Je sais où Jeanne d'Arc est née. **12.** Je vais vous poser des questions.

VI. *Combinez deux phrases en une seule, en employant* **ne . . . ni . . . ni.**

Ex.:—Il ne fait pas chaud. Il ne fait pas froid.
   —**Il ne fait ni chaud ni froid.**

1. Il ne fait pas trop chaud. Il ne fait pas trop froid. **2.** Elle n'est pas petite. Elle n'est pas grande. **3.** Elle n'est pas brune. Elle n'est pas blonde. **4.** Je ne parle pas français. Je ne parle pas anglais. **5.** Je n'ai pas de tabac.* Je n'ai pas de cigarettes. **6.** Nous n'avons pas de vin rouge. Nous n'avons pas de vin blanc. **7.** Nous n'avons pas de pommes. Nous n'avons pas de bananes. **8.** Il n'y a pas d'hôtel ici. Il n'y a pas de restaurant ici.

VII. Dictée d'après le dialogue, p. 33.

VIII. Conversations.

(1)

"Do you want to take a walk this afternoon?"
"Yes, I am willing, if it is not raining."
"At what time?"
"At half-past four."
"All right. See you this afternoon."

(2)

"Do you want to go to the movies (**au cinéma**)?"
"Yes, I am willing. Must one take a raincoat?"
"No. It isn't worthwhile. It isn't going to rain."

---

* With **ne . . . ni . . . ni,** nouns are used without a definite article and without the preposition de. Ex.: **Elle n'a ni frères ni sœurs.**

Which Season Do You Prefer?

ROGER —[1]Regardez la neige!

JOHN —[2]Tiens! C'est la première fois qu'il neige* cette année.

ROGER —[3]Je n'aime pas du tout l'hiver. [4]On ne peut même pas sortir.

JOHN —[5]Mais si. [6]En hiver on peut sortir. [7]Et puis, on peut patiner, faire du ski, aller au théâtre, au bal, etc.

ROGER —[8]Oui, mais l'hiver dure trop longtemps.

JOHN —[9]Quelle saison préférez-vous, alors?

ROGER —[10]Je crois que je préfère l'été. [11]J'aime voir des feuilles sur les arbres, [12]et des fleurs dans les jardins.

JOHN —[13]Mais la campagne est aussi belle en automne qu'en été, [14]et il fait moins chaud.

ROGER —[15]Oui. L'automne commence bien, [16]mais il finit mal. [17]J'aime mieux le printemps.

JOHN —[18]Vous avez raison. [19]Tout le monde est content de voir venir le printemps.

ROGER —[1]Look at the snow!

JOHN —[2]Well! It is the first time it has snowed this year.

ROGER —[3]I don't like winter at all. [4]You can't even go out.

JOHN —[5]Yes, you can. [6]You can go out in winter. [7]And besides, you can skate, ski, go to the theatre, to dances, etc.

ROGER —[8]Yes, but winter lasts too long.

JOHN —[9]What season do you prefer, then?

ROGER —[10]I think I prefer summer. [11]I like to see leaves on the trees, [12]and flowers in the gardens.

JOHN —[13]But the country is as beautiful in the fall as in the summer, [14]and it is not so hot.

ROGER —[15]Yes. The fall begins well, [16]but it ends badly. [17]I like the spring better.

JOHN —[18]You are right. [19]Everyone is glad to see the spring come.

---

* Note that in French, the present tense is used in this phrase although in English we normally use the present perfect to express the same idea.

I. SUBSTITUTIONS. *Répétez les phrases suivantes en substituant les mots indiqués:*

  1. Je n'aime pas du tout [l'hiver].
  la neige/ les bananes/ le vent/ le mois de février

  2. Je n'aime pas du tout [faire du ski].
  sortir en hiver/ patiner/ aller au théâtre/ aller à la campagne

  3. J'aime voir venir [le printemps].
  l'été/ l'automne/ l'hiver/ le beau temps

  4. On peut aller au théâtre [en hiver].
  au printemps/ en été/ en automne/ au mois de janvier

  5. Il pleut beaucoup [en hiver].
  au printemps/ en été/ en automne/ au mois d'avril

  6. [La campagne est aussi belle] en automne qu'en été.
  Les fleurs sont aussi belles/ Les feuilles sont aussi belles/ Les arbres sont aussi beaux/ Les jardins sont aussi beaux/ Le ciel est aussi beau/ Il fait aussi beau

II. *Répondez en français à chacune des questions suivantes:*

  1. Quel temps fait-il? **2.** Est-ce la première fois qu'il neige cette année? **3.** Est-ce que Roger aime l'hiver? **4.** Pourquoi n'aime-t-il pas l'hiver? **5.** Est-ce qu'on peut sortir en hiver? **6.** Qu'est-ce qu'on peut faire en hiver? **7.** Est-ce que l'hiver dure longtemps ici? **8.** Quelle saison préférez-vous? **9.** Pourquoi Roger préfère-t-il l'été? **10.** En quelle saison y a-t-il des fleurs dans les jardins? **11.** En quelle saison y a-t-il des feuilles sur les arbres? **12.** Y a-t-il des feuilles sur les arbres en hiver? **13.** Aimez-vous la campagne en automne? **14.** Est-ce que la campagne est belle en automne? **15.** Est-ce que la campagne est aussi belle en automne qu'en été? **16.** Est-ce qu'il fait moins chaud en automne qu'en été? **17.** Est-ce que l'automne commence bien? **18.** Est-ce que l'automne finit bien?

III. *Demandez à quelqu'un:*

  1. quel temps il fait. **2.** s'il pleut. **3.** s'il neige. **4.** si c'est la première fois qu'il neige cette année. **5.** si Roger aime l'hiver. **6.** si on peut sortir en hiver. **7.** ce qu'on peut faire en hiver (*what one can do in winter*). **8.** si l'hiver dure trop longtemps ici. **9.** quelle saison il préfère. **10.** pourquoi Roger préfère l'été. **11.** si la campagne est belle en automne. **12.** s'il fait moins chaud en automne qu'en été. **13.** si tout le monde est content de voir venir le printemps. **14.** quand commence le printemps. **15.** quand finit le printemps.

IV. DICTÉE D'APRÈS LES DIALOGUES, pp. 41-42, pp. 50-51.

V. CONVERSATION.

"I don't like winter at all."

"Why not (**Pourquoi pas**)?"

"Because it is too cold. And besides, winter lasts too long. I like spring better."

"You are right. I prefer spring too. It begins badly, but it ends well."

Interrogative, Demonstrative and Possessive Adjectives

22. Interrogative adjectives.

—**Quel** âge avez-vous?	How old are (*what* age have) you?
—**Quelle** heure est-il?	*What* time is it?
—**Quelle** est votre adresse?	*What* is your address?
—A **quelle** heure arrive le train?	At *what* time does the train come?
—**Quels** sont les mois de l'année?	*What* are the months of the year?

A. Forms.

The forms of the interrogative adjective are:

	SINGULAR	PLURAL
MASCULINE:	quel?	quels?
FEMININE:	quelle?	quelles?

B. Agreement.

Like all adjectives, they agree in gender and number with the noun which they modify.

C. Use.

Do not confuse **Quel? Quelle?** etc., with **Que? Qu'est-ce que?**. As **quel? quelle?** etc., are forms of the interrogative *adjective,* they are used only to modify nouns. The noun modified may stand next to the adjective (**Quel âge . . . ? Quelle heure . . . ?**) or it may be separated from it by a form of the verb **être** (**Quelle est votre adresse?**). But **Que?** (**Qu'est-ce que?**) is a pronoun and can not of course modify a noun. Ex.: **Que** pensez-vous de Charles? or **Qu'est-ce que** vous pensez de Charles?

66

23. Demonstrative adjectives.

—Quel temps fait-il **ce** matin?   How is the weather *this* morning?
—Êtes-vous libre **cet** après-midi?   Are you free *this* afternoon?
—C'est la première fois qu'il neige   It is the first time it has snowed *this*
   cette année.   year.
—Je n'aime pas **ces** cigarettes.   I don't like *these* cigarettes.

A. Forms.

The forms of the demonstrative adjective are:

	SINGULAR	PLURAL
MASCULINE:	ce, (cet)	ces
FEMININE:	cette	ces

B. Use.

Ce is used before masculine singular nouns beginning with a consonant.
Cet is used before those beginning with a vowel or mute *h*. Ex.: **Ce**
matin. **Ce** soir. BUT: **Cet** après-midi. **Cet** hôtel.

The suffix **-là** is often added to the noun following a demonstrative
adjective—especially with expressions of time. The difference between
ce matin and **ce matin-là** is *this* morning and *that* morning. Compare:
cet été and **cet été-là**, **cette année** and **cette anné-là**.

The suffix **-ci** is seldom used except in contrast to demonstrative
pronouns (§ 80).

24. Possessive adjectives.

—Où habitent **vos** parents?   Where do *your* parents live?
—**Mes** parents habitent à Paris.   *My* parents live in Paris.
—Voulez-vous **mon** imperméable?   Do you want *my* raincoat?

A. Forms.

The forms of the possessive adjectives are:

SINGULAR		PLURAL	
MASCULINE	FEMININE	MASCULINE AND FEMININE	
mon	ma (mon)	mes	*my*
ton	ta (ton)	tes	*your*
son	sa (son)	ses	*his, her, its*
notre	notre	nos	*our*
votre	votre	vos	*your*
leur	leur	leurs	*their*

B. Agreement and use.

Possessive adjectives agree in gender and number with the noun they modify. Ex.:

—Roger parle de **son** père et de **sa** mère.

Roger speaks of *his* father and mother.

—Marie parle de **son** père et de **sa** mère.

Mary speaks of *her* father and mother.

Note especially the difference between the possessive adjective of the third person singular (**son, sa, ses**) and that of the third person plural (**leur, leurs**):

(1) In referring to one person, you would use the third person singular forms:

—Où demeure **son** père? Where does *his* (*her*) father live?
—Où demeure **sa** mère? Where does *his* (*her*) mother live?
—Où demeurent **ses** parents? Where do *his* (*her*) parents live?

(2) In referring to two or more persons, you would use the third person plural forms:

—Où demeure **leur** père? Where does *their* father live?
—Où demeure **leur** mère? Where does *their* mother live?
—Où demeurent **leurs** parents? Where do *their* parents live?

(3) The forms **ma, ta, sa,** are used before feminine singular nouns beginning with a consonant, the **mon, ton, son** forms before those beginning with a vowel or mute **h.**

ma sœur, **ma** petite sœur BUT: **mon** autre sœur
ma petite auto BUT: **mon** auto
ma nouvelle adresse BUT: **mon** adresse

I. *Demandez en français à quelqu'un:*

1. quelle heure il est. **2.** quel temps il fait. **3.** quel âge il a. **4.** quel jour nous sommes. **5.** quelle saison il préfère. **6.** à quelle heure il va déjeuner. **7.** à quelle heure le train arrive. **8.** à quelle gare le train arrive. **9.** à quel restaurant il déjeune d'habitude. **10.** en quelle saison il y a des fleurs dans les jardins. **11.** en quel mois nous sommes. **12.** en quelle année il est né. **13.** quelle est son adresse. **14.** sa nationalité. **15.** sa profession. **16.** la date de son anniversaire. **17.** quels sont les jours de la semaine. **18.** quels sont les mois de l'année. **19.** quel est le premier jour de la semaine. **20.** quel est le dernier mois de l'année.

II. EXERCICES D'APPLICATION.

A. *Répétez chacun des mots suivants, en employant un adjectif démon-stratif:*

(a) Ex.:—le matin,
   —**ce matin.**

I. le soir, le journal, les journaux, le château, le cheval, les chevaux, le jardin. **2.** l'été, l'hôtel, les hôtels, l'hôpital, les hôpitaux, l'arbre, les arbres, l'après-midi, l'hiver, l'automne. **3.** la fleur, les fleurs, l'année, la rue, la jeune fille, les jeunes filles, l'adresse, la cigarette, les cigarettes, la semaine.

(b) Ex.:—ce matin (this morning)
   —**ce matin-là** (that morning)

I. ce soir. **2.** cet après-midi. **3.** cette nuit. **4.** cette semaine. **5.** cette année. **6.** cet hiver. **7.** cet été. **8.** Aujourd'hui (ce jour-là).

B. *Répétez les phrases suivantes, en employant l'adjectif possessif:*

Ex.:—le frère de Marie,
   —**son frère;**
   —le frère de John,
   —**son frère.**

I. le père de Marie. **2.** le père de Roger. **3.** la mère de Roger. **4.** la mère de Marie. **5.** la sœur de John. **6.** la sœur de Marie. **7.** l'adresse de Marie. **8.** l'adresse de Roger. **9.** les parents de John. **10.** les parents de Marie. **11.** la fiancée de Charles. **12.** les yeux de Louise. **13.** les yeux de Charles. **14.** les cheveux de Louise. **15.** les parents de Roger et de Marie. **16.** les cousines de Roger et de Marie. **17.** la nationalité de Roger et de Marie. **18.** la profession de John et de Roger. **19.** les promenades de Roger et de Marie. **20.** les heures de laboratoire de John et de Roger.

C. *Dites au pluriel:*

Ex.:—votre frère,
   —**vos frères.**

I. mon cousin, ma cousine, mon journal, ma cigarette. **2.** votre cousin, votre cousine, votre journal, votre cigarette. **3.** notre cousin, notre cousine, notre journal, notre cigarette.

III. *Répondez en français à chacune des questions suivantes, en employant l'adjectif possessif convenable:*

I. Où demeurent vos parents? **2.** Où habitent les parents de John? **3.** Où habite le père de John? **4.** Est-ce que la mère de John est morte? **5.** Est-ce que les frères de John sont en Amérique? **6.** Est-ce que ses sœurs sont aussi en Amérique?   **7.** Comment s'appelle la fiancée de Charles Dupont?   **8.** Connaissez-vous l'emploi du temps de John?   **9.** Savez-vous l'adresse de Charles Dupont?   **10.** Savez-vous l'adresse de Louise Bedel?

IV. *En commençant votre question par "**Qu'est-ce que**", demandez en français à quelqu'un:*

Ex.:—ce qu'il a comme dessert.
   —**Qu'est-ce que vous avez comme dessert?**

1. ce qu'il veut comme dessert.   **2.** ce qu'il veut comme plat de viande.
3. ce qu'il veut comme vin.   **4.** ce qu'il a comme hors-d'œuvre.   **5.** ce qu'il a comme fruits.   **6.** ce qu'il pense de Charles.   **7.** ce qu'il pense de Marie.
8. ce qu'il sait de Jeanne d'Arc.   **9.** ce qu'il sait du 14 juillet.   **10.** ce qu'on peut faire en hiver.   **11.** ce qu'on peut faire au printemps.   **12.** ce qu'on peut faire quand il neige.

V. *Dites en français à quelqu'un:*

Ex.:—de vous donner son adresse.
   —**Donnez-moi votre adresse.**

1. de vous donner son imperméable.   **2.** d'apporter son imperméable.   **3.** de vous donner son emploi du temps.   **4.** de vous donner son adresse.   **5.** de vous donner l'adresse de ses parents.   **6.** de vous donner ses cigarettes.

VI. *Dites en français:*

1. You are right.   **2.** He is lucky.   **3.** As usual.   **4.** Not yet.   **5.** Not at all.
6. When is your cousin going to be married?   **7.** Winter lasts too long.   **8.** Have you (the) change for one hundred francs?   **9.** American tobacco costs 2 francs 50 per package.   **10.** What color are her eyes?   **11.** In the nineteenth century.   **12.** In 1793.   **13.** In the month of December.   **14.** In the month of August.   **15.** What is the date of the French national holiday?   **16.** Do you want some coffee?   **17.** Don't you want some coffee?   **18.** It is the first time it has snowed this year.   **19.** The last time.

Errands

JOHN —[1]J'ai des courses à faire. [2]Je veux d'abord acheter du pain. [3]On vend du pain à l'épicerie, n'est-ce pas?

MARIE —[4]Non. Il faut aller à la boulangerie.

JOHN —[5]Ensuite, je veux acheter de la viande.

MARIE —[6]Quelle espèce de viande?

JOHN —[7]Du bœuf et du porc.

MARIE —[8]Pour le bœuf, allez à la boucherie. [9]Pour le porc, allez à la charcuterie.

JOHN —[10]Faut-il aller à deux magasins différents?

MARIE —[11]Oui. En France, les charcutiers vendent du porc. [12]Les bouchers vendent les autres espèces de viande.

JOHN —[13]Je veux acheter aussi du papier à lettres. [14]On vend du papier à lettres à la pharmacie, n'est-ce pas?

MARIE —[15]Non. Les pharmaciens ne vendent que des médicaments.

JOHN —[16]Où faut-il aller, alors?

MARIE —[17]Allez à la librairie ou au bureau de tabac.

JOHN —[1]I have some errands to do. [2]First I want to buy some bread. [3]They sell bread at the grocery store, don't they?

MARIE —[4]No. You have to go to the bakery.

JOHN —[5]Then, I want to buy some meat.

MARIE —[6]What sort of meat?

JOHN —[7]Some beef and pork.

MARIE —[8]For beef, go to the butcher's. [9]For pork, go to the pork butcher's.

JOHN —[10]Must one go to two different stores?

MARIE —[11]Yes. In France, pork butchers sell pork. [12]Butchers sell the other kinds of meat.

JOHN —[13]I want also to buy some stationery. [14]They sell stationery at the drug store, don't they?

MARIE —[15]No. The pharmacists sell only medicines.

JOHN —[16]Where must one go, then?

MARIE —[17]Go to the bookstore or the tobacco shop.

JOHN —[18]Ainsi, les bouchers ne vendent pas de porc, les pharmaciens ne vendent que des médicaments, et on vend du papier à lettres dans les bureaux de tabac!

JOHN —[18]Thus, the butchers don't sell pork, the pharmacists sell only medicines, and they sell stationery in the tobacco shops!

MARIE —[19]Vous pouvez aller au Super-marché, si vous voulez.

MARIE —[19]You can go to the Super-market if you want to.

JOHN —[20]Oh non! J'aime bien causer avec les marchands.

JOHN —[20]Oh no! I like to chat with the shopkeepers.

I. SUBSTITUTIONS. *Répétez les phrases suivantes en substituant les mots indiqués:*

1. Il faut aller [à la boulangerie].
   à l'épicerie/ à la boucherie/ à la charcuterie/ à la pharmacie/ à la librairie

2. Où faut-il aller pour acheter [du pain]?
   du boeuf/ du porc/ des médicaments/ du papier à lettres/ un journal/ des cigarettes

3. Qu'est-ce qu'on vend [à la boulangerie]?
   à la boucherie/ à la charcuterie/ à la pharmacie/ à la librairie/ au bureau de tabac

4. J'aime bien [causer avec les marchands].
   causer avec mes amis/ faire des courses/ aller au théâtre/ voir venir le printemps

5. J'aime bien [les pommes].
   la neige/ le beau temps/ l'hiver/ les blondes

II. *Répondez en français à chacune des questions suivantes:*

1. Avez-vous des courses à faire? 2. Que voulez-vous acheter d'abord? 3. Est-ce qu'on vend du pain à l'épicerie? 4. Où faut-il aller pour acheter du pain? 5. Qu'est-ce que vous voulez acheter ensuite? 6. Quelle espèce de viande voulez-vous acheter? 7. Où faut-il aller pour acheter du boeuf? 8. Où est-ce qu'il faut aller pour acheter du porc? 9. Est-ce que les charcutiers vendent du boeuf? 10. Est-ce que les bouchers vendent du porc? 11. Où est-ce qu'on vend du papier à lettres? 12. Qu'est-ce que les pharmaciens vendent?

III. *Demandez à quelqu'un:*

1. s'il a des courses à faire. 2. où l'on vend du pain. 3. si l'on vend du pain à l'épicerie. 4. quelle espèce de viande il veut acheter. 5. où il faut aller pour acheter du boeuf. 6. où il faut aller pour acheter du porc. 7. si le charcutier vend du boeuf. 8. si le boucher vend du porc. 9. s'il faut aller

à deux magasins différents. **10.** si l'on vend du papier à lettres à la pharmacie. **11.** où il faut aller pour acheter du papier à lettres. **12.** ce qu'on vend à la boulangerie. **13.** ce qu'on vend à la boucherie. **14.** ce qu'on vend à la charcuterie. **15.** ce qu'on vend à la pharmacie en France. **16.** ce qu'on vend au bureau de tabac.

IV. *Répétez les phrases suivantes en employant* **ne . . . que . . .** (only, nothing but).

Ex.:—Les pharmaciens vendent des médicaments.
—**Les pharmaciens ne vendent que des médicaments.**

1. Les charcutiers vendent du porc. **2.** Les bouchers vendent de la viande. **3.** Mme Cochet a des cigarettes françaises. **4.** John aime les cigarettes américaines. **5.** John a un billet de cent francs. **6.** Il y a un restaurant sur la place.

V. *Dites en français:*

1. First I want to buy some bread. Then I want to buy some meat. **2.** First you have to go to the bakery. Then you have to go to the butcher's. **3.** Pharmacists don't sell stationery. Then(in that case) I am going to the bookstore. **4.** Butchers don't sell pork. Then I am going to the pork butcher's. **5.** The weather is fine. Then I am going to take a walk. **6.** Then (afterwards) I am going to have dinner at the White Horse Inn.

VI. Dictée d'après le dialogue, p. 53.

VII. Conversations.

(1) Vous voulez acheter un journal, du papier à lettres et de l'aspirine. Vous demandez à quelqu'un où l'on vend ces différents articles.
(2) Vous voulez faire un pique-nique. Vous demandez à quelqu'un où l'on vend les provisions que vous voulez acheter.

Descriptive Adjectives

25. Forms and agreement of adjectives.

Un **petit** garçon	A *little* boy
Une **petite** fille	A *little* girl
Deux **petits** garçons	Two *little* boys
Deux **petites** filles	Two *little* girls

A. Agreement.

Adjectives agree in gender and number with the noun modified.

B. Forms.

When the masculine singular form of an adjective ends in a consonant, you can often find the feminine by adding an **e** to the masculine singular. In these adjectives, the final consonant, which is normally silent in the masculine form, is pronounced in the feminine forms. Ex.: **content-contente, grand-grande, français-française.**

Many adjectives do not follow this pattern. The forms of the commonest ones will be taken up in the following paragraph.

If the masculine singular of an adjective ends in -**e**, the masculine and feminine forms are identical. Ex.: **un jeune homme, une jeune fille.**

You usually obtain the plural form of adjectives by adding an -**s** to the singular forms. Ex.: **petit-petits** (*m.*), **petite-petites** (*f.*). This **s** is pronounced only in linking.

26. Position of adjectives.

Contrary to English usage, the great majority of adjectives follow the noun modified. However, some of the commonest ones normally precede the noun.

A. Adjectives which precede the noun modified:

—Est-ce que c'est un **bon** restaurant?	Is it a *good* restaurant?
—C'est un **grand jeune** homme.	He is a *tall young* man.
—C'est une **petite jeune** fille.	She is a *small* girl.

| —C'est un **vieux** monsieur. | He is an *old* gentleman. |
| —C'est un **bel** enfant. | He is a *good looking* child. |

The following descriptive adjectives normally precede the noun they modify:

| | SINGULAR | | PLURAL | |
MASCULINE	FEMININE	MASCULINE	FEMININE
beau (bel)	belle	beaux	belles (*beautiful*)
bon	bonne	bons	bonnes (*good*)
mauvais	mauvaise	mauvais	mauvaises (*bad*)
joli	jolie	jolis	jolies (*pretty*)
grand	grande	grands	grandes (*large, tall*)
long	longue	longs	longues (*long*)
petit	petite	petits	petites (*small*)
jeune	jeune	jeunes	jeunes (*young*)
vieux (vieil)	vieille	vieux	vieilles (*old*)
nouveau (nouvel)	nouvelle	nouveaux	nouvelles (*new*)

The masculine forms **bel, vieil,** and **nouvel** are used only before masculine words beginning with a vowel or mute **h.**

B. Adjectives which follow the noun modified:

—Elle a les yeux **bleus.**	She has *blue* eyes.
—L'hôtel du Cheval **blanc.**	The *White* Horse Inn.
—Elle a les cheveux **blonds.**	She has *blond* hair.
—C'est un ingénieur **français.**	He is a *French* engineer.

Forms of a few adjectives which follow the noun modified:

(1) ADJECTIVES OF COLOR

blanc, blanche, blancs, blanches (*white*)
bleu, bleue, bleus, bleues (*blue*)
jaune, jaune, jaunes, jaunes (*yellow*)
noir, noire, noirs, noires (*black*)
rouge, rouge, rouges, rouges (*red*)
vert, verte, verts, vertes (*green*)

(2) ADJECTIVES OF NATIONALITY

américain, américaine, américains, américaines (*American*)
français, française, français, françaises (*French*)
italien, italienne, italiens, italiennes (*Italian*)
russe, russe, russes, russes (*Russian*)
allemand, allemande, allemands, allemandes (*German*)

27. Comparative of adjectives: regular.

A. Superiority is expressed by **plus ... que** *

John est **plus grand que** sa sœur.	John is *taller than* his sister.
Il fait **plus froid** aujourd'hui **qu'hier.**	It is *colder* today *than* yesterday.

B. Equality is expressed by **aussi ... que**

Roger est **aussi intelligent que** John.	Roger is *as intelligent as* John.
La campagne est **aussi belle** en automne **qu'au** printemps.	The country is *as beautiful* in fall *as* in spring .

C. Inferiority is expressed by **moins ... que**

Marie est **moins grande que** son frère.	Marie is *less tall than* her brother.
En automne, il fait **moins chaud qu'en** été.	In fall, it is *cooler (less hot) than* in summer.

28. Superlative of adjectives: regular.

A. le plus (la plus, les plus)

Marie est **la plus jolie** jeune fille de la classe.	Mary is *the prettiest* girl in the class.
Henri est l'étudiant **le plus intelligent.**	Henry is *the most intelligent* student.
Ce sont les étudiants **les plus gentils.**	They are *the nicest* students.

B. le moins (la moins, les moins)

L'hiver est **la moins belle** saison de l'année.	Winter is *the least beautiful* season of the year.
C'est aussi **la moins agréable.**	It is also *the least agreeable.*

(1) To express the superlative degree of adjectives, you insert the appropriate definite article before the comparative form. The comparative and superlative of the adjective **grand** *(tall)* have the following forms:

---

* It is necessary to distinguish between **plus ... que,** which is used in comparisons, and **plus de** which is an expression of quantity. Ex.: Marie a **plus de dix** cousins. Marie has *more than ten* cousins.

COMPARATIVE		SUPERLATIVE	
plus grand	*taller*	le plus grand	*the tallest*
plus grande		la plus grande	
plus grands		les plus grands	
plus grandes		les plus grandes	
moins grand	*less tall*	le moins grand	*the least tall*
moins grande		la moins grande	
moins grands		les moins grands	
moins grandes		les moins grandes	

(2) Superlative forms of adjectives normally stand in the same position in relation to the noun modified as their positive forms.

(*a*) ADJECTIVES WHICH PRECEDE:

Le **petit** garçon   **Le plus petit** garçon
La **jolie** jeune fille   **La plus jolie** jeune fille

(*b*) ADJECTIVES WHICH FOLLOW:

L'étudiant **intelligent**   L'étudiant **le plus intelligent**
La chambre **agréable**   La chambre **la plus agréable**

Note that when the superlative form of an adjective which follows the noun modified is used, the definite article is used twice—once before the noun, and once as a part of the superlative form of the adjective.

29. Irregular comparative and superlative of adjective **bon** and adverb **bien.**

A. Adjective **bon:**

—L'hôtel Continental est un **bon** hôtel.   The Continental is a *good* hotel.

—L'hôtel du Cheval blanc est **meilleur.**   The White Horse Inn is *better.*

—C'est **le meilleur** hôtel de la ville.   It is *the best* hotel in town.

The forms are:

bon (*good*)	meilleur (*better*)	le meilleur (*best*)
bonne	meilleure	la meilleure
bons	meilleurs	les meilleurs
bonnes	meilleures	les meilleures

B. Adverb **bien:**

On mange **bien** à l'hôtel Continental.	The food is *good* at the Continental. (You eat *well* at the Continental.)
On mange **mieux** chez Jacques.	The food is *better* at Jack's.
C'est là qu'on mange **le mieux.**	That is where the food is *best*.
Je vais **bien.**	I am *well*.
Je vais **mieux.**	I am *better*.
Je vais **le mieux** du monde.	I couldn't possibly be better.

The forms are: **bien** *(well)*   **mieux** *(better)*   **le mieux** *(best)*.

Note that in English the comparative and superlative of the adjective *good* and the adverb *well* are identical. We say *good, better, best,* and *well, better, best;* consequently we do not have to know whether *best* is an adjective or an adverb in such sentences as: *Spring is the best season,* and *It is the season I like best.* But in French you have to know whether the adjective or the adverb is called for in order to choose the correct form.

> Le printemps est **la meilleure** saison *(adj.)*.
> C'est la saison que j'aime **le mieux** *(adv.)*.

I. EXERCICES D'APPLICATION.

> **A.** *Employez la forme convenable de l'adjectif indiqué avec chacun des mots suivants:*

1. Beau, bel, belle.

Ex.:—un château.

> —**C'est un beau château.**

une jeune fille/ un arbre/ un hôtel/ une maison/ un printemps/ un été

2. Vieux, vieil, vieille.

Ex.:—une église.

> —**C'est une vieille église.**

un restaurant/ un arbre/ un hôtel/ une maison/ une rue/ un ami

3. Bon petit, bonne petite.

Ex.:—un restaurant.

> —**C'est un bon petit restaurant.**

un garçon/ une fille/ une jeune fille/ un vin blanc/ un hôtel/ une librairie

B. *Substituez* **mauvais, mauvaise** *à* **bon, bonne:**

1. C'est un bon garçon. **2.** C'est un bon hôtel. **3.** C'est un bon restaurant. **4.** C'est un bon journal. **5.** C'est une bonne saison. **6.** C'est une bonne histoire *(story)*.

C. *Mettez au pluriel:*

Ex.:—C'est un joli château.

  —**Ce sont de jolis châteaux.**

1. C'est une jolie jeune fille. **2.** C'est un vieil ami. **3.** C'est un bel enfant.
4. C'est une longue histoire. **5.** C'est un mauvais restaurant.

D. *Répétez les phrases suivantes en substituant les mots indiqués:*

1. Marie a une nouvelle robe [blanche].
rouge/ noire/ bleue/ rose/ jaune

2. Nous n'avons pas de journaux [américains].
russes/ allemands/ anglais/ italiens

3. Il fait [plus beau] aujourd'hui qu'hier.
plus chaud/ plus mauvais/ plus froid/ plus de vent/ moins chaud/ moins froid/
moins de vent

4. Marie est plus [grande] que sa cousine.
jeune/ jolie/ intelligente/ gentille/ agréable

5. Louise est moins [grande] que sa cousine.
jolie/ gentille/ intelligente

E. *Répétez, en employant le superlatif et* **de la ville:**

Ex:.—C'est un bon restaurant.

  —**C'est le meilleur restaurant de la ville.**

C'est un bon hôtel/ C'est une bonne boulangerie/ C'est une belle place/ C'est une
longue rue/ C'est un joli jardin.

F. *Répétez les phrases suivantes en substituant les mots indiqués:*

1. Aujourd'hui, je vais [bien].
mal/ très mal/ mieux qu'hier/ moins bien qu'hier/ le mieux du monde

2. Ici, on mange [bien].
mieux qu'à l'autre hôtel/ beaucoup mieux qu'à l'autre hôtel/ moins bien qu'à l'autre
hôtel/ beaucoup moins bien qu'à l'autre hôtel

3. J'aime mieux [les pommes] que [les bananes].
le printemps . . . l'hiver/ les arbres . . . les fleurs/ les blondes . . . les brunes/ le vin
blanc . . . le vin rouge/ le tabac américain . . . le tabac français

G. *Répétez en remplaçant* **aussi bon(s), aussi bonne(s)** *par* **meilleur(s),
meilleure(s):**

Ex.:—Les cigarettes américaines sont aussi bonnes que les cigarettes françaises.

  —**Les cigarettes américaines sont meilleures que les cigarettes françaises.**

1. Le vin blanc est aussi bon que le vin rouge. **2.** Le tabac américain est aussi
bon que le tabac français. **3.** Les blondes sont aussi bonnes que les brunes.
4. Le pain américain n'est pas aussi bon que le pain français. **5.** La cuisine
anglaise n'est pas aussi bonne que la cuisine française.

II. *Répondez en français à chacune des questions suivantes:*

1. De quelle couleur sont les feuilles (*f.*) en été? **2.** De quelle couleur sont-elles en automne? **3.** De quelle couleur est le ciel quand il fait beau? **4.** Est-ce que la campagne est blanche en hiver? **5.** Est-ce que la campagne est aussi belle au printemps qu'en automne? **6.** Est-ce qu'il fait plus froid aujourd'hui qu'hier (*yesterday*)? **7.** Est-ce qu'il fait plus chaud aujourd'hui qu'hier? **8.** Quel est le mois le plus chaud de l'année? **9.** Quelle est la plus belle saison de l'année? **10.** Quelle est la plus mauvaise saison? **11.** Quelle est la meilleure saison pour faire du ski? **12.** Est-ce qu'il fait moins chaud au mois d'octobre qu'au mois de juin? **13.** Aimez-vous mieux le printemps que l'été? **14.** Aimez-vous mieux les blondes que les brunes? **15.** Déjeunez-vous mieux le dimanche que les autres jours de la semaine? **16.** Quel est le meilleur hôtel de la ville? **17.** Quels sont les meilleurs étudiants de la classe? **18.** Est-ce que John est aussi grand que sa sœur? **19.** Marie est-elle aussi intelligente que son frère?

III. *Dites en français:*

1. What do you think of *Le Figaro?* **2.** I like *Le Figaro* a lot. **3.** It's one of the best French newspapers. **4.** I like *Le Figaro* better than *Le Monde.* **5.** French papers are smaller than American papers, aren't they? **6.** Are they as good as American papers? **7.** Certainly. **8.** Then, give me *Le Figaro,* please.

An Invitation

JOHN —[1]Je suis invité chez les Brown. [2]Les connaissez-vous?

ROGER —[3]Non, je ne les connais pas. [4]Est-ce que ce M. Brown est Américain?

JOHN —[5]Oui, il est Américain, mais sa femme est Française.

ROGER —[6]Quand M. Brown est-il venu en France?

JOHN —[7]Il est venu en France il y a cinq ou six ans.

ROGER —[8]Est-il venu directement* des États-Unis?

JOHN —[9]Non, je crois qu'il a passé deux ou trois ans en Angleterre.

ROGER —[10]Où demeure M. Brown?

JOHN —[11]Il demeure près du Bois de Boulogne.†

ROGER —[12]Qu'est-ce qu'il fait?

JOHN —[13]Il est banquier. [14]Sa banque se trouve près de l'Opéra.††

ROGER —[15]Comment avez-vous fait sa connaissance?

JOHN —[1]I am invited to the Browns'. [2]Do you know them?

ROGER —[3]No, I do not know them. [4]Is this Mr. Brown American?

JOHN —[5]Yes, he is American, but his wife is French.

ROGER —[6]When did Mr. Brown come to France?

JOHN —[7]He came to France five or six years ago.

ROGER —[8]Did he come directly from the United States?

JOHN —[9]No, I think he spent two or three years in England.

ROGER —[10]Where does Mr. Brown live?

JOHN —[11]He lives near the Bois de Boulogne.

ROGER —[12]What does he do?

JOHN —[13]He is a banker. [14]His bank is near the Opera.

ROGER —[15]How did you meet him?

---

* Adverbs are often formed by adding -ment to the feminine of an adjective.
† The Bois de Boulogne is a large and beautiful park west of Paris.
†† The Great Opera House, which dominates the Place de l'Opéra, the Grands Boulevards, and the Avenue de l'Opéra, is in the heart of the shopping district.

JOHN —[16]C'est un vieil ami de mon père. [17]Il est venu souvent chez nous à Philadelphie.

JOHN —[16]He's an old friend of my father. [17]He often came to our house in Philadelphia.

ROGER —[18]Êtes-vous déjà allé chez les Brown?

ROGER —[18]Have you been (gone) to the Browns' before?

JOHN —[19]Oui, je suis allé chez eux plusieurs fois. [20]Sa femme et lui ont été très aimables pour moi.

JOHN —[19]Yes, I have gone to their house several times. [20]His wife and he have been very nice to me.

I. SUBSTITUTIONS. *Répétez les phrases suivantes en substituant les mots indiqués:*

1. Je suis invité [chez les Brown].
chez eux/ chez Marie/ chez Roger/ chez ma cousine

2. Il est venu en France il y a [cinq ou six ans].
quatre ou cinq ans/ deux ou trois ans/ deux ou trois mois/ deux ou trois semaines/ cinq ou six semaines

3. Il a passé deux ou trois [ans] en Angleterre.
mois/ semaines/ jours/ heures

4. Où se trouve [sa banque]?
sa maison/ le Bois de Boulogne/ l'Opéra/ l'avenue de l'Observatoire

5. C'est un [vieil] ami de mon père.
grand/ bon/ nouvel/ jeune

6. Êtes-vous déjà allé [chez les Brown]?
chez eux/ en Angleterre/ en France/ à Paris/ à Philadelphie

7. Je suis allé chez eux [plusieurs fois].
deux fois/ cinq ou six fois/ le semaine dernière/ dimanche dernier/ au mois d'octobre

8. Sa femme et lui ont été aimables [pour moi].
pour nous/ pour eux/ pour John/ pour nos amis

II. *Répondez en français à chacune des questions suivantes:*

1. Chez qui John est-il invité? **2.** Est-ce que Roger connaît les Brown? **3.** Est-ce que ce M. Brown est Américain? **4.** Est-ce que sa femme est Américaine? **5.** Quand M. Brown est-il venu en France? **6.** Est-il venu directement des États-Unis? **7.** Où les Brown demeurent-ils? **8.** Que fait M. Brown? **9.** Où se trouve sa banque? **10.** Comment John a-t-il fait sa connaissance? **11.** Où habite John? **12.** Est-ce que John est déjà allé chez les Brown? **13.** Est-ce que M. et Mme Brown ont été aimables pour John?

III. *Demandez à un autre étudiant (à une autre étudiante):*

1. chez qui John est invité. **2.** si Roger connaît les Brown. **3** si ce M. Brown
est Américain. **4.** quand M. Brown est venu en France. **5.** s'il est venu directement des États-Unis. **6.** où demeurent les Brown. **7.** ce que fait M. Brown.
8. où se trouve sa banque. **9.** comment John a fait sa connaissance. **10.** où
habite John. **11.** si John est allé chez les Brown. **12.** si M. et Mme Brown
ont été aimables pour John.

IV. *Dites en français:*

1. How did you meet him? **2.** How did you meet her? **3.** Where did you
meet him? **4.** Where did you meet her? **5.** When did you meet him? **6.**
When did you meet her? **7.** How did you meet them? **(leur).** **8.** Where
did you meet them? **9.** When did you meet them?

V. Dictée d'après le dialogue, p. 60.

VI. Conversation.

Vous expliquez à un ami (une amie) pourquoi vous ne pouvez pas
accepter son invitation à dîner.

The *Passé Composé*

30. Meaning and formation of the **passé composé.**

The *passé composé* (compound past) tense is used to indicate that the action described by the verb took place in the past. It corresponds both to the English present perfect (*I have eaten lunch*) and the simple past (*I ate lunch*).

This tense is a combination of the past participle of a verb and the present indicative of an auxiliary verb. While in English the compound tenses of all verbs use the auxiliary verb *to have,* in French some verbs are conjugated with **avoir** and some with **être.** The first group is much more numerous than the second.

31. **Passé composé** of verbs conjugated with auxiliary **avoir.**

A. *Passé composé* of **être,** *to be:* Irregular:

—**Avez-vous** été malade la semaine dernière?   *Were you* sick last week?
—Oui, **j'ai été** malade.   Yes, *I was* sick.

(1) The forms of the *passé composé* of **être** are:
J'ai été, *I was, I have been,* tu as été, il(elle) a été, nous avons été, vous avez été, ils(elles) ont été.

(2) This tense is composed of the present indicative of **avoir** and the past participle of **être,** i.e., **été.**

(3) For the negative of the *passé composé* of **être,** you use the negative form of the present indicative of **avoir** with the past participle **été.** Ex.: **Je n'ai pas été.**

(4) For the interrogative of this tense, you use the interrogative of the auxiliary with the past participle **été.** Ex.: **Avez-vous été?**

B. *Passé composé* of **avoir,** *to have:* Irregular:

—**Avez-vous eu** le temps de déjeuner à midi?   *Did you have time* to lunch at noon?

—Non, **je n'ai pas eu** le temps de déjeuner.   No, *I didn't have* time to lunch.

(1) The forms of the *passé composé* of **avoir** are:
J'ai eu, *I had, I have had,* tu as eu, il (elle) a eu, nous avons eu, vous avez eu, ils (elles) ont eu.

(2) This tense is composed of the present indicative of **avoir** and the past participle of **avoir,** i.e., **eu.**

(3) For the negative and interrogative forms, you use the negative and interrogative forms of the auxiliary verb. Ex.: **Je n'ai pas eu. Avez-vous eu?**

C. *Passé composé* of **déjeuner,** *to lunch:* First Conjugation:

—**Avez-vous déjeuné** à midi?	*Did you lunch* at noon?
—Non, **j'ai déjeuné** à midi et demi.	No. *I lunched* at half past twelve.
—A quelle heure Roger **a-t-il dîné?**	*What time did* Roger *have dinner?*
—**Il a dîné** à six heures et quart.	*He had dinner* at a quarter past six.
—**Avez-vous acheté** un journal?	*Did you buy* a paper?
—Oui, **j'ai acheté** le Figaro.	Yes, *I bought Le Figaro.*

(1) The forms of the *passé composé* of **déjeuner** are: **J'ai déjeuné,** *I had lunch, I have had lunch, I ate lunch, I have eaten lunch,* **tu as déjeuné, il (elle) a déjeuné, nous avons déjeuné, vous avez déjeuné, ils (elles) ont déjeuné.**

(2) This tense is composed of the present tense of the verb **avoir** and the past participle of **déjeuner,** i.e., **déjeuné.**

(3) You can always find the past participle of regular verbs of the first conjugation by substituting **-é** for the **-er** ending of the infinitive.

(4) For the negative and interrogative forms, you use the negative and interrogative of the auxiliary. Ex.: **Je n'ai pas déjeuné. Avez-vous déjeuné?**
The following regular verbs with which you are familiar will be used in the oral practice exercises: **dîner,** *to dine;* **acheter,** *to buy;* **parler,** *to speak;* **habiter, demeurer,** *to live in;* **apporter,** *to bring;* **commencer,** *to begin;* **donner,** *to give;* etc.

32. Passé composé of verbs conjugated with auxiliary être.

—Quand êtes-vous arrivé à Paris?	When *did you get* to Paris?
—Je suis arrivé hier.	*I arrived* yesterday.
—Quand **M. Brown est-il venu** en France?	When *did* Mr. Brown come to France?
—Il est venu en France il y a deux ou trois ans.	*He came* to France two or three years ago.
—Êtes-vous déjà allé chez les Brown?	*Have you been (gone)* to the Browns' before?
—Oui, je suis allé chez eux plusieurs fois.	Yes, *I have been* to their house several times.

Aside from all reflexive verbs (which will be studied later), the following verbs are the only common ones which are conjugated with **être**:

INFINITIVE	PAST PARTICIPLE
aller *(to go)*	allé
venir *(to come)*	venu
entrer *(to go in)*	entré
sortir *(to go out)*	sorti
partir *(to leave)*	parti
arriver *(to arrive)*	arrivé
rester *(to stay)*	resté
monter *(to go up)*	monté
descendre *(to go down)*	descendu
tomber *(to fall)*	tombé
naître *(to be born)*	né
devenir *(to become)*	devenu
mourir *(to die)*	mort
retourner *(to return)*	retourné

(1) Note also that **revenir,** *to come back;* **rentrer,** *to go back in, to go back home,* and other compounds of the verbs listed above are normally conjugated with **être.**

(2) The forms of the *passé composé* of **aller,** if the subject is masculine, are: **Je suis allé,** *I went, I have gone,* **tu es allé, il est allé, nous sommes allés, vous êtes allé(s), ils sont allés.**

(3) In compound tenses of the verbs listed above, the past participle agrees in gender and number with the subject of the verb. The feminine and plural forms of the participle follow the pattern of adjectives. Ex.: **Il est allé. — Elle est allée. — Ils sont allés. — Elles sont allées.**

I. Exercices d'application.

A. *Mettez les phrases suivantes à la forme négative:*

Ex.:—J'ai dîné.
    —**Je n'ai pas dîné.**

I. J'ai déjeuné à midi. **2.** Le garçon a apporté la carte. **3.** Il a parlé à Roger. **4.** Il a donné l'addition à Roger. **5.** Nous avons déjeuné. **6.** Nous avons parlé français. **7.** Nous avons habité à Paris. **8.** Nous avons été malades. **9.** Ils ont commencé à parler français. **10.** Ils ont passé trois ans en Angleterre. **11.** Il a neigé ce matin. **12.** Il a apporté son imperméable. **13.** Je suis allé à la gare. **14.** Il est allé à la gare. **15.** Il est arrivé hier. **16.** Nous sommes arrivés hier. **17.** Il est venu chez nous. **18.** Il est né en France. **19.** Nous sommes nés en France. **20.** Il est venu directement des États-Unis.

B. *Mettez les phrases suivantes à la forme interrogative:*

Ex.:—Roger a dîné.
    —**Roger a-t-il dîné?**

I. Roger a déjeuné à midi. **2.** Roger a acheté un journal. **3.** Le garçon a apporté la carte. **4.** Le garçon a donné l'addition. **5.** John a parlé à la concierge. **6.** John et Roger ont dîné au restaurant. **7.** John est allé à la préfecture de police. **8.** John est déjà allé chez les Brown. **9.** M. Brown est venu des États-Unis. **10.** John est né à Philadelphie. **11.** Sa mère est morte. **12.** Louis XIV est mort en 1715.

C. *Mettez les phrases suivantes au passé composé:*

Ex.:—Je déjeune à midi.
    —**J'ai déjeuné à midi.**

I. J'achète un journal. **2.** Nous parlons français. **3.** Il apporte la carte. **4.** John demande l'addition. **5.** John est malade. **6.** Il a le temps de déjeuner. **7.** Il va chez les Brown. **8.** Nous allons au bal. **9.** Il arrive à cinq heures. **10.** Le train part à six heures. **11.** Nous rentrons à cinq heures. **12.** Je dîne à sept heures.

II. *Répondez en français à chacune des questions suivantes:*

I. A quelle heure avez-vous déjeuné? **2.** A quelle heure êtes-vous venu(e) à l'université? **3.** A quelle heure avez-vous dîné hier? **4.** A quelle heure êtes-vous entré(e) dans la classe de français? **5.** A quelle heure les autres étudiants sont-ils entrés dans la classe de français? **6.** Avez-vous acheté un journal aujourd'hui? **7.** Avez-vous commencé à parler français? **8.** Avez-vous donné votre adresse à la concierge? **9.** Êtes-vous allé(e) à New York l'été dernier? **10.** Êtes-vous venu(e) à l'université hier? **11.** Avez-vous eu le temps de déjeuner? **12.** Avez-vous été malade hier? **13.** Les étudiants ont-ils commencé à parler français? **14.** Avez-vous patiné l'hiver dernier? **15.** A-t-il beaucoup neigé au mois de novembre?

III. *Répondez négativement:*

1. Avez-vous acheté un journal ce matin? **2.** Avez-vous passé deux ans en Angleterre? **3.** Avez-vous été malade l'été dernier? **4.** Êtes-vous allé(e) au laboratoire hier après-midi? **5.** Roger a-t-il acheté des cigarettes? **6.** Avez-vous apporté votre imperméable? **7.** Marie a-t-elle apporté son imperméable? **8.** Vos parents sont-ils allés en France? **9.** Êtes-vous sorti(e) hier soir? **10.** Êtes-vous rentré(e) à dix heures?

IV. *Demandez à quelqu'un:*

1. s'il a acheté un journal aujourd'hui. **2.** s'il est né à Chicago. **3.** s'il a donné son adresse à la concierge. **4.** s'il a eu le temps de déjeuner à midi. **5.** si son père est allé à Paris. **6.** où il est né. **7.** où son père est né. **8.** à quelle heure il a dîné hier soir. **9.** à quelle heure il a déjeuné aujourd'hui. **10.** quand Napoléon est mort. **11.** comment John a fait la connaissance des Brown.

Shopping

JOHN —[1]Où êtes-vous allée cet après-midi?

MARIE —[2]Je suis allée en ville.

JOHN —[3]Qu'est-ce que vous avez fait?

MARIE —[4]J'ai fait des courses.

JOHN —[5]Qu'est-ce que vous avez acheté?

MARIE —[6]Beaucoup de choses. [7]Je suis d'abord allée au Prisunic.

JOHN —[8]Qu'est-ce que c'est qu'un Prisunic?

MARIE —[9]C'est un magasin où l'on vend de tout, [10]à bon marché. [11]Ensuite, je suis allée chez la modiste.*

JOHN —[12]Quoi faire?

MARIE —[13]Acheter un chapeau.

JOHN —[14]Le chapeau que vous avez sur la tête?

MARIE —[15]Oui. Est-ce qu'il vous plaît?

JOHN —[16]Certainement. [17]Il est un peu drôle, [18]mais il vous va très bien.

MARIE —[19]J'ai marché tout l'après-midi. [20]Je suis un peu fatiguée.

JOHN —[21]Êtes-vous allée en ville à pied?

JOHN —[1]Where have you been this afternoon?

MARIE —[2]I went downtown.

JOHN —[3]What did you do?

MARIE —[4]I did some errands.

JOHN —[5]What did you buy?

MARIE —[6]Many things. [7]I went to the ten cent store first.

JOHN —[8]What is a Prisunic?

MARIE —[9]It is a store where they sell all sorts of things, [10]cheap. [11]Then I went to the milliner's.

JOHN —[12]What for?

MARIE —[13]To buy a hat.

JOHN —[14]The hat which you have on (your head)?

MARIE —[15]Yes. Do you like it (does it please you)?

JOHN —[16]Certainly. [17]It is a little funny, [18]but it is very becoming.

MARIE —[19]I walked all the afternoon. [20] I am a little tired.

JOHN —[21]Did you walk downtown?

---

* **Chez** means *at* (or *to*) *the house of, at* (or *to*) *the shop of* and is used only of persons. One says: **à la pharmacie,** but: **chez le pharmacien.**

MARIE —²²Oui, j'ai voulu profiter du beau temps. ²³En tout cas, cette promenade m'a fait beaucoup de bien.

MARIE —²²Yes, I wanted to take advantage of the fine weather. ²³In any case, that walk did me a lot of good.

I. SUBSTITUTIONS. *Répétez les phrases suivantes en substituant les mots indiqués:*

1. Qu'est-ce que c'est qu'[un Prisunic]?
   un bureau de tabac/ une modiste/ une charcuterie/ une épicerie/ une librairie

2. Qu'est-ce qu'on achète [chez la modiste]?
   chez le pharmacien/ à la pharmacie/ au Prisunic/ chez le boucher/ à la boucherie

3. Est-ce que [mon chapeau] vous plaît?
   mon nouveau chapeau/ ma nouvelle robe/ ce journal/ ce magasin/ mon papier à lettres

4. Est-ce que [mon chapeau] me va bien?
   ma nouvelle robe/ cette couleur/ mon imperméable/ mon nouvel imperméable/ l'imperméable que j'ai acheté

5. [Votre chapeau] vous va très bien.
   Votre nouvelle robe/ Cette couleur/ Votre manteau/ Le rouge/ Le bleu

6. En tout cas, [cette promenade] m'a fait beaucoup de bien.
   le beau temps/ le soleil/ cet après-midi en ville/ cette promenade à la campagne/ ce médicament

II. *Répétez chacune des phrases suivantes en ajoutant* **et je suis un peu fatigué(e):**

1. J'ai marché tout l'après-midi . . . 2. Je suis allé(e) en ville . . . 3. Je suis allé(e) en ville à pied . . . 4. J'ai passé tout l'après-midi en ville . . . 5. J'ai passé plusieurs heures en ville . . . 6. Je suis allé(e) à plusieurs magasins différents . . . 7. J'ai parlé français tout l'après-midi . . .

III. *Répondez en français, d'après le texte, à chacune des questions suivantes:*

1. Où Marie est-elle allée cet après-midi? 2. Qu'est-ce qu'elle a fait? 3. Qu'est-ce qu'elle a acheté? 4. Qu'est-ce que c'est qu'un Prisunic? 5. Où Marie est-elle allée ensuite? 6. Quoi faire? 7. Qu'est-ce que John pense du chapeau de Marie? 8. Pourquoi Marie est-elle fatiguée? 9. Comment est-elle allée en ville? 10. Pourquoi est-elle allée en ville à pied? 11. Est-ce que cette promenade lui a fait du bien?

IV. *Demandez à quelqu'un:*

1. où il est allé cet après-midi. **2.** ce qu'il a fait en ville. **3.** ce qu'il a acheté. **4.** où il est allé ensuite. **5.** pourquoi il est allé au Prisunic. **6.** s'il a marché tout l'après-midi. **7.** s'il est allé en ville à pied. **8.** s'il a voulu profiter du beau temps.

V. *Répondez en français à chacune des questions suivantes:*

1. Qu'est-ce que c'est qu'une boulangerie? **2.** Qu'est-ce que c'est qu'une charcuterie? **3.** une boucherie? **4.** une pharmacie? **5.** un bureau de tabac? **6.** Qu'est-ce qu'on vend dans une boucherie? **7.** Qu'est-ce qu'on vend dans un Prisunic? **8.** Qu'est-ce qu'on achète chez la modiste? **9.** Où est-ce qu'on achète de la viande? **10.** des médicaments? **11.** du papier à lettres? **12.** des journaux?

VI. Dictée d'après le dialogue, p. 63 et pp. 71-72.

VII. Conversation.

"What did you do yesterday afternoon?"
"I went downtown."
"What for?"
"To do some errands."
"To what stores did you go?"
"To the milliner's. Do you like my hat?"
"Yes, it is very becoming."

Troisième Lecture Illustrée, p. 17, *Scènes parisiennes.*

Present Indicative and *Passé Composé*
Second and Third Conjugations,
and Reflexive Verbs

33. Present indicative of **finir** *(to finish)*: second conjugation, regular.

—A quelle heure **finissez-vous** votre travail?	At what time *do you finish* your work?
—**Je finis** vers cinq heures, mais les autres étudiants **finissent** d'habitude avant moi.	*I finish* around five o'clock, but the other students usually *finish* before I do.
—**J'obéis** à la loi.	*I obey* the law.

(1) The affirmative forms of the present indicative of **finir** are: **Je finis,** *I finish, I am finishing,* **tu finis, il (elle) finit, nous finissons, vous finissez, ils (elles) finissent.**

(2) The negative and interrogative forms follow the usual pattern. Ex.: **Il ne finit pas. Finit-il?**

(3) There are relatively few common verbs which belong to the second conjugation. **Choisir,** *to choose,* and **obéir à,** *to obey,* which are conjugated like **finir,** will be used in the oral practice exercises.

34. Passé composé of finir.

—A quelle heure **avez-vous fini** votre travail hier soir?	At what time *did you finish* your work last night?
—**J'ai fini** mon travail vers onze heures.	*I finished* my work at about eleven o'clock.

(1) The forms of the *passé composé* of **finir** are: **J'ai fini,** *I finished, I have finished,* **tu as fini, il a fini, nous avons fini, vous avez fini, ils ont fini.**

(2) For the negative and interrogative forms, you use the negative and interrogative of the auxiliary verb. Ex.: **Avez-vous fini? — Non, je n'ai pas fini.**

(3) The past participle of **finir** and other regular verbs of the second conjugation is found by substituting the ending **-i** for the infinitive ending **-ir.**

35. Present indicative of **répondre** *(to answer):* third conjugation, regular.

—**Répondez-vous** toujours aux lettres de vos amis?   *Do you* always *reply* to the letters of your friends?

—Oui, **je réponds** toujours à leurs lettres.   Yes, *I* always *answer* their letters.

(1) The affirmative forms of the present indicative of **répondre** are: **je réponds,** *I answer, I am answering,* **tu réponds, il répond, nous répondons, vous répondez, ils répondent.**

(2) The negative and interrogative forms follow the usual pattern. Note, however, that in **répond-il?** the **d** is linked and pronounced **t.**

(3) There are relatively few very common verbs which belong to the third conjugation. **Vendre,** *to sell,* and **entendre,** *to hear,* which are conjugated like **répondre,** will be used in the oral practice exercises.

36. Passé composé of **répondre.**

—**Avez-vous répondu** à la demande de M. Duval?   *Have you answered* Mr. Duval's request?

—Oui, **j'ai répondu** à sa demande.   Yes, *I answered* his request.

(1) The forms of the *passé composé* of **répondre** are: **J'ai répondu,** *I answered, I have answered,* **tu as répondu, il a répondu, nous avons répondu, vous avez répondu, ils ont répondu.**

(2) The past participle of regular verbs of the third conjugation is found by substituting the ending **-u** for the infinitive ending **-re.**

37. Present indicative of **se dépêcher** *(to hurry):* reflexive first conjugation, regular.

—**Vous dépêchez-vous** pour arriver à l'heure à l'université?   *Do you hurry* to get to the University on time?

—Beaucoup d'étudiants **se dépêchent,** mais **je ne me dépêche pas.**   Many students *hurry,* but *I do not hurry.*

(1) A reflexive verb always has a pronoun object which refers to the subject of the verb. We have a few reflexive verbs in English (I hurt myself, you hurt yourself, etc.), but in French they are very common.

(2) The forms of the present indicative of **se dépêcher** are:

AFFIRMATIVE	NEGATIVE
Je me dépêche, *I hurry*	Je ne me dépêche pas
Tu te dépêches	Tu ne te dépêches pas
Il se dépêche	Il ne se dépêche pas
Nous nous dépêchons	Nous ne nous dépêchons pas
Vous vous dépêchez	Vous ne vous dépêchez pas
Ils se dépêchent	Ils ne se dépêchent pas

INTERROGATIVE

Est-ce que je me dépêche?
Te dépêches-tu?
Se dépêche-t-il?
Nous dépêchons-nous?
Vous dépêchez-vous?
Se dépêchent-ils?

Note that in the affirmative forms both the pronoun subject (**il**) and the pronoun object (**se**) precede the verb. In the negative forms, **ne** follows the subject (**il**) and **pas** follows the verb—as you would expect. In the interrogative forms, the pronoun object (**se**) remains before the verb and the pronoun subject (**il**) follows the verbs according to the usual pattern.

(3) When the subject of a reflexive verb is a noun, it of course takes the place of the pronoun subject (**il, elle, on**); but the pronoun object (**se**) must always be expressed. Ex.: **Charles ne se dépêche pas. Charles se dépêche-t-il?**

(4) There are reflexive verbs in all conjugations, but in the oral practice exercises only the following ones will be used: **se coucher,** *to lie down, to go to bed;* **se lever,** *to get up, to rise;* **se réveiller,** *to wake up;* **s'habiller,** *to dress* and **s'appeler,** *to be named.*

38. Passé composé of se dépêcher.

—**Vous êtes-vous dépêché** pour finir votre travail?   *Did you hurry* to finish your work?

—**Oui, je me suis dépêché.**   Yes, *I hurried.*

All reflexive verbs are conjugated with **être**. The easiest way to get the forms of the *passé composé* clearly in mind is to think of the auxiliary verb **être** as a reflexive verb (**je me suis**) and place the past participle (**dépêché**) after it.

(1) The forms of the *passé composé* of **se dépêcher** for MASCULINE subject* are:

AFFIRMATIVE	INTERROGATIVE
Je me suis dépêché, *I hurried*	Est-ce que je me suis dépêché?
Tu t'es dépêché	T'es-tu dépêché?
Il s'est dépêché	S'est-il dépêché?
Nous nous sommes dépêchés	Nous sommes-nous dépêchés?
Vous vous êtes dépêché(s)	Vous êtes-vous dépêché(s)?
Ils se sont dépêchés	Se sont-ils dépêchés?

NEGATIVE

Je ne me suis pas dépêché
Tu ne t'es pas dépêché
etc.

(2) If the subject is a noun, you follow the same word order as for the present tense (see par. 37). Of course the past participle comes at the end. Ex.: **Charles s'est dépêché. Charles ne s'est pas dépêché. Charles s'est-il dépêché?**

I. EXERCICES D'APPLICATION.

A. *Répondez au singulier, puis au pluriel:*

Ex.:—Finissez-vous?
    —**Je finis.   Nous finissons.**

1. Choisissez-vous?   2. Obéissez-vous?   3. Finit-il?   4. Choisit-il?   5. Obéit-il?

B. *Répétez, puis dites négativement:*

Ex.:—Je finis.
    —**Je finis.   Je ne finis pas.**

1. Il finit.   2. Il choisit.   3. Il obéit.   4. Nous finissons.   5. Nous choisissons.
6. Nous obéissons.   7. Vous finissez.   8. Vous choisissez.   9. Vous obéissez.
10. Ils finissent.

---

* As the rule for agreement of the past participle in compound tenses of reflexive verbs is complicated (and of comparatively little importance for practical purposes), there is no point in trying to master it at this time.

C. *Répondez au singulier, puis au pluriel:*

1. Répondez-vous? **2.** Vendez-vous? **3.** Entendez-vous? **4.** Répond-il? **5.** Vend-il? **6.** Entend-il?

D. *Répétez, puis dites négativement:*

1. Je réponds. **2.** Je vends. **3.** J'entends. **4.** On répond. **5.** On vend. **6.** On entend. **7.** Nous répondons. **8.** Nous entendons. **9.** Vous répondez. **10.** Vous vendez. **11.** Vous entendez. **12.** Ils répondent. **13.** Ils entendent. **14.** Ils vendent.

E. *Mettez les phrases suivantes au passé composé:*

1. Je finis à cinq heures. **2.** J'obéis à la loi. **3.** Je choisis du papier à lettres. **4.** Nous obéissons à la loi. **5.** Nous répondons aux lettres. **6.** Je réponds au téléphone. **7.** Il répond à sa demande. **8.** Il vend son auto. **9.** Entendez-vous le téléphone? **10.** Répondez-vous au téléphone? **11.** Je ne vends pas de journaux. **12.** Ils n'obéissent pas.

F. *Répondez:*

Ex.:—Vous dépêchez-vous?
    —**Je me dépêche.**

1. Vous couchez-vous? **2.** Comment vous appelez-vous? **3.** Se dépêche-t-il? **4.** Se couche-t-il? **5.** Se lève-t-il? **6.** S'habille-t-il? **7.** Comment s'appelle-t-il?

G. *Répétez, puis dites négativement:*

Ex.:—Je me dépêche.
    —**Je me dépêche.   Je ne me dépêche pas.**

1. Je me couche. **2.** Je me lève. **3.** Il se couche. **4.** Il se réveille. **5.** Elle se lève. **6.** Nous nous dépêchons. **7.** Nous nous levons. **8.** Nous nous couchons. **9.** Ils se lèvent *(pl.)* **10.** Il se dépêche. **11.** Je m'habille. **12.** Il s'habille.

H. *Mettez les phrases suivantes au passé composé:*

Ex.:—Je me lève à sept heures.
    —**Je me suis levé(e) à sept heures.**

1. Je me couche à minuit. **2.** Il se couche à minuit. **3.** Elle se réveille vers huit heures. **4.** Elle se lève. **5.** Elle se dépêche. **6.** Elle s'habille. **7.** Nous nous dépêchons. **8.** Nous nous habillons. **9.** Vous dépêchez-vous? **10.** Vous levez-vous? **11.** Vous couchez-vous? **12.** Se couchent-ils?

II. *Répondez en français à chacune des questions suivantes:*

(*a*) 1. A quelle heure vous êtes-vous couché hier soir? 2. A quelle heure vous êtes-vous levé ce matin? 3. A quelle heure vous êtes-vous réveillé ce matin? 4. A quelle heure avez-vous fini votre travail hier soir? 5. A quelle heure êtes-vous venu à l'université? 6. Vous êtes-vous dépêché pour arriver à l'heure à l'université?

(*b*) 1. A quelle heure vous levez-vous le* dimanche? 2. Est-ce que vous vous habillez le dimanche? 3. A quelle heure vous couchez-vous d'habitude? 4. A quelle heure finissez-vous votre travail? 5. Est-ce que vous obéissez à vos parents? 6. Répondez-vous aux lettres de vos amis? 7. Est-ce qu'on vend du pain à l'épicerie? 8. Est-ce qu'en France les pharmaciens vendent des journaux?

III. *Demandez à quelqu'un:*

(*a*) 1. comment il s'appelle. 2. à quelle heure il se couche d'habitude. 3. à quelle heure il se réveille le dimanche. 4. à quelle heure il se lève le dimanche. 5. à quelle heure il se lève les autres jours de la semaine.

(*b*) 1. comment s'appelle sa sœur. 2. s'il se dépêche pour arriver à l'heure à l'université. 3. à quelle heure il s'est couché hier soir. 4. à quelle heure il s'est levé ce matin. 5. ce qu'on vend dans un Prisunic. 6. si en France les pharmaciens vendent des cigarettes. 7. à quelle heure il finit d'habitude son travail.

---

* **Le dimanche** means *on Sunday* or *on Sundays*. This use of the definite article is explained in par. 113.

Renting a Room

JOHN —[1]Bonjour, madame. Avez-vous une chambre meublée à louer?

MME DUVAL —[2]Oui, monsieur. J'en ai une au premier.*

JOHN —[3]Est-ce que je peux la voir?

MME DUVAL —[4]Mais oui, monsieur. Par ici. [5]C'est la première porte à droite, en †haut de l'escalier. [6]Voulez-vous bien monter?

JOHN —[7]Volontiers.

MME DUVAL —[8]Voici la chambre. Comment la trouvez-vous?

JOHN —[9]Je la trouve vraiment très agréable.

MME DUVAL —[10]Et elle est très tranquille. [11]Il n'y a jamais de bruit dans le quartier.

JOHN —[12] Tant mieux, [13]car j'ai besoin de travailler le soir.

MME DUVAL —[14]Voici la salle de bain, avec eau chaude toute la journée.

JOHN —[15]Quel est le loyer, s'il vous plaît?

MME DUVAL —[16]Cent cinquante francs par mois, monsieur.

JOHN —[1]Good morning, Madam. Have you a furnished room for rent?

MRS. DUVAL —[2]Yes, sir. I have one (of them) on the second floor.

JOHN —[3]May I see it?

MRS. DUVAL —[4]Why of course, sir. This way. [5]It is the first door on the right at the top of the stairs. [6]Would you like to (will you please) go up?

JOHN —[7]Yes, I'll be glad to.

MRS. DUVAL —[8]Here is the room. How do you like it?

JOHN —[9]I think it is really very nice.

MRS. DUVAL —[10]And it is very quiet. [11]There is never any noise in this part of town.

JOHN —[12]So much the better, [13]for I have to (I need to) work in the evening.

MRS. DUVAL —[14]Here is the bathroom, with hot water all day.

JOHN —[15]What is the rent, please?

MRS. DUVAL —[16]One hundred and fifty francs a month, sir.

---

* **Le premier (étage)** is one flight up from the ground floor.
† The **h** of the word **haut** is aspirate, therefore the **n** is not linked.

JOHN —[17]Je crois que cette chambre me convient tout à fait. [18]Quand sera-t-elle prête?

MME DUVAL —[19]Est-ce que demain matin vous convient?

JOHN —[20] Oui, parfaitement.

MME DUVAL —[21]C'est entendu.

JOHN —[22]A demain, madame.

JOHN —[17]I think that this room suits me perfectly. [18]When will it be ready?

MRS. DUVAL —[19]Does tomorrow morning suit you?

JOHN —[20]Yes, perfectly.

MRS. DUVAL —[21]All right.

JOHN —[22]See you tomorrow, Madam.

I. SUBSTITUTIONS. *Répétez les phrases suivantes en substituant les mots indiqués:*

1. Avez-vous [une chambre] à louer?
   des chambres/ un appartement/ une maison

2. Avez-vous [une maison] à vendre?
   des fleurs/ une auto/ un cheval

3. J'en ai [une] au premier.
   deux/ trois/ quatre/ plusieurs

4. Voulez-vous bien [monter]?
   entrer/ choisir/ vous asseoir/ *(with impatience implied)* vous dépêcher/ finir/ répondre à cette question/ rentrer à l'heure

5. Je crois que [cette chambre] me convient tout à fait.
   cet appartement/ cette maison/ ce quartier/ cette auto/ ce chapeau/ cet hôtel

6. J'ai besoin de travailler [le soir].
   toute la soirée/ le matin/ toute la matinée/ l'après-midi/ tout l'après-midi/ la nuit/ toute la nuit/ le jour/ toute la journée

II. *Répétez, en remplaçant le nom par* **le, la, les:**

Ex.:—Comment trouvez-vous la chambre?
    —**Comment la trouvez-vous?**

1. Comment trouvez-vous la maison? 2. Comment trouvez-vous ma robe?
3. Comment trouvez-vous le rosbif? 4. Comment trouvez-vous ce raisin?
5. Comment trouvez-vous mon chapeau? 6. Comment trouvez-vous les hors-d'œuvre? 7. Comment trouvez-vous ces poires?

III. *Répondez, d'après le texte, à chacune des questions suivantes:*

1. Avez-vous une chambre meublée à louer? 2. Est-ce que je peux la voir?
3. Comment trouvez-vous la chambre? 4. Est-ce que la chambre est tranquille? 5. Y a-t-il du bruit dans le quartier? 6. Est-ce que John a besoin de travailler le soir? 7. Y a-t-il une salle de bain? 8. Y a-t-il de l'eau chaude toute la journée? 9. Quel est le loyer? 10. Quand la chambre sera-t-elle prête?

IV. *Demandez à quelqu'un:*

1. s'il a une chambre meublée à louer. **2.** si vous pouvez voir la chambre.
3. si la chambre est au premier. **4.** où se trouve la porte de la chambre.
5. comment il trouve la chambre. **6.** si la chambre est tranquille. **7.** s'il y a
du bruit dans le quartier. **8.** quand la chambre sera prête.

V. *Répétez chacune des phrases suivantes en remplaçant* **ne . . . pas** *par*
ne . . . jamais.

Ex.:—Je n'ai pas d'argent.
—**Je n'ai jamais d'argent.**

1. Il n'y a pas de bruit dans le quartier. **2.** Ma tante n'est pas à l'heure.
3. Ils ne sont pas à la maison. **4.** Je ne réponds pas aux lettres. **5.** Nous ne
travaillons pas la nuit. **6.** John et Roger ne vont pas à la campagne. **7.** Ils
n'entendent pas le téléphone. **8.** Je ne suis pas allé(e) en Angleterre. **9.** Il
n'est pas venu me voir. **10.** Je ne me dépêche pas. **11.** Je ne me suis pas
levé(e) avant sept heures. **12.** Je ne me suis pas couché(e) avant minuit.

VI. Dictée d'après le dialogue, pp. 81-82.

VII. Conversation.

"Have you a room for rent?"
"Yes. I have two: one on the second floor and one on the third."
"What is the rent of the room?"
"The rent of the room on the second floor is 125 francs per month. The
rent of the other is 110 francs per month."
"I prefer the room on the second floor."

Unstressed Forms of Personal Pronouns

39. Remarks about the forms of personal pronouns.

The French personal pronouns have two sets of forms: the unstressed forms, which are used only in conjunction with verbs (i.e., as subject or object of verbs), and the stressed forms, which will be studied later. The unstressed forms are sometimes called "conjunctive" pronouns and the stressed forms "disjunctive" pronouns.

40. Unstressed forms of personal pronouns used as subjects of a verb.

—**Je** vais à l'hôtel.	*I* am going to the hotel.
—**Il** est Américain.	*He* is an American.
—Qu'est-ce que **vous** voulez?	What do *you* want?

The subject forms are: **je, tu, il (elle, on), nous, vous, ils (elles).**

41. Personal pronouns used as direct objects of a verb.

—Allez-vous venir **me** voir?	Are you going to come to see *me?*
—Oui, je vais venir **vous** voir.	Yes, I am going to come to see *you.*
—Voici la chambre. Comment **la** trouvez-vous?	Here is the room. How do you like *it?*
—Je **la** trouve très agréable.	I think *it* is very nice.
—Aimez-vous les pommes?	Do you like apples?
—Oui, je **les** aime beaucoup.	Yes, I like *them* very much.

A. Forms.

The direct object forms are: **me, te, le (la), nous, vous, les.**

B. Use and position.

(1) **Le, la,** and **les** refer either to persons or things. Ex.: Comment trouvez-vous **la chambre?** — Je la trouve très agréable. Comment trouvez-vous **Marie?** — Je **la** trouve très gentille.

(2) The direct object pronoun precedes the verb.* In compound tenses it precedes the auxiliary verb.

 Personal pronouns used as indirect objects of a verb—referring only to persons.

—Avez-vous donné votre adresse à la concierge?   Did you give your address to the concierge?

—Oui, je **lui** ai donné mon adresse.   Yes, I have given *her* my address.

—Avez-vous parlé aux étudiants?   Did you speak to the students?

—Oui, je **leur** ai parlé.   Yes, I spoke *to them*.

Note that in «Je lui ai donné mon adresse», **lui** is the indirect object of **J'ai donné**, *I gave to her;* in «Je leur ai parlé», **leur** is the indirect object of **J'ai parlé**, *I spoke to them*.

A. Forms.

The indirect object forms used to refer to persons are: **me, te, lui, nous, vous, leur.**

Note that **lui, leur,** replace either a masculine or feminine noun. Thus: «**Je lui ai donné mon adresse**» answers both the question «**Avez-vous donné votre adresse à Charles?**» and the question «**Avez-vous donné votre adresse à Marie?**»

B. Position.

The pronoun indirect object precedes the verb.† When the verb is in a compound tense, the pronoun object precedes the auxiliary verb. Ex.: **Je lui ai donné mon adresse.**

(1) When you have both a direct and indirect object pronoun, **me, te, nous, vous** (the indirect object forms) precede **le, la, les** (the direct object forms). Ex.: — **Est-ce qu'il vous a donné son adresse?** — **Oui, il me l'a donnée.** — **Est-ce que vous m'avez donné votre adresse?** — **Oui, je vous l'ai donnée.** — **Est-ce que vous m'avez donné les livres** *(the books)?* — **Oui, je vous les ai donnés.**

(2) When you have a direct and an indirect object pronoun, both of which are in the third person, **le, la, les,** the direct object forms, precede

---

* The only exception, that of affirmative imperative, will be studied in paragraph 52.
† Except affirmative imperatives.

lui, leur, the indirect object forms. Ex.: — **Est-ce que vous avez donné votre adresse à Marie?** — Oui, je **la lui** ai donnée. — **Est-ce que vous avez donné les livres à Roger?** — Oui, je **les lui** ai donnés. — **Est-ce que vous avez donné les livres à Marie et à Roger?** — Oui, je **les leur** ai donnés.

43. Personal pronoun **y** used as indirect object of a verb—referring only to things.

—Avez-vous répondu à la lettre?	Did you answer the letter?
—Oui, j'y ai répondu.	Yes, I answered (replied to) *it*.
—Avez-vous répondu aux lettres?	Did you answer the letters?
—Oui, j'y ai répondu.	Yes, I answered (replied to) *them*.

44. Use of **en** as a partitive pronoun.

A. To replace nouns in a partitive sense.

En is used here * as a pronoun object to replace nouns which are taken in a partitive sense (**du pain, de la viande, des pommes**):

—Avez-vous du pain?	Have you any bread?
—Oui, j'en ai.	Yes, I have *some* (of it).
—Avez-vous acheté de la viande?	Have you bought any meat?
—Oui, j'en ai acheté.	Yes, I bought *some* (of it).
—Voici des pommes. **En** voulez-vous?	Here are some apples. Do you want *any* (of them)?

B. With expressions of quantity.

If you use expressions of quantity (**beaucoup, un peu, pas,** etc.) or numbers in such phrases, **en** must still be expressed:

—Avez-vous une chambre à louer?	Have you a room for rent?
—Oui, j'en ai **une.**	Yes, I have *one* (of them).
—Avez-vous des cousins?	Have you any cousins?
—Oui, j'en ai **beaucoup.**	Yes, I have *a lot* (of them).
—Voici des pommes.	Here are some apples.
—**En** voulez-vous **une?**	Do you want *one* (of them)?

C. Position.

When there is another personal pronoun before the verb, the pronoun **en** always comes last. Ex.: **Est-ce qu'il vous a donné des poires?** — Oui, il **m'en** a donné. — **Est-ce que vous avez donné des pommes à Charles?** — Oui, je **lui en** ai donné.

---

* **En** used to replace a noun object of the preposition **de** will be studied in par. 52.

I. Exercices d'application. *Répétez en remplaçant les mots en italique* (in italics) *par un pronom personnel:*

A. le, la, les

1. Je trouve *la chambre* très agréable.   **2.** J'aime bien *les cigarettes* françaises. **3.** Je n'aime pas *les bananes*.   **4.** John trouve *le chapeau de Marie* un peu drôle.   **5.** Il connaît *Louise Bedel*.   **6.** Il connaît très bien *les Brown*. **7.** Roger ne connaît pas *les Brown*.   **8.** Comment avez-vous trouvé *la chambre?*   **9.** J'ai trouvé *la chambre* agréable.   **10.** Comment John et Roger ont-ils trouvé *le dîner?*   **11.** Ils ont trouvé *le dîner* très bon.   **12.** Le garçon apporte *la carte.*

B. en

1. J'ai *des fruits*.   **2.** Je n'ai pas *de fruits*.   **3.** Roger n'a pas *de frères*.   **4.** Mme Cochet n'a pas *de cigarettes américaines*.   **5.** Elle a *du tabac français*. **6.** John n'a pas acheté *de tabac français*.   **7.** Avez-vous *des cousins?*   **8.** A-t-il *des cousins?*   **9.** Combien *de cousins* a-t-il?   **10.** Il n'y a pas *de hors-d'œuvre*. **11.** Il n'y a plus *de hors-d'œuvre*.

C. en . . . une, plusieurs, *etc.*

1. J'ai *une chambre* au premier.   **2.** J'ai acheté *un journal*.   **3.** J'ai acheté *deux journaux*.   **4.** J'ai acheté beaucoup *de fruits*.   **5.** Je n'ai pas acheté beaucoup *de papier à lettres*.   **6.** Il y a *une table* là-bas.   **7.** Il y a *deux tables* par ici.   **8.** John a mangé un peu *de viande*.   **9.** Il a mangé un peu *de salade*.   **10.** Il a mangé plusieurs *olives*.   **11.** Roger a plusieurs *frères*. **12.** Marie a plusieurs *chapeaux*.

D. lui, leur

1. J'ai parlé *à la concierge*   **2.** J'ai parlé *à John*.   **3.** J'obéis *à mon père*. **4.** J'obéis *à mes parents*.   **5.** John a dit bonjour *à la concierge*.   **6.** Il a dit au revoir *à Roger*.   **7.** Il a dit au revoir *à ses cousins*.   **8.** J'ai répondu *au professeur*.   **9.** J'ai répondu *à mes parents*.

E. y

1. J'ai répondu *à la lettre*.   **2.** Je n'ai pas répondu *à la lettre*.   **3.** Je n'ai pas répondu *aux questions*.   **4.** Je vais *à la gare*.   **5.** Je suis allé *à la gare*.   **6.** A quelle heure allez-vous *à la gare?*   **7.** Quand allez-vous répondre *à cette lettre?* (y répondre).   **8.** Je vais répondre *à cette lettre* demain matin.

II. Exercices d'application. *Compléments directs et indirects.*

A. *Répétez les phrases suivantes en substituant les mots indiqués et puis en remplaçant les noms par des pronoms personnels:*

Ex.:—Il m'a donné le paquet.
    —**Il me l'a donné.**

1. Il m'a donné [le journal].
    la carte/ les fleurs/ des fleurs/ ma monnaie

2. Il nous a donné [le journal].
    la carte/ les fleurs/ des fleurs/ notre monnaie

3. Vous a-t-il donné [le journal]?
    la carte/ les fleurs/ des fleurs/ votre monnaie

B. *Répétez en remplaçant les noms par deux pronoms personnels:*

Ex.:—J'ai donné le journal à mon père.
    —**Je le lui ai donné.**

1. J'ai donné ma nouvelle adresse à la concierge. **2.** J'ai donné ma nouvelle adresse à mes amis. **3.** Il a apporté la carte à John et à Roger. **4.** Il a apporté des hors-d'œuvre à John et à Roger. **5.** J'ai donné les roses à ma mère. **6.** J'ai donné des roses à ma mère.

III. *Répondez en français en remplaçant les noms par les pronoms convenables:*

1. Connaissez-vous Louise Bedel? **2.** Connaissez-vous M. Brown? **3.** Connaissez-vous les Brown? **4.** Avez-vous apporté votre imperméable? **5.** Avez-vous des frères? **6.** Combien de frères avez-vous? **7.** Avez-vous acheté des journaux aujourd'hui? **8.** Y a-t-il des feuilles sur les arbres en été? **9.** Y a-t-il des feuilles sur les arbres en hiver? **10.** Avez-vous des parents en France? **11.** Est-ce que John a parlé au pharmacien? **12.** Est-ce que John a parlé à Mme Cochet? **13.** Est-ce que vous avez répondu à la concierge? **14.** Avez-vous répondu au télégramme? **15.** John a-t-il répondu aux questions du commissaire de police? **16.** Allez-vous au cinéma ce soir? **17.** Êtes-vous allé au cinéma hier soir? **18.** Avez-vous donné votre nom à l'agent de police? **19.** Avez-vous donné votre adresse à l'agent de police? **20.** Avez-vous donné vos papiers à l'agent de police? **21.** Avez-vous donné de l'argent à l'agent de police? **22.** Est-ce que votre père vous a donné de l'argent? **23.** Est-ce que le boulanger vous a donné votre monnaie? **24.** Vous a-t-il donné de la monnaie?

IV. CONVERSATION.

"I want to buy a sandwich. Is there a drug store near by (near here)?"

"There is a drug store over there on the square. But druggists do not sell sandwiches . . ."

"What do they sell, then?"

"Medicines."

"Where do they sell sandwiches?"

"At the restaurant near the station."

Plans for the Afternoon

Roger —[1]Où irez-vous cet après-midi?

Marie —[2]J'irai en ville.

Roger —[3]Qu'est-ce que vous ferez?

Marie —[4]Je ferai des courses.

Roger —[5]Qu'est-ce que vous achèterez?

Marie —[6]J'achèterai un manteau et une robe.

Roger —[7]Comment irez-vous en ville?

Marie —[8]J'irai à pied, s'il fait beau.

Roger —[9]Vous serez bientôt fatiguée. [10]Pourquoi ne prenez-vous pas l'autobus?

Marie —[11]Je n'aime pas prendre l'autobus. [12]Il y a trop de monde.

Roger —[13]Qu'est-ce que vous ferez s'il pleut?

Marie —[14]S'il pleut, je prendrai un taxi.

Roger —[15]A quelle heure rentrerez-vous?

Marie —[16]Je rentrerai de bonne heure, avant cinq heures.

Roger —[17]N'oubliez pas notre rendez-vous pour ce soir.

Marie —[18]Je n'oublierai pas. [19]A quelle heure finirez-vous votre travail?

Roger —[1]Where are you going this afternoon?

Marie —[2]I am going downtown.

Roger —[3]What are you going to do?

Marie —[4]I shall do some errands.

Roger —[5]What are you going to buy?

Marie —[6]I shall buy a coat (lady's coat) and a dress.

Roger —[7]How will you go downtown?

Marie —[8]I shall walk, if the weather is fine.

Roger —[9]You will soon be tired. [10]Why don't you take the bus?

Marie —[11]I don't like to take the bus. [12]There are too many people.

Roger —[13]What will you do if it rains?

Marie —[14]If it rains, I'll take a taxi.

Roger —[15]What time will you get home?

Marie —[16]I'll get back early, before five o'clock.

Roger —[17]Don't forget our date for this evening.

Marie —[18]I won't forget. [19]What time will you finish your work?

ROGER —[20]Je finirai vers six heures.	ROGER —[20]I'll finish at about six o'clock.
MARIE —[21]A ce soir.	MARIE —[21]I'll see you this evening.
ROGER —[22]Entendu. Je viendrai vous chercher à huit heures précises.	ROGER —[22]All right. I'll come for you (to get you) at eight o'clock on the dot.

I. SUBSTITUTIONS. *Répétez les phrases suivantes en substituant les mots indiqués:*

   1. Je rentrerai [de bonne heure].

     à sept heures du soir/ à quatre heures moins le quart/ vers cinq heures et quart/ vers minuit/ à minuit

   2. Je viendrai vous chercher [à huit heures précises].

     à sept heures précises/ à neuf heures précises/ à cinq heures précises/ à quatre heures précises

II. *Répétez en remplaçant les noms par les pronoms convenables:*

   Ex.:—Je viendrai chercher John.
     —**Je viendrai le chercher.**

   1. Je viendrai chercher [Roger].

     Marie/ John et Roger/ Marie et Louise/ les Brown

   2. J'irai chercher [les Brown].

     Louise Bedel/ Charles Dupont/ ma mère/ mes cousines/ mon imperméable

III. *Répondez en français, d'après le texte, à chacune des questions suivantes:*

   1. Où irez-vous cet après-midi? **2.** Qu'est-ce que vous ferez? **3.** Qu'est-ce que vous achèterez? **4.** Comment irez-vous en ville? **5.** Pourquoi ne prenez-vous pas l'autobus? **6.** Qu'est-ce que vous ferez s'il pleut? **7.** A quelle heure rentrerez-vous? **8.** A quelle heure finirez-vous votre travail? **9.** Est-ce que vous oublierez notre rendez-vous pour ce soir? **10.** A quelle heure viendrez-vous me chercher?

IV. *Demandez à quelqu'un:*

   1. où il ira cet après-midi. **2.** ce qu'il fera en ville. **3.** ce qu'il achètera. **4.** comment il ira en ville. **5.** ce qu'il fera s'il pleut. **6.** à quelle heure il rentrera. **7.** à quelle heure il (elle) finira son travail. **8.** s'il oubliera son rendez-vous pour ce soir.

V. Révision. *Pronoms personnels. Répétez en remplaçant les noms par les pronoms convenables:*

Ex.:—La concierge m'a donné la lettre.
    —**Elle me l'a donnée.**

1. J'ai acheté le journal. **2.** Je l'ai donné à John. **3.** J'ai acheté les journaux. **4.** J'ai acheté des journaux. **5.** J'ai acheté deux journaux. **6.** J'ai acheté un journal. **7.** Le marchand *(merchant)* m'a donné le journal. **8.** Le marchand vous a donné le journal. **9.** La concierge m'a donné la lettre. **10.** Elle vous a donné la lettre. **11.** Elle vous a donné les lettres. **12.** Elle vous a donné des lettres.

VI. Exercices d'application. *Verbes pronominaux.*

A. *Répétez les phrases suivantes en substituant les mots indiqués:*

1. Je vais [me coucher].
me lever/ m'habiller/ me dépêcher

2. Il va [se coucher].
se lever/ s'habiller/ se dépêcher

3. Nous allons [nous coucher].
nous lever/ nous habiller/ nous dépêcher

B. *Demandez en français à quelqu'un:*

1. comment il s'appelle. **2.** à quelle heure il s'est couché hier soir. **3.** à quelle heure il se couche d'habitude. **4.** à quelle heure il se lève d'habitude. **5.** à quelle heure il s'est levé ce matin. **6.** à quelle heure il s'habille le dimanche. **7.** à quelle heure il s'est habillé ce matin. **8.** s'il se dépêche le dimanche matin. **9.** s'il va se lever de bonne heure demain. **10.** s'il veut s'habiller pour aller en ville. **11.** s'il se dépêche le dimanche matin. **12.** si les étudiants se couchent de bonne heure le samedi soir.

VII. Dictée d'après le dialogue, pp. 89-90 et pp. 98-99.

VIII. Conversation.

"What are you going to do Saturday afternoon?"
"I am going to the movies."
"What time are you going?"
"At about two-thirty."
"I'll go with you if you wish."
"All right. I'll see you Saturday."

Note on the *Thèmes d'imitation*

The *Thèmes d'imitation* which will be found in each Grammar Unit from now on, are little themes that are based upon one or more of the dialogs you have already studied. Their purpose is to give you additional practice in using authentic French word patterns. They are scarcely more difficult than the dialogs you have been doing orally; but they call for more conscious effort because they call into play a greater variety of expressions and make use of longer sentences.

The best way to turn out a good, correct, and idiomatic French *Thème* is to work through it orally, sentence by sentence, before putting pen to paper. When you can not recall the right word or phrase, it is better to try to find it in a dialog than in the vocabulary; for if an expression is used in a dialog, you know precisely what it means and how it is used. When you *do* refer to the vocabulary, look for ways to express what you are trying to say. You can not possibly produce a good *Thème* by merely "looking up" all the words and copying them down. YOU HAVE TO THINK THE THING THROUGH IN FRENCH.

When you have worked on a sentence orally until it sounds right to you, write it down, taking care to spell words correctly, to use the proper forms, etc. Then after you have written each sentence, reread it to be sure it expresses the idea you set out to express.

Future Tense and Imperative

45. Formation of the future of regular verbs.

—**Déjeunerez-vous** en ville?	*Will you have lunch* in town?
—Oui, **je déjeunerai** à l'hôtel du Cheval blanc.	Yes, *I shall have lunch* at the White Horse Inn.
—Quand **finirez-vous** votre travail?	When *shall you finish* your work?
—**Je finirai** de bonne heure.	*I shall finish* early.
—**Je finirai** tard.	*I shall finish* late.
—**Je finirai** avant minuit.	*I'll finish* before midnight.
—**Je finirai** après minuit.	*I'll finish* after midnight.
—**Répondrez-vous** à sa lettre?	*Shall you answer* his (her) letter?
—Oui, **je répondrai** bientôt à sa lettre.	Yes, *I shall answer* his (her) letter soon.
—**Vous dépêcherez-vous** de finir votre travail?	*Will you hurry* to finish your work?
—Oui, **je me dépêcherai.**	Yes, *I shall hurry.*

The forms of the future tense of regular verbs are:

FIRST CONJUGATION	SECOND CONJUGATION	THIRD CONJUGATION
je déjeunerai	je finirai	je répondrai
I shall have lunch	*I shall finish*	*I shall answer*
tu déjeuneras	tu finiras	tu répondras
il déjeunera	il finira	il répondra
nous déjeunerons	nous finirons	nous répondrons
vous déjeunerez	vous finirez	vous répondrez
ils déjeuneront	ils finiront	ils répondront

(1) The future tense of regular verbs may be found by adding the future endings **-ai, -as, -a, -ons, -ez, -ont** to the infinitive, except that in the case of verbs of the third conjugation (ending in **-re**) the final **e** is omitted.

(2) Reflexive verbs follow the usual pattern. Ex.: **Je me dépêcherai, tu te dépêcheras, il se dépêchera,** etc.

111

(3) Although the use of *shall* and *will* in English is somewhat delicate, the future tense in French simply denotes futurity. **Irez-vous** and **Voulez-vous aller . . .** are quite different in meaning; the former ind: cates futurity and the latter indicates willingness.

46. Future tense of être and avoir.

—Vos parents **seront** contents de vous voir.　　Your parents *will be* glad to see you.

—**Je serai** content aussi de les voir.　　*I'll be glad* to see them too.

—Est-ce que **j'aurai** le temps de déjeuner?　　*Will I have* time to have lunch?

The forms of the future of **être** and **avoir** are:

être
- je serai, *I shall be*
- tu seras
- il sera
- nous serons
- vous serez
- ils seront

avoir
- j'aurai, *I shall have*
- tu auras
- il aura
- nous aurons
- vous aurez
- ils auront

47. Use of the future tense.

—**Je ferai** des courses demain.　　*I shall do* some errands tomorrow.

—S'il pleut, **je prendrai** un taxi.　　If it rains, *I'll take* a taxi.

(1) Generally speaking, the future tense is used as in English. Note particularly that it is used in the result clause of conditional sentences which express what will happen if a given condition is fulfilled. Ex.: **Je prendrai un taxi** *(the result),* **s'il pleut** *(the condition).*

(2) Contrary to English usage, however, the future tense is always used in temporal clauses introduced by **quand,** *when;* **lorsque,** *when,* etc., if the future time is implied. Ex.: Je déjeunerai **quand je rentrerai.** I shall have lunch, *when I get home.* **Lorsqu'il neigera,** je ferai du ski. *When it snows,* I shall go skiing.

(3) As in English, the present tense is frequently used for the immediate future. Ex.: **Je vais à la gare à midi.**

48. Formation and use of the imperative.

A. Imperative of regular verbs:

—**Regardez** la neige!	*Look at* the snow!
—**Répondez** tout de suite à sa lettre.	*Reply* to his letter at once.
—J'ai faim. **Allons** déjeuner.	I'm hungry. *Let's go* to lunch.
—Voici un restaurant. **Entrons.**	Here's a restaurant. *Let's go in.*
—Garçon, **donnez-moi** la carte, s'il vous plaît.	Waiter, *give me* the menu, please.

(1) Forms of the imperative of regular verbs:

FIRST CONJUGATION		SECOND CONJUGATION	
regarde(s) *	*look* (**tu** form)	finis	*finish* (**tu** form)
regardons	*let's look*	finissons	*let's finish*
regardez	*look* (**vous** form)	finissez	*finish* (**vous** form)

THIRD CONJUGATION	
réponds	*answer* (**tu** form)
répondons	*let's answer*
répondez	*answer* (**vous** form)

(2) The imperative of regular verbs is the same as the second person singular * and the first and second person plural of the present indicative without the subject pronoun.

B. Imperative of reflexive verbs:

—Dépêchez-vous!	*Hurry!*
—Asseyez-vous.	*Sit down.*

(1) Forms of the imperative of reflexive verbs:

dépêche-toi	*hurry* (**tu** form)
dépêchons-nous	*let's hurry*
dépêchez-vous	*hurry* (**vous** form)

(2) The reflexive object must always be expressed. With affirmative imperative, the object follows (dépêchez-**vous**); with negative imperative, the object precedes the verb (ne **vous** dépêchez pas).

---

* The **tu** form of the imperative of the first conjugation has an s only when it is followed by **y** or **en**.

C. Imperative of **être** and **avoir:**

(1) Forms of the imperative of **être** and **avoir:**

sois	*be* (**tu** form)		aie	*have* (**tu** form)
soyons	*let's be*		ayons	*let's have*
soyez	*be* (**vous** form)		ayez	*have* (**vous** form)

(2) The imperative of **être** and **avoir** is used primarily in set expressions such as:

—Soyez le bienvenu! *Welcome!*

—Ayez la bonté de . . . *Please (i.e., Have the kindness to . . .)*

I. EXERCICES D'APPLICATION.

A. *Mettez les formes suivantes au pluriel:*

Ex.:—Je déjeunerai. **Nous déjeunerons.**

I. Je parlerai. **2.** Je rentrerai. **3.** Je me coucherai. **4.** Je m'habillerai. **5.** Je finirai. **6.** J'obéirai. **7.** Je choisirai. **8.** Je répondrai. **9.** Je vendrai. **10.** J'entendrai. **11.** J'irai. **12.** Je ferai. **13.** Je serai. **14.** Je prendrai. **15.** J'aurai.

B. *Mettez au pluriel:*

Ex.:—Il parlera. **Ils parleront.**

I. Il dînera. **2.** Il rentrera. **3.** Il se couchera. **4.** Il s'habillera. **5.** Il finira. **6.** Il achètera. **7.** Il donnera. **8.** Il partira. **9.** Il arrivera. **10.** Il prendra. **11.** Il aura. **12.** Il sera. **13.** Il regardera. **14.** Il fera. **15.** Il se lèvera.

C. *Mettez chacune des phrases suivantes au futur:*

I. Je prends un taxi. **2.** Il fait beau. **3.** Il fait des courses. **4.** Il a vingt et un ans. **5.** Il vend son auto. **6.** Il est ici. **7.** Nous avons faim. **8.** Il va en ville. **9.** Le train part à cinq heures. **10.** Je déjeune à la maison. **11.** Il y a de la neige en hiver. **12.** Y a-t-il beaucoup de monde? **13.** Avez-vous le temps d'aller au bureau de poste? **14.** A-t-il besoin de son auto? **15.** Est-il content de vous voir?

D. *Dites en français à quelqu'un:*

Ex.:—de se lever. **Levez-vous.**

—de ne pas se lever. **Ne vous levez pas.**

I. d'entrer. **2.** de parler français. **3.** de regarder. **4.** de rentrer de bonne heure. **5.** d'aller à la charcuterie. **6.** de finir son travail. **7.** de se dépêcher.

8. de s'habiller. **9.** de s'asseoir. **10.** de ne pas entrer. **11.** de ne pas aller au cinéma ce soir. **12.** de ne pas oublier votre rendez-vous. **13.** de ne pas se dépêcher. **14.** de ne pas vendre son auto.

II. *Répondez en français à chacune des questions suivantes:*

(*a*) **1.** Qu'est-ce que Marie fera cet après-midi? **2.** Où ira-t-elle? **3.** Qu'est-ce qu'elle achètera? **4.** Comment ira-t-elle en ville? **5.** Qu'est-ce qu'elle fera s'il pleut? **6.** A quelle heure rentrera-t-elle? **7.** Qu'est-ce que Roger fera cet après-midi? **8.** A quelle heure finira-t-il son travail?

(*b*) **1.** Qu'est-ce que Marie fera s'il pleut? **2.** Qu'est-ce qu'elle fera si elle ne trouve pas de taxi? **3.** Qu'est-ce qu'elle fera quand elle rentrera? **4.** Qu'est-ce que vous ferez quand vous rentrerez ce soir? **5.** Où irez-vous cet après-midi s'il fait beau? **6.** Qu'est-ce que vous ferez cet hiver quand il neigera?

III. *Répétez chacune des phrases suivantes en remplaçant* **quand** *par* **lorsque:**

1. Quand il neigera, je ferai du ski. **2.** Quand j'irai en ville, je ferai des courses. **3.** Je serai content quand l'été arrivera. **4.** Soyez prêt quand je viendrai vous chercher. **5.** Je serai prêt quand vous viendrez me chercher.

IV. *Répétez en remplaçant* **si** *et le présent par* **quand** *et le futur:*

Ex.:—. . . si je suis . . ., **quand je serai . . .**

1. S'il fait beau, je ferai une promenade. **2.** Si nous avons le temps, nous irons au cinéma. **3.** Si je suis libre, je viendrai vous voir. **4.** Si John vient me voir, je serai content. **5.** S'il y a de la neige, je ferai du ski. **6.** J'irai en France si j'ai de l'argent. **7.** Parlerez-vous français si vous allez en France? **8.** Il finira son travail s'il a le temps.

V. RÉVISION. *Dites en français:*

1. At first. **2.** Afterwards. **3.** In that case. **4.** The first time. **5.** Once. **6.** Once a (*par*) week. **7.** Several times. **8.** Several times a day. **9.** Several times a week. **10.** I haven't time. **11.** What time is it? **12.** How is the weather? **13.** A long time. **14.** Too long. **15.** Two years ago. **16.** In the evening. **17.** In the morning. **18.** All day long. **19.** All afternoon. **20.** Sunday. **21.** Next Sunday. **22.** Early. **23.** Late. **24.** Soon.

VI. Thème d'imitation:

John Hughes is a young American chemical engineer. He lives in Paris. He has rented a room near the Observatory, in the Latin Quarter, in the house of an old lady, Mrs. Duval. She is seventy years old, she has white hair, and she is very nice to John, because she likes Americans. John is happy. He likes (**Il aime bien**) his room, and autumn in Paris is one of the most beautiful seasons of the year. The trees of the Avenue of the Observatory are very beautiful in the month of October. The month of November is usually less pleasant, because it is cold and it rains a good deal. But John forgets the bad weather and he thinks he is lucky to be (**d'être**) in Paris.

A Trip

Au guichet, à la Gare de l'Est

ROGER —[1]Je voudrais un billet aller et retour pour Reims.

L'EMPLOYÉ —[2]Quelle classe, monsieur?

ROGER —[3]Seconde, s'il vous plaît. [4]Combien de temps ce billet est-il bon?

L'EMPLOYÉ —[5]Quinze jours,* monsieur.

ROGER —[6]Est-ce que je dois changer de train en route?

L'EMPLOYÉ —[7]Oui, vous devez changer à Épernay.

ROGER —[8]Combien de temps faut-il attendre la correspondance?

L'EMPLOYÉ —[9]Vous aurez à peu près une demi-heure à Épernay.

Sur le quai, à Épernay

ROGER —[10] Pardon, sur quelle voie le train de Reims arrive-t-il?

L'EMPLOYÉ —[11]Ici, monsieur, sur la première voie.

ROGER —[12]Le train est-il à l'heure?

L'EMPLOYÉ —[13]Non, monsieur. Il est en retard de dix minutes.

At the Ticket Window of the Eastern Railway Station

ROGER —[1]I should like a round-trip ticket to Rheims.

THE EMPLOYEE —[2]Which class, sir?

ROGER —[3]Second, please. [4]How long is this ticket good?

THE EMPLOYEE —[5]Two weeks, sir.

ROGER —[6]Do I have to change trains on the way?

THE EMPLOYEE —[7]Yes, you have to change trains at Epernay.

ROGER —[8]How long do you have to wait for the connection?

THE EMPLOYEE —[9]You will have about half an hour at Epernay.

On the Platform at Epernay

ROGER —[10]Pardon me. On which track does the Rheims train come in?

THE EMPLOYEE —[11]Here, sir. On the first track.

ROGER —[12]Is the train on time?

THE EMPLOYEE —[13]No, sir. It is ten minutes late (late by ten minutes).

---

* The French say **quinze jours** (15 days) for "two weeks" and **huit jours** for "a week."

ROGER —¹⁴Est-ce que j'aurai le temps d'aller au buffet?

L'EMPLOYÉ —¹⁵Vous pouvez essayer, mais dépêchez-vous. ¹⁶Le train s'arrête seulement trois minutes. ¹⁷Si vous manquez ce train, vous serez obligé de passer la nuit à Épernay.

ROGER —¹⁴Will I have time to go to the lunchroom?

THE EMPLOYEE —¹⁵You can try it, but hurry. ¹⁶The train stops just three minutes. ¹⁷If you miss this train, you will have to spend the night at Epernay.

I. SUBSTITUTIONS. *Répétez les phrases suivantes en substituant les mots indiqués:*

1. Je voudrais un billet aller et retour pour [Reims].
   Lyon/ Marseille/ Bruxelles/ Rome

2. Je voudrais bien [aller en France].
   faire une promenade/ rentrer chez moi/ lui parler/ le voir/ leur parler/ les voir

3. Est-ce que je dois changer [de train]?
   de gare/ de chambre/ d'hôtel/ de robe/ de chapeau

4. Vous devez changer [de train].
   de gare/ de chambre/ d'hôtel/ de robe/ de chapeau

5. Le train est en retard de [dix minutes].
   trois minutes/ vingt minutes/ une demi-heure/ deux heures

II. *Répondez en français, d'après le texte, à chacune des questions suivantes:*

1. Où va Roger? 2. Quelle espèce de billet veut-il? 3. Quelle classe? 4. Combien de temps son billet est-il bon? 5. Est-ce qu'il doit changer de train en route? 6. Combien de temps faut-il attendre la correspondance? 7. De combien de minutes le train est-il en retard? 8. Est-ce que Roger aura le temps d'aller au buffet? 9. Qu'est-ce qu'il sera obligé de faire s'il manque la correspondance? 10. Combien de temps le train s'arrête-t-il?

III. *Demandez à quelqu'un:*

1. un billet aller et retour pour Reims. 2. combien de temps votre billet est bon. 3. si vous devez changer de train en route. 4. où vous devez changer de train. 5. combien de temps il faut attendre la correspondance. 6. sur quelle voie arrive le train de Reims. 7. si le train est à l'heure. 8. si le train est en retard. 9. si le train est en retard d'une demi-heure. 10. s'il s'arrête dix minutes. 11. si vous aurez le temps d'aller au buffet. 12. ce que c'est que le buffet d'une gare.

IV. Exercices d'application.

A. *Posez la question à laquelle répond chacune des phrases suivantes, en commençant par* **combien de temps:**

Ex.:—Il faut attendre vingt minutes.
    —**Combien de temps faut-il attendre?**

1. Il faut travailler deux heures. **2.** Monsieur Brown a passé deux ans en Angleterre. **3.** Ce billet est bon quinze jours. **4.** Je serai ici deux jours. **5.** L'hiver dure longtemps. **6.** Il faut une demi-heure pour aller en ville. **7.** Il faut cinq minutes pour aller à la pharmacie.

B. *Répétez en remplaçant* **à** (at) *par* **vers** (at about):

1. Il arrive à cinq heures. **2.** Je déjeune à midi. **3.** Je me couche à onze heures. **4.** Je vais rentrer à six heures.

C. *Répétez en employant* **à peu près** (about) *devant le nombre indiqué:*

1. Vous aurez vingt minutes à Épernay. **2.** Il a passé dix ans en Angleterre. **3.** Il faut une heure pour dîner. **4.** Il est venu en France il y a cinq ans.

D. *Remplacez l'impératif par* **vous devez** *et l'infinitif:*

Ex.:—Parlez français.
    —**Vous devez parler français.**

1. Allez à la boulangerie. **2.** Finissez votre travail. **3.** Couchez-vous de bonne heure. **4.** Dépêchez-vous. **5.** Soyez à l'heure. **6.** Ne soyez pas en retard. **7.** Commencez tout de suite.

V. Dictée d'après le dialogue, pp. 107-108.

VI. Conversation.

"What time does the train to Rheims arrive here?"
"At 21:37."
"At what time will it get to Rheims?"
"At 22:59."
"Is there a good hotel near the station?"
"Yes, you can spend the night at the Hôtel des Voyageurs."

At the Haberdasher's

ROGER —[1]Combien coûtent ces mouchoirs?

LE VENDEUR —[2]Vingt francs la douzaine, monsieur.

ROGER —[3]Donnez-m'en une douzaine, s'il vous plaît. [4]Combien coûte cette paire de gants?

LE VENDEUR —[5]Vingt-cinq francs, monsieur.

ROGER —[6]Ces gants sont-ils de bonne qualité?

LE VENDEUR —[7]Certainement, monsieur. [8]Vous ne trouverez rien de meilleur.

ROGER —[9]En avez-vous d'autres?

LE VENDEUR —[10]Oui, monsieur. En voici des gris.

ROGER —[11]Bon. Donnez-les-moi. [12]Quel est le prix de ce pardessus?

LE VENDEUR —[13]Deux cent cinquante francs, monsieur. [14]Voulez-vous l'essayer?

ROGER —[15]Volontiers.

LE VENDEUR —[16]Il vous va très bien. [17]Le voulez-vous?

ROGER —[18]Oui. Mettez-le dans un carton, s'il vous plaît.

LE VENDEUR —[19]Voulez-vous l'emporter tout de suite?

ROGER —[20]Non, je ne rentre pas chez moi maintenant.

ROGER —[1]How much do these handkerchiefs cost?

THE SALESMAN —[2]Twenty francs a dozen, sir.

ROGER —[3]Give me a dozen, please. [4]How much is this pair of gloves?

THE SALESMAN —[5]Twenty-five francs, sir.

ROGER —[6]Are these gloves of good quality?

THE SALESMAN —[7]Certainly, sir. [8]You won't find anything better.

ROGER —[9]Have you any others?

THE SALESMAN —[10]Yes, sir. Here are some gray ones.

ROGER —[11]All right. Give them to me. [12]What is the price of this topcoat?

THE SALESMAN —[13]Two hundred and fifty francs, sir. [14]Do you want to try it on?

ROGER —[15]Yes. I'll be glad to.

THE SALESMAN —[16]It looks very well on you. [17]Do you want it?

ROGER —[18]Yes, put it in a box (cardboard), please.

THE SALESMAN —[19]Do you want to take it with you?

ROGER —[20]No, I am not going home now.

Le vendeur —²¹Eh bien, je pourrai vous le faire envoyer cet après-midi.

The Salesman —²¹Well, I can have it sent to you this afternoon.

Roger —²²Je n'ai pas d'argent sur moi . . .

Roger —²²I haven't any money on me . . .

Le vendeur —²³Cela ne fait rien, monsieur. ²⁴Nous vous enverrons la facture.

The Salesman —²³That doesn't make any difference, sir. ²⁴We will send you the bill.

I. Substitutions. *Répétez les phrases suivantes en substituant les mots indiqués:*

1. (a) [Ces gants] sont-ils de bonne qualité?
   Ces mouchoirs/ Ces imperméables/ Ces cravates

   (b) [Ce pardessus] est-il de bonne qualité?
   Ce chapeau/ Cet imperméable/ Ce papier à lettres

2. Vous ne trouverez rien [de meilleur].
   de plus joli/ de meilleur marché/ de plus beau/ de plus élégant/ de plus chaud

3. Je ne rentre pas chez moi [maintenant].
   tout de suite/ à midi/ pour déjeuner/ après déjeuner/ avant minuit

4. Je pourrai vous le faire envoyer [cet après-midi].
   bientôt/ tout de suite/ vers cinq heures/ avant cinq heures/ avant midi

5. Il y a [une douzaine] de personnes dans l'avion.
   une demi-douzaine/ une dizaine/ une vingtaine/ une centaine

6. Voilà de belles pommes. Donnez m'en [une].
   une douzaine/ une demi-douzaine/ deux/ deux douzaines/ deux kilos

II. *Répondez en français, d'après le texte:*

1. Combien coûtent ces mouchoirs? 2. Combien de mouchoirs Roger achète-t-il? 3. Combien coûte cette paire de gants? 4. Ces gants sont-ils de bonne qualité? 5. Est-ce que le vendeur en a d'autres? 6. De quelle couleur sont-ils? 7. Quel est le prix de ce pardessus? 8. Est-ce que ce pardessus va bien à Roger? 9. Où Roger dit-il de mettre le pardessus? 10. Pourquoi ne l'emporte-t-il pas tout de suite? 11. Quand le vendeur pourra-t-il envoyer le pardessus?

III. *Répondez en français:*

1. Irez-vous en ville cet après-midi? 2. A quelle heure rentrerez-vous? 3. Dînerez-vous en ville? 4. Dînerez-vous quand vous rentrerez? 5. Pourrez-vous m'acheter un journal? 6. Irez-vous au cinéma si vous avez le temps? 7. Pourrez-vous venir me chercher? 8. A quelle heure viendrez-vous me chercher?

IV. *Répétez en remplaçant l'impératif par* **voulez-vous bien** *avec l'infinitif:*

Ex.:—Donnez-moi la carte.
   —**Voulez-vous bien me donner la carte?**

1. Entrez. **2.** Envoyez-moi la facture. **3.** Envoyez-la-moi. **4.** Essayez-le. **5.** Donnez-moi votre adresse. **6.** Donnez-la-moi. **7.** Donnez-lui votre adresse. **8.** Attendez deux minutes.

V. *Répétez les phrases suivantes en remplaçant le nom par le pronom convenable:*

Ex.:—Avez-vous d'autres * gants?
   —**En avez-vous d'autres?**

1. Avez-vous des gants gris? * **2.** Avez-vous des gants de meilleure qualité? **3.** Voici d'autres gants. **4.** Voilà de beaux mouchoirs. **5.** Voilà des mouchoirs de belle qualité. **6.** Mettez le pardessus dans un carton. **7.** Mettez la paire de gants dans le carton. **8.** Mettez les mouchoirs dans le carton. **9.** Voilà les gants. **10.** Voilà la paire de gants.

VI. Dictée d'après le dialogue, pp. 117-118.

VII. Conversation.

"How much are these oranges (**oranges,** *f.*)?"
"Two francs a dozen."
"These oranges are too small and they are green. Have you others?"
"Here are some very beautiful ones at 3 fr. 50."
"Good. Give me a dozen."

---

* Note that with adjectives that precede nouns, you normally say **de** (Avez-vous **d'autres** gants? En avez-vous **d'autres?**); but with adjectives that follow nouns, you say **du, de la,** or **des** (Avez-vous **des** gants gris? En avez-vous **des** gris?).

Stressed Forms of Personal Pronouns

49. Distinction between stressed forms and unstressed forms of personal pronouns.

The stressed forms of personal pronouns differ from the unstressed forms in both form and usage. You have learned that the unstressed forms are ordinarily used as subject, direct object, and indirect object of verbs. The stressed forms are commonly used after prepositions and, in certain circumstances, with verbs.

50. Stressed forms of personal pronouns.

—Où allez-vous?	Where are you going?
—Je vais **chez moi.**	I am going *home.*
—Allez-vous chez M. Brown?	Are you going to Mr. Brown's?
—Oui, je vais **chez lui.**	Yes, I am going *to his house.*
—Êtes-vous déjà allé chez les Brown?	Have you been to the Browns' before?
—Oui, je suis déjà allé **chez eux.**	Yes, I have already been *to their house.*
—Êtes-vous allé au bal avec Marie?	Did you go to the dance with Mary?
—Oui, j'y suis allé **avec elle.**	Yes, I went *with her.*

The stressed forms of personal pronouns are: **moi, toi, lui (elle), nous, vous, eux (elles).**

Note carefully that the third person of stressed forms has different forms for masculine and feminine (**lui** and **elle, eux** and **elles**), whereas the third person of unstressed forms has only one form (**lui**) for the singular and one form (**leur**) for the plural.

51. Use of the stressed forms of personal pronouns.

A. As object of a preposition (**de, avec, sans, chez, pour,** etc.):

—Voulez-vous venir **avec moi?**	Do you want to go along *with me?*
—Si Marie ne rentre pas, je déjeunerai **sans elle.**	If Mary does not come back, I will have lunch *without her.*
—Connaissez-vous ses cousines?	Do you know his (*or* her) cousins?
—Oui, je suis allé **chez elles** plusieurs fois.	Yes, I have gone *to their house* several times.
—Avez-vous peur de votre père?	Are you afraid of your father?
—Non, je n'ai pas peur **de lui.**	No, I am not afraid *of him.*

The stressed forms are generally used only to refer to persons:

—Parlez-vous de **Charles?** —Oui, nous parlons de **lui.**
—Parlez-vous de **Marie?** —Oui, nous parlons d'**elle.**
—Avez-vous besoin de **moi?** —Non, je n'ai pas besoin de **vous.**

When speaking of things, instead of the prepositions **de** with a stressed form of the personal pronoun, you use the pronoun **en** (*of it, of them*).

—Parlez-vous **de votre voyage?** —Oui, nous **en** parlons.
—Avez-vous besoin **de gants?** —Oui, **j'en** ai besoin.
—Avez-vous peur **des examens?** —Non, je n'**en** ai pas peur.

B. After **c'est, ce sont** (whether expressed or understood):

—Qui est là? —C'est **moi.** (or **Moi.**)	Who is there? It's *I.* (or *I.*)
—Qui a écrit cette lettre?	Who wrote that letter?
—C'est **elle.** (or **Elle.**)	It was *she.* (or *She did.*)
—Qui sont ces jeunes filles? Est-ce que ce sont vos cousines?	Who are those girls? Are they your cousins?—Yes, it is *they.*
—Oui, ce sont **elles.**	

C. To specify the persons indicated by a plural form of a personal pronoun:

—**Elle et moi,** nous sommes allés au cinéma ensemble.	*She and I* (we) went to the movies together.
—**Lui et elle** sont allés en ville.	*He and she* went downtown.

D. In addition to, or instead of, an unstressed form of personal pronouns, for emphasis:

—**Moi,** je ne sais pas.	*I* don't know.
—**Moi,** je suis Américain.	*I* am an American.
—**Lui** aussi est Américain.	*He too* is an American.

52. Use of personal pronouns with the imperative.

A. With the affirmative imperative:

Personal pronoun objects follow the affirmative imperative:
>—Mettez-**le** dans un carton. *(dir. obj.)*
>—Donnez-**en** aussi à Roger. *(dir. obj. partitive)*
>—Garçon, donnez-**moi** des hors-d'œuvre. *(indir. obj.)*

(1) For direct object you use **le, la, les; en.** For indirect object you use **moi (m'), toi (t'), lui, nous, vous, leur.**

(2) When you have both a direct and an indirect object pronoun, the indirect object comes last except when **en** is used. Ex.: Montrez-moi votre carte d'identité. Montrez-**la-moi.** Montrez-**la-lui.** Apportez-nous les fruits. Apportez-**les-nous.** Apportez-**les-leur.** Achetez-moi des cigarettes. Achetez-**m'en.** Achetez-**lui-en.**

B. With the negative imperative:

With negative imperatives, the unstressed forms of personal pronouns are used and stand in order of pronoun objects which is normal in the declarative sentences (Par. 42.). Ex.: Vous me donnez votre adresse. Vous me la donnez. **Ne me la donnez pas.** *(neg. imper.)* Vous lui donnez la carte. Vous la lui donnez. **Ne la lui donnez pas.** *(neg. imper.)* Vous m'apportez du café. Vous m'en apportez. **Ne m'en apportez pas.** *(neg. imper.)*

I. Exercices d'application.

A. *Répétez en remplaçant les noms par les pronoms convenables:*

Ex.:—Je suis allé chez les Brown.
   —**Je suis allé chez eux.**

1. J'ai passé la journée chez mon oncle.   **2.** J'ai passé la journée chez mes parents.   **3.** John est allé au bal avec Marie.   **4.** Il est allé au bal avec ses cousines.   **5.** Je suis parti sans mon père.   **6.** Je suis parti sans les jeunes filles.

B. *Répétez en remplaçant les noms par* **en** *ou* **y:**
1. Nous avons parlé de nos voyages.   **2.** Nous avons parlé de notre promenade.
3. Avez-vous répondu à sa lettre?   **4.** Avez-vous répondu aux questions?
5. Je n'ai pas peur des examens.   **6.** Je n'ai pas peur de la neige.

II. *Répondez affirmativement en français à chacune des questions suivantes, en remplaçant les noms par les pronoms convenables:*

1. Êtes-vous déjà allé(e) chez M. Brown? **2.** Êtes-vous allé(e) au cinéma avec Marie? **3.** Êtes-vous déjà allé(e) chez Marie et chez Alice? **4.** Est-ce que vous avez déjeuné avec Roger? **5.** Avez-vous déjeuné avec votre ami? **6.** Êtes-vous allé(e) au bal samedi soir avec Marie? **7.** Êtes-vous parti(e) sans Marie? **8.** Avez-vous fait des courses pour votre mère? **9.** Avez-vous acheté des gants pour votre mère? **10.** Avez-vous confiance en votre père? **11.** Est-ce que John a loué une chambre chez Mme Duval?

III. *Répondez négativement, en employant le pronom convenable:*

1. Avez-vous besoin de moi? **2.** Avez-vous besoin de mon frère? **3.** Avez-vous besoin de mon auto? **4.** Est-ce que vous avez parlé de l'examen? **5.** Avez-vous parlé de votre travail? **6.** Avez-vous parlé de John et de Roger? **7.** Avez-vous peur de votre père? **8.** Avez-vous peur de vos parents? **9.** Avez-vous peur des trains? **10.** Avez-vous peur des agents de police? **11.** Avez-vous peur des taxis? **12.** Avez-vous confiance en moi? **13.** Est-ce que Marie a confiance en John? **14.** Est-ce que John a loué une chambre chez Mme Cochet?

IV. Exercices d'application. *Impératif.*

A. *Répétez en remplaçant les noms par les pronoms convenables:*

Ex.:—Apportez-moi les fruits.
    —**Apportez-les-moi.**

1. Apportez-moi l'addition. **2.** Apportez-moi les hors-d'œuvre. **3.** Apportez-nous le plat de viande. **4.** Apportez-nous du raisin. **5.** Apportez-moi de la crème. **6.** Apportez-nous des fruits.

B. *Mettez les phrases suivantes à la forme négative:*

Ex.:—Donnez-moi la carte.
    —**Ne me donnez pas la carte.**

1. Donnez-lui l'addition. **2.** Envoyez-lui la facture. **3.** Envoyez-lui de l'argent. **4.** Apportez-nous du café. **5.** Donnez-moi du café.

V. *Dites à quelqu'un:*

Ex.:—de vous donner une paire de gants. **Donnez-moi une paire de gants.**
    —de vous en donner une paire. **Donnez-m'en une paire.**

1. de vous donner une douzaine de mouchoirs. **2.** de vous en donner une douzaine. **3.** de vous apporter une pomme. **4.** de vous en apporter une. **5.** de

vous en apporter une demi-douzaine. **6.** de vous donner un peu de café. **7.** de vous en donner un peu. **8.** de ne pas vous en donner beaucoup. **9.** de ne pas vous donner de crème. **10.** de ne pas vous en donner trop.

VI. Révision. *Dites en français:*

A. venir chercher

1. What time must I come for you? **2.** I am going to come for you at a quarter to one. **3.** What time did he come for you? **4.** He came for me at half past one.

B. aller chercher

1. We went for them yesterday. **2.** He went for her in a taxi. **3.** Have you your tickets?—Yes, we went for them yesterday.

VII. Thème d'imitation:

Friday afternoon, John and Roger did some errands. They went into several stores. Then John told Roger that he wanted [1] to go to a drugstore to buy some writing paper and some post cards. They went into a drugstore and John said to the druggist: "I would like some writing paper and some post cards." The pharmacist said to him: "We sell neither [2] writing paper nor post cards, sir. If you need those things, go to the bookstore or the tobacco shop. They do not sell medicines in tobacco shops, and I have neither writing paper nor post cards." Roger thought [3] the incident [4] very funny; [5] but John thought it was less amusing.

---

[1] voulait (imperfect). [2] **Cf.** Il ne fait **ni trop froid** ni trop chaud. [3] a trouvé. [4] l'incident (*m.*).
[5] amusant.

Going Downtown

A l'arrêt de l'autobus

ROGER —[1]Bonjour, John. Qu'est-ce que vous faites ici?

JOHN —[2]Vous voyez, j'attends l'autobus.

ROGER —[3]Est-ce que vous l'attendez* depuis longtemps?

JOHN —[4]Je l'attends depuis un quart d'heure.

ROGER —[5]Vraiment? Vous n'avez pas vu d'autobus depuis† un quart d'heure?

JOHN —[6]Si. Un autobus est venu.

ROGER —[7]Pourquoi ne l'avez-vous pas pris?

JOHN —[8]Je n'ai pas pu monter. [9]Il était complet.

ROGER —[10]Voici un autre autobus qui arrive.

JOHN —[11]Je vois des gens debout.

ROGER —[12]Ça ne fait rien. [13]Montons tout de même.

Dans l'autobus

JOHN —[14]Il n'y a pas beaucoup de place . . .

ROGER —[15]Il y aura de la place plus loin, quand les gens commenceront à descendre.

At the Bus Stop

ROGER —[1]Good morning, John. What are you doing here?

JOHN —[2]You see, I am waiting for the bus.

ROGER —[3]Have you been waiting for it long?

JOHN —[4]I have been waiting for it for a quarter of an hour.

ROGER —[5]Really? You haven't seen a bus for a quarter of an hour?

JOHN —[6]Yes, I have. A bus came.

ROGER —[7]Why didn't you take it?

JOHN —[8]I couldn't get on. [9]It was full.

ROGER —[10]Here comes another bus.

JOHN —[11]I see people standing.

ROGER —[12]That makes no difference. [13]Let's get on anyway.

On the Bus

JOHN —[14]There is not much room . . .

ROGER —[15]There will be room further on, when people begin to get off.

---

* When the present indicative of the verb is used with **depuis,** it indicates that the action began in the past and is still going on at the time the statement is made.

† When the **passé composé** is used with **depuis,** it indicates a simple past action.

JOHN —[16]Je l'espère. [17]Où descendez-vous?

ROGER —[18]Je descends à l'arrêt de la rue de la Paix. [19]Je vais chez le coiffeur.

JOHN —[20]Moi aussi. Si vous voulez, j'irai avec vous.

ROGER —[21]Entendu. Nous pourrons y aller ensemble.

JOHN —[16]I hope so. [17]Where are you getting off?

ROGER —[18]I am getting off at the Rue de la Paix. [19]I am going to the barber's.

JOHN —[20] So am I. I'll go with you, if you don't mind.

ROGER —[21]O.K. We can go there together.

I. SUBSTITUTIONS. *Répétez les phrases suivantes en substituant les mots indiqués:*

1. [J'attends l'autobus] depuis un quart d'heure.
   Je suis ici/ Il pleut/ Marie parle/ Nous sommes ici

2. Depuis combien de temps [attendez-vous]?
   êtes-vous ici/ fait-il froid/ parlez-vous français/ demeurez-vous ici

3. Depuis quand [attendez-vous]?
   êtes-vous ici/ fait-il froid/ parlez-vous français/ demeurez-vous ici

4. Je n'ai pas pu [monter].
   déjeuner à midi/ arriver à l'heure/ aller au buffet/ y aller/ venir vous chercher

5. Je descends à l'arrêt de [la rue de la Paix].
   la rue de la Nation/ la rue de la Gare/ la rue de l'Hôpital/ la rue de la Poste

II. *Répondez en français à chacune des questions suivantes, d'après le texte:*

(a) 1. Bonjour. Qu'est-ce que vous faites ici?   2. Est-ce que vous attendez l'autobus depuis longtemps?   3. N'avez-vous pas vu d'autobus depuis un quart d'heure?   4. Pourquoi n'avez-vous pas pris l'autobus?   5. Y a-t-il des gens debout dans l'autobus?   6. Quand y aura-t-il de la place dans l'autobus? 7. Où descendez-vous?   8. Où allez-vous?

(b) 1. Où John attend-il l'autobus?   2. L'attend-il depuis longtemps?   3. Est-ce qu'un autobus est venu?   4. Pourquoi John n'a-t-il pas pu monter? 5. Y a-t-il beaucoup de gens dans l'autobus qui arrive?   6. Où Roger va-t-il descendre?   7. Où va-t-il?

III. *Demandez à quelqu'un:*

1. ce qu'il fait ici.   2. s'il attend l'autobus depuis longtemps.   3. s'il n'a pas vu d'autobus depuis un quart d'heure.   4. pourquoi il n'a pas pris l'autobus. 5. s'il y a des gens debout dans l'autobus.   6. quand il y aura de la place dans l'autobus.   7. où il descend.   8. où il va.

IV. *Répétez chacune des phrases suivantes en ajoutant* **depuis longtemps:**

Ex.:—Je n'ai pas vu d'autobus.
—**Je n'ai pas vu d'autobus depuis longtemps.**

I. Je n'ai pas vu mon père.   **2.** Je ne suis pas allé(e) au cinéma.   **3.** John n'est pas allé chez les Brown.   **4.** Je n'ai pas pris l'autobus.   **5.** Je n'ai pas fait de longue promenade.   **6.** Nous n'avons pas écrit de lettres.   **7.** Nous ne sommes pas sorti(e)s.   **8.** Je ne suis pas allé(e) chez le coiffeur.

V. *Dites en français:*

A. depuis

I. I have been here for three months.   **2.** I have been here for half an hour.
3. I have been living here for a long time.   **4.** I have been living here since the 20th of September.   **5.** I have been speaking French since the 20th of September.   **6.** I have been speaking French for three months.

B. de la place

I. There is not much room.   **2.** There is room on the bus.   **3.** There is no room on the bus.   **4.** There is no more room on the bus.   **5.** There is no more room.   **6.** There will be room further on.   **7.** There won't be any more room.

C. temps, fois

I. How many times do you go to the movies per month?   **2.** How long does winter last?   **3.** How long do you have to work tonight?   **4.** How long does the train stop?   **5.** This is the first time it has snowed this year.   **6.** This is the first time I have been skiing this year.   **7.** This is the second time I have gone to the movies this week.

VI. Révision.

Répondez en français à chacune des questions suivantes, en rem-plaçant les mots en italiques par l'adverbe **y** (there).

Ex.:—Allez-vous *à la gare?*
—**Oui, j'y vais.**

I. Allez-vous *chez le coiffeur?*   **2.** Allez-vous *au bureau de tabac?*   **3.** Allez-vous *à la banque* ce matin?   **4.** Allez-vous *au cinéma* demain soir?   **5.** Roger va-t-il *chez le coiffeur?*   **6.** Marie va-t-elle *chez la modiste?*   **7.** Avez-vous besoin d'aller *chez le coiffeur?*   **8.** Avez-vous besoin d'aller *à la banque?*
9. John et Roger sont-ils montés *dans l'autobus?*   **10.** John et Roger sont-ils allés *en ville ensemble?*   **11.** Irez-vous *au cinéma* ce soir? Answer: Oui, j'irai.
(Y is omitted before the future of **aller.)**

VII. Dictée d'après le dialogue, pp. 120-121.

VIII. Conversation.

"Did you go downtown yesterday?"
"Yes, I went (there)."
"How did you go?"
"I went on the bus **(en autobus).**"
"Were there many people when you got on?"
"Yes, there were people standing."
"Where did you get off?"
"I got off at the bus stop of the Rue de la Paix."

Quatrième Lecture Illustrée, p. 24, *Voyage à Reims.*

Talking Over School Days

JOHN —[1]A quelle école alliez-vous, quand vous aviez douze ans?

ROGER —[2]J'allais au collège,* c'est-à-dire à l'école secondaire.

JOHN —[3]Où habitiez-vous à ce moment-là?

ROGER —[4]J'habitais une petite ville des Alpes.

JOHN —[5]C'est une région très pittoresque, n'est-ce pas?

ROGER —[6]Oui, mais cette ville a bien changé depuis. [7]On y a construit des usines de produits chimiques. [8]Le progrès, vous savez . . .

JOHN —[9]Qu'est-ce que vous faisiez à l'école?

ROGER —[10]Je travaillais neuf heures par jour.

JOHN —[11]Quoi?

ROGER —[12]J'y allais tous les matins à sept heures, et j'en sortais à quatre heures de l'après-midi.

JOHN —[13]Est-ce qu'il y avait beaucoup d'élèves dans cette école?

ROGER —[14]Non. Il n'y avait guère plus de cent élèves.

JOHN —[1]To what school did you go, when you were twelve years old?

ROGER —[2]I went to the "collège," that is to say, to the secondary school.

JOHN —[3]Where did you live at that time?

ROGER —[4]I was living in a little city in the Alps.

JOHN —[5]That's a very picturesque region, isn't it?

ROGER —[6]Yes, but that city has changed a great deal since. [7]They have built chemical factories there. [8]Progress, you know . . .

JOHN —[9]What did you do at school?

ROGER —[10]I worked nine hours per day.

JOHN —[11]What?

ROGER —[12]I went (there) every morning at seven o'clock, and I got out at four o'clock in the afternoon.

JOHN —[13]Were there many pupils in that school?

ROGER —[14]No. There were hardly more than a hundred pupils.

---

* The secondary schools in France are called **Lycées** if they are entirely supported by the State, and **Collèges** if they are supported by a municipality, a church, etc.

John —[15]Je crois qu'on travaillait trop dans cette école.

Roger —[16]Je ne suis pas tout à fait de votre avis, John. [17]Je crois que cette école m'a fait beaucoup de bien.

John —[15]I think that they worked too hard in that school.

Roger —[16]I don't quite agree with you, John. [17]I think that school did me a great deal of good.

I. Substitutions. *Répétez les phrases suivantes en substituant les mots indiqués:*

1. A quelle école alliez-vous quand vous aviez [douze ans]?
dix ans/ quinze ans/ huit ans

2. Où habitiez-vous [à ce moment-là]?
l'année dernière/ il y a deux ans/ quand vous aviez cinq ans

3. On y a construit [des usines].
de grandes usines/ de nouvelles usines/ des usines de produits chimiques/ des usines d'automobiles

4. Il n'y avait guère plus de [cent] élèves.
cent cinquante/ deux cents/ trois cents/ cinq cents

5. Il n'y avait guère moins de [cent] élèves.
deux mille/ trois mille/ cinq mille/ cinq cents

II. *Répétez les phrases suivantes en remplaçant le complément par* y:

Ex.:—J'allais à l'école tous les matins.
    —**J'y allais tous les matins.**

1. J'allais à l'école tous les jours. **2.** J'allais à la pharmacie tous les soirs. **3.** J'allais à la campagne tous les ans. **4.** J'allais au cinéma tous les samedis. **5.** J'allais en ville tous les huit jours. **6.** J'allais chez le coiffeur tous les quinze jours.

III. *Répondez en français à chacune des questions suivantes, d'après le texte:*

1. A quelle école alliez-vous quand vous aviez douze ans? **2.** Où habitiez-vous à ce moment-là? **3.** Est-ce que la région des Alpes est très pittoresque? **4.** Pourquoi la ville a-t-elle changé depuis ce moment-là? **5.** Qu'est-ce que vous faisiez à l'école? **6.** A quelle heure y alliez-vous? **7.** A quelle heure en sortiez-vous? **8.** Alliez-vous à l'école à pied? **9.** Alliez-vous à l'école tous les matins? **10.** Y avait-il beaucoup d'élèves dans cette école? **11.** Est-ce que John croit qu'on travaillait trop dans cette école? **12.** Est-ce que Roger est de son avis?

IV. *Demandez à quelqu'un:*

1. à quelle école il allait quand il avait douze ans. 2. où il habitait à ce moment-là. 3. à quelle heure il allait à l'école. 4. combien d'heures par jour il passait à l'école. 5. à quelle heure il en sortait. 6. s'il allait à l'école à pied. 7. si l'école était près de la maison. 8. s'il allait à l'école tous les jours. 9. s'il y avait beaucoup d'élèves dans cette école. 10. si John croit qu'on travaillait trop dans cette école. 11. s'il est de l'avis de John.

V. *Répondez en français à chacune des questions personnelles suivantes:*

1. A quelle école alliez-vous quand vous aviez quatorze ans? 2. Comment s'appelait cette école? 3. Combien d'élèves y avait-il dans cette école? 4. Est-ce que vous aimiez bien cette école? 5. Est-ce que vous aviez beaucoup de travail dans cette école? 6. Est-ce que l'école était loin de chez vous?

VI. *Dites en français:*

1. Five or six years ago, Roger lived in Chambéry. 2. He lives in Paris now. 3. He has been living in Paris for several years. 4. He came to Paris five or six years ago. 5. He spent two years in England. 6. He thinks the little school in Chambéry did him a lot of good. 7. I used to go to school every morning at seven. 8. I used to go to school every day. 9. I used to go to work every evening. 10. I used to go to Paris every year.

VII. Dictée d'après le dialogue, pp. 128-129.

VIII. Conversation.

Talking over school days.

The Imperfect Tense

53. Remark about the imperfect tense.

Generally speaking, the French imperfect tense expresses habitual actions in the past (**A quelle école alliez-vous . . .**) or a state of affairs in the past (**quand vous aviez douze ans?**).

In order to distinguish clearly between the imperfect and the *passé composé,* you could say that the *passé composé* expresses WHAT HAPPENED and that the imperfect describes the CIRCUMSTANCES or STATE OF AFFAIRS at the time. Examples:

Dimanche dernier, j'ai fait une promenade *(what happened).* Il faisait beau *(state of the weather)* et j'avais l'intention *(state of mind)* de faire le tour du lac. Mais j'ai rencontré Marie *(what happened)* qui m'a dit *(what happened)* qu'il y avait un excellent film *(state of affairs at the local movie house)* au Rivoli . . . Nous y sommes allés ensemble *(what happened).* Le film était en effet très amusant *(state of affairs as to the particular film).* Nous avons passé un excellent après-midi *(what happened).*

54. Imperfect of regular verbs.

—Où **déjeuniez-vous** quand **vous étiez** à Paris?	Where *did you use to have lunch* when *you were* in Paris?
—A quelle heure **finissiez-vous** d'habitude votre travail?	What time *did you* usually *finish* your work?
—**Je finissais** vers six heures.	*I used to finish* around six.
—John est entré pendant que **je répondais** à sa lettre.	John came in as *I was answering* his letter.
—**Nous nous dépêchions** tous les matins pour prendre l'autobus de sept heures.	*We used to hurry* every morning in order to get the seven-o'clock bus.

A. The forms of the imperfect tense are:

FIRST CONJUGATION	SECOND CONJUGATION	THIRD CONJUGATION
je déjeunais	je finissais	je répondais
I was having lunch,	*I was finishing,*	*I was answering,*
I used to have lunch,	*I used to finish,*	*I used to answer,*
etc.	*etc.*	*etc.*
tu déjeunais	tu finissais	tu répondais
il déjeunait	il finissait	il répondait
nous déjeunions	nous finissions	nous répondions
vous déjeuniez	vous finissiez	vous répondiez
ils déjeunaient	ils finissaient	ils répondaient

B. The imperfect tense is formed as follows:

(1) The imperfect stem is the same as that of the first person plural of the present indicative.

EXAMPLES: **déjeunons, déjeun-; finissons, finiss-; répondons, répond-.**

(2) The endings are: **-ais, -ais, -ait, -ions, -iez, -aient.** Thus, if you know the present indicative, you can always figure out the imperfect. For example:

PRESENT: **Nous déjeunons, nous finissons, nous répondons.**
IMPERFECT: **Nous déjeunions, nous finissions, nous répondions.**

Note that the three persons of the singular and the third person plural of the imperfect are pronounced alike, except in linking.

C. Reflexive verbs follow the usual pattern.

EXAMPLES: **Je me dépêchais, tu te dépêchais, etc.**

55. Imperfect of **être** and **avoir.**

The forms of the imperfect of **être** and **avoir** are:

être		**avoir**	
j'étais	nous étions	j'avais	nous avions
I was	vous étiez	*I had, I used to have, etc.*	vous aviez
tu étais	ils étaient	tu avais	ils avaient
il était		il avait	

56. The commonest uses of the imperfect.

A. To describe a habitual action in the past (English *used to):*

—**J'allais** à l'école à sept heures du matin.   *I used to go* to school at seven o'clock in the morning.

—**Je me levais** à six heures.   *I used to get up* at six o'clock.

B. To describe what was going on when an action took place (English progressive past):

—**J'allais** en ville quand je l'ai rencontré.   *I was going* downtown when I met him.

—**Il pleuvait** quand j'ai quitté la maison.   *It was raining* when I left home.

—**Il faisait beau** quand je suis rentré(e).   *It was fine weather* when I got home.

Note that in these examples, **je l'ai rencontré, j'ai quitté la maison** and **je suis rentré(e)** are simple past actions, which are expressed by the *passé composé.* **J'allais en ville, il pleuvait** and **il faisait beau** describe what was going on when the specific action took place.

C. To describe a situation which existed in the past:

—**L'école n'était pas** loin de la maison.   The school *was not* far from my house.

—**Il n'y avait pas** beaucoup d'élèves dans cette école.   *There were not* many pupils in that school.

—Franklin **vivait** au dix-huitième siècle.   Franklin *lived* in the eighteenth century.

D. To describe the way a person felt, looked, etc., in the past, especially with the verbs **croire,** *to believe, to think;* **penser,** *to think;* **espérer,** *to hope,* and with many expressions containing **être** or **avoir** (**être content, avoir froid,** etc.):

—**Je croyais** que **vous étiez** malade.   *I thought* that *you were* sick.

—**J'espérais** vous voir au bal samedi soir.   *I was hoping* to see you at the dance Saturday evening.

—**J'étais** content de voir venir le printemps.   *I was* glad to see spring come.

E. With **depuis** and an expression of time, to report an action that had been going on for a specified period when another action took place.

—John **attendait** l'autobus **depuis un quart d'heure** quand Roger est arrivé. John *had been waiting* for the bus *for a quarter of an hour* when Roger arrived.

—Il **neigeait depuis une demi-heure** quand je me suis levé. *It had been snowing for a half-hour* when I got up.

I. EXERCICES D'APPLICATION.

A. *Répondez au singulier, puis au pluriel:*

Ex.:—Déjeuniez-vous?
   —**Je déjeunais.   —Nous déjeunions.**

I. Parliez-vous?   **2.** Habitiez-vous?   **3.** Finissiez-vous?   **4.** Obéissiez-vous?   **5.** Répondiez-vous?   **6.** Attendiez-vous?   **7.** Étiez-vous?   **8.** Aviez-vous?   **9.** Vous couchiez-vous?   **10.** Vous leviez-vous?   **11.** Vous dépêchiez-vous?

B. *Répondez au singulier, puis au pluriel:*

Ex.:—Parlait-il?
   —**Il parlait.   —Ils parlaient.**

I. Dînait-il?   **2.** Habitait-il?   **3.** Allait-il?   **4.** Obéissait-elle?   **5.** Entrait-elle?   **6.** Attendait-elle?   **7.** Se couchait-il?   **8.** S'habillait-il?   **9.** Avait-il?   **10.** Était-elle?

C. *Mettez les phrases suivantes à l'imparfait:*

Ex.:—Je parle.
   —**Je parlais.**

I. Je demeure à Paris.   **2.** Je me lève à sept heures et demie.   **3.** Il a dix-huit ans.   **4.** Je finis à six heures.   **5.** Combien d'élèves y a-t-il?   **6.** Je ne suis pas de votre avis.   **7.** Il attend l'autobus.   **8.** Il attend l'autobus depuis un quart d'heure.   **9.** Qu'est-ce que vous faites?   **10.** Il ne travaille pas.   **11.** Il fait beau.   **12.** Nous allons à l'école.

D. *Répétez les phrases suivantes en ajoutant les mots* **depuis un quart d'heure.**

Ex.:—J'attendais l'autobus quand vous êtes arrivé.
   —**J'attendais l'autobus depuis un quart d'heure quand vous êtes arrivé.**

I. J'étais à la maison quand vous avez téléphoné.   **2.** Je travaillais quand vous êtes arrivé(e).   **3.** Il neigeait quand je me suis couché(e).   **4.** Il pleuvait quand je suis rentré(e).   **5.** Le train était en gare quand je suis arrivé(e).

II. *Répondez en français:*

1. A quelle heure avez-vous quitté la maison ce matin? 2. Est-ce qu'il pleuvait quand vous avez quitté la maison? 3. Est-ce qu'il faisait beau quand vous vous êtes levé(e)? 4. Quel temps faisait-il quand êtes arrivé(e) à l'université? 5. Est-ce qu'il a neigé hier? 6. Est-ce qu'il neigeait quand vous êtes rentré(e) hier soir? 7. Êtes-vous allé(e) au cinéma hier? 8. Est-ce que le film était bon? 9. Y avait-il beaucoup de monde au cinéma? 10. Aviez-vous faim quand vous êtes rentré(e)? 11. A quelle heure vous êtes-vous couché(e) hier soir? 12. Étiez-vous fatigué(e) quand vous vous êtes couché(e)?

III. *Demandez à quelqu'un:*

1. s'il connaît l'histoire des États-Unis. 2. s'il sait quand vivait Franklin 3. où demeurait Franklin. 4. ce que faisait Franklin. 5. si Franklin est allé en France. 6. si Franklin parlait français. 7. combien de temps Franklin est resté en France. 8. où Franklin est allé quand il était en France. 9. si La Fayette vivait à ce moment-là. 10. si Louis XVI était roi (*king*) de France à ce moment-là. 11. si Marie-Antoinette était reine (*queen*) de France.

IV. *Dites en français:*

1. I went downtown yesterday afternoon. 2. When I left home the weather was fine. 3. I had several errands to do. 4. I took a bus as far as the square. 5. I went first to the bank. 6. And as **(pendant que)** I was waiting at the window **(au guichet)**, Roger Duplessis came (arrived). 7. He and I went shopping together. 8. We were tired and we came home in a taxi.

V. Thème d'imitation:

Last week, John and Roger took a trip [1] to Rheims. They took the train at the Eastern Railroad Station, and arrived at Epernay two hours later. John was hungry, and he went to the lunchroom of the station. Roger told him that the train stopped only three minutes and that they were going to miss the connection. That is [2] what they did, and as there were no more trains for Rheims that day, they had to spend the night in the hotel . . . When they arrived in Rheims, they went through [3] the cathedral [4]. John thought it was admirable [5]. Then they saw the cellars [6] where champagne is made [7]. There were many bottles [8], kilometers of bottles, and John was greatly impressed [9]. They returned to Paris, very happy about [10] their trip.

---

[1] the trip, **le voyage.** [2] that is, **c'est.** [3] to go through, **visiter.** [4] the cathedral, **la cathédrale.** [5] Use *passé composé* of **trouver.** Before he went there he thought (**pensait**) that it was a fine cathedral, but after seeing it he thought (**a trouvé**) that is was marvelous. He saw it, he went through it, he reacted to it. [6] the cellar, **la cave.** [7] *Lit.* one makes the wine of Champagne. [8] the bottle, **la bouteille.** [9] **a été très impressionné.** [10] happy about, **content de.**

A Long Walk in the Snow

JOHN —[1]Bonjour, Marie. [2]Je ne vous ai pas vue au bal* samedi dernier. [3]J'espérais pourtant vous y voir.

MARIE —[4]Je suis restée à la maison ce soir-là. [5]Je ne me sentais pas très bien, [6]et je me suis couchée de bonne heure.

JOHN —[7]J'espère que cela n'était rien.

MARIE —[8]Je l'espérais aussi. [9]Mais le lendemain, [10]j'avais mal à la gorge.

JOHN —[11]Avez-vous fait venir le médecin?

MARIE —[12]Non. C'était tout simplement un rhume.

JOHN —[13]J'espère que ce n'était pas grave.

MARIE —[14] Non. Je suis restée au lit deux jours. [15]Maintenant, je vais beaucoup mieux.

JOHN —[16] Mais comment avez-vous attrapé cela?

MARIE —[17]Vendredi, Roger et moi avons fait une longue promenade. [18]Il faisait beau, mais assez froid. [19]Nous avons marché dans

JOHN —[1]Hello, Marie. [2]I did not see you at the dance last Saturday. [3]I was hoping (however) to see you there.

MARIE —[4]I stayed at home that evening. [5]I didn't feel very well, [6]so I went to bed early.

JOHN —[7]I hope it was not anything serious.

MARIE —[8]I hoped so too. [9]But the next day [10]I had a sore throat.

JOHN —[11]Did you send for the doctor?

MARIE —[12]No. It was just a cold.

JOHN —[13]I hope that it was not serious.

MARIE —[14]No. I stayed in bed for two days. [15]Now I am much better.

JOHN —[16]But how did you catch it (that)?

MARIE —[17]Friday, Roger and I took a long walk. [18]It was fine weather, but pretty cold. [19]We walked in the snow until night-fall. [20]I was

* un bal is a large dance. A small informal dance is une sauterie.

140

la neige jusqu'à la nuit. ²⁰J'avais   cold when I got home.
froid quand je suis rentrée.

JOHN —²¹Vous ferez bien de vous   JOHN —²¹You'd better get a good
reposer.   rest (You will do well to rest.)

MARIE —²²Oh! Je n'en mourrai pas!   MARIE —²²Oh! I won't die of it!

I. SUBSTITUTIONS. *Répétez les phrases suivantes en substituant les mots indiqués:*

  1. [Je suis resté(e) à la maison] parce que je ne me sentais pas très bien.
     Je ne suis pas allé(e) au bal/ Je me suis couché(e) de bonne heure/ J'ai fait venir le médecin/ Je suis resté(e) au lit deux jours/ Je suis resté(e) au lit plusieurs jours

  2. Je ne suis pas sorti(e) hier soir parce qu'[il neigeait].
     j'étais fatigué(e)/ je n'avais pas le temps/ j'avais du travail à faire/ Je voulais écrire des lettres/ il faisait trop froid

  3. J'avais [froid] quand je suis rentré(e).
     chaud/ faim/ soif *thirst*/ un rhume

  4. Mais le lendemain j'avais mal [à la gorge].
     à la tête/ aux yeux/ aux dents *(teeth)*/ à l'estomac *(stomach)*

  5. Vous ferez bien de [vous reposer].
     vous coucher de bonne heure/ rester au lit/ ne pas sortir/ ne pas aller à la sauterie/ ne pas marcher dans la neige jusqu'à la nuit

II. *Répondez en français à chacune des questions suivantes:*

  1. Est-ce que John a vu Marie au bal samedi soir? 2. Est-ce qu'il espérait l'y voir? 3. Pourquoi Marie est-elle restée à la maison ce soir-là? 4. Est-ce qu'elle se sentait bien? 5. Est-ce qu'elle s'est couchée tard ce soir-là? 6. Pourquoi s'est-elle couchée de bonne heure? 7. Est-ce qu'elle allait mieux le lendemain? 8. Qu'est-ce qu'elle avait le lendemain? 9. A-t-elle fait venir le médecin? 10. Est-ce qu'elle était très malade? 11. Combien de temps est-elle restée au lit? 12. Est-ce qu'elle va mieux maintenant? 13. Avec qui a-t-elle fait une promenade vendredi? 14. Quel temps faisait-il ce jour-là? 15. Qu'est-ce que Marie et Roger ont fait jusqu'à la nuit? 16. Est-ce que Marie avait chaud quand elle est rentrée? 17. Est-ce que Marie fera bien de se reposer? 18. Qu'est-ce qu'il faut faire quand on est fatigué?

III. *Demandez en français:*

  1. si Marie était au bal samedi soir. 2. pourquoi Marie n'y était pas. 3. si John espérait l'y voir. 4. pourquoi Marie s'est couchée de bonne heure ce soir-là. 5. si Marie avait mal à la gorge quand elle s'est couchée. 6. pourquoi

Marie n'a pas fait venir le médecin.   **7.** si Marie est restée longtemps au lit. **8.** comment Marie a attrapé un rhume.   **9.** si Marie va mieux maintenant. **10.** si Marie fera bien de se reposer.   **11.** ce qu'il faut faire quand on est fatigué.

IV. *Dites en français:*

A. avoir froid, avoir chaud, etc.

I. She was cold.   **2.** I am cold.   **3.** Are you cold?   **4.** Are you warm?   **5.** I was warm.   **6.** I was hungry.   **7.** Were you hungry?   **8.** Was he hungry? **9.** He had a sore throat.   **10.** Did you have a sore throat?   **11.** No, I had a headache.   **12.** I haven't a headache.   **13.** I have a cold.   **14.** She has a cold. **15.** She had a cold yesterday.

B. aller, faire venir

I. How are you?   **2.** I am well.   **3.** I am better.   **4.** I was better.   **5.** I wasn't better.   **6.** I hope you'll be better soon.   **7.** Did you send for the doctor?   **8.** Yes, I sent for the doctor.   **9.** I sent for him.   **10.** I didn't send for him.

C. jusqu'à

I. We walked in the snow until nightfall.   **2.** I am wet to the bones.   **3.** I worked until midnight.   **4.** I will go with you as far as the square.   **5.** I will go with you that far (**jusque là**).   **6.** I will stay at home until five o'clock.   **7.** I will rest until noon.

V. Dictée d'après le dialogue, pp. 132-133.

VI. Conversation.

You make alternate plans for a walk depending upon the weather.

Où est ma cravate?

ROGER —[1]Serez-vous bientôt prêt, John?

JOHN —[2]Oui, tout à l'heure. [3]Je cherche ma cravate rouge, mais je ne sais pas où je l'ai mise.*

ROGER —[4]Je peux vous prêter une des miennes.

JOHN —[5]Non, merci. Je n'aime pas les vôtres.

ROGER —[6]Vous êtes bien aimable. [7]Vous voulez dire que je n'ai pas de goût, n'est-ce pas?

JOHN —[8]Je veux dire seulement que j'aime mieux mes cravates que les vôtres.

ROGER —[9]Eh bien, cherchez-les, puisque vous les aimez tant!

JOHN —[10]Est-ce que je peux porter une cravate verte avec un complet bleu?

ROGER. —[11]Cela m'est égal . . . [12]Mais avez-vous regardé dans votre tiroir?

JOHN —[13]Oui, j'ai cherché partout.

ROGER —[14]Je vais regarder dans le mien. [15]Tiens! Cette cravate rouge n'est pas à moi. [16]Est-ce qu'elle est à vous, par hasard?

ROGER —[1]Will you soon be ready, John?

JOHN —[2]Yes, in a moment. [3]I am looking for my red tie, but I don't know where I put it.

ROGER —[4]I can lend you one of mine.

JOHN —[5]No, thank you. I don't like yours.

ROGER —[6]I like that! [7]You mean that I have poor taste, I suppose!

JOHN —[8]I just mean that I like my ties better than yours.

ROGER —[9]Well, look for them, since you like them so much!

JOHN —[10]Can I wear a green tie with a blue suit?

ROGER —[11]It's all right with me . . . [12]But have you looked in your drawer?

JOHN —[13]Yes, I have looked everywhere.

ROGER —[14]I am going to look in mine. [15]Well! This red tie is not mine. [16]Is it yours, by chance?

---

* For the agreement of the past participle, see pp. 178-179.

JOHN —[17]Mais oui, elle est à moi. [18]C'est la cravate que je cherchais. [19]Pourquoi était-elle avec les vôtres?

JOHN —[17]Why yes, it's mine. [18]It's the tie I was looking for. [19]Why was it with yours?

ROGER —[20]Je crois que la bonne admire tant vos cravates, qu'elle a essayé de m'en donner une!

ROGER —[20]I think the maid admires your ties so much that she tried to give me one of them!

I. SUBSTITUTIONS. *Répétez les phrases suivantes en substituant les mots indiqués:*

  1. Je cherche ma cravate [rouge].
  jaune/ bleue/ noire/ grise/ blanche

  2. Je veux dire seulement que j'aime mieux [mes cravates] que les vôtres.
  mes gants/ mes cigarettes/ mes mouchoirs/ mes complets/ mes robes

  3. Est-ce qu'on peut porter [une cravate verte] avec [un complet bleu]?
  une cravate rouge . . . un complet gris/ un chapeau rouge . . . une robe grise/ des gants jaunes . . . une robe verte/ des gants blancs . . . un manteau noir

  4. Je crois que la bonne admire tant [vos cravates] qu'elle a essayé de m'en donner [une].
  vos gants . . . une paire/ vos mouchoirs . . . un/ vos robes . . . une/ vos chapeaux . . . un

II. *Répondez en français à chacune des questions suivantes:*

  1. Quand Roger sera-t-il prêt? **2.** Où a-t-il mis sa cravate rouge? **3.** Est-ce que Roger veut bien lui prêter une cravate? **4.** Est-ce que John aime bien les cravates de Roger? **5.** Est-ce que John a cherché partout? **6.** A-t-il regardé dans son tiroir? **7.** Est-ce que sa cravate rouge y est? **8.** Où Roger va-t-il regarder? **9.** Qu'est-ce qu'il trouve dans son tiroir? **10.** Est-ce que la cravate qu'il trouve est à lui? **11.** Est-ce que John sait pourquoi sa cravate est dans le tiroir de Roger?

III. *Demandez à quelqu'un:*

  1. s'il sera bientôt prêt. **2.** s'il veut bien vous prêter des gants. **3.** ce que cherche John. **4.** si l'on peut porter une cravate jaune avec un complet noir. **5.** si John a regardé dans son tiroir. **6.** si John a cherché partout. **7.** ce que Roger trouve dans son tiroir. **8.** si c'est la cravate que cherchait John. **9.** de quelle couleur est cette cravate. **10.** qui a mis cette cravate dans ce tiroir.

IV. *Dites en français:*

A. beaucoup, tant, trop

1. John has many ties.   **2.** He has too many of them.   **3.** Have you many (of them)?   **4.** No, I haven't many.   **5.** I am very fond of ties.   **6.** John likes ties so much he buys too many.

B. chercher, regarder

1. I am looking for my gloves.   **2.** Have you looked in your drawer?   **3.** Yes, they are not there.   **4.** Have you looked in mine?   **5.** Yes, I have looked in yours, too.   **6.** I have looked everywhere.

C. vouloir dire, aimer mieux

1. Do you mean I have poor taste?   **2.** Do you mean she has no taste?   **3.** What do you mean?   **4.** I mean I do not like her hats.   **5.** I mean I like my ties better than yours.   **6.** I mean I like my hats better than yours.   **7.** Do you like your hats better than mine?   **8.** I like red ties better than green ones.

V. Dictée d'après le dialogue, pp. 140-141.

VI. Conversation.

Borrowing a raincoat.

Possessive Pronouns

57. Remark on possessive adjectives and possessive pronouns.

Possessive adjectives and possessive pronouns differ both in form and use. You have learned that possessive adjectives (**mon, ton, son,** etc.) are used TO MODIFY NOUNS. These words correspond to English forms *my, your, her,* etc.

Possessive pronouns are used AS EQUIVALENT OF NOUNS MODIFIED BY A POSSESSIVE ADJECTIVE. They correspond to the English forms *mine, yours, his, hers,* etc. Ex.: **My** (*adj.*) father is a doctor. **Mine** (*pron.*) is an engineer.

58. Forms and use of possessive pronouns.

—Voici mon adresse.	Here is my address.
—Donnez-moi **la vôtre.**	Give me *yours.*
—J'ai mes gants. Où sont **les vôtres?**	I have my gloves. Where are *yours?*
—**Les miens** sont dans ma poche.	*Mine* are in my pocket.
—Est-ce que Marie a **les siens?**	Does Marie have *hers?*
—Roger a apporté son imperméable.	Roger brought his raincoat.
—Marie a laissé **le sien** à la maison.	Marie left *hers* at home.

The forms of the possessive pronouns are:

SINGULAR		PLURAL		
MASCULINE	FEMININE	MASCULINE	FEMININE	
le mien	la mienne	les miens	les miennes	*(mine)*
le tien	la tienne	les tiens	les tiennes	*(yours)*
le sien	la sienne	les siens	les siennes	*(his, hers, its)*
le nôtre	la nôtre	les nôtres	les nôtres	*(ours)*
le vôtre	la vôtre	les vôtres	les vôtres	*(yours)*
le leur	la leur	les leurs	les leurs	*(theirs)*

They agree in gender and number with the things possessed. Ex.: In answer to the question: — Avez-vous **vos gants?**, either John or Mary could answer: — Oui, j'ai **les miens.**

146

59. Possessive pronouns with preposition à or de.

—J'ai écrit à mes parents.	I have written to my parents.
—Avez-vous écrit **aux vôtres?**	Have you written to *yours?*
—J'ai besoin de mon imperméable, et Marie a besoin **du sien.**	I need my raincoat and Mary needs *hers.*

When used with the preposition **à** or **de** the forms are:

du mien, de la mienne, des miens, des miennes, etc.

au mien, à la mienne, aux miens, aux miennes, etc.

60. Use of être à to express possession.

—Ces gants **ne sont pas à moi.**	These gloves *are not mine* (lit.: to me).
—**Sont-ils à vous?**	*Are they yours* (lit.: to you)?
—Non. Je crois **qu'ils sont à Charles.**	No. I think *they are Charles'* (lit.: to Charles).

In phrases in which the verb **être** is used, possession is normally expressed by preposition **à** with the name of a person (**Ces gants sont à Charles**) or **à** with a personal pronoun (**Ces gants sont à lui**). After the preposition you use the stressed forms **moi, toi, lui, elle,** etc.

I. *Répétez les phrases suivantes en remplaçant le nom par le pronom possessif:*

Ex.:—J'ai mon imperméable.

—J'ai le mien.

(*a*) 1. J'ai ma cravate. 2. J'ai mon chapeau. 3. J'ai mon tabac. 4. J'ai mes gants. 5. J'ai mes cigarettes. 6. Roger a son imperméable. 7. Il a sa cravate. 8. Il a son chapeau. 9. Il a son tabac. 10. Il a ses gants. 11. Il a ses cigarettes.

(*b*) 1. Je peux vous prêter mon pardessus. 2. Je peux vous prêter mon auto. 3. Je peux vous prêter mes skis. 4. Je peux vous prêter une de mes cravates. 5. Je peux vous prêter une de mes paires de gants.

(*c*) 1. Où avez-vous acheté votre journal? 2. Où avez-vous acheté votre papier à lettres? 3. Où avez-vous acheté votre tabac? 4. Où avez-vous acheté vos cigarettes? 5. Où avez-vous acheté vos mouchoirs?

(*d*) 1. J'ai besoin de mes gants. 2. Roger a besoin de ses gants. 3. Marie a besoin de ses gants. 4. Nous avons besoin de nos gants. 5. Avez-vous besoin de vos gants?

II. *Dites en français:*

(*a*) (**une auto**) 1. Is this automobile yours? 2. No, it belongs to Charles. 3. Where is yours? 4. Mine is over there. 5. What color is yours? 6. Mine

is black.   **7.** His is yellow.   **8.** Hers is white.   **9.** Ours is blue.   **10.** Theirs
is red.   **11.** Yours is blue, isn't it?

(*b*) **1.** He's a friend of mine.   **2.** It's one of my books.   **3.** It's one of my
ties.   **4.** He's one of my professors.   **5.** He's one of my cousins.   **6.** She's one
of my cousins.

III. *Répondez à chacune des questions suivantes, en remplaçant le nom*
   par le pronom possessif:

Ex.:—Roger a-t-il son imperméable?

   —**Oui, il a le sien.**

1. Marie a-t-elle son imperméable?   **2.** Marie a-t-elle ses gants?   **3.** Avez-
vous vos gants?   **4.** Avez-vous besoin de vos gants?   **5.** Roger a-t-il besoin
de ses gants?   **6.** John et Roger ont-ils besoin de leurs gants?   **7.** Où avez-vous
acheté votre tabac?   **8.** Où John et Roger ont-ils acheté leur tabac?   **9.** Où
avez-vous acheté vos cigarettes?   **10.** Où John a-t-il acheté ses cigarettes?
11. Où Marie a-t-elle acheté ses cigarettes?   **12.** Est-ce que votre chambre
vous plaît?

IV. Révision des dialogues, pp. 117-118 et pp. 120-121.

1. Quelle espèce de billet John demande-t-il pour aller à Reims?   **2.** En quelle
classe voyage-t-il?   **3.** Combien de temps son billet est-il bon?   **4.** Est-ce que
le train qu'il prend va directement à Reims?   **5.** A quelle ville doit-il changer
de train?   **6.** Combien de temps doit-il attendre la correspondance?   **7.** Est-ce
que son train est à l'heure?   **8.** Qu'est-ce qu'il veut faire avant l'arrivée du
train?   **9.** Qu'est-ce qui arrivera s'il manque son train?   **10.** De combien de
mouchoirs Roger a-t-il besoin?   **11.** Quel est le prix de la paire de gants qu'il
veut acheter?   **12.** De quelle couleur sont les gants qu'il achète?   **13.** Est-ce
que le chapeau qu'il essaie lui va bien?   **14.** Pourquoi n'emporte-t-il pas ses
achats?   **15.** Pourquoi ne paye-t-il pas tout de suite ses achats?   **16.** Quand
les payera-t-il?

V. Thème d'imitation:

Yesterday John did not feel very well. Winter in Paris is often [1] cold and
damp [2]. John took a long walk, and he was cold and (he was) wet when he
got home. Roger said to him: "Go to bed, pal [3]. I am going to send for the
doctor. It is probably [4] not very serious, but you never can tell . . .[5] " The
doctor came a half-hour later. He was an elderly [6] gentleman, dressed in
black and very friendly. He took John's temperature [7], looked at his throat
and said to him: "You have a little fever [8], but it is nothing serious. Stay
in bed until tomorrow and rest. You will not die of it." Today, John is
much better. He is going to get up tomorrow morning and go to his
laboratory as usual.

---

[1] often, **souvent.**   [2] damp, **humide.**   [3] pal, old man, etc., **mon vieux.**   [4] probably, **sans doute.**
[5] you never can tell, **on ne sait jamais.**   [6] elderly, **d'un certain âge.**   [7] la température.   [8] la fièvre.

Retour des vacances

JOHN —[1]Tiens, bonsoir, Marie! Vous êtes de retour? [2]Je suis content de vous revoir. [3]Avez-vous passé de bonnes vacances de Noël en Bretagne?

MARIE —[4]Oui, excellentes, merci; mais trop courtes, comme toutes les vacances. *Congé — vacation — 2 wks, etc*

JOHN —[5]Quand êtes-vous revenue?

MARIE —[6]Je suis revenue hier soir à onze heures.

JOHN —[7]Avez-vous fait bon voyage?

MARIE —[8]Oh! ne m'en parlez pas! [9]A Rennes, l'express de Paris était bondé, [10]et j'ai à peine pu trouver une place. [11]Et puis, il faisait horriblement chaud dans le compartiment.

JOHN —[12]Vous n'avez pas de chance!

MARIE —[13]J'ai dîné au wagon restaurant. [14]C'est la seule partie du voyage qui était supportable.

JOHN —[15]Aimez-vous dîner au wagon-restaurant?

MARIE —[16]Assez. C'est une façon de passer une demi-heure.

JOHN —[17]Qu'est-ce que vous avez fait le jour de Noël?

JOHN —[1]Well, good evening, Marie! Are you back? [2]I am glad to see you again. [3]Did you have a good Christmas vacation in Britanny?

MARIE —[4]Yes, excellent, thank you; but too short, like all vacations.

JOHN —[5]When did you get back?

MARIE —[6]I got back last night at 11 o'clock.

JOHN —[7]Did you have a good trip?

MARIE—[8]Oh! Don't even mention it! [9]At Rennes the Paris express was crowded, [10]and I could scarcely find a seat. [11]And then, it was terrifically hot in the compartment.

JOHN —[12]Tough luck!

MARIE —[13]I had dinner in the diner. [14]That's the only part of the trip which was bearable.

JOHN —[15]Do you like to dine in the diner?

MARIE —[16]Pretty well. It's a way of spending half an hour.

JOHN —[17]What did you do on Christmas day?

149

MARIE —¹⁸Ce qu'on fait partout ce jour-là. ¹⁹Nous sommes allés à la messe de minuit. ²⁰ Nous avons fait le réveillon* chez les Kerguélen. ²¹Je me suis bien amusée.

MARIE —¹⁸What one does everywhere on that day. ¹⁹We went to midnight mass. ²⁰We had a réveillon at the Kerguélens'. ²¹I had a good time.

I. SUBSTITUTIONS. *Répétez les phrases suivantes en substituant les mots indiqués:*

1. Je suis revenu(e) [hier soir à onze heures].
   hier soir à huit heures et demie/ hier matin/ hier après-midi/ avant-hier *(day before yesterday)*/ la semaine dernière

2. Je suis de retour depuis [hier soir à onze heures].
   hier soir à huit heures et demie/ hier matin/ hier après-midi/ avant-hier/ la semaine dernière

3. J'ai à peine pu [trouver une place.]
   trouver un taxi/ monter dans l'autobus/ aller en ville/ marcher

II. *Répondez en français à chacune des questions suivantes:*

1. Où Marie a-t-elle passé les vacances de Noël?   2. A-t-elle passé de bonnes vacances?   3. Est-ce qu'elle a trouvé les vacances trop courtes?   4. Quand est-elle revenue?   5. A-t-elle fait bon voyage?   6. Y avait-il beaucoup de monde dans l'express de Paris?   7. A-t-elle pu facilement *(easily)* trouver une place?   8. Est-ce qu'il faisait chaud dans le compartiment?   9. Où Marie a-t-elle dîné?   10. Pourquoi Marie aime-t-elle dîner au wagon-restaurant?   11. Qu'est-ce qu'elle a fait le jour de Noël?   12. A quelle heure est-elle allée à la messe?   13. Chez qui est-elle allée faire le réveillon?   14. Est-ce que Marie s'est bien amusée le jour de Noël?

III. *Demandez à quelqu'un:*

1. si Marie a passé de bonnes vacances.   2. où Marie a passé les vacances de Noël.   3. quand Marie est revenue.   4. si elle a trouvé les vacances trop courtes.   5. si elle a fait bon voyage.   6. s'il y avait beaucoup de monde dans l'express de Paris.   7. si elle a pu facilement trouver une place.   8. s'il faisait chaud dans le compartiment.   9. où Marie a dîné.   10. pourquoi elle aime dîner au wagon-restaurant.   11. ce qu'elle a fait le jour de Noël.   12. si elle est allée à la messe de minuit.   13. chez qui elle est allée faire le réveillon.   14. si elle s'est bien amusée le jour de Noël.

---

* Repas fait au milieu de la nuit, surtout la nuit de Noël. La pièce de résistance est d'ordinaire une oie *(goose)*, une dinde *(turkey)*, ou un jambon *(ham)*.

IV. *Répétez en remplaçant le passé composé par le passé composé de* **pouvoir** *et l'infinitif:*

Ex.:—Il n'a pas déjeuné ce matin.
   —**Il n'a pas pu déjeuner ce matin.**

1. Il n'a pas fait ses courses.   **2.** Il n'a pas travaillé hier soir.   **3.** Il n'a pas été à l'heure.   **4.** Il n'a pas trouvé de place.   **5.** Il ne s'est pas levé de bonne heure.   **6.** Il ne s'est pas couché avant minuit.

V. *Demandez à quelqu'un ce qu'il a fait:*

1. le jour de Noël.   **2.** le matin de Noël.   **3.** le soir de Noël.   **4.** le lendemain de Noël.   **5.** la veille de Noël (*Christmas Eve*).   **6.** le 4 juillet.   **7.** le premier janvier (le jour de l'An).

VI. *Répondez affirmative aux questions suivantes en remplaçant les noms par les pronoms convenables:*

1. Avez-vous écrit à vos parents hier?   **2.** Êtes-vous allé(e) au cinéma samedi dernier?   **3.** Avez-vous parlé du film à votre frère?   **4.** Est-ce que Roger vous a parlé du film?   **5.** Est-ce que Marie vous a parlé de ses vacances?   **6.** Est-ce qu'elle a pu trouver une place dans le train?   **7.** Êtes-vous allé(e) au cinéma avec Roger?   **8.** Êtes-vous allé(e) au cinéma avec Roger et John?   **9.** Êtes-vous allé(e) au cinéma avec Marie?   **10.** Avez-vous parlé de Charles?   **11.** Avez-vous parlé de Marie?   **12.** Marie s'est elle bien amusée chez les Kerguélen?

VII. Dictée d'après le dialogue, pp. 143-144.

VIII. Conversation.

Two friends talk over their vacation.

Si j'étais riche

JOHN —[1]Qu'est que vous feriez si vous étiez riche, Roger?

ROGER —[2]Je ne sais pas.

JOHN —[3]Ne voudriez-vous pas voyager?

ROGER —[4]Si. Je voudrais visiter plusieurs pays étrangers.

JOHN —[5]Où iriez-vous?

ROGER —[6]J'irais en Italie, visiter Florence et Rome, [7]aux États-Unis, voir les gratte-ciel, [8]et en Russie, voir ce qui se passe là-bas.

JOHN —[9]Est-ce que c'est tout?

ROGER —[10]Non. J'achèterais une grosse automobile, [11]et j'irais m'amuser au bord de la mer.

JOHN —[12]J'espère que vous ne serez jamais riche, Roger.

ROGER —[13]Pourquoi dites-vous cela?

JOHN —[14]Parce que vous seriez malheureux. [15] Vous ne sauriez pas dépenser votre argent.

ROGER —[16]Vous avez peut-être raison. [17]Je voudrais seulement être riche de temps en temps.

JOHN —[18]J'ai une idée, Roger!

ROGER —[19]Laquelle?

JOHN —[20]Cherchez un millionnaire qui pense comme vous. [21]Vous pourriez changer de rôle [22]tous les six mois, par exemple!

JOHN —[1]What would you do if you were rich, Roger?

ROGER —[2]I don't know.

JOHN —[3]Wouldn't you like to travel?

ROGER —[4]Yes. I'd like to visit several foreign countries.

JOHN —[5]Where would you go?

ROGER —[6]I'd go to Italy, to visit Florence and Rome, [7]to the United States, to see the skyscrapers, [8]and to Russia, to see what's happening there.

JOHN —[9]Is that all?

ROGER —[10]No. I would buy a big car, [11]and I would go to the seashore to have a good time.

JOHN —[12]I hope you will never be rich, Roger.

ROGER —[13]Why do you say that?

JOHN —[14]Because you would be unhappy. [15]You would not know how to spend your money.

ROGER —[16]You are perhaps right. [17]I'd like to be rich only from time to time.

JOHN —[18]I have an idea, Roger!

ROGER —[19]What is it?

JOHN —[20]Look for a millionaire who thinks as you do. [21]You could change places [22]every six months, for example!

I. Substitutions. *Répétez les phrases suivantes en substituant les mots indiqués:*

    1. Qu'est-ce que vous feriez [si vous étiez riche]?
      si vous étiez millionnaire/ si vous étiez en France/ si vous n'aviez pas d'argent/ si vous aviez mal à la gorge/ s'il y avait de la neige

    2. Si j'étais riche, [j'irais en Italie].
      j'irais aux États-Unis/ j'irais en Russie/ je voudrais visiter plusieurs pays étrangers/ j'achèterais une grosse automobile/ j'irais m'amuser au bord de la mer

    3. Vous pourriez changer [de rôle].
      de train/ d'autobus/ de robe/ de chapeau/ d'hôtel

II. *Répondez en français à chacune des questions suivantes:*

    1. Êtes-vous allé(e) au bord de la mer l'été dernier? **2.** Est-ce que vous voudriez voyager en Europe? **3.** Avez-vous déjà visité des pays étrangers? **4.** Êtes-vous jamais allé(e) en France? **5.** Êtes-vous déjà allé(e) en Angleterre? **6.** Voudriez-vous aller en Russie? **7.** Voudriez-vous aller en Italie? **8.** Voudriez-vous aller en Espagne? **9.** Voudriez-vous aller en Belgique? **10.** Quelles villes européennes voudriez-vous visiter? **11.** Est-ce que vous voudriez passer quelques semaines à Paris? **12.** Où iriez-vous si vous étiez riche? **13.** Iriez-vous à Versailles si vous étiez en France? **14.** Seriez-vous malheureux (malheureuse) si vous étiez riche? **15.** Voudriez-vous changer de rôle avec un millionnaire tous les six mois? **16.** Aimez-vous dépenser de l'argent?

III. *Demandez à quelqu'un:*

    1. ce qu'il ferait s'il était riche. **2.** s'il ne voudrait pas voyager. **3.** s'il voudrait visiter des pays étrangers. **4.** où il irait. **5.** s'il voudrait aller en Italie. **6.** pourquoi il voudrait aller en Italie. **7.** pourquoi il voudrait aller en Russie. **8.** s'il achèterait une automobile. **9.** où il irait s'amuser. **10.** s'il saurait dépenser son argent. **11.** ce qu'il ferait s'il était millionnaire.

IV. *Dites en français:*

    A. Révision des pronoms possessifs.

    1. These gloves are not mine. **2.** Are they yours? **3.** Where are yours? **4.** Mine are at home. **5.** Ours are at home. **6.** His are at home. **7.** Roger likes his hat better than mine. **8.** Henry studied his lessons but Alice didn't study hers. **9.** I study mine every day. **10.** Alice is going to study hers right away.

B. se passer

1. I would like to go to Russia to see what is going on there. 2. I don't know what is going on here. 3. Do you know what is going on in Paris? 4. I don't know what happened last Saturday.

V. Dictée d'après le dialogue, pp. 149-150.

VI. Conversation.

"How are you?"
"So-so (**comme ci comme ça**)."
"What did you say? (i.e. What do you say?)"
"I am not very well today".
"Why do you say that?"
"If I didn't have an examination, I would be better."

Cinquième Lecture Illustrée, p. 32, *En province*.

The Conditional

61. Conditional of regular verbs.

—**Je déjeunerais** à la maison, si j'avais le temps de rentrer. — *I would lunch* at home, if I had time to go home.

—**Je finirais** plus tôt, si je commençais plus tôt. — *I would finish* sooner, if I began sooner.

—**Je répondrais** à sa lettre, si j'avais son adresse. — *I would answer* his letter, if I had his address.

—**Je me dépêcherais,** si j'étais à votre place. — *I would hurry,* if I were in your place.

The forms of the conditional of regular verbs are:

FIRST CONJUGATION	SECOND CONJUGATION	THIRD CONJUGATION
je déjeunerais	je finirais	je répondrais
I would (should*) lunch	*I would (should*) finish*	*I would (should*) answer*
tu déjeunerais	tu finirais	tu répondrais
il déjeunerait	il finirait	il répondrait
nous déjeunerions	nous finirions	nous répondrions
vous déjeuneriez	vous finiriez	vous répondriez
ils déjeuneraient	ils finiraient	ils répondraient

The forms of the conditional of regular verbs may be found by adding the endings **-ais, -ais, -ait, -ions, -iez, -aient** to the infinitive, except that in the case of verbs of the third conjugation (ending in **-re**) the final **e** of the infinitive is omitted. As the endings are the same as those of the imperfect indicative, you should be able to learn the forms of the conditional at a glance.

---

* Very careful speakers are likely to say *I should, you would,* etc., although most people say *I would, you would,* etc. Whatever pattern you happen to follow in English, you say **je finirais, tu finirais,** etc., in French. There is no alternative.

Note that the three forms of the singular and the third person plural are all pronounced alike except for linking.

The conditional of reflexive verbs follows the usual pattern: **Je me dépêcherais, tu te dépêcherais,** etc.

62. Conditional of **être** and **avoir**.

—**Vous seriez** malheureux, si vous étiez riche.　　*You would be* unhappy, if you were rich.

—**J'aurais** le temps, si je me levais de bonne heure.　　*I would have time,* if I got up early.

The forms of the conditional of **être** and **avoir** are:

être	avoir
je serais	j'aurais
I would (should) be	*I would (should) have*
tu serais	tu aurais
il serait	il aurait
nous serions	nous aurions
vous seriez	vous auriez
ils seraient	ils auraient

63. Commonest uses of the conditional.

(1) The conditional is used in the result clause of certain conditional sentences:

—**Je répondrais** à sa lettre, si j'avais son adresse.　　*I would answer* his letter, if I had his address.

—**Je travaillerais** davantage, si j'étais à votre place.　　*I would work* more, if I were in your place.

In conditional sentences which describe *what would happen* if a certain condition were fulfilled, the conditional is used in the result clause (**Je répondrais à sa lettre**) and the imperfect is used in the if-clause (**si j'avais son adresse**).

Note the difference between this conditional sentence and those you have seen (see par. 47), which describe *what will happen* if a certain condition is fulfilled. Ex.: **Je prendrai un taxi** *(fut.)* **s'il pleut** *(present).*

(2) The conditional is often used even though the if-clause is omitted. Ex.: **Vous ne sauriez pas** dépenser votre argent. *You would not know* how to spend your money (i.e., if you were rich).

—**A** votre place, **je travaillerais** davantage.　　(If I were) in your place, *I would work* harder.

(3) To express future action in indirect discourse which depends upon a verb in a past tense:

—Il a dit qu'**il irait** en Italie.   He said *he would go* to Italy.
—Elle a dit qu'**elle ferait** des courses.   She said *she would do* some errands.

Note that this use of the conditional is parallel to English usage. If someone said: *I shall go to Italy,* you could report it by a direct quotation (direct discourse), or by an indirect quotation (indirect discourse). For example:

DIRECT: He said, *"I shall go to Italy."* Il a dit —**J'irai** en Italie.
INDIRECT: He said *he would go* to Italy. Il a dit qu'**il irait** en Italie.

64. Remark about English *should* and *would*.

While it is generally bad practice to think of French words and phrases in terms of their supposed English equivalents, it is particularly dangerous in the case of *should* and *would*. While these words are indeed used to form a conditional in English, they have other very common meanings which have nothing whatever to do with the conditional.

(1) *Should* denoting obligation (meaning "ought to"): To express in French "I should go to the library" (i.e. I ought to go to the library), you use a form of the verb **devoir.** This verb will be studied later. Meanwhile, remember that the conditional forms themselves carry no suggestion of obligation.

(2) *Would* denoting habitual action (meaning "used to"): You have seen in paragraph 56 that habitual action in the past is expressed in French by the imperfect indicative. Ex.:

—**Il allait** au cinéma tous les soirs   He *would go* (used to go) to the
   après le dîner.   movies every evening after dinner.

I. EXERCICES D'APPLICATION.

   A. Répétez, en remplaçant le futur par le conditionnel:

1. Je lui parlerai.   2. J'irai en ville.   3. Je n'aurai pas le temps.   4. Achèterez-vous ces gants?   5. Déjeunerez-vous en ville?   6. Lui répondrez-vous?   7. Il se dépêchera.   8. Vous dépêcherez-vous?   9. Ils commenceront tout de suite. 10. A quelle heure finiront-ils?   11. Y aura-t-il de la place?   12. Qu'est-ce que vous achèterez?

B. *Répétez, en remplaçant le présent par le conditionnel:*

1. J'achète le journal.   **2.** Je me lève de bonne heure.   **3.** Il obéit à la loi.
4. Il est à l'heure.   **5.** Vous avez le temps.   **6.** Nous n'avons pas le temps.
7. Ils vont en Italie.   **8.** Ils font du ski.   **9.** Que faites-vous?   **10.** Je ne sais
pas.   **11.** Ne voulez-vous pas aller à Versailles?   **12.** Pouvez-vous m'envoyer
son adresse?

C. *Répétez les phrases suivantes, en remplaçant le présent et le futur*
par l'imparfait et le conditionnel:

Ex.:—Si je commence plus tôt, je finirai plus tôt.
   —Si je commençais plus tôt, je finirais plus tôt.

1. Si j'ai le temps de rentrer, je déjeunerai à la maison.   **2.** S'il fait beau, j'irai
en ville.   **3.** Si mon père m'envoie un chèque, j'achèterai un manteau.   **4.**
Nous monterons s'il y a de la place.   **5.** S'il neige, je prendrai un taxi.
6. Si je me couche de bonne heure, je me lèverai de bonne heure.   **7.** Si je
n'ai pas de cigarettes, j'irai au bureau de tabac.   **8.** Si Roger ne finit pas son
travail, il ne sera pas content.

D. *Mettez les phrases suivantes à la forme indirecte.*

Ex.:—Il a dit: J'irai en Italie.
   —Il a dit qu'il irait en Italie.

1. Il a dit: Je rentrerai à midi.   **2.** Je lui ai dit: Je ferai des courses cet
après-midi.   **3.** Je lui ai dit: Je me coucherai de bonne heure.   **4.** Il m'a dit:
Je me dépêcherai.   **5.** Ils nous ont dit: Nous serons à l'heure.

II. *(Exercice sur le conditionnel et sur l'imparfait) Dites en français:*

1. (*a*) I would (or should) be. (*b*) I was. (*c*) If I were . . .   **2.** (*a*) He would
have. (*b*) He had. (*c*) If he had . . .   **3.** (*a*) We would have lunch. (*b*) We
were having lunch. (*c*) If we were having lunch . . .   **4.** (*a*) You would finish.
(*b*) You were finishing. (*c*) If you finished (If you were to finish) (If you
should finish) . . .   **5.** (*a*) They would answer. (*b*) They were answering.
(*c*) If they answered (If they were to answer) (If they should answer) . . .
6. (*a*) I would go. (*b*) I was going. (*c*) If I were going (If I were to go) (If
I should go) (If I went) . . .

III. *Demandez à quelqu'un:*

1. s'il déjeunerait à la maison, s'il avait le temps de rentrer.   **2.** s'il achèterait
une grosse auto, s'il était riche.   **3.** s'il saurait dépenser son argent, s'il était
millionnaire.   **4.** s'il ferait une promenade, s'il faisait beau.   **5.** ce qu'il ferait,
s'il avait faim.   **6.** ce qu'il ferait, s'il était fatigué.   **7.** ce qu'il ferait, s'il était
malade.   **8.** ce qu'il achèterait, si son père lui envoyait un chèque de cinquante
dollars.   **9.** s'il serait heureux de passer quelques semaines à Paris, s'il avait
le temps.

IV. *Dites en français:*

1. You are right. **2.** I hope it will snow. **3.** I hoped it would snow. **4.** Will you go skiing if it snows? **5.** Will you go skiing when it snows? **6.** Would you go skiing if it snowed? **7.** He said he would go skiing if it snowed. **8.** He always goes skiing when there is enough snow **(assez de neige).** **9.** He always went skiing when there was enough snow.

V. Révision des dialogues, pp. 128-129 et pp. 132-133.

1. Qu'est-ce que John fait à l'arrêt de l'autobus? **2.** Depuis combien de temps attend-il l'autobus? **3.** Est-ce qu'il y avait beaucoup de monde dans l'autobus qui est arrivé? **4.** Y a-t-il des gens debout dans l'autobus qui arrive? **5.** Est-ce qu'il y a de la place dans l'autobus? **6.** Est-ce que John et Roger sont montés tout de même? **7.** Quand est-ce qu'il y aura de la place? **8.** Pourquoi Roger descend-il à l'arrêt de la rue de la Paix? **9.** Où Roger habitait-il quand il avait douze ans? **10.** A quelle école allait-il? **11.** Dans quelle région se trouve la ville où il habitait? **12.** A quelle heure partait-il pour l'école? **13.** A quelle heure en sortait-il? **14.** Y avait-il beaucoup d'élèves dans cette école? **15.** Croyez-vous que les élèves de cette école travaillaient trop?

VI. Thème d'imitation:

Today is Christmas Day. After Midnight Mass, John and Roger went to the Christmas-Eve Party [1] at the Browns. On the table there was a beautiful turkey, and John, who had not seen turkey since his last Thanksgiving [2] in America, thought [3] that turkey (was) delicious.[4] I won't mention [5] the wines of all sorts, red and white.

John and Roger got home at five o'clock in the morning! When John woke up several hours later, he said to Roger: "Santa Claus [6] brought me a sure enough headache,[7] but that's all right because I had a very good time. The Browns are very nice and their food is excellent, isn't it?"

---

[1] to go to the Christmas-Eve Party, **aller faire le réveillon.** [2] **n'avait pas vu de dinde depuis son dernier Thanksgiving.** [3] use *passé composé* because it describes John's reaction. [4] delicious, **délicieux** *m.*, **délicieuse** *f.* [5] *Lit.* I do not speak. [6] Santa Claus, **le Père Noël.** [7] **un bon mal de tête.**

A Versailles

JOHN —¹Je ne croyais pas Versailles si grand. ²Tout est majestueux: les vastes salles du château, les longues allées du parc, les pièces d'eau, les jardins, les fontaines . . .

ROGER —³Louis XIV aimait la splendeur. ⁴Maintenant, comprenez-vous pourquoi on l'appelait le Grand Roi?

JOHN —⁵Oui, je comprends.

ROGER —⁶«Noblesse oblige,» vous savez.

JOHN —⁷Je sais que Louis XIV a fait construire Versailles. ⁸Mais qui est-ce qui l'a construit pour lui?

ROGER —⁹Un des architectes était Mansard.

JOHN —¹⁰J'ai entendu parler de lui. ¹¹Nous avons en anglais le mot «mansard.»

ROGER —¹²Tiens! Qu'est-ce que cela veut dire?

JOHN —¹³Je crois que c'est une espèce de toit.

ROGER —¹⁴Le mot «mansarde» existe aussi en français.

JOHN —¹⁵Qu'est-ce que c'est qu'une «mansarde?»

JOHN —¹I did not think Versailles was so large. ²Everything is majestic: the enormous rooms of the château, the long walks of the park, the ornamental pools, the gardens, the fountains . . .

ROGER —³Louis XIV went in for magnificence. ⁴Now do you understand why they called him the Great King?

JOHN —⁵Yes, I understand.

ROGER —⁶"Noblesse oblige",* you know.

JOHN —⁷I know that Louis XIV had Versailles built. ⁸But who built it for him?

ROGER —⁹Mansard was one of the architects.

JOHN —¹⁰I have heard of him. ¹¹We have the word "mansard" in English.

ROGER —¹²Really! What does that mean?

JOHN —¹³I think it is a sort of roof.

ROGER —¹⁴We also have the word "mansarde" in French.

JOHN —¹⁵What is a "mansarde"?

---

* Nobility imposes obligations (i.e. it is up to persons of high birth, rank, or position to live up to their position in every way).

ROGER —[16]C'est d'ordinaire une chambre sous le toit. [17]C'est là qu'on met les vieux meubles, les chaises cassées, les tapis usés, et cætera. [18]Le sort est parfois ironique.

JOHN —[19]Qu'est-ce qui vous fait dire cela?

ROGER —[20]Mansard a passé sa vie à construire des palais, [21]et il a laissé son nom à une humble chambre.

ROGER —[16]It is usually a room under the roof (i.e. a garret room). [17]That's where we put pieces of old furniture, broken chairs, worn-out carpets, etc. [18]Fate is sometimes ironical.

JOHN —[19]What makes you say that?

ROGER —[20]Mansard spent his life building palaces, [21]and (yet) he left his name to a humble room.

I. SUBSTITUTIONS. *Répétez les phrases suivantes en substituant les mots indiqués:*

1. Je ne croyais pas [Versailles si grand].
   les jardins si beaux/ les salles si vastes/ les allées si longues/ les allées si larges *(wide)*/ Mansard si bon architecte

2. Louis XIV a fait construire [Versailles].
   une belle chapelle/ de beaux châteaux/ plusieurs palais/ de beaux monuments

3. [Nous avons] fait construire une maison.
   J'ai/ Ma sœur a/ Mes parents ont/ Avez-vous/ Votre père a-t-il

4. J'ai entendu parler [de lui].
   de Mansard/ des Brown/ d'eux/ de Jeanne d'Arc/ d'elle

5. Il a passé [sa vie à construire des palais].
   l'après-midi à faire des courses/ la soirée à travailler/ le week-end à faire du ski/ trois jours à se reposer/ l'été à visiter l'Italie

II. *Répondez à chacune des questions suivantes en remplaçant le nom par le pronom convenable.*

Ex.:—Avez-vous entendu parler de Mansard?
   —Oui, j'ai entendu parler de lui.
   —Avez-vous entendu parler de Versailles?
   —Oui, j'en ai entendu parler.

1. Avez-vous entendu parler [de Louis XIV]?
   des Brown/ de Napoléon/ de Jeanne d'Arc/ des rois de France

2. Avez-vous entendu parler [du château de Versailles]?
   des fontaines de Versailles/ du parc de Versailles/ de la chapelle de Versailles/ des mansardes

III. *Répondez à chacune des questions suivantes:*

1. De quel château parlent John et Roger? **2.** Est-ce que John croyait que Versailles était si grand? **3.** Qu'est-ce qu'on trouve dans le château? **4.** Qu'est-ce qu'il y a dans le parc? **5.** Comment appelait-on Louis XIV? **6.** Est-ce qu'il aimait la splendeur? **7.** Comprenez-vous la phrase "Noblesse oblige"? **8.** Qui a fait construire Versailles? **9.** Qui est-ce qui a construit le château pour Louis XIV? **10.** Avez-vous entendu parler de Mansard? **11.** Avez-vous entendu parler des allées du parc? **12.** Avez-vous entendu parler des fontaines de Versailles? **13.** Connaissez-vous le mot anglais "mansard"? **14.** Qu'est-ce que cela veut dire? **15.** Est-ce que le mot "mansarde" existe aussi en français? **16.** Qu'est-ce que c'est qu'une mansarde? **17.** Qu'est-ce qu'on met dans les mansardes? **18.** Qu'est-ce que Mansard a fait pendant sa vie? **19.** A quoi a-t-il laissé son nom?

IV. *Demandez à quelqu'un:*

1. s'il y a beaucoup de fontaines à Versailles. **2.** comment on appelait Louis XIV. **3.** ce que veut dire "Noblesse oblige". **4.** qui a fait construire le château de Versailles. **5.** qui a construit le château. **6.** s'il a entendu parler de Mansard. **7.** s'il connaît le mot anglais "mansard". **8.** si le mot "mansarde" existe aussi en français. **9.** ce que veut dire le mot anglais "mansard". **10.** où l'on met les vieux meubles. **11.** ce qu'on met dans les mansardes. **12.** si le sort est parfois ironique. **13.** comment Mansard a passé sa vie. **14.** à quoi il a laissé son nom.

V. RÉVISION. *Verbes pronominaux. Demandez à quelqu'un:*

1. comment il s'appelle. **2.** s'il se lève tard pendant les vacances. **3.** à quelle heure il se lève pendant les vacances. **4.** à quelle heure il s'est levé ce matin. **5.** à quelle heure il s'est couché hier soir. **6.** s'il s'est bien reposé dimanche dernier. **7.** comment s'appelle son professeur de français. **8.** s'il s'est bien amusé samedi soir.

VI. DICTÉE D'APRÈS LE DIALOGUE, p. 152.

VII. CONVERSATION.

"Do you know who planned (**dessiner**) the Versailles gardens?"
"No, I don't know. Who was it?"
"It was Le Nôtre."
"Oh yes. I think I have heard of him. His gardens are majestic, aren't they?"

Qu'est-ce que vous avez?

ROGER —[1]Qu'est-ce que vous avez, Marie?

MARIE —[2]Je n'ai rien du tout, je vous assure.

ROGER —[3]Mais si, vous avez quelque chose. [4]Vous avez l'air triste. [5]A quoi pensez-vous?

MARIE —[6]Je pense à Jeanne. La connaissez-vous?

ROGER —[7]Non, je ne crois pas. Qui est-ce?

MARIE —[8]C'est une de mes cousines.

ROGER —[9]Vous avez tant de cousines! [10]Laquelle de vos cousines est-ce?

MARIE —[11]C'est ma cousine qui demeure à Reims.

ROGER —[12]Oh oui! vous m'avez déjà parlé d'elle. [13]Qu'est-ce qui lui est arrivé?

MARIE —[14]J'ai reçu hier une lettre de ma tante Ernestine. [15]Elle m'écrit que Jeanne va se marier jeudi prochain.

ROGER —[16]Quoi? Est-ce que cette nouvelle vous rend triste?

MARIE —[17]Non, au contraire.

ROGER —[18]Qu'est-ce qui vous ennuie, alors?

ROGER —[1]What is the matter with you, Marie?

MARIE —[2]Nothing is the matter, really.

ROGER —[3]Yes there is. Something is wrong. [4]You look very sad. [5]What are you thinking about?

MARIE —[6]I am thinking of Jane. Do you know her?

ROGER —[7]No, I don't think so. Who is she?

MARIE —[8]She's a cousin of mine.

ROGER —[9]You have so many cousins! [10]Which of your cousins is she?

MARIE —[11]She's my cousin who lives in Rheims.

ROGER —[12]Oh yes! You have already spoken to me about her. [13]What has happened to her?

MARIE —[14]I had a letter from my aunt Ernestine yesterday. [15]She writes me that Jane is going to get married next Thursday.

ROGER —[16]What? Does that news make you sad?

MARIE —[17]No. On the contrary.

ROGER —[18]What is bothering you then?

MARIE —[19]Je ne pourrai pas aller à son mariage.

ROGER —[20]C'est dommage, en effet. [21]Avec qui votre cousine se marie-t-elle?

MARIE —[22]Avec un jeune homme que je connaissais quand il avait dix ans. [23]Comme le temps passe!

MARIE —[19]I cannot go to her wedding.

ROGER —[20]It's indeed too bad. [21]To whom is your cousin getting married?

MARIE —[22]To a young man I knew when he was ten years old. [23]How time flies!

I. SUBSTITUTIONS. *Répétez les phrases suivantes en substituant les mots indiqués:*

1. Il a l'air [triste].
   fatigué/ content/ jeune/ agréable/ gentil/ intelligent
2. Vous avez l'air d'avoir [chaud].
   froid/ faim/ soif *(thirsty)*/ quelque chose/ très chaud
3. Est-ce que [cette nouvelle] vous rend triste?
   la neige/ le travail/ la pluie *(rain)*/ un bon dîner

II. *Répondez affirmativement, puis négativement à chacune des questions suivantes:*

Ex.:—Avez-vous acheté quelque chose?
   —**Oui, j'ai acheté quelque chose.**
   —**Non, je n'ai rien acheté.**

1. Avez-vous reçu quelque chose? 2. Avez-vous trouvé quelque chose? 3. Avez-vous entendu quelque chose? 4. Avez-vous envoyé quelque chose? 5. Avez-vous fait quelque chose? 6. Avez-vous quelque chose à faire? 7. Avez-vous quelque chose?

III. *Remplacez le nom par le pronom convenable dans les phrases suivantes:*

A. penser à*

Ex.:—Je pense à Jeanne. **Je pense à elle.**
   —Je pense à mes examens. **J'y pense.**

1. Je pense à mes parents. 2. Je pense à mon examen. 3. Roger pense à son père. 4 Il pense à son travail. 5 Nous pensons à nos amis. 6. Nous pensons à votre demande. 7. Pensez-vous à cette lettre? 8. Pensez-vous à votre mère? 9. Il faut penser à vos examens.

---

* It is important to distinguish between **penser à** and **penser de.** While both are translated "to think of" in English, **penser à** means *to think of* a person or a thing, and **penser de** means *to think something about* a person or a thing, i.e. to hold an opinion.
Penser à. When the object of **penser à** is a personal pronoun which refers to a person or persons, the stressed form of the personal pronoun is used: Pensez-vous à **Marie?** Oui, je pense à **elle.** When the object of **penser à** is a pronoun referring to things, the form **y** is used: Pensez-vous à **vos examens?** Oui, j'y pense.

B. penser de*

Ex.:—Que pensez-vous de Jeanne?   **Que pensez-vous d'elle?**
    —Que pensez-vous de ce journal?   **Qu'en pensez-vous?**

1. Que pensez-vous de Louis XIV? **2.** Que pensez-vous de Versailles? **3.**
Qu'est-ce que John pense de Versailles? **4.** Que pense-t-il de son auto?
5. Que pensez-vous de ce film? **6.** Que pensez-vous de mes cousins? **7.** Que
pensez-vous de mon chapeau? **8.** Que pensez-vous des Brown?

IV. *Répondez en français à chacune des questions suivantes:*

1. Qu'est-ce qu'a Marie? **2.** A-t-elle l'air triste? **3.** A quoi pense-t-elle?
4. Est-ce que Roger connaît Jeanne? **5.** Qui est Jeanne? **6.** Est-ce que Marie
a beaucoup de cousines? **7.** Où Jeanne demeure-t-elle? **8.** Est-ce que Marie
a déjà parlé d'elle à Roger? **9.** De qui Marie a-t-elle reçu une lettre hier?
10. Qu'est-ce que sa tante Ernestine lui dit dans sa lettre? **11.** Est-ce que
cette nouvelle la rend triste? **12.** Qu'est-ce qui ennuie Marie? **13.** Avec qui
sa cousine se marie-t-elle? **14.** Quel âge avait le fiancé de Jeanne quand
Marie le connaissait?

V. *Demandez à quelqu'un:*

1. ce qu'il a. **2.** s'il a quelque chose. **3.** pourquoi il a l'air triste. **4.** à quoi
il pense. **5.** s'il connaît Jeanne. **6.** si Marie a beaucoup de cousines. **7.** si
Marie a déjà parlé de sa cousine à Roger. **8.** de qui Marie a reçu une lettre
hier. **9.** quand Jeanne va se marier. **10.** si cette nouvelle le rend triste.
11. avec qui se marie sa cousine. **12.** pourquoi Marie ne peut pas aller
au mariage de sa cousine.

VI. *Dites en français:*

A. qu'est-ce que? (object form)

1. What's the matter with you? **2.** What's the matter with him? **3.** What's
the matter with her? **4.** What's the matter with them? **5.** What was the
matter with them? **6.** What was the matter with him?

---

* **Penser de.** When the object of **penser de** is a personal pronoun which refers to a person or
persons, the stressed form of the personal pronoun is used: Qu'est-ce que vous pensez **d'elle?**
Je pense beaucoup de bien **d'elle.** When the object of **penser de** is a personal pronoun refer-
ing to things, the form **en** is used: Qu'est-ce que vous pensez **de ce livre?** Qu'est-ce que vous
en pensez?

B. qu'est-ce qui? (subject form)

I. What happened to her?   **2.** What happened to him?   **3.** What happened to them?   **4.** What happened to you?   **5.** What happened to Marie?   **6.** What happened?   **7.** What's bothering you?   **8.** What's bothering her?   **9.** What's bothering them?

VII. DICTÉE D'APRÈS LE DIALOGUE, pp. 160-161.

VIII. CONVERSATION.

"Did you get a letter this morning?"
"Yes. My cousin writes me she is getting married."
"Are you going *(fut.)* to the wedding?"
"No. I can't go *(there)*."
"It's too bad."

Interrogative Pronouns

65. Interrogative pronouns referring to persons.

A. Subject forms: **qui?** or **qui est-ce qui?** *who?*:

—**Qui** a dit cela?   *Who* said that?
    OR
—**Qui est-ce qui** a dit cela?

B. Object forms: **qui?** and **qui est-ce que?** *whom?*:

—**Qui** avez-vous vu?   *Whom* did you see?
    OR
—**Qui est-ce que** vous avez vu?

—**A qui** avez-vous parlé?   *To whom* did you speak?
    OR
—**A qui est-ce que** vous avez parlé?

—**Avec qui** votre cousine se ma-   *To whom* is your cousin getting mar-
    rie-t-elle?   ried?
    OR
—**Avec qui est-ce que** votre cou-
    sine se marie?

—**De qui** parlez-vous?   *About whom* are you talking?
    OR
—**De qui est-ce que** vous parlez?

Note that when **Qui?** is used as object of a verb or preposition, you invert the order of subject and verb. With **Qui est-ce qui?** or **Qui est-ce que?** you use normal word order.

C. **à qui?** *whose?*:

—**A qui** sont ces gants?   *Whose* gloves are these?
—**A qui** est ce chapeau?   *Whose* hat is this?

Note that **à qui?** is the interrogative form corresponding to **à moi, à vous,** etc., which you have seen in paragraph 60.

66. Interrogative pronouns referring to things, etc. (i.e., not persons).

A. Subject form: **qu'est-ce qui?** *What?:*

   —**Qu'est-ce qui** se passe?   *What* is happening?

   —**Qu'est-ce qui** lui est arrivé?   *What* happened to him (*or* to her)?

The alternate subject form **que?** can be used in some cases but not always, whereas **qu'est-ce qui?** is always safe as a subject form.

B. Direct object form: **que?** and **qu'est-ce que?**, *what?:*

   —**Que** vous a-t-il dit?   *What* did he say to you?

        OR

   —**Qu'est-ce qu'**il vous a dit?

   —**Que** lui avez-vous répondu?   *What* did you reply to him?

        OR

   —**Qu'est-ce que** vous lui avez ré-
     pondu?

   —**Qu'**avez-vous?   *What* *is* the matter with you?

        OR

   —**Qu'est-ce que** vous avez?

The only difference between **que?** and **qu'est-ce que?** is that with **que?** you use inverted word order.

C. Object of a preposition: **quoi?**, *what?:*

   —**A quoi** pensez-vous?   *What* are you thinking *of?*

        OR

   —**A quoi est-ce que** vous pensez?

   —**De quoi** parlez-vous?   *What* are you talking *about?*

        OR

   —**De quoi est-ce que** vous parlez?

   —**De quoi** avez-vous besoin?   *What* do you need?

        OR

   —**De quoi est-ce que** vous avez be-
     soin?

Since the verb **penser à** means to *think of,* you naturally say: **A quoi pensez-vous?** (Cf. note on p. 164.)

67. Qu'est-ce que c'est que . . . ? *What is . . . ?*

—Qu'est-ce que c'est qu'un Prisunic?   *What is* a "Prisunic"?
—Qu'est-ce que c'est que cela?   *What is* that?

You use **Qu'est-ce que c'est que . . .?** to ask for a description or a definition.

68. Interrogative pronoun **lequel? laquelle? lesquels? lesquelles?** *which? which one? which ones?* (persons or things).

A. Subject or object:

—**Laquelle** de vos cousines va se   *Which one* of your cousins is get-
    marier?   ting married?
—Voici des livres. **Lesquels** voulez-   Here are some books. *Which ones*
    vous?   do you want?

(1) **Lequel? laquelle?**, etc. are used to distinguish between two or more persons or things within a group. Ex.: *Who* are those people? **Qui** sont ces gens?'BUT: *Which one* is Mr. Duval? **Lequel** est M. Duval?

(2) These forms agree in gender and number with the nouns to which they refer.

B. With prepositions **à** or **de:**

—Voici deux livres. **Duquel** avez-   Here are two books. *Which one* do
    vous besoin?   you need?
—**A laquelle** de vos cousines avez-   *To which one* of your cousins did
    vous écrit?   you write?

In combination with prepositions **à** and **de** the forms of **lequel?** etc. are:

auquel? à laquelle? auxquels? auxquelles?
duquel? de laquelle? desquels? desquelles?

I. EXERCICES D'APPLICATION.

A. *Posez la question à laquelle répond chacune des phrases suivantes en remplaçant le sujet par* **Qui?** *puis par* **Qui est-ce qui?**

Ex.:—Mon père a dit cela.
    —**Qui a dit cela? Qui est-ce qui a dit cela?**

1. Roger est allé au bal. 2. La bonne a sa cravate. 3. Mansard a construit ce château. 4. John a acheté ce journal. 5. Je suis allé à la gare. 6. Elle est venue chez eux. 7. Roger veut du café. 8. Je connais Louise Bedel. 9. Je sais la date de la prise de la Bastille.

B. *Posez la question à laquelle répond chacune des phrases suivantes en remplaçant le complément par* **Qui?** *puis par* **Qui est-ce que?**

Ex.:—J'ai vu Marie.

—**Qui avez-vous vu?   Qui est-ce que vous avez vu?**

1. J'ai rencontré Marie.   2. J'ai parlé à Marie.   3. Je suis sorti avec elle.
4. J'ai écrit à M. Brown.   5. Roger a écrit à ses parents.   6. Il a acheté des fleurs pour Marie.   7. Il est allé au bal avec elle.   8. Il a envoyé chercher le médecin.   9. Nous avons envoyé des gants à ma mère.

C. *Posez la question à laquelle répond chacune des phrases suivantes en employant* **à qui . . .?**

Ex.:—Ces gants sont à moi.

—**A qui sont ces gants?**

1. Ce pardessus est à Charles.   2. Ces mouchoirs sont à moi.   3. Cette auto est à mon père.   4. Cet imperméable est à mon frère.   5. Cette cravate est à lui.

D. *Posez la question à laquelle répond chacune des phrases suivantes en remplaçant le sujet par* **Qu'est-ce qui?**

Ex.:—Le vent fait ce bruit.

—**Qu'est-ce qui fait ce bruit?**

1. Mon auto fait ce bruit.   2. Cette nouvelle me rend triste.   3. Cette nouvelle m'ennuie.   4. La neige me rend triste.   5. Rien ne m'ennuie.   6. Rien ne me plaît.   7. Rien ne se passe.   8. Quelque chose de terrible est arrivé.
9. Rien ne lui est arrivé.   10. Ce mauvais café m'a rendu malade.

E. *Posez la question à laquelle répond chacune des phrases suivantes en remplaçant le complément par* **Qu'est-ce que?** *puis par* **Que?**

Ex.:—J'ai fait des courses.

—**Qu'est-ce que vous avez fait?   Qu'avez-vous fait?**

1. J'ai acheté des bonbons.   2. Il a dit bonjour.   3. Il a apporté des hors-d'œuvre.   4. Elle n'a rien dit.   5. Je n'ai rien du tout.   6. Nous avons fait une promenade cet après-midi.   7. J'ai mangé une pomme.   8. J'ai choisi une belle cravate.

F. *Posez la question à laquelle répond chacune des phrases suivantes en remplaçant le complément par* **quoi?**

Ex.—Je pense à l'examen.

—**A quoi pensez-vous?**

1. Je pense à mes examens.   2. J'ai besoin de papier à lettres.   3. J'ai besoin d'un journal.   4. J'ai besoin d'argent.   5. Nous parlons de notre voyage.
6. Je commencerai par des hors-d'œuvre.   7. Je finirai par des fruits.   8. Je pense à l'été prochain.

G. *Posez le question à laquelle répond chacune des phrases suivantes en remplaçant le nom par* **lequel? laquelle?** etc.

Ex.:—Voilà plusieurs jeunes filles. Jeanne est la plus grande.
   —**Laquelle est la plus grande?**

I. Marie est la plus jolie.   **2.** Alice est la plus intelligente.   **3.** Hélène et Marguerite sont blondes.   **4.** Je préfère Marie.   **5.** J'ai parlé de Louise.   **6.** Je pense à Louise.

II. *Demandez à quelqu'un:*

I. qui a construit le château de Versailles.   **2.** pour qui le château a été construit.   **3.** ce que c'est qu'un château.   **4.** laquelle des villes de France est la plus grande.   **5.** de qui Marie a reçu une lettre hier.   **6.** à qui pense Marie.   **7.** ce qui ennuie Marie.   **8.** ce que la tante de Marie a dit dans sa lettre.   **9.** lesquelles des villes d'Italie Roger aimerait visiter.   **I0.** ce que Roger voudrait voir aux États-Unis.

III. Révision des dialogues, pp. 140-141 et pp. 143-144.

I. Pourquoi Marie n'est-elle pas allée au bal samedi dernier?   **2.** Comment se sentait-elle ce soir-là?   **3.** Est-ce qu'elle était très malade?   **4.** A-t-elle fait venir le médecin?   **5.** Comment va-t-elle maintenant?   **6.** Est-ce qu'il faisait très froid le jour où elle a fait une longue promenade?   **7.** Avait-elle froid en rentrant?   **8.** Est-ce qu'elle fera bien de se reposer?   **9.** Pourquoi John n'est-il pas prêt à sortir?   **I0.** Pourquoi John n'accepte-t-il pas la cravate de Roger?   **II.** Est-ce qu'on pourrait porter une cravate verte avec un complet bleu?   **I2.** Est-ce que John a cherché dans son tiroir?   **I3.** Où Roger trouve-t-il la cravate de John?   **I4.** Pourquoi la bonne a-t-elle mis la cravate de John avec celles de Roger?

IV. Thème d'imitation:

Louis XIV was [1] not the best king of France, but he is certainly the most famous [2]. He was born in 1643 and he died in 1715. The first part [3] of his reign [4] was probably the greatest period [5] of the history of France. He had * an enormous château built at Versailles. The work took [6] more than [7] forty years, and the best artists [8] of the seventeenth century worked at Versailles. The long buildings [9], the beautiful walks in the park, the gardens, everything gives an impression [10] of splendor and harmony [11]. Louis XIV had the sun as an emblem [12]. It is at Versailles that you [13] understand why he is often called [13] the Sun-King [14].

---

[1] present tense. [2] famous, **célèbre.** [3] part, **la partie.** [4] reign, **le règne.** [5] period, **la période.** [6] *Lit.* lasted. [7] With numbers you say **plus de.** [8] artist, **artiste** *(m.).* [9] building, **le bâtiment.** [10] une impression. [11] **harmonie** *(f.).* [12] as an emblem, **comme emblème.** [13] Use pronoun **on** with both verbs. [14] **le Roi-Soleil.**

* Use **passé composé.** Remember that the **passé composé** is the normal past tense. It tells the story. The imperfect is used to describe the circumstances or state of affairs as the story unfolds.

Un accident

Au commissariat de police	**At the Police Station**

LE COMMISSAIRE DE POLICE —[1]Vous êtes bien M. John Hughes, ingénieur-chimiste, [2]demeurant 15, avenue de l'Observatoire?

JOHN —[3]Oui, monsieur le commissaire.

LE COMMISSAIRE DE POLICE —[4]Hier après-midi, vous avez été témoin de l'accident [5]au cours duquel le docteur Lambert a été blessé?

JOHN —[6]Oui, monsieur le commissaire.

LE COMMISSAIRE DE POLICE —[7] Où étiez-vous au moment où l'auto du docteur, [8]qui suivait la rue de Vaugirard, [9]est entrée en collision avec un camion [10]venant de l'avenue Pasteur?

JOHN —[11]J'étais devant l'Institut Pasteur.*

LE COMMISSAIRE DE POLICE —[12]Comment l'accident a-t-il eu lieu?

JOHN —[13]La chaussée était très glissante, [14]car il avait plu. [15]Le docteur Lambert, dont l'auto allait très vite, [16]n'a pas pu s'arrêter à temps.

THE COMMISSAIRE DE POLICE —[1]You are indeed Mr. John Hughes, a chemical engineer, [2]who lives at 15 Avenue de l'Observatoire?

JOHN —[3]Yes, sir.

THE COMMISSAIRE DE POLICE —[4]Yesterday afternoon you were a witness of the accident [5]in the course of which Dr. Lambert was hurt?

JOHN —[6]Yes, sir.

THE COMMISSAIRE DE POLICE — [7]Where were you at the moment when the doctor's car, [8]which was going along Vaugirard Street, [9]collided with a truck [10]coming from Pasteur Avenue?

JOHN —[11]I was in front of the Pasteur Institute.

THE COMMISSAIRE DE POLICE — [12]How did the accident take place?

JOHN —[13]The street was very slippery, [14]for it had been raining. [15]Dr. Lambert, whose car was going very fast, [16]couldn't stop in time.

---

* The Institut Pasteur, founded by the great Pasteur, consists of a hospital, a museum, and a research institute for biological chemistry.

LE COMMISSAIRE DE POLICE —[17]A quelle vitesse le camion allait-il [18]quand l'accident a eu lieu?

JOHN —[19]A environ 30 kilomètres à l'heure.

LE COMMISSAIRE DE POLICE —[20]Je vous remercie, monsieur. [21]Ce que vous venez de dire [22]est d'accord avec les renseignements que nous avons déjà.

THE COMMISSAIRE DE POLICE — [17]How fast was the truck going [18]when the accident took place?

JOHN —[19]About 30 kilometers per hour.

THE COMMISSAIRE DE POLICE — [20]I thank you, sir. [21]What you have said [22]agrees with the information we already have.

I. SUBSTITUTIONS. *Répétez les phrases suivantes en substituant les mots indiqués:*

1. [Le docteur Lambert] a été blessé.
   Un passant/ Un médecin/ Un agent de police/ Un vieux monsieur

2. . . . l'accident au cours duquel [le docteur Lambert] a été blessé.
   un passant/ un médecin/ un agent de police/ un vieux monsieur

3. Vous avez été témoin de l'accident au cours duquel [le docteur Lambert] a été blessé.
   un passant/ un médecin/ un agent de police/ un vieux monsieur

4. Le docteur Lambert, dont l'auto allait [très vite], n'a pas pu s'arrêter à temps.
   assez vite/ trop vite/ beaucoup trop vite/ à trente kilomètres à l'heure

5. Où étiez-vous au moment où [l'accident] a eu lieu?
   la collision/ l'incident/ la bataille/ la querelle/ la dispute

6. Où étiez-vous au moment de [l'accident]?
   la collision/ l'incident/ la bataille/ la querelle/ la dispute

7. Ce que vous venez de [dire] . . .
   faire/ acheter/ manger/ répondre/ chercher/ regarder

II. *Répondez en français à chacune des questions suivantes:*

I. A qui John parle-t-il? **2.** Où la conversation a-t-elle lieu? **3.** Que fait John Hughes? **4.** Où demeure-t-il? **5.** De quoi a-t-il été témoin? **6.** Quand l'accident a-t-il eu lieu? **7.** Qui a été blessé au cours de l'accident? **8.** Quelle rue suivait l'auto du docteur Lambert? **9.** D'où venait le camion? **10.** Où était John au moment de l'accident? **11.** Pourquoi la chaussée était-elle glissante? **12.** Pourquoi le docteur Lambert n'a-t-il pas pu s'arrêter à temps? **13.** A quelle vitesse le camion allait-il quand l'accident a eu lieu? **14.** A quelle vitesse allait l'auto du docteur au moment de l'accident? **15.** Est-ce que le commissaire a déjà parlé à des témoins de l'accident? **16.** Qu'est-ce que le commissaire a dit à John en le remerciant?

III. *Demandez à quelqu'un:*

1. à qui parle John Hughes. **2.** pourquoi le commissaire a fait venir John Hughes. **3.** l'adresse de John. **4.** sa profession. **5.** de quoi il a été témoin. **6.** où l'accident a eu lieu. **7.** quand l'accident a eu lieu. **8.** pourquoi l'accident a eu lieu. **9.** comment l'accident a eu lieu. **10.** s'il avait plu avant l'accident. **11.** pourquoi la chaussée était glissante. **12.** à quelle vitesse allait le camion au moment de l'accident.

IV. *Répétez, en remplaçant le passé composé par* **Je viens de** (I have just) *avec l'infinitif.*

Ex.:—J'ai déjeuné.
—**Je viens de déjeuner.**

1. J'ai acheté un journal. **2.** J'ai trouvé ma cravate. **3.** J'ai fini ma lettre. **4.** Je suis allé(e) à la pharmacie. **5.** Je me suis levé(e). **6.** Je me suis habillé(e). **7.** J'ai été témoin de l'accident.

V. Dictée d'après le dialogue, pp. 163-164.

VI. Conversation.

"What's your name?"
"My name is Henri Duval."
"What do you do?"
"I am a student."
"Did you see the accident?"
"Yes. I was on the corner of the Rue de la Paix."
"How fast was Dr. Lambert's car going?"
"It wasn't going very fast."

The *Passé Simple* and the Pluperfect, Future Perfect and Conditional Perfect

69. Meaning and use of the *passé simple*.

The names *passé simple* (simple past) and *passé composé* (compound past) are used to distinguish two tenses which, generally speaking, have the same meaning: both tenses are used to express simple past actions.

You have seen that the *passé composé* is commonly used in conversation. The *passé simple* is used only in literary narrative style and in rather formal speech.

EXAMPLE OF THE USE OF THE PASSÉ SIMPLE

A cette époque, il y **eut** une épidémie dans le pays des Troglodytes. Un médecin habile **arriva** du pays voisin et **donna** ses remèdes. Quand il **demanda** à ses clients de lui payer ses services, il ne **trouva** que des refus.

Le médecin **retourna** dans son pays et il y **arriva** très fatigué. Il **apprit** bientôt après que la même maladie ravageait de nouveau le pays des Troglodytes. Ils **allèrent** à lui tout de suite lui demander de revenir avec ses remèdes.

Le médecin **refusa.** Les Troglodytes **moururent** et **furent** victimes de leurs propres injustices.

At that time there *was* an epidemic in the land of the Troglodytes. A skillful doctor *arrived* from the neighboring country and *gave* his remedies. When he *asked* his patients to pay him for his services he *received* only refusals.

The doctor *returned* to his own country and he *arrived* there very tired. He *learned* soon afterwards that the same disease was again ravaging the land of the Troglodytes. They *went* to him immediately to ask him to come back with his remedies.

The doctor *refused.* The Troglodytes *died* and they *were* victims of their own injustice.

70. Forms of the **passé simple.**

A. Regular verbs:

FIRST CONJUGATION	SECOND CONJUGATION	THIRD CONJUGATION
je déjeunai	je finis	je répondis
I lunched	*I finished*	*I answered*
tu déjeunas	tu finis	tu répondis
il déjeuna	il finit	il répondit
nous déjeunâmes	nous finîmes	nous répondîmes
vous déjeunâtes	vous finîtes	vous répondîtes
ils déjeunèrent	ils finirent	ils répondirent

B. Être and **avoir:**

être	avoir
je fus	j'eus
I was	*I had*
tu fus	tu eus
il fut	il eut
nous fûmes	nous eûmes
vous fûtes	vous eûtes
ils furent	ils eurent

(As the **passé simple** *is primarily used in writing, it will be used only for aural practice and will appear only in exercise I, A.)*

71. Pluperfect **(plus-que-parfait)** of regular verbs and of **avoir** and **être.**

—**J'avais** déjà **accepté** l'invitation de Robert, quand j'ai reçu la vôtre.

I had already *accepted* Robert's invitation when I received yours.

—La chaussée était très glissante, car **il avait plu.**

The surface of the street was very slippery, for *it had been raining.*

—**Il était** déjà **parti,** quand je lui ai téléphoné.

He had already *left,* when I telephoned him.

The forms of the pluperfect indicative are:

J'avais déjeuné, etc. *I had lunched, etc.*
J'avais fini, etc. *I had finished, etc.*
J'avais répondu, etc. *I had answered, etc.*
J'avais été, etc. *I had been, etc.*
J'avais eu, etc. *I had had, etc.*
J'étais arrivé(e), etc. *I had arrived, etc.*
Je m'étais levé(e), etc. *I had got up, etc.*

(1) The pluperfect is formed like the *passé composé* except that the imperfect of the auxiliary is used.

(2) As in English, the pluperfect tense expresses an action which had already taken place when another past action took place.

72. Future perfect tense (futur antérieur).

—J'aurai fini mon travail quand il   *I shall have finished* my work when
    arrivera.   he arrives.

The future perfect is formed like the other compound tenses except that the future of the auxiliary verb is used.

J'aurai déjeuné, etc. *I shall have lunched, etc.*
Je serai arrivé(e), etc. *I shall have arrived, etc.*

As in English, the future perfect tense is used to express an action which will take place in the future before another future action takes place. In sentences in which you use a future perfect in one clause, the verb in the other clause is always in the future tense (cf. paragraph 47). Ex.: **Je serai parti** quand elle **recevra** ma lettre. *I shall have left* when she gets my letter *(will receive)*.

73. The conditional perfect (conditionnel passé).

—Si nous avions eu le temps, **nous**   If we had had time, *we would have*
    serions allés au bal.   *gone* to the dance.
—Je serais volontiers **allé** avec lui,   *I would have* gladly *gone* with him if
    si je n'avais pas eu mal à la tête.   I hadn't had a headache.

The conditional perfect is formed like the other compound tenses except that the conditional of the auxiliary verb is used.

J'aurais déjeuné, etc. *I would have lunched, etc.*
J'aurais répondu, etc. *I would have answered, etc.*
Je serais arrivé(e), etc. *I would have arrived, etc.*
Je me serais levé(e), etc. *I would have got up, etc.*

It is most commonly used in conditional sentences in which the verb in the if-clause is in the pluperfect. It expresses an action which would have taken place, if another action had taken place (cf. paragraph 63).

74. Agreement of the past participle* in compound tenses.

A. Verbs conjugated with **avoir:**

—J'ai planté des fleurs dans mon I have planted flowers in my garden.
  jardin.
—Les fleurs que j'ai plantées n'ont The flowers I planted did not grow.
  pas poussé.

When a verb is conjugated with **avoir,** the participle agrees in gender and number with a preceding direct object. If the direct object follows the participle, or if the verb has no direct object, there is of course no agreement and the masculine singular form of the participle is used.

Thus in **J'ai planté des fleurs,** there is no agreement because the direct object follows the participle.

In **Les fleurs que j'ai plantées n'ont pas poussé,** the participle **plantées** is feminine plural because the direct object **que,** which precedes the verb, refers to **les fleurs,** which is feminine plural. In the same sentence, **poussé** has no direct object and therefore cannot agree.

B. Verbs conjugated with **être** (not including reflexives):

—**John** est allé en ville.   John went downtown.
—**Marie** est allée en ville.   Marie went downtown.
—**Ils** sont arrivés à dix heures.   They *(masc.)* arrived at ten o'clock.
—**Elles** sont arrivées à neuf heures. They *(fem.)* arrived at nine o'clock.

Except for reflexive verbs, when a verb is conjugated with **être,** the past participle agrees in gender and number with the subject of the verb. **Vous** may of course be masculine or feminine, singular or plural. Ex.: **Marie, êtes-vous allée au cinéma? Henri, êtes-vous allé au cinéma? Êtes-vous allés au cinéma ensemble?**

C. Reflexive verbs:

—Roger s'est levé à sept heures.   Roger got up at seven o'clock.
—Marie s'est levée à neuf heures.   Marie got up at nine o'clock.

---

* The agreement of the past participle is purely a matter of spelling in most cases and is therefore of comparatively little importance in spoken French.

Although reflexive verbs are conjugated with **être**, their past participles agree as if they were conjugated with **avoir**, i.e. they agree with a preceding direct object. In the preceding examples, **se** is the preceding direct object in each case. In the first example, it refers to Roger and the agreement is masculine. In the second it refers to Marie and the agreement is feminine.

I. EXERCICES D'APPLICATION.

A. *Indiquez le temps de chacune des formes suivantes:*

Ex.:—Il arriva: **passé simple.** Il arrivera: **futur.** Il arrive: **présent.**

1. Il entra. **2.** Il se leva. **3.** Il se lèvera. **4.** Il répondit. **5.** Il répond. **6.** Il répondra. **7.** Il acheta. **8.** Ils achètent. **9.** Ils achetèrent. **10.** Ils choisissent. **11.** Ils choisirent. **12.** Ils entrèrent. **13.** Ils entreront. **14.** Il eut. **15.** Il vendit. **16.** Ils finirent. **17.** Ils furent. **18.** Ils auront. **19.** Ils eurent. **20.** Il ne fut pas.

B. *Mettez les phrases suivantes au plus-que-parfait:*

Ex.:—Il a plu.
   —**Il avait plu.**

1. J'ai répondu à sa lettre. **2.** Il a fini son dîner. **3.** Nous avons fait nos courses. **4.** Le train est déjà parti. **5.** Nous sommes allés en ville. **6.** Je me suis couché de bonne heure. **7.** Ils sont arrivés en retard. **8.** J'ai toujours obéi à la loi. **9.** J'ai acheté une auto. **10.** A-t-il neigé?

C. *Répétez les phrases suivantes en substituant les mots indiqués:*

1. [J'avais fini mon travail] quand vous avez téléphoné.
   Je m'étais couché (e) / J'étais sorti (e) / Je n'avais pas fini mon travail/ Je n'avais pas encore dîné/ Je n'avais pas reçu votre lettre

2. [Il aurait fait des courses] s'il avait eu le temps.
   Il serait allé en ville/ Il aurait répondu à cette lettre/ Il aurait fait une promenade/ Il se serait bien amusé à Paris

D. *Employez le plus-que-parfait et le conditionnel passé dans les phrases suivantes:*

Ex.:—Si j'avais de l'argent, j'irais en Italie.
   —**Si j'avais eu de l'argent, je serais allé(e) en Italie.**

1. S'il faisait beau, j'irais en ville. **2.** S'il pleuvait, je prendrais un taxi. **3.** Si j'avais des courses à faire, je prendrais mon auto. **4.** Je répondrais à sa lettre, si j'avais son adresse. **5.** Elle irait au bal, si elle n'avait pas mal à la gorge. **6.** Si nous manquions notre train, nous passerions la nuit à Épernay.

E. *Répétez la phrase suivante en substituant les mots indiqués:*

J'aurai fini mon travail [quand vous arriverez].
quand vous serez prêt/ quand Marie sera prête/ quand vous viendrez me chercher/ quand John viendra me chercher

II. *Répondez en français à chacune des questions suivantes:*

1. Si vous aviez eu le temps, est-ce que vous seriez allé au cinéma hier soir? **2.** Est-ce que la chaussée aurait été glissante s'il n'avait pas plu? **3.** Étiez-vous parti ce matin quand il a commencé à pleuvoir? **4.** Est-ce que vous aviez fini votre travail hier soir quand je vous ai téléphoné? **5.** Est-ce que vous aurez fini votre travail à cinq heures et demie? **6.** Est-ce que vous aurez fini votre travail quand votre frère arrivera?

III. Révision. *Répondez en français à chacune des phrases suivantes:*

1. A quelle heure avez-vous déjeuné? **2.** A quelle heure dînerez-vous ce soir? **3.** A quelle heure dîneriez-vous si vous alliez en ville? **4.** A quelle heure dînez-vous le dimanche? **5.** A quelle heure dîniez-vous pendant les vacances? **6.** Est-ce que vous vous couchez de bonne heure le dimanche? **7.** Est-ce que vous vous couchez plus tard en été qu'en hiver? **8.** Vous êtes-vous levé(e) de bonne heure ce matin? **9.** Vous êtes-vous couché(e) tard hier soir? **10.** Est-ce que vous vous couchiez tard pendant les vacances? **11.** Est-ce que vous vous coucherez tard ce soir? **12.** Est-ce que vous vous coucheriez tard si vous aviez un examen demain?

IV. Révision des dialogues, pp. 149-150 et p. 152.

1. Où Marie est-elle allée passer ses vacances de Noël? **2.** Comment est-elle revenue de Bretagne? **3.** Y avait-il beaucoup de monde dans l'express de Paris? **4.** Comment dit-on en français "You are lucky"? **5.** Comment dit-on en français "You are out of luck"? **6.** Chez qui Marie a-t-elle fait le réveillon? **7.** Est-ce qu'elle s'est bien amusée pendant les vacances? **8.** Qu'est-ce que vous feriez si vous étiez riche? **9.** Quels pays voudriez-vous visiter? **10.** Qu'est-ce que vous achèteriez si vous alliez en France? **11.** Voudriez-vous changer de rôle tous les six mois avec un millionnaire? **12.** Savez-vous ce qui se passe en Europe?

V. Thème d'imitation:

Two days ago, in front of the Pasteur Institute, John witnessed an accident in the course of which Dr. Lambert was hurt. The car in which Dr. Lambert was [1] collided with a truck. When the truck-driver [2] saw the doctor's car, he tried to stop, but it was too late . . . At the noise of the accident, the passers-by came to see what was happening [3] and to help [4] the victims [5] if there were any. When he tried [6] to get out of his car, Dr. Lambert couldn't walk. [7] He had a [8] broken leg. [9] A policeman arrived and they took [10] Dr. Lambert to the hospital.

That afternoon, John went to the police station and the police commissioner asked him [11] all sorts of questions which [12] he answered the best he could. [13]

---

[1] French word order: in which was Dr. Lambert. [2] driver, **chauffeur.** [3] Imperfect of **arriver** or **se passer.** [4] to help, **aider.** [5] victim, **la victime.** [6] Use preposition **de** after **essayer** and after **sortir.** [7] Imperfect or *passé composé.* [8] Use definite article. [9] leg, **la jambe.** [10] **on a emporté** or **emmené.** [11] Use **poser.** [12] which, **auxquelles.** [13] the best he could, **de son mieux.**

Chez l'horloger

L'HORLOGER* —¹Qu'est-ce qu'il y a, monsieur?

JOHN —²Je voudrais faire réparer cette montre. ³Je l'ai laissée tomber hier, ⁴et elle ne marche plus.

L'HORLOGER —⁵Où avez-vous acheté cette montre-là?

JOHN —⁶Je l'ai achetée en Amérique.

L'HORLOGER —⁷Je m'en doutais. ⁸Je n'ai jamais vu une montre comme ça.

JOHN —⁹Est-ce que vous pourrez la réparer tout de même?

L'HORLOGER —¹⁰Je crois. Il s'agit d'une réparation simple. ¹¹Mais je serai obligé de faire venir un ressort.

JOHN —¹²Pouvez-vous me dire quand ma montre sera prête?

L'HORLOGER —¹³Voyons . . . Je vais commander aujourd'hui le ressort dont j'ai besoin. ¹⁴ Je le recevrai sans doute vers le milieu de la semaine prochaine.

JOHN —¹⁵Je voudrais bien avoir ma montre le plus tôt possible.

L'HORLOGER —¹⁶Revenez d'aujourd'hui en huit.

JOHN —¹⁷Bon. J'attendrai jusque là.

THE JEWELER —¹What can I do for you, sir?

JOHN —²I'd like to have this watch repaired. ³I dropped it yesterday, ⁴and now it won't run.

THE JEWELER —⁵Where did you buy that watch?

JOHN —⁶I bought it in America.

THE JEWELER —⁷I rather thought so. ⁸I have never seen a watch like that.

JOHN —⁹Can you repair it anyway?

THE JEWELER —¹⁰I think so. It is a question of a simple repair job. ¹¹But I'll have to send for a spring.

JOHN —¹²Can you tell me when my watch will be ready?

THE JEWELER —¹³Let's see . . . Today I'll order the spring I need. ¹⁴I'll probably get it toward the middle of next week.

JOHN —¹⁵I'd certainly like to have my watch as soon as possible.

THE JEWELER —¹⁶Come back a week from today.

JOHN —¹⁷Okay. I'll wait till then.

---

* Un horloger est une personne qui fait, répare, vend des horloges, des pendules et des montres.

I. Substitutions. *Répétez les phrases suivantes en substituant les mots indiqués:*

1. Je voudrais faire réparer [cette montre].
   cette auto/ cette pendule/ ce tapis/ cette chaise cassée/ le toit de ma maison

2. Il s'agit [d'une réparation simple].
   d'une vieille maison/ d'un vieux toit/ d'une montre qui ne marche plus/ d'une auto qui ne marche plus

3. Il s'agissait *(It was a question of)* [d'une réparation difficile].
   d'une montre américaine/ d'un ressort cassé/ d'un ami de mon père/ tout simplement d'un rhume

4. Il s'agit [de réparer cette montre].
   de construire une maison/ de faire des courses/ de trouver ma cravate/ de s'arrêter à temps

5. Je voudrais bien avoir ma montre [le plus tôt possible].
   d'aujourd'hui en huit/ d'aujourd'hui en quinze/ de vendredi en huit/ lundi prochain/ vers le milieu de la semaine prochaine

6. Je vais commander aujourd'hui [le ressort] dont j'ai besoin.
   les livres/ les chaises/ les meubles/ le tapis/ les journaux

II. *Répondez en français à chacune des questions suivantes:*

1. Pourquoi John va-t-il chez l'horloger? 2. Qu'est-ce que c'est qu'un horloger? 3. Est-ce que la montre de John marche toujours *(still)*? 4. Pourquoi ne marche-t-elle plus? 5. Où John a-t-il acheté sa montre? 6. Est-ce que l'horloger a déjà vu une montre comme ça? 7. Est-ce qu'il pourra la réparer tout de même? 8. Est-ce qu'il s'agit d'une réparation simple? 9. Qu'est-ce que l'horloger sera obligé de faire venir? 10. Pourquoi sera-t-il obligé de faire venir un ressort? 11. Est-ce que l'horloger peut dire à John quand sa montre sera prête? 12. Quand va-t-il commander le ressort dont il a besoin? 13. Quand pense-t-il le recevoir? 14. Quand dit-il à John de revenir? 15. Est-ce que John sera obligé d'attendre longtemps? 16. Quand John reviendra-t-il chez l'horloger? 17. Quand voudrait-il bien avoir sa montre?

III. *Demandez en français à quelqu'un:*

1. s'il a jamais laissé tomber sa montre. 2. si sa montre s'est arrêtée. 3. si une montre peut marcher sans ressort. 4. ce qui fait marcher une montre. 5. ce qui se passe quand le ressort d'une montre est cassé. 6. si l'horloger peut réparer la montre de John. 7. s'il s'agit d'une réparation difficile. 8. ce que l'horloger va commander. 9. de quoi il aura besoin. 10. quand il recevra le ressort.

IV. *Répondez en français:*

1. Avez-vous fait réparer votre montre? **2.** Avez-vous fait réparer votre auto?
3. Marie a-t-elle fait venir le médecin? **4.** L'horloger a-t-il fait venir un
ressort? **5.** Allez-vous faire venir un taxi? **6.** Allez-vous faire construire une
maison? **7.** Qui a fait construire Versailles? **8.** Où John fera-t-il réparer sa
montre?

V. DICTÉE D'APRÈS LE DIALOGUE, pp. 172-173.

VI. CONVERSATION.

You have broken your glasses (**lunettes,** *f.*). You need new lenses (**verres,**
m.). You want your glasses repaired as soon as possible. You can't see without glasses, etc. The oculist (**l'oculiste**) answers that he is very busy (**très
occupé**), he has many customers (**clients,** *m.*), but that you can come back
Saturday afternoon at 5:00.

Relative Pronouns

75. Subject form qui, *who, which.*

The form **qui** is used as the subject of a verb and may refer to either persons or things:

—C'est ma cousine **qui** demeure à Reims.　She's my cousin *who* lives in Rheims.

—Voici un autre autobus **qui** arrive.　Here comes another bus.

76. Direct object form que, *whom, which.*

The form **que** is used as the direct object of a verb and may refer to either persons or things:

—C'est un jeune homme **que** je connaissais quand j'avais dix ans.　He's a young man I used to know when I was ten.

—Voici la cravate **que** je cherchais.　Here is the tie I was looking for.

In English the object form of the relative pronoun is practically always omitted: we say "He's a boy I used to know" rather than "He's a boy *whom* I used to know"; but in French the relative pronoun must always be expressed in relative clauses.

77. Relative pronoun dont, *whose, of whom, of which.*

Dont is used in place of a relative pronoun preceded by the preposition **de**. It may refer to persons or things.

—Le docteur Lambert, **dont** l'auto allait très vite, n'a pas pu s'arrêter à temps.　Dr. Lambert, *whose* car was going very fast, could not stop in time.

—Je vais commander aujourd'hui le ressort **dont** j'ai besoin.　I am going to order today the spring *which* I need (*of which* I have need).

185

78. Relative pronouns used with prepositions other than **de.**

A. qui, *whom:*

To refer to *persons,* **qui** is the form of the relative which is ordinarily used after prepositions other than **de,** such as: **à, avec, chez,** etc.

—Le docteur Lambert, **à qui** j'ai parlé, est un bon médecin.	Doctor Lambert, *to whom* I spoke, is a good doctor.
—La dame **chez qui** je demeure a des chambres à louer.	The lady *at whose house* I live has rooms to rent.

B. lequel, laquelle, lesquels, lesquelles, *which:*

To refer to *things,* **lequel,** etc. is the relative pronoun you use after prepositions other than **de,** such as: **à, avec, dans, pour, sans,** etc.

—L'auto **dans laquelle** il était est entrée en collision avec un camion.	The car *in which* he was collided with a truck.
—La lettre, **à laquelle** j'ai déjà répondu, est sur mon bureau.	The letter, *to which* I have already replied, is on my desk.

(1) Note that in clauses indicating time or place, **où** is ordinarily used instead of **auquel, dans lequel,** etc. Thus it corresponds to English *when* as well as *where.* Ex.: La ville **où** je suis né. The city *in which* I was born.

(2) With the prepositional expressions **à côté de, près de, autour de, au cours de, au-dessus de,** etc., the form **lequel,** etc. must be used. **Dont** cannot be used with these expressions. Ex.: l'accident au cours **duquel. . .** ; la maison près **de laquelle. . .**

79. Use of **ce qui, ce que,** *what (that which).*

A. Subject form **ce qui:**

—J'irais en Russie voir **ce qui** se passe là-bas.	I'd go to Russia to see *what* is going on there.
—Savez-vous **ce qui** se passe en Russie?	Do you know *what* is going on in Russia?

Ce qui is the relative pronoun which corresponds to the interrogative pronoun **Qu'est-ce qui?** Ex.: **Qu'est-ce qui** se passe en Russie? *(interrogative)* — Je ne sais pas **ce qui** se passe en Russie. *(relative)*

B. Direct object form **ce que:**

—**Ce que** vous venez de me dire est   *What* you have just told me is quite
   très vrai.   true.
—**Ce qu'**il dit est absurde.   *What* he says is absurd.

Ce que is the relative pronoun which corresponds to the interrogative
form **Qu'est-ce que?** Ex.: —**Qu'est-ce que** vous avez dit? *(interrog.)*
Je n'ai pas entendu **ce que** vous avez dit. *(relative)*

Note that the entire clause **ce qui se passe en Russie** is the direct object
of **voir** and **savez-vous. Ce qui** is of course the subject of **se passe.**
Likewise the clause **Ce qu'il dit** is the subject of **est;** but **ce qu'** is the
object of **dit.**

I. EXERCICES D'APPLICATION.

A. *Répétez les phrases suivantes en employant* **Voilà . . . qui . . . :**

Ex.:—Un autobus arrive.
    —**Voilà un autobus qui arrive.**

I. Ma cousine demeure à Reims. **2.** Mon ami va se marier. **3.** Un taxi
s'arrête. **4.** Un avion passe. **5.** Le printemps arrive. **6.** Les feuilles tom-
bent. **7.** Le vent se lève. **8.** Les enfants s'amusent.

B. *Répétez les phrases suivantes en employant* **Voilà le (la, les) . . .
que . . . :**

Ex.:—J'ai acheté des gants.
    —**Voilà les gants que j'ai achetés.**

I. J'ai acheté des cigarettes. **2.** J'ai planté des fleurs. **3.** J'ai reçu une lettre.
4. Je cherchais ma cravate. **5.** Nous avons trouvé de l'argent. **6.** Nous avons
commandé un ressort. **7.** Il a fait réparer cette montre. **8.** Il m'a donné
cette adresse.

C. *Répétez les phrases suivantes en employant* **Voilà le (la, les) . . .
dont . . . :**

Ex.:—J'ai besoin de papier à lettres.
    —**Voilà le papier à lettres dont j'ai besoin.**

I. J'ai besoin de gants. **2.** J'ai besoin d'argent. **3.** Il a besoin de monnaie.
4. Il a besoin d'un ressort. **5.** Je vous ai parlé de cette jeune fille. **6.** Il vous
a parlé de ce musée. **7.** J'ai entendu parler de ce château. **8.** Il s'agit de ce
journal. **9.** Il s'agissait de cette montre.

D. *Répétez en employant* **Voilà le (la, les) . . . (à, pour, avec, chez) qui . . . :**

Ex.:—Je suis allé(e) au cinéma avec cette jeune fille.
   —**Voilà la jeune fille avec qui je suis allé(e) au cinéma.**

I. J'ai parlé à cet agent de police. **2.** J'ai envoyé des fleurs à cette jeune fille.
3. J'ai donné le journal à cet étudiant. **4.** J'ai demandé des renseignements à cet agent de police. **5.** Je suis allé(e) au bal avec ce jeune homme. **6.** J'ai fait une promenade avec ce petit garçon. **7.** Je demeure chez cette dame.
8. J'ai acheté des bonbons pour ces enfants.

E. *Répétez en employant* **Voilà le (la, les) . . . (à, dans, pour, sur) lequel (laquelle, lesquels, lesquelles) . . . :**

Ex.:—Il était dans cette auto.
   —**Voilà l'auto dans laquelle il était.**

I. Il était dans ce taxi. **2.** J'ai répondu à cette lettre. **3.** Nous avons répondu à ces questions. **4.** Je pensais à ce restaurant. **5.** J'ai acheté un ressort pour cette montre. **6.** J'ai commandé un tapis pour cette chambre. **7.** J'ai posé mes lunettes sur cette table. **8.** J'ai mis mes cigarettes sur cette chaise.

II. *Répondez à chacune des questions suivantes en commençant par* **Je ne sais pas ce qui . . . :**

Ex.:—Qu'est-ce qui se passe?
   —**Je ne sais pas ce qui se passe.**

I. Qu'est-ce qui s'est passé? **2.** Qu'est-ce qui arrive? **3.** Qu'est-ce qui est arrivé? **4.** Qu'est-ce qui lui est arrivé? **5.** Qu'est-ce qui ennuie Marie? **6.** Qu'est-ce qui l'ennuie? **7.** Qu'est-ce qui la rend triste? **8.** Qu'est-ce qui l'a rendue malade?

III. *Répondez à chacune des questions suivantes en commençant par* **Je ne sais pas ce qu(e) . . . :**

Ex.:—Qu'est-ce qu'il a dit?
   —**Je ne sais pas ce qu'il a dit.**

I. Qu'est ce qu'il a acheté? **2.** Qu'est-ce qu'il a fait? **3.** Qu'est-ce que vous ferez ce soir? **4.** Qu'est-ce que l'horloger a commandé? **5.** Qu'est-ce qu'il a reçu? **6.** Qu'est-ce que vous feriez si vous étiez riche? **7.** Qu'est-ce que c'est qu'un Prisunic? **8.** Qu'est-ce que c'est qu'une charcuterie? **9.** Que veut dire "Noblesse oblige"? **10.** Que veut dire le mot "mansarde"?

IV. *Répondez en français à chacune des questions suivantes:*

1. Comment s'appelle la dame chez qui John demeure? 2. Est-ce que la chambre que John a louée est agréable? 3. Croyez-vous tout ce que disent *(say)* les journaux? 4. Savez-vous avec qui Charles ira en vacances? 5. Avez-vous entendu ce que je vous ai dit? 6. Quel est le nom de la ville où vous habitez? 7. Y avait-il beaucoup de monde à l'endroit où vous êtes monté dans l'autobus? 8. Quel temps faisait-il le jour où l'accident a eu lieu? 9. D'où venait le camion? 10. Avez-vous été témoin de l'accident dont nous avons parlé?

V. *Dites en français:*

1. "Who told you that?" "It's my father who told me that." 2. "Whom did you see at the dance?" "I saw a girl you know." 3. "To whom did you talk?" "The person I talked to is named Charles." 4. "About whom are you talking?" "The person we are talking about is Dr. Lambert." 5. "What's the matter with you?" "I don't know what's the matter with me." 6. "Whose book is this?" "I don't know whose book it is."

VI. Thème d'imitation:

Yesterday, Roger told Marie and John that there was a good film at the Cinéma Marignan and he asked them if they wanted to go to see it. It was an American film which John had already seen in the United States; but as he had thought [1] the film excellent, he gladly accepted Roger's invitation. John thought [1] that the film was in English, and he was very much surprised [2] when he heard Hollywood actors and actresses, whom he had so often [3] seen in America, talking [4] French perfectly [5] and with the best accent. Very much interested [6], John looked attentively [7] at the actors' lips. They seemed [8] to be speaking French. John thinks now that the cinema is a fine invention [9].

---

[1] Note the difference between the meaning of "thought" in the two sentences. [2] surprised, **surpris** (*p. part. of* **surprendre**). [3] so often, **si souvent**. [4] Use infinitive. [5] perfectly, **parfaitement**. [6] interested, **intéressé**. [7] attentively, **attentivement**. [8] Use **avoir l'air de** with infinitive. [9] invention, **l'invention** (*f.*).

Au Bon Marché*

LA VENDEUSE —[1]Qu'est-ce que vous désirez, mademoiselle?

MARIE —[2]Je voudrais une écharpe.

LA VENDEUSE —[3]Choisissez, mademoiselle. Nous avons un excellent choix.

MARIE —[4]Une de mes amies en a une que j'aime beaucoup. [5]Elle l'a achetée ici, je crois.

LA VENDEUSE —[6]De quelle couleur est celle de votre amie?

MARIE —[7]C'est une écharpe de soie blanche.

LA VENDEUSE —[8]Que pensez-vous de cette écharpe-ci, mademoiselle?

MARIE —[9]Combien est-ce?

LA VENDEUSE —[10]Vingt francs.

MARIE —[11]Et celle-là?

LA VENDEUSE —[12]Vingt-trois francs.

MARIE —[13]C'est un peu cher. [14]Avez-vous quelque chose de meilleur marché?

LA VENDEUSE —[15]Mais oui, mademoiselle. Celle-ci ne coûte que dix-huit francs.

MARIE —[16]Je crois que j'aime mieux celle que vous m'avez montrée tout à l'heure.

LA VENDEUSE —[17]Laquelle, mademoiselle?

THE SALESGIRL —[1]Something for you, Mademoiselle?

MARY —[2]I'd like a scarf.

THE SALESGIRL —[3]Choose, Mademoiselle. We have an excellent selection.

MARY —[4]A friend of mine has one which I like very much. [5]She bought it here, I think.

THE SALESGIRL —[6]What color is your friend's?

MARY —[7]It's a white silk scarf.

THE SALESGIRL —[8]What do you think of this scarf, Mademoiselle?

MARY —[9]How much is it?

THE SALESGIRL —[10]Twenty francs.

MARY —[11]And that one?

THE SALESGIRL —[12]Twenty-three francs.

MARY —[13]It's rather expensive. [14]Have you something cheaper?

THE SALESGIRL —[15]Oh yes, Mademoiselle. This one costs only eighteen francs.

MARY —[16]I think I prefer the one which you showed me a moment ago.

THE SALESGIRL —[17]Which one, Mademoiselle?

---

* Well-known department store in Paris.

190

MARIE —[18]Celle-ci. Voulez-vous bien la mettre dans une boîte?

LA VENDEUSE —[19]Volontiers. Désirez-vous autre chose, mademoiselle?

MARIE —[20]Je voudrais aussi des mouchoirs.

LA VENDEUSE —[21]Aimez-vous ceux-ci?

MARIE —[22]Quel en est le prix?

LA VENDEUSE —[23]Deux francs cinquante la pièce.

MARIE —[24]J'en prendrai une demi-douzaine.

LA VENDEUSE —[25]Voulez-vous bien payer la caissière, mademoiselle? [26]Vous trouverez vos achats à la caisse.

MARY —[18]This one. Will you please put it in a box?

THE SALESGIRL —[19]Certainly. Do you wish something else, Mademoiselle?

MARY —[20]I'd also like some handkerchiefs.

THE SALESGIRL —[21]Do you like these?

MARY —[22]What is the price of them?

THE SALESGIRL —[23]Two francs fifty apiece.

MARY —[24]I'll take a half dozen of them.

THE SALESGIRL —[25]Will you please pay the cashier, Mademoiselle? [26]You will find your purchases at the cashier's window.

I. SUBSTITUTIONS. *Répétez les phrases suivantes en substituant les mots indiqués:*

1. Une de mes amies en a [une] que j'aime beaucoup.
   un/ une paire/ plusieurs/ deux ou trois

2. Avez-vous quelque chose [de meilleur marché]?
   de meilleure qualité/ d'autre/ de moins cher/ de plus clair (*light color*) / de plus foncé (*dark*)

3. Nous n'avons rien [de meilleur marché].
   de meilleure qualité/ d'autre/ de moins cher/ de plus clair/ de plus foncé

4. Cette écharpe-ci est [meilleur marché] que celle-là.
   moins chère/ plus chère/ plus originale/ plus jolie/ de meilleure qualité

II. *Répondez à chacune des questions suivantes, d'après le texte:*

1. A qui parle Marie? 2. Qu'est-ce que c'est qu'une vendeuse? 3. Dans quel magasin la conversation a-t-elle lieu? 4. Qu'est-ce que Marie veut acheter? 5. Y a-t-il beaucoup d'écharpes dans ce magasin? 6. Où l'amie de Marie a-t-elle acheté la sienne? 7. De quelle couleur est cette écharpe? 8. Com-

bien d'écharpes la vendeuse montre-t-elle à Marie? **9.** Quel est le prix de l'écharpe que la vendeuse lui montre? **10.** Est-ce que la vendeuse a quelque chose de meilleur marché? **11.** Quelle écharpe Marie achète-t-elle? **12.** Est-ce que Marie achète autre chose? **13.** Combien de mouchoirs prend-elle? **14.** Où est-ce qu'elle trouvera ses achats? **15.** Qui est-ce qu'elle payera?

III. *Répondez à chacune des questions suivantes, affirmativement, puis négativement en employant* **rien . . . d'autre:**

Ex.:—Avez-vous acheté autre chose?
—**Oui, nous avons acheté autre chose.**
—**Non, nous n'avons rien acheté d'autre.**

1. Avez-vous trouvé autre chose? **2.** Marie a-t-elle trouvé autre chose? **3.** Avez-vous vu autre chose? **4.** Marie a-t-elle vu autre chose? **5.** Avez-vous cherché autre chose? **6.** Avez-vous autre chose?

IV. *Dites en français:*

A. il s'agit de

1. It's a matter of a simple repair. **2.** It's a question of a white silk scarf. **3.** What's up (Of what is it a question)? **4.** It's just a question of giving your address to the postman **(au facteur).**

B. rendre

5. Does that make you sad? **6.** That letter made me happy. **7.** That long walk in the snow made me sick. **8.** The postman brought me a letter which made me sad.

C. venir de

9. What you have just said is true. **10.** Marie has just arrived from Brittany. **11.** I have just finished my work. **12.** The postman has just brought me a letter.

D. de quelle couleur

13. What color is your scarf? **14.** What color are your gloves? **15.** What color is her car? **16.** I don't know what color it is.

V. Dictée d'après le dialogue, p. 182.

VI. Révision des dialogues, pp. 160-161 et pp. 163-164.

1. Où se trouve Versailles? **2.** Qu'est-ce qu'il y a de célèbre à Versailles? **3.** Qui est-ce qui a fait construire le château de Versailles? **4.** Quand le château a-t-il été construit? **5.** Avez-vous entendu parler de la Galerie des

Glaces *(Hall of Mirrors)?* **6.** Comprenez-vous la phrase "Noblesse oblige"? **7.** Qui était Mansard? **8.** Qu'est-ce que c'est qu'une mansarde? **9.** Qu'est-ce qu'on met dans les mansardes? **10.** Qui est-ce qui a dessiné les jardins de Versailles? **11.** Avez-vous entendu parler des pièces d'eau et des fontaines de Versailles? **12.** Pourquoi Marie a-t-elle l'air triste? **13.** Qu'est-ce qu'elle a? **14.** A qui pense-t-elle? **15.** Comment sait-elle que sa cousine va se marier? **16.** Est-ce que sa cousine Jeanne va bientôt se marier? **17.** Avec qui doit-elle se marier? **18.** Est-ce que la nouvelle du mariage la rend triste? **19.** Qu'est-ce qui l'ennuie? **20.** Est-ce qu'elle voudrait bien aller au mariage de Jeanne?

VII. CONVERSATIONS.

(1) Conversation avec une vendeuse au sujet d'une écharpe—le prix, la couleur, si l'écharpe vous va bien, etc.

(2) Conversation avec un vendeur au sujet d'une paire de chaussures *(a pair of shoes)*—le prix, la pointure *(size)*. Vous pouvez dire que les chaussures sont trop étroites *(narrow)*, trop longues, trop courtes, qu'elles vous font mal aux pieds *(hurt your feet)*, etc.

Sixième Lecture Illustrée, p. 40, *Versailles*.

Demonstrative Pronouns

80. Forms and use of celui-ci, *this one*, celui-là, *that one*, etc.

—Je voudrais acheter une écharpe.	I'd like to buy a scarf.
—Que pensez-vous de **celle-ci?**	What do you think of *this one?*
—Combien est-ce?	How much is it?
—Vingt francs.	Twenty francs.
—Et **celle-là?**	And *that one?*

The forms of **celui-ci,** *etc.* are:

SINGULAR		PLURAL	
celui-ci *(m.)*	*this one*	ceux-ci *(m.)*	*these*
celle-ci *(f.)*		celles-ci *(f.)*	
celui-là *(m.)*	*that one*	ceux-là *(m.)*	*those*
celle-là *(f.)*		celles-là *(f.)*	

You use **celui-ci, celui-là,** etc. to distinguish between persons or things within a group. They agree in gender and number with the word to which they refer.

81. Use of celui, celle, *the one;* ceux, celles, *the ones.*

These forms, as opposed to the forms **celui-ci,** etc. are always modified by a relative clause or a prepositional phrase.

A. Modified by a relative clause:

—J'ai plusieurs cousins. **Celui qui** habite à Paris s'appelle Lambert.	I have several cousins. *The one* who lives in Paris is named Lambert.
—**Ceux qui** habitent à Tours s'appellent Dupuy.	*The ones* who live in Tours are named Dupuy.
—**Celui dont** je vous ai parlé hier va se marier.	*The one* I mentioned (of whom I spoke to you) yesterday is going to get married.

194

The commonest combinations of **celui,** etc. with relative pronouns are:

(masculine singular) celui qui, celui que, celui dont, celui auquel, etc.

(feminine singular) celle qui, celle que, celle dont, celle à laquelle, etc.

(masculine plural) ceux qui, ceux que, ceux dont, ceux auxquels, etc.

(feminine plural) celles qui, celles que, celles dont, celles auxquelles, etc.

B. Modified by a prepositional phrase beginning with **de:**

—Une de mes amies a une jolie écharpe. / One of my friends has a pretty scarf.

—De quelle couleur est **celle de votre amie?** / What color is *your friend's?*

—Je n'aime pas ce chapeau. / I don't like that hat.

—**Celui de Marie** est plus joli. / *Mary's* is prettier.

(1) In English we say: *My book and my friend's.* In French you say: **Mon livre et celui de mon ami** *(that of my friend).*

(2) Note that **l'un** *(the one)* is not a demonstrative pronoun and can not be used in place of **celui, celle,** etc.

82. Use of **ceci,** *this* and **cela, ça,*** *that.*

Unlike the other demonstrative pronouns, **ceci** and **cela** are used to refer to something which has not been specifically named. They never refer to persons. They are used:

A. To refer to an idea, a statement, or a situation:

—**Cela** m'est égal. / *That* (or *It*) is all the same to me.

—Est-ce que **cela** vous rend triste? / Does *that* make you sad?

—Pourquoi dites-vous **cela (ça)?** / Why do you say *that?*

—**Ceci** est très important. / *This* is very important.

B. To refer to objects which have not been specifically named:

—Qu'est-ce que c'est que **cela (ça)?** / What is *that?*

—J'ai acheté **ceci** pour mon frère et **cela** pour ma sœur. / I bought *this* for my brother and *that* for my sister.

---

* **Cela** and **ça** have the same use and meaning, but **ça** is a bit less formal.

I. EXERCICES D'APPLICATION.

Répétez les phrases suivantes, en remplaçant le nom par le pronom démonstratif.

A. Ex.:—Envoyez-moi cette écharpe-ci.
   —**Envoyez-moi celle-ci.**

I. Envoyez-moi ce chapeau-là. **2.** Envoyez-moi ces mouchoirs-ci. **3.** Envoyez-moi cette photo-ci. **4.** Envoyez-moi ces photos-là. **5.** Envoyez-moi ces gants-là. **6.** Envoyez-moi ce livre-ci.

B. Ex.:—J'ai acheté ces gants à Paris.
   —**J'ai acheté ceux-ci (ou ceux-là) à Paris.**

I. J'ai acheté cette robe à Paris. **2.** J'ai acheté cette auto à Paris. **3.** J'ai acheté ce chapeau à Paris. **4.** J'ai acheté ces cravates à Paris. **5.** J'ai acheté ce pardessus à Paris. **6.** J'ai acheté ces montres à Paris.

C. Ex.:—Ma cousine qui demeure à Reims s'appelle Duval.
   —**Celle qui demeure à Reims s'appelle Duval.**

I. Mes cousines qui demeurent à Paris s'appellent Dupuy. **2.** Mes cousins qui demeurent à Lyon s'appellent Dupont. **3.** Mon cousin qui demeure à Philadelphie s'appelle Hughes. **4.** Mon cousin dont nous parlions habite à Rome. **5.** Ma cousine que vous avez vue au bal est gentille. **6.** Mon cousin dont vous avez fait la connaissance hier est ici. **7.** Ma cousine à qui j'ai écrit hier va se marier. **8.** Voilà le livre dont j'ai besoin.

D. Ex.:—Voilà le livre de John.
   —**Voilà celui de John.**

I. Voilà les livres de John. **2.** Voilà les livres de Marie. **3.** Voilà la cravate de Roger. **4.** Voilà l'auto de mon frère. **5.** Voilà le journal de mon père. **6.** Voilà la plume de ma tante.

II. *Dites en français:*

Ex.:—My book and my friend's.
   —**Mon livre et celui de mon ami.**

I. My watch and my friend's. **2.** My gloves and my friend's. **3.** Her scarf and her friend's. **4.** My scarf and Marie's. **5.** My car and my brother's. **6.** Our parents and our friend's. **7.** Our parents and our friends' *(plural).*

III. *Répétez chacune des phrases suivantes en remplaçant le nom par le pronom démonstratif convenable:*

1. Pourriez-vous m'envoyer cette écharpe-ci ce soir? **2.** Les photos que j'ai prises hier ne sont pas très bonnes. **3.** J'ai acheté le livre dont je vous ai parlé. **4.** Comment trouvez-vous l'auto de M. Duval? **5.** Les gants que j'ai achetés hier sont très chauds. **6.** Donnez-moi ce livre-ci et gardez (*keep*) ce livre-là.

(not for specific objects)

IV. *Dites en français en employant* **ceci, cela (ça):** *cela?*

Qu'est-ce que c'est que cela

1. What's that? **2.** It (that) makes no difference. (It's all the same to me). **3.** It makes me sad. **4.** Who told you that? **5.** Why do you say that? **6.** This is very important. **7.** Where did you buy that? **8.** I bought this for you. **9.** I can have that sent to you this afternoon.

V. *Répondez en français, en employant un pronom démonstratif:*

Ex.:—Voilà deux écharpes. Laquelle préférez-vous?
—Je préfère **celle-ci.**

1. Voilà deux mouchoirs. Lequel préférez-vous? **2.** Voilà des cartes-postales. Lesquelles allez-vous acheter? **3.** Cette jeune fille-ci est-elle aussi grande que cette jeune fille-là? **4.** Est-ce que ce livre-ci est aussi gros que ce livre-là? **5.** Est-ce que le château de Chantilly est aussi grand que le château de Versailles? (Non . . .) **6.** Est-ce que les tragédies de Marlowe sont aussi belles que les tragédies de Shakespeare? (Non . . .) **7.** Aimez-vous mieux les romans (*novels*) de Dumas que les romans de Balzac? **8.** Préférez-vous la musique de Debussy ou la musique de Berlioz?

VI. Révision des dialogues, pp. 172-173 et p. 182.

1. Pourquoi le commissaire de police a-t-il fait venir John Hughes? **2.** De quel accident a-t-il été témoin? **3.** Pourquoi l'accident a-t-il eu lieu? **4.** Est-ce qu'il avait plu ce jour-là? **5.** Où était John au moment de l'accident? **6.** Est-ce que le camion allait vite au moment de l'accident? **7.** A quelle vitesse allait-il? **8.** Est-ce que le commissaire de police avait déjà parlé à d'autres témoins de l'accident? **9.** Qu'est-ce que c'est qu'un horloger? **10.** Pourquoi John porte-il sa montre chez l'horloger? **11.** Pourquoi sa montre ne marche-t-elle plus? **12.** Pourquoi l'horloger se doute-t-il que John a acheté sa montre en Amérique? **13.** Quand l'horloger va-t-il commander le ressort dont il a besoin? **14.** Quand est-ce qu'il espère recevoir (*to receive*) le ressort? **15.** Quand dit-il à John de revenir? **16.** Pourquoi John voudrait-il bien avoir sa montre le plus tôt possible?

VII. Thème d'imitation:

John and Roger spent the afternoon in the Jardin du Luxembourg, near the University. There were many students there with their girl friends [1], many children with their nurses [2], and many Parisians who had come there to look at the people, the sky, the flowers, and the trees.

John was looking at an elderly gentleman dressed in black who was giving bread to the birds [3]. He had birds on his [4] head, on his shoulders [5], on his hands [6], everywhere. Suddenly [7] an old lady came and said to John: "Sir, will you please [8] pay me for your chair [9]? It's ten centimes." Roger told John that in the public parks [10] in Paris, you rent a chair for the afternoon. "After all, you rent a room for a week or for a month", said John to himself [11]. "Why should one not rent [12] a chair for an afternoon?" And he gave the old lady the ten centimes she was asking for.

---

[1] girl friend, **une amie.** [2] nurse, **la bonne.** [3] bird, **l'oiseau—les oiseaux**(*m.*). [4] Cf. Le chapeau que vous avez sur la tête? [5] shoulder, **une épaule.** [6] hand, **la main.** [7] suddenly, **tout à coup.** [8] **Voulez-vous bien.** [9] chair, **la chaise.** [10] **dans les jardins publics.** [11] **s'est dit John.** Note that in French, after a direct quotation the subject of the verb said, answered, asked, etc., always follows the verb. Ex.: **a dit Roger, a-t-il dit, a demandé Marie, a répondu Roger,** etc. [12] Why should one not rent, **Pourquoi ne pas louer.**

Excursion à la campagne

ROGER —[1]Il y a presque deux heures que nous avons quitté Melun.

JOHN —[2]Je commence à avoir mal aux jambes. [3]Je n'ai pas l'habitude d'aller à bicyclette.

ROGER —[4]Je crois que nous avons pris la mauvaise route.

JOHN —[5]J'en ai peur.

ROGER —[6]Voilà un homme qui travaille dans son champ. [7]Il pourra nous donner des renseignements.

ROGER (à l'homme) —[8]Est-ce que nous sommes loin de Fontainebleau?*

L'HOMME —[9]Mais oui, mon pauvre monsieur. [10]Je suis fâché de vous apprendre [11]que vous vous êtes trompé de route.

ROGER —[12]Quelle route faut-il prendre, alors?

L'HOMME —[13]Vous voyez ce village, là-bas? [14]C'est Barbizon.† Allez-y. [15]A la sortie, prenez le premier chemin à gauche. [16]Il vous mènera à Fontainebleau.

ROGER —[17]A quelle distance est-ce d'ici?

ROGER —[1]We left Melun almost two hours ago.

JOHN —[2]My legs are beginning to hurt. [3]I am not used to bicycling.

ROGER —[4]I think we took the wrong road.

JOHN —[5]I'm afraid so.

ROGER —[6]There's a man working in his field. [7]He can give us information.

ROGER (to the man) —[8]Are we far from Fontainebleau?

THE MAN —[9]You certainly are, sir. [10]I am sorry to tell you [11]that you took the wrong road.

ROGER —[12]Which road must we take then?

THE MAN —[13]You see that village over there? [14]It's Barbizon. Go to it. [15]As you leave the village, take the first road on the left. [16]It will take you to Fontainebleau.

ROGER —[17]How far is it from here?

---

* Fontainebleau, célèbre pour son château de la Renaissance et sa belle forêt, est à une cinquantaine de kilomètres au sud-est de Paris.

† Barbizon est un village près de Fontainebleau. Au XIXème siècle, ce village a été la résidence favorite de plusieurs peintres célèbres, entre autres Corot et Millet.

L'HOMME —[18]C'est à sept ou huit kilomètres.

ROGER —[19]Zut alors! Par cette chaleur, ce n'est pas drôle!

L'HOMME —[20]Si vous avez chaud et si vous avez soif, [21]vous pourrez vous arrêter à Barbizon. [22]C'est ma femme qui tient l'auberge [23]juste en face de l'église.

THE MAN —[18]It's seven or eight kilometers.

ROGER —[19]Well confound it! In such hot weather, that's not funny!

THE MAN —[20]If you are hot and if you are thirsty, [21]you can stop at Barbizon. [22]My wife runs the inn [23]right across the street from the church.

I. SUBSTITUTIONS. *Répétez les phrases suivantes en substituant les mots indiqués:*

1. Il y a presque deux heures que [nous avons quitté Melun].
   nous avons quitté la maison/ nous sommes arrivé (e) s/ je suis parti (e) / John et Roger sont partis

2. Répétez chacune des phrases précédentes en remplaçant **Il y a . . . que** par **Voilà . . . que** (which has the same use and meaning as **il y a . . . que**).*

3. Je commence à avoir mal [aux jambes].
   à la tête/ aux yeux/ aux dents (*teeth*) / aux pieds/ à la gorge

4. Je n'ai pas l'habitude [d'aller à bicyclette].
   de marcher/ de travailler le soir/ de me lever de bonne heure/ de me coucher tard

5. Je suis fâché de vous apprendre [que vous vous êtes trompé (s) de route].
   que vous êtes sur la mauvaise route/ que vous n'êtes pas sur la bonne route/ que vous avez pris la mauvaise route/ que Fontainebleau est à 7 ou 8 kilomètres d'ici

6. A la sortie, prenez [le premier chemin à gauche].
   le premier chemin à droite/ la première route à gauche/ la première rue à droite/ la grande avenue à gauche

---

* Il y a . . . que, voilà . . . que as expressions of time: When **il y a . . . que, voilà . . . que** are used with a *passé composé*, they mean *ago.* Ex.: **Il y a deux heures que nous avons quitté Melun. Voilà deux heures que nous avons quitté Melun.**
When used with a present indicative, **il y a . . que, voilà . . . que** indicate that the action began in the past and is still going on at the time the statement is made. They have practically the same meaning as **depuis.**

{ —Depuis combien de temps attendez-vous l'autobus?
            OR
  —Combien de temps y a-t-il que vous attendez l'autobus?

{ —Je l'attends depuis un quart d'heure.
            OR
  —Voilà un quart d'heure que je l'attends.

II. *Répondez en français à chacune des questions suivantes:*

1. Où vont Roger et John? **2.** Comment voyagent-ils? **3.** Combien de temps y a-t-il qu'ils ont quitté Melun? **4.** Est-ce que John est fatigué? **5.** Pourquoi a-t-il mal aux jambes? **6.** Est-ce qu'ils sont sur la bonne route? **7.** A qui Roger demande-t-il des renseignements? **8.** Qu'est-ce qu'il demande à l'homme qui travaille dans son champ? **9.** Est-ce qu'ils sont près d'un village? **10.** Comment s'appelle ce village? **11.** Quelle route l'homme leur dit-il de prendre à la sortie du village? **12.** Où cette route les mènera-t-elle? **13.** A quelle distance de Barbizon est Fontainebleau? **14.** Pourquoi Roger dit-il que ce n'est pas drôle? **15.** Où pourront-ils s'arrêter s'ils ont chaud?

III. *Demandez à quelqu'un:*

1. s'il y a longtemps que John et Roger ont quitté Melun. **2.** pourquoi John commence à avoir mal aux jambes. **3.** ce que fait l'homme à qui Roger demande des renseignements. **4.** pourquoi Roger demande des renseignments. **5.** ce que Roger demande. **6.** si John et Roger sont sur la mauvaise route. **7.** quel chemin il faut prendre à la sortie de Barbizon. **8.** à quelle distance est Fontainebleau de Barbizon. **9.** quel temps il fait ce jour-là.

IV. *Dites en français, en employant* **se tromper:**

1. You took the wrong road (you were mistaken about the road). **2.** You were mistaken. **3.** I was mistaken. **4.** He was mistaken. **5.** He is mistaken. **6.** I think he is mistaken. **7.** I think you are mistaken.

V. *Répondez en français à chacune des questions suivantes:*

A. quitter, partir de

1. A quelle heure avez-vous quitté la maison ce matin? **2.** A quelle heure êtes-vous parti de la maison ce matin? **3.** Êtes-vous parti sans déjeuner? **4.** Avez-vous quitté la maison sans déjeuner? **5.** Y a-t-il longtemps que John et Roger ont quitté Melun? **6.** Y a-t-il longtemps qu'ils sont partis de Melun?

B. combien de temps y a-t-il que . . . ? depuis quand?

7. Combien de temps y a-t-il que vous attendez l'autobus? **8.** Combien de temps y a-t-il que vous étudiez le français? **9.** Combien de temps y a-t-il que vous êtes à l'Université? **10.** Depuis quand êtes-vous à l'Université? **11.** Depuis quand étudiez-vous le français?

VI. DICTÉE D'APRÈS LE DIALOGUE, pp. 190-191.

VII. CONVERSATION.

Vous vous êtes égaré(e) *(lost)* dans la forêt de Fontainebleau. Vous demandez le chemin de Barbizon à un peintre qui travaille dans la forêt.

Irregular Verbs in *-er* and in *-ir*

83. Remarks about irregular verbs.

The easiest and quickest way to learn irregular verbs is to examine their forms carefully, note which forms are irregular, and practice using them in exercises such as those suggested below. It is perhaps useful to note:

A. PRESENT INDICATIVE:

The only tense of irregular verbs which is practically always irregular is the present indicative.

(1) STEM: Instead of having one stem throughout the tense like **parler** (PARL-,)—irregular verbs generally have two stems, one for the first and second person plural and another for the other persons. Sometimes this difference is very striking (**je vais, nous allons**) and sometimes it is scarcely noticeable (**je connais, nous connaissons**).

(2) ENDINGS: Practically all irregular verbs have the present indicative endings **-s, -s, -t, -ons, ez, -ent,** but a few have **-e, -es, -e** in the singular.

B. FUTURE:

Very few irregular verbs have an irregular future (and conditional). Those which *are* irregular are irregular only as to the stem: **faire— je ferai,** etc.

C. IMPERFECT:

Except for **être,** the imperfect always follows the pattern of regular verbs (see paragraph 54).

D. PAST PARTICIPLE:

The past participle of irregular verbs follows several different patterns. Those following the same pattern are grouped together in this book.

84. Irregular verbs ending in -er.

There are only two irregular verbs in this group: **aller,** *to go,* and **envoyer,** *to send.* **Renvoyer,** *to send back, to send away,* is of course conjugated like **envoyer.**

85. Aller, *to go.*

—Où **allez-vous** ce soir?	Where *are you going* this evening?
—**Je vais** au cinéma.	*I am going* to the movies.
—Où **êtes-vous allé(e)** l'été dernier?	Where *did you go* last summer?
—**Je suis allé(e)** à la campagne.	*I went* to the country.
—Comment **irez-vous** en ville?	How *will you go* downtown?
—**J'irai** à pied.	*I shall* walk.

PRÉSENT: Je vais, tu vas, il va, nous allons, vous allez, ils vont.
IMPARFAIT: J'allais.
PASSÉ COMPOSÉ: Je suis allé(e).
FUTUR: J'irai.

86. Special uses of **aller,** *to go,* and s'en aller, *to leave, to go away.*

—**Je vais** chercher mon pardessus.	*I am going* to get my overcoat.
—A quelle heure **allez-vous** à la gare?	At what time *are you going* to the station?
—**J'y vais** à cinq heures.	*I am going (there)* at five o'clock.
—Quand **partez-vous?**	When are you leaving?
—**Je m'en vais** demain soir.	*I am leaving* tomorrow evening.

Note that **s'en aller** and **partir** have practically the same meaning and use except that **s'en aller** is rarely used in compound tenses. It is conjugated like **aller** except that it is reflexive: **Je m'en vais, il s'en va,** etc.

87. Envoyer, *to send.*

—**Envoyez-vous** des cartes-postales à vos amis quand vous voyagez?	*Do you send* post cards to your friends when you travel?
—Oui, **j'en envoie** quelquefois.	Yes, *I send* some occasionally.
—**J'ai envoyé** hier des fleurs à ma grand-mère.	*I sent* some flowers to my grand-mother yesterday.
—**Nous vous enverrons** la facture.	*We shall send* you the bill.
—**J'ai envoyé** chercher le journal.	*I sent* for the paper.
—Je pourrai vous **le faire envoyer** cet après-midi.	I can *have it sent* to you this afternoon.

PRÉSENT: J'envoie, tu envoies, il envoie, nous envoyons, vous envoyez, ils
  envoient.
IMPARFAIT: J'envoyais, etc.
PASSÉ COMPOSÉ: J'ai envoyé, etc.
FUTUR: J'enverrai, etc.

88. First group of irregular verbs in -ir: partir, sortir, sentir, servir, dormir, etc.

The characteristics of this group are that they all have two stems in the
present indicative; par— part—, sor— sort—, sen— sent—, etc., and a
past participle ending in -i.

A. Partir, *to leave:*

—Quand **partez-vous?**	When *are you leaving?*
—Mon train **part** à neuf heures.	My train *leaves* at nine o'clock.
—**Je partirai** de la maison à huit heures et demie.	*I shall leave* the house at 8:30.

PRÉSENT: Je pars, tu pars, il part, nous partons, vous partez, ils partent.
IMPARFAIT: Je partais. PASSÉ COMPOSÉ: Je suis parti(e). FUTUR: Je partirai.

B. Sortir, *to go out* (intransitive), *to take out* (transitive):

—**Est-ce que vous sortez** souvent le soir?	*Do you go out* often in the evening?
—Oui, **je sors** assez souvent.	Yes, *I go out* rather often.

PRÉSENT: Je sors, tu sors, il sort, nous sortons, vous sortez, ils sortent.
IMPARFAIT: Je sortais. PASSÉ COMPOSÉ: Je suis sorti(e). FUTUR: Je sortirai.

C. Sentir, *to smell;* **se sentir,** *to feel:*

—**Sentez-vous** ces roses?	*Do you smell* those roses?
—Oui, elles **sentent** très bon.	Yes, *they smell* very good.
—**Je ne me sens pas** très bien.	*I don't feel* very well.

PRÉSENT: Je sens, tu sens, il sent, nous sentons, vous sentez, ils sentent.
IMPARFAIT: Je sentais. PASSÉ COMPOSÉ: J'ai senti. FUTUR: Je sentirai.

D. Servir, *to serve;* **se servir de,** *to use, to help oneself:*

—**Vous êtes-vous servi de** votre auto hier soir?	*Did you use* your car last night?
—Voici les hors-d'œuvre. **Servez-vous.**	Here are the hors d'oeuvres. *Help yourself.*

PRÉSENT: Je sers, tu sers, il sert, nous servons, vous servez, ils servent.
IMPARFAIT: Je servais. PASSÉ COMPOSÉ: J'ai servi. FUTUR: Je servirai.

E. dormir, *to sleep;* **s'endormir,** *to fall asleep:*

—**Avez-vous** bien **dormi** cette nuit?	*Did you sleep* well last night?
—Oui, **je me suis endormi(e)** à dix heures, et **j'ai dormi** toute la nuit.	Yes, *I went to sleep* at ten o'clock, and *I slept* all night.

PRÉSENT: Je dors, tu dors, il dort, nous dormons, vous dormez, ils dorment.
IMPARFAIT: Je dormais. PASSÉ COMPOSÉ: J'ai dormi. FUTUR: Je dormirai.

Compounds of these verbs follow the same pattern of conjugation.
Ex.: **sentir - consentir** *(to consent).*

89. Second group of irregular verbs in **-ir: venir, tenir.**

The characteristics of this group are that they have two stems for the present indicative **(viens-venons),** an irregular future **(viendrai),** and a past participle in **-u (venu).**

A. venir, *to come:*

—D'où **venez-vous?**	Where have you been? (From where *do you come*)?
—**Je viens** de la gare.	I've been to the station. (*I come* from the station).
—**Il est venu** nous chercher en auto.	*He came* for us in his car.
—**Nous viendrons** vous voir à cinq heures.	*We shall come* to see you at 5:00.

B. venir de + infinitive = *to have just* + past participle:

—Ce que **vous venez de dire** est vrai.	What *you have just said* is true.
—Le docteur **vient d'arriver.**	The doctor *has just come.*

PRÉSENT: Je viens, tu viens, il vient, nous venons, vous venez, ils viennent.
IMPARFAIT: Je venais. PASSÉ COMPOSÉ: Je suis venu(e). FUTUR: Je viendrai.

C. tenir, *to hold, to keep:*

—C'est ma femme qui **tient** l'auberge.	My wife *runs* the inn.
—**Tenez** la porte ouverte, s'il vous plaît.	*Hold* the door open, please.

PRÉSENT: Je tiens, tu tiens, il tient, nous tenons, vous tenez, ils tiennent.
IMPARFAIT: Je tenais. PASSÉ COMPOSÉ: J'ai tenu. FUTUR: Je tiendrai.

Revenir, *to come back;* **devenir,** *to become;* **se souvenir (de),** *to remember,* **prévenir,** *to warn;* **appartenir (à),** *to belong to,* and other compounds are conjugated like **venir.**

90. Third group of irregular verbs in -ir: ouvrir, *to open*, etc.

The characteristics of this group are that the past participle ends in **-ert** and that the endings of the singular of the present indicative are **-e, -es, -e**.

—A quelle heure le bureau de poste ouvre-t-il?	What time *does* the post office *open?*
—Il ouvre à neuf heures du matin.	*It opens* at 9:00 A.M.
—Qui a ouvert la fenêtre?	Who *opened* the window?

PRÉSENT: J'ouvre, tu ouvres, il ouvre, nous ouvrons, vous ouvrez, ils ouvrent.
IMPARFAIT: J'ouvrais. PASSÉ COMPOSÉ: J'ai ouvert. FUTUR: J'ouvrirai.

Offrir, *to offer;* **souffrir,** *to suffer;* **couvrir,** *to cover;* and compounds of **ouvrir** and **couvrir** are conjugated according to the same pattern.

I. EXERCICES D'APPLICATION.

A. *Mettez les formes suivantes au singulier.*

Ex.:—Nous allons: **Je vais.**
    —Ils vont: **Il va.**

1. Nous envoyons. **2.** Nous partons. **3.** Elles sortent. **4.** Nous ouvrons. **5.** Nous dormons. **6.** Nous venons. **7.** Ils viennent. **8.** Nous tenons. **9.** Nous devenons. **10.** Nous souffrons. **11.** Ils dorment. **12.** Nous nous en allons. **13.** Ils s'endorment. **14.** Nous nous endormons. **15.** Nous nous souvenons. **16.** Elles se souviennent. **17.** Nous nous sentons. **18.** Elles se sentent.

B. *Mettez les formes suivantes au futur.*

Ex.:—Je vais.
    —J'irai.

1. Il va. **2.** Ils vont. **3.** J'envoie. **4.** Ils envoient. **5.** Envoie-t-il? **6.** Nous partons. **7.** Je m'endors. **8.** Il ouvre. **9.** Nous venons. **10.** Vous venez. **11.** Il devient. **12.** J'offre. **13.** Je m'en vais. **14.** Je me souviens.

C. *Mettez les formes suivantes au passé composé.*

Ex.:—Nous allons.
    —**Nous sommes allé(e)s.**

1. Il va. **2.** Il envoie. **3.** Il dort. **4.** Il s'endort. **5.** Je sens. **6.** Il part. **7.** Elle sort. **8.** Je viens. **9.** Il devient. **10.** Il ouvre. **11.** Nous ouvrons. **12.** Il souffre. **13.** J'offre. **14.** Ouvre-t-il? **15.** Dort-il?

D. *Répétez les phrases suivantes en substituant les mots indiqués.*

1. Je vais chercher [des cigarettes] *(I am going to get).*
les billets/ le journal/ les journaux/ un agent de police/ mon ami

2. J'enverrai chercher [le médecin] *(I'll send for).*
les billets/ les journaux/ des cigarettes/ un agent de police/ mon ami

II. *Répondez affirmativement:*

1. Allez-vous dîner à la maison ce soir?   **2.** Envoyez-vous des cartes-postales à vos amis quand vous voyagez?   **3.** Est-ce que vous sortez souvent le soir? **4.** Êtes-vous sorti(e) hier soir?   **5.** Avez-vous bien dormi cette nuit?   **6.** Vous êtes-vous endormi(e) de bonne heure?   **7.** Envoyez-vous des fleurs à vos parents pour leur anniversaire *(birthday)*?   **8.** Partez-vous aujourd'hui pour le week-end?   **9.** Venez-vous à l'université à pied?   **10.** Viendrez-vous me voir dimanche?

III. *Remplacez le passé composé par* **venir de** *et l'infinitif:*

Ex.:—J'ai fini.
    —**Je viens de finir.**

1. Le train est parti.   **2.** Il s'est endormi.   **3.** Elle est sortie.   **4.** Elles sont sorties.   **5.** J'ai ouvert la fenêtre.   **6.** J'ai envoyé chercher le journal.   **7.** Il est revenu.   **8.** Il m'a offert son auto.

IV. *Dites en français:*

A. sortir (de)

1. The doctor has gone out.   **2.** He went out five minutes ago.   **3.** He goes out every morning.   **4.** He used to go out at night (le soir ou la nuit).   **5.** You can't go out in winter.   **6.** If you go out, bring me a sandwich.   **7.** The train was pulling out of the station when I arrived.   **8.** Go out!   **9.** Don't go out.

B. partir (de)

1. What time does the train leave Rheims?   **2.** It left five minutes ago.   **3.** It just left.   **4.** I left early.   **5.** I shall leave tomorrow.   **6.** Are you going away for the week end?   **7.** When are you leaving?   **8.** Leave!   **9.** Don't leave.

C. se servir (de)

1. Are you using your car this afternoon?   **2.** I am using my bicycle.   **3.** John used the bus.   **4.** He used to use his bicycle when he was twelve.   **5.** Do you want to use my car?   **6.** Use my car.   **7.** Don't use my car.   **8.** Help yourself.

V. Révision du dialogue, pp. 190-191.

1. Pourquoi Marie va-t-elle au Bon Marché? **2.** Est-ce qu'elle achète une écharpe comme celle de son amie? **3.** De quelle couleur est l'écharpe de son amie? **4.** Est-ce que les premières écharpes qu'on lui montre sont trop chères? **5.** Est-ce que la vendeuse a quelque chose de meilleur marché? **6.** Après avoir choisi une écharpe, est-ce que Marie veut acheter autre chose? **7.** Est-ce que Marie paye la vendeuse? **8.** Où trouvera-t-elle ses achats?

VI. Thème d'imitation:

In the United States, children ride bicycles; then when they are seventeen or eighteen years old, they get into their car and stay in it [1]. But nearly [2] all French people, young and old, ride bicycles. The distances are not too great, the roads are excellent, and if you choose country roads [3] where there are not too many cars, it is very pleasant to travel by bicycle. You [4] see many interesting things in the villages, you can stop where you wish and when you wish. If you take the train you can even take along [5] your bicycle. Of course you [6] have to have good legs! But with a little practice [7], you can do fifty or seventy-five kilometers without needing to send for the doctor . . .

---

[1] *lit.* descend from it no more. [2] nearly, **presque.** [3] country road, **le chemin.** [4] Use **vous** in this passage. To repeat **on** so many times would sound awkward. [5] take along, **emmener.** [6] Use **il faut** + infinitive. [7] practice, **l'habitude** *(f.).*

Arrivée à la ferme des Deschamps

ROGER —¹Bonjour, ma cousine.

MME DESCHAMPS —²Tiens! bonjour, Roger. ³Quelle bonne surprise!

ROGER —⁴Permettez-moi de vous présenter John Hughes. ⁵C'est mon meilleur ami.

MME DESCHAMPS —⁶Je suis heureuse* de faire votre connaissance, monsieur. ⁷Roger m'a souvent parlé de vous.

JOHN —⁸Nous avons décidé de profiter du beau temps pour venir vous voir.

MME DESCHAMPS —⁹C'est une excellente idée. ¹⁰Avez-vous fait bon voyage?

ROGER —¹¹Oui. Mais nous sommes assez fatigués.

MME DESCHAMPS —¹²Asseyez-vous et reposez-vous. ¹³Voulez-vous prendre quelque chose?

ROGER —¹⁴Je prendrai de la bière, si vous en avez.

MME DESCHAMPS —¹⁵Et vous, monsieur?

JOHN —¹⁶Je prendrai un verre d'eau fraîche.

MME DESCHAMPS —¹⁷Ne préférez-vous pas autre chose?

ROGER —¹Hello, cousin!

MRS. DESCHAMPS —²Well! Hello, Roger. ³What a pleasant surprise!

ROGER —⁴May I introduce John Hughes? ⁵He's my best friend.

MRS. DESCHAMPS —⁶I am happy to meet you, sir. ⁷Roger has often spoken of you.

JOHN —⁸We decided to take advantage of the fine weather to come to see you.

MRS. DESCHAMPS —⁹It's an excellent idea. ¹⁰Did you have a good trip?

ROGER —¹¹Yes. But we are rather tired.

MRS. DESCHAMPS —¹²Sit down and rest. ¹³Will you have something to eat or drink?

ROGER —¹⁴I'll have some beer, if you have some.

MRS. DESCHAMPS —¹⁵And what about you, sir?

JOHN —¹⁶I'll have a glass of cold water.

MRS. DESCHAMPS —¹⁷Wouldn't you rather have something else?

* On répond aussi couramment «Enchanté, monsieur», «Enchanté, madame.»

ROGER —[18]Mais non, ma cousine. John est Américain. [19]Il ne boit que de l'eau.

MME DESCHAMPS —[20]J'espère bien que vous allez passer quelques jours avec nous.

JOHN —[21]Nous ne voulons pas vous déranger. [22]Nous avons l'intention de repartir ce soir.

MME DESCHAMPS —[23]Vous n'êtes pas pressés. [24]Restez quelques jours ici. [25]C'est le moment de la moisson. [26]Si vous voulez, vous pourrez nous aider.

ROGER —[18]Oh no. John is an American. [19]He drinks only water.

MRS. DESCHAMPS —[20]I certainly hope you are going to spend a few days with us.

JOHN —[21]We don't want to put you out (inconvenience you). [22]We are intending to go back this evening.

MRS. DESCHAMPS —[23]You are not in a hurry. [24]Stay here a few days. [25]It's harvest time. [26] If you want to, you can help us.

I. EXERCICES D'APPLICATION. *Répétez les phrases suivantes en substituant les mots indiqués:*

1. Nous avons décidé de profiter du beau temps pour [venir vous voir].
   aller à la campagne/ faire une excursion/ faire une promenade à bicyclette/ jouer au tennis

2. Je prendrai [un verre d'eau fraîche].
   un verre de lait/ un peu de lait/ une tasse de café/ un peu de café/ une bouteille de bière/ un peu de bière

3. Nous avons l'intention de [repartir ce soir].
   partir demain soir/ quitter Fontainebleau demain/ rester quelques jours ici/ nous reposer aujourd'hui

4. C'est le moment [de la moisson].
   de partir/ de vous lever/ de nous en aller/ de rentrer

5. Il ne boit pas [d'eau].
   de vin/ de bière/ de café/ de lait/ de thé

6. Il ne boit que [de l'eau].
   du vin/ de la bière/ du café/ du lait/ du thé

II. *Répondez en français à chacune des questions suivantes:*

1. Où John et Roger viennent-ils d'arriver? 2. Qui est Madame Deschamps? 3. Est-ce qu'elle attendait l'arrivée de John et Roger? 4. Est-ce qu'elle a déjà fait la connaissance de John? 5. Est-ce que Roger a parlé de

John à sa cousine? **6.** Pourquoi John et Roger ont-ils décidé de venir voir les Deschamps? **7.** Est-ce que leur voyage à bicyclette les a fatigués? **8.** Que veut dire «prendre quelque chose»? **9.** Que prend Roger? **10.** Et John? **11.** Quand John et Roger ont-ils l'intention de repartir? **12.** Est-ce qu'ils ont peur de déranger les Deschamps? **13.** Est-ce qu'ils sont pressés? **14.** Qu'est-ce que leur dit Madame Deschamps pour les faire rester?

III. *Répondez en français à chacune des phrases impératives suivantes:*

1. Présentez un étudiant (une étudiante) à un autre (à une autre). **2.** Dites à un autre étudiant qu'on vous a souvent parlé de lui. **3.** Demandez à un autre étudiant s'il a fait bon voyage. **4.** Dites-lui de s'asseoir. **5.** Dites-lui de se reposer. **6.** Demandez-lui s'il veut prendre quelque chose. **7.** Demandez-lui ce qu'il veut prendre. **8.** Demandez-lui s'il ne préfère pas autre chose. **9.** Dites-lui que vous prendrez un verre d'eau fraîche.

IV. Dictée d'après le dialogue, pp. 199-200.

V. Conversation.

Vous faites une promenade à bicyclette et vous vous arrêtez dans une ferme pour demander un verre d'eau.

Dans la forêt de Fontainebleau

ROGER —[1]Je vois des champignons au bord de la route. [2]Il doit y en avoir beaucoup dans le bois. [3]Si nous en rapportions quelques-uns à la maison?

JOHN —[4]Est-ce que vous connaissez les champignons?

ROGER —[5]Plus ou moins. [6]Ramassez seulement ceux-ci. [7]Ils sont très faciles à reconnaître. [8]Le dessus est brun et le dessous est jaune.

JOHN —[9]Bon. Mais je ne sais pas où les mettre.

ROGER —[10]Tenez, mettez-les dans ce sac.

JOHN —[11]Est-ce que celui-ci est bon?

ROGER —[12]Oui.

JOHN —[13]Et celui-là?

ROGER —[14]Excellent.

JOHN —[15]Oh! J'en vois beaucoup au pied de cet arbre. [16]Apportez votre sac, voulez-vous?

ROGER —[17]Faites attention! [18]Est-ce que vous voulez empoisonner toute la famille?

JOHN —[19]Mais ces champignons ressemblent à ceux que vous m'avez montrés.

ROGER —[1]I see some mushrooms on the side of the road. [2]There must be lots of them in the woods. [3]Suppose we take a few of them back home (How about taking a few of them home)?

JOHN —[4]Do you know mushrooms?

ROGER —[5]More or less. [6]Just pick these. [7]They are very easy to recognize. [8]The upper surface is brown and the under side is yellow.

JOHN —[9]O.K. But I do not know where to put them.

ROGER —[10]Here, put them in this bag.

JOHN —[11]Is this one good?

ROGER —[12]Yes.

JOHN —[13]And that one?

ROGER —[14]Excellent.

JOHN —[15]Oh! I see lots of them at the foot of this tree. [16]Bring your bag over, will you?

ROGER —[17]Watch out! [18]Do you want to poison the entire family?

JOHN —[19]Well, these mushrooms are like those you showed me.

Roger —²⁰Les mauvais champignons ressemblent beaucoup aux bons.

Roger —²⁰The poisonous mushrooms look very much like the good ones.

John —²¹Vous auriez dû me dire ça plus tôt.

John —²¹You should have told me so sooner.

Roger —²²J'ai eu tort de ne pas vous prévenir. ²³En tout cas, il vaut mieux laisser ceux dont vous n'êtes pas sûr . . .

Roger —²²I was wrong not to warn you. ²³In any case, it is better to leave those you are not sure of . . .

I. Substitutions. *Répétez les phrases suivantes en substituant les mots indiqués:*

   1. Je vois [des champignons] au bord de la route.
   des fleurs/ un homme/ des gens/ des enfants

   2. Si nous en rapportions quelques-uns [à la maison]?
   à ma cousine/ à nos cousins/ dans ce sac/ sur nos bicyclettes

   3. J'ai eu tort [de ne pas vous prévenir].
   de ne pas vous dire au revoir/ de ne pas faire mes courses/ de ne pas travailler hier soir/ de ne pas écrire à mon père

   4. Vous avez eu tort [de ramasser de mauvais champignons].
   de dépenser tout votre argent/ de sortir hier soir/ de dormir tout l'après-midi/ de vous coucher si tard

   5. Vous auriez dû *(should have)* [me dire ça] plus tôt.
   me prévenir/ venir me voir/ revenir/ rentrer/ commencer à travailler

II. *Répondez en français à chacune des questions suivantes:*

   1. Qu'est-ce que Roger voit au bord de la route? **2.** Qu'est-ce qu'il propose de faire? **3.** Est-ce que Roger connaît les champignons? **4.** Est-ce que Roger dit à John de ramasser tous les champignons? **5.** Pourquoi ces champignons-là sont-ils faciles à reconnaître? **6.** De quelle couleur est le dessus des champignons dont il s'agit? **7.** De quelle couleur est le dessous des champignons dont il s'agit? **8.** Où Roger dit-il de les mettre? **9.** Qu'est-ce que John trouve au pied d'un arbre? **10.** Qu'est-ce qu'il demande à Roger de lui apporter? **11.** Pourquoi Roger lui dit-il de faire attention? **12.** Est-ce que John veut empoisonner toute la famille? **13.** Alors, pourquoi a-t-il ramassé de mauvais champignons? **14.** Qu'est-ce que Roger aurait dû lui dire plus tôt? **15.** Est-ce qu'il a eu raison de ne pas lui dire cela plus tôt? **16.** Est-ce qu'il vaut mieux laisser les champignons dont on n'est pas sûr? **17.** Est-ce qu'il vaut mieux ramasser seulement les champignons dont on est sûr?

III. *Demandez à quelqu'un:*

1. s'il connaît les champignons. 2. s'il va quelquefois ramasser des champignons à la campagne. 3. ce que Roger voit au bord de la route. 4. si les bons champignons sont difficiles à reconnaître. 5. si on peut ramasser tous les champignons qu'on trouve. 6. de quelle couleur est le dessus des champignons dont parle Roger. 7. pourquoi il faut faire attention en ramassant des champignons. 8. si les mauvais champignons ressemblent beaucoup aux bons. 9. s'il est dangereux de ramasser des champignons qu'on ne connaît pas.

IV. Exercices d'application.

A. *Remplacez* **il y a** *par* **il doit y avoir** (there must be) *dans chacune des phrases suivantes.*

Ex.:—Il y a des champignons dans le bois.
   —**Il doit y avoir des champignons dans le bois.**

1. Il y a beaucoup de champignons dans le bois. 2. Il y en a beacoup dans le bois. 3. Il y en a quelques-uns dans le bois. 4. Il y a un train cet après-midi. 5. Il y en a un cet après-midi. 6. Il y en a plusieurs cet après-midi.

B. *Répétez, en remplaçant l'impératif par* **si nous** *avec l'imparfait.*

Ex.:—Rapportons des champignons à la maison.
   —**Si nous rapportions des champignons à la maison?**

1. Ramassons des champignons. 2. Ramassons des fraises des bois *(wild strawberries).* 3. Allons à la campagne pour le week-end. 4. Allons chercher des fleurs sauvages. 5. Partons ce soir. 6. Quittons la maison de bonne heure.

C. *Répondez négativement aux questions suivantes:*

1. Ressemblez-vous à votre père? 2. Les enfants ressemblent-ils toujours à leurs parents? 3. Est-ce que votre frère vous ressemble? 4. Est-ce que votre sœur vous ressemble? 5. Est-ce que les jumeaux *(twins)* se ressemblent toujours? 6. Est-ce que les mauvais champignons ressemblent toujours aux bons?

V. Dictée d'après le dialogue, pp. 209-210.

VI. Conversation.

Au cours d'une promenade dans une forêt, vous parlez avec un ami de ce que vous voyez.

Irregular Verbs in *-re*

91. First group: past participle in **u.**

A. connaître, *to know, to be acquainted with:*

—**Connaissez-vous** Roger Duplessis?   *Do you know* Roger Duplessis?
—Oui, **je** le **connais** un peu.   Yes, *I know* him slightly.
—Où **l'avez-vous connu?**   Where *did you know* him?
—**Je l'ai connu** à Paris.   *I knew* him in Paris.

PRÉSENT: Je connais, tu connais, il connaît, nous connaissons, vous connaissez, ils connaissent.
IMPARFAIT: Je connaissais. PASSÉ COMPOSÉ: J'ai connu. FUTUR: Je connaîtrai.

B. croire, *to believe:*

—**Croyez-vous** ce que disent les journaux?   *Do you believe* what the papers say?
—**Je ne crois pas** tout ce qu'ils disent.   *I do not believe* all they say.
—**Je n'ai pas cru** ce qu'il m'a dit.   *I did not believe* what he told me.

PRÉSENT: Je crois, tu crois, il croit, nous croyons, vous croyez, ils croient.
IMPARFAIT: Je croyais. PASSÉ COMPOSÉ: J'ai cru. FUTUR: Je croirai.

C. boire, *to drink:*

—**Buvez-vous** du café?   *Do you drink* coffee?
—Non, **je** ne **bois** que du lait.   No, *I drink* only milk.
—Qu'est-ce que John **a bu?**   What *did* John *drink?*
—**Il a bu** de l'eau fraîche.   *He drank* some cold water.

PRÉSENT: Je bois, tu bois, il boit, nous buvons, vous buvez, ils boivent.
IMPARFAIT: Je buvais. PASSÉ COMPOSÉ: J'ai bu. FUTUR: Je boirai.

D. lire, *to read:*

—**Lisez-vous** la *Nouvelle Revue Française?*   *Do you read* the NRF?
—Oui, je la **lis** quelquefois.   Yes, *I read* it sometimes.
—**Avez-vous lu** des romans de Balzac?   *Have you read* any novels of Balzac?
—Oui, **j'en ai lu** deux ou trois.   Yes, *I have read* two or three of them.

PRÉSENT: Je lis, tu lis, il lit, nous lisons, vous lisez, ils lisent.
IMPARFAIT: Je lisais. PASSÉ COMPOSÉ: J'ai lu. FUTUR: Je lirai.

92. Second group: past participle in -i, -is, or -it.

A. dire, *to say, to tell:*

—Qu'est-ce que **vous dites?**	What's that (What *do you say*)?
—**Je dis** que je ne crois pas ce que le marchand m'**a dit.**	*I say* I don't believe what the store-keeper *told me.*

PRÉSENT: Je dis, tu dis, il dit, nous disons, vous dites, ils disent.
IMPARFAIT: Je disais. PASSÉ COMPOSÉ: J'ai dit. FUTUR: Je dirai.

B. écrire, *to write:*

—**Écrivez-vous** souvent à votre mère?	*Do you write* to your mother often?
—**Je** lui **écris** tous les huit jours.	*I write* her every week.
—**Je** lui **ai écrit** dimanche.	*I wrote* her Sunday.

PRÉSENT: J'écris, tu écris, il écrit, nous écrivons, vous écrivez, ils écrivent.
IMPARFAIT: J'écrivais. PASSÉ COMPOSÉ: J'ai écrit. FUTUR: J'écrirai.

C. suivre, *to follow, to take (a course):*

—**Suivez-vous** les conseils de vos parents?	*Do you follow* the advice of your parents?
—Oui, **je** les **suis** toujours.	Yes, *I* always *follow* it (them).
—**Avez-vous suivi** un cours d'histoire?	*Did you take* a history course?
—Oui, **j'en ai suivi** plusieurs.	Yes, *I took* several of them.

PRÉSENT: Je suis, tu suis, il suit, nous suivons, vous suivez, ils suivent.
IMPARFAIT: Je suivais. PASSÉ COMPOSÉ: J'ai suivi. FUTUR: Je suivrai.

D. prendre, *to take:*

—Est-ce que **vous prenez** l'autobus?	*Are you taking* the bus?
—Non, **je prends** le train.	No, *I am taking* the train.
—**J'ai** déjà **pris** mon billet.	*I have* already *gotten* (taken) my ticket.
—**Prenez-vous** du sucre?	*Do you take* sugar?
—Non, **je prends** un peu de crème.	No, *I take* a little cream.

PRÉSENT: Je prends, tu prends, il prend, nous prenons, vous prenez, ils prennent.
IMPARFAIT: Je prenais. PASSÉ COMPOSÉ: J'ai pris. FUTUR: Je prendrai.

E. mettre, *to put, to put on;* **se mettre à,** *to begin:*

—Où **mettez-vous** votre argent?	Where *do you put* your money?
—**Je** le **mets** dans mon porte-mon-naie.	*I put* it in my pocketbook.
—Je ne sais pas où **j'ai mis** ma cravate.	I do not know where *I put* my tie.
—Marie **a mis** sa nouvelle robe.	Marie *put on* her new dress.
—**Nous nous sommes mis** à travailler à une heure et demie.	*We started* to work at 1:30.

PRÉSENT: Je mets, tu mets, il met, nous mettons, vous mettez, ils mettent.
IMPARFAIT: Je mettais. PASSÉ COMPOSÉ: J'ai mis. FUTUR: Je mettrai.

93. Faire, *to do, to make,* etc.

A. Normal uses of **faire:**

—Qu'est-ce que **vous faites** (pres.) ce soir?	What *are you doing* tonight?
—Je ne sais pas ce que **je ferai** (fut.).	I don't know what *I shall do.*
—Je n'ai rien à **faire.**	I have nothing *to do.*
—Cela ne **fait** rien.	That *makes* no difference.

B. Special uses of **faire:**

(1) Impersonal:

Il fait beau.	*It's* fine weather.
Il fait bon (jour, nuit, etc.)	*It's* pleasant (light, dark, etc.)

(2) **faire** + an infinitive = *to have* + past participle:

—Qui **a fait construire** ce château?	Who *had* this château *built?*
—**J'ai fait réparer** ma montre.	*I had* my watch *repaired.*

PRÉSENT: Je fais, tu fais, il fait, nous faisons, vous faites, ils font.
IMPARFAIT: Je faisais. PASSÉ COMPOSÉ: J'ai fait. FUTUR: Je ferai.

94. Plaindre, *to pity;* se plaindre, *to complain.*

—De quoi **vous plaignez-vous?**	What *are you complaining* about?
—Je ne me **plains** pas.	*I am not complaining.*

PRÉSENT: Je plains, tu plains, il plaint, nous plaignons, vous plaignez, ils plaignent.
IMPARFAIT: Je plaignais, etc. PASSÉ COMPOSÉ: J'ai plaint, etc. FUTUR: Je plaindrai, etc.

Craindre, *to fear,* is conjugated like **plaindre.** Ex.: Qu'est-ce que **vous craignez? Je** ne **crains** rien.

A few verbs ending in **-eindre** and **-oindre** are conjugated like **plaindre** except that the vowel **e** or **o** of the ending remains **e** and **o** respectively: **atteindre**, *to reach, to attain;* **éteindre**, *to extinguish;* **peindre**, *to paint;* **rejoindre**, *to meet, to catch up with;* etc.

I. Exercices d'application.

A. *Répondez affirmativement:*

Ex:.—Connaissez-vous?
   —Je connais.

1. Croyez-vous? **2.** Lisez-vous? **3.** Connaissez-vous? **4.** Buvez-vous? **5.** Dites-vous? **6.** Écrivez-vous? **7.** Suivez-vous? **8.** Prenez-vous? **9.** Mettez-vous? **10.** Faites-vous? **11.** Plaignez-vous? **12.** Vous plaignez-vous? **13.** Craignez-vous? **14.** Peignez-vous? **15.** Rejoignez-vous?

B. *Mettez les phrases suivantes au passé composé:*

Ex.:—Je suis un cours de chimie.
   —J'ai suivi un cours de chimie.

1. Je ne bois pas de café. **2.** Je ne prends pas de crème. **3.** Je ne crois pas ce qu'il m'a dit. **4.** Nous ne lisons pas le journal. **5.** Qu'est-ce que vous lui dites? **6.** Nous ne disons rien. **7.** A qui écrivez-vous? **8.** Que faites-vous? **9.** Qu'est-ce que vous craignez? **10.** Où rejoignez-vous vos amis? **11.** Il suit mes conseils.

C. *Mettez les phrases suivantes à l'imparfait en commençant par* **A ce moment-là:**

Ex.:—Je ne connais pas Paris.
   —A ce moment-là, je ne connaissais pas Paris.

1. Je crois tout ce qu'on me dit. **2.** Je ne bois pas de vin. **3.** Je ne lis pas le journal. **4.** Il n'écrit pas beaucoup. **5.** Il suit les conseils de ses parents. **6.** Il ne prend pas de café. **7.** Il fait du ski. **8.** Il se plaint tout le temps.

D. *Répétez en remplaçant* **commencer** *par* **se mettre à:**

Ex.:—Je commence à travailler à huit heures.
   —Je me mets à travailler à huit heures.

1. A quelle heure commencez-vous à travailler? **2.** Il a commencé à lire. **3.** Nous avons commencé à écrire des lettres. **4.** Il a commencé à pleuvoir. **5.** J'ai commencé à acheter de vieux livres. **6.** Ils ont commencé à ramasser des champignons.

II. *Demandez à quelqu'un:*

Ex.:—s'il prend du sucre dans son café.
   —**Prenez-vous du sucre dans votre café?**

l. s'il connaît Versailles. **2.** s'il croit qu'il va pleuvoir. **3.** s'il boit du lait.
4. s'il lit beaucoup de romans. **5.** ce qu'il dit. **6.** s'il écrit beaucoup de
lettres. **7.** quels cours il suit. **8.** ce qu'il prend comme dessert. **9.** où il met
son argent. **l0.** s'il se plaint. **ll.** s'il craint la pluie. **l2.** ce qu'il fait le
dimanche. **l3.** quel temps il faisait hier. **l4.** à quelle heure il fait nuit en
hiver. **l5.** où Roger a fait réparer sa montre. **l6.** ce qu'on fait réparer dans
un garage.

III. *Dites en français:*

l. I took the train at Épernay. **2.** I got my ticket in Paris. **3.** I took a
chemistry course last year. **4.** I took (followed) his advice. **5.** I had some
coffee at noon. **6.** She put on her new dress. **7.** He put on his hat. **8.** They
started to work early. **9.** They will start to work tomorrow. **l0.** Have you
read what they wrote? **ll.** Do you believe what they said? **l2.** What are
you doing this evening? **l3.** I have nothing to do. **l4.** I have something to
do. **l5.** I have a great deal to do. *Je n'ai rien à faire*

J'ai beaucoup à faire

IV. Révision des dialogues, pp. 199-200 et pp. 209-210.

l. Comment John et Roger vont-ils à la campagne? **2.** Pourquoi craignent-ils
d'avoir pris la mauvaise route? **3.** Qu'est-ce que demande Roger à l'homme
qui travaille dans son champ? **4.** Où cet homme leur dit-il d'aller? **5.** Quel
chemin doivent-ils prendre à la sortie de Barbizon? **6.** A quelle distance est
Barbizon de Fontainebleau? **7.** Savez-vous ce que c'est qu'un kilomètre? **8.**
Savez-vous combien il y a de mètres dans un kilomètre? **9.** Pourquoi Roger
a-t-il chaud? **l0.** Pourquoi John a-t-il mal aux jambes? **ll.** A qui Roger
présente-t-il John? **l2.** Qu'est-ce que vous diriez pour présenter quelqu'un?
l3. Qu'est-ce que vous dites quand on vous présente quelqu'un? **l4.** Qu'est-ce
que Mme Deschamps demande à John et à Roger? **l5.** Est-ce que John boit
de la bière? **l6.** Qu'est-ce qu'il prend? **l7.** Pourquoi John et Roger ont-ils
l'intention de repartir le même soir? **l8.** Est-ce qu'ils sont pressés? **l9.** Pourquoi les Deschamps avaient-ils besoin d'aide à ce moment-là? **20.** Avez-vous
jamais travaillé dans une ferme au moment de la moisson?

V. THÈME D'IMITATION:

As [1] they were bicycling in the Fontainebleau Forest, Roger saw some mushrooms on the side of the road. "What luck [2]", said he to John. "I'm crazy about [3] mushrooms. Let's pick some. I'll give them to my cousin, and we'll eat them this evening." "Pick all the mushrooms you wish," answered John, "and eat them. *I* shall not eat any." "Why?" asked Roger. "There is no danger [4] when you just pick the mushrooms you know." "Do you think (so)?" said John. "In America, my father knew a professor of botany [5] who had spent his life studying [6] mushrooms. Do you know how the poor man died? He died of mushroom poisoning [7] . . ."

Roger picked mushrooms all the same; but that evening he didn't have much appetite.

---

[1] as, **comme.**   [2] what luck, **quelle chance,** or **quelle veine.**   [3] to be crazy about, **adorer.**
[4] danger, **le danger.**   [5] botany, **la botanique.**   [6] à **étudier.**   [7] *lit.* poisoned by mushrooms.

A l'église du village

ROGER —[1]Bonjour, monsieur le curé.

LE CURÉ —[2]Bonjour, mes amis. [3]Entrez donc. [4]J'étais en train de travailler dans mon jardin quand vous avez sonné.

JOHN —[5]Nous nous excusons de vous déranger quand vous êtes occupé.

LE CURÉ —[6]Vous ne me dérangez pas du tout. [7]Je viens de tailler mes rosiers, [8]et je suis à votre disposition.

ROGER —[9]Nous avons entendu dire que vous avez une très belle église, [10]et nous avons envie de la visiter.

LE CURÉ —[11]Je me ferai un plaisir de vous accompagner dans votre visite. [12]Mais je crains que vous ne * soyez un peu déçus. [13]Bien qu'elle soit classée «monument historique», [14]c'est une simple église de village.

JOHN —[15]J'ai lu quelque part que votre église date du douzième siècle.

ROGER —[1]Good morning, sir.

LE CURÉ —[2]Good morning, my friends. [3]Do come in. [4]I was busy working in my garden, when you rang.

JOHN —[5]We apologize for bothering you when you are busy.

LE CURÉ —[6]You aren't bothering me at all. [7]I have just trimmed my rosebushes, [8]and I am at your service.

ROGER —[9]We have heard that you have a very beautiful church, [10]and we are eager to go through it.

LE CURÉ —[11]I shall take pleasure in showing you through it. [12]But I'm afraid you'll be a little disappointed. [13]Although it is classified as a "historical monument," [14]it's a simple village church.

JOHN —[15]I have read somewhere that your church dates from the XIIth century.

---

* When a subordinate clause depends upon **craindre** used affirmatively (and a few other expressions), the subordinate clause is introduced by **que . . . ne** instead of **que** alone. This pleonastic **ne,** as it is called, is meaningless and is frequently omitted in conversation.

Craindre
avoir peur de
de peur que

LE CURÉ —[16]Une partie seulement de l'édifice actuel date de l'époque romane.* [17]L'église a été brûlée en 1392 [18]et a été en partie reconstruite au siècle suivant.

ROGER —[19]J'ai entendu parler des vitraux de votre église. [20]On dit qu'ils sont très vieux.

LE CURÉ —[21]Je ne crois pas qu'il y ait plus de deux ou trois vitraux vraiment anciens. [22]La plupart d'entre eux** sont relativement modernes . . . [23]Voulez-vous bien entrer par cette porte? [24]L'intérieur de l'église est un peu sombre, [25]mais vos yeux s'habitueront vite à l'obscurité.

LE CURÉ —[16]Just a part of the present building dates from the romanesque period. [17]The church was burned in 1392 [18]and was partly rebuilt in the following century.

ROGER —[19]I have heard of the stained-glass windows of your church. [20]They say they are very old.

LE CURÉ —[21]I don't believe there are more than two or three of the stained-glass windows which are really old. [22]Most of them are relatively modern . . . [23]Will you come in through this door? [24]The inside is a little dark, [25]but your eyes will quickly get used to the darkness.

I. SUBSTITUTIONS. *Répétez les phrases suivantes en substituant les mots indiqués:*

1. J'étais en train de [travailler dans mon jardin] quand vous avez sonné.
   tailler mes rosiers/ lire le journal/ réparer mon auto/ écrire des lettres

2. Nous nous excusons [de vous déranger].
   de ne pas être à l'heure/ d'être en retard/ d'être en avance (*ahead of time*) / d'avoir oublié notre rendez-vous

3. Nous avons entendu dire que [vous avez une très belle église].
   les Brown sont de retour/ Louise Bedel va se marier/ elle va habiter dans notre quartier/ l'église a été construite au douzième siècle

4. J'ai entendu parler [des vitraux de votre église].
   des fontaines de Versailles/ de Mansard/ de lui/ de Jeanne d'Arc/ d'elle

---

* Les plus vieilles églises françaises datent de l'époque romane, c'est-à-dire des onzième et douzième siècles. L'architecture de cette époque est caractérisée par l'emploi fréquent de l'arc en demi-cercle. Les murs très épais n'ont que de rares fenêtres, ce qui explique l'obscurité de l'intérieur de ces églises.
** Note that you say la **plupart d'entre eux,** not la **plupart d'eux.** The same is true for **beaucoup, quelques-uns, plusieurs.**

II. *Répondez en français à chacune des questions suivantes:*

1. Qu'est-ce que Roger a dit quand le curé a ouvert la porte? **2.** Que faisait le curé quand Roger a sonné? **3.** De quoi Roger s'excuse-t-il? **4.** Qu'est-ce que répond le curé? **5.** Que vient-il de faire dans son jardin? **6.** Qu'est-ce que Roger a entendu dire à propos de l'église? **7.** Pourquoi John et Roger sont-ils venus voir le curé? **8.** Qu'est-ce que le curé offre de faire? **9.** Pourquoi le curé dit-il: «Je crains que vous ne soyez un peu déçus»? **10.** Est-ce que cette église est classée «monument historique»? **11.** Où Roger a-t-il lu que l'église date du douzième siècle? **12.** Est-ce que tout l'édifice actuel date de l'époque romane? **13.** En quelle année l'église a-t-elle été brûlée? **14.** Quand a-t-elle été reconstruite? **15.** Est-ce que Roger a entendu parler des vitraux de l'église? **16.** Qu'est-ce qu'il a entendu dire à leur sujet? **17.** Est-ce que la plupart des vitraux de l'église sont anciens? **18.** Est-ce que la plupart d'entre eux sont modernes? **19.** Est-ce que l'intérieur de l'église est sombre? **20.** Est-ce que les yeux de John et de Roger s'habitueront vite à l'obscurité?

III. *Répétez les phrases suivantes, en remplaçant le nom par le pronom personnel:*

Ex.:—La plupart des vitraux sont relativement modernes.
     —**La plupart d'entre eux sont relativement modernes.**

1. Quelques-uns des vitraux sont relativement modernes. **2.** Plusieurs des vitraux sont relativement modernes. **3.** La plupart des statues *(f.)* sont relativement modernes. **4.** Quelques-unes des statues sont relativement modernes. **5.** Plusieurs des statues sont relativement modernes.

IV. *Dites en français:*

A. avoir envie de

1. We are eager to visit your church. **2.** I'd like to see the stained-glass windows. **3.** Are you interested in seeing Florence and Rome? **4.** I felt like working in my garden.

B. Je crains que

1. I am afraid you will be a little disappointed. **2.** I am afraid you will be a little tired. **3.** I am afraid you will be a little late. **4.** I am afraid you will be a little early.

C. Bien qu'elle soit

1. Although it is classified as a historical monument, it's a simple village church.   2. Although she is tired, she will go to the dance tonight.   3. Although she is busy, she will be glad to see you.

D. s'habituer à

1. Your eyes will quickly get used to the darkness.   2. Your eyes will quickly get used to it.   3. I am not used to riding a bicycle, but I shall get used to it.
4. I am not used to drinking black coffee, but I shall get used to it.

V. RÉVISION DE L'IMPÉRATIF. *Dites à quelqu'un:*

1. d'entrer.   2. de ne pas entrer.   3. de s'asseoir.   4. de ne pas s'asseoir.
5. de se dépêcher.   6. de ne pas se dépêcher.   7. de ne pas se déranger.   8.
de vous excuser.   9. de prendre l'autobus.   10. de faire attention.   11. de
faire venir le médecin.   12. de ne pas croire tout ce que disent les journaux.
13. de s'en aller.   14. de ne pas partir.

VI. DICTÉE D'APRÈS LE DIALOGUE, pp. 212-213.

VII. CONVERSATION.

Vous demandez des renseignements à un guide au sujet d'un château de la Renaissance que vous voulez visiter (date de construction, nom de l'architecte, jours et heures de visite, etc.).

Au jardin

MME DESCHAMPS —[1]Il faut que j'aille au jardin cueillir des fleurs.

ROGER —[2]Voulez-vous que nous vous aidions?

MME DESCHAMPS —[3]Mais oui. Faites attention de bien fermer la porte. [4]Je ne veux pas que les poules puissent entrer. [5]Elles mangent à peu près toute ma salade.

ROGER —[6]Quelles fleurs allez-vous cueillir?

MME DESCHAMPS —[7]J'ai besoin de roses et d'œillets. [8]J'en ferai un bouquet pour la salle à manger.

ROGER —[9]Vous avez un très beau jardin.

MME DESCHAMPS —[10]Je devrais m'en occuper davantage, [11]mais je n'ai pas le temps.

ROGER —[12]Est-ce que vous avez du maïs?

MME DESCHAMPS —[13]Non, je n'en ai pas. [14]D'ailleurs, l'été est trop frais [15]pour que le maïs puisse mûrir ici.

JOHN —[16]Je m'en doutais un peu.

ROGER —[17]Regardez ces pois, ces *haricots verts et ces choux. [18]Ils poussent à merveille.

MRS. DESCHAMPS —[1]I must go to the garden to pick some flowers.

ROGER —[2]Do you want us to help you?

MRS. DESCHAMPS —[3]Why yes. Be careful to close the garden gate properly. [4]I don't want the hens to be able to get in. [5]They eat practically all my salad greens.

ROGER —[6]What flowers are you going to pick?

MRS. DESCHAMPS —[7]I need roses and carnations. [8]I'll make a bouquet of them for the dining room.

ROGER —[9]You have a very fine garden.

MRS. DESCHAMPS —[10]I ought to take care of it better (more), [11]but I haven't the time.

ROGER —[12]Have you got any corn?

MRS. DESCHAMPS —[13]No, I haven't any. [14]Anyway, the summer is too cool [15]for corn to mature here.

JOHN —[16]I rather thought so.

ROGER —[17]Look at those peas, green beans, and cabbages. [18]They certainly are growing.

---

* The h of haricots is aspirate.

MME DESCHAMPS —[19]Oui, mais il n'a guère plu cette année. [20]Une bonne pluie ferait du bien à mes légumes.

JOHN —[21]Voulez-vous que nous les arrosions?

MME DESCHAMPS —[22]Je crois qu'il vaut mieux attendre [23]jusqu'à ce qu'il fasse moins chaud . . .

MRS. DESCHAMPS —[19]Yes; but it hasn't rained much this year. [20]A good rain would do a good deal for my vegetables.

JOHN —[21]Do you want us to water them?

MRS. DESCHAMPS —[22]I think it's better to wait [23] till it's cooler . . .

I. SUBSTITUTIONS. *Répétez les phrases suivantes en substituant les mots indiqués:*

1. Faites attention [de bien fermer la porte].
   de ne pas laisser la porte ouverte/ de ne pas laisser entrer les poules/ de ne pas être en retard/ de ne pas manquer votre avion (*plane*)

2. J'ai besoin [de roses et d'œillets].
   de papier à lettres/ d'une nouvelle auto/ de cigarettes/ d'argent/ de monnaie

3. Je devrais [m'en occuper] davantage, mais je n'ai pas le temps.
   me reposer/ m'amuser/ travailler/ dormir

4. Je crois qu'il vaut mieux attendre jusqu'[à la nuit].
   à demain/ à six heures/ à la semaine prochaine/ à l'été prochain/ à dimanche

5. Je crois qu'il vaut mieux attendre jusqu'à ce qu'il fasse [moins chaud].
   plus chaud/ moins froid/ plus froid/ beau

II. *Répondez en français à chacune des questions suivantes:*

1. Pourquoi faut-il que Mme Deschamps aille au jardin? 2. Est-ce qu'elle veut que John et Roger l'aident? 3. Pourquoi faut-il qu'ils fassent attention de bien fermer la porte du jardin? 4. Pourquoi Mme Deschamps ne veut-elle pas que les poules puissent entrer dans son jardin? 5. Quelles fleurs veut-elle cueillir? 6. Qu'est-ce qu'elle fera de ces fleurs? 7. Comment Roger trouve-t-il le jardin de Mme Deschamps? 8. Est-ce que Mme Deschamps devrait s'occuper davantage de son jardin? 9. Pourquoi ne peut-elle pas s'en occuper davantage? 10. Est-ce que Mme Deschamps a du maïs dans son jardin? 11. Pourquoi le maïs ne peut-il pas mûrir dans le Nord de la France? 12. Quels légumes y a-t-il dans le jardin? 13. Est-ce qu'ils poussent bien? 14. Est-ce qu'il a beaucoup plu cette année-là? 15. Pourquoi Mme Deschamps voudrait-elle une bonne pluie? 16. Qu'est-ce que John propose de faire? 17. Est-ce que Mme Deschamps croit qu'il faut arroser tout de suite? 18. Jusqu'à quand dit-elle d'attendre? 19. Savez-vous vous occuper d'un jardin? 20. Qu'est-ce qu'il faut faire s'il ne pleut pas? 21. Est-ce qu'il vaut mieux arroser le matin ou le soir? 22. Est-ce qu'on peut avoir un beau jardin si on ne s'en occupe pas?

III. *Demandez à quelqu'un:*

1. s'il doit aller au jardin cueillir des fleurs.   **2.** s'il veut bien fermer la porte.
3. s'il veut bien vous aider.   **4.** quelles fleurs Mme Deschamps veut cueillir.
5. s'il sait s'occuper d'un jardin.   **6.** s'il vaut mieux arroser les légumes quand
il fait chaud ou quand il fait frais.

IV. Exercices d'application.

A. *Répétez les phrases suivantes en remplaçant* **Je vais** *par* **Il faut que**
j'aille:

1. Je vais au jardin cueillir des fleurs.   **2.** Je vais à la gare.   **3.** Je vais au
restaurant.   **4.** Je vais en ville faire des courses.   **5.** Je vais voir ce film.
6. Je vais à la banque toucher un chèque.   **7.** Je vais au bureau de tabac
chercher un journal.   **8.** Je vais mettre une lettre à la poste *(mail a letter)*.
9. Je vais à la maison.pour le week-end.

B. *Répétez les phrases suivantes en remplaçant* **ne . . . pas** *par* **ne . . .**
guère:

1. Il n'a pas plu cette année.   **2.** Je n'ai pas travaillé aujourd'hui.   **3.** Je n'ai
pas dormi la nuit dernière.   **4.** Il n'a pas neigé cet hiver.   **5.** Je ne me suis
pas amusé cet hiver.   **6.** Je ne me suis pas reposé pendant le week-end.   **7.** Je
n'ai pas l'habitude d'aller à bicyclette.   **8.** Je n'ai pas le temps de m'occuper
de mon jardin.

V. Dictée d'après le dialogue, pp. 221-222.

VI. Conversation.

Un ami vient vous voir et vous l'invitez à voir votre jardin. Il y a dans votre
jardin des choux *(m.)*, des tomates *(f.)*, des asperges *(f.) (asparagus)*, des
pommes de terre *(f.)*, de la laitue *(lettuce)*, des pivoines *(f.) (peonies)*, des
marguerites *(f.) (daisies)*, des violettes *(f.)* et des pensées *(f.) (pansies)*.

Septième Lecture Illustrée, p. 46, *A la campagne.*

The Subjunctive

95. Present subjunctive of être and avoir, and of regular verbs.

A. être:

que je sois, que tu sois, qu'il soit, que nous soyons, que vous soyez, qu'ils soient.

B. avoir:

que j'aie, que tu aies, qu'il ait, que nous ayons, que vous ayez, qu'ils aient.

C. Regular verbs:

donner: que je donne, que tu donnes, qu'il donne, que nous donnions, que vous donniez, qu'ils donnent.

finir: que je finisse, que tu finisses, qu'il finisse, que nous finissions, que vous finissiez, qu'ils finissent.

répondre: que je réponde, que tu répondes, qu'il réponde, que nous répondions, que vous répondiez, qu'ils répondent.

(1) The endings of the present subjunctive of all verbs (except **être** and **avoir**) are: **-e, -es, -e, -ions, -iez, -ent.**

(2) The stem of the present subjunctive of regular verbs is the same as that of the first person plural of the present indicative. Ex.: PRES. IND. **Nous finissons.** PRES. SUBJ. **je finisse,** etc.

96. Commonest uses of the present subjunctive.

A. —Il faut que **je donne** mon adresse à la concierge.

I must *give* my address to the concierge.

—Il faut que **je finisse** mon travail.

I must *finish* my work.

—Il faut que **je réponde** à cette lettre.

I must *answer* this letter.

—Il faut que **je sois** à la gare à 4 heures.

I must *be* at the station at 4 o'clock.

—Il vaut mieux que **vous finissiez** votre travail.

It's better for *you* to *finish* your work.

—Voulez-vous que **nous** vous **aidions?**

Do you want *us to help* you?

—J'aime mieux qu'**il attende** jus-   I prefer for *him to wait* until this
    qu'à ce soir.   evening.

—Je regrette que **vous ayez** mal à   I am sorry *you have* a headache.
    la tête.

—J'ai peur que **vous** ne **soyez** un   I am afraid *you will be* a little dis-
    peu déçu.   appointed.

—Je suis content que **vous ayez**   I am glad *you have answered* that
    répondu à cette lettre.   letter.

—Je suis content que **vous soyez**   I am glad *you have come.*
    arrivé.

(1) For all practical purposes there is no difference between the meaning of the indicative and the subjunctive.

(2) The subjunctive is used in subordinate clauses introduced by **que**
and depending upon certain verbs which express wishing, wanting,
desiring; joy, sorrow, happiness, regret, fear; approval or disapproval,
etc. Among the verbs of this group which may take the subjunctive,
the following are the most frequently used; **vouloir, désirer; aimer
mieux; préférer; souhaiter,** *to wish;* **craindre,** *to fear;* **être content;
être heureux; avoir peur,** etc., and a number of impersonal expressions
such as **Il faut que . . . , Il vaut mieux que . . . ,** etc.

But while the subjunctive is used in SUBORDINATE CLAUSES which
depend upon these verbs, these verbs may also be followed by an infinitive if the verb and infinitive have the same subject. Ex.:—Do *you*
want to water the garden *(yourself)?* **Voulez-vous arroser le jardin?**
(infinitive) —Do *you* want *us* to water the garden? **Voulez-vous que
nous arrosions le jardin?** (subjunctive)

(3) If the verb depending upon **Il faut . . .** etc. has an expressed subject
(whether noun or pronoun), the subjunctive is used in the subordinate
clause; if the dependent verb has no expressed subject, the infinitive
is used. Ex.:—**Il faut que vous travailliez davantage.** *You must work
harder.* BUT: **Il faut travailler davantage.** *One must work harder.*

B. —Croyez-vous **qu'il y ait** de la place   Do you think *there will be* room on
    dans l'autobus?   the bus?

—Pensez-vous **que je sois** en retard?   Do you think *I'll be* late?

—Non, je ne pense pas **que vous**   No, I don't think *you'll be* late.
    soyez en retard.

Croire and **penser** do not always take the subjunctive. For these verbs
and other expressions which express belief (**être sûr, il me semble,**
etc.), it is necessary to observe:

(1) the indicative is used in clauses depending upon AFFIRMATIVE FORMS (**Je crois qu'il y aura** de la place);

(2) the indicative or subjunctive may be used in clauses depending upon the interrogative or negative forms. Generally speaking, the subjunctive in such clauses is supposed to express a greater degree of uncertainty than the indicative. **Je ne crois pas qu'il y aura de la place** means *I rather doubt that there will be any room.* However, the difference between **Croyez-vous qu'il y aura de la place?** and **Croyez-vous qu'il y ait de la place?** is scarcely perceptible. In conversation most people simply use the indicative after all forms of **croire** and **penser.**

C. —Bien qu'elle **soit** classée monument historique . . .   Although *it is classed* as a historical monument . . .

—Il vaut mieux attendre jusqu'à ce qu'il **ait répondu** à votre lettre.   It is better to wait until *he has answered* your letter.

The subjunctive must be used in clauses introduced by certain conjunctive expressions of which the following are the most frequently used: **à moins que,** *unless;* **avant que,** *before;* **bien que,** *although;* **jusqu'à ce que,** *until;* **pour que,** *so that;* **de peur que,** *for fear that; etc.*

D. —C'est le meilleur roman que **j'aie lu.**   That's the best novel *I've read.*

—Henri est le seul étudiant **qui soit** absent.   Henry is the only student *who is* absent.

The subjunctive is used in relative clauses whose antecedent is modified by a superlative or by the word **seul.** *premiere + derniere*

97. Present subjunctive of the commonest irregular verbs.

—Il faut que **j'aille** à un de mes champs.   I must *go* to one of my fields.

—Je ne veux pas que les poules **puissent** entrer.   I don't want the hens *to be able* to get in.

—Il vaut mieux que nous attendions jusqu'à ce qu'il **fasse** moins chaud.   It's better for us to wait until *it is* cooler.

—Je ne crois pas qu'il **sache** mon adresse.   I don't think *he knows* my address.

A. The commonest irregular verbs whose present subjunctive has two stems are:

> **aller:** aille, ailles, aille, **allions, alliez,** aillent.
> **boire:** boive, boives, boive, **buvions, buviez,** boivent
> **croire:** croie, croies, croie, **croyions, croyiez,** croient
> *to owe* **devoir:** doive, doives, doive, **devions, deviez,** doivent
> **envoyer:** envoie, envoies, envoie, **envoyions, envoyiez,** envoient
> **prendre:** prenne, prennes, prenne, **prenions, preniez,** prennent
> **recevoir:** reçoive, reçoives, reçoive, **recevions, receviez,** reçoivent
> **tenir:** tienne, tiennes, tienne, **tenions, teniez,** tiennent
> **venir:** vienne, viennes, vienne, **venions, veniez,** viennent
> **voir:** voie, voies, voie, **voyions, voyiez,** voient
> **vouloir:** veuille, veuilles, veuille, **voulions, vouliez,** veuillent

B. The commonest irregular verbs whose present subjunctive has a single irregular stem:

> **faire:** fasse, fasses, fasse, fassions, fassiez, fassent
> **pouvoir:** puisse, etc.
> **savoir:** sache, etc.

C. The commonest irregular verbs whose present subjunctive follows the pattern of regular verbs and can be found from the first person plural of the present indicative (see paragraph 95) are: **connaître, dire, dormir, écrire, lire, mettre, partir, plaindre, sentir, servir, sortir, suivre.**

98. Formation and use of the **passé composé*** of the subjunctive.

A. Formation:

The *passé composé* of the subjunctive is composed of the present subjunctive of the auxiliary verb and the past participle of the verb. Ex.:

> **être:** j'aie été, tu aies été, il ait été, nous ayons été, vous ayez été, ils aient été.
>
> **avoir:** j'aie eu, tu aies eu, etc.
> **donner:** j'aie donné, tu aies donné, etc.
> **arriver:** je sois arrivé(e), tu sois arrivé(e), etc.

---

* As the imperfect and pluperfect subjunctive are purely literary tenses, they will appear only in the verb tables in the Appendix.

If a verb has 2 stems in the indicative, it will have 2 stems in the subjunctive

B. Use:

Generally speaking, the *passé composé* of the subjunctive is used like the present subjunctive except that it expresses actions that have already taken place. Ex.:

> Je regrette que l'accident **ait eu** lieu. I am sorry the accident *took* place.
>
> Nous sommes contents qu'il **soit arrivé.** We are glad he *has arrived.*
>
> Je ne crois pas que vous **ayez lu** ce roman. I don't think you *have read* this novel.

I. *Dites en français chacune des phrases suivantes, en employant* **il faut que:**

1. Je donne mon adresse à la concierge. 2. Vous donnez votre adresse à la concierge. 3. Je finis mon travail à onze heures. 4. Nous finissons notre travail à minuit. 5. Je réponds à la lettre de mon cousin. 6. Vous répondez à la lettre de votre cousin. 7. Je suis toujours à l'heure. 8. Il est toujours à l'heure. 9. Nous sommes toujours à l'heure. 10. Vous vous couchez de bonne heure. 11. Je vais à la bibliothèque. 12. Je vais chercher un journal. 13. Je fais mon travail. 14. Nous faisons notre travail. 15. J'écris à ma mère. 16. Je prends le train à quatre heures. 17. Il part aujourd'hui. 18. Je mets la lettre à la poste. 19. Vous venez me voir. 20. Nous savons l'heure de son arrivée. 21. Vous dites ce que vous pensez. 22. Il ouvre la fenêtre.

II. *Dites en français chacune des phrases suivantes, en employant l'expression indiquée:*

A. Il vaut mieux que:

1. Nous parlons français. 2. Vous finissez votre travail avant de vous coucher. 3. Nous attendons l'arrivée du train. 4. Vous buvez un verre d'eau fraîche. 5. Il prend une tasse de café. 6. Il se sert de mon auto. 7. Vous dormez jusqu'à huit heures. 8. Je suis les conseils de mes parents. 9. Nous sommes toujours à l'heure.

B. Voulez-vous que?:

1. Nous arrosons le jardin. 2. Nous vous envoyons la facture. 3. Nous rentrons de bonne heure. 4. Nous prenons nos billets aujourd'hui. 5. Je viendrai vous voir dimanche. 6. Je tiens la porte ouverte.

C. J'aime mieux que:

1. Vous parlez français. 2. Nous ne parlons pas anglais. 3. Vous choisissez votre écharpe. 4. Vous commencez tout de suite. 5. Vous n'êtes pas en retard.

D. J'ai peur que . . . ne: *I am afraid . . .*

1. Vous serez un peu déçu. **2.** Il n'y aura pas de place dans l'autobus. **3.** Il est malade. **4.** Il fera froid demain. **5.** Il boit trop de café. **6.** Il ne croit pas ce que je lui dis. **7.** Nous avons suivi la mauvaise route. **8.** Nous sommes en retard.

E. Je regrette que:

1. Vous avez mal à la tête. **2.** Votre mère est malade. **3.** Vous n'êtes pas venu me voir. **4.** Il ne m'a pas écrit. **5.** L'accident a eu lieu. **6.** Vous avez répondu à cette lettre. **7.** Il n'a pas pu s'arrêter à temps.

F. Je ne crois pas que:

1. Il peut aller en ville. **2.** Il a lu tous les romans de Balzac. **3.** Il est allé voir le Panthéon. **4.** Il sait le grec *(Greek)*. **5.** Vous pouvez finir aujourd'hui. **6.** Il recevra ma dépêche *(telegram)* avant six heures.

III. *Répétez les phrases suivantes en remplaçant l'infinitif par* **qu'il** *et le subjonctif:*

Ex.:—Je regrette d'être en retard.

—Je regrette qu'il soit en retard.

1. Il faut être toujours à l'heure. **2.** Il faut venir me voir. **3.** Il vaut mieux aller à l'hôpital. **4.** Je veux savoir ce qui se passe. **5.** J'aime mieux boire du lait. **6.** J'ai peur de ne pas avoir le temps. **7.** Je ne crois pas pouvoir finir aujourd'hui. **8.** Je suis content d'être arrivé. **9.** Je suis content d'avoir vu Versailles. **10.** Je ne veux pas faire cela.

IV. *Dites en français:*

1. She's (**C'est**) the prettiest girl I know. **2.** That's (**C'est**) the most beautiful château I have seen. **3.** The most interesting novel I have read is *Les Trois Mousquetaires*. **4.** It's the best novel I have read. **5.** It's the only French novel I know. **6.** That's the only advice I can give you.

V. Révision du dialogue, pp. 212-213.

1. Où John a-t-il vu des champignons? **2.** Est-ce que Roger connaît les champignons? **3.** Est-ce que les mauvais champignons ressemblent aux bons? **4.** Est-ce qu'il vaut mieux laisser ceux dont on n'est pas sûr? **5.** Est-ce qu'on risque de s'empoisonner si on mange des champignons des bois? **6.** Que feriez-vous si vous trouviez des fraises des bois? **7.** Est-ce que vous cueillez des fleurs sauvages *(wild)* quand vous en trouvez dans les bois? **8.** En quelle saison trouve-t-on le plus de fleurs sauvages?

VI. Thème d'imitation:

Mrs. Deschamps said to Roger and John "Do you want to come to the garden with me? I have to pick some green beans. It is already six o'clock. If I do not hurry, dinner will never be ready by [1] seven o'clock and my husband [2] will not be happy." Roger opened the garden gate. "What a [3] fine garden (you have), cousin! How do you have time to take care of it, with all the work of the harvest?" "It's a question [4] of finding time," answered Mrs. Deschamps. "I get up every morning at five o'clock to water my garden before the heat of the day . . . Be careful to close the gate properly, Roger. If you leave it open, the hens get into the garden. Do you see that one over there? She is busy [5] eating my salad greens! Chase her out, [6] will you? I am no longer young and I do not like to chase hens." Roger shooed the hen out. Then he began [7] to pick green beans so that [8] dinner would be ready on time and so that Mr. Deschamps would be happy.

---

[1] i.e. at seven o'clock.   [2] husband, **le mari.**   [3] After **quel!** the noun is used without an article.
[4] **il s'agit de.**   [5] **en train de.**   [6] chase, chase out, shoo out, **chasser.**   [7] **se mettre à.**   [8] **pour que.**

Une partie de pêche

ROGER —[1]Si nous allions à la pêche demain matin?

JOHN —[2]A quoi bon? Nous n'attraperons rien.

ROGER —[3]Je n'y vais pas pour attraper quelque chose.

JOHN —[4]Pourquoi y allez-vous alors?

ROGER —[5]J'y vais parce que j'aime être [6]au bord de l'eau, à l'ombre des grands arbres. [7]Êtes-vous jamais allé à la pêche le matin de bonne heure?

JOHN —[8]Oui, j'y suis allé quelquefois.

ROGER —[9]N'aimez vous pas être en plein air?

JOHN —[10]Si. Mais je ne prends jamais de poissons.

ROGER —[11]Moi non plus, mais cela ne fait rien. [12]Si l'on en prend, tant mieux, [13]si l'on n'en prend pas, tant pis.

JOHN —[14]Où voulez-vous aller?

ROGER —[15]Je connais un endroit sous le vieux pont, [16]de l'autre côté de la rivière, [17]où il y a des poissons gros comme ça!

JOHN —[18]Ceux que vous manquez?

ROGER —[19]Ne vous moquez pas de moi . . .

ROGER —[1]How about going fishing tomorrow morning?

JOHN —[2]What's the use? We won't catch anything.

ROGER —[3]I don't go to catch anything.

JOHN —[4]Why do you go then?

ROGER —[5]I go because I like to be [6]beside the water, in the shade of the tall trees. [7]Have you ever gone fishing in the early morning?

JOHN —[8]Yes, I've gone occasionally.

ROGER —[9]Don't you like to be in the open air?

JOHN —[10]Yes. But I never catch any fish.

ROGER —[11]Neither do I, but that makes no difference. [12]If you catch some, so much the better, [13]if you don't catch any, so much the worse.

JOHN —[14]Where shall we go?

ROGER —[15]I know a place under the old bridge [16]on the other side of the creek, [17]where there are fish as large as that! (gesture)

JOHN —[18]The ones which get away?

ROGER —[19]Do not make fun of me . . .

JOHN —[20]A quelle heure avez-vous l'intention de partir?

JOHN —[20]What time do you plan to leave?

ROGER —[21]De bonne heure. Il faudra que nous nous levions à 4 heures du matin.

ROGER —[21]Early. We'll have to get up at 4:00 A.M.

JOHN —[22]Mais il ne fait pas encore jour à cette heure-là!

JOHN —[22]But it isn't yet daylight at that time!

ROGER —[23]Justement! Nous verrons le soleil se lever sur la rivière. [24]De quoi vous plaignez-vous?

ROGER —[23]Precisely! We shall see the sun rise over the creek. [24]What are you complaining about?

I. SUBSTITUTIONS. *Répétez les phrases suivantes en substituant les mots indiqués:*

1. Je n'y vais pas pour [attraper quelque chose].
   prendre des poissons/ voir le soleil se lever/ manquer des poissons/ manquer les gros poissons

2. J'y vais parce que j'aime être [au bord de l'eau].
   à l'ombre des grands arbres/ en plein air/ à la campagne/ au bord de la rivière

3. Si l'on en [prend], tant mieux, si l'on n'en [prend] pas, tant pis.
   attrape/ voit/ a pour le dîner/ rapporte à la maison

4. Il faudra que [nous nous couchions] de bonne heure.
   nous nous levions/ nous nous habillions/ nous nous mettions en route/ nous nous mettions à pêcher

II. *Répondez en français:*

1. Où Roger propose-t-il d'aller demain matin? 2. Est-ce que John espère attraper quelque chose? 3. Est-ce que Roger va à la pêche pour attraper quelque chose? 4. Alors, pourquoi y va-t-il? 5. Est-ce que John est jamais allé à la pêche le matin de bonne heure? 6. A-t-il l'habitude de prendre beaucoup de poissons? 7. Et Roger? 8. Est-ce que Roger est content quand il prend des poissons? 9. Est-ce qu'il est mécontent (*unhappy*) quand il n'en prend pas? 10. Est-ce qu'il connaît un endroit où il y a de gros poissons? 11. Où se trouve cet endroit? 12. A quelle heure faudra-t-il qu'ils se lèvent? 13. Est-ce qu'il fait déjà jour à cette heure-là? 14. Pourquoi Roger veut-il partir de si bonne heure? 15. Avez-vous de la chance quand vous allez à la pêche? 16. Croyez-vous toujours ce que disent les pêcheurs?

III. *Demandez à quelqu'un:*

I. s'il aime voir le soleil se lever sur la rivière.   **2.** s'il aime voir le soleil se coucher sur le lac.   **3.** s'il a jamais attrapé des poissons.   **4.** s'il connaît un endroit où il y a de gros poissons.   **5.** s'il croit tout ce que disent les pêcheurs. **6.** à quelle heure il part quand il va à la pêche.   **7.** de quoi il se plaint.   **8.** s'il fait jour à quatre heures du matin.   **9.** à quelle heure il fait jour au mois de mai.   **10.** s'il vaut mieux pêcher le matin ou le soir.

IV. *Répétez chacune des phrases suivantes en remplaçant les mots en italiques par l'adverbe* **y:**

Ex.:—Êtes-vous allé *à la pêche?*
   —**Y êtes-vous allé?**

I. Êtes-vous allé *à la pêche* ce matin?   **2.** Allez-vous souvent *à la pêche?* **3.** Êtes-vous jamais allé *à la pêche?*   **4.** N'êtes-vous jamais allé *à la pêche?* **5.** Voulez-vous aller *en ville* cet après-midi?   **6.** Voulez-vous que j'aille *en ville* avec vous?   **7.** Croyez-vous que les Brown soient allés *en Angleterre* cet été? **8.** Sont-ils jamais allés *au bord de la mer?*   **9.** Ne sont-ils pas allés *au bord de la mer?*   **10.** Ne sont-ils jamais allés *au bord de la mer?*   **11.** Allons à *la pêche.*   **12.** N'allez pas *au cinéma* ce soir.

V. *Répondez négativement en employant* **ne ... jamais:**

I. Avez-vous jamais vu Versailles?   **2.** Avez-vous jamais lu *Les Trois Mous-quetaires?*   **3.** Avez-vous jamais été à l'hôpital?   **4.** Avez-vous jamais entendu parler des vitraux de Chartres?   **5.** Êtes-vous jamais allé à Marseille?   **6.** Vous êtes-vous jamais occupé d'un jardin?

VI. *Dites en français:*

I. That makes no difference.   **2.** What's the use?   **3.** It's too bad.   **4.** You are lucky.   **5.** Don't make fun of me.   **6.** The ones that get away (that you miss)?   **7.** A fish *that big* got away (I missed a fish *that big*.)   **8.** I never catch any fish.   **9.** Neither do I.   **10.** Neither does he.   **11.** Neither do they. **12.** Precisely.

VII. Dictée d'après le dialogue, pp. 225-226.

VIII. Conversation.

Vous parlez d'une partie de pêche que vous avez faite.

Arrivée à la gare de Lyon

MARIE —[1]Bonjour, John. Bonjour, Roger. Je suis heureuse de vous revoir.

ROGER —[2]Nous aussi, nous sommes enchantés de vous revoir, Marie.

JOHN —[3]Vous nous avez manqué beaucoup, vous savez.

MARIE —[4]Flatteur!

ROGER —[5]C'est gentil de votre part d'être venue nous attendre à la gare.

MARIE —[6]Je me demande si vous vous rendez compte que j'ai fait pour vous un grand sacrifice. [7]Je devais jouer au tennis ce matin. [8]Mais quand j'ai appris que vous deviez revenir aujourd'hui, j'ai décidé de venir vous attendre ici.

ROGER —[9]Quand avez-vous reçu notre dépêche?

MARIE —[10]Il y a à peu près une heure. [11]Mais vous auriez dû me dire l'heure exacte de votre arrivée.

ROGER —[12]Nous ne la savions pas nous-mêmes. [13]Nous n'étions pas sûrs d'attraper le train de huit heures et demie.

MARIE —[14]John, votre concierge m'a téléphoné qu'un câblogramme pour vous est arrivé ce matin.

MARY —[1]Hello, John. Hello, Roger. I am glad to see you again.

ROGER —[2]We are delighted to see you again too, Mary.

JOHN —[3]We have missed you very much, you know.

MARY —[4]Flatterer!

ROGER —[5]It's nice of you to have come to meet us at the station.

MARY —[6]I wonder if you realize that I made a great sacrifice for you. [7]I was to play tennis this morning. [8]But when I found out that you were to come back today, I decided to come to meet you here.

ROGER —[9]When did you get our wire?

MARY —[10]About an hour ago. [11]But you should have told me the exact time of your arrival.

ROGER —[12]We didn't know it ourselves. [13]We were not sure of catching the eight-thirty train.

MARY —[14]John, your concierge telephoned me that a cable came for you this morning.

Joyeux Noël + Heureuse Nouvelle Année
r Heureux Novel An

John —¹⁵Oh! Je sais ce que c'est. ¹⁶Hélène Frazer doit arriver ces jours-ci. ¹⁷Elle m'indique sans doute le jour de son arrivée.

Marie —¹⁸Tiens, tiens! Qui est cette Hélène?

John —¹⁹C'est une jeune Américaine de mes amies qui est actuellement à Londres. ²⁰Elle m'a demandé de lui servir de guide à Paris.

John —¹⁵Oh! I know what it is. ¹⁶Helen Frazer is to arrive some time soon. ¹⁷She's doubtless telling me the date of her arrival.

Mary —¹⁸Aha! Who is this Helen?

John —¹⁹She is a friend of mine, an American girl who is in London at present. ²⁰She asked me to act as guide for her in Paris.

I. Substitutions. *Répétez les phrases suivantes en substituant les mots indiqués:*

1. C'est gentil de votre part [d'être venu(e) nous attendre à la gare].

   de nous inviter à dîner/ de nous avoir invités à dîner/ de m'avoir envoyé des fleurs/ d'être venu(e) nous chercher

2. C'est gentil de sa part (*of him, of her*) [de venir nous voir].

   de nous prêter son appartement/ de nous offrir ce tableau/ de vous donner sa place/ de nous accompagner

3. [Je sais] ce que c'est.

   Je me demande/ Savez-vous/ Ne savez-vous pas/ Je ne sais pas/ Ils ne savent pas

II. *Répondez en français à chacune des questions suivantes:*

1. A quelle gare John et Roger arrivent-ils?   **2.** Qui est venu les attendre à la gare?   **3.** Comment Marie savait-elle qu'ils allaient arriver ce matin-là?   **4.** Savait-elle l'heure exacte de leur arrivée?   **5.** Quand a-t-elle reçu leur dépêche?   **6.** Pourquoi John et Roger n'ont-ils pas indiqué l'heure exacte de leur arrivée?   **7.** Qu'est-ce que Marie devait faire ce matin-là?   **8.** Qu'est-ce qu'elle a décidé de faire quand elle a reçu leur télégramme?   **9.** Est-ce que John et Roger se rendent compte du sacrifice qu'elle a fait?   **10.** Étaient-ils sûrs d'attraper le train de huit heures et demie?   **11.** Comment Marie a-t-elle appris qu'il y a un câblogramme pour John?   **12.** Quand ce câblogramme est-il arrivé?   **13.** Est-ce que John sait ce que c'est?   **14.** Quand Hélène doit-elle arriver?   **15.** Qu'est-ce que dit Marie quand elle entend parler d'Hélène?   **16.** D'où vient Hélène?   **17.** Qu'est-ce qu'elle a demandé à John?   **18.** Où est-elle actuellement?

III. Exercices d'application.

A. *Répétez en remplaçant la forme négative du passé composé par* **Je devais** (I was supposed to) *et l'infinitif:*

Ex.:—Je n'ai pas joué au tennis ce matin.
— **Je devais jouer au tennis ce matin.**

I. Je ne suis pas allé(e) au bal.   **2.** Je n'ai pas travaillé hier soir.   **3.** Je n'ai pas vu ce film.   **4.** Je ne suis pas rentré(e) à midi.   **5.** Je ne me suis pas levé(e) de bonne heure.   **6.** Je ne suis pas parti(e) hier soir.

B. *Répétez en remplaçant la forme négative du passé composé par* **Vous auriez dû** (You should have) *et l'infinitif:*

Ex.:—Vous ne m'avez pas dit l'heure exacte de votre arrivée.
— **Vous auriez dû me dire l'heure exacte de votre arrivée.**

I. Vous ne m'avez pas donné votre adresse.   **2.** Vous ne m'avez pas téléphoné.
3. Vous ne m'avez pas prévenu.   **4.** Vous n'avez pas écrit à votre mère.   **5.** Vous ne m'avez pas indiqué le jour de votre arrivée.   **6.** Vous n'êtes pas parti hier soir.

IV. *Dites en français:*

A. se rendre compte (que)

I. I wonder if you realize that I made a great sacrifice for you.   **2.** Do you realize that the church is very old?   **3.** Do you realize that the stained-glass windows are very beautiful?   **4.** Do you realize that I am very tired?   **5.** Do you realize that I was supposed to play tennis this morning?   **6.** Do you realize that it is midnight?

B. manquer (à)   *English object becomes Fr. subject*

I. We missed you very much.   **2.** I missed you very much.   **3.** I missed him. (*lit.* He was missing to me).   **4.** I missed her very much.   **5.** I missed John.
6. I missed my mother.

V. Dictée d'après le dialogue, pp. 235-236.

VI. Narration.

Racontez ce que vous avez fait au cours d'un séjour dans une ferme. Dans cette ferme il y avait des vaches (f.) (cows), des porcs (m.) (pigs), des bœufs (m.) (oxen), des chevaux (horses), des moutons (m.) (sheep), des oies (f.) (geese). Dans les champs, dont le sol (soil) était très fertile, il y avait du blé (wheat), du foin (hay), de l'avoine (f.) (oats), des betteraves à sucre (sugar beets), etc.

Irregular Verbs in *-oir*

99. Remarks about verbs in **-oir.**

The characteristics of this group are that they have two stems in the present indicative (**pouvoir: peu-pouv-**), an irregular future (**je pourrai**), and a past participle in **-u** (except **s'asseoir**).

As **pouvoir** corresponds to English *to be able, may, might, can,* and *could,* it is necessary to study with the greatest attention the use and meaning of the different tenses of this verb. **Devoir** is equally complicated and **vouloir** is only slightly less so.

100. Pouvoir, *to be able.*

PRÉSENT: *may, can*

—Est-ce que **je peux** voir la chambre?	*May I* see the room? OR *Can I* see the room?
—Oui, **vous pouvez** la voir.	Yes, *you may* see it.

PASSÉ COMPOSÉ: *could, was able to*

—**Je n'ai pas pu** trouver une place dans l'autobus.	*I couldn't* find a seat in the bus.

FUTUR: *may, can*

—**Vous pourrez** revenir dans huit jours.	*You may* come back in a week.

CONDITIONNEL: *could, might*

—**Vous pourriez** changer de rôle avec un millionnaire.	*You could* change places with a millionaire.

PRÉSENT: Je peux, tu peux, il peut, nous pouvons, vous pouvez, ils peuvent. *I may; I can; I am able.*

IMPARFAIT: Je pouvais, etc. *I was able, I could.* PASSÉ COMPOSÉ: J'ai pu, etc. *I have been able, I could.*

FUTUR: Je pourrai, etc. *I shall be able, I can, I may.* CONDITIONNEL: Je pourrais, etc. *I could, I might.*

101. Vouloir, *to want.*

PRÉSENT: *want*

—**Voulez-vous** essayer ce chapeau?   *Do you want* to try on this hat?
—Roger **veut** aller à la pêche.   Roger *wants* to go fishing.
—John **ne veut pas** y aller.   John *refuses* to go.

IMPARFAIT: *wanted*

—**Je voulais** faire une promenade hier, mais il a plu toute la journée.   *I wanted to* (but didn't necessarily act on my desire) take a walk, but it rained all day.

PASSÉ COMPOSÉ: *wanted, decided*

—**J'ai voulu** profiter du beau temps.   *I decided* to take advantage of the fine weather (and did so).

—Marie **n'a pas voulu** sortir.   Marie *refused* to go out.

CONDITIONNEL: *would like, want*

—**Je voudrais** un billet aller et retour pour Reims.   *I would like* a round-trip ticket to Rheims.
—**Je voudrais** partir le plus tôt possible.   *I would like* to leave as soon as possible.

PRÉSENT: Je veux, tu veux, il veut, nous voulons, vous voulez, ils veulent. *I want; I will (i.e. I insist).*

IMPARFAIT: Je voulais, etc. *I wanted, I intended.* PASSÉ COMPOSÉ: J'ai voulu, etc. *I wanted, I decided.*

FUTUR: Je voudrai, etc. *I shall want,* etc. CONDITIONNEL: Je voudrais, etc. *I would like, I want.*

102. Expressions with **vouloir.**

A. vouloir bien *to be willing:*

—**Je veux bien.**   *I am willing.*
—**Voulez-vous bien** payer la caissière?   *Will you please* pay the cashier?
—**Voulez-vous bien** monter?   *Will you please* go up?
—**Je voudrais bien** avoir ma montre le plus tôt possible.   *I would like* to have my watch as soon as possible.

B. vouloir dire, *to mean:*

—Que **voulez-vous dire?**   What *do you mean?*
—Que **veut dire** «déçu»?   What *does* "déçu" *mean?*

103. Devoir.*

A. Present tense:

The present tense is used to express:

(1) probability:

—**Il doit être** chez lui en ce moment.   *He must be (probably is)* at home now.

—**Il doit y avoir** un train vers 8 heures.   *There must be* a train around 8:00.

(2) an action which one expects to fulfill:

—Quand est-ce que **vous devez être** de retour?   When *are you supposed to be* back?

—**Je dois être** de retour demain.   *I am supposed to be* back tomorrow.

(3) necessity:

—**Vous devez changer** de train à Épernay.   *You have to change* trains at Epernay.

B. Imperfect tense:

The imperfect is most commonly used to express an action which was expected to take place but which did not necessarily take place:

—**Je devais** jouer au tennis ce matin, mais j'ai décidé de venir vous attendre à la gare.   *I was to (was supposed to)* play tennis this morning but I decided to come to meet you at the station.

C. *Passé composé:*

The *passé composé* is most commonly used to express probability (past):

—Où est votre livre?   Where is your book?

—Je ne sais pas. **J'ai dû** le laisser dans l'autobus.   I don't know. *I must have* left it in the bus.

D. Conditional:

The conditional is used to express the speaker's judgment as to the desirability or propriety of an action (present or future):

—**Vous devriez** travailler davantage.   *You should* work harder.

—**Vous ne devriez pas** faire cela.   *You ought not* to do that.

---

* **Devoir** is also used as a transitive verb meaning "to owe". Ex.: Vous me devez mille francs.

E. Conditional perfect:

The conditional perfect is used to express the speaker's judgment (disapproval) of:

(1) something which has been done:

—**Vous n'auriez pas dû** faire cela.   *You ought not to have* done that.

(2) something which has not been done:

   Vous auriez dû me dire l'heure   *You should have* told me the exact
   exacte de votre arrivée.   time of your arrival.

PRÉSENT: Je dois, tu dois, il doit, nous devons, vous devez, ils doivent.

IMPARFAIT: Je devais, etc. PASSÉ COMPOSÉ: J'ai dû, etc. FUTUR: Je devrai, etc.

104. Falloir, *to have to, must,* etc.: impersonal.

—**Il faut que** j'aille en ville faire   *I must* go downtown to do some
   des courses.   errands.

—**Il a fallu que** nous attendions la   *We had to* wait for the connection.
   correspondance.

—**Il faudra que** nous nous levions   *We shall have to* get up early.
   de bonne heure.

—**Il ne faut pas** faire cela.   *You must not* do that.

—**Il faut** une heure pour aller de   *It takes* an hour to go from Paris
   Paris à Versailles.   to Versailles.

PRÉSENT: Il faut *(must)*. IMPARFAIT: Il fallait *(had to, should have)*. PASSÉ COMPOSÉ: Il a fallu *(had to)*. FUTUR: Il faudra *(will have to)*.

105. Valoir* mieux, *to be better:* impersonal.

—**Il vaut mieux** laisser ceux dont   *It is better* to leave the ones about
   vous n'êtes pas sûr.   which you are not sure.

—**Il vaudrait mieux** faire venir le   *It would be better* to send for the
   médecin.   doctor.

PRÉSENT: Il vaut mieux *(It is better)*. IMPARFAIT: Il valait mieux. PASSÉ COMPOSÉ: Il a mieux valu. FUTUR: Il vaudra mieux.

106. Pleuvoir, *to rain:* impersonal.

—**S'il pleut,** je prendrai un taxi.   *If it rains,* I'll take a taxi.

—**Il pleuvait** quand j'ai quitté la   *It was raining* when I left the house.
   maison.

—**Il a plu** cette nuit.   *It rained* last night.

---

* **Valoir** is also used as a transitive verb meaning "to be worth". Ex.: Cette montre vaut mille francs.

PRÉSENT: Il pleut. *It rains, it is raining.* IMPARFAIT: Il pleuvait. *It was rain-ing.* PASSÉ COMPOSÉ: Il a plu. *It rained.* FUTUR: Il pleuvra. *It will rain.*

107. Voir, *to see.*

—Vous voyez ce village là-bas?	*You see* that village over yonder?
—Je vois des champignons au bord de la route.	*I see* some mushrooms on the side of the road.
—Il y a longtemps que je ne vous ai pas vu.	*I haven't seen* you a long time.
—Je vois venir le facteur.	*I see* the postman *coming.*

PRÉSENT: Je vois, tu vois, il voit, nous voyons, vous voyez, ils voient. *I see,* etc.
IMPARFAIT: Je voyais, etc. *I saw,* etc. PASSÉ COMPOSÉ: J'ai vu, etc. *I saw, I have seen,* etc. FUTUR: Je verrai, etc. *I shall see, I'll see,* etc.

108. Savoir, *to know, to know how.*

—Savez-vous quand vivait Jeanne d'Arc?	*Do you know* when Joan of Arc lived?
—Je sais qu'elle est morte en 1431.	*I know* that she died in 1431.
—Je vous le dirai aussitôt que je le saurai.	I shall tell you as soon as *I find out.*
—Vous ne sauriez pas dépenser votre argent.	*You wouldn't know how* to spend your money.
—Savez-vous conduire une auto?	*Do you know how* to drive a car?

PRÉSENT: Je sais, tu sais, il sait, nous savons, vous savez, ils savent. *I know,* etc.

IMPARFAIT: Je savais, etc. *I knew,* etc. PASSÉ COMPOSÉ J'ai su, etc. *I knew, I found out,* etc. FUTUR: Je saurai, etc. *I shall know how, I shall find out.*

I. EXERCICES D'APPLICATION.

A. *Répondez affirmativement:*

1. Pouvez-vous? 2. Pourriez-vous? 3. Avez-vous pu? 4. Voudriez-vous? 5. A-t-il voulu? 6. Devez-vous? 7. Deviez-vous? 8. Devriez-vous? 9. Au-riez-vous dû? 10. Voyez-vous? 11. Savez-vous? 12. Saviez-vous?

B. *Remplacez le présent par le conditionnel:*

1. Je peux. 2. Nous pouvons. 3. Je veux. 4. Nous voulons. 5. Je dois. 6. Nous devons. 7. Il vaut mieux. 8. Il faut. 9. Vous voulez. 10. Vous voyez. 11. Vous ne savez pas. 12. Vous pouvez.

C. *Remplacez l'imparfait par le passé composé:*

1. Je voulais. 2. Il voulait bien. 3. Je ne pouvais pas. 4. Il fallait. 5. Il pleuvait. 6. Je savais. 7. Il savait. 8. Il voyait.

II. EMPLOI DU VERB **devoir.**

A. *Répétez en remplaçant le présent et* **sans doute** *par le présent de* **devoir** *et l'infinitif.*

Ex.:—Il est sans doute chez lui en ce moment.
   —**Il doit être chez lui en ce moment.**

1. Il arrive sans doute ce soir. 2. Le bureau de poste est sans doute ouvert en ce moment. 3. Nous avons sans doute le temps d'aller au buffet. 4. Ils sont sans doute en vacances. 5. Il y a sans doute des champignons dans le bois. 6. Il y a sans doute un train vers 8 heures.

B. *Répétez en remplaçant le passé composé et* **sans doute** *par le passé composé de* **devoir** *et l'infinitif.*

Ex.:—J'ai sans doute laissé mon livre dans l'autobus.
   —**J'ai dû laisser mon livre dans l'autobus.**

1. Elle a sans doute attrapé un rhume. 2. Nous avons sans doute pris la mauvaise route. 3. J'ai sans doute laissé mon portefeuille *(wallet)* à la maison. 4. Ils ont sans doute manqué leur train. 5. Il a sans doute plu cette nuit. 6. Elle a sans doute reçu* un chèque de son père. 7. Vous avez sans doute entendu parler de lui.

C. *Répétez en remplaçant* **Je crois** *et le présent de* **devoir** *par le conditionnel de* **devoir.**

Ex.:—Je crois que vous devez répondre à cette lettre.
   —**Vous devriez répondre à cette lettre.**

1. Je crois que vous devez travailler davantage. 2. Je crois que vous ne devez pas sortir ce soir. 3. Je crois qu'elle doit s'occuper davantage de son jardin. 4. Je crois que nous devons partir de bonne heure. 5. Je crois que nous devons nous mettre en route tout de suite. 6. Je crois qu'elle doit partir plus tôt.

D. *Répétez en remplaçant le conditionnel de* **devoir** *et* **aujourd'hui** *par le conditionnel passé de* **devoir** *et* **hier.**

Ex.:—Vous devriez répondre à cette lettre aujourd'hui.
   —**Vous auriez dû répondre à cette lettre hier.**

---

* For the forms of **recevoir** *(to receive)* see p. 359.

I. Vous devriez travailler aujourd'hui. **2.** Vous ne devriez pas sortir aujour-d'hui. **3.** Il devrait rester à la maison. **4.** Nous devrions partir aujourd'hui. **5.** Ils devraient se mettre en route aujourd'hui. **6.** Vous ne devriez pas boire tant de café aujourd'hui.

III. *Répondez en français:*

I. Savez-vous conduire une auto? **2.** Savez-vous jouer au tennis? **3.** Si vous étiez riche, sauriez-vous dépenser votre argent? **4.** Avez-vous lu le journal d'aujourd'hui? **5.** Quand est-ce que vous verrez Paris? **6.** Quand est-ce que vous reverrez vos parents? **7.** Est-ce que vous recevez souvent des nouvelles de vos amis? **8.** Est-ce que vous avez jamais reçu des cartes-postales de Paris? **9.** Est-ce que vous devez aller à la campagne pour le week-end? **10.** Qu'est-ce que Marie devait faire le jour où elle a reçu la dépêche de Roger? **11.** Comment a-t-elle appris que ses amis devaient revenir ce jour-là? **12.** Qu'est-ce que Roger aurait dû lui dire dans sa dépêche?

IV. *Dites en français:*

I. Can I see the room? **2.** May I see the room? **3.** Could you tell me the time? **4.** I could send it to you. **5.** I could not *(passé composé)* find it. **6.** I'd like to see you. **7.** I'd like to talk to you. **8.** I want (would like) some handkerchiefs. **9.** I am willing. **10.** I won't! **11.** Let's see. **12.** I'll see. **13.** I should work harder. **14.** You should go to spend a few days in the country. **15.** I must have left my book in the bus. **16.** They ought to have sent the telegram sooner.

V. Révision du dialogue, pp. 221-222.

I. Qu'est-ce que le curé était en train de faire quand Roger a sonné? **2.** De quoi John s'excuse-t-il? **3.** Pourquoi John a-t-il envie de visiter l'église? **4.** Qu'est-ce que le curé venait de faire? **5.** Pourquoi le curé craint-il qu'ils ne soient un peu déçus? **6.** A quelle époque l'église a-t-elle été cons-truite? **7.** Est-ce que Roger a entendu parler des vitraux de l'église? **8.** Est-ce que la plupart d'entre eux sont anciens? **9.** Combien y a-t-il de vitraux vraiment anciens? **10.** Pourquoi l'intérieur des églises romanes est-il d'ordinaire sombre?

VI. Thème d'imitation:

"I must tell you what happened to me last Saturday, John. That day I went fishing near the old bridge on the other side of the creek. You know the place, don't you? . . . Suddenly, I felt a fish on the end of my line [1]. I pulled it in to the bank [2] and I was going to take him out [3] of the water, when a fish *that big,* which was following mine, opened its enormous mouth [4], took my fish, and went away with it [5]." "You ought to put that in the paper," said John. "You caught the big fish, didn't you?" "No," Roger replied, "he broke my line." "That's really too bad," said John. "It's the sad story of the big fish that gets away [6]." "Don't make fun of me," answered Roger. "Big fish are much harder to catch than little ones, because they are larger. People [7] do not believe fishermen. They say: "Oh! that's a fish story! [8] Believe, me, those who say that do not know what they are saying."

---

[1] on the end of my line, **au bout de ma ligne.** [2] Use **amener au bord.** [3] take out, **sortir** (**Sortir** is used either as a transitive or intransitive verb). [4] its enormous mouth, **une bouche énorme.** [5] Omit *it.* Never mind if your sentence ends with **avec.** In such phrases, **avec** is regarded by grammarians as an adverb. [6] *lit.:* that one misses. [7] people, **les gens.** [8] *lit.:* a story of fishermen.

A la terrasse d'un café

JOHN —¹Asseyons-nous à la terrasse de ce café. ²Nous pourrons voir passer les gens.

HÉLÈNE —³Quel est ce monument là-bas, au bout de la rue?

JOHN —⁴Vous devriez le reconnaître. C'est le Panthéon.

HÉLÈNE —⁵Oh! je m'en souviens. ⁶C'est l'endroit où l'on enterre les grands hommes, n'est-ce pas?

JOHN —⁷Oui, quelques-uns d'entre eux. ⁸On trouve là notamment les tombeaux de Voltaire et de Victor Hugo.

HÉLÈNE —⁹Pourquoi appelle - t - on cette partie de Paris le Quartier Latin?

JOHN —¹⁰Parce que c'est le quartier de l'université, et que le latin était autrefois la langue de l'université.

HÉLÈNE —¹¹Où est donc la Sorbonne?

JOHN —¹²A deux pas d'ici. ¹³Nous irons tout à l'heure, si vous voulez.

HÉLÈNE —¹⁴Pourquoi appelle - t - on l'université de Paris la Sorbonne? ¹⁵J'ai lu l'explication quelque part, mais je ne me la rappelle pas.

JOHN —¹Let's sit down in this sidewalk café. ²We can see the people go by.

HELEN —³What is that monument over there at the end of the street?

JOHN —⁴You ought to recognize it. It's the Pantheon.

HELEN —⁵Oh! I remember (it). ⁶It's the place where they bury the great men, isn't it?

JOHN —⁷Yes, some of them. ⁸In particular, there are the tombs of Voltaire and Victor Hugo.

HELEN —⁹Why do they call this part of Paris the Latin Quarter?

JOHN —¹⁰Because it is the quarter of the University, and that Latin was formerly the language of the University.

HELEN —¹¹Well, where is the Sorbonne?

JOHN —¹²Just a few steps from here. ¹³We'll go there after a while if you wish.

HELEN —¹⁴Why do they call the University of Paris the Sorbonne? ¹⁵I read the explanation somewhere, but I don't remember it.

JOHN —[16]C'est qu'au temps de Saint Louis,* un certain Robert de Sorbon a fondé un collège pour les étudiants de théologie. [17]Ce collège, appelé la Sorbonne, est devenu la Faculté des Lettres et la Faculté des Sciences.

HÉLÈNE —[18]Tous ces étudiants ont l'air sérieux et préoccupé . . .

JOHN —[19]Il y a de quoi. [20]Ils sont en train de passer leurs examens et les examens, en France, ne sont pas faciles.

JOHN —[16]It's that in the time of Saint Louis, a man named Robert de Sorbon founded a college for theology students. [17]This college, called the Sorbonne, has become the Faculty of Letters and the Faculty of Sciences.

HELEN —[18]All these students look serious and worried . . .

JOHN —[19]There is reason for it. [20]They are busy taking their examinations, and in France examinations are not easy.

I. SUBSTITUTIONS. *Répétez les phrases en substituant les mots indiqués:*

1. Nous pourrons [voir passer les gens].
   voir venir l'avion/ voir arriver le train/ regarder passer les gens/ entendre parler le Président

2. La Sorbonne a été fondée [au temps de Saint Louis].
   au treizième siècle/ au cours du treizième siècle/ au moment des croisades/ en 1253.

II. *Répondez en français à chacune des questions suivantes:*

1. Où sont assis John et Hélène? 2. Dans quel quartier se trouve la terrasse où ils sont assis? 3. Quel monument voit-on de la terrasse de ce café? 4. Qu'est-ce que c'est que le Panthéon? 5. Connaissez-vous des hommes célèbres qui sont enterrés au Panthéon? 6. Pourquoi appelle-t-on cette partie-là de Paris le Quartier Latin? 7. Saviez-vous qu'autrefois tous les étudiants de l'université parlaient latin? 8. En quelle langue les professeurs faisaient-ils leurs conférences *(lectures)*? 9. Qui a fondé la Sorbonne? 10. Quand vivait Robert de Sorbon? 11. Qu'est-ce que c'était autrefois que la Sorbonne? 12. Qu'est-ce que c'est maintenant que la Sorbonne? 13. Où Hélène a-t-elle lu l'explication du nom «Sorbonne»? 14. Est-ce qu'elle se rappelle cette explication? 15. Pourquoi les étudiants ont-ils l'air sérieux et préoccupé? 16. Est-ce qu'il y a un Panthéon en Amérique? 17. Où est-ce qu'on enterre

---

* Saint Louis (Louis IX), roi de France de 1226 à 1270. Il a fondé un hôpital pour trois cents chevaliers devenus aveugles au cours des croisades, d'où le nom de Quinze-Vingts donné à cet hôpital, qui existe toujours à Paris. On lui doit aussi la construction de la Sainte-Chapelle, un des plus élégants monuments de l'art gothique. La ville de Saint-Louis aux États-Unis, a été nommée d'après lui.

les grands hommes aux États-Unis? **18.** Où est enterré George Washington? **19.** Où est enterré Victor Hugo? **20.** Croyez-vous que ce soit une bonne idée d'enterrer les grands hommes dans un monument comme le Panthéon? **21.** Vous souvenez-vous de la date de la mort de Louis XIV?

III. *Demandez à quelqu'un:*

1. ce que c'est que ce monument là-bas au bout de la rue. **2.** quelle langue on parlait autrefois dans les universités. **3.** ce qu'est devenu le collège fondé par Robert de Sorbon. **4.** dans quel siècle la Sorbonne a été fondée. **5.** s'il savait pourquoi on appelle l'Université de Paris «la Sorbonne.»

IV. Exercices d'application.

A. *Répétez les phrases suivantes, en remplaçant* **être** *par* **avoir l'air:**

Ex.:—Il est préoccupé.
    —Il a l'air préoccupé.

1. Vous êtes préoccupé. **2.** Elle est fatiguée.* **3.** Ils sont heureux. **4.** Tous ces étudiants sont sérieux et préoccupés. **5.** Cette jeune fille est triste. **6.** Les Brown sont très gentils.

B. *Répétez les phrases suivantes, en remplaçant* **avoir** *par* **avoir l'air d'avoir:**

Ex.:—Il a faim.
    —Il a l'air d'avoir faim.

1. Il a froid. **2.** Vous avez chaud. **3.** John a soif. **4.** Il a mal à la tête. **5.** Il a un rhume. **6.** Les Brown ont beaucoup d'argent.

V. *Dites en français:*

A. il y a de quoi

1. There is good reason. **2.** There is reason to be worried. **3.** There is no reason to be worried. **4.** There is no reason to thank me. **5.** You are welcome (**Il n'y a pas de quoi**).

B. au temps de . . . , au . . . , en . . . ,

1. In the time of Louis XIV. **2.** In the seventeenth century. **3.** In 1657. **4.** In the time of François Premier. **5.** In the sixteenth century. **6.** In 1525. **7.** In the time of Saint Louis. **8.** In the thirteenth century. **9.** In 1253.

---

* Either: Elle a l'air **fatigué** or **fatiguée** may be used.

C. se rappeler, se souvenir de

(1) *Employez* **se rappeler** *dans chacune des phrases suivantes:*
I. I read the explanation somewhere, but I don't remember it.   **2.** I saw that explanation somewhere, but I don't remember it.   **3.** I used to know his address, but I don't remember it.   **4.** Do you remember it?   **5.** I do not remember it any longer.

(2) *Employez* **se souvenir de** *dans chacune des phrases précédentes:*

VI. Dictée d'après le dialogue, pp. 238-239.

Le long des quais

HÉLÈNE —[1]Que regardent ces gens-là, le long de la Seine?

JOHN —[2]Ils examinent les étalages des bouquinistes.

HÉLÈNE —[3]Que vendent ces bouquinistes?

JOHN —[4]Toute sorte de choses. [5]Les uns vendent de vieilles estampes, d'autres des timbres-poste, d'autres de vieilles pièces de monnaie, mais la plupart font le commerce des livres d'occasion.

HÉLÈNE —[6]Mon frère m'a demandé de lui envoyer des timbres. [7]Traversons la rue. [8]Nous pourrons jeter un coup d'œil sur les étalages.

JOHN —[9]Savez-vous quels timbres votre frère veut se procurer?

HÉLÈNE —[10]Oui, j'ai dans mon sac une liste qu'il a dressée.

HÉLÈNE (au bouquiniste) —[11]Avez-vous les timbres indiqués sur cette liste?

LE BOUQUINISTE —[12]Voyons un peu . . . Martinique, 1886; Second Empire, 1853; Sénégal, 1903; etc. [13]Oui, mademoiselle. Je crois les avoir tous, sauf les timbres du Second Empire, série 1853. [14]Il ne m'en reste aucun.

HELEN —[1]What are those people looking at along the Seine?

JOHN —[2]They are examining the displays of the old-book dealers.

HELEN —[3]What do those old-book dealers sell?

JOHN —[4]All sorts of things. [5]Some sell old prints, others postage stamps, others old coins, but most of them deal in second-hand books.

HELEN —[6]My brother asked me to send him some stamps. [7]Let's cross the street. [8]We can take a look at the displays.

JOHN —[9]Do you know what stamps your brother wants to get?

HELEN —[10]Yes. I have in my bag a list which he drew up.

HELEN —[11]Have you the stamps noted on this list?

LE BOUQUINISTE —[12]Let's take a look . . . Martinique, 1886; Second Empire, 1853; Senegal, 1903; etc. [13]Yes, Mademoiselle, I think I have them all, except the 1853 series of the Second Empire. [14]I haven't a one of them left.

HÉLÈNE —[15]Tant pis.

LE BOUQUINISTE —[16]Voulez-vous consulter cet album? [17]Vous y trouverez peut-être certains timbres qui vous intéressent.

HÉLÈNE. —[18]Je ne connais pas grand-chose aux timbres-poste.

JOHN —[19]Vous n'avez qu'à choisir les plus jolis!

HÉLÈNE —[20]Oh non! Il y a quelque temps, j'ai envoyé plusieurs timbres à mon frère. [21]J'avais choisi les plus jolis. [22] Mais il avait déjà la plupart d'entre eux, et il m'a dit que mon choix ne valait* rien.

HELEN —[15]Too bad.

LE BOUQUINISTE —[16]Do you want to look at this album? [17]You will perhaps find in it certain stamps which interest you.

HELEN —[18]I don't know much about postage stamps.

JOHN —[19]All you have to do is to choose the prettiest (ones).

HELEN —[20]Oh no! Some time ago, I sent several stamps to my brother. [21]I had chosen the prettiest. [22]But he already had most of them and he told me my selection was no good (was worth nothing).

I. SUBSTITUTIONS. *Répétez les phrases suivantes, en substituant les mots indiqués:*

1. Nous pourrons jeter un coup d'œil [sur les étalages].
   sur les journaux/ sur les revues (*magazines*) / sur les estampes/ sur les livres d'occasion

2. Il ne m'en reste [aucun].
   pas/ pas beaucoup/ plus/ plus du tout/ guère/ qu'un/ que deux

3. Vous n'avez qu'à [choisir les plus jolis].
   traverser la rue/ consulter cet album/ téléphoner à vos parents/ appeler un taxi/ suivre cette rue

II. *Répondez en français à chacune des questions suivantes:*

1. Où sont les étalages des bouquinistes? 2. Que vendent les bouquinistes? 3. Où iriez-vous si vous vouliez acheter des livres d'occasion? 4. Qui est-ce qui a demandé à Hélène de lui envoyer des timbres? 5. Pourquoi Hélène propose-t-elle de traverser la rue? 6. Comment sait-elle quels timbres son frère veut se procurer? 7. Où a-t-elle mis la liste qu'il lui a envoyée? 8. Connaissez-vous quelques-uns des timbres qu'il voudrait se procurer? 9. Est-ce que le bouquiniste a tous les timbres qu'Hélène voudrait acheter? 10. Est-ce qu'il lui reste des timbres du Second Empire, série 1853? 11. Qu'est-ce que

---

* From **valoir**, used here as transitive verb meaning "to be worth."

c'est qu'un album? **12.** Pourquoi Hélène ne sait-elle pas quels timbres choisir dans l'album? **13.** Quels timbres John lui dit-il de choisir? **14.** Pourquoi ne suit-elle pas son conseil? **15.** Est-ce que vous collectionnez les timbres-poste? **16.** Est-ce que vous collectionnez autre chose? **17.** Est-ce que tous les vieux timbres valent quelque chose?

III. *Demandez à quelqu'un:*

1. ce que vendent la plupart des bouquinistes. **2.** où l'on vend des timbres-poste. **3.** s'il connaît des gens qui font collection de vieilles estampes. **4.** s'il reste au marchand des timbres du Second Empire. **5.** si Hélène sait quels timbres son frère veut se procurer. **6.** si Hélène s'est déjà procuré des timbres pour son frère. **7.** ce qu'on met dans un album. **8.** ce qu'Hélène a envoyé à son frère il y a quelque temps. **9.** s'il a déjà entendu parler des bouquinistes de Paris.

IV. Exercices d'application.

A. *Répétez les phrases suivantes en employant l'infinitif:*

Ex.:—Je crois que je les ai tous.
  —**Je crois les avoir tous.**

1. Je crois que je les connais tous. **2.** Je crois que je sais son adresse. **3.** Je crois que je peux venir vous chercher. **4.** Je ne crois pas que je puisse partir aujourd'hui. **5.** Je ne crois pas que je sache son adresse. **6.** Je ne crois pas que j'irai en ville cet après-midi.

B. *Répétez en remplaçant* **rien** *par* **pas . . . grand-chose**:

Ex.:—Il ne m'a rien dit.
  —**Il ne m'a pas dit grand-chose.**

1. Il ne me reste rien. **2.** Je n'ai rien trouvé. **3.** Il n'a rien à faire. **4.** Je ne connais rien aux timbres. **5.** Nous ne connaissons rien à l'art gothique. **6.** Nous n'avons rien fait.

C. *Employez* **la plupart** *dans chacune des expressions suivantes:*

Ex.:—Beaucoup de bouquinistes.
  —**La plupart des bouquinistes.**

1. Beaucoup de gens. **2.** Beaucoup d'entre eux. **3.** Beaucoup d'églises gothiques. **4.** Beaucoup d'entre elles. **5.** Quelques-uns des timbres. **6.** Quelques-uns d'entre eux. **7.** Plusieurs des estampes. **8.** Plusieurs d'entre elles.

V. *Dites en français:*

A. valoir

1. My choice was no good.   **2.** Most stamps are worthless.   **3.** Most old books are worthless.   **4.** This old book is worthless.   **5.** This old book is not worth much.   **6.** That old book is worth 500 francs.   **7.** It is better not to buy it.

B. il (me) reste

1. I haven't a one of them left.   **2.** I have several (of them) left.   **3.** I have one left.   **4.** I have two Martinique stamps left.   **5.** Have you any Second Empire stamps left?   **6.** How many of them do you have left?

C. le long de

1. Along the quais.   **2.** Along the Seine.   **3.** Along the street.   **4.** Along the roads.   **5.** Along the Grands Boulevards.

VI. Dictée d'après le dialogue, pp. 249-250.

VII. Conversation.

Vous voyez à la devanture *(shop window)* d'un magasin où l'on vend des objets d'art, une série de gravures *(engravings)* représentant des coins du vieux Paris. Vous demandez des renseignements sur l'auteur de ces gravures, la date, etc., et vous discutez du prix avec le marchand.

Indefinite Adjectives and Pronouns;
Use of Articles and Prepositions Summarized

109. Indefinite adjectives and pronouns.

The word "indefinite" when applied to adjectives and pronouns means that the adjective or pronoun concerned does not define or determine the person or thing to which it refers. The corresponding indefinite adjectives and pronouns in English are: *each, every, several, all, no, such, same,* etc.

110. Commonest indefinite adjectives and pronouns which have the same form.

—Avez-vous **tous** ces timbres? *(adj.)*	Have you got *all* these stamps?
—Oui, je crois les avoir presque **tous.** *(pron.)*	Yes, I think I have almost *all* of them.
—J'ai envoyé **plusieurs** timbres à mon frère. *(adj.)*	I sent *several* stamps to my brother.
—Je lui en ai envoyé **plusieurs.** *(pron.)*	I sent him *several*.
—Il ne me reste **aucun** timbre du Second Empire. *(adj.)*	I haven't *a single* Second Empire stamp left.
—Il ne m'en reste **aucun.** *(pron.)*	I haven't *a single one* left.
—Avez-vous d'**autres** journaux? *(adj.)*	Have you *other* papers?
—Non, je n'en ai pas d'**autres.** *(pron.)*	No, I have no *others*.
—C'est la **même** écharpe que celle de mon amie. *(adj.)*	It is the *same* scarf as my friend's.
—C'est la **même** que la sienne. *(pron.)*	It is the *same* as hers.

257

The forms of these adjectives and pronouns are:

> tout, toute, tous,* toutes: *all, every*
> plusieurs: *several*
> aucun, aucune: ADJ. *no, not a;* PRON. *none, not a one*
> autre, autres: ADJ. *other;* PRON. *another one, others*
> même, mêmes: ADJ. *same;* PRON. *same one, same ones*

When **aucun** is used with a verb, the verb must be preceded by **ne**. Note, however, that **pas** is not used with **aucun**.

111. Commonest indefinite adjective and pronouns whose corresponding forms are different.

—Il pleut **chaque** fois que je vais à la pêche. *(adj.)*	It rains *each* time I go fishing.
—**Chacun** de ces timbres vaut dix francs. *(pron.)*	*Each* of these stamps is worth ten francs.
—J'espère que vous allez passer **quelques** jours avec nous *(adj.)*	I hope you are going to spend *a few* days with us.
—Voilà des champignons. Si nous en rapportions **quelques-uns** à la maison? *(pron.)*	There are some mushrooms. What if we took home *a few* of them?
—Avez-vous **quelque** chose de meilleur? *(adj.)*	Have you *some*thing better?
—Est-ce que **quelqu'un** est venu? *(pron.)*	Did *anyone* come?

(1) The corresponding forms of these adjectives and pronouns are:

> ADJECTIVE: chaque, *each*
> PRONOUN: chacun, chacune, *each, each one*
>
> ADJECTIVE: quelque, quelques, *some, a few*
> PRONOUN: quelqu'un, quelques-uns, quelques-unes, *somebody, someone; some, a few*

(2) They of course agree in gender and number with the noun to which they refer; but **quelqu'un** in the singular is usually thought of as neither masculine nor feminine.

---

* When **tous** is used as a pronoun, the final **s** is pronounced.

(3) When **quelque chose** or **rien** is followed by an adjective, the adjective is preceded by **de** and has the masculine form. Ex.: **quelque chose de bon,** *something good;* **rien d'intéressant,** *nothing interesting.*

112. Indefinite pronouns which have no corresponding indefinite adjective.

—**On** trouve des bouquinistes le long de la Seine.
You find secondhand book dealers along the Seine.

—Est-ce que John est venu me voir?
Did John come to see me?

—Non, **personne n'**est venu.
No, *no one* came.

—Je **n'**ai vu **personne.**
I have not seen *anyone.*

—Êtes-vous occupé ce soir?
Are you busy this evening?

—Non, je **n'**ai **rien** à faire.
No, I have *nothing* to do.

—**Rien** du tout.
Nothing at all.

—Je **n'**ai trouvé **rien** d'intéressant dans ce journal.
I didn't find *anything* interesting in that paper.

—**Les uns** vendent de vieilles estampes, d'autres des timbres-poste et d'autres de vieilles pièces de monnaie.
Some sell old prints, others postage stamps, and others old coins.

—Avez-vous ces deux timbres?
Have you these two stamps?

—Non, je n'ai **ni l'un ni l'autre.**
No, I have *neither.*

(1) The forms of these pronouns are:

l'un, l'une, les uns, les unes, *the one, the ones*
on, *one, you, we, they, people, someone, anybody*
personne, *no one, nobody*
rien, *nothing*

Note that **l'un, l'une,** etc. are always used in opposition to **l'autre,** etc. For **celui qui,** *the one who,* see p. 194.

(2) When **rien** or **personne** is used with a verb, the verb is preceded by **ne. Pas** is not used with **rien** or **personne.**

113. Use of definite article in French contrary to English usage.

A. With nouns which indicate profession or official function:

—**Le docteur** Lambert n'a pas pu s'arrêter à temps.
Doctor Lambert couldn't stop in time.

—Bonjour, **monsieur le curé.**
Good morning, *sir (to a priest).*

B. With parts of the body, when the person concerned is clearly identified by the context:

—Elle a **les yeux bleus.**	She has *blue eyes.*
—Je commence à avoir mal **aux jambes.**	*My legs* are beginning to hurt.
—Le chapeau que vous avez **sur la tête.**	The hat you have *on your head.*
—Je **me** suis lavé **les mains.**	I washed *my hands.*

C. With the names of the days of the week, to indicate habitual occurrence:

—Je vais à la pêche le samedi.	I *usually* go fishing *on Saturday.*
BUT: Je vais à la pêche samedi.	I am going fishing Saturday (i.e. next Saturday).

D. In the expressions **le matin, l'après-midi, le soir, la nuit,** meaning *in the:*

—Je me lève **le** matin de bonne heure.	I get up early *in the* morning.
—Je vais au laboratoire **l'après-midi.**	I go to the laboratory *in the* afternoon.

E. With expressions of measure in specifying the price:

—Les œufs coûtent trois francs **la douzaine.**	Eggs cost three francs *a dozen.*
—Le lait coûte soixante centimes **le litre.**	Milk costs sixty centimes *a liter.*
—Ce tabac coûte un franc cinquante **le paquet.**	This tobacco costs one franc fifty *a package.*
—Cette étoffe coûte cinq francs **le mètre.**	This material costs five francs *per meter.*
—Le beurre coûte quatre francs cinquante **la livre.**	Butter costs four francs fifty *per pound.*

Note that you say **deux francs pièce,** *two francs apiece* or *each;* and that with the expressions of time, you use **par** when the price is being specified. Ex.: — **Quel est le loyer?** — **Cent cinquante francs par mois.**

F. With nouns taken in a general sense:

L'homme est mortel.	Man is mortal.
Vive **la** liberté!	Hurrah for liberty!
La vie est chère.	Living is high.
La viande est chère.	Meat is expensive.
Je n'aime pas **le** café.	I don't like coffee.

114. Omission of indefinite article in French contrary to English usage.

A. When a noun, especially a proper name, is followed by a second noun which is added to explain the first one, the second noun ordinarily has no article:

—Vous êtes bien M. John Hughes, ingénieur-chimiste?

Are you (indeed) Mr. John Hughes, *a* chemical engineer?

—C'est le Louvre, ancien palais royal.

It is the Louvre, *a* former royal palace.

B. When a noun (or personal pronoun) referring to a person is followed by the verb **être** and a noun indicating profession or nationality, the latter is used without an article:

—Il est Américain, mais sa femme est Française.

He is *an American,* but his wife is French.

—M. Brown est banquier.

Mr. Brown is *a* banker.

Do not forget that a noun following **c'est** always has a modifier. Ex.: **C'est un banquier. C'est un** Américain. **C'est ma** bicyclette.

115. Use of prepositions and definite articles with geographical names.

A. With names of continents and countries which are feminine:

—J'irais **en** Suisse et **en** Belgique.

I would go *to* Switzerland and *to* Belgium.

—J'irais **en** Amérique et **en** Afrique.

I would go *to* America and *to* Africa.

—Les olives viennent **de** France, **d'**Espagne et **d'**Afrique.

Olives come *from* France, Spain and Africa.

With the name of a continent or a country which is feminine, you use **en** without an article to express *to* or *in,* and **de** without an article to express *from:* **en** France, **de** France. If the geographical name has a modifier (l'Amérique **du Sud**), careful speakers often use **dans** WITH THE ARTICLE to express *to* or *in* and **de** WITH THE ARTICLE to express *from* but **en** and **de** (without the article) are also used:

—Ces oranges viennent **de l'**Afrique du Nord *or* **d'**Afrique du Nord.

These oranges come *from* North Africa.

—Un de mes oncles habite **dans l'**Amérique du Sud *or* **en** Amérique du Sud.

One of my uncles lives *in* South America.

B. With names of countries which are masculine:

—Il demeure **au** Canada.	He lives *in* Canada.
—Il vient **du** Mexique.	He comes *from* Mexico.
—J'irais **aux** États-Unis voir les gratte-ciel.	I would go *to the* United States to see the skyscrapers.

You always use the article in combination with **à** or **de** with the names of countries which are masculine.

C. With names of cities:

—Il demeure à Clermont-Ferrand.	He lives *in* Clermont-Ferrand.
—Je suis né à Rouen.	I was born *in* Rouen.
—Mon père vient de Paris.	My father comes *from* Paris.
—Êtes-vous allé à Versailles?	Have you been *to* Versailles?

You never use an article with the name of a city except with **Le Havre** and a few other cities in which the article is a part of the name. Ex.:
— Connaissez-vous **Le Havre?** Êtes-vous allé à **La Nouvelle-Orléans?**

I. Substitutions. *Répétez les phrases suivantes, en substituant les mots indiqués:*

1. Je ne vais pas souvent en ville [le samedi], mais j'irai [samedi (prochain)].
   l'après-midi . . . cet après-midi/ le matin . . . ce matin/ le soir . . . ce soir/ le vendredi . . . vendredi

2. Je ne vais pas souvent en ville [le samedi], mais j'y suis allé [samedi dernier].
   le matin . . . hier matin/ l'après-midi . . . hier après-midi/ le soir . . . hier soir/ le vendredi soir . . . vendredi soir

3. Elle doit passer quelques jours à [Londres].
   Paris/ Rome/ (Le) Havre/ (Le) Mans

4. Elle est actuellement [en Angleterre (au Canada)].
   (la) Normandie/ (l') Italie/ (l') Europe/ (la) Suisse/ (le) Canada/ (les) États-Unis/ (le) Mexique/ (le) Japon

5. Elle revient ces jours-ci d'[Angleterre].
   Bretagne/ Italie/ Allemagne/ Rome/ Paris/ Amsterdam/ (le) Canada/ (les) États-Unis/ (le) Mexique/ (Le) Havre

II. Exercices d'application.

A. *Répondez affirmativement à chacune des questions suivantes, en employant le pronom indéfini convenable:*

Ex.:—Est-ce qu'il reste au marchand des timbres du Second Empire?
   —**Oui, il lui en reste quelques-uns.**

I. Est-ce qu'Hélène a envoyé plusieurs timbres à son frère? **2.** Est-ce que le marchand a tous les timbres qu'Hélène voudrait acheter? **3.** A-t-il d'autres timbres? **4.** Avez-vous trouvé toutes les estampes que vous vouliez acheter? **5.** Avez-vous vu quelques-unes des estampes de Daumier? **6.** Est-ce qu'il reste au marchand des timbres de la Martinique?

B. *Répondez négativement à chacune des questions suivantes, en employant le pronom indéfini convenable:*

Ex.:—Avez-vous acheté quelque chose au Bon Marché?
   —**Non, je n'ai rien acheté au Bon Marché.**

I. Est-ce qu'il vous reste des timbres du Second Empire? **2.** Est-ce que le marchand a tous les timbres qu'Hélène voudrait acheter? **3.** Est-ce qu'il a d'autres timbres à vendre? **4.** Avez-vous vu quelqu'un devant la maison? **5.** Est-ce que quelqu'un a téléphoné? **6.** Avez-vous quelque chose à faire ce soir? **7.** Avez-vous trouvé quelque chose d'intéressant?

C. *Répondez négativement, en employant* **ni l'un ni l'autre:**

I. Avez-vous ces deux timbres? **2.** Voulez-vous du thé ou du café? **3.** Avez-vous acheté du pain ou de la viande? **4.** Avez-vous un frère ou une sœur? **5.** Avez-vous choisi un fruit ou une pâtisserie *(French pastry)*?

III. *Dites en français:*

A. tout
I. All the stamps. **2.** Every day. **3.** Every week. **4.** Every Thursday.

B. fois
I. Sometimes. **2.** Each time. **3.** Several times. **4.** Once. **5.** Twice.

C. quelque chose, rien
I. Something. **2.** Something good. **3.** Something better. **4.** Something else (quelque chose d'autre, autre chose). **5.** Nothing. **6.** Nothing interesting. **7.** Nothing else. **8.** Nothing important.

D. le, la
I. Eggs cost 3 francs a dozen. **2.** Sugar costs 25 centimes per pound. **3.** Potatoes cost 25 centimes per kilo. **4.** Milk costs 50 centimes a litre. **5.** Good wine costs 10 francs per bottle. **6.** This material costs 5 francs per meter.

IV. Révision des dialogues, pp. 225-226 et pp. 235-236.

I. Pourquoi Madame Deschamps veut-elle aller au jardin? **2.** Qu'est-ce que Roger offre de faire? **3.** Pourquoi Madame Deschamps lui dit-elle de bien

fermer la porte?   4. Qu'est-ce qu'elle fera des fleurs qu'elle va cueillir?   5.
Pourquoi ne s'occupe-t-elle pas davantage de son jardin?   6. Pourquoi n'y
a-t-il pas de maïs dans son jardin?   7. Est-ce qu'il a beaucoup plu cette
année-là?   8. Pourquoi ne veut-elle pas que John arrose le jardin tout de
suite?   9. A quel moment de la journée vaut-il mieux arroser un jardin?
10. Quand Roger veut-il aller à la pêche?   11. Pourquoi John ne veut-il pas
y aller?   12. Est-ce que Roger prend d'habitude beaucoup de poissons?   13.
Où se trouve l'endroit où il y a de gros poissons?   14. Pourquoi John se
moque-t-il de Roger?   15. A quelle heure faudra-t-il qu'ils se lèvent?   16.
Aimez-vous mieux la pêche ou la chasse *(hunting)*?   17. En quelle saison la
chasse est-elle ouverte?

V. Thème d'imitation:

Along the Seine, especially near the Ile de la Cité, are [1] the displays of
the old-book dealers. Those dealers in old books are ordinarily elderly
people. Each of them has one or two boxes [2] which he opens in the morning
and closes in the evening. Nearly all of them buy and sell secondhand books.
The Parisians, in particular those who like old books, enjoy spending [3] an
afternoon looking at the displays. A hundred years ago, you could get rare
books for almost nothing. But things have changed a great deal since. Rare
books are becoming rarer and rarer [4] and the dealers in old books know the
value of what they sell. However, you still find things worth buying [5] in
their displays, which are [6] a part of the Parisian landscape like Notre-
Dame or the Eiffel Tower.

---

[1] Use **se trouver.** [2] box, **la boîte.** [3] enjoy spending, **passent volontiers.** [4] rarer and rarer,
de plus en plus rares. [5] worth buying, **intéressant.** [6] to be a part of, **faire partie de.**

Aux Tuileries

JOHN —[1]Maintenant entrons dans le Jardin des Tuileries.* [2]Que pensez-vous de ce coin de Paris?

HÉLÈNE —[3]Je suis étonnée de trouver tant d'espace au cœur même de la ville. [4]Je n'avais pas la moindre idée de l'étendue de la Place de la Concorde.** [5]Mais, dites-moi, quel est ce grand bâtiment devant nous?

JOHN —[6]C'est le Louvre, ancien palais royal.***

HÉLÈNE —[7]Est-ce que c'est là qu'est le musée du Louvre?

JOHN —[8]Oui; mais le musée n'occupe qu'une partie de l'édifice. [9]Le reste est occupé par des bureaux des ministères.

HÉLÈNE —[10]Et voilà l'Arc de Triomphe.† [11]D'après les photographies que j'ai vues, je le croyais plus grand.

JOHN —[12]C'est l'Arc de Triomphe du Carrousel que vous voyez là. [13]L'autre, celui de l'Étoile,† est

JOHN —[1]Now, let's go into the Tuileries Gardens. [2]What do you think of this section of Paris?

HELEN —[3]I am astonished to find so much (open) space in the very heart of the city. [4]I didn't have the slightest idea of the size of the Place de la Concorde. [5]But, tell me, what is this great building in front of us?

JOHN —[6]It's the Louvre, a former royal palace.

HELEN —[7]Is that where the Louvre Museum is?

JOHN —[8]Yes; but the museum occupies only a part of the building. [9]The rest is occupied by offices of ministries.

HELEN —[10]And there is the Arch of Triumph. [11]From the photographs I have seen, I thought it was larger.

JOHN —[12]That's the Arch of Triumph of the Carrousel that you see there. [13]The other one, that

* Jardin d'un ancien palais habité par Napoléon et détruit par le feu en 1871.
** La vaste Place de la Concorde, dont le centre est occupé par un obélisque, est entourée de statues monumentales symbolisant les principales villes de France.
*** La construction du Louvre actuel, commencée au XVIème siècle, n'a été terminée que vers la fin XIXème siècle.
† Arc de Triomphe, dédié aux armées de Napoléon Ier. Il doit son nom aux douze avenues qui rayonnent autour de la place, formant une étoile dont il occupe le centre.

au bout de l'avenue des Champs-Élysées.† [14]Si vous vous retournez, vous pourrez le voir là-bas ...

HÉLÈNE —[15]Regardez cette petite fille qui pleure, John. [16]Le vent a emmené son bateau à voile au milieu du bassin. [17]Est-ce que vous pouvez l'aider?

JOHN —[18]J'aurais beau faire. [19]Le bateau est trop loin pour que je puisse l'atteindre. [20]Le vent finira sans doute par le ramener au bord.

HÉLÈNE —[21]J'ai envie de cueillir une de ces fleurs comme souvenir de notre promenade.

JOHN —[22]Gardez-vous-en bien. [23]Si un agent de police vous voyait, il pourrait bien vous faire un procès-verbal!

of the Étoile, is at the end of the Champs-Élysées. [14]If you turn around, you can see it over there ...

HELEN —[15] Look at this little girl who is crying, John. [16]The wind has carried her sailboat to the middle of the pool. [17]Can you help her?

JOHN —[18]Whatever I would do would be in vain. [19]The boat is too far for me to be able to reach it. [20]The wind will finally bring it back to the edge, no doubt.

HELEN —[21]I wish I could pick one of those flowers as a souvenir of our walk.

JOHN —[22]Don't do anything of the kind. [23]If a policeman should see you, he might very well give you a ticket!

I. SUBSTITUTIONS. *Répétez les phrases suivantes, en substituant les mots indiqués:*

1. [Je n'avais pas la moindre idée] de l'étendue de la Place de la Concorde.
   Je n'avais pas idée/ Je n'avais aucune idée/ Je ne me rendais pas compte/ Je ne me rendais pas du tout compte

2. [D'après les photos que j'ai vues], je le croyais plus grand.
   D'après les cartes-postales que j'ai vues/ D'après ce que j'ai lu/ D'après ce qu'on m'a dit/ D'après ce que j'ai entendu dire

3. Le vent a emmené son bateau à voile [au milieu du bassin].
   au beau milieu du bassin/ de l'autre côté du bassin/ loin du bord/ près de l'autre bord

4. Le vent finira sans doute par le ramener [au bord].
   près du bord/ de notre côté/ près de nous/ de ce côté

II. *Répétez en employant* **finir par** *avec l'infinitif:*

Ex.:—J'irai en Europe.

    —**Je finirai par aller en Europe.**

1. Je trouverai mon porte-monnaie. **2.** Elle ira en France. **3.** Vos yeux s'habitueront à l'obscurité. **4.** Il a répondu à ma lettre. **5.** J'ai trouvé le

† Belle avenue qui va de la Place de la Concorde à la Place de l'Étoile.

j'ai fini d'étudier
↳ finished studying

j'ai fini par étudier
↳ ended up studying
(means to end up doing something
we hadn't planned on)

(a fini par venir)

timbre que je cherchais. **6.** La jeune fille que j'attendais est venue. **7.** J'ai trouvé un taxi. **8.** L'autobus est arrivé. **9.** Je me suis souvenu de son adresse.

III. *Répondez en français à chacune des questions suivantes:*

1. Où John et Hélène entrent-ils? **2.** Qu'est-ce que c'est que le Jardin des Tuileries? **3.** De quoi Hélène est-elle étonnée? **4.** Est-ce qu'elle croyait que la Place de la Concorde était aussi vaste? **5.** Quel est le grand bâtiment qu'elle voit devant elle? **6.** Qu'est-ce que c'est que le Louvre? **7.** Où se trouve le musée du Louvre? **8.** Est-ce que le musée occupe tout l'édifice? **9.** Qu'est-ce qui occupe le reste de l'édifice? **10.** Combien y a-t-il d'arcs de triomphe à Paris? **11.** Qui les a fait construire? (Napoléon.) **12.** Où se trouve l'Arc de Triomphe de l'Étoile? **13.** Pourquoi la petite fille pleure-t-elle? **14.** Qu'est-ce qu'Hélène demande à John de faire? **15.** Qu'est-ce que répond John? **16.** Pourquoi ne peut-il pas atteindre le petit bateau? **17.** Comment le bateau reviendra-t-il au bord? **18.** Pourquoi Hélène a-t-elle envie de cueillir une fleur? **19.** Pourquoi John lui dit-il de ne pas le faire?

IV. *Répondez en français à chacune des questions suivantes:*

1. Avez-vous jamais entendu parler du Louvre? **2.** Avez-vous jamais entendu parler du Jardin des Tuileries? **3.** Avez-vous vu des photographies de l'Arc de Triomphe de l'Étoile? **4.** Connaissez-vous quelques tableaux *(pictures)* qui sont au Louvre? **5.** Y a-t-il des arcs de triomphe en Amérique? **6.** Est-ce que vous avez jamais cueilli des fleurs dans un jardin public? **7.** Est-ce qu'un agent de police vous a jamais fait un procès-verbal? **8.** Êtes-vous jamais allé dans un bateau à voile?

V. *Dites en français:*

A. avoir beau faire, avoir beau essayer

1. Whatever I would do would be in vain. **2.** Whatever we would do would be in vain. **3.** Whatever you would do would be in vain. **4.** Whatever I did was in vain. **5.** Whatever we did was in vain. **6.** Whatever you did was in vain. **7.** Whatever I do will be in vain. **8.** Whatever we do will be in vain. **9.** Whatever you do will be in vain. **10.** It will be no use for me to try. **11.** It will be no use for him to try. **12.** It will be no use for her to try.

B. Emploi ou omission de l'article.

1. What is that large building in front of us? It's the Louvre, a former royal palace. **2.** What is that book you have in your hand (**à la main**)? It's *Le Père Goriot,* a novel of Balzac. **3.** Who's the gentleman with whom you were talking? It's Mr. Lejeune, a former cabinet minister (**ministre**). **4.** It's Mr. Bedel, a former professor at the Sorbonne.

VI. Dictée d'après le dialogue, pp. 253-254.

VII. Conversation.

"Have you been to the Louvre?"

"Yes. I have just visited a part of the museum."

"Which part?"

"The picture galleries (**Les galeries de peinture**)."

"Did you see the Mona Lisa (**la Joconde**)?"

"Yes. I looked for it everywhere. But it was no use looking. I couldn't find it. I finally asked the guard (**le gardien**) . . ."

"What do you think of it?"

"It's doubtless a very fine picture. But I don't know much about pictures."

A Notre-Dame

JOHN —[1]Nous sommes maintenant dans l'Île de la Cité.*

HÉLÈNE—[2]Est-ce qu'on n'appelle pas aussi cette île l'Île-de-France?

JOHN —[3]J'ai peur que vous ne confondiez vos îles, Hélène. [4]L'Île-de-France est la région autour de Paris. [5]L'Île de la Cité est une île au milieu de la Seine.

HÉLÈNE—[6]Je reconnais, à droite, les tours de Notre-Dame. [7]Si nous visitions Notre-Dame?

JOHN —[8]Mais oui. Traversons la place et entrons dans la cathédrale.

HÉLÈNE —[9]Attendez que je prenne une photo.

JOHN —[1]We are now on the Island of the City.

HELEN —[2]Don't they also call this island the Island of France?

JOHN —[3]I am afraid you are confusing your islands, Helen. [4]The Île-de-France is the region around Paris. [5]The Île de la Cité is an island in the middle of the Seine.

HELEN —[6]I recognize on the right the towers of Notre-Dame. [7]Suppose we visit Notre-Dame.

JOHN —[8]Certainly. Let's cross the square and go into the cathedral.

HELEN —[9]Wait for me to take a picture.

Dans Notre-Dame

HÉLÈNE —[10]Comme l'intérieur est vaste et silencieux! [11]On ose à peine parler, même à voix basse. [12]Je voudrais bien assister à une messe à Notre-Dame.

JOHN —[13]Si vous voulez, nous reviendrons dimanche prochain. [14]Vous pourrez entendre les grandes orgues.

HÉLÈNE —[15]Est-ce qu'on peut monter en †haut des tours?

In Notre-Dame

HELEN —[10]How large and silent the interior is! [11]You hardly dare speak, even in a low voice. [12]I would like to go to a service at Notre-Dame.

JOHN —[13]If you want to, we will come back next Sunday. [14]You will be able to hear the great organ.

HELEN —[15]Can you go up to the top of the towers?

---

* Le mot **cité** est employé à Paris, comme à Londres, pour désigner la partie la plus ancienne et la plus centrale de la ville.

† Aspirate **h.**

JOHN —[16]Rien de plus facile. [17]Cet escalier en colimaçon nous y conduira. [18]En arrivant en haut, vous pourrez prendre d'autres photos.

JOHN —[16]Nothing is easier. [17]This spiral staircase will take us up there. [18]When we get up to the top, you can take some more pictures.

En haut d'une des tours de Notre-Dame

At the top of one of the towers of Notre-Dame

HÉLÈNE —[19]Je suis essoufflée . . . [20]Mais quel panorama! On voit Paris tout entier.

HELEN —[19]I am out of breath . . . [20]But what a panorama! You can see all Paris.

JOHN —[21]Devant vous, vous avez la Sainte-Chapelle, le Louvre et les Champs-Élysées; sur la rive gauche, le Quartier Latin et la Sorbonne; et sur la rive droite, les grands boulevards et Montmartre.

JOHN —[21]In front of you, you have the Sainte-Chapelle, the Louvre and the Champs-Élysées; on the left bank, the Latin Quarter and the Sorbonne; and on the right bank, the great boulevards and Montmarte.

HÉLÈNE —[22]J'ai hâte de visiter les quartiers de Paris que je ne connais pas encore.

HELEN —[22]I am very eager to visit the parts of Paris with which I am not yet acquainted.

I. SUBSTITUTIONS. *Répétez les phrases suivantes, en substituant les mots indiqués:*

1. Je voudrais bien assister [à une messe à Notre-Dame].
   à une représentation à la Comédie-Française/ à un concert à la Salle Pleyel/ à une conférence à la Sorbonne/ aux courses à Chantilly

2. Ils ont assisté [à une représentation à l'Opéra].
   au match de football/ au mariage de Louise/ à la cérémonie/ à la messe de minuit

(Note that **assister à** means *to go to* or *to attend* a specific event or performance but that you don't use **assister à** with places, schools, etc.)

3. Je voudrais bien aller [à Notre-Dame].
   à la Comédie-Française/ à l'Opéra/ à la Sorbonne/ au cinéma

4. Mon oncle est allé [à l'école en France].
   au Lycée Henri Quatre/ à l'université de Rennes/ à la Sorbonne/ au Collège de France

II. *Répondez en français à chacune des questions suivantes:*

1. Où sont John et Hélène maintenant? **2.** Qu'est-ce que c'est que l'Île-de-France? **3.** Où se trouve l'Île de la Cité? **4.** Que confond Hélène? **5.** Qu'est-ce qu'elle voit à droite? **6.** Qu'est-ce qu'elle propose de faire? **7.** Qu'est-ce qu'Hélène veut faire avant d'entrer dans la cathédrale? **8.** Comment trouve-t-elle l'intérieur de la cathédrale? **9.** A quoi Hélène voudrait-elle assister? **10.** Quand John propose-t-il de revenir? **11.** Pourquoi propose-t-il de revenir ce jour-là? **12.** Est-ce qu'on peut monter en haut des tours de Notre-Dame? **13.** Comment y monte-t-on? **14.** Qu'est-ce qu'Hélène pourra faire en arrivant en haut? **15.** Comment se sent-elle en arrivant en haut? **16.** Qu'est-ce qu'on voit du haut des tours de Notre-Dame? **17.** Qu'est-ce qu'on voit sur la rive gauche? **18.** Qu'est-ce qu'on voit sur la rive droite? **19.** Qu'est-ce qu'Hélène a hâte de visiter? **20.** Quels quartiers de Paris a-t-elle déjà visités?

III. *Demandez à quelqu'un:*

1. s'il voudrait assister à une messe à Notre-Dame. **2.** s'il voudrait voir la Place de la Concorde. **3.** s'il voudrait voir l'Arc de Triomphe. **4.** s'il voudrait visiter le Musée du Louvre. **5.** s'il sait conduire une auto. **6.** s'il aime bien conduire une auto. **7.** s'il voudrait conduire une auto à Paris.

IV. EXERCICES D'APPLICATION.

A. *Répétez les phrases suivantes, en remplaçant* **craindre (que) (de)** *par*

(1) **avoir peur que:**

1. Je crains que vous ne confondiez vos îles. **2.** Je crains que vous ne soyez en retard. **3.** Je crains que vous ne soyez pas à l'heure. **4.** Nous craignons que vous ne soyez un peu déçus. **5.** Nous craignons que vous ne soyez pas contents.

(2) **avoir peur de:**

1. Je crains la pluie. **2.** Il craint le froid. **3.** Elle ne craint rien. **4.** Qu'est-ce que vous craignez? (De quoi . . .) **5.** Je crains d'être en retard. **6.** Je crains de ne pas arriver à l'heure. **7.** Vous craignez tout.

B. *Répétez les phrases suivantes, en employant* **attendez que** *et le subjonctif:*

Ex.:—Je vais prendre une photo.

—**Attendez que je prenne une photo.**

attendez que

1. Je vais acheter des cigarettes.   **2.** Je vais jeter un coup d'œil sur le journal.
3. Je vais finir cette histoire.   **4.** Je vais boire mon café.   **5.** Je vais finir mon
travail.   **6.** Je vais ouvrir la fenêtre.

C. *Répétez en remplaçant* **avoir envie** (to feel like) *par* **avoir hâte** (to
be eager to): *(Jean hardly wait) (avoir hâte is a stronger verb of feeling
than avoir envie)*

1. J'ai envie de visiter les quartiers de Paris que je ne connais pas encore.
2. J'ai envie d'aller à la campagne.   **3.** J'ai envie de partir en vacances.   **4.**
Nous avons envie de déjeuner.   **5.** Nous avons envie de voir la Sainte-
Chapelle.   **6.** Nous avons envie d'assister à une représentation à la Comédie-
Française.

J'ai envie de visiter la cathédral (I feel like visiting)

V. *Dites en français:*   *J'ai hâte de vister -- (I am eager to visit)*

1. There are many factories around Paris.   **2.** There used to be a château in
the middle of the Garden of the Tuileries.   **3.** There is an Egyptian Obelisk
(**un obélisque égyptien**) in the middle of the Place de la Concorde.   **4.** Have
you ever been up (**monter**) to the top of the towers of Notre-Dame?   **5.** I
would like to go up to the top of the Eiffel Tower.   **6.** From the top of the
towers of Notre-Dame, you can see all of Paris.

VI. Dictée d'après le dialogue, pp. 265-266.

VII. Conversation.

Vous montez avec un ami (une amie) en haut d'un gratte-ciel de New-York.
Vous prenez l'ascenseur (*elevator*). Arrivé(e) en haut, vous attirez l'attention
de votre ami(e) sur le port, les grands bateaux, le musée Métropolitain, le
Parc Central, etc.

Huitième Lecture Illustrée, p. 55, *De retour à Paris.*

Use of Infinitives and Present Participles

116. Verbs which may take infinitives.

A. Verbs and verbal expressions followed by the preposition **de** which take infinitives:

—**Permettez-moi de** vous présenter mon ami John Hughes.	*Allow me to* introduce my friend John Hughes.
—**Vous serez obligé de** passer la nuit à Épernay.	*You will be obliged to* spend the night at Épernay.
—**Je regrette d'être** en retard.	*I am sorry to* be late.
—**Nous avons décidé de** profiter du beau temps.	*We decided to* take advantage of the fine weather.
—**J'ai demandé** à mon père **de** m'envoyer un chèque.	*I asked* my father *to* send me a check.
—**Il m'a dit de** ne pas l'attendre.	*He told* me *not to* wait for him.

(1) The commonest verbs followed by **de** which may take infinitives are: **décider de, se dépêcher de, dire de, essayer de, être obligé de, permettre de, refuser de,** etc., and such expressions as **avoir besoin de, avoir l'habitude de, être en train de,** etc.

(2) You have seen that some of these verbs may govern a subordinate clause. Ex.: —**Il m'a dit qu'il reviendrait. Je regrette qu'il soit venu.**

B. Verbs followed by the preposition **à** which take infinitives:

—**Il a commencé à** pleuvoir.	*It began to* rain.
—**Avez-vous appris à** parler français?	*Have you learned to* speak French?
—**Nous avons continué à** marcher.	*We kept on* walking.
—**Vous n'avez qu'à** traverser la rue.	*You have only to cross* the street.

The commonest verbs followed by the preposition **à** which take infinitives are: **aider à,** *to help;* **apprendre à,** *to learn;* **commencer à; réussir à,** *to succeed;* **inviter à,** to invite; **se mettre à,** *to begin;* **avoir à,** *to have to,* etc.

C. Verbs which may take infinitives without a preposition:

—**Je vais faire** des courses cet après-midi.	*I am going to do* some errands this afternoon.
—**Pouvez-vous** me **donner** votre adresse?	*Can you give* me your address?
—**Je dois partir** par le train de sept heures.	*I am to leave* by the seven o'clock train.
—**Voulez-vous faire** une promenade avec moi?	*Do you want to take* a walk with me?
—**Faut-il changer** de train en route?	*Must one change* trains on the way?

The commonest verbs which may take an infinitive without a preposition are: **aller; devoir; faire; falloir (il faut,** etc.**); oser,** *to dare;* **pouvoir; savoir; venir; vouloir.**

117. Forms of the verb used after prepositions.

A. Present infinitive after prepositions **par, pour, sans,** and expressions such as **avant de:**

—Il m'a envoyé une dépêche **avant de partir.**	He sent me a wire *before leaving.*
—Il est parti **sans dire** au revoir.	He left *without saying* good-bye.
—Le vent finira **par le ramener** au bord.	The wind will finally *bring* it *back* to the edge.
—Nous ne l'attendrons pas **pour déjeuner.**	We will not wait lunch for him (We will not wait for him *to have lunch*).
—**Pour arriver** à l'heure, j'ai quitté la maison à sept heures.	*So as to arrive* on time, I left home at seven o'clock.
—Il faut manger **pour vivre** . . .	You must eat *to live* . . .

Pour is generally used with an infinitive to express the idea *so as to* or *in order to;* but when it is used after **aller** with an infinitive, it has the meaning *for the express purpose of.* Ex.:

—Je vais en ville **faire** des courses.	I am going downtown *to do* some errands.
—Je vais en ville **pour faire** des courses.	I am going downtown *for the express purpose of doing* some errands.

B. Perfect infinitive after **après:**

—**Après avoir visité** Versailles, nous sommes allés à Fontainebleau.

After visiting (having visited) Versailles, we went to Fontainebleau.

—**Après être allé** en Normandie, John est allé en Bretagne.

After going (having gone) to Normandy, John went to Brittany.

C. Present participle after **en:**

—**En partant** à cinq heures, vous serez chez vous à sept heures.

By leaving at five o'clock, you will be home at seven.

—**En arrivant** en haut, vous pourrez prendre d'autres photos.

On arriving at the top, you can take some more pictures.

The present participle of verbs may be found by adding the ending **-ant** to the stem of the first person plural of the present indicative, except for the verbs **avoir, être,** and **savoir** whose present participles are, respectively, **ayant, étant,** and **sachant.**

I. SUBSTITUTIONS. *Répétez les phrases suivantes en substituant les mots indiqués:*

1. Il [a décidé] de partir ce soir.
a refusé/ a été obligé/ a regretté/ m'a demandé/ m'a dit

2. Elle [a besoin] de faire des courses.
a l'habitude/ est en train/ est contente/ a envie

3. Nous avons [commencé] à parler français.
continué/ réussi/ appris

II. EXERCICES D'APPLICATION.

A. *Répétez les phrases suivantes, en remplaçant le passé composé, et le mot* **puis** *par le passé de l'infinitif:*

Ex.:—Nous avons visité Versailles, puis nous sommes allés à Fontainebleau.
   —**Après avoir visité Versailles, nous sommes allés à Fontainebleau.**

1. Elle a visité l'Angleterre, puis elle est allée en France. **2.** Elle est allée à Rouen, puis elle est allée à Paris. **3.** Elle a déjeuné, puis elle a jeté un coup d'œil sur le journal. **4.** Il a regardé les étalages des bouquinistes, puis il a acheté des timbres. **5.** Il s'est couché, puis il s'est endormi tout de suite.

B. *Employez le participe présent dans chacune des phrases suivantes:*

Ex.:—Si vous partez à cinq heures, vous serez chez vous à sept heures.
   —**En partant à cinq heures, vous serez chez vous à sept heures.**

I. Si nous partons maintenant, nous arriverons à l'heure.   **2.** Quand nous irons au Panthéon, nous verrons le Quartier latin.   **3.** Quand je regardais les étalages des bouquinistes, j'ai trouvé une belle estampe.   **4.** Quand nous irons à l'Île de la Cité, nous traverserons le Pont-Neuf.*   **5.** Quand nous traverserons le Pont-Neuf, nous jetterons un coup d'œil sur la Seine.   **6.** Quand vous arriverez en haut de la tour, vous pourrez prendre d'autres photos.

III. *Répondez en français:*

I. Vous êtes-vous dépêché(e) de déjeuner ce matin?   **2.** Avez-vous regretté de ne pas vous être levé(e) plus tôt?   **3.** Avez-vous l'habitude de vous dépêcher le matin?   **4.** Qu'est-ce que vous avez à faire cet après-midi?   **5.** Prenez-vous l'autobus pour rentrer chez vous?   **6.** Est-ce que vous attendez qu'il fasse chaud pour aller nager *(to swim)?*   **7.** Avez-vous l'intention d'aller en France un de ces jours?   **8.** Est-ce qu'Hélène a réussi à trouver les timbres qu'elle cherchait?   **9.** Seriez-vous content(e) de passer quelques jours dans une ferme?   **10.** Quels quartiers de Paris Hélène a-t-elle vus avant de visiter Notre-Dame?

IV. *Dites en français:*

(*a*) I. I am glad to know it.   **2.** I am glad you know it.   **3.** I am sorry to leave.   **4.** I am sorry he has left.   **5.** Helen wants to go to the Louvre.   **6.** She wants me to go with her.   **7.** I shall wait for you until noon.   **8.** I shall wait for you until you come.   **9.** I am sending him a wire to announce my arrival.   **10.** I am sending him a wire so he will know I am coming.

(*b*) I. He finally sent me his address.   **2.** We finally decided to stay at home.   **3.** I finally found the Mona Lisa (**la Joconde**).   **4.** He left without leaving his address.   **5.** That goes without saying.   **6.** "One must eat to live, not (**et non pas**) live to eat."   **7.** He told me to wait for him.   **8.** He told me not to wait for him.   **9.** He told me to hurry.   **10.** He told me not to hurry.   **11.** He told me not to bother.   **12.** I took a taxi so as not to be late.   **13.** He asked me not to leave before seeing him.   **14.** I told you not to pick those mushrooms.

---

* Le Pont-Neuf *(The New Bridge)* est le plus célèbre des ponts de Paris. Bien qu'il ait été construit au commencement du dix-septième siècle, on l'appelle toujours le Pont-Neuf.

V. RÉVISION DES DIALOGUES, pp. 238-239 ET pp. 249-250.

1. Qui est venu attendre John et Roger à la gare? **2.** Est-ce que Marie leur a manqué? **3.** Qu'est-ce que Marie devait faire le jour de leur arrivée? **4.** Comment a-t-elle appris qu'ils devaient arriver? **5.** Qu'est-ce qu'ils auraient dû lui dire dans leur dépêche? **6.** Pourquoi ne lui ont-ils pas dit l'heure exacte de leur arrivée? **7.** Est-ce qu'ils se rendent compte du sacrifice qu'elle a fait? **8.** Comment John a-t-il appris qu'Hélène Frazer devait arriver ces jours-ci? **9.** Dans quel quartier se trouve le Panthéon? **10.** Connaissez-vous quelques-uns des livres de Victor Hugo? **11.** Est-ce que la Sorbonne est loin du Panthéon? **12.** A quelle époque Saint Louis était-il roi de France? **13.** Quand Robert de Sorbon a-t-il fondé son collège? **14.** Est-ce que vous vous rappelez le nom de l'hôpital fondé à Paris par Saint Louis? **15.** De quel style d'architecture est la Sainte-Chapelle? **16.** Connaissez-vous d'autres monuments en France qui datent de l'époque gothique?

ILLUSTRATED READINGS

En France

Le Sacré-Coeur de Montmartre

La Place de la Concorde

L'Île de la Cité

Arrivée à Paris

(Conversations 1–5)

John Hughes, jeune ingénieur-chimiste américain,
arrive à Paris pour travailler
dans les laboratoires d'une compagnie américaine
établie en France. Il va en taxi
au numéro quinze, avenue de l'Observatoire,
fait la connaissance de la concierge
et s'installe dans sa nouvelle chambre.
Il passe les premiers jours à voir
les endroits célèbres de la capitale,
l'Île de la Cité, la Place de la Concorde,
les Champs-Élysées, Montmartre, etc.
Tout est nouveau pour lui, et les premiers jours
dans un pays étranger
sont toujours difficiles, même
s'ils sont très intéressants.

Habiter un pays où tout le monde
parle français, même les enfants
qui ne vont pas encore à l'école,
est pour John une expérience nouvelle.

Notre-Dame

4

Un jour qu'il visite Notre-Dame, John va à la préfecture
de police, voisine de la cathédrale,
se procurer la carte d'identité obligatoire
pour les étrangers qui habitent en France.
Le commissaire lui demande son âge, sa profession,
son adresse à Paris, le nom et l'adresse de ses parents.
Avec sa carte d'identité dans sa poche,
John a la satisfaction d'être en règle avec la police française.

Au cours de sa première visite au laboratoire,
John fait la connaissance d'un jeune chimiste français,
Roger Duplessis. Les deux jeunes chimistes
sont bientôt de bons amis.
Un jour, Roger invite John à aller avec lui à Chantilly
voir les célèbres courses de chevaux.
Un autobus conduit les deux jeunes gens à la Gare du Nord.
Une heure plus tard, le train arrive à Chantilly.
Le château est situé près d'une rivière et le champ de courses
est près du château. « C'est un endroit magnifique

pour des courses de chevaux, pense John. Le beau château,
les jardins, les chevaux, tout donne l'impression
d'une autre époque et d'un autre monde ».
John remarque dans l'assistance des femmes très chics,
qui attirent l'attention des spectateurs. « Ce sont
des mannequins des grandes maisons de couture parisiennes,
explique Roger. Les courses de chevaux sont un rendez-vous
de la société élégante, et par conséquent un excellent endroit
pour lancer les nouvelles modes ».
John conclut qu'après tout l'élégance n'est pas encore morte.

7

ROTIS

ENTRECOTE BORDELAISE. — Côte de bœuf bien mortifiée cuite au gril sur br
sarments, accompagnée des trois sauces (Bercy, Béarnaise et Marchand de Vin).

CONFITS D'OIES MAISON. — Quartiers cuits et conservés dans leur graisse. Rissol
servir et accompagnés de pommes Henri IV.

LÉGUMES

CÈPES BORDELAISE. — Têtes sautées à l'huile, pieds hachés, avec léger parfum d'ail

FONDS D'ARTICHAUTS RÉCAMIER. — Fonds pochés au vin blanc, farcis aux cha
gras, avec sauce crème.

CHAMPIGNONS FARCIS PÉRIGOURDINE. — Jeunes champignons de couche farc
truffes, braisés au four.

ENTREMETS

CRÊPES JEANNETTE. — Crêpes aux liqueurs bordelaises, fourrées de crème pâtiss
aux Marques.

ANANAS CHATEAU TROMPETTE. — Tranches d'ananas, biscuits à la cuiller parfu
recouverts de crème pâtissière et d'amandes pilées, Glacé au four et servi flambant.

SOUFFLÉ DU CHATEAU. — Mariage forcé de la glace et du feu. Plat délicie
recommandé. (Commander vingt minutes à l'avance.)

(Conversations 6–10)

Roger et John dînent ensemble dans un des grands restaurants de la capitale. Leur table est près d'une fenêtre, d'où ils ont une belle vue sur la Seine. Le garçon apporte la carte avec tout le sérieux d'un diplomate. John examine le menu avec curiosité.

—Je suis toujours surpris du talent des Français dans la présentation des plats, dit-il à son ami. Aux États-Unis, les noms des plats sont d'habitude purement descriptifs, sans aucun ornement. Ici, ils font venir l'eau à la bouche. Voici par exemple, dans la liste des plats de poisson, l'indication « Filets de Sole Tante-Marie ». Quelle différence entre « Filets de Sole Tante-Marie » et simplement « Fillet of Sole »! Un appel au sentiment familial, une allusion à la chère tante Marie, de son vivant si bonne cuisinière, et les filets de sole deviennent quelque chose de rare, d'unique. Les gens qui inventent de telles appellations sont certes d'excellents psychologues.

La cuisine française

—Puisque vous parlez de l'art de présenter les plats, répond Roger, regardez dans les « Spécialités recommandées ». Il y a là un soufflé avec la description suivante:

9

«Mariage forcé de la glace et du feu. Plat délicieux spécialement recommandé. (Commander vingt minutes à l'avance)» ... Ce «mariage forcé de la glace et du feu» est une jolie invention. Cela fait penser aux quatre éléments, à l'hostilité traditionnelle de l'eau et du feu, aux volcans couverts de neige de l'Islande. Le plaisir qu'on a à manger ce soufflé est à la fois d'ordre corporel et d'ordre spirituel!

Le repas terminé, John et Roger quittent le restaurant,
très satisfaits spirituellement et corporellement. Ils s'arrêtent un instant devant un kiosque à journaux. John remarque qu'il y a là des journaux et des revues de tous les

grands pays du monde, journaux américains, anglais, allemands, russes, italiens. Plusieurs sont dans une langue qu'il
ne peut pas même identifier. Après tout, pense-t-il, Paris
est une ville si cosmopolite qu'il y a des gens pour les
acheter, et pour les lire.

Le Jardin du Luxembourg

Scènes parisiennes

(Conversations 11–15)

Marie et John marchent ensemble dans le Jardin du Luxembourg. C'est un beau jardin près de l'Université, qui a été dessiné au dix-septième siècle et qui maintenant est très fréquenté par les étudiants.

17

Nous sommes à la fin de septembre. C'est le moment où l'été finit et où l'automne commence. Les feuilles des arbres sont déjà jaunes et la terre est couverte de feuilles mortes. Il y a un de ces légers brouillards si fréquents à Paris en automne, et l'humidité est assez pénétrante. Cependant l'automne parisien est d'ordinaire une saison charmante, juste assez triste pour être poétique.

John demande à Marie s'il fait froid à Paris pendant l'hiver.

—Pas particulièrement, répond Marie. La température ne descend pas souvent au dessous de zéro degré centigrade et il neige rarement. Mais le ciel est souvent couvert et les pluies sont fréquentes, de sorte que l'hiver à Paris paraît plus froid qu'il ne l'est véritablement. Par

contre, le printemps est une très jolie saison. Beaucoup des avenues parisiennes sont plantées de marronniers, et lorsqu'au printemps ces marronniers sont couverts de fleurs blanches et roses, c'est un spectacle magnifique.

Quittant le Jardin du Luxembourg, John et Marie descendent vers Saint-Germain-des-Prés. En face de la vieille église, John s'arrête un instant à la vitrine d'un libraire pour regarder les livres nouveaux.

—La plupart de ces livres ont une apparence bien austère, dit-il à Marie. Sur la couverture en papier jaune ou gris, il n'y a guère que le nom de l'auteur et le titre du livre. Aux États-Unis, il y a presque toujours sur la couverture de nos livres une image destinée à attirer l'attention, une jolie femme autant que possible . . .

—On achète un livre pour le lire et non pas pour la jolie femme sur la couverture, répond Marie. Les illustrations, même sur la couverture, sont réservées d'ordinaire aux livres de voyages et aux livres sur l'art, pour lesquels ces illustrations ont une espèce de valeur documentaire. Mais à quoi bon avoir une image sur la couverture d'un roman?

—Simplement parce que la figure ou la silhouette d'une jolie femme est toujours agréable à contempler, répond John.

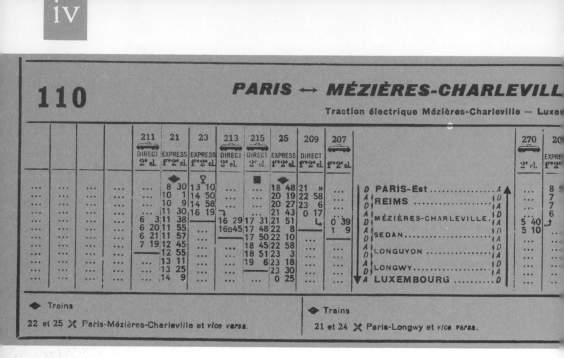

Voyage à Reims

(Conversations 16–20)

John et Roger ont décidé de profiter des derniers beaux
jours de l'automne pour faire un petit voyage en province.
Ils n'ont pas l'intention d'aller très loin,
car ils ne disposent que de deux ou trois jours.
Finalement, leur choix s'arrête sur Reims. John n'a jamais vu
la cathédrale de Reims, et Reims est juste à la distance convenable.

Roger consulte l'horaire des chemins de fer.

—Tout s'arrange admirablement, dit-il à John.

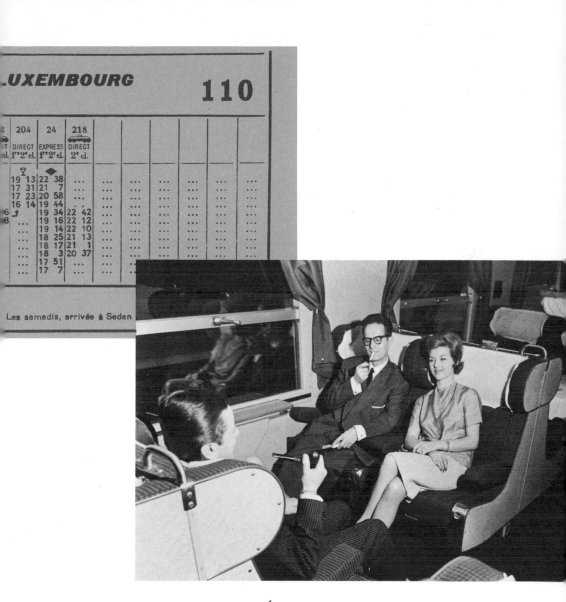

	204	24	218						
	DIRECT 1re 2e cl.	EXPRESS 1re 2e cl.	DIRECT 2e cl.							
	19 13	22 38	...	...	...	...	...	...	...
	17 31	21 7	...	...	...	...	...	...	...
	17 23	20 58	...	...	...	...	...	...	...
	16 14	19 44	...	...	...	...	...	...	...
6 ♪		19 34	22 42	...	...	...	...	...	...
8 ...		19 16	22 12	...	...	...	...	...	...
...		19 14	22 10	...	...	...	...	...	...
...		18 25	21 13	...	...	...	...	...	...
...		18 17	21 1	...	...	...	...	...	...
...		18 3	20 37	...	...	...	...	...	...
...		17 51	...	...	...	...	...	...	...
...		17 7	...	...	...	...	...	...	...

Les samedis, arrivée à Sedan

Nous n'aurons pas besoin d'aller à Épernay et d'y attendre
la correspondance. La ligne Mézières-Charleville
passe par Reims. Si nous prenons l'express qui quitte Paris
à 8h. 30, nous arriverons à notre destination à 10h.
Et l'horaire du retour est tout aussi commode. En quittant
Reims à 21h. 7, nous serons à Paris à 22h. 38, assez tôt
pour avoir une bonne nuit de sommeil et être frais et disposé
pour le travail de lundi.

Le lendemain matin, nos deux amis prennent le train
à la gare de l'Est. Le compartiment où ils s'installent est
très confortable. L'express roule à toute vitesse. Au delà
des maisons grises de la capitale, il traverse
la banlieue parisienne, avec ses jardins potagers
et ses jolies maisons de pierre blanche, puis l'agréable et
paisible campagne de l'Île-de-France, avec ses champs fertiles,
ses arbres verts et ses petits villages aux toits rouges
groupés autour de leur vieux clocher. Dans le voisinage de Reims,
les vignes couvrent le flanc des collines.
C'est la saison des vendanges, et partout au milieu des vignes,
hommes et femmes sont en train de cueillir les lourdes
grappes de raisin.

    —Savez-vous que le vin de champagne est en grande partie
fabriqué avec du raisin rouge? dit Roger.
Pour avoir un vin blanc, il suffit de laisser fermenter le jus
du raisin sans la peau. C'est elle qui contient les pigments.

Tout de suite après leur arrivée
à Reims, John et Roger vont voir
la cathédrale. John est très impressionné.
Malheureusement, une partie de la façade
est cachée par des échafaudages.
—Je n'ai jamais encore vu
une seule cathédrale sans échafaudages,
remarque Roger.
On est toujours en train de travailler
quelque part, de réparer quelque chose,
et ici encore plus qu'ailleurs.
A la fin de la première guerre mondiale,
la pauvre cathédrale de Reims,
brûlée, mutilée, était presque en ruines.
A travers d'énormes trous dans la voûte,
on pouvait voir le ciel.
Même maintenant, bien des statues,
bien des sculptures portent encore
des traces de ces mauvais jours.
Et malgré tout, la vieille cathédrale
des rois de France est toujours debout.

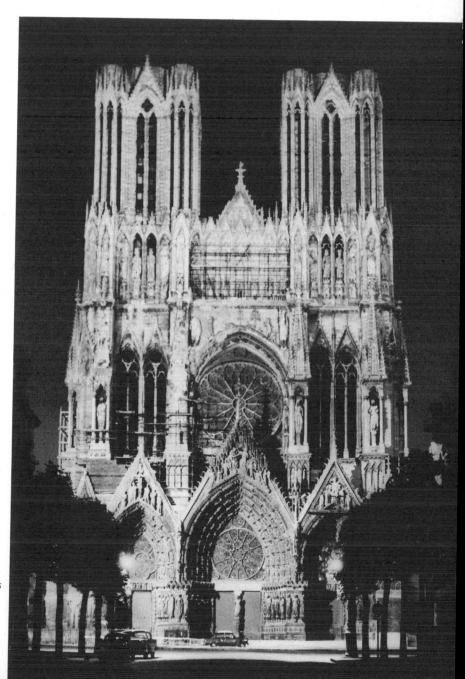

cathédrale de Reims

Le lendemain, les deux jeunes gens visitent
les vastes caves souterraines d'une des maisons de champagne.
Un guide leur explique comment on prépare le vin de champagne,
comment les bouteilles sont laissées un certain temps
dans une certaine position, puis placées dans une autre.
John ne savait pas que la préparation du champagne était une
opération si longue et si compliquée.

Leur visite terminée, John et Roger dînent dans un des bons
restaurants de la ville. Puis ils vont prendre le train
qui les ramènera à Paris.

Les Alpes

Le Mont-Saint-Michel

En province

La côte bretonne

Un village des Alpes

V

(Conversations 21–25)

Marie et Roger sont de retour à Paris, à la fin des vacances de Noël. Marie est allée passer ses vacances en Bretagne, où elle a de la famille, et Roger est allé revoir la petite ville des Alpes où il est né. Le lendemain de leur retour, John demande à ses amis leurs impressions.

Saint-Malo

—J'adore la Bretagne, dit Marie. Mon oncle et ma tante habitent à Saint-Malo, dans la partie de la ville encore entourée de vieilles fortifications. Leur maison est une de ces grandes et belles demeures construites par les marchands d'autrefois, au temps où Saint-Malo était une ville prospère, enrichie par son commerce et par ses corsaires.

34

Évidemment, Saint-Malo n'est plus ce qu'il était il y a deux ou trois siècles. Les corsaires ont disparu. Tout ce qui reste à l'heure actuelle pour donner au port animation et couleur, du moins en été, ce sont de braves pêcheurs bretons. Pourtant, même en hiver, la ville a son charme, un charme un peu triste.

—Vraiment, je ne sais pas si je choisirais la Bretagne pour y passer mes vacances de Noël, remarque John. Il y a des endroits plus gais.

—En réalité, continue Marie, mes vacances m'ont beaucoup plu. Nous avons fait le réveillon chez des amis, les Kerguélen, qui ont un vieux château à quelque distance de

Une ville bretonne: Fougères

Saint-Malo, près du Mont-Saint-Michel. Quand vous irez
au Mont-Saint-Michel, n'oubliez pas d'aller jusqu'à Saint-
Malo. Vous ne regretterez rien.

—Entendu, répond John. Et vous, Roger, racontez-nous
un peu ce que vous avez fait pendant vos vacances dans
les Alpes.

Le Mont-Saint-Michel

—J'avais quitté ma ville natale lorsque j'étais enfant, et je n'y étais jamais retourné. Je ne m'attendais pas aux changements que j'y ai trouvés. On était en train de démolir l'école où j'allais lorsque j'avais douze ans pour installer à cet endroit les bureaux d'une compagnie d'électricité qui exploite l'énergie d'un grand barrage construit dans le voi-

sinage. Cela m'a fait quelque chose de voir disparaître mon ancienne école. Comme le temps passe!

—Que voulez-vous, Roger, c'est la vie!, répond John. Marie a vu la France d'autrefois, celle de la Bretagne et des vieux châteaux, et vous, vous avez vu la France d'aujourd'hui, celle des barrages et des grandes usines.

vi

Versailles

Un bel après-midi de mai, John et Roger ont décidé d'aller visiter le château de Versailles. John connaissait l'histoire de l'ancienne résidence royale, dont il avait vu des photographies. Mais il faut aller à Versailles pour se rendre compte de ce qu'est vraiment le palais de Louis XIV. L'ensemble est si vaste que la photographie ordinaire ne peut en donner qu'une vue fragmentaire — une pièce d'eau, une allée dans le parc, un coin du palais ou d'un des Trianons. Si la photographie aérienne peut donner une vue d'ensemble, elle ne donne ni échelle, ni perspective, ni détails. John ne s'attendait pas à trouver des vues si lointaines et si habilement ménagées.

A ce moment de l'année, les touristes, encore peu nombreux, semblaient perdus dans l'immensité des jardins et du parc, parmi les statues impassibles des dieux et des déesses. A l'intérieur du palais, John trouva la décoration des grandes galeries un peu lourde, un peu trop somptueuse, avec tous ces guerriers musclés et cuirassés, ces armes, ces plumes, ces chevaux impétueux. Cela ne l'empêcha pas d'être fort impressionné. On peut ne pas aimer Versailles, le trouver trop froid et trop majestueux. Personne ne peut nier que c'est une étonnante œuvre d'art.

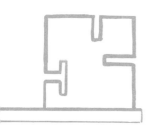

Le château de Versailles

La chambre de Louis XIV

La bibliothèque de Louis XVI

Le Grand Trianon

Le lendemain matin, de retour à Paris, John va chez un horloger faire réparer sa montre. Arrivé au coin d'une rue, il entend tout à coup un grand bruit métallique. Une auto vient d'entrer en collision avec un camion. Le chauffeur descend de son camion sain et sauf. L'automobiliste a eu moins de chance: il est sans connaissance au volant de son auto. Aussitôt les passants s'assemblent à l'endroit où l'accident a eu lieu, et plusieurs d'entre eux s'occupent de la victime. Deux agents arrivent. L'un d'eux s'approche de John et tire un petit carnet de sa poche.

—C'est toujours à moi que ces choses arrivent, se dit John. Vingt personnes au moins ont été témoins de l'accident, et je suis celui que l'agent choisit pour avoir des renseignements!

Néanmoins, John donne volontiers tous les détails qu'il peut donner. Après avoir indiqué son nom et son adresse, il donne sa version de l'accident. Il lui a semblé que l'automobiliste allait trop vite, car il avait plu et la chaussée était fort glissante.

—Je vous remercie, monsieur, dit l'agent de police en remettant son petit carnet dans sa poche. Le commissaire de police du XVe arrondissement vous enverra une convocation s'il a besoin de renseignements supplémentaires.

—Zut alors! pense John. Maintenant, je vais être obligé d'aller au commissariat de police du XVe arrondissement! Quelle barbe!

A la campagne

(Conversations 31–35)

Ce matin, John et Roger ont quitté Paris de bonne heure pour aller voir des cousins de Roger, les Deschamps, qui habitent dans un petit village près de Fontainebleau. Ils ont pris le train jusqu'à Melun.

Le château de Fontainebleau

Là, ils ont descendu leurs bicyclettes du fourgon, pour faire à bicyclette le reste du voyage. A dix heures du matin, ils sont en train de pédaler le long d'une jolie route, heureux de l'ombre des arbres qui la bordent, car la journée est chaude et le soleil haut dans le ciel.

46

—Voilà une auberge qui a l'air sympathique, dit John à Roger au moment où ils traversent la place d'un village. Si nous nous arrêtions pour prendre quelque chose, un bon verre de bière bien fraîche par exemple? Je meurs de soif et j'ai un peu mal aux jambes, car je n'ai pas l'habitude d'aller à bicyclette.

—Ne voulez-vous pas attendre jusqu'à ce que nous soyons arrivés chez mes cousins? répond Roger. Nous serons à leur ferme dans un quart d'heure. Si vous buvez maintenant un verre de bière, vous aurez encore plus chaud qu'auparavant et vos jambes vous abandonneront tout à fait.

—Eh bien, répond Roger avec résignation, j'attendrai jusque là.

Un quart d'heure plus tard, nos deux amis arrivent à la grille de la ferme. Mme Deschamps, qui les voit arriver, vient à leur rencontre. Les présentations faites, elle conduit les visiteurs dans la vaste cuisine, qui depuis les temps les plus anciens est la salle familiale des fermes françaises. John remarque la haute cheminée et les vieux ustensiles de cuivre accrochés au mur. On les distingue à peine dans la demi-obscurité, car Mme Deschamps tient les volets fermés à cause de la chaleur.

—Vous allez prendre quelque chose, n'est-ce pas? leur dit-elle. Par cette chaleur, vous devez en avoir besoin.

John boit enfin son verre de bière.

—Il faut que j'aille au jardin chercher des légumes et cueillir des fleurs, dit Mme Deschamps aux jeunes gens lorsqu'ils sont un peu reposés de leur fatigue. Voulez-vous m'accompagner?

Comme beaucoup de jardins en France, le jardin des Deschamps est entouré de murs et ces murs sont couverts d'espaliers d'où pendent des poires magnifiques. Le jardin lui-même est divisé en carrés séparés les uns des autres par de petites allées.

—Cette symétrie, ces arbres taillés en espalier, ces fleurs, ces allées de sable, tout cela me rappelle un peu Versailles, dit en riant John à Mme Deschamps.

—Après tout, pourquoi ne pas joindre l'utile à l'agréable? répond-elle.

On se partage le travail. Tandis que Mme Deschamps cueille des roses et des œillets, John cueille des haricots verts et Roger choisit quelques pieds de salade.

Puis tout le monde revient à la maison attendre le retour de M. Deschamps. Il est avec son tracteur dans un champ près du village et il a promis de revenir à midi et quart ou à midi et demi, au plus tard.

Le Panthéon

De retour à Paris

(Conversations 36–41)

Si nous visitions le Panthéon? dit un jour John à Roger.
Je n'y suis jamais allé.

Les deux jeunes gens se dirigent donc vers le Panthéon.
A quelque distance, ils s'arrêtent un instant pour regarder
la façade de l'édifice.

—Vous voyez là-haut la Patrie entre la Liberté et l'Histoire
en train de distribuer des prix aux grands hommes, explique Roger.
Lisez l'inscription : AUX GRANDS HOMMES LA PATRIE RECONNAISSANTE.

Tout en montant l'escalier, Roger lui dit un mot de l'histoire
du Panthéon. C'est une ancienne église du dix-huitième siècle
que la Révolution a transformée en temple destiné à servir de lieu
de sépulture à ses grands hommes.
La Révolution y a mis Voltaire et Rousseau.
On y a enterré ensuite des hommes politiques ou des écrivains
plus ou moins continuateurs de la tradition révolutionnaire,
Hugo et Zola par exemple.

A l'intérieur, un guide explique aux visiteurs les peintures murales
qui représentent des scènes de la vie de sainte Geneviève.
C'était une jeune fille qui vivait il y a quinze cents ans
et qui, selon la légende, a sauvé Paris d'Attila et de ses Huns.

—Elle est devenue la patronne de la ville, continue le guide.
En son honneur, on appelait autrefois le quartier de l'Université
la Montagne Sainte-Geneviève.

—Voilà une montagne facilement accessible, dit John à son ami.
Le boulevard Saint-Michel vous mène tout droit au sommet.

—Rappelez-vous qu'une partie du vignoble champenois
est sur des collines appelées la Montagne de Reims.
Il y a montagnes et montagnes, des grandes et des petites . . .

—Après tout, Mount Vernon n'est qu'une simple colline.

Le guide conduit ensuite les visiteurs
dans la galerie souterraine où se trouvent les tombeaux.
D'une voix monotone, il récite des phrases apprises par cœur.

Arrivé devant le tombeau de Jean-Jacques Rousseau,
il explique que « par la porte entr'ouverte du tombeau sort
une main tenant une torche allumée ». Symbolisme assez lugubre,
pense John, mais fort clair.

Après leur visite, les deux jeunes gens descendent le
boulevard Saint-Michel jusqu'à la Seine. Arrivés en vue de
Notre-Dame, ils tournent à gauche. Les rues
le long de la Seine dominent le fleuve, et c'est sur le
parapet du fleuve, à l'ombre des arbres, que les bouquinistes
ont installé leurs boîtes. John s'étonne un peu
du choix de cet endroit.

—Vous avez peut-être vu de vieilles estampes représentant
le Pont-Neuf tel qu'il était il y a trois siècles,
avec des boutiques de chaque côté, explique Roger. Le pont

Le Pont-Neuf

La boutique d'un bouquiniste

était toute la journée couvert de monde et c'était
naturellement un excellent endroit pour le commerce
des livres, des modes, etc. Chassés du pont, les commerçants
se sont installés au bord du fleuve.

Tout en marchant, John jette un coup d'œil sur les étalages.
Il voit là toute sorte de choses, livres anciens
et modernes, timbres-poste et vieilles pièces de monnaie
pour les collectionneurs. Dans une boutique
du quai Malaquais, il achète une paire de vieux pistolets
—« pour ma chambre en Amérique », explique-t-il à Roger.
Il met l'un des pistolets dans la poche droite,
l'autre dans la poche gauche de son pardessus.

—Attention! lui dit en riant son ami.
Si un agent de police vous voyait, il pourrait bien
vous faire un procès-verbal : Vous avez sur vous
des armes prohibées!

Un peintre parisien

Les deux amis continuent leur promenade, traversent la Seine,
la Place de la Concorde et finissent l'après-midi à la terrasse d'un café
sur les Grands Boulevards.

La Place de la Concorde

La terrasse d'un café

Questions on Readings

I. ARRIVÉE À PARIS *(Conversations 1-5)*

1. Quelle est la nationalité de John Hughes? **2.** Quelle est sa profession? **3.** Pourquoi est-il à Paris? **4.** Où demeure John? **5.** Où habitent ses parents? **6.** Pourquoi est-ce que John va à la préfecture de police? **7.** Est-ce que la préfecture de police est loin de Notre-Dame? **8.** Qui est Roger Duplessis? **9.** Où est situé le château de Chantilly? **10.** Est-ce que le champ de courses est loin du château?

II. LA CUISINE FRANÇAISE *(Conversations 6-10)*

1. Où John et Roger dînent-ils ensemble? **2.** Où est leur table? **3.** Qu'est-ce que le garçon apporte à John et à Roger? **4.** Quel plat de poisson y a-t-il sur la carte? **5.** Quelle description la carte donne-t-elle du soufflé? **6.** Quand John et Roger quittent-ils le restaurant? **7.** Sont-ils satisfaits de leur dîner? **8.** Où s'arrêtent-ils un instant? **9.** Qu'est-ce que John remarque quand il est devant le kiosque à journaux? **10.** Est-ce qu'il peut identifier tous les journaux? **11.** Quels journaux peut-il identifier? **12.** Est-ce que Paris est une ville très cosmopolite?

III. SCÈNES PARISIENNES *(Conversations 11-15)*

1. Où se trouve le Jardin du Luxembourg? **2.** Quand a-t-il été dessiné? **3.** Par qui est-il fréquenté? **4.** Quand commence l'automne? **5.** Quel temps fait-il ce jour-là? **6.** Est-ce qu'il neige souvent à Paris pendant l'hiver? **7.** En quelle saison les marronniers sont-ils en fleurs? **8.** De quelle couleur sont les fleurs des marronniers? **9.** Où vont John et Marie lorsqu'ils quittent le Jardin du Luxembourg? **10.** Pourquoi John s'arrête-t-il un instant à la vitrine d'un libraire? **11.** Pourquoi dit-il que les livres français ont une apparence bien austère? **12.** Qu'est-ce qu'il y a souvent sur la couverture des livres aux États-Unis?

IV. VOYAGE À REIMS *(Conversations 16-20)*

1. Pourquoi John et Roger n'ont-ils pas l'intention de faire un long voyage? **2.** Comment iront-ils à Reims? **3.** A quelle heure quitteront-ils Paris? **4.** A quelle gare vont-ils le lendemain? **5.** Qu'est-ce qu'il y a dans la banlieue parisienne? **6.** Où se trouvent les vignes de champagne? **7.** Pourquoi y a-t-il beaucoup d'hommes et de femmes au milieu des vignes? **8.** Est-ce que le vin de champagne est toujours fabriqué avec des raisins blancs? **9.** Qu'est-ce qu'il y a sur la façade de la cathédrale de Reims? **10.** Pourquoi y a-t-il souvent des échafaudages sur les cathédrales? **11.** Est-ce que la cathédrale de Reims a beaucoup souffert de la première guerre mondiale? **12.** Est-ce que la préparation du vin de champagne est une opération simple?

V. EN PROVINCE *(Conversations 21-25)*

1. Où Marie est-elle allée passer les vacances de Noël? **2.** Quels parents a-t-elle en Bretagne? **3.** Dans quelle partie de Saint-Malo son oncle et sa tante habitent-ils? **4.** Quand Saint-Malo était-elle une ville très prospère? **5.** Qu'est-ce qui faisait à ce moment-là la prospérité de la ville? **6.** Qu'est-ce que Marie pense de ses vacances? **7.** Où Marie dit-elle à John d'aller quand il ira au Mont-Saint-Michel? **8.** Qu'est-ce que Roger a fait pendant ses vacances de Noël? **9.** Est-ce qu'il s'attendait aux changements qu'il a trouvés dans sa ville natale? **10.** Qu'est-ce qu'on était en train de faire à ce moment-là? **11.** Pourquoi démolissait-on son ancienne école? **12.** Est-ce que ça lui a fait quelque chose de voir disparaître son ancienne école?

VI. À VERSAILLES *(Conversations 26-30)*

1. Est-ce que John avait entendu parler du château de Versailles? **2.** Est-ce qu'il avait vu des photographies du château? **3.** Y avait-il beaucoup de touristes le jour où il est allé à Versailles? **4.** Qu'est-ce qu'il a pensé de la décoration des galeries? **5.** Est-ce que cela l'a empêché d'être impressionné? **6.** Qu'est-ce que John a fait le lendemain matin? **7.** Qu'est-ce qui s'est passé quand il est arrivé au coin d'une rue? **8.** Est-ce que le chauffeur du camion a été blessé au cours de l'accident? **9.** Comment a-t-on trouvé l'automobiliste après l'accident? **10.** Qui s'est occupé de la victime? **11.** Qu'est-ce que l'agent de police a demandé à John? **12.** Qu'est-ce que John pense de ce qui lui est arrivé?

VII. À LA CAMPAGNE *(Conversations 31-35)*

1. Qui sont les Deschamps? **2.** Comment John et Roger sont-ils allés à Melun? **3.** Comment font-ils le reste du voyage? **4.** Qu'est-ce que John propose à Roger de faire au moment où ils traversent la place d'un village? **5.** Pourquoi voudrait-il boire un verre de bière bien fraîche? **6.** Pourquoi Roger lui dit-il d'attendre jusqu'à ce qu'ils soient arrivés à la ferme? **7.** Qui vient à leur rencontre? **8.** Où Mme Deschamps conduit-elle ses visiteurs? **9.** Pourquoi tient-elle fermés les volets de la cuisine? **10.** Pourquoi faut-il que Mme Deschamps aille à son jardin? **11.** Qu'est-ce qu'il y a sur les murs du jardin? **12.** A quelle heure M. Deschamps a-t-il promis de revenir?

VIII. DE RETOUR À PARIS *(Conversations 36-41)*

1. Quelle est l'inscription sur la façade du Panthéon? **2.** Connaissez-vous des grands hommes qui sont enterrés au Panthéon? **3.** Que représentent les peintures murales à l'intérieur du Panthéon? **4.** Quand vivait sainte Geneviève? **5.** Pourquoi est-elle devenue la patronne de Paris? **6.** Où le guide conduit-il les visiteurs? **7.** Où les bouquinistes ont-ils installé leurs boîtes? **8.** Qu'est-ce qu'il y avait autrefois de chaque côté du Pont-Neuf? **9.** Qu'est-ce que John achète dans une boutique du quai Malaquais? **10.** Où met-il les pistolets qu'il achète? **11.** Pourquoi Roger lui dit-il de faire attention? **12.** Comment les deux amis finissent-ils l'après-midi?

Credits and Notes on Illustrations

(Numbers refer to pages. Credits are listed in order of appearance on a page, from left to right, from top to bottom.)

1—*Wheat fields in La Beauce,* photo Languepin from Rapho Guillumette Pictures; *detail from Renoir's «Bal à Bougival»,* courtesy of The Museum of Fine Arts, Boston; *gas lamppost at the entrance to the Louvre,* photo Sanford H. Roth from Rapho Guillumette Pictures; *daisies,* photo Izis from Rapho Guillumette Pictures. **2**—*Taxi driver,* French Government Tourist Office; *Le Sacré-Cœur,* French Government Tourist Office; *La Place de la Concorde,* photo Pierre Belzeaux from Rapho Guillumette Pictures. **3**—*Avenue de l'Observatoire,* photo Peter Buckley; *l'Île de la Cité,* French Embassy Press and Information Division. **4**—*Parisian children,* photo Henri Cartier-Bresson, Magnum Photos; *Notre-Dame,* photo Pierre Belzeaux from Rapho Guillumette Pictures. **5**—*Flower vendor,* photo Izis from Rapho Guillumette Pictures. **6**—*Bus stop in Paris,* photo Georges Viollon from Rapho Guillumette Pictures; *detail from an illuminated manuscript (Musée Condé du Château de Chantilly),* French Government Tourist Office. **7**—*Château de Chantilly,* photo Yvon; *horse races,* French Government Tourist Office. **8**—*Outdoor restaurant at the Place du Tertre, Paris,* photo Silberstein from Rapho Guillumette Pictures. **9**—*The Seine,* photo Albert Monier. **10**—*Chef preparing «Sole normande»,* photo Feher, French Government Tourist Office. **11**—*Drawing* by Georgette de Lattre; *headwaiter at the Café de Paris,* photo David Seymour, Magnum Photos. **12**—*Bakery,* photo Sanford H. Roth from Rapho Guillumette Pictures; *boy carrying bread,* photo Robert Doisneau from Rapho Guillumette Pictures; *vegetable stall,* French Government Tourist Office. **13**—*Girl with bread,* photo Janine Niepce from Rapho Guillumette Pictures; *in a restaurant,* photo David Seymour, Magnum Photos. **14**—*In front of a restaurant,* photo Henri Cartier-Bresson, Magnum Photos. **15**—*Newspaper display,* photo Ken Heyman from Rapho Guillumette Pictures; *newsstand,* photo Ciccione from Rapho Guillumette Pictures. **16**—*Le Jardin du Luxembourg (seventeenth-century engraving),* courtesy New York Public Library, Prints Division. **17**—*Mother and child in the Jardin du Luxembourg,* photo Fritz Henle from Monkmeyer; *students seated under statue,* photo Three Lions. **18**—*Notre-Dame,* photo Albert Monier. **19**—*La Place de la Concorde in autumn,* photo Seeberger from Rapho Guillumette Pictures. **20**—*Chestnut tree,* photo Messager from Rapho Guillumette Pictures. **21**—*Detail from a sixteenth-century tapestry,* courtesy of the Metropolitan Museum of Art, Gift of George Blumenthal, 1941; *view of the Seine and the Eiffel Tower,* photo Davis Pratt from Rapho Guillumette Pictures. **22**—*Church of Saint-Germain-des-Prés reflected in a bookstore window,* French Cultural Services. **23**—*Bus stop at Saint-Germain-des-Prés,* photo Dennis Stock, Magnum Photos. **25**—*On a train,* photo French National Railroads. **26**—*A village in Île-de-France,* photo Henri Cartier-Bresson, Magnum Photos. **27**—*Vineyards, Champagne region,* photo Robert Doisneau from Rapho Guillumette Pictures. **28**—*Detail of the Smiling Angel,* Reims cathedral, photo Yvon; *outline of a thirteenth-century stained-glass window,* photo Giraudon; *statues, Reims cathedral,* French Government Tourist Office. **29**—*Reims cathedral,* photo Goursat from Rapho Guillumette Pictures. **30**—*Changing position of champagne bottles in a wine cellar,* photo Kayfetz from Monkmeyer; *wine-tasting,* photo Fritz Henle from Monkmeyer. **31**—*Paris railway station,* photo Sabine Weiss from Rapho Guillumette Pictures. **32**—*Mont-Saint-Michel,* photo Yvon; *Chamonix,* photo Yvon. **33**—*Brittany,* photo Feher, French Government Tourist Office; *village in the Alps,* photo André de Dienes from Rapho Guillumette Pictures. **34**—*A Breton woman,* photo Ergy Landau from Rapho Guillumette Pictures; *Saint-Malo,* photo Karquel, French Government Tourist Office. **35**—*Fishermen,* photo Henri Cartier-Bresson, Magnum Photos. **36**—*Fougères,* French Cultural Services; *swan boat, woodcut from* «*Vergier d'honneur*» (1496), courtesy Walters Art Gallery, Baltimore. **37**—*Mont-Saint-Michel,* photo Yvon. **38**—*Elementary school,* French Embassy Press & Information Division; *the Alps,* French Government Tourist Office. **39**—*Dam in the Alps,* photo Doumic, French Government Tourist Office. **41**—*Aerial view of Versailles,* French Government Tourist Office; *old engraving of Versailles,* photo Yvon; *Versailles at night,* photo Ciccione from Rapho Guillumette Pictures. **42**—*The main front of the palace of Versailles,* photo Three Lions; *the library of Louis XVI,* French Embassy Press & Information Division; *the bedroom of Louis XIV,* French Embassy Press & Information Division. **43**—*Grand Trianon,* photo Yvon. **44**—*Man carrying bread,* photo Robert Doisneau from Rapho Guillumette Pictures; *mailman,* photo Janine Niepce from Rapho Guillumette Pictures; *a spectator,* photo Denis Brihat from Rapho Guillumette Pictures; *Parisian policemen in front of the Opera,* photo Janine Niepce from Rapho Guillumette Pictures. **45**—*Spectators,* photo Robert Doisneau from Rapho Guillumette Pictures. **46**—*Fontainebleau,* photo Yvon. **47**—*A road in Fontainebleau forest,* French Government Tourist Office. **48**—*Country inn,* Cultural Services of the French Embassy. **49**—*Drawing by Georgette de Lattre; farm scene,* French Government Tourist Office; *a village in Île-de-France,* photo Henri Cartier-Bresson, Magnum Photos. **50**—*Country house and garden,* French Government Tourist Office. **51**—*Girl with flowers,* photo Ergy Landau from Rapho Guillumette Pictures. **52**—*In the field,* photo Ergy Landau from Rapho Guillumette Pictures. **53**—*Landscape,* photo Ciccione from Rapho Guillumette Pictures. **54**—*The Pantheon (1836 engraving),* French

Embassy Press & Information Division; *The Pantheon*, French Cultural Services. **56**—*Rue de Seine*, photo Erich Hartmann, Magnum Photos. **57**—*Sidewalk café near the Pantheon*, photo Inge Mörath, Magnum Photos; *Pont-Neuf, engraving*, Bibliothèque Nationale, Cabinet des Estampes. **58**—*Bookstalls along the Seine near Notre-Dame*, photo Albert Monier. **59**—*L'Île Saint Louis*, photo Marton, French Government Tourist Office. **60**—*Bird, by Henri Matisse*, French Cultural Services; *Parisian street artist*, photo Ken Heyman from Rapho Guillumette Pictures. **61**—*Roofs of Paris, with the Eiffel Tower in the background*, photo Izis from Rapho Guillumette Pictures; *chimneys*, photo Ergy Landau from Rapho Guillumette Pictures. **62**—*Pont des Invalides*, photo Sabine Weiss from Rapho Guillumette Pictures; *La Place de la Concorde*, photo Gene Badger from Rapho Guillumette Pictures. **63**—*Sidewalk café on the Champs-Élysées*, photo Fritz Henle from Monkmeyer; *drawing* by Georgette de Lattre. **64**—*Daisies*, photo Izis from Rapho Guillumette Pictures; *lampposts*, photo Sanford H. Roth from Rapho Guillumette Pictures.

REFERENCE MATERIALS

Table of Sounds of the French Language

As Represented by Symbols of the International Phonetic Alphabet

	Bi-labial	Labio-dental	Dental and Alveolar	Palato-alveolar	Palatal	Velar	Uvular
CONSONANTS							
Plosive	p b		t d			k g	
Nasal	m		n		ɲ		
Lateral			l				
Rolled			r*				ʀ
Fricative		f v	s z	ʃ ʒ			
Semi-vowels	w ɥ				j (ɥ)	(w)	
VOWELS					*Front Central Back*		
Close					i y	u	
Half-close					e ø ə	o õ	
Half-open					ɛ̃ ɛ œ œ̃	ɔ	
Open					a	a ɑ̃	

* The symbols [ʀ] and [r] represent two ways of producing "r" in French. The [ʀ] is produced between the back of the tongue and the soft palate, the [r] with the tip of the tongue against the teeth or gums. Only the [ʀ] is used in the phonetic transcriptions in this book, but the alveolar [r] is quite commonly used in many parts of France.

How to Get a Good French Accent

I. INTRODUCTION

In this section, and in the vocabulary, we indicate the pronunciation of French words by symbols of the International Phonetic Alphabet. It looks confusing at first: indeed, when you see that **Bonjour, monsieur,** for example, is pronounced [bõ ʒuʀ məsjø] you may think that the transcription is worse than the French spelling! But at least you can see clearly and immediately that the **n** of **bon** is not sounded, that **mon** is not pronounced **mŏn,** that **sieur** is not pronounced **shur,** and so on. With a little practice, you will find that the transcriptions are invaluable for pronunciation exercises. If you refer to the Key whenever you do not understand what a symbol indicates, you will quickly learn what each of the 36 symbols represents. In the Key, we use only French words to illustrate the sounds that the symbols represent instead of trying to explain the sounds of French in terms of English. The reason for this is (1) it is misleading, if not downright false, to say that any French sound is the same as any English sound, and (2) the easiest and most direct way of knowing what a given symbol represents is to hear it in a familiar word or phrase. (The key can be found on p. 290.)

You don't need to memorize the symbols before you begin using them—any more than you would memorize all the diacritical marks in an English dictionary before looking up a word. And you don't need to write in phonetic symbols any more than you need to be able to write diacritical marks in English—at least not at first.

II. TRANSCRIPTIONS AND EXERCISES

A.   THE FIRST STEP

The first step in getting a good French accent is to *hear* how French phrases really sound. If you listen carefully to your instructor and the voices on the tapes, you will quickly realize that the rhythm and intonation of French phrases are entirely different from English. In saying "Where is the restaurant?" for example, most of us would put strong accents on *where* and on the syllable *rest–,* and we would enunciate the vowels quite clearly; but we would pronounce the rest of the words of the phrase with so little stress that the vowels *e, au,* and *a* would all sound very much alike. A French person who is not familiar with our system of accented and unaccented syllables, however, would say something like: "Wear eez zee res-tau-rant?" in six clear syllables of equal length. You are so used to hearing certain syllables stressed and others unstressed, that you would *think* the Frenchman is merely accenting the wrong syllables. But that is not what he is doing: he is really giving each syllable equal stress as he would in speaking French—where there are no accented syllables and, consequently, no unaccented ones. To make things even worse, he is using French sounds because in French there is no *wh* (as in *where*), no *ĭ* (as in *is*), and no *th* (as in *the*). Moreover the French "R" is entirely different from ours.

Once you accept the idea that French people really give equal stress to each pronounced syllable, you can quickly catch the rhythm of simple French phrases and you are ready to do the first rhythm exercises. Don't worry about the individual sounds for the moment. It will be much easier to learn them after you catch the rhythm of a few complete phrases.

B.   KEY TO PHONETIC ALPHABET

CONSONANTS		VOWELS	
[p]	*as in* parlez-vous?	[i]	*as in* voici
[b]	*as in* bonjour	[y]	*as in* sur la place
[t]	*as in* tout droit	[e]	*as in* allez-vous?
[d]	*as in* de rien	[ø]	*as in* un peu
[k]	*as in* comment?	[ə]	*as in* de rien
[g]	*as in* la gare	[ɛ]	*as in* êtes-vous?
[m]	*as in* monsieur	[ɛ̃]	*as in* vin
[n]	*as in* une banane	[œ]	*as in* onze heures
[ɲ]	*as in* à la campagne	[œ̃]	*as in* un restaurant
[l]	*as in* le château	[a]	*as in* à la gare
[ʀ]	*as in* bonjour	[ɑ]	*as in* là-bas
[f]	*as in* en face	[ɑ̃]	*as in* en France
[v]	*as in* au revoir	[ɔ]	*as in* le bureau de poste
[s]	*as in* s'il vous plaît	[o]	*as in* l'hôtel
[z]	*as in* pas‿encore	[õ]	*as in* bonjour
[ʃ]	*as in* à gauche	[u]	*as in* bonjour
[ʒ]	*as in* je vais		

SEMI-VOWELS

[w]   *as in* oui   [j]   *as in* bien   [ɥ]   *as in* huit

CONVERSATION 1

IPA Transcription of Dialog

1. bɔ̃ʒuʀ, məsjø. 2. bɔ̃ʒuʀ, madam. 3. ɛtvu məsjø yg? 4. wi, madam,
ʒəsɥi məsjø yg. 5. kɔmɑ̃talevu, məsjø? 6. bjɛ̃, mɛʀsi. evu? 7. pɑmal, mɛʀsi.
8. paʀlevu ɑ̃glɛ? 9. nɔ̃, ʒən paʀl pɑ(z)ɑ̃glɛ. 10. mɛ vu paʀle fʀɑ̃sɛ, nɛspa?
11. wi, madam, ʒpaʀl œ̃pø fʀɑ̃sɛ. 12. vwasi yn lɛtʀ puʀ vu. 13. mɛʀsi boku.
14. dəʀjɛ̃, məsjø. 15. oʀvwaʀ, madam. 16. oʀvwaʀ, məsjø.

I. Exercices de rythme (Rhythm exercises) :

The first exercise contains phrases of four syllables. You first listen to
the instructor or the voices on the tape. Then you establish the
rhythm for yourself by tapping four sharp, even taps on the table or
repeating four times a syllable such as *toc, toc, toc, toc*. Then you
repeat the phrases several times in the same rhythm without accenting
any syllable and without slighting any syllable.

A. *Repeat in four short, equally stressed syllables:*

1. Bonjour monsieur (madame).   [bɔ̃ ʒuʀ mə sjø (ma dam).]
2. Merci monsieur (madame).   [mɛʀ si mə sjø.]
3. De rien monsieur (madame).   [də ʀjɛ̃ mə sjø.]
4. Au revoir monsieur (madame).   [oʀ vwaʀ mə sjø.]

B. *Repeat in five short, equally stressed syllables:*

(a) 1. Bonjour mademoiselle.   [bɔ̃ ʒuʀ mad mwa zɛl.]
    2. Merci mademoiselle.   [mɛʀ si mad mwa zɛl.]
    3. De rien mademoiselle   [də ʀjɛ̃ mad mwa zɛl.]
    4. Au revoir mademoiselle.   [oʀ vwaʀ mad mwa zɛl.]

(b) 1. Êtes-vous Monsieur Hughes? [ɛt vu mə sjø yg?]
    2. Comment allez-vous?   [kɔ mɑ̃ ta le vu?]
    3. Parlez-vous français?   [paʀ le vu fʀɑ̃ sɛ?]
    4. Je ne parle pas français.   [ʒən paʀl pɑ fʀɑ̃ sɛ.]
    5. Parlez-vous anglais?   [paʀ le vu ɑ̃ glɛ?]
    6. Je ne parle pas anglais.   [ʒən paʀl pɑ ɑ̃ glɛ.]
    7. Je parle un peu français.   [ʒpaʀl œ̃ pø fʀɑ̃ sɛ.]
    8. Je parle un peu anglais.   [ʒpaʀl œ̃ pø ɑ̃ glɛ.]

C. *Repeat in six short, equally stressed syllables:*

1. Merci beaucoup monsieur.	[mɛr si bo ku mə sjø.]
2. Merci beaucoup madame.	[mɛr si bo ku ma dam.]
3. Voici une lettre pour vous.	[vwa si yn lɛtr pur vu.]
4. Mais vous parlez français.	[mɛ vu par le frɑ̃ sɛ.]
5. Mais vous parlez anglais.	[mɛ vu par le ɑ̃ glɛ.]

D. *Repeat in seven short, equally stressed syllables:*

1. Vous parlez français n'est-ce pas?	[vu par le frɑ̃ sɛ nɛs pɑ?]
2. Vous parlez anglais n'est-ce pas?	[vu par le ɑ̃ glɛ nɛs pɑ?]
3. Je parle un peu français monsieur.	[ʒparl œ̃ pø frɑ̃ sɛ mə sjø.]
4. Je parle un peu français madame.	[ʒparl œ̃ pø frɑ̃ sɛ ma dam.]
5. Je parle un peu anglais monsieur.	[ʒparl œ̃ pø ɑ̃ glɛ mə sjø.]
6. Je parle un peu anglais madame.	[ʒparl œ̃ pø ɑ̃ glɛ ma dam.]
7. Je ne parle pas français monsieur.	[ʒən parl pɑ frɑ̃ sɛ mə sjø.]
8. Je ne parle pas français madame.	[ʒən parl pɑ frɑ̃ sɛ ma dam.]
9. Je ne parle pas anglais monsieur.	[ʒən parl pɑ ɑ̃ glɛ mə sjø.]
10. Je ne parle pas anglais madame.	[ʒən parl pɑ ɑ̃ glɛ ma dam.]

II. PRONUNCIATION EXERCISES.

A. French uvular "R".

Your natural reaction to the letter "r" is to turn the tip of your tongue up as you do in pronouncing an r in English; but if you turn the tip of your tongue up, you will simply...produce an English r! So in learning the French uvular "ʀ", you first put the tip of your tongue against your lower front teeth and *hold it there firmly.* Then you pronounce the English words *Ah!* and *agog,* noting that the "g" is pronounced in the back of your mouth by raising the back of your tongue until it touches your palate. Next you move your tongue a little farther back than the position in which you pronounce this [g] and pronounce very lightly each of the following French words: **art** [aʀ], **rat** [ʀa], **gare** [gaʀ], **rare** [ʀaʀ]. Repeat this series a dozen times, keeping the tip of your tongue down, using as little breath as possible, and pronouncing the "ʀ" as lightly as you can. Avoid gargling the "ʀ"! Many people pronounce it so lightly that Americans can scarcely hear it at all.

Now repeat three times each of the following words and expressions—giving equal stress to each syllable and producing the uvular "ʀ" with care:

1. Une lettre [yn lɛtʀ]. **2.** Voilà une lettre pour vous [vwa la yn lɛtʀ puʀ vu]. **3.** Bonjour [bõ ʒuʀ]. **4.** Au revoir [oʀ vwaʀ]. **5.** Merci [mɛʀ si.]

6. De rien [də ʀjɛ̃].   **7.** Parlez-vous français? [paʀ le vu fʀɑ̃ sɛ?]   **8.** Je parle un peu français [ʒpaʀl œ̃ pø fʀɑ̃ sɛ].

Repeat this exercise several times each day until you can produce the sound lightly, elegantly, and unselfconsciously. Never under any circumstances substitute an American **r** or a Spanish **r** for the uvular "ʀ". If you pronounce French words and phrases wrong even *a few times,* it makes it much more difficult to get a good French accent.

B. Exercise on the French *"u".* (Represented by the symbol [y]).

When you see the letter "u" you will naturally put your tongue in position to say "oo" as in English; but if you put your tongue in that position, you will just say "oo". So in learning to pronounce the French [y], the first step is to put your tongue in the position to say "ee" in English or [i] in French *and keep it there.*

Now you say: **Voici, i, i, i,** several times, keeping the vowel [i] short.

Next you say [i] several times and round your lips while repeating the sound [i]. If you do this, you will produce a proper French [y].

Now repeat several times: [i], [y], [i], [y] very crisply and without moving your tongue.

Now say: Voici une lettre pour vous [vwa si yn lɛtʀ puʀ vu] several times.

If you still have trouble producing the French [y], you put your hands at the corners of your mouth, say **i, i, i, i,** while moving your lips forwards and backwards so that you can't help saying [i] [y], [i] [y].

Repeat this exercise daily until you can produce this sound easily. Always think of the sound [i] as in **voici** and avoid thinking of [u] as in **vous.**

CONVERSATION 2

IPA TRANSCRIPTION OF DIALOG

a la gaʀ

1. u ɛl ʃato, silvuplɛ?   **2.** (œ̃nɑ̃plwaje) tudʀwɑ, məsjø.   **3.** u ɛl myze? **4.** lmy ze ɛ dɑl ʃa to.   **5.** jatil œ̃ʀɛstɔʀɑ̃ pʀɛ dy ʃato?   **6.** wi, məsjø. ilja œ̃ ʀɛstɔʀɑ̃ pʀɛ dy ʃato.   **7.** mɛʀsi boku.   **8.** dəʀjɛ̃, məsjø.

dɑ̃ la ʀy

9. (a œ̃pasɑ̃) paʀdõ, məsjø. u ɛl byʀod pɔst?   **10.** syʀ la plas, la bɑ, a goʃ. **11.** jatil œ̃ byʀod taba pʀɛdisi?   **12.** mɛ wi, məsjø. ilja œ̃ byʀod taba dɑ̃ laʀyd la pɛ.   **13.** uɛ laʀyd lapɛ?   **14.** a dʀwat, məsjø.   **15.** mɛʀsi boku.

I. Exercices de rythme:

    A. *Répétez en quatre syllabes:*

    1. Où est le château?   [u ɛl ʃɑ to?]
    2. Où est le musée?   [u ɛl my ze?]

    B. *Répétez en cinq syllabes:*

    1. Où est le bureau de poste?   [u ɛl by ʀod pɔst?]
    2. Où est le restaurant?   [u ɛl ʀɛs tɔ ʀɑ̃?]
    3. Dans la rue de la Paix.   [dɑ̃ la ʀyd la pɛ.]

    C. *Répétez en six syllabes:*

    1. Où est le bureau de tabac?   [u ɛl by ʀod ta ba?]
    2. Où est la rue de la Paix?   [u ɛ la ʀyd la pɛ?]
    3. Y a-t-il un restaurant . . . ?   [ja ti lœ̃ ʀɛs tɔ ʀɑ̃ . . . ?]
    4. Il y a un restaurant . . .   [il ja œ̃ ʀɛs tɔ ʀɑ̃ . . .]

II. Exercices de prononciation:

    A. Exercise on **e** [e] as in **allez-vous** and **eu** [ø] as in **un peu.**

    1. Say [e] as in allez; **e, e, e.** Keep the vowel short and clear.

    Répétez: (1) Comment allez-vous?   (2) un employé.   (3) le musée.   (4) **et vous?**   (5) un étudiant.

    2. *Say* [e], [e], [e]. Keep repeating this sound, holding the tip of your tongue against your lower front teeth and rounding your lips until you produce the sound [ø] as in **un peu.**

    Répétez: [e], [e], [e]; [ø], [ø], [ø].   (1) un **peu.**   (2) monsieur.   (3) deux.

    B. Review exercises on [R] and [y] from Conversation I.

III. Note on linking:

When a final consonant that is normally silent is pronounced with the initial vowel sound of the following word, linking (*liaison*) is said to take place: you say, of course, **les/Français** (without linking) but **les‿Américains** (with linking). It is important to note at once that linking does not take place before all words that begin with a vowel sound, but only between words that are naturally grouped together— such as the subject of a sentence and its modifiers or the verb and words immediately associated with it.

Nevertheless, linking is very tricky: while in certain cases it *must* be made and in others it would be a dreadful mistake to make it, there are many cases where linking is correct in formal speaking and inappropriate in everyday, friendly conversation. In the transcriptions of the dialogs, we have tried to indicate the way the dialogs would be spoken in a friendly, natural, and correct conversation. Here are a few additional suggestions for those who are interested:

A. Linking does take place:

NOUNS: between articles and nouns, between articles and adjectives that precede nouns, and between nouns and the adjectives that precede them:

les‿étudiants, les bons‿étudiants, des‿étudiants, deux‿étudiants, un‿autre étudiant, mes‿étudiants, mon‿étudiant.

PRONOUNS: between personal pronouns (including **y** and **en**) and verbs, and between pronouns:

ils‿ont, ont‿ils? vous‿êtes, vous‿allez. Je les‿ai achetés. Nous‿en‿avons. Donnez - nous‿en. Allez‿y.

PREPOSITIONS: between preposition and object:

dans‿un mois, en‿Italie, en‿hiver, sans‿effort, chez‿eux.

ADVERBS: between certain adverbs (the short ones) and adjectives:

très‿agréable, plus‿amusant, moins‿utile, bien‿aimable.

B. Linking does not normally take place:

NOUNS: (*a*) before nouns beginning with aspirate "h":

des/hors-d'œuvre, en/haut de l'escalier

(*b*) between nouns and adjectives that follow them:

un étudiant/américain, des cigarettes/américaines.

VERBS: between noun subject and verb:

Le train/arrive. Jean/habite à Paris. Paris/est une belle ville. Les Français/aiment les sports.

C. Linking is impossible:

before the word **huit** (tous les/huit jours); before the word **oui** (mais/oui, il a dit/oui); before or after the word **et** (Jean/et/ Hélène); in the number **cent/un.** You do not link **les/onze** or **dans/onze,** but you may say **il est‿onze heures.**

D. Linking is optional in innumerable cases.

However, optional linkings are generally to be avoided except in formal conversation, in singing, and in reading poetry. For example, we do not recommend that the following optional linkings after verbs be made in everyday conversation:

Je vais/à la gare. Je suis/à la maison. Vous parlez/anglais.
Je ne parle pas/anglais. Vous avez/un frère.

Even if you prefer to make such linkings after the verb, you should avoid linking after the inverted form between a personal pronoun and prepositions, nouns, or articles:

Allez-vous/à la gare? Parlez-vous/anglais? Avez-vous/un frère?

Such linkings would sound bookish or affected to many French people today. (For a detailed treatment of optional linking, see three articles of Pierre Delattre in the *French Review*, XXX (1956), pp. 48-54; XXIX (1955), pp. 42-49; XXI (1947), pp. 148-157.)

CONVERSATION 3

IPA TRANSCRIPTION OF DIALOG

dɑ̃laʀy

1. paʀdõ, uɛ lotɛl dyʃvalblɑ̃? 2. syʀ la plas, məsjø. 3. ɛskəsɛ lwɛ̃disi? 4. nõ, snɛpɑ lwɛ̃disi. 5. ɛskəsɛtœ̃ bɔnotɛl? 6. wi, məsjø, sɛtœ̃ tʀɛ bɔnotɛl. 7. ɛskə la kɥizin ɛ bɔn? 8. sɛʀtɛnmɑ̃, məsjø. la kɥizin ɛtɛksɛlɑ̃t. 9. jatil œ̃notʀotɛl isi? 10. wi, ilja œ̃notɛl ɑ̃ fas də legliz. 11. mɛʀsi boku. 12. dəʀjɛ̃, məsjø.

a lotɛl dyʃvalblɑ̃

13. kɛl ɛl pʀid la pɑ̃sjõ? 14. vɛ̃t sɛ̃ fʀɑ̃ paʀ ʒuʀ. 15. kɛl ɛl pʀi deʀpɑ? 16. katʀ fʀɑ̃ puʀ ləpti deʒœne, 17. ɥi fʀɑ̃ puʀl deʒœne, 18. e ɥi fʀɑ̃ puʀl dine.

I. EXERCICE DE RYTHME:

Répétez en six syllabes:

1. Est-ce que c'est près d'ici?	[ɛs kə sɛ pʀɛ di si?]
2. Est-ce que c'est loin d'ici?	[ɛs kə sɛ lwɛ̃ di si?]
3. Est-ce que c'est près de la gare?	[ɛs kə sɛ pʀɛd la gaʀ?]
4. Est-ce que c'est loin de la gare?	[ɛs kə sɛ lwɛ̃d la gaʀ?]
5. Est-ce que c'est sur la place?	[ɛs kə sɛ syʀ la plas?]

II. EXERCICES DE PRONONCIATION:

A. Exercise on the mute **e**:

Répétez en deux syllabes:

Le musée	[lmy ze]
Le château	[lʃɑ to]

Répétez en quatre syllabes:

Le prix de la pension	[lpʀid la pɑ̃ sjõ]

Répétez en cinq syllabes:

Quel est le prix des repas?	[kɛ lɛl pʀi deʀ pa?]

B. Exercise on French **"ui"** (Represented by the symbols [ɥi]).

When you see the letters **ui**, you will probably want to put your lips in position to pronounce a [w] as in the English words *suite, cuirass,* etc. So you have to avoid advancing your lips; because if you advance your lips as if to say [w], it will be difficult not to say it.

To pronounce the French [ɥi], you first repeat several times:

[i] [y], [i] [y].

Then you say, several times:

[y] [i], [y] [i]

without pausing between the two sounds and without pronouncing a [w].

Then you pronounce the two sounds in one syllable several times and you will get a proper [ɥi]. This sound is very close to the sound (yē) that is often heard in English phrases such as "Are you eating?" which, when pronounced rapidly, sounds something like (yeeting?).

Now repeat each of the following, taking care not to insert a [w] after the "s":

Je suis Monsieur Hughes.	[ʒə sɥi mə sjø yg.]
Je ne suis pas Monsieur Hughes.	[ʒən sɥi pɑ mə sjø yg.]
Je suis Américain.	[ʒə sɥi(z) a me ʀi kɛ̃.]
Je ne suis pas Américain.	[ʒən sɥi pɑ a me ʀi kɛ̃.]

CONVERSATION 4

IPA Transcription of Dialog

alɔtɛl

1. kɛl œʀ ɛtil? **2.** ilɛ(t)õzœʀ. **3.** ɛskəldeʒœne ɛ pʀɛ? **4.** nõ, məsjø, pɑzãkɔʀ.
5. a kɛl œʀ vulevu deʒœne? **6.** a õzœʀ e kaʀ, **7.** u a õzœʀ edmi. **8.** a
kɛlœʀ alevu a la gaʀ? **9.** ʒvea la gaʀ a midi. **10.** lə tʀɛ̃ puʀ paʀi aʀiv a
midi e kaʀ, nɛspa? **11.** nõ, məsjø. ilaʀiv a døzœʀ mwɛ̃lkaʀ. **12.** alɔʀ, ʒvɛ
deʒœne a midi, kɔm dabityd. **13.** ɛskəl byʀod pɔst ɛtuvɛʀ sɛtapʀɛmidi?
14. wi, məsjø. **15.** iletuvɛʀ də ɥitœʀ dy matɛ̃ a sɛtœʀ dy swaʀ.

I. Exercice de rythme:

A. *Répétez en sept syllabes:*

Est-cᴇ que lᴇ déjeuner est prêt?   [ɛs kəl de ʒœ ne ɛ pʀɛ?]
Jᴇ vais à la gare à midi.   [ʒvɛ a la gaʀ a mi di.]
Jᴇ vais déjeuner à midi.   [ʒvɛ de ʒœ ne a mi di.]

B. *Répétez en huit syllabes:*

Est-cᴇ que lᴇ bureau dᴇ postᴇ est ouvert?   [ɛs kəl by ʀod pɔst ɛ tu vɛʀ?]

C. *Répétez en dix ou onze syllabes:*

Est-cᴇ que lᴇ bureau dᴇ postᴇ est   [ɛs kəl by ʀod pɔst ɛ tu veʀ sma tɛ̃
    ouvert cᴇ matin?   *or* sə matɛ̃?]

II. Exercice de prononciation: [ɛ] (**quelle**) and [œ] (**heure**).

A. *Répétez:*
Quelle heure est-il?

B. *Dites:*
Quelle, [ɛ], [ɛ], [ɛ]. Keep the vowel short and clear.

C. *Répétez:*
1. Cet après-midi. **2.** N'est-ce pas? **3.** Sept. **4.** Prêt. **5.** Près d'ici.

D. *Dites:*
Quelle heure ... ? [œ], [œ], [œ].

E. *Répétez:*

1. Quelle heure est-il? [kɛl œʀ ɛ til?] **2.** Neuf heures [nœ vœʀ]. **3.** Neuf [nœf]. **4.** Le déjeuner [lde ʒœ ne]. **5.** Je vais déjeuner [ʒvɛ de ʒœ ne].

GRAMMAR UNIT 1

III. EXERCISE ON THE FRENCH [t]

The first step in learning to pronounce the French [t] is to hear (1) that it is produced with much less flow of air than the corresponding English sound and (2) to note that it is completely articulated in all positions.

Compare English *tent* and French **tente:** in *tent,* the first "t" is produced with a puff of air and the second one is hardly articulated at all; in **tente,** the first "t" is pronounced without the puff of air and the second is clearly articulated.

Next, note that the English "t" is produced with the tip of the tongue against the alveolar (the ridge behind the front teeth) but that the French "t" is produced with the tip of the tongue against the front teeth and the upper surface of the tongue against the alveolar.

Now hold your hand (or a strip of paper) in front of your mouth and say the following pairs of words, moving your tongue back for each English word and forward for each French word. Use as little breath as possible for the French words. (*a*) tobacco, **le tabac.** (*b*) tea, **le thé.** (*c*) two, **tout.** (*d*) toot, **toute.** (*e*) toe, **-teau.** Repeat this exercise until you can say the French words without feeling a puff of air on your hand (or seeing the paper move).

Finally, repeat each of the following, pronouncing the "t" with as little breath as possible:

1. du tabac. **2.** des cigarettes. **3.** les hôtels. **4.** le petit hôtel. **5.** le petit déjeuner. **6.** le château. **7.** près du château. **8.** tout droit. **9.** à droite. **10.** il est ouvert. **11.** huit heures du matin. **12.** Comment allez-vous?

CONVERSATION 5

IPA Transcription of Dialog

a la pRefɛktyRd pɔlis

1. kɔmɑ̃ vɯzaplevu, məsjø? **2.** ʒmapɛl ʒɑ̃ yg. **3.** kɛl ɛ vɔtR(ə) nasjɔnalite?
4. ʒsɥizamerikɛ̃. **5.** u ɛt vu ne? **6.** ʒsɥi ne a filadɛlfi. **7.** kɛl aʒ avevu?
8. ʒe vɛ̃teɶ̃enɑ̃. **9.** kɛl ɛ vɔtR prɔfɛsjɔ̃? **10.** ʒsɥizɛ̃ʒenjɶR ʃimist.
11. udmɶRevu? **12.** ʒədmɶR a paRi. **13.** kɛl ɛ vɔtR adRɛs a paRi? **14.** kɛ̃z,
avnyd lɔpsɛRvatwaR. **15.** u abit vo paRɑ̃? **16.** mɔ̃ pɛR abit a filadɛlfi.
17. ma mɛR ɛ mɔRt. **18.** avevu de paRɑ̃ ɑ̃ fRɑ̃s? **19.** nɔ̃, ʒnepɑd paRɑ̃ ɑ̃
fRɑ̃s. **20.** vwa la vɔtR(ə) kaRt didɑ̃tite. **21.** mɛRsi, məsjø.

Exercise on the French [l] (*l'hôtel*).

The French "l", like the French "t" is produced with the tip of the tongue against the front teeth.

Compare English *eel* (ēŭl) **in two syllables and French il** [il] **in** one syllable.

Now pronounce English *eel* and French **il** several times, moving the tongue forward for the French word each time and giving the French word a very brief, light utterance.

Now pronounce the following with the tongue against the front teeth for all the *t's* and *l's:*

1. l'hôtel. **2.** la lettre. **3.** Pas mal. **4.** le tabac. **5.** l'hôtel Continental.
6. l'hôtel du Cheval blanc. **7.** Quelle heure est-il? **8.** Comment s'appelle-t-il?
9. Comment s'appelle-t-elle? **10.** Quel âge a-t-il? **11.** Quel âge a-t-elle?

CONVERSATION 6

IPA Transcription of Dialog

1. ʒe fɛ̃. **2.** mwa osi. **3.** alɔ̃ deʒɶne. **4.** vwasi ɶ̃ RɛstɔRɑ̃. ɑ̃tRɔ̃. **5.** vwala
yn tablə libR. asejevu. **6.** gaRsɔ̃, dɔne mwa la kaRt, silvuplɛ. **7.** vwasi, məsjø.
vulevu de ɔRdɶvR? **8.** wi, apɔRte mwa de ɔRdɶvR. **9.** vulevu dy vɛ̃ blɑ̃ u
dy vɛ̃ Ruʒ? **10.** dy vɛ̃ Ruʒ, silvuplɛ. **11.** kɛskə vuvule kɔm pladvjɑ̃d? **12.** dy
Rɔsbif e de pɔmdətɛR fRit. **13.** kɛskə vuvule kɔm desɛR? **14.** kɛskə vuzave?
15. nuzavɔ̃ de pɔm, de banan, de pwaR e dy Rezɛ̃. **16.** apɔRte mwa yn pwaR.
17. vulevu dy kafe? **18.** wi, dɔnemwa dykafenwaR. **19.** evu, məsjø? **20.**
mɛRsi, ʒənɛmpɑl kafe. **21.** gaRsɔ̃, ladisjɔ̃, silvuplɛ. **22.** tutsɥit, məsjø.

EXERCISE ON THE FRONT [a] (**la gare**), AND THE BACK [ɑ] (**pas**).

A. *Répétez:*

la gare, [a], [a], [a].

B. *Répétez:*

1. la carte. **2.** la table. **3.** la banane. **4.** la poire. **5.** à la gare. **6.** quatre heures et quart. **7.** le café noir.

C. *Répétez:*

n'est-ce pas? [ɑ], [ɑ], [ɑ].

D. *Répétez:*

1. trois. **2.** là-bas [la bɑ]. **3.** le château. **4.** pas encore. **5.** tout droit.
6. Quel âge avez-vous?

GRAMMAR UNIT 2

I. EXERCICES DE RYTHME:

Répétez:

A. QUATRE SYLLABES.

J'ai du café.	[ʒe dy ka fe.]
Je n'ai pas de café.	[ʒne pɑd ka fe.]
J'ai de la monnaie.	[ʒed la mɔ nɛ.]
Je n'ai pas de monnaie.	[ʒne pɑd mɔ nɛ.]

B. SIX SYLLABES.

J'ai des parents en France.	[ʒe de pa rɑ̃ ɑ̃ frɑ̃s.]
Je n'ai pas de parents en France.	[ʒne pɑd pa rɑ̃ ɑ̃ frɑ̃s.]

C. SEPT SYLLABES.

J'ai une carte d'identité.	[ʒe yn kart di dɑ̃ ti te.]
Je n'ai pas de carte d'identité.	[ʒne pɑd kart di dɑ̃ ti te.]

II. EXERCICES DE PRONONCIATION SUR [ɔ] (**la pomme**) ET [o] (**l'hôtel**).

A. *Répétez:* la pomme [ɔ], [ɔ], [ɔ].

Répétez:

1. un restaurant. **2.** le bureau de poste. **3.** comme d'habitude. **4.** votre profession. **5.** votre nationalité. **6.** du rosbif. **7.** la monnaie. **8.** octobre.
9. pas encore. **10.** alors. **11.** hors-d'œuvre.

Note that the **o**'s in **octobre** are both [ɔ] [ɔk tɔbʀ], that they are not pronounced like either of the o's in English *October.* The nearest English equivalent is the short **ŭ** in Eng. *duck.*

B. *Répétez:*

l'hôtel, [o], [o], [o]. Keep the vowel short and clear.

Répétez:

1. beaucoup. **2. au** revoir. **3.** le châte**au**. **4.** le bure**au**. **5.** l'autre hôtel. **6.** v**o**s parents. **7. au**jourd'hui. **8.** de l'**eau**. **9.** l'hôtelier.

CONVERSATION 7

IPA Transcription of Dialog

1. kɛlɛladat oʒuʀdɥi? **2.** sɛtoʒuʀdɥi lə tʀɑ̃t sɛptɑ̃bʀ. **3.** kɑ̃(t) alevu amaʀsɛj? **4.** o mwadɔktɔbʀ. **5.** vwasi mɔ̃nɑ̃plwa dytɑ̃: **6.** ɔktɔbʀ e nɔvɑ̃bʀ amaʀsɛj; **7.** desɑ̃bʀ, ʒɑ̃vje e fevʀie apaʀi; **8.** maʀs e avʀil a ljõ; **9.** mɛ, ʒɥɛ̃, ʒɥije, e u apaʀi... **10.** ɛskə vuzɛt libʀ lasmɛn prɔʃɛn? **11.** vwajõ... kɛl ʒuʀ sɔm nu oʒuʀdɥi? **12.** sɛtoʒuʀdɥi vɑ̃dʀədi. **13.** ʒvɛ olabɔʀatwaʀ lœ̃di, maʀdi, mɛʀkʀədi e ʒœdi. **14.** ʒsɥi libʀ vɑ̃dʀədi, samdi e dimɑ̃ʃ. **15.** vulevuvniʀ a ʀwɑ̃ avɛkmwa? **16.** vɔlõtje. a kɛlœʀ paʀtevu? **17.** lə tʀɛ̃ paʀ a sɛ̃kœʀ. **18.** sɛtɑ̃tɑ̃dy. a ʒœdi apʀɛmidi.

Exercise on the French mute "e" as in **le cheval.**

A. *Repeat:*

le cheval [lə ʃval], [ə], [ə], [ə].
Note that the [ə] is produced with the tip of the tongue against the lower front teeth and the lips slightly rounded.

2. *Now repeat the following expressions with a mute "e":*

1. le cheval [lə ʃval]. **2.** le repas [lər pɑ]. **3.** le petit déjeuner [lə pti de ʒœ ne]. **4.** Je ne parle pas français [ʒən paʀl pɑ frɑ̃ sɛ]. **5.** De rien, monsieur [də ʀjɛ̃ mə sjø]. **6.** est-ce que [ɛskə].

B. *Repeat the following phrases and note that the mute "e's" are entirely silent.*

1. *Répétez en quatre syllabes:*

| Où est le̸ château? | [u ɛl ʃa to?] |
| Où est le̸ musée? | [u ɛl my ze?] |

La rue de la Paix.	[la ʁyd la pɛ.]
Je vais à la gare.	[ʒve a la gaʁ.]
Je n'aime pas le café.	[ʒnɛm pɑl ka fe.]
Le bureau de tabac.	[lby ʁod ta ba.]
Je m'appelle John Hughes.	[ʒma pɛl ʒɑ̃ yg.]

2. *Répétez en cinq syllabes:*

Où est le bureau de poste?	[u ɛl by ʁod pɔst?]
Je parle un peu français.	[ʒpaʁl œ̃ pø fʁɑ̃ sɛ.]
Je déjeune à midi.	[ʒde ʒœn a mi di.]
Je dîne au restaurant.	[ʒdin o ʁɛs tɔ ʁɑ̃.]
L'hôtel du Cheval blanc.	[lo tɛl dy ʃval blɑ̃.]

NOTE. Don't imagine it is difficult to pronounce French words such as **Je déjeune, Je m'appelle, Je n'aime pas,** *etc.* without sounding the mute e's. You produce these—and more difficult—combinations in English all the time without thinking about it. You have no trouble saying something like: "Zydad back" for "Is your dad back?" or "Dymother come" for "Did your mother come?" or "Zyname Percy?" for "Is your name Percy?" and so on.

GRAMMAR UNIT 3

Nasal Vowels

As English is very rich in nasal vowels, the only difficulty the French nasal vowels present is that they must be sounded without actually pronouncing the consonant **n**—except, of course, in linking.

I. EXERCICE SUR [ɛ̃] (*ingénieur*).

Répétez:

1. Très bien [ɛ], [ɛ̃]. **2.** bien. [ɛ̃], [ɛ̃], [ɛ̃]. **3.** loin. **4.** de rien. **5.** cinq heures moins le quart. **6.** vingt-cinq. **7.** Américain.

II. EXERCICE SUR [ɑ̃] (**par****e****nts**).

Répétez:

1. Des parents en France. [ɑ̃], [ɑ̃], [ɑ̃]. **2.** cent francs. **3.** cent ans. **4.** le restaurant. **5.** du vin blanc. **6.** un plat de viande. **7.** l'anglais. **8.** entendu.

III. Exercice sur [õ] (*non*).

Répétez:

1. Pardon! [õ], [õ], [õ]. **2.** bonjour. **3.** à onze heures. **4.** allons. **5.** entrons. **6.** votre profession. **7.** le garçon. **8.** un bon dîner. **9.** nous avons. 10. ils ont.

IV. Exercice sur [œ̃] (*un* **restaurant**).

Répétez:

1. **un** restaurant [œ̃], [œ̃], [œ̃]. **2. un** musée. **3. un** agent de police. **4.** lundi. **5. un** an.

Note that many French people usually substitute [ɛ̃] for [œ̃] so that **un** rhymes with **vin.** We do not recommend that students follow this practice but that they be prepared to understand words like [ɛ̃frã] (**un franc**) or [lɛ̃di] (**lundi**) when they hear them.

CONVERSATION 8

IPA Transcription of Dialog

1. ualevu? **2.** ʒveaʃte œ̃ zuʀnal. **3.** uvãtõ de ʒuʀno? **4.** õ vã deʒuʀno obyʀodtaba. **5.** avevu deʒuʀno, madam? **6.** wi, məsjø. le vwala. **7.** dɔnemwal figaʀo, silvuplɛ. **8.** ləvwasi, məsjø. **9.** kõbjɛ̃(n)es? **10.** vɛt sɛ̃ sã tim. **11.** vwa la œ̃ frã. **12.** vwala la mɔnɛː swa sãt kɛz sã tim. **13.** avevu desigaʀɛtameʀiken? **14.** ʒəʀgʀɛt, məsjø. **15.** nunavõpɑd sigaʀɛtameʀiken. **16.** ʒnɛm pɑ le sigaʀɛt frãsez. **17.** nuzavõ dytaba ameʀikɛ̃. **18.** kõbjɛ̃ kuttil? **19.** il kut də frã sɛ̃ kɑt lə pakɛ. **20.** vwa la œ̃ bijɛd sã frã. **21.** avevu la mɔnɛd sã frã? **22.** ʒkʀwakwi. la vwala. **23.** ɛstu, məsjø? **24.** wi, sɛtu puʀoʒuʀdμi.

Exercise on [ʃ] as in **le *ch*âteau** and [ʒ] as in **le dé*j*euner.**

These sounds are so much like those we produce in the words *sh*allow and ple*as*ure, that most students never bother to pronounce them as the French do. But if you pronounce them with the tip of the tongue turned up—as in English, it is very difficult to pronounce correctly such words as **je, juin, chercher,** etc.

Repeat the following words, trying hard to keep the tip of the tongue DOWN:

A. [ʃ] **1.** chercher. **2.** le château. **3.** la chambre. **4.** la chaise. **5.** je cherche.

B. [ʒ] **1.** le déjeuner. **2.** je déjeune. **3.** jeudi. **4.** le huit juin. **5.** je sais (*slowly*) [ʒə sɛ]. **6.** je sais (*quickly*) [ʒsɛ]. **7.** je suis (*slowly*) [ʒə sɥi]. **8.** je suis (*quickly*) [ʒsɥi]. **9.** Je suis ingénieur-chimiste. **10.** le quatorze juillet. **11.** Jeudi, je déjeune avec Jeanne. **12.** Je vais acheter un journal. **13.** Je crois que oui.

GRAMMAR UNIT 4

Cardinal Numbers

DATES, NUMBERS, COUNTING.

A. In dates, street numbers, telephone numbers, in counting, etc. the cardinal numbers are pronounced as follows:

1. œ̃	**11.** ɔ̃z	**21.** vɛ̃teœ̃
2. dø	**12.** duz	**22.** vɛ̃tdø
3. tʀwɑ	**13.** tʀɛz	**23.** vɛ̃ttʀwɑ
4. katʀ	**14.** katɔrz	**24.** vɛ̃tkatʀ
5. sɛ̃k	**15.** kɛ̃z	**25.** vɛ̃tsɛ̃k
6. sis	**16.** sɛz	**26.** vɛ̃tsis
7. sɛt	**17.** disset	**27.** vɛ̃tsɛt
8. ɥit	**18.** dizɥit	**28.** vɛ̃tɥit
9. nœf	**19.** diznœf	**29.** vɛ̃tnœf
10. dis	**20.** vɛ̃	

30. tʀɑ̃t	**31.** tʀɑ̃teœ̃	**32.** tʀɑ̃tdø, etc.
40. kaʀɑ̃t	**41.** kaʀɑ̃teœ̃	**42.** kaʀɑ̃tdø, etc.
50. sɛ̃kɑ̃t	**51.** sɛ̃kɑ̃teœ̃	**52.** sɛ̃kɑ̃tdø, etc.
60. swasɑ̃t	**61.** swasɑ̃teœ̃	**62.** swasɑ̃tdø, etc.
70. swasɑ̃tdis	**71.** swasɑ̃teɔz	**72.** swasɑ̃tduz, etc.

80. katʀəvɛ̃		**81.** katʀəvɛ̃œ̃, etc.
90. katʀəvɛ̃dis		**91.** katʀəvɛ̃ɔz, etc.
100. sɑ̃		**101.** sɑ̃ œ̃ **102.** sɑ̃ dø, etc.
500. sɛ̃sɑ̃		**501.** sɛ̃sɑ̃ œ̃, etc.
600. sisɑ̃		**601.** sisɑ̃ œ̃, etc.
700. sɛtsɑ̃		**701.** sɛtsɑ̃ œ̃, etc.
800. ɥisɑ̃		**801.** ɥisɑ̃ œ̃, etc.
900. nœfsɑ̃		**901.** nœfsɑ̃ œ̃

1000. mil, **1001.** mil ɛ̃, etc.		**5000.** sɛ̃mil	
1100. õzsɑ̃ *or* milsɑ̃		**6000.** simil	
1200. duzsɑ̃ *or* mildøsɑ̃		**7000.** sɛtmil	
1300. trɛzsɑ̃ *or* miltʀwɑsɑ̃, etc.		**8000.** ɥimil	
2000. dø mil		**9000.** nœfmil	
2100. dømil sɑ̃		**10.000.** dimil	
2200. dømildøsɑ̃		**500.000.** sɛ̃sɑ̃mil	
2300. dømiltʀwɑsɑ̃, etc.		**1.000.000.** ɛ̃miljõ	

B. When cardinal numbers are used purely as adjectives and are immediately followed by the nouns they modify,

(1) their final consonants are linked to a word beginning with a vowel:

1. un enfant	ɛ̃nɑ̃fɑ̃
2. deux enfants	døzɑ̃fɑ̃
3. trois enfants	trwɑzɑ̃fɑ̃
5. cinq enfants	sɛ̃kɑ̃fɑ̃
6. six enfants	sizɑ̃fɑ̃
7. sept enfants	sɛtɑ̃fɑ̃
8. huit enfants	ɥitɑ̃fɑ̃
9. neuf* enfants	nœfɑ̃fɑ̃
10. dix enfants	dizɑ̃fɑ̃

(2) the final consonant of 2, 3, 5, 6, 8, 10, is silent before a word beginning with a consonant:

2. deux francs	døfʀɑ̃
3. trois francs	tʀwɑfʀɑ̃
5. cinq francs	sɛ̃fʀɑ̃
6. six francs	sifʀɑ̃
8. huit francs	ɥifʀɑ̃
10. dix francs	difʀɑ̃

(3) the pronunciation of the final consonant of 7 and 9 before a word beginning with a consonant is optional but most people pronounce it:

7. sept francs	sɛtfʀɑ̃
dix-sept francs	dissɛtfʀɑ̃
9. neuf francs	nœffʀɑ̃
dix-neuf francs	diznœffʀɑ̃

---

* Note that in **neuf ans** and **neuf heures**, the **f** is pronounced **v**.

CONVERSATION 9

IPA Transcription of Dialog

1. kɔnɛsevu listwaʀ də fʀɑ̃s? 2. sɛʀtɛnmɑ̃. ʒkɔnɛ ʒandaʀk e napɔleõ. 3. kɛskə vusaved ʒandaʀk? 4. ʒsɛ kɛlɛne a dõremi. 5. savevu u ɛ ne napɔleõ? 6. ilɛ ne ɑ̃ kɔʀs, o dizɥitjɛm sjɛkl. 7. kɛlɛladat dəlabata:j də vatɛʀlo? 8. dizɥisɑ̃kɛz ɛ ladat dəla bata:j dəvatɛʀlo. 9. napɔleõ ɛmɔʀ œ̃ pø plytaʀ. 10. ɑ̃ kɛlane lwi katɔʀz ɛtilmɔʀ? 11. il ɛmɔʀ ɑ̃ dissɛtsɑ̃kɛz. 12. vu kɔnɛsel katɔʀz ʒɥijɛ, nɛspɑ? 13. bjɛ̃nɑ̃tɑ̃dy. sɛl ʒuʀd la fɛt nasjɔnal ɑ̃fʀɑ̃s. 14. savevu puʀkwa? 15. paʀskə sɛl ʒuʀd la pʀiz dəla bastij, 16. lə katɔʀz ʒɥijɛ, dissɛtsɑ̃ katʀəvɛ̃nœf. 17. ʒən vɛ ply vu pozed kɛstjõ. 18. vusavetu!

Exercises on [s], [z], [d], [n].

As for French [t] and [l], the tip of the tongue should be against or near the front teeth to pronounce [s], [z], [d], and [n], and less breath is used than in pronouncing the equivalent consonants in English.

With the tip of your tongue against or near the front teeth, repeat each of the following:

A. [s] and [z]:

1. Est-ce tout [ɛs tu]? 2. Vous savez tout. 3. Des cigarettes. 4. Six cents. 5. Seize cents. 6. dix-sept [dis sɛt]. 7. Ils sont [il sõ]. 8. Ils ont [il zõ].

B. [d] and [n]:

1. des bananes. 2. la date. 3. la date de la fête nationale. 4. bien entendu. 5. Suzanne n'aime pas les bananes. 6. la date de la bataille de Waterloo.

CONVERSATION 10

IPA Transcription of Dialog

1. kɔnɛsevu lwiz bədɛl? 2. nõ, ʒən la kɔnɛpɑ. 3. mɛ si. vuzave fɛ sa kɔnɛsɑ̃s ʃemaʀi samdi dɛʀnje. 4. ɛs yn pətit ʒœnfij bʀyn? 5. mɛ nõ. sɛtyn gʀɑ̃d ʒœnfij blõd. 6. də kɛl kulœʀ sõ sezjø? 7. ɛl a lezjøblø, kɔm tut leblõd. 8. o! vupaʀled la ʒœnfij abije ɑ̃ blø? 9. ɛla leʃvø blõ, leʒu ʀoz e le lɛvʀ(ə) ʀuʒ, nɛspɑ? 10. wi, sɛsa. 11. e bjɛ̃? 12. ɛl vasmaʀje ʒødi pʀɔʃɛ̃. 13. avɛk ki? 14. avɛk ʃaʀldypõ. 15. ʒkɔnɛ tʀɛbjɛ̃ ʃaʀl. 16. kɛskilfɛ? 17. ilɛtɛ̃ʒɛnjœʀ. 18. kə pɑ̃sevud ʃaʀl? 19. ʒpɑ̃s kiladlaʃɑ̃s. 20. safjɑ̃se ɛʒɔli e ɛlɛ tʀɛ ʒɑ̃tij.

Note that **Louise** is pronounced [lwiz] in one syllable. Compare: **oui** [wi]. *Repeat also:* **Louis Quatorze** [lwi ka tɔʀz] in three syllables; **Louisiane** [lwi zjan] in two syllables.

CONVERSATION 11

IPA Transcription of Dialog

I. vulevu fɛʀ ynpʀɔmnad? **2.** ʒvø bjɛ̃. kɛltɑ̃fɛtil? **3.** ilfɛbo. **4.** mɛilfɛ dyvɑ̃.
5. ɛskilfɛfʀwɑ? **6.** nõ, pɑdytu. **7.** ilnəfɛ nitʀɔʃo nitʀɔfʀwɑ. **8.** sɛtœ̃botɑ̃
puʀ ynpʀɔmnad. **9.** fotil pʀɑ̃dʀ œ̃nẽpɛʀmeabl? **10.** snɛ pɑ lapɛn. **11.** il
nə vapɑ plœvwaʀ. **12.** ɛtvusyʀ kilnɔvapɑ plœvwaʀ? **13.** wi. ləsjɛlɛblø e
ilfɛdysɔlɛj. **14.** ʒvukʀwa. **15.** ʒəkõfjɑ̃s ɑ̃vu.

(ynœʀ plytaʀ)

16. il plø; il plø(t)avɛʀs. **17.** ʒsɥi muje ʒyskozo. **18.** sɛ vɔtʀə fot. **19.** ma
fot? kɔmɑ̃ sla? **20.** vusavebjɛ̃. ʒne ply kõfjɑ̃s ɑ̃vu.

EXERCISE ON [u] (*vous*) AND [y] (*sûr*).

A. *Repeat each of the following words and phrases, making it a point
to sound the* [u] *clearly—without sounding an* **i** *or* **e** *before the* [u]
or [ŭ] *after it.*

I. Bonjour. **2.** beaucoup. **3.** Voulez-vous faire une promenade? **4.** douze.
5. C'est tout.

B. Note that the jaws are close together and the lips are rounded for
both [u] (*tout*) and [y] (*du*) : the difference between the two sounds
is made by putting the tongue forward in the mouth for [y] and
dropping it back for [u]. *Repeat slowly and carefully:*

[u] [y], [u] [y], *several times, putting your tongue forward for* [y] *and
retracting it for the* [u].

Repeat the following with great care several times:

I. [y] [u]. **2.** du tout. **3.** [ɑ] [y] [u]. **4.** pas du tout. **5.** Êtes-vous sûr?
6. Je n'ai plus confiance en vous. **7.** le musée du Louvre.

CONVERSATION 12

IPA Transcription of Dialog

I. ʀgaʀde lanɛʒ! **2.** tjɛ̃! sɛ lɑpʀəmjɛʀfwa kilnɛʒ sɛtane. **3.** ʒnɛm pɑdytu
livɛʀ. **4.** õnpømempɑ sɔʀtiʀ. **5.** mɛ si. **6.** ɑ̃nivɛʀ õpøsɔʀtiʀ. **7.** e pɥi, õ
pøpatine, fɛʀdyski, aleoteatʀ, obal, ɛtsetera. **8.** wi, mɛ livɛʀ dyʀ tʀɔ lõtɑ̃.
9. kɛl sɛzõ pʀefeʀevu, alɔʀ? **10.** ʒkʀwa kəʒ pʀɛfɛʀ lete. **11.** ʒɛm vwaʀ de
fœj syʀ lezaʀbʀ, **12.** e deflœʀ dɑ̃leʒaʀdɛ̃. **13.** mɛ la kɑ̃paɲ ɛtosi bɛl ɑ̃notɔn
kɑ̃nete, **14.** e ilfɛ mwɛ̃ʃo. **15.** wi. lotɔn kɔmɑ̃s bjɛ̃, **16.** mɛ il finimal.
17. ʒɛm mjøl pʀɛtɑ̃. **18.** vuzave ʀezõ. **19.** tulmõd ɛ kõtɑ̃d vwaʀ vəniʀ lə
pʀɛtɑ̃.

EXERCISE ON [p], [f], [k].

These consonants are much like their English equivalents except that they are pronounced with noticeably less breath.

Pronounce each of the following with as little breath as possible:

A. [p]: **1.** le papier. **2.** on peut. **3.** on ne peut pas. **4.** Et puis, on peut patiner. **5.** On peut patiner un peu. **6.** un peu plus tard.

B. [f]: **1.** des fleurs. **2.** faire du ski. **3.** je préfère. **4.** des feuilles. **5.** la première fois.

C. [k]: **1.** Quelle heure est-il? **2.** la campagne. **3.** le café. **4.** Quelle est votre profession? **5.** Quand allez-vous à Caen [kɑ̃]? **6.** Quand allez-vous à Cannes [kan]?

NOTE: One way to avoid putting too much stress on initial consonants is to practice putting the consonant at the end of the preceding word:

[ləp apje] le papier; [def lœʀ] des fleurs; [lək afe] le café.

CONVERSATION 13

IPA TRANSCRIPTION OF DIALOG

1. ʒedekuʀsafɛʀ. **2.** ʒvødabɔʀ aʃtɛ dypɛ̃. **3.** õvɑ̃dypɛ̃ alepisʀi, nɛspɑ? **4.** nõ. ilfotale ala bulɑ̃ʒʀi. **5.** ɑ̃sч̥it, ʒvø(z)aʃted lavjɑ̃d. **6.** kɛlɛspɛs dəvjɑ̃d? **7.** dybœf e dypɔʀ. **8.** puʀ ləbœf, ale(z)ala buʃʀi. **9.** puʀ ləpɔʀ, ale(z)ala ʃaʀkytʀi. **10.** fotil ale a dø magazɛ̃ difeʀɑ̃? **11.** wi. ɑ̃fʀɑ̃s, leʃaʀkytje vɑ̃d dypɔʀ. **12.** lebuʃe vɑ̃d lezotʀəzɛspɛs dəvjɑ̃d. **13.** ʒvø(z)aʃte osi dypapje alɛtʀ. **14.** õvɑ̃ dypapjealɛtʀ alafaʀmasi, nɛspɑ? **15.** nõ. lefaʀmasjɛ̃ vɑ̃d kədemedikamɑ̃. **16.** u fotilale alɔʀ? **17.** ale(z)ala libʀɛʀi u o byʀodtaba. **18.** ɛ̃si, lebuʃen vɑ̃d pɑdpɔʀ, lefaʀmasjɛ̃ vɑ̃d kə demedikamɑ̃, e õvɑ̃ dypapjealɛtʀ dɑ̃lebyʀod taba! **19.** vu pu ve(z)a le o sypɛʀ maʀʃe, si vu vule. **20.** o nõ! ʒɛm bjɛ̃ koze avɛk le maʀʃɑ̃.

CONVERSATION 14

IPA TRANSCRIPTION OF DIALOG

1. ʒsч̥izɛ̃vite ʃe le bʀun. **2.** le kɔnɛsevu? **3.** nõ, ʒən le kɔnɛpɑ. **4.** ɛskəs məsjø bʀun ɛtameʀikɛ̃? **5.** wi, il ɛtameʀikɛ̃, mɛ safam ɛfʀɑ̃sez. **6.** kɑ̃ məsjø bʀun ɛtilvəny ɑ̃fʀɑ̃s? **7.** ilɛvny ɑ̃fʀɑ̃s ilja sɛkusizɑ̃. **8.** ɛtil vəny diʀɛktəmɑ̃ dezetazyni? **9.** nõ, ʒkʀwa kilapɑse dø(z)utʀwazɑ̃ ɑ̃nɑ̃glətɛʀ. **10.** udmœʀ

məsjø bʀun? 11. ildəmœʀ pʀɛ dy bwɑdbulɔɲ. 12. kɛskilfɛ? 13. ilɛbɑ̃kje.
14. sabɑ̃k sətʀuv pʀɛdlɔpeʀɑ. 15. kɔmɑ̃ avevufɛ sakɔnɛsɑ̃s? 16. sɛtœ̃
vjɛjamid mõpɛʀ. 17. ilɛvny suvɑ̃ ʃenu afiladɛlfi. 18. ɛtvudeʒa ale ʃelebʀun?
19. wi, ʒsɥizale ʃezø plyzjœʀfwa. 20. safam elɥi õtete tʀɛzɛmabl puʀ mwa.

NOTE: French people who know English would be likely to pronounce *Brown* [braun], but others would say [brun] just as they pronounce the English word *clown* [klun].

CONVERSATION 15

IPA TRANSCRIPTION OF DIALOG

1. uɛtvuzale sɛtapʀemidi? 2. ʒsɥizale ɑ̃vil. 3. kɛskə vuzavefɛ? 4. ʒefɛde
kuʀs. 5. kɛskəvuzave(z) aʃte? 6. bokud ʃoz. 7. ʒsɥi dabɔʀ ale o pʀizunik.
8. kɛskəse kɑ̃̃epʀizunik? 9. sɛtœ̃magazɛ̃ ulõvɑ̃ dətu, 10. a bõ marʃe.
11. ɑ̃sɥit, ʒsɥizale ʃelamɔdist. 12. kwafɛʀ? 13. aʃte œ̃ ʃapo. 14. ləʃapok(ə)
vuzave syʀlatɛt? 15. wi. ɛskilvuplɛ? 16. sɛʀtenmɑ̃. 17. ilɛtœ̃pødʀol,
18. mɛ ilvuvatʀɛbjɛ̃. 19. ʒemarʃe tulapʀemidi. 20. ʒsɥi(z) œ̃pøfatige.
21. ɛtvuale ɑ̃vil apje? 22. wi, ʒevuly pʀɔfite dybotɑ̃. 23. ɑ̃tuka, sɛtpʀɔmnad
mafɛ bokudbjɛ̃.

CONVERSATION 16

IPA TRANSCRIPTION OF DIALOG

1. bõʒuʀ, madam. avevuynʃɑ̃bʀə mœble alwe? 2. wi, məsjø. ʒɑ̃neyn opʀəmje.
3. ɛskəʒpø lavwaʀ? 4. mɛwi, məsjø. paʀisi. 5. sɛlapʀəmjɛʀpɔʀtadʀwat ɑ̃
odlɛskalje. 6. vulevu bjɛ̃ mõte? 7. vɔlõtje. 8. vwasi la ʃɑ̃bʀ. kɔmɑ̃ latru-
vevu? 9. ʒlatʀuv vʀɛmɑ̃ tʀɛzagʀeabl. 10. e ɛlɛ tʀɛtʀɑ̃kil. 11. ilnja
ʒamɛdbʀɥi dɑ̃lkaʀtje. 12. tɑ̃mjø, 13. kaʀ ʒebɔzwɛ̃d tʀavajelswaʀ. 14. vwasi
lasaldəbɛ̃, avɛk oʃod tutlaʒuʀne. 15. kɛle l(ə) lwaje, silvuplɛ? 16. sɑ̃ sɛ̃ kɑ̃t
fʀɑ̃ paʀmwɑ, məsjø. 17. ʒkʀwaksetʃɑ̃bʀə m(ə) kõvjɛ̃ tutafɛ. 18. kɑ̃sʀatɛl
pʀɛt? 19. ɛskədmɛ̃ matɛ̃ vukõvjɛ̃? 20. wi, paʀfɛtmɑ̃. 21. sɛtɑ̃tɑ̃dy.
22. admɛ̃, madam.

CONVERSATION 17

IPA TRANSCRIPTION OF DIALOG

1. u iʀevu sɛtapʀemidi? 2. ʒiʀe ɑ̃vil. 3. kɛskəvufʀe? 4. ʒ(ə)fʀe dekuʀs.
5. kɛskəvuzaʃetʀe? 6. ʒaʃɛtʀe œ̃ mɑ̃to e ynʀɔb. 7. kɔmɑ̃iʀevu ɑ̃vil? 8. ʒiʀe

apje, silfɛbo. **9.** vusʀe bjɛ̃to fatige. **10.** puʀkwan pʀənevupɑ lɔtɔbys?
11. ʒnɛmpɑ pʀɑ̃dʀə lɔtɔbys. **12.** ilja tʀɔdmõd. **13.** kɛskəvufʀe silplø?
14. silplø, ʒpʀɑ̃dʀecɛ̃taksi. **15.** akɛlœʀ ʀɑ̃tʀəʀevu? **16.** ʒ(ə)ʀɑ̃tʀəʀed bɔnœʀ,
avɑ̃ sɛ̃k œʀ. **17.** nubliepɑ nɔtʀə ʀɑ̃devu puʀ səswaʀ. **18.** ʒnubliʀepɑ.
19. akɛlœʀ finiʀevu vɔtʀə tʀavaj? **20.** ʒfiniʀe vɛʀ sizœʀ. **21.** a səswaʀ.
22. ɑ̃tɑ̃dy. ʒvjɛ̃dʀe vu ʃɛʀʃe a ɥitœʀ pʀesiz.

If you can produce a French uvular [ʀ] easily and naturally before
and after all the vowels you do not need to do the following exercise.
But if you are still having a little trouble with it, this is the point
beyond which you should no longer postpone mastering it.

A. *Review the exercise on* [ʀ] *from the first pronunciation exercise on
pp. 292-3.*

B. *Repeat carefully each of the following:*

1. le rat, l'art, la gare, rare, une orange.
2. près, très, rester, l'air, la guerre.
3. répéter, je ferai, je serai, rentrer, je rentrerai.
4. Paris, Américain, j'écrirai, j'irai, je rirai *(I shall laugh)*.
5. l'heure, l'aurore, l'horreur, des roses, la route.
6. la rue, le fruit, le bruit, on construit, je crois, j'ai cru.
7. (*a*) A quelle heure finirez-vous votre travail?
    (*b*) Je rentrerai de bonne heure.
    (*c*) Je n'oublierai pas notre rendez-vous.

CONVERSATION 18

IPA Transcription of Dialog

o giʃe, a la gaʀ də lɛst

1. ʒvudʀe œ̃ bije ale ɛʀtuʀ puʀ ʀɛ̃s. **2.** kɛl klas, məsjø? **3.** s(ə)gõd, silvuplɛ.
4. kõbjɛ̃dtɑ̃sbijɛ ɛtilbõ? **5.** kɛz ʒuʀ, məsjø. **6.** ɛskəʒdwa ʃɑ̃ʒedtʀɛ̃ ɑ̃ʀut?
7. wi, vudve ʃɑ̃ʒe a epɛʀnɛ. **8.** kõbjɛ̃dtɑ̃ fotilatɑ̃dʀ lakɔʀɛspõdɑ̃s? **9.** vuzɔʀe
apøpʀe yn dəmi œ̃ʀ a epɛʀnɛ.

syʀ ləke a epɛʀnɛ

10. paʀdõ. syʀ kɛl vwa lətʀɛ̃dʀɛs aʀivtil? **11.** isi, məsjø, syʀ la pʀəmjɛʀ vwa.
12. l(ə)tʀɛ̃ ɛtilalœʀ? **13.** nõ, məsjø. ilɛtɑ̃ʀtaʀ də diminyt. **14.** ɛske ʒɔʀeltɑ̃
dale obyfɛ? **15.** vupuve(z) ɛsɛje, mɛ depeʃevu. **16.** l(ə)tʀɛ̃ saʀɛt sœlmɑ̃ tʀwa
minyt. **17.** sivumɑ̃kestʀɛ̃, vusʀezɔbliʒed paselanɥi a epɛʀnɛ.

CONVERSATION 19

IPA Transcription of Dialog

1. kɔ̃bjɛ̃ kut semuʃwaʀ? 2. (ləvɑ̃dœʀ) vɛ̃ fʀɑ laduzɛn, məsjø. 3. dɔnemɑ̃ ynduzɛn, silvuplɛ. 4. kɔ̃bjɛ̃ kut sɛt pɛʀ də gɑ̃? 5. vɛt sɛ̃ fʀɑ, məsjø. 6. segɑ̃sɔ̃til dəbɔnkalite? 7. sɛʀtɛnmɑ̃, məsjø. 8. vun tʀuvʀe ʀjɛ̃d mɛjœʀ. 9. ɑ̃navevu dotʀ? 10. wi, məsjø. ɑ̃vwasidegʀi. 11. bɔ̃. dɔnelemwa. 12. kɛlɛl pʀid sə paʀdəsy? 13. də sɑ̃ sɛ̃kɑ̃t fʀɑ, məsjø. 14. vulevu lɛsɛje? 15. vɔlɔ̃tje. 16. ilvuvatʀɛbjɛ̃. 17. ləvulevu? 18. wi. mɛtelə dɑ̃zœ̃kaʀtɔ̃, silvuplɛ. 19. vulevu lɑ̃pɔʀte tutsɥit? 20. nɔ̃, ʒən ʀɑ̃tʀəpɑ ʃemwa mɛ̃tnɑ. 21. e bjɛ̃, ʒpuʀe vulfeʀɑ̃vwaje sɛtapʀemidi. 22. ʒnepadaʀʒɑ̃ syʀmwa . . . 23. slanfɛʀjɛ̃, məsjø. 24. nuvuzɑ̃veʀɔ̃ lafaktyʀ.

CONVERSATION 20

IPA Transcription of Dialog

a la ʀɛd lɔtɔbys

1. bɔ̃ʒuʀ ʒɑ̃. kɛskəvufɛtisi? 2. vuvwaje, ʒatɑ̃ lɔtɔbys. 3. ɛskə vu latɑ̃dedpɥi lɔ̃tɑ̃? 4. ʒlatɑ̃dpɥi(z)œ̃kaʀ dœʀ. 5. vʀɛmɑ̃? vunavepavy dɔtɔbys dəpɥi(z) œ̃kaʀdœʀ? 6. si. œ̃nɔtɔbys ɛvny. 7. puʀkwan lavevupɑ pʀi? 8. ʒnepɑ pymɔ̃te. 9. iletɛ kɔ̃plɛ. 10. vwasi œ̃nɔtʀ ɔtɔbys ki aʀiv. 11. ʒvwa de ʒɑ̃dbu. 12. sanfɛʀjɛ̃. 13. mɔ̃tɔ̃ tudmɛm.

dɑ̃ lɔtɔbys

14. ilnjapɑ bokudplas . . . 15. iljɔʀadlaplas ply lwɛ̃, kɑ̃ leʒɑ̃ kɔmɑ̃sʀɔa desɑ̃dʀ. 16. ʒlɛspɛʀ. 17. u desɑ̃devu? 18. ʒdesɑ̃ a laʀɛd laʀydlapɛ. 19. ʒvɛʃelkwafœʀ. 20. mwa osi. sivuvule, ʒiʀeavɛkvu. 21. ɑ̃tɑ̃dy. nupuʀɔ̃ziale ɑ̃sɑ̃bl.

CONVERSATION 21

IPA Transcription of Dialog

1. a kɛlekɔl aljevu, kɑ̃ vuzavje duzɑ̃? 2. ʒalɛ(z)okɔlɛʒ, sɛtadiʀ a lekɔls(ə) gɔ̃dɛʀ. 3. u abitjevu asmɔmɑ̃la? 4. ʒabitɛzyn pətitvil dezalp. 5. sɛtyn ʀeʒjɔ̃ tʀɛ pitɔʀɛsk, nɛspɑ? 6. wi, mɛ sɛtvil a bjɛ̃ ʃɑ̃ʒed(ə)pɥi. 7. ɔ̃ni a kɔ̃stʀɥi dezyzin də pʀɔdɥi ʃimik. 8. l(ə) pʀɔgʀɛ, vusave . . . 9. kɛskəvufɔzje(z) alekɔl? 10. ʒtʀavaje nœvœʀ paʀ ʒuʀ. 11. kwa? 12. ʒi alɛ tulematɛ̃ a sɛtœʀ, e ʒɑ̃ sɔʀte a katʀœʀ dəlapʀemidi. 13. ɛskiljavɛ bokudelɛv dɑ̃setekɔl? 14. nɔ̃. ilnjavegɛʀ plydsɑ̃telɛv. 15. ʒkʀwakɔ̃tʀavajetʀɔ dɑ̃setekɔl. 16. ʒənsɥipɑ tutafɛdvɔtʀavi, ʒɑ̃. 17. ʒkʀwaksetekɔl mafebokudbjɛ̃.

CONVERSATION 22

IPA TRANSCRIPTION OF DIALOG

1. bõʒuʀ, maʀi.   2. ʒənvuzepɑvy obal samdidɛʀnje.   3. ʒɛspeʀɛ puʀtɑ̃ vuzi vwaʀ.   4. ʒsɥi ʀɛste alamɛzõ səswaʀla.   5. ʒənmə sɑ̃tɛpɑ tʀɛbjẽ,   6. e ʒəmsɥi kuʃedbɔnœʀ.   7. ʒɛspɛʀ kə sla netɛʀjẽ.   8. ʒ(ə)lɛspeʀɛ osi.   9. mɛl(ə) lɑ̃dmẽ,   10. ʒavɛ malalagɔʀʒ.   11. avevufɛvniʀl(ə) mɛtsẽ?   12. nõ. setɛ tusẽpləmɑ œrym.   13. ʒɛspɛʀ kəsnetɛpɑ gʀav.   14. nõ. ʒsɥi ʀɛsteoli døʒuʀ.   15. mẽtnɑ̃ ʒvɛbokumjø.   16. mɛ kɔmɑ̃ avevu(z)atʀape sla?   17. vɑ̃dʀədi, ʀɔʒe e mwa avõfe ynlõg pʀɔmnad.   18. ilfəzɛbo, mɛ ase fʀwa.   19. nuza-võmaʀʃe dɑ̃lanɛʒ ʒyskalanɥi.   20. ʒavɛfʀwɑ kɑ̃ʒsɥi ʀɑ̃tʀe.   21. vufʀe bjẽd vuʀpoze.   22. o! ʒnɑ̃muʀʀepɑ.

CONVERSATION 23

IPA TRANSCRIPTION OF DIALOG

u ɛ makʀavat?

1. sʀevu bjẽtopʀɛ, ʒɑ̃?   2. wi, tutalœʀ.   3. ʒ(ə) ʃɛʀʃ ma kʀavat ʀuʒ, mɛ ʒɔnsɛpɑ u ʒle miz.   4. ʒpø vupʀɛte yndemjɛn.   5. nõ, mɛʀsi. ʒnɛmpɑ levotʀ.   6. vuzɛt bjẽnɛmabl.   7. vuvulediʀ kəʒnepadgu, nɛspɑ?   8. ʒvødiʀ sœlmɑ̃ kəʒɛm mjø mekʀavat kəlevotʀ.   9. e bjẽ, ʃɛʀʃele, pɥiskə vulezɛmetɑ̃.   10. ɛskəʒpø pɔrte ynkʀavat vɛrt avɛk œ̃ kõplɛblø?   11. slametegal . . .   12. mɛ avevuʀgaʀde dɑ̃ vɔtʀətiʀwaʀ?   13. wi, ʒeʃɛʀʃe paʀtu.   14. ʒveʀgaʀde dɑ̃lmjẽ.   15. tjẽ! sɛtkʀavatʀuʒ nɛpɑzamwa.   16. ɛskɛlɛtavu, paʀazaʀ?   17. mɛ wi, ɛlɛtamwa.   18. sɛlakʀavat kəʒ(ə)ʃɛʀʃe.   19. puʀkwa etetɛl avɛklevotʀ?   20. ʒkʀwak labɔn admiʀtɑ̃ vokʀavat, kɛlaɛsɛjed mɑ̃dɔne yn!

CONVERSATION 24

IPA TRANSCRIPTION OF DIALOG

ʀətuʀ de vakɑ̃s

1. tjẽ, bõswaʀ, maʀi! vuzɛt dəʀtuʀ?   2. ʒsɥi kõtɑ̃d vuʀvwaʀ.   3. avevupased-bɔnvakɑ̃s dənɔel ɑ̃bʀətaɲ?   4. wi, ɛksɛlɑ̃t, mɛʀsi; mɛ tʀɔkuʀt, kɔm tutlevakɑ̃s.   5. kɑ̃ɛtvu ʀəvny?   6. ʒsɥi ʀəvny jɛʀswaʀ aõzœʀ.   7. avevu fɛbõvwajaʒ?

8. o! nə mã paʀlepɑ! 9. a ʀɛn, lɛkspʀɛsdəpaʀi etɛbõde, 10. e ʒe apɛn pytʀuve ynplas. 11. e pɥi, ilfɔzɛ(t)ɔʀiblɔmã ʃo dãlkõpaʀtimã. 12. vunave padʃãs. 13. ʒedine ovagõ ʀɛstɔʀã. 14. sɛ la sœlpaʀti dyvwajaʒ kietɛ sypɔʀtabl. 15. ɛmevu dine ovagõ ʀɛstɔʀã? 16. ase. sɛtynfasõd pɑse yndəmiœʀ. 17. kɛskəvuzavefɛ l(ə)ʒuʀ dənɔɛl? 18. skõfɛ paʀtu səʒuʀla. 19. nusɔmzale alamɛsdəminɥi. 20. nuzavõfɛlʀevɛjõ ʃe le kɛʀgelɛn. 21. ʒəmsɥi bjɛ̃namyze.

CONVERSATION 25

IPA Transcription of Dialog

si ʒetɛ ʀiʃ

1. kɛskəvufəʀje sivuzetjeʀiʃ, ʀɔʒe? 2. ʒənsɛpɑ. 3. nə vudʀievupɑ vwajaʒe? 4. si, ʒvudʀɛ vizite plyzœʀ pei(z)etʀãʒe. 5. u iʀjevu? 6. ʒiʀɛ(z)ãnitali, vizite flɔʀãs e ʀɔm, 7. ozetazyni, vwaʀ legʀatsjɛl, 8. e ãʀysi vwaʀ skispɑs labɑ. 9. ɛskəsetu? 10. nõ. ʒaʃetʀeyn gʀos ɔtɔmɔbil, 11. e ʒiʀɛ mamyze obɔʀdlamɛʀ. 12. ʒɛspeʀ kəvunsʀeʒameʀiʃ, ʀɔʒe. 13. puʀkwa ditvu sla? 14. paʀskə vusəʀje malœʀø. 15. vunsɔʀjepɑ depãse vɔtʀaʀʒã. 16. vuzave pøtɛtʀə ʀezõ. 17. ʒvudʀɛ sœlmã ɛtʀəʀiʃ də tãzãtã. 18. ʒə ynide, ʀɔʒe. 19. lakɛl? 20. ʃɛʀʃe ɶ̃ miljɔnɛʀ kipãs kɔmvu. 21. vupuʀje ʃã̃zedʀol 22. tulesimwa, paʀɛgzãpl!

CONVERSATION 26

IPA Transcription of Dialog

a vɛʀsɑj

1. ʒənkʀwajɛpɑ vɛʀsɑj si gʀã. 2. tut ɛ maʒɛstɥø: le vastə saldyʃato, le lõgzale dypaʀk, le pjɛsdo, leʒaʀdɛ̃, lefõten... 3. lwikatɔʀz ɛmɛ lasplãdœɛʀ. 4. mɛtnã, kõpʀənevu puʀkwa õ laplɛ l(ə) gʀã ʀwa? 5. wi, ʒkõpʀã. 6. nɔblɛs ɔbliʒ, vusave. 7. ʒsɛk(ə) lwikatɔʀz a fɛkõstʀɥiʀ vɛʀsɑj. 8. mɛ kiɛski lakõstʀɥi puʀ lɥi? 9. ɶ̃ dezaʀʃitɛkt ete mãsaʀ. 10. ʒe ãtãdy paʀledlɥi. 11. nuzavõ(z) ãnãglɛlmo «mænsard». 12. tjɛ̃! kɛskəsla vødiʀ? 13. ʒkʀwak(ə)sɛt ynɛspɛs dətwa. 14. l(ə)mo «mãsaʀd» ɛgzistosi ãfʀãse. 15. kɛskəse kynmãsaʀd? 16. sedɔʀdineʀ ynʃãbʀ(ə) sultwa. 17. sɛlakõmɛ levjəmœbl, leʃezkɑse, letapiyze, ɛtsetera. 18. ləsɔʀ epaʀfwa iʀɔnik. 19. kɛski vufɛdiʀ sla? 20. mãsaʀ apɑsesavi akõstʀɥiʀepalɛ, 21. e ilalɛse sõnõ aynɶ̃bləʃãbʀ.

CONVERSATION 27

IPA Transcription of Dialog

keskəvuzave?

1. keskəvuzave, maʀi? 2. ʒneʀjẽdytu, ʒvuzasyʀ. 3. mɛsi, vuzave kɛlkəʃoz. 4. vuzavelɛʀ tʀist. 5. akwapɑ̃sevu? 6. ʒpɑ̃s a ʒan. lakɔnɛsevu? 7. nõ, ʒənkʀwapɑ. ki ɛs? 8. sɛtyn dəmekuzin. 9. vuzave tɑ̃dkuzin. 10. lakɛl dəvokuzin ɛs? 11. sɛmakuzin kidmœʀ aʀɛs. 12. o wi! vumavedeʒapaʀledɛl. 13. kɛski lч̩ietaʀive? 14. ʒeʀsy jɛʀ ynlɛtʀ də matɑ̃t ɛʀnɛstin. 15. ɛlmekʀi k(ə) ʒanvasmaʀje ʒ̈ødipʀɔʃẽ. 16. kwa? ɛskə sɛtnuvɛl vuʀɑ̃tʀist? 17. nõ, okõtʀɛʀ. 18. keskivuzɑ̃nч̩i, alɔʀ? 19. ʒənpuʀepɑzale asõmaʀjaʒ. 20. sɛdɔmaʒ, ɑ̃nefɛ. 21. avɛk ki vɔtʀəkuzin s(ə)maʀitɛl? 22. avɛkõ̃eʒœnɔm kəʒkɔnɛsɛ kɑ̃tilavedizɑ̃. 23. kɔmlətɑ̃pɑs!

CONVERSATION 28

IPA Transcription of Dialog

õ̃enaksidɑ̃

o kɔmisaʀjadpɔlis

1. (lkɔmisɛʀ d(ə) pɔlis) vuzɛt bjẽ məsjø ʒɑ̃ yg, ẽʒenjœʀʃimist, 2. dəmœʀɑ̃ kẽz, avnyd lɔpsɛʀvatwaʀ? 3. wi, məsjølkɔmisɛʀ. 4. jɛʀapʀemidi, vuzavezete temwẽdlaksidɑ̃ 5. okuʀdykɛl lədɔktœʀ lɑ̃bɛʀ aeteblese? 6. wi, məsjø lkɔmisɛʀ. 7. u etjevu omɔmɑ̃ u lɔto dydɔktœʀ, 8. ki sч̩ive laʀydvoʒiʀaʀ, 9. ɛtɑ̃tʀe ɑ̃kɔlizjõ avɛkõ̃e kamjõ 10. vənɑ̃dlavny pastœʀ? 11. ʒetedvɑ̃ lẽstity pastœʀ. 12. kɔmɑ̃ laksidɑ̃ atilyljø? 13. laʃose ete tʀeglisɑ̃t, 14. kaʀ ilavɛply. 15. lədɔktœʀlɑ̃bɛʀ, dõlɔtoale tʀevit, 16. napɑpy saʀetc atɑ̃. 17. akelvitɛs ləkamjõ alɛtil 18. kɑ̃ laksidɑ̃ ayljø? 19. a ɑ̃viʀõ tʀɑ̃t kilɔmetʀalœʀ. 20. ʒvuʀmɛʀsi, məsjø. 21. skəvuvneddiʀ 22. ɛdakɔʀ avɛk leʀɑ̃sɛɲmɑ̃k nuzavõ deʒa.

CONVERSATION 29

IPA Transcription of Dialog

ʃe lɔʀlɔʒe

1. keskilja, məsjø? 2. ʒvudʀe fɛʀ ʀepaʀe sɛt mõtʀ. 3. ʒle lesetõbe jɛʀ, 4. e ɛlnəmaʀʃ ply. 5. u avevuzaʃtesɛtmõtʀəla? 6. ʒleaʃte ɑ̃nameʀik.

7. ʒmɑ̃dutɛ. **8.** ʒne ʒame vy ynmõtʀ kɔmsa. **9.** ɛskəvupuʀe laʀepaʀe tud mɛm? **10.** ʒkʀwa. ilsaʒi dynʀepaʀɑsjõ sɛpl. **11.** mɛ ʒəsʀe ɔbliʒɛd fɛʀvəniʀ œ̃ʀsɔʀ. **12.** puvevumdiʀ kɑ̃ mamõtʀəsʀapʀɛt? **13.** vwajõ ... ʒvɛkɔmɑ̃de oʒuʀdɥi ləʀsɔʀ dõʒebəzwɛ̃. **14.** ʒəlʀəsəvʀe sɑ̃dut vɛʀ ləmiljødlasmɛnpʀɔʃɛn. **15.** ʒvudʀɛ bjɛ̃navwaʀ mamõtʀ lə plyto pɔsibl. **16.** ʀəvne doʒuʀdɥi ɑ̃ ɥit. **17.** bõ. ʒatɑ̃dʀe ʒyskə la.

CONVERSATION 30

IPA TRANSCRIPTION OF DIALOG

o bõmaʀʃe

1. (lavɑ̃døz) kɛskəvudezire, madmwazɛl? **2.** ʒvudʀɛ(z) yneʃaʀp. **3.** ʃwazise, madmwazɛl. nuzavõ(z) œ̃nɛksɛlɑ̃ ʃwa. **4.** yndəmezami ɑ̃nayn kəʒɛmboku. **5.** ɛl la aʃte isi, ʒ(ə) kʀwa. **6.** də kɛl kulœʀ ɛ sɛldəvɔtʀami? **7.** sɛtyneʃaʀp dəswablɑ̃ʃ. **8.** kəpɑ̃sevud sɛteʃaʀpsi, madmwazɛl? **9.** kõbjɛ̃(n)ɛs? **10.** vɛ̃ fʀɑ̃. **11.** e sɛl la? **12.** vɛ̃t tʀwɑ fʀɑ̃. **13.** sɛtœ̃pøʃɛʀ. **14.** avevu kɛlkəʃoz dəmɛjœʀmaʀʃe? **15.** mɛwi, madmwazɛl. sɛlsi nəkutkə dizɥi fʀɑ̃. **16.** ʒkʀwak(ə) ʒɛm mjø sɛlkə vumavemõtʀe tutalœʀ. **17.** lakɛl, madmwazɛl? **18.** sɛlsi. vulevu bjɛ̃ lamɛtʀ dɑ̃zynbwat? **19.** vɔlõtje. deziʀevu otʀəʃoz, madmwazɛl? **20.** ʒvudʀɛ(z)osi demuʃwaʀ. **21.** ɛmevu søsi? **22.** kɛlɑ̃nɛlpʀi? **23.** dø fʀɑ̃ sɛ̃kɑ̃t lapjɛs. **24.** ʒɑ̃pʀɑ̃dʀe yndəmiduzɛn **25.** vulevubjɛ̃ pɛje lakɛsjɛʀ, madmwazɛl? **26.** vutʀuvʀe vozaʃa alakɛs.

CONVERSATION 31

IPA TRANSCRIPTION OF DIALOG

ɛkskyʀsjõ ala kɑ̃paɲ

1. ilja pʀɛskədøzœʀ kənuzavõkite məlœ̃. **2.** ʒkɔmɑ̃s a avwaʀ maloʒɑ̃b. **3.** ʒnepɑ labityd dale abisiklɛt. **4.** ʒkʀwak(ə)nuzavõpʀi lamɔvezʀut. **5.** ʒɑ̃ne pœʀ. **6.** vwala œ̃nɔm kitʀavaj dɑ̃sõʃɑ̃. **7.** ilpuʀa nudɔne deʀɑ̃seɲmɑ̃. **8.** (alɔm) ɛskə nu sɔm lwɛ̃dfõtɛnblo? **9.** mɛwi, mõpovʀ məsjø. **10.** ʒsɥifaʃed vuzapʀɑ̃dʀ **11.** kə vuvuzɛt tʀõpe dʀut. **12.** kɛlʀut fotil pʀɑ̃dʀ, alɔʀ? **13.** vuvwajes vilaʒ, labɑ? **14.** sɛ baʀbizõ. alezi. **15.** alasɔʀti, pʀɑnel pʀəmje ʃmɛ̃ agoʃ. **16.** il vu mɛnʀa afõtɛnblo. **17.** a kɛldistɑ̃s ɛsdisi? **18.** sɛtasɛt u ɥi kilɔmɛtʀ. **19.** zytalɔʀ! paʀsɛtʃalœʀ, snɛpɑdʀol! **20.** sivuzaveʃo e sivu zaveswaf, **21.** vupuʀe vuzaʀɛte a baʀbizõ. **22.** sɛmafam ki tjɛ̃ lobɛʀʒ **23.** ʒyst ɑ̃fas dəleɡliz.

CONVERSATION 32

IPA Transcription of Dialog

aʀive ala fɛʀm dedeʃã

1. bõʒuʀ, makuzin. 2. tjɛ̃! bõʒuʀ, ʀɔʒe. 3. kɛl bɔnsyʀpʀiz! 4. pɛʀmɛtemwad vupʀezɑ̃te ʒɑ̃ yg. 5. sɛ mõ mɛjœʀ ami. 6. ʒsɥizœʀøz dəfɛʀ vɔtʀ(e)kɔnɛsɑ̃s, məsjø. 7. ʀɔʒe masuvɑ̃ paʀledvu. 8. nuzavõndesided pʀɔfite dybotɑ̃ puʀ v(ə)niʀvuvwaʀ. 9. sɛtynɛksɛlɑ̃tide. 10. avevu fɛbõvwajaʒ? 11. wi. mɛ nusɔmzasefatige. 12. asɛjevu ɛʀpozevu. 13. vulevu pʀɑ̃dʀ(ə) kɛlkəʃoz? 14. ʒpʀɑ̃dʀed labjɛʀ, sivuzɑ̃nave. 15. evu, məsjø? 16. ʒpʀɑ̃dʀe œ̃vɛʀ dofʀɛʃ. 17. n(ə) pʀefeʀevupɑotʀəʃoz? 18. mɛnõ, makuzin. ʒɑ̃ ɛtameʀikɛ̃. 19. ilnə bwakədlo. 20. ʒɛspɛʀ bjɛ̃k(ə) vuzale pɑse kɛlkəʒuʀ avɛknu. 21. nunvulõpɑ vudeʀɑ̃ʒe. 22. nuzavõ lɛ̃tɑ̃sjõ dəʀpaʀtiʀ səswaʀ. 23. vunɛtpɑ pʀɛse. 24. ʀɛste kɛlkəʒuʀ(z)isi. 25. sɛlmɔmɑ̃d lamwasõ. 26. sivuvule, vupuʀe nuzɛde.

CONVERSATION 33

IPA Transcription of Dialog

dɑ̃ lafɔʀed fõtɛnblo

1. ʒvwa deʃɑpiɲõ obɔʀdlaʀut. 2. il dwatjɑ̃navwar boku dɑ̃l bwa. 3. si nuzɑ̃rapɔʀtjõ kɛlkəzœ̃ alamɛzõ? 4. ɛskəvukɔnɛse leʃɑpiɲõ? 5. plyz u mwɛ̃. 6. ʀamɑse sœlmɑ̃ søsi. 7. ilsõ tʀɛfasil aʀkɔnɛtʀ. 8. lədsy ɛ bʀœ̃ e lədsu ɛ ʒon. 9. bõ. mɛ ʒənsɛpa u lemɛtʀ. 10. təne, mɛtele dɑ̃səsak. 11. ɛskə səlɥisi ɛbõ? 12. wi. 13. e səlɥila? 14. ɛksɛlɑ̃. 15. o! ʒɑ̃vwaboku opjedsɛtaʀbʀ. 16. apɔʀte vɔtʀəsak, vulevu? 17. fɛt(z)atɑ̃sjõ! 18. ɛskəvuvule(z)ɑ̃pwazɔne tutlafamij? 19. mɛ seʃɑpiɲõ ʀəsɑ̃bl a søkvumave mõtʀe. 20. lemɔvɛ ʃɑpiɲõ ʀəsɑ̃bl(ə) boku obõ. 21. vuzɔʀjedym diʀsa plyto. 22. ʒe y tɔʀ dən pɑ vu pʀevniʀ. 23. ɑ̃tukɑ, ilvomjø lɛse sø dõvunɛtpɑsyʀ.

CONVERSATION 34

IPA Transcription of Dialog

a legliz dyvilaʒ

1. bõʒuʀ, məsjølkyʀe. 2. bõʒuʀ, mezami. 3. ɑ̃tʀedõ(k). 4. ʒetezɑ̃tʀɛd tʀavaje dɑ̃mõʒaʀdɛ̃ kɑ̃vuzavesɔne. 5. nunuzɛkskyzõd vudeʀɑ̃ʒe kɑ̃vuzɛt(z)ɔkype. 6. vun mədeʀɑ̃ʒe pɑdytu. 7. ʒvjɛ̃d taje meʀozje, 8. eʒsɥiza

vɔtʀ(ə) dispɔzisjõ. **9.** nuzavõzãtãdydiʀ kəvuzave yn tʀɛbɛlegliz, **10.** e nuzavõ(z)ãvid lavizite, **11.** ʒəmfʀɛ œ̃plɛzir dəvuzakõpaɲe dãvɔtʀ(ɔ)visit. **12.** mɛʒkʀɛ̃ k(ə)vunswaje œ̃pødesy. **13.** bjɛ̃kɛl swaklase mɔnymãistɔʀik, **14.** sɛtyn sɛ̃plegliz dəvilaʒ. **15.** ʒely kɛlkəpaʀ kəvɔtʀɛgliz datdyduzjemsjɛkl. **16.** ynpaʀti sœlmã dəledifisaktɥɛl dat də lepɔkʀɔman. **17.** legliz aetebʀyle ãtʀɛzsãkatʀəvẽduz **18.** e aete ãpaʀti ʀkõstʀɥit osjɛkləsɥivã. **19.** ʒeãtãdy paʀle devitʀo dvɔtʀegliz. **20.** õdi kilsõ tʀɛvjø. **21.** ʒənkʀwapɑ kiljɛplyd dø(z)utʀwɑvitʀo vʀɛmã ãsjɛ̃. **22.** laplypaʀdãtʀø sõ ʀ(ɔ)lativmã mɔdɛʀn. **23.** vulevubjɛ̃(n)ãtʀe paʀsɛtpɔʀt? **24.** lɛ̃teʀjœʀ d(ə)legliz ɛtœ̃pøsõbʀ, **25.** mɛ vozjø sabityʀõvit alɔpskyʀite.

CONVERSATION 35

IPA Transcription of Dialog

o ʒaʀdɛ̃

1. ilfok(ə)ʒajoʒaʀdɛ̃ kœjiʀdeflœʀ. **2.** vulevuk(ə)nuvuzɛdjõ? **3.** mɛwi. fɛt(z)atãsjõd bjɛ̃fɛʀmelapɔʀt. **4.** ʒənvøpak lepul pɥisãtʀe. **5.** ɛlmãʒapøpʀɛ tutmasalad. **6.** kɛlflœʀ alevukœjiʀ? **7.** ʒe bəzwɛ̃ dʀoz e dœjɛ. **8.** ʒãfʀe œ̃bukɛ puʀ lasalamãʒe. **9.** vuzave œ̃tʀɛboʒaʀdɛ̃. **10.** ʒədvʀe mãnɔkype davãtaʒ, **11.** mɛ ʒne pɑltã. **12.** ɛskəvuzave dymais? **13.** nõ, ʒnãnepɑ. **14.** dajœʀ, lete ɛtʀɔfʀɛ **15.** puʀkəl mais pɥis myʀiʀisi. **16.** ʒmãdute œ̃pø. **17.** ʀəgaʀde sepwɑ, seaʀikovɛʀ eseʃu. **18.** ilpus amɛʀvej. **19.** wi, mɛ ilnagɛʀply sɛtane. **20.** ynbɔnplɥi fʀɛdybjɛ̃ amelegym. **21.** vulevuk(ə) nulezaʀozjõ? **22.** ʒkʀwakil vomjø(z)atãdʀ **23.** ʒyskaskilfas mwɛ̃ʃo.

CONVERSATION 36

IPA Transcription of Dialog

ynpaʀtid pɛʃ

1. si nuzaljõ(z)alapɛʃ dəmɛ̃matɛ̃? **2.** akwabõ? nunatʀapʀõ ʀjɛ̃. **3.** ʒnivepɑ puʀatʀape kɛlkəʃoz. **4.** puʀkwa ialevu alɔʀ? **5.** ʒive paʀskə ʒemɛtʀ **6.** obɔʀdəlo, alõbʀədegʀãzaʀbʀ. **7.** ɛtvuʒamezale alapɛʃ ləmatɛ̃dbɔnœʀ? **8.** wi, ʒisɥizale kɛlkəfwa. **9.** nɛmevupɑ(z) ɛtʀãplenɛʀ? **10.** si. mɛ ʒənpʀã ʒamɛdpwasõ. **11.** mwa nõply, mɛ slanfɛʀjɛ̃. **12.** silõnãpʀã, tãmjø, **13.** si-lõnãpʀãpɑ, tãpi. **14.** u vulevu(z)ale? **15.** ʒkɔnɛ(z)œ̃nãdʀwa sulvjøpõ, **16.** dəlotʀkoted laʀivjɛʀ, **17.** u iljadepwasõ gʀokɔmsa! **18.** søk vumãke? **19.** nəvumɔkepɑdmwa... **20.** akɛlœʀ avevulɛtãsjõd paʀtir? **21.** dəbɔnœʀ. ilfodʀak nunuləvjõ akatʀœʀ dymatɛ̃. **22.** mɛil nəfepɑ(z)ãkɔʀ ʒuʀ asɛtœʀla. **23.** ʒystəmã! nuvɛʀõlsɔlej səlve syʀlaʀivjɛʀ. **24.** dəkwa vuplɛɲevu?

CONVERSATION 37

IPA TRANSCRIPTION OF DIALOG

aʀive alagaʀ dəljõ

1. bõʒuʀ, ʒɑ̃. bõʒuʀ, ʀɔʒe. ʒsɥizœʀøz dəvuʀvwaʀ.   **2.** nu(z)osi, nusɔmzɑ̃ʃɑ̃ted vuvʀwaʀ, maʀi.   **3.** vunuzave mɑ̃ke boku, vusave.   **4.** flatœʀ!   **5.** seʒɑ̃tid vɔtʀ(ə) paʀ dɛtʀ(ə) vny nuzatɑ̃dʀalagaʀ.   **6.** ʒəmdəmɑ̃d sivuvuʀɑ̃dekõt kə ʒe fɛ puʀ vu œ̃ gʀɑ̃ sakʀifis.   **7.** ʒədvɛ ʒwe otɛnis s(ə)matɛ̃.   **8.** mɛ kɑ̃ ʒeapʀik vudəvje ʀəvniʀ oʒuʀdɥi, ʒedesided vəniʀ vuzatɑdʀisi.   **9.** kɑ̃(t)avevuʀsy nɔtʀə depɛʃ?   **10.** ilja apøpʀe ynœʀ.   **11.** mɛvuzɔʀjedym diʀ lœʀɛgzakt dəvɔtʀaʀive.   **12.** nunlasavjõpɑ numɛm.   **13.** nunetjõpɑsyʀ datʀapeltʀɛ̃ də ɥitœʀedmi.   **14.** ʒɑ̃, vɔtʀəkõsjɛʀʒ matelefɔne kœ̃ kablɔgʀam puʀvu ɛtaʀivesmatɛ̃.   **15.** o! ʒsɛskəsɛ.   **16.** elɛnfʀɑzɛʀdwataʀive seʒuʀsi.   **17.** ɛlmɛ̃dik sɑ̃dut ləʒuʀd(ə) sõnaʀive.   **18.** tjɛ̃, tjɛ̃! ki ɛ sɛt elɛn?   **19.** sɛtynʒœnameʀikɛn dəmezami kiɛtaktɥɛlmɑ̃ a lõdʀ.   **20.** ɛlmadmɑ̃ded lɥisɛʀviʀdəgid apaʀi.

CONVERSATION 38

IPA TRANSCRIPTION OF DIALOG

alatɛʀas dœ̃kafe

1. asejõnu(z)alatɛʀas dəskafe.   **2.** nupuʀõ vwaʀpɑse leʒɑ̃.   **3.** kɛl ɛsmɔnymɑ̃ lɑbɑ, ɔbudlaʀy?   **4.** vudəvʀije ləʀkɔnɛtʀ. sɛl pɑteõ.   **5.** o! ʒmɑ̃ suvjɛ̃.   **6.** selɑ̃dʀwa u lõnɑ̃tɛʀ legʀɑ̃zɔm, nɛspɑ?   **7.** wi, kɛlkəzœ̃ dɑ̃tʀø.   **8.** õtʀuvla nɔtamɑ̃ letõbodvɔltɛʀ ed viktɔʀygo.   **9.** puʀkwa apɛltõ sɛtpaʀtidpaʀi l(ə) kaʀtjelatɛ̃?   **10.** paʀskə sɛlkaʀtjedlyniveʀsite, ekl(ə)latɛ̃ etɛtotʀəfwa la lɑ̃gdə lyniveʀsite.   **11.** u ɛ dõk lasɔʀbɔn?   **12.** adøpɑ disi.   **13.** nuziʀõ tutalœʀ, sivuvule.   **14.** puʀkwa apɛltõ lyniveʀsitedpaʀi la sɔʀbɔn?   **15.** ʒely lɛksplikasjõ kɛlkəpaʀ, mɛ ʒɑ̃n məlaʀapɛlpɑ . . .   **16.** sɛkotɑ̃d sɛlwi, œ̃sɛʀtɛ̃ ʀɔbɛʀd(ə) sɔʀbõ afõde œ̃kɔlɛʒ puʀ lezetydjɑ̃d teɔlɔʒi.   **17.** sə kɔlɛʒ, aple lasɔʀbɔn, ɛ dəvny lafakyltedelɛtʀ e lafakyltedesjɑ̃s.   **18.** tusezetydjɑ̃ õlɛ̃ʀ seʀjø e pʀeɔkype . . .   **19.** iljadkwa.   **20.** ilsõtɑ̃tʀɛ̃dpɑse lœʀzɛgzamɛ̃ e lezegzamɛ̃, ɑ̃fʀɑ̃s, nəsõpɑ fasil.

CONVERSATION 39

IPA TRANSCRIPTION OF DIALOG

ləlõdeke

1. kəʀgaʀd seʒɑ̃la, ləlõd lasen?   **2.** ilzegzamin lezetalaʒ debukinist.   **3.** kəvɑ̃d sebukinist?   **4.** tutsɔʀtdəʃoz.   **5.** lezœ̃vɑ̃d dəvjejzɛstɑ̃p, dotʀə detɛ̃bʀəpɔst,

dotʀə dəvjɛj pjɛsdəmɔnɛ, mɛlaplypaʀ fõlkɔmɛʀs delivʀ(ə) dɔkɑzjõ. **6.** mõ-
fʀɛʀ madmãded lчi ãvwaje detẽbʀ. **7.** tʀavɛʀsõlaʀy. **8.** nupuʀõʒte ǿkudœj
syʀlezetalaʒ. **9.** savevu kɛltẽbʀə vɔtʀ(ə)fʀɛʀ vøspʀɔkyʀe? **10.** wi, ʒedãmõsak
ynlist kiladʀɛse. **11.** (o bukinist) avevu letẽbʀəẽdike syʀsɛt list? **12.** vwa-
jõzǿpø...maʀtinik dizчisãkatʀəvẽsis; s(ə)gõtãpiʀ, dizчisãsẽkãttʀwa; senegal,
diznœfsãtʀwa; ɛtseteʀa. **13.** wi, madmwazɛl. ʒkʀwa lezavwaʀ tus, sɔf letẽbʀə
dysgõtãpiʀ, seʀi dizчisãsẽkãttʀwa. **14.** il nəmãʀɛst okǿ. **15.** tãpi. **16.** vulevu kõsylte sɛtalbɔm? **17.** vuzitʀuvʀe pøtɛtʀ sɛʀtẽ tẽbʀ kivuzẽteʀɛs.
18. ʒənkɔnɛpa gʀãʃoz otẽbʀəpɔst. **19.** vunaveka ʃwazir leplyʒɔli. **20.** o nõ!
iljakɛlkətã, ʒe ãvwaje plyzjœʀ tẽbʀ amõfʀɛʀ. **21.** ʒavɛʃwazi leplyʒɔli.
22. mɛ ilavɛ deʒa laplypaʀ dãtʀø, e ilmadik mõʃwan valɛʀjẽ.

CONVERSATION 40

IPA Transcription of Dialog

o tчilʀi

1. mẽtnã, ãtʀõ dãlʒaʀdẽ detчilʀi. **2.** kə pãsevudsəkwẽd paʀi? **3.** ʒsчizetɔned
tʀuve tãdɛspas okœʀmɛm dəlavil. **4.** ʒnavɛ pɑ lamwẽdʀided(ə) letãdyd
laplasd(ə)lakõkɔʀd. **5.** mɛ, ditmwa, kɛlɛsgʀãbatimãdvãnu? **6.** sɛl(ə)luvʀ,
ãsjẽpalɛ ʀwajal. **7.** ɛskəsela kɛl myzedy luvʀ? **8.** wi; mɛl myze nɔkyp
kynpaʀtid ledifis. **9.** ləʀɛst ɛtɔkype paʀ debyʀo deministɛʀ. **10.** e vwala
laʀk də tʀiõf. **11.** dapʀe lefɔtɔgʀafik ʒevy, ʒəl kʀwaje plygʀã. **12.** se
laʀkdətʀiõf dykaʀuzɛl kəvuvwajela. **13.** lotʀ, selчid letwal, ɛtobudlavny de
ʃãzelize. **14.** sivuvuʀtuʀne, vupuʀelvwaʀ labɑ... **15.** ʀ(ə)gaʀde sɛt pətitfij
kiplœʀ, ʒã. **16.** ləvã a ãmne sõbatoavwal omiljø dybasẽ. **17.** ɛskəvupuve
lɛde? **18.** ʒɔʀɛ bo fɛʀ. **19.** l(ə)bato ɛtʀɔlwẽ puʀkəʒpчis latẽdʀ. **20.** ləvã
finiʀɑ sã dut paʀ ləʀamneobɔʀ. **21.** ʒe ãvidkœjiʀ yndəsefloeʀ kɔmsuvniʀ
dənɔtʀ(ə) pʀɔmnad. **22.** gaʀdevuzã bjẽ. **23.** si ǿenaʒãdpɔlis vuvwajɛ,
ilpuʀɛ bjẽ vufɛʀ ǿepʀɔsevɛʀbal.

CONVERSATION 41

IPA Transcription of Dialog

anɔtʀədam

1. nusɔm mẽtnã dã lildɔlasite. **2.** ɛskõnapɛlpɑzosi sɛtil lildəfʀãs? **3.** ʒe pœʀ
kə vun kõfõdje vozil, elɛn. **4.** lildəfʀãs ɛ laʀeʒjõ otuʀd(ə)pari. **5.** lildəlasite
ɛtynil omiljød lasen. **6.** ʒəʀkɔnɛ, adʀwat, letuʀ d(ə) nɔtʀədam. **7.** sinuvizitjõ
nɔtʀədam? **8.** mɛwi. tʀavɛʀsõ laplas e ãtʀõ dãlakatedʀal. **9.** atãdekəʒpʀɛn
ynfɔto.

(dɑ̃ nɔtʀədam)

10. kɔm lɛ̃teʀjœʀ ɛvast esilɑ̃sjø!   11. õnozapɛnpaʀle, mɛmavwabɑs.   12. ʒvudʀɛ bjẽnasiste aynmɛs anɔtʀədam.   13. sivuvule, nuʀvjẽdʀõ dimɑ̃ʃpʀɔʃɛ̃. 14. vupuʀezɑ̃tɑ̃dʀə legʀɑ̃dzɔʀg.   15. ɛskõpømõte ɑ̃ o detuʀ?   16. ʀjẽd plyfasil. 17. sɛtɛskalje ɑ̃kɔlimasõ nuzikõdɥiʀa.   18. ɑ̃naʀivɑ̃ ɑ̃ o, vupuʀepʀɑ̃dʀə dotʀəfɔto.

(ɑ̃ o dyndetuʀ dənɔtʀədam)

19. ʒsɥizesufle . . .   20. mɛ kɛlpanɔʀama! õvwapaʀi tutɑ̃tje.   21. dəvɑ̃vu, vuzave la sɛ̃tʃapɛl, ləluvʀ eleʃɑ̃zelize; syʀlaʀivgoʃ, ləkaʀtjelatɛ̃ e lasɔʀbɔn; esyʀlaʀiv dʀwat, legʀɑ̃bulvaʀ emõmaʀtʀ.   22. ʒe ɑt dəvizite lekaʀtjedpaʀik(ə) ʒən kɔnɛpɑzɑ̃kɔʀ.

The Relation Between French Spelling and French Pronunciation

When students first begin to read French on their own, they sometimes seem to forget all they have learned about French pronunciation. They often even mispronounce words they have been using and pronouncing correctly for several weeks.

In order to combat this tendency, it is useful to explain what reading in a foreign language means (pp. xvi-xviii, Introduction) and give the students information about diacritical marks and about the way the various combinations of vowels and consonants are pronounced. The following section contains the material we have found most effective. Useful as this information may be, however, rather than have students study the entire section at once, we try to introduce each item at a moment when it will actually clarify a difficulty which comes up in a reading exercise. For example, the moment at which the student will perhaps be most receptive to the statement that **-ien** is pronounced [jɛ̃] as in **bien, rien, le chien** is when he stumbles on the pronunciation of a form such as **Je viendrai.**

I. DIACRITICAL SIGNS

The following typographical signs are used (*a*) to distinguish between two or more possible pronunciations of a letter, or (*b*) to distinguish between two words which are pronounced alike, and, except for the diacritical marks, are spelled alike. *In no case do these signs indicate that a syllable should be stressed.*

A. The acute accent (´) (**accent aigu**) is used only on the vowel e: l'été, espérer. The **é** is usually pronounced [e].

B. The grave accent (`) (**accent grave**) is used mostly on e followed by a final s or -re: très, près, après-midi; père, frère, j'espère, ils allèrent. The **è** is always pronounced [ɛ].

This accent is also used on the **a** in the preposition **à,** *to,* to distinguish it from the third person singular of the present indicative of **avoir.** Likewise it is used on the **a** of the adverb **là,** *there,* to distinguish it from the article **la,** *the,* as well as on the **u** of the adverb **où,** *where,* to distinguish it from the conjunction **ou,** *or.*

C. The circumflex accent (ˆ) (**accent circonflexe**) is found on all the vowels (except the semi-vowel **y**) : âme, même, île, hôtel, sûr. An **â** is usually pronounced [ɑ], **ê** [ɛ], **î** [i], **ô** [o], **û** [y].

D. The cedilla (¸) (**cédille**) under **c** indicates that the letter is pronounced [s].

E. When a diaeresis (¨) (**tréma**) is placed over the second of two vowels, it indicates that the vowel so marked begins a new syllable. **Noël, naïf.**

Note, however, that the name **Saint-Saëns** is pronounced [sɛ̃ sɑ̃s].

II. ELISION

When a vowel is dropped out before a word beginning with a vowel or mute **h,** elision (**élision**) is said to take place. You can't just assume that *any* final vowel is elided before any initial vowel. Elision takes place in the following cases:

A. When the article **le** or **la** is immediately followed by a noun or adjective beginning with a vowel sound, the **e** (or **a**) of the article is elided.

B. When **je, me, te, se, ce, le, la, ne, que** are immediately followed by a verb that begins with a vowel sound or the word **en,** the **e** is elided.

C. The **i** of **si** is elided when it is followed by **il, ils.** This vowel is not elided elsewhere: you write (and say) **si elle, si un homme, si on,** etc.

D. When **entre, que, parce que, puisque, lorsque** are followed by a pronoun beginning with a vowel, the final **e** is elided.

Note that before the words **huit** and **onze, le** is not elided: **le huit septembre, le onze mars.**

Remember also that the demonstrative adjective **ce** is not elided but is replaced by the form **cet** before nouns beginning with a vowel sound.

III. SYLLABICATION

In dividing French words into syllables, in so far as possible each syllable should begin with a consonant and end in a vowel.

A. When a single consonant stands between two vowels, the consonant goes with the vowel which follows it: **bu·reau, ta·bac, hô·tel, ga·re, vou·lez.**

B. When a double consonant (**tt, dd, pp,** etc.) stands between two vowels:

(1) in most cases it represents a single sound and stands in the following syllable: **donnez** [dɔ-ne], **allez** [a-le], **excellent** [ɛk-sɛ-lɑ̃], **addition** [a-di-sjɔ̃]:

(2) in some cases it represents two consonants, one of which is pronounced with the previous vowel and one with the following one: **accident** [ak-si-dɑ̃], **suggérer** [syg-ʒe-ʀe].

C. When two or more different consonants stand between vowels:

(1) one consonant may go with the vowel which precedes and one with the one which follows: **mer·ci, par·lez, res·tau·rant, ob·ser·va·toire;**

(2) two consonants may form a consonant cluster* and stand together at the beginning of the following syllable: **ta·ble, li·bre, a·près, qua·tre;**

(3) one consonant may go with the preceding vowel and a consonant cluster* may stand together at the beginning of the next syllable: **en·ten·dre, or·ches·tre, mal·gré, em·ploi.**

The digraphs **ch, ph, th, gn** (each of which of course represents a single sound) always stand with the vowel which follows.

Repeat the following pairs of words and note especially the way the French words are divided: *American,* **A·mé·ri·cain;** *nationality,* **na·tio·na·li·té;** *profession,* **pro·fe·ssion;** *democratic,* **dé·mo·cra·tique;** *Philadelphia,* **Phi·la·del·phie.**

Note that **n, m** behave one way when they are followed by a vowel (**i·nutile**) and another when they are not (**in·telligent, j'ai faim**), but in both cases the principle that syllables tend to begin with a consonant and end with a vowel is preserved: [i-ny-til], [ɛ̃-tɛ-li-ʒɑ̃], [ʒe fɛ].

---

* The following are the consonant clusters which occur commonly: **bl, cl, fl, gl, pl; br, cr, dr, gr, pr, tr, vr.**

IV. CONSONANTS

LETTER   PRONUNCIATION

b	[b]	in practically all cases: une banane, le bébé.
	[p]	when followed by **t** or **s**: absurde, absent, absolument, obtenir.
		Silent when final: les soldats de plomb.
c	[k]	when followed by **a, o, u,** or **l, r**: le café, le corps, la curiosité, je crois.
	[s]	when followed by **e, i, y**: c'est, certainement, ici, la bicyclette.
	[k]	usually when final: avec, le sac.
		Silent in: le tabac, franc, blanc, le porc.
	[g]	in: second, secondaire, anecdote.
ç	[s]	Used only before **a, o, u**: le français, le garçon, j'ai reçu.
cc	[k]	except when followed by **e, i, y**: accorder.
	[ks]	when followed by **e, i, y**: accepter, accident.
ch	[ʃ]	usually: chercher, le chimiste, chez, Charles.
	[k]	sometimes: un orchestre, le chœur.
d	[d]	in practically all cases: dans, l'addition, madame, le sud.
		Usually silent when final: le pied, le nid, le hasard, le nord.
	[t]	in: tout de suite, le médecin, quand il . . .
f	[f]	in practically all cases: franc, le café.
	[f]	usually when final: le chef, neuf, le rosbif, un œuf.
		Silent in: les œufs, les bœufs, la clef.
	[v]	in: neuf heures, neuf ans.
g	[g]	when followed by **a, o, u,** or **l, r**: la gare, grand.
	[ʒ]	when followed by **e, i, y**: gentil, les gens, la girafe, le gymnase.
gg	[gʒ]	when followed by **e, i, y**: suggérer.
gn	[ɲ]	la campagne, la Bretagne, la vigne.
gu	[g]	in: la guerre, le guide.
	[gɥ]	in: aiguille.
	[gy]	in: aigu.
h		Always silent: l'homme, l'hôtel, les hors-d'œuvre.
j	[ʒ]	janvier, je déjeune.
k	[k]	le kilo.
l	[l]	usually pronounced even when final: l'hôtel, le cheval.
		Silent in: gentil, le fusil, le fils, le pouls.
	[j]	when preceded by **ai** or **ei**: le travail, le soleil, vieil, etc.
ll	[j]	when preceded by **ai, ei, ui**: travailler, vieille.
	[j]	usually when preceded by **i**: la fille, gentille, juillet, la famille.
	[l]	in: ville, village, mille, tranquille, illustrer, etc.

LETTER   PRONUNCIATION

m	[m]	at the beginning of a syllable: aimer, madame, calme. When final in a syllable, **m** causes the preceding vowel to be nasalized but is not otherwise pronounced: faim [fɛ̃], chambre [ʃɑ̃bʀ], ensemble [ɑ̃sɑ̃bl], important [ɛ̃pɔʀtɑ̃].
mm	[m]	l'homme, comme, comment.
n	[n]	at the beginning of a syllable; nous, une, inutile. When final in a syllable or when followed by a consonant, **n** nasalizes a preceding vowel but is not otherwise pronounced: bon [bõ], vingt [vɛ̃], enfant [ɑ̃fɑ̃], intelligent [ɛ̃tɛliʒɑ̃], la France [lafʀɑ̃s]. Silent in **-ent** verb endings.
nn	[n]	bonne, sonner, donnez, l'année.
p	[p]	in practically all cases: le papier, le départ, l'aptitude, le pneu, la psychologie, le psaume. Usually silent when final: trop, beaucoup. Silent in: le temps, compter, la sculpture, etc.
q, qu	[k]	in practically all cases: qui, que, quel, le coq.
qu	[kw]	in: une aquarelle, un aquarium.
r	[ʀ]	in practically all cases: la rue, très, l'art, vers. Pronounced when final in: le fer, la mer, fier, cher, car, pour, l'hiver, etc. Silent in infinitive ending **-er,** and in: boucher, boulanger, charcutier, épicier, monsieur, léger, premier, volontiers, etc.
s	[s]	at beginning of a word or when preceded or followed by a consonant: absent, sang, aspect, etc.
	[z]	when between vowels: la raison, la maison, les roses.
	[z]	when linked: vous‿avez. Usually silent when final: les, tables, lesquels.
	[s]	in: le fils, mars, le sens, tous (*pronoun*), omnibus, autobus, Reims, Saint-Saëns, etc.
sc	[sk]	when followed by **a, o, u,** or **l, r:** la sculpture, scolaire.
	[s]	when followed by **e, i, y:** la science, le scénario.
ss	[s]	assez, aussi, essayer.
t	[t]	at beginning of a syllable: le temps, l'été, l'amitié. Silent when final in verb forms (except in linking) and in most nouns and adjectives: le lit, le restaurant, élégant, différent, cent, vingt, excellent, tout, etc.
	[t]	in: l'est, l'ouest, net, la dot, Brest, tact, intact, exact.
th	[t]	le thé, le théâtre.

LETTER	PRONUNCIATION	
ti	[s]	in -tion ending, and in: démocratie, initial, patience, etc.
v	[v]	in all cases: voulez-vous? avez-vous?
w	[v]	in: le wagon, Waterloo.
	[w]	in: le tramway, le sandwich.
x	[ks]	in: excellent, le luxe, l'index.
	[gz]	in: exact, exemple, examen.
	[s]	in: soixante; and in dix, six when final in a phrase.
	[z]	in: dix, six when linked: dix ‿ enfants.
		Silent in: dix, six, when followed by a word beginning with a pronounced consonant: dix francs; and in: paix, voix, etc.
y	[j]	in: les yeux, payer, il y a, envoyer.
z	[z]	le zéro, le gaz, zut!
		Silent in -ez verb ending and in: chez (except in linking).

V. VOWELS

LETTER	PRONUNCIATION	
a, à	[a]	in most cases: la gare, l'accident, la table, à Paris.
	[ɑ]	in: pas, phrase, vase, etc.
â	[ɑ]	in most cases: âge, âme, pâle, château.
ai	[ɛ]	except when final: j'avais, il avait, il fait, ils avaient.
	[ə]	in: nous faisons, je faisais, tu faisais, etc.
	[e]	when final: j'ai, j'irai.
au	[o]	in most cases: au Canada, haut, il faut, chaud.
	[ɔ]	in: j'aurai, le restaurant, Paul.
ay	[ɛj]	in: essayer, payer, ayez.
	[ei]	in: le pays.
	[aj]	in: La Fayette.
è, ê	[ɛ]	je me lève, le père, la tête, vous êtes.
	[e]	l'été, espérer, allé.
e	[ɛ]	when followed by two consonants or in final syllable when followed by a single pronounced consonant: rester, verte, avec, mettre; and in: il est.
	[e]	in final syllable when followed by silent d, f, r, z: pied, la clef, le boucher, allez; and in: et, and les, mes, etc.
	[ə]	in the words je, me, te, se, ce, le, de, ne, que; and in the first syllable of many words such as: venir, demander, demain, cheval, etc.

This [ə] is usually omitted in conversation if the phrase is easily pronounced without the vowel.

Silent in words of more than one syllable when final or when followed by silent s or nt: ville, robes, parle, parles, parlent. |

LETTER	PRONUNCIATION	
eau	[o]	le bureau, l'eau, le veau.
ei	[ɛ]	la neige, la peine.
ey	[ɛj]	asseyez-vous.
eu	[œ]	in most cases when followed in the same word by a pronounced consonant: neuf, leur, jeune, Europe.
	[ø]	when final, or when followed by the sound [z] or a silent final consonant: un peu, deux, il veut, les yeux, heureuse.
	[y]	in *passé simple,* imperfect subjunctive, and past participle of avoir: j'eus, etc.; il eût, etc.; il a eu, etc.
i	[i]	ici.
o	[ɔ]	except when followed by a silent final consonant or the sound [z] or [sj]: notre, joli, l'école, objet, hors-d'œuvre, les pommes, la note, la dot, la robe.
	[o]	when followed by a silent final consonant or the sound [z] or [sj]: mot, dos, nos, gros, la rose, poser, motion.
ô	[o]	le nôtre, table d'hôte, ôter.
œu	[œ]	when followed in the same word by a pronounced consonant: la sœur, hors-d'œuvre, un œuf, le bœuf.
	[ø]	in the plural forms œufs [ø], bœufs [bø].
oi	[wa]	moi, une poire, la boîte, une fois.
	[wɑ]	trois, le mois, le bois, les pois, le roi, froid.
ou, où	[u]	nous, voulez-vous? toujours, où? ou.
oui	[wi]	Louis, oui.
oy	[waj]	loyer, soyons, voyons.
u	[y]	sur, plus, une, la rue, du café.
ua	[ɥa]	nuage.
ue	[ɥɛ]	actuel, actuellement.
ui	[ɥi]	puis, huit, je suis, la nuit, lui, le bruit, juillet.
uy	[yj]	gruyère.
	[ɥij]	fuyez, ennuyer, appuyer.
y	[i]	in: j'y vais, le pays, la bicyclette, Égypte, Ypres.

VI. NASAL VOWELS

A. Generally speaking, when vowels are followed in the same syllable by **m, n,** the vowel is nasalized and the **m** or **n** is not pronounced.

LETTER	PRONUNCIATION	
a	[ã]	quand, sans, grand, l'anglais, la chambre, allemand.
ae	[ã]	Caen, Saint-Saëns.
ai	[ɛ̃]	le pain, le bain, la faim, la main.
ao	[ã]	Laon, le paon.

LETTER	PRONUNCIATION	
e	[ɑ̃]	en, ensemble, le temps, le membre, la dent, vendre, emmener [ɑ̃mne], l'ennui, évident.
	[a]	évidemment, solennel, la femme.
	[ɛ̃]	examen, européen, le citoyen.
i	[ɛ̃]	la fin, le vin, vingt, impossible.
ie	[jɛ̃]	bien, rien, le chien, ancien, il tient, vous viendrez, etc.
	[i]	in: ils étudient.
	[jɑ̃]	in: patience, orient, science.
o	[ɔ̃]	on, bon, non, sont, onze, l'oncle, le nom, le nombre, compter.
	[ə]	in: monsieur.
oi	[wɛ̃]	loin, moins, le coin, le point.
u	[œ̃]	un, chacun, lundi, le parfum.
	[ɔ]	in a few Latin words: album, postscriptum, maximum.
ui	[ɥɛ̃]	juin.

B. Vowels followed by **mm, nn** are usually not nasalized.

a	[a]	année, constamment, élégamment.
e	[ɛ]	ennemi, prennent, tiennent, viennent.
o	[ɔ]	comme, comment, bonne, sonner, l'homme, nommer, le sommeil, Sorbonne, la monnaie.

Verb Forms

I. REGULAR VERBS

118. Formation of regular verbs from key forms.

All the forms of regular verbs can be derived from the following key forms: the present infinitive, the present indicative, the past participle, and the *passé simple*. The following paragraphs contain an explanation of the way the various forms can be derived.

119. Forms which can be derived from the infinitive.

A. To form the future tense, add to the infinitive* the endings: **-ai, -as, -a, -ons, -ez, -ont.** Examples:

donner	je donnerai	*I shall give*
finir	je finirai	*I shall finish*
vendre	je vendrai	*I shall sell*

B. To form the present conditional, add to the infinitive* the endings: **-ais, -ais, -ait, -ions, -iez, -aient.** Examples:

donner	je donnerais	*I should* or *would give*
finir	je finirais	*I should* or *would finish*
vendre	je vendrais	*I should* or *would sell*

120. Forms which can be derived from the present indicative.†

A. To form *the present participle,* drop the **-ons** of the first person plural of the present indicative and add the ending **-ant.** Examples:

nous donnons	donnant	*giving*
nous finissons	finissant	*finishing*
nous vendons	vendant	*selling*

B. To form *the imperfect indicative,* drop the **-ons** of the first person plural of the present indicative and add the endings: **-ais, -ais, -ait, -ions, -iez, -aient.** Examples:

---

* For infinitives of the third conjugation, the **-e** of the **-re** ending is omitted. Ex.: je vendrai, je répondrai, etc.

† For the formation of the present indicative of regular verbs, see paragraph 14 (2); paragraph 33 (1); and paragraph 35 (1).

nous donnons	je donnais	*I was giving, etc.*
nous finissons	je finissais	*I was finishing, etc.*
nous vendons	je vendais	*I was selling, etc.*

C. To form *the imperative,* use the following forms of the present indicative without the pronoun subject: the second person singular, the first person plural, and the second person plural. Examples:

tu donnes	donne(s)*	*give*
tu finis	finis	*finish*
tu vends	vends	*sell*
nous donnons	donnons	*let's give*
nous finissons	finissons	*let's finish*
nous vendons	vendons	*let's sell*
vous donnez	donnez	*give*
vous finissez	finissez	*finish*
vous vendez	vendez	*sell*

D. To form *the present subjunctive* drop the **-ons** of the first person plural of the present indicative and add the endings: **-e, -es, -e, -ions, -iez, -ent.** Examples:

nous donnons	je donne	*I give*†
nous finissons	je finisse	*I finish*
nous vendons	je vende	I sell

121. Forms in which the past participle** is used.

A. The past participle is used in conjunction with the different tenses of the auxiliary verb **avoir** (in a few cases **être,** see paragraph 32) to form the compound tenses of verbs.

(1) To form the *passé composé,* use the present tense of the auxiliary verb with the past participle of the verb. Examples:

| **j'ai** donné | *I gave, I have given* |
| **je suis** arrivé | *I arrived, I have arrived* |

(2) To form *the pluperfect,* use the imperfect tense of the auxiliary verb with the past participle of the verb. Examples:

| **j'avais** donné | *I had given* |
| **j'étais** arrivé | *I had arrived* |

---

* In the verbs of the first conjugation, the **s** of the second singular ending is used only when followed by the word **y** or **en.**

† The subjunctive forms are translated in several different ways, depending upon the context.

** For the formation of the past participle, see paragraphs 31 (C), 34 (3), 36 (2).

(3) To form *the past anterior* (a literary tense which is approximately equivalent to the pluperfect), use the *passé simple* of the auxiliary verb with the past participle of the verb. Examples:

j'eus donné	*I had given*
je fus arrivé	*I had arrived*

(4) To form *the future perfect,* use the future tense of the auxiliary verb with the past participle of the verb. Examples:

j'aurai donné	*I shall have given*
je serai arrivé	*I shall have arrived*

(5) To form *the conditional perfect,* use the present conditional of the auxiliary verb with the past participle of the verb. Examples:

j'aurais donné	*I should or would have given*
je serais arrivé	*I should or would have arrived*

(6) To form *the **passé composé** of the subjunctive,* use the present subjunctive of the auxiliary verb with the past participle of the verb. Examples:

j'aie donné	*I have given, etc.*
je sois arrivé	*I have arrived, etc.*

(7) To form *the pluperfect of the subjunctive,* use the imperfect subjunctive of the auxiliary verb with the past participle of the verb. Examples:

j'eusse donné	*I had given, etc.*
je fusse arrivé	*I had arrived, etc.*

(8) To form *the perfect infinitive,* use the present infinitive of the auxiliary verb and the past participle of the verb. Examples:

avoir donné	*to have given*
être arrivé	*to have arrived*

B. The past participle is used in conjunction with the different tenses of the auxiliary verb **être** to form the tenses of the passive voice of transitive verbs (i.e. of verbs normally conjugated with **avoir**). Examples:

PRESENT INDIC.	**je suis** flatté	*I am flattered*
IMPERFECT	**j'étais** flatté	*I was flattered*
FUTURE	**je serai** flatté	*I shall or will be flattered*
CONDITIONAL	**je serais** flatté	*I should or would be flattered*
PASSÉ COMPOSÉ	**j'ai été** flatté	*I was or have been flattered*
PLUPERFECT	**j'avais été** flatté	*I had been flattered*
PAST ANTERIOR	**j'eus été** flatté	*I had been flattered*

Although some of the forms of the passive voice look very complicated, they present no real difficulty either from the point of view of form or meaning. When broken down into their component parts and translated literally into English, they practically always make good sense *and good English*. Examples:

Il avait été tué.	*He had*	*been*	*killed.*
Vous auriez été étonné.	*You would have*	*been*	*surprised.*

The English passive voice is by no means always rendered in French by the passive voice. (See *use of* **faire** *with an infinitive* 93 (B).)

122. Forms which can be derived from the **passé simple.***

To form the imperfect subjunctive, drop the last letter of the first person singular of the *passé simple,* and add the endings: -sse, -sses, -^t, -ssions, -ssiez, -ssent.

PASSÉ SIMPLE		IMPERFECT SUBJ.
je donnai	*I gave*	je donnasse
je finis	*I finished*	je finisse
je vendis	*I sold*	je vendisse

The vowel preceding the **t** of the third person singular of the imperfect subjunctive always has a circumflex accent. Ex.: donn**â**t, fin**î**t, vend**î**t, e**û**t, f**û**t, etc.

123. Regular conjugations.

A. Infinitive and tenses formed on it:

FUTURE

I	II	III
donner	**finir**	**vendre**
je donnerai	je finirai	je vendrai
tu donneras	tu finiras	tu vendras
il donnera	il finira	il vendra
nous donnerons	nous finirons	nous vendrons
vous donnerez	vous finirez	vous vendrez
ils donneront	ils finiront	ils vendront

---

* For the formation of the *passé simple,* see paragraph 70.

CONDITIONAL

je donnerais	je finirais	je vendrais
tu donnerais	tu finirais	tu vendrais
il donnerait	il finirait	il vendrait
nous donnerions	nous finirions	nous vendrions
vous donneriez	vous finiriez	vous vendriez
ils donneraient	ils finiraient	ils vendraient

B. Present indicative and tenses which can be formed from it:

PRESENT INDICATIVE

je donne	je finis	je vends
tu donnes	tu finis	tu vends
il donne	il finit	il vend
nous **donnons**	nous **finissons**	nous **vendons**
vous donnez	vous finissez	vous vendez
ils donnent	ils finissent	ils vendent

IMPERATIVE

donne (s)	finis	vends
donnons	finissons	vendons
donnez	finissez	vendez

PRESENT PARTICIPLE

donnant	finissant	vendant

IMPERFECT

je donnais	je finissais	je vendais
tu donnais	tu finissais	tu vendais
il donnait	il finissait	il vendait
nous donnions	nous finissions	nous vendions
vous donniez	vous finissiez	vous vendiez
ils donnaient	ils finissaient	ils vendaient

PRESENT SUBJUNCTIVE

je donne	je finisse	je vende
tu donnes	tu finisses	tu vendes
il donne	il finisse	il vende
nous donnions	nous finissions	nous vendions
vous donniez	vous finissiez	vous vendiez
ils donnent	ils finissent	ils vendent

C. Past participle and tenses in which past participle appears:

(1)   Verbs conjugated with **avoir:**

PAST PARTICIPLE

donné	fini	vendu

PASSÉ COMPOSÉ

j'ai donné, etc.	j'ai fini, etc.	j'ai vendu, etc.

PLUPERFECT

j'avais donné, etc.	j'avais fini, etc.	j'avais vendu, etc.

PAST ANTERIOR

j'eus donné, etc.	j'eus fini, etc.	j'eus vendu, etc.

FUTURE PERFECT

j'aurai donné, etc.	j'aurai fini, etc.	j'aurai vendu, etc.

CONDITIONAL PERFECT

j'aurais donné, etc.	j'aurais fini, etc.	j'aurais vendu, etc.

PASSÉ COMPOSÉ SUBJUNCTIVE

j'aie donné, etc.	j'aie fini, etc.	j'aie vendu, etc.

PLUPERFECT SUBJUNCTIVE

j'eusse donné, etc.	j'eusse fini, etc.	j'eusse vendu, etc.

PERFECT INFINITIVE

avoir donné	avoir fini	avoir vendu

PERFECT PARTICIPLE

ayant donné	ayant fini	ayant vendu

(2)   Verbs conjugated with **être:**

PAST PARTICIPLE	**arrivé** (*from* arriver)
PASSÉ COMPOSÉ	je suis arrivé (e) , etc.
PLUPERFECT	j'étais arrivé (e) , etc.
PAST ANTERIOR	je fus arrivé (e) , etc.
FUTURE PERFECT	je serai arrivé (e) , etc.
CONDITIONAL PERFECT	je serais arrivé (c) , etc.
PASSÉ COMPOSÉ SUBJUNCTIVE	je sois arrivé (e), etc.
PLUPERFECT SUBJUNCTIVE	je fusse arrivé (e) , etc.
PERFECT INFINITIVE	être arrivé (e)(s)
PERFECT PARTICIPLE	étant arrivé (e)(s)

D. *Passé simple* and imperfect subjunctive

PASSÉ SIMPLE

je donnai	je finis	je vendis
tu donnas	tu finis	tu vendis
il donna	il finit	il vendit
nous donnâmes	nous finîmes	nous vendîmes
vous donnâtes	vous finîtes	vous vendîtes
ils donnèrent	ils finirent	ils vendirent

IMPERFECT SUBJUNCTIVE

je donnasse	je finisse	je vendisse
tu donnasses	tu finisses	tu vendisses
il donnât	il finît	il vendît
nous donnassions	nous finissions	nous vendissions
vous donnassiez	vous finissiez	vous vendissiez
ils donnassent	ils finissent	ils vendissent

124. Verbs of the first conjugation which are regular except for a slight variation in their stem.

A. Verbs whose stem vowel is a mute **e** (ach**e**ter, app**e**l**e**r) have two stems.

(1) Whenever in conjugation the mute **e** of the stem vowel is followed by a syllable containing a mute **e**, the **e** of the stem vowel is pronounced [ɛ]. This occurs in the following forms: the first, second, and third person singular and the third person plural of the present indicative and the present subjunctive (**e, -es, -e, -ent**); the second person singular of the imperative (**-e** or **-es**); and the six forms of both the future and conditional (**-erai**, etc., **-erais**, etc.) .

(2) Whenever the mute **e** of the stem vowel is followed by a syllable containing any vowel other than a mute **e**, it is pronounced [ə] as in the infinitive. This phenomenon is reflected in the spelling as follows:

(*a*) In **acheter**, *to buy;* **lever**, *to raise;* **mener**, *to lead;* and a few other verbs, the stem vowel is written **è** when followed by a syllable containing a mute **e**. Ex.: PRESENT: **J'**ach**ète**, tu *achètes*, il *achète*, nous **achetons, vous achetez, ils** *achètent;* FUTURE: *j'achèterai*, etc.; CONDITIONAL: *j'achèterais*, etc.

(*b*) In **appeler**, *to call;* **jeter**, *to throw;* and a few other verbs ending in **-eler, -eter**, the final l or t of the stem is doubled when followed by a mute syllable. Ex.: PRESENT: **J'**appelle, tu *appelles*, il *appelle*, **nous appelons, vous appelez, ils** *appellent;* FUTUR: *j'appellerai*, etc.

B. Verbs whose stem vowel is **é:**

In **espérer,** *to hope;* **céder,** *to yield;* **préférer,** *to prefer* and a few other verbs whose stem vowel is **é,** the stem vowel is written **è** and pronounced [ɛ] in the present indicative (and present subjunctive) when followed by a mute syllable. Ex.: PRESENT: **J'espère, tu espères, il espère,** nous espérons, vous espérez, ils *espèrent.* (In the future and conditional, however, the stem vowel of these verbs is written **é.** Ex.: **J'espérerai.**)

C. Verbs ending in **-cer, -ger, -yer** show a slight variation in the spelling of the stem *but not in its pronunciation.*

(1) In **commencer, avancer,** etc., the final **c** of the stem is written **ç** whenever in conjugation it is followed by an **a** or **o.** Ex.: PRESENT: **Je commence, tu commences, il commence, nous** *commençons,* **vous commencez, ils commencent;** PRESENT PART.: *commençant;* IMPERFECT: je *commençais,* tu *commençais,* il *commençait,* **nous commencions, vous commenciez, ils** *commençaient;* PASSÉ SIMPLE: **je** *commençai,* etc.

(2) In **manger,** *to eat,* and other verbs ending in **-ger,** you write **ge** instead of **g** whenever the following vowel is **a** or **o.** Ex.: PRESENT: **je mange, tu manges, il mange, nous** *mangeons,* **vous mangez, ils mangent;** IMPERFECT: **je** *mangeais,* etc.; PASSÉ SIMPLE: **je** *mangeai,* etc.

(3) In **ennuyer,** *to bother,* and other verbs ending in **-oyer, -uyer,** you write **i** instead of **y** whenever the following letter is a mute **e.** Ex.: **il** *ennuie,* **but nous** *ennuyons.*

(4) In **payer,** *to pay,* and other verbs ending in **-ayer, -eyer,** you may write **y** throughout the verb, or, if you prefer, you may write **i** instead of **y** whenever the following letter is a mute **e.** Ex.: **Je paye** *or* **je pa***i***e,** *but* **nous payons.**

II. AUXILIARY VERBS

125. Conjugation of auxiliary verbs **être** and **avoir.**

Simple tenses

INFINITIVE

être, *to be*   **avoir,** *to have*

Present Indicative

je suis, *I am*	j'ai, *I have*
tu es	tu as
il est	il a
nous sommes	nous avons
vous êtes	vous avez
ils sont	ils ont

Imperfect

j'étais, *I was*	j'avais, *I had*
tu étais	tu avais
il était	il avait
nous étions	nous avions
vous étiez	vous aviez
ils étaient	ils avaient

Passé Simple

je fus, *I was*	j'eus, *I had*
tu fus	tu eus
il fut	il eut
nous fûmes	nous eûmes
vous fûtes	vous eûtes
ils furent	ils eurent

Future

je serai, *I shall* or *will be*	j'aurai, *I shall* or *will have*
tu seras	tu auras
il sera	il aura
nous serons	nous aurons
vous serez	vous aurez
ils seront	ils auront

Conditional

je serais, *I should* or *would be*	j'aurais, *I should* or *would have*
tu serais	tu aurais
il serait	il aurait
nous serions	nous aurions
vous seriez	vous auriez
ils seraient	ils auraient

PRESENT SUBJUNCTIVE

je sois, *I am,* etc.	j'aie, *I have,* etc.
tu sois	tu aies
il soit	il ait
nous soyons	nous ayons
vous soyez	vous ayez
ils soient	ils aient

IMPERFECT SUBJUNCTIVE

je fusse, *I was,* etc.	j'eusse, *I had,* etc.
tu fusses	tu eusses
il fût	il eût
nous fussions	nous eussions
vous fussiez	vous eussiez
ils fussent	ils eussent

IMPERATIVE

sois, *be*	aie, *have*
soyons	ayons
soyez	ayez

PRESENT PARTICIPLE

étant	ayant

Compound tenses

PAST PARTICIPLE

été	**eu**

PASSÉ COMPOSÉ

j'ai été, *I was, I have been,* etc.	j'ai eu, *I had, I have had,* etc.

PLUPERFECT

j'avais été, *I had been,* etc.	j'avais eu, *I had had,* etc.

PAST ANTERIOR

j'eus été, *I had been,* etc.	j'eus eu, *I had had,* etc.

FUTURE PERFECT

j'aurai été, *I shall have been,* etc.	j'aurai eu, *I shall have had,* etc.

CONDITIONAL PERFECT

j'aurais été, *I should* or *would*   j'aurais eu, *I should* or *would*
    have been, etc.   *have had,* etc.

PASSÉ COMPOSÉ SUBJUNCTIVE

j'aie été, *I have been,* etc.   j'aie eu, *I have had,* etc.

PLUPERFECT SUBJUNCTIVE

j'eusse été, *I had been,* etc.   j'eusse eu, *I had had,* etc.

PERFECT INFINITIVE

avoir été, *to have been*   avoir eu, *to have had*

PERFECT PARTICIPLE

ayant été, *having been*   ayant eu, *having had*

III. IRREGULAR VERBS

126. Formation of irregular verbs.

Although the rules for deriving the forms of regular verbs (see paragraphs 118-122) do not apply strictly to all irregular verbs, they do apply to a substantial proportion of their forms.

127. Reference list of commonest irregular verbs.

abattre	*see* battre	131	astreindre	*see* craindre	138
s'abstenir	*see* tenir	167	atteindre	*see* craindre	138
abstraire	*see* traire	168	avoir		125
accourir	*see* courir	137	battre		131
accueillir	*see* cueillir	141	boire		132
acquérir		128	bouillir	*see* dormir	144
admettre	*see* mettre	152	combattre	*see* battre	131
aller		129	commettre	*see* mettre	152
apercevoir	*see* recevoir	161	comprendre	*see* prendre	160
apparaître	*see* connaître	135	compromettre	*see* mettre	152
appartenir	*see* tenir	167	concevoir	*see* recevoir	161
apprendre	*see* prendre	160	conclure		133
assaillir	*see* cueillir	141	conduire		134
s'asseoir		130	connaître		135

conquérir	*see* acquérir	128	enfreindre	*see* craindre	138
consentir	*see* dormir	144	s'enfuir	*see* fuir	149
construire	*see* conduire	134	entreprendre	*see* prendre	160
contenir	*see* tenir	167	entretenir	*see* tenir	167
contraindre	*see* craindre	138	entrevoir	*see* voir	174
contredire	*see* dire	143	entr'ouvrir	*see* ouvrir	156
contrefaire	*see* faire	147	envoyer		146
convaincre	*see* vaincre	169	éteindre	*see* craindre	138
convenir	*see* venir	171	être		125
coudre		136	exclure	*see* conclure	133
courir		137	extraire	*see* traire	168
couvrir	*see* ouvrir	156	faire		147
craindre		138	falloir		148
croire		139	feindre	*see* craindre	138
croître		140	fuir		149
cueillir		141	geindre	*see* craindre	138
se débattre	*see* battre	131	haïr		150
décevoir	*see* recevoir	161	inclure	*see* conclure	133
découvrir	*see* ouvrir	156	inscrire	*see* écrire	145
décrire	*see* écrire	145	interdire	*see* dire	143
se dédire	*see* dire	143	intervenir	*see* venir	171
déduire	*see* conduire	134	introduire	*see* conduire	134
défaire	*see* faire	147	joindre	*see* craindre	138
démentir	*see* dormir	144	lire		151
dépeindre	*see* craindre	138	maintenir	*see* tenir	167
déplaire	*see* plaire	157	maudire	*see* dire	143
déteindre	*see* craindre	138	médire	*see* dire	143
détenir	*see* tenir	167	mentir	*see* dormir	144
détruire	*see* conduire	134	mettre		152
devenir	*see* venir	171	mourir		153
devoir		142	mouvoir		154
dire		143	naître		155
discourir	*see* courir	137	obtenir	*see* tenir	167
disparaître	*see* connaître	135	offrir	*see* ouvrir	156
distraire	*see* traire	168	omettre	*see* mettre	152
dormir		144	ouvrir		156
écrire		145	paraître	*see* connaître	135
élire	*see* lire	151	parcourir	*see* courir	137
émettre	*see* mettre	152	partir	*see* dormir	144
émouvoir	*see* mouvoir	154	parvenir	*see* venir	171
endormir	*see* dormir	144	peindre	*see* craindre	138
s'endormir	*see* dormir	144	percevoir	*see* recevoir	161

128. acquérir, to acquire.

FUTURE
  j'acquerrai, etc.; COND. j'acquerrais, etc.

PRESENT INDICATIVE
  j'acquiers, tu acquiers, il acquiert,
  nous acquérons, vous acquércz, ils acquièrent.

IMPERATIVE
  acquiers, acquérons, acquérez.

PRES. PART.
  acquérant; IMPERFECT j'acquérais, etc.

PRES. SUBJ.
  j'acquière, tu acquières, il acquière,
  nous acquérions, vous acquériez, ils acquièrent.

PAST PARTICIPLE
  acquis; PASSÉ COMPOSÉ j'ai acquis, etc.

PASSÉ SIMPLE
  j'acquis, etc.; IMPER. SUBJ. j'acquisse, etc.

129. aller, to go.

FUTURE
  j'irai, etc.; COND. j'irais, etc.

PRESENT INDICATIVE
  je vais, tu vas, il va,
  nous allons, vous allez, ils vont.

IMPERATIVE
  va (s) , allons, allez.

PRES. PART.
  allant; IMPERFECT j'allais, etc.

PRES. SUBJ.
  j'aille, tu ailles, il aille,
  nous allions, vous alliez, ils aillent.

PAST PARTICIPLE
  allé; PASSÉ COMPOSÉ je suis allé, etc.

PASSÉ SIMPLE
  j'allai, etc; IMPERF. SUBJ. j'allasse, etc.

130. s'asseoir, to sit down.

FUTURE
je m'assiérai, etc.; COND. je m'assiérais, etc.

PRESENT INDICATIVE
je m'assieds, tu t'assieds, il s'assied,
nous nous asseyons, vous vous asseyez, ils s'asseyent.

IMPERATIVE
assieds-toi, asseyons-nous, asseyez-vous.

PRES. PART.
s'asseyant; IMPERFECT je m'asseyais, etc.

PRES. SUBJ.
je m'asseye, tu t'asseyes, il s'asseye,
nous nous asseyions, vous vous asseyiez, ils s'asseyent.

PAST PARTICIPLE
assis; PASSÉ COMPOSÉ je me suis assis, etc.

PASSÉ SIMPLE
je m'assis, etc.; IMPERF. SUBJ. je m'assisse, etc.

Alternate form of **s'asseoir.**

FUTURE
je m'assoirai, etc. *or* je m'asseyerai, etc.

CONDITIONAL
je m'assoirais, etc. *or* je m'asseyerais, etc.

PRESENT INDICATIVE
je m'assois, tu t'assois, il s'assoit,
nous nous assoyons, vous vous assoyez, ils s'assoient.

PRES. PART.
s'assoyant; IMPERFECT je m'assoyais, etc.

PRES. SUBJ.
je m'assoie, tu t'assoies, il s'assoie,
nous nous assoyions, vous vous assoyiez, ils s'assoient.

asseoir, *to seat* is conjugated like **s'asseoir,** but it takes the auxiliary verb **avoir.**

131. battre, to beat.

All forms are regular except:

PRESENT INDICATIVE—je bats, tu bats, il bat, nous battons, vous battez, ils battent.

Like **battre: abattre,** *to fell, to beat down;* **combattre,** *to fight,* and **se débattre,** *to struggle.*

132. boire, to drink.

FUTURE and COND. regular.

PRESENT INDICATIVE
je bois, tu bois, il boit,
nous buvons, vous buvez, ils boivent.

IMPERATIVE
bois, buvons, buvez.

PRES. PART.
buvant; IMPERFECT je buvais, etc.

PRES. SUBJ.
je boive, tu boives, il boive,
nous buvions, vous buviez, ils boivent.

PAST PARTICIPLE
bu; PASSÉ COMPOSÉ j'ai bu, etc.

PASSÉ SIMPLE
je bus, etc.; IMPERF. SUBJ. je busse, etc.

133. conclure, to conclude.

FUTURE and COND. regular.

PRESENT INDICATIVE
je conclus, tu conclus, il conclut,
nous concluons, vous concluez, ils concluent.

IMPERATIVE
conclus, concluons, concluez.

PRES. PART.
concluant; IMPERFECT je concluais, etc.

PRES. SUBJ.
je conclue, etc.

PAST PARTICIPLE
conclu; PASSÉ COMPOSÉ j'ai conclu, etc.

PASSÉ SIMPLE
je conclus, etc.; IMPERF. SUBJ. je conclusse, etc.

Like **conclure: exclure,** *to exclude,* and **inclure,** *to include,* except that the past participle of the latter is **inclus.**

134. conduire, to conduct, to drive.

FUTURE and COND. regular.

PRESENT INDICATIVE
je conduis, tu conduis, il conduit,
nous conduisons, vous conduisez, ils conduisent.

IMPERATIVE
conduis, conduisons, conduisez.

PRES. PART.
conduisant; IMPERFECT je conduisais, etc.

PRES. SUBJ.
je conduise, etc.

PAST PARTICIPLE
conduit; PASSÉ COMPOSÉ j'ai conduit, etc.

PASSÉ SIMPLE
je conduisis, etc.; IMPERF. SUBJ. je conduisisse, etc.

Like **conduire: construire,** *to construct;* **déduire,** *to deduce;* **détruire,** *to destroy;* **introduire,** *to introduce;* **produire,** *to produce;* **reconduire,** *to lead back;* **réduire,** *to reduce;* **séduire,** *to seduce, to please;* **traduire,** *to translate;* etc.

135. connaître, to know, to be acquainted with.

FUTURE and COND. regular.

PRESENT INDICATIVE
je connais, tu connais, il connaît,
nous connaissons, vous connaissez, ils connaissent.

IMPERATIVE
connais, connaissons, connaissez.

PRES. PART.
connaissant; IMPERFECT je connaissais, etc.

PRES. SUBJ.
je connaisse, etc.

PAST PARTICIPLE
connu; PASSÉ COMPOSÉ j'ai connu, etc.

PASSÉ SIMPLE
je connus, etc.; IMPERF. SUBJ. je connusse, etc.

Like **connaître: apparaître,** *to appear;* **disparaître,** *to disappear;* **paraître,** *to appear;* **reconnaître,** *to recognize;* etc.

136. coudre, to sew.

FUTURE and COND. regular.

PRESENT INDICATIVE
je couds, tu couds, il coud,
nous cousons, vous cousez, ils cousent.

IMPERATIVE
couds, cousons, cousez.

PRES. PART.
cousant; IMPERFECT je cousais, etc.

PRES. SUBJ.
je couse, etc.

PAST PARTICIPLE
cousu; PASSÉ COMPOSÉ j'ai cousu, etc.

PASSÉ SIMPLE
je cousis, etc.; IMPERF. SUBJ. je cousisse, etc.

137. courir, to run.

FUTURE
je courrai, etc.; COND. je courrais, etc.

PRESENT INDICATIVE
je cours, tu cours, il court,
nous courons, vous courez, ils courent.

IMPERATIVE
cours, courons, courez.

PRES. PART.
courant; IMPERFECT je courais, etc.

PRES. SUBJ.
je coure, etc.

PAST PARTICIPLE
couru; PASSÉ COMPOSÉ j'ai couru, etc.

PASSÉ SIMPLE
je courus, etc.; IMPERF. SUBJ. je courusse, etc.

Like **courir: accourir,** *to hasten;* **discourir,** *to discourse;* **parcourir,** *to go over;* **secourir,** *to help;* etc.

138. craindre, to fear.

FUTURE and COND. regular.

PRESENT INDICATIVE
   je crains, tu crains, il craint,
   nous craignons, vous craignez, ils craignent.

IMPERATIVE
   crains, craignons, craignez.

PRES. PART.
   craignant; IMPERFECT je craignais, etc.

PRES. SUBJ.
   je craigne, etc.

PAST PARTICIPLE
   craint; PASSÉ COMPOSÉ j'ai craint, etc.

PASSÉ SIMPLE
   je craignis, etc.; IMPERF. SUBJ. je craignisse, etc.

Like **craindre**: **astreindre**, *to compel;* **atteindre**, *to attain;* **contraindre**, *to compel;* **dépeindre**, *to depict;* **déteindre**, *to fade;* **enfreindre**, *to infringe;* **éteindre**, *to extinguish;* **feindre**, *to feign;* **geindre**, *to groan;* **joindre**, *to join;* **peindre**, *to paint;* **plaindre**, *to pity;* **se plaindre**, *to complain;* **rejoindre**, *to rejoin, to meet;* **restreindre**, *to restrain;* **teindre**, *to dye;* etc.

139. croire, to believe.

FUTURE and COND. regular.

PRESENT INDICATIVE
   je crois, tu crois, il croit
   nous croyons, vous croyez, ils croient.

IMPERATIVE
   crois, croyons, croyez.

PRES. PART.
   croyant; IMPERFECT je croyais, etc.

PRES. SUBJ.
   je croie, tu croies, il croie,
   nous croyions, vous croyiez, ils croient.

PAST PARTICIPLE
   cru; PASSÉ COMPOSÉ j'ai cru, etc.

PASSÉ SIMPLE
   je crus, etc.; IMPERF. SUBJ. je crusse, etc.

140. croître, to grow.

FUTURE and COND. regular.

PRESENT INDICATIVE
je croîs, tu croîs, il croît,
nous croissons, vous croissez, ils croissent.

IMPERATIVE
croîs, croissons, croissez.

PRES. PART.
croissant; IMPERFECT je croissais, etc.

PRES. SUBJ.
je croisse, etc.

PAST PARTICIPLE
crû; PASSÉ COMPOSÉ j'ai crû, etc.

PASSÉ SIMPLE
je crûs, etc.; IMPERF. SUBJ. je crusse, etc.

141. cueillir, to pick, to gather.

FUTURE
je cueillerai, etc.; COND. je cueillerais, etc.

PRESENT INDICATIVE
je cueille, tu cueilles, il cueille,
nous cueillons, vous cueillez, ils cueillent.

IMPERATIVE
cueille (s) , cueillons, cueillez.

PRES. PART.
cueillant; IMPERFECT je cueillais, etc.

PRES. SUBJ.
je cueille, etc.

PAST PARTICIPLE
cueilli; PASSÉ COMPOSÉ j'ai cueilli, etc.

PASSÉ SIMPLE
je cueillis, etc.; IMPERF. SUBJ. je cueillisse, etc.

Like **cueillir**: **accueillir**, *to welcome;* and **recueillir**, *to gather, to collect.*
assaillir, *to assail* and **tressaillir**, *to start,* etc. are like **cueillir** except that
the future and conditional are regular.

142. devoir, must, etc.

FUTURE
   je devrai, etc.; COND. je devrais, etc.

PRESENT INDICATIVE
   je dois, tu dois, il doit,
   nous devons, vous devez, ils doivent.

IMPERATIVE
   ——

PRES. PART.
   devant; IMPERFECT je devais, etc.

PRES. SUBJ.
   je doive, tu doives, il doive,
   nous devions, vous deviez, ils doivent.

PAST PARTICIPLE
   dû; PASSÉ COMPOSÉ j'ai dû, etc.

PASSÉ SIMPLE
   je dus, etc.; IMPERF. SUBJ. je dusse, etc.

143. dire, to say.

FUTURE and COND. regular.

PRESENT INDICATIVE
   je dis, tu dis, il dit,
   nous disons, vous dites, ils disent.

IMPERATIVE
   dis, disons, dites.

PRES. PART.
   disant; IMPERFECT je disais, etc.

PRES. SUBJ.
   je dise, etc.

PAST PARTICIPLE
   dit; PASSÉ COMPOSÉ j'ai dit, etc.

PASSÉ SIMPLE
   je dis, etc.; IMPERF. SUBJ. je disse, etc.

Like dire: redire, *to say again.*

The following verbs are like **dire** except that the 2nd person plural of the present indicative ends in **-disez: contredire,** *to contradict;* **se dédire,** *to retract;* **interdire,** *to prohibit;* **médire,** *to slander;* **prédire,** *to predict.* **maudire,** *to curse* is conjugated like **finir.**

144. dormir, to sleep.

Future and Cond. regular.

PRESENT INDICATIVE
je dors, tu dors, il dort,
nous dormons, vous dormez, ils dorment.

IMPERATIVE
dors, dormons, dormez.

PRES. PART.
dormant; IMPERFECT je dormais, etc.

PRES. SUBJ.
je dorme, etc.

PAST PARTICIPLE
dormi; PASSÉ COMPOSÉ j'ai dormi, etc.

PASSÉ SIMPLE
je dormis, etc.; IMPERF. SUBJ. je dormisse, etc.

Like **dormir: endormir,** *to put to sleep;* **s'endormir,** *to fall asleep;* etc.

The following verbs are conjugated like **dormir** but the present indicative of each is given in full:

bouillir, *to boil:* bous, bous, bout, bouillons, bouillez, bouillent.

mentir, *to lie,* and **démentir,** *to contradict:* mens, mens, ment, mentons, mentez, mentent.

partir, *to leave,* and **repartir,** *to leave again:* pars, pars, part, partons, partez, partent. (Conjugated with auxiliary **être.**)

se repentir, *to repent:* repens, repens, repent, repentons, repentez, repentent.

sentir, *to feel, to smell;* **consentir,** *to consent;* **pressentir,** *to have a presentiment;* **ressentir,** *to feel:* sens, sens, sent, sentons, sentez, sentent.

servir, *to serve;* **se servir de,** *to use:* sers, sers, sert, servons, servez, servent.

sortir, *to go out:* sors, sors, sort, sortons, sortez, sortent. (Conjugated with auxiliary **être.**)

145. écrire, to write.

FUTURE and COND. regular.

PRESENT INDICATIVE
j'écris, tu écris, il écrit,
nous écrivons, vous écrivez, ils écrivent.

IMPERATIVE
écris, écrivons, écrivez.

PRES. PART.
écrivant; IMPERFECT j'écrivais, etc.

PRES. SUBJ.
j'écrive, etc.

PAST PARTICIPLE
écrit; PASSÉ COMPOSÉ j'ai écrit, etc.

PASSÉ SIMPLE
j'écrivis, etc.; IMPERF. SUBJ. j'écrivisse, etc.

Like écrire: décrire, *to describe;* inscrire, *to inscribe;* prescrire, *to prescribe;*
proscrire, *to proscribe;* souscrire, *to subscribe;* etc.

146. envoyer, to send.

FUTURE
j'enverrai, etc.; COND. j'enverrais, etc.

PRESENT INDICATIVE
j'envoie, tu envoies, il envoie,
nous envoyons, vous envoyez, ils envoient.

IMPERATIVE
envoie (s) , envoyons, envoyez.

PRES. PART.
envoyant; IMPERFECT j'envoyais, etc.

PRES. SUBJ.
j'envoie, tu envoies, il envoie,
nous envoyions, vous envoyiez, ils envoient.

PAST PARTICIPLE
envoyé; PASSÉ COMPOSÉ j'ai envoyé, etc.

PASSÉ SIMPLE
j'envoyai, etc.; IMPERF. SUBJ. j'envoyasse, etc.

Like envoyer: renvoyer, *to send back, to send away.*

147. faire, to do, to make.

FUTURE
je ferai, etc.; COND. je ferais, etc.

PRESENT INDICATIVE
je fais, tu fais, il fait,
nous faisons, vous faites, ils font.

IMPERATIVE
fais, faisons, faites.

PRES. PART.
faisant; IMPERFECT je faisais, etc.

PRES. SUBJ.
je fasse, etc.

PAST PARTICIPLE
fait; PASSÉ COMPOSÉ j'ai fait, etc.

PASSÉ SIMPLE
je fis, etc., IMPERF. SUBJ. je fisse, etc.

Like **faire**: **contrefaire,** *to imitate;* **défaire,** *to undo;* **satisfaire,** *to satisfy;*
etc.

148. falloir, must, etc. (impersonal).

FUTURE
il faudra; COND. il faudrait.

PRESENT INDICATIVE
il faut.

IMPERATIVE
——

PRES. PART.
—— IMPERFECT il fallait.

PRES. SUBJ.
il faille.

PAST PARTICIPLE
fallu; PASSÉ COMPOSÉ il a fallu.

PASSÉ SIMPLE
il fallut; IMPERF. SUBJ. il fallût.

149. fuir, to flee.

FUTURE and COND. regular.

PRESENT INDICATIVE
  je fuis, tu fuis, il fuit,
  nous fuyons, vous fuyez, ils fuient.

IMPERATIVE
  fuis, fuyons, fuyez.

PRES. PART.
  fuyant; IMPERFECT je fuyais, etc.

PRES. SUBJ.
  je fuie, tu fuies, il fuie,
  nous fuyions, vous fuyiez, ils fuient.

PAST PARTICIPLE
  fui; PASSÉ COMPOSÉ j'ai fui, etc.

PASSÉ SIMPLE
  je fuis, etc.; IMPERF. SUBJ. je fuisse, etc.

Like **fuir:** s'enfuir, *to flee, to escape.*

150. *haïr, to hate.

FUTURE and COND. regular.

PRESENT INDICATIVE
  je hais, tu hais, il hait,
  nous haïssons, vous haïssez, ils haïssent.

IMPERATIVE
  hais, haïssons, haïssez.

PRES. PART.
  haïssant; IMPERFECT je haïssais, etc.

PRES. SUBJ.
  je haïsse, etc.

PAST PARTICIPLE
  haï; PASSÉ COMPOSÉ j'ai haï, etc.

PASSÉ SIMPLE
  je haïs, tu haïs, il haït,
  nous haïmes, vous haïtes, ils haïrent.

IMPERF. SUBJ. je haïsse, tu haïsses, il haït, etc.

---

* The **h** is aspirate in all the forms of **haïr.**

151. lire, to read.

FUTURE and COND. regular.

PRESENT INDICATIVE
je lis, tu lis, il lit,
nous lisons, vous lisez, ils lisent.

IMPERATIVE
lis, lisons, lisez.

PRES. PART.
lisant; IMPERFECT je lisais, etc.

PRES. SUBJ.
je lise, etc.

PAST PARTICIPLE
lu; PASSÉ COMPOSÉ j'ai lu, etc.

PASSÉ SIMPLE
je lus, etc.; IMPERF. SUBJ. je lusse, etc.

Like lire: élire, to elect.

152. mettre, to put.

FUTURE and COND. regular.

PRESENT INDICATIVE
je mets, tu mets, il met,
nous mettons, vous mettez, ils mettent.

IMPERATIVE
mets, mettons, mettez.

PRES. PART.
mettant; IMPERFECT je mettais, etc.

PRES. SUBJ.
je mette, etc.

PAST PARTICIPLE
mis; PASSÉ COMPOSÉ j'ai mis, etc.

PASSÉ SIMPLE
je mis, etc.; IMPERF. SUBJ. je misse, etc.

Like mettre: admettre, to admit; commettre, to commit; compromettre, to compromise; émettre, to put out, to emit; omettre, to omit; permettre, to permit; promettre, to promise; remettre, to put back, to hand to; soumettre, to submit; transmettre, to transmit; etc.

153. mourir, to die.

FUTURE
je mourrai, etc.; COND. je mourrais, etc.

PRESENT INDICATIVE
je meurs, tu meurs, il meurt,
nous mourons, vous mourez, ils meurent.

IMPERATIVE
meurs, mourons, mourez.

PRES. PART.
mourant; IMPERFECT je mourais, etc.

PRES. SUBJ.
je meure, tu meures, il meure,
nous mourions, vous mouriez, ils meurent.

PAST PARTICIPLE
mort; PASSÉ COMPOSÉ je suis mort (e) , etc.

PASSÉ SIMPLE
je mourus, etc.; IMPERF. SUBJ. je mourusse, etc.

154. mouvoir, to move.

FUTURE
je mouvrai, etc.; COND. je mouvrais, etc.

PRESENT INDICATIVE
je meus, tu meus, il meut,
nous mouvons, vous mouvez, ils meuvent.

IMPERATIVE
meus, mouvons, mouvez.

PRES. PART.
mouvant; IMPERFECT je mouvais, etc.

PRES. SUBJ.
je meuve, tu meuves, il meuve,
nous mouvions, vous mouviez, ils meuvent.

PAST PARTICIPLE
mû; PASSÉ COMPOSÉ j'ai mû, etc.

PASSÉ SIMPLE
je mus, etc.; IMPERF. SUBJ. je musse, etc.

Like **mouvoir**: émouvoir, *to stir;* **s'émouvoir,** *to be stirred;* etc., except that
the past participle is **ému**—without the circumflex accent.

155. naître, to be born.

FUTURE and COND. regular.

PRESENT INDICATIVE
je nais, tu nais, il naît,
nous naissons, vous naissez, ils naissent.

IMPERATIVE
nais, naissons, naissez.

PRES. PART.
naissant; IMPERFECT je naissais, etc.

PRES. SUBJ.
je naisse, etc.

PAST PARTICIPLE
né; PASSÉ COMPOSÉ je suis né (e) , etc.

PASSÉ SIMPLE
je naquis, etc.; IMPERF. SUBJ. je naquisse, etc.

Like naître: renaître, *to be reborn.*

156. ouvrir, to open.

FUTURE and COND. regular.

PRESENT INDICATIVE
j'ouvre, tu ouvres, il ouvre,
nous ouvrons, vous ouvrez, ils ouvrent.

IMPERATIVE
ouvre (s) , ouvrons, ouvrez.

PRES. PART.
ouvrant; IMPERFECT j'ouvrais, etc.

PRES. SUBJ.
j'ouvre, etc.

PAST PARTICIPLE
ouvert; PASSÉ COMPOSÉ j'ai ouvert, etc.

PASSÉ SIMPLE
j'ouvris, etc.; IMPERF. SUBJ. j'ouvrisse, etc.

Like ouvrir: couvrir, *to cover;* découvrir, *to discover;* entr'ouvrir, *to open slightly;* offrir, *to offer, to give;* souffrir, *to suffer,* etc.

157. plaire, to please.

FUTURE and COND. regular.

PRESENT INDICATIVE
je plais, tu plais, il plaît,
nous plaisons, vous plaisez, ils plaisent.

IMPERATIVE
plais, plaisons, plaisez.

PRES. PART.
plaisant; IMPERFECT je plaisais, etc.

PRES. SUBJ.
je plaise, etc.

PAST PARTICIPLE
plu; PASSÉ COMPOSÉ j'ai plu, etc.

PASSÉ SIMPLE
je plus, etc.; IMPERF. SUBJ. je plusse, etc.

Like plaire: déplaire, *to displease.*

taire, *to say nothing about,* and **se taire,** *to be silent,* are conjugated like
plaire except that the 3rd person singular of the present indicative is
written without the circumflex accent.

158. pleuvoir, to rain (impersonal).

FUTURE
il pleuvra; COND. il pleuvrait.

PRESENT INDICATIVE
il pleut.

PRES. PART.
pleuvant; IMPERFECT il pleuvait.

PRES. SUBJ.
il pleuve.

PAST PARTICIPLE
plu; PASSÉ COMPOSÉ il a plu.

PASSÉ SIMPLE
il plut; IMPERF. SUBJ. il plût.

159. pouvoir, to be able, can, etc.

FUTURE
  je pourrai, etc.; COND. je pourrais, etc.

PRESENT INDICATIVE
  je peux (je puis) , tu peux, il peut,
  nous pouvons, vous pouvez, ils peuvent.

PRES. PART.
  pouvant; IMPERFECT je pouvais, etc.

PRES. SUBJ.
  je puisse, tu puisses, il puisse,
  nous puissions, vous puissiez, ils puissent.

IMPERATIVE
—— —— ——

PAST PARTICIPLE
  pu; PASSÉ COMPOSÉ j'ai pu, etc.

PASSÉ SIMPLE
  je pus, etc.; IMPERF. SUBJ. je pusse, etc.

160. prendre, to take.

FUTURE and COND. regular.

PRESENT INDICATIVE
  je prends, tu prends, il prend,
  nous prenons, vous prenez, ils prennent.

IMPERATIVE
  prends, prenons, prenez.

PRES. PART.
  prenant; IMPERFECT je prenais, etc.

PRES. SUBJ.
  je prenne, tu prennes, il prenne,
  nous prenions, vous preniez, ils prennent.

PAST PARTICIPLE
  pris; PASSÉ COMPOSÉ j'ai pris, etc.

PASSÉ SIMPLE
  je pris, etc.; IMPERF. SUBJ. je prisse, etc.

Like prendre: apprendre, *to learn;* comprendre, *to understand;* entrepren-
dre, *to undertake;* reprendre, *to take again,* etc.; surprendre, *to surprise;*
etc.

161. recevoir, to receive.

FUTURE
> je recevrai, etc.; COND. je recevrais, etc.

PRESENT INDICATIVE
> je reçois, tu reçois, il reçoit,
> nous recevons, vous recevez, ils reçoivent.

IMPERATIVE
> reçois, recevons, recevez.

PRES. PART.
> recevant; IMPERFECT je recevais, etc.

PRES. SUBJ.
> je reçoive, tu reçoives, il reçoive,
> nous recevions, vous receviez, ils reçoivent.

PAST PARTICIPLE
> reçu; PASSÉ COMPOSÉ j'ai reçu, etc.

PASSÉ SIMPLE
> je reçus, etc.; IMPERF. SUBJ. je reçusse, etc.

Like **recevoir: apercevoir,** *to catch a glimpse of;* **concevoir,** *to conceive;* **décevoir,** *to deceive;* **percevoir,** *to collect;* etc.

162. résoudre, to resolve, to solve.

FUTURE and COND. regular.

PRESENT INDICATIVE
> je résous, tu résous, il résoud,
> nous résolvons, vous résolvez, ils résolvent.

IMPERATIVE
> résous, résolvons, résolvez.

PRES. PART.
> résolvant; IMPERFECT je résolvais, etc.

PRES. SUBJ.
> je résolve, etc.

PAST PARTICIPLE
> résolu; PASSÉ COMPOSÉ j'ai résolu, etc.

PASSÉ SIMPLE
> je résolus, etc.; IMPERF. SUBJ. je résolusse, etc.

163. rire, to laugh.

FUTURE and COND. regular.

PRESENT INDICATIVE
   je ris, tu ris, il rit,
   nous rions, vous riez, ils rient.

IMPERATIVE
   ris, rions, riez.

PRES. PART.
   riant; IMPERFECT je riais, etc.

PRES. SUBJ.
   je rie, tu ries, il rie,
   nous riions, vous riiez, ils rient.

PAST PARTICIPLE
   ri; PASSÉ COMPOSÉ j'ai ri, etc.

PASSÉ SIMPLE
   je ris, etc.; IMPERF. SUBJ. je risse, etc.

Like rire: sourire, *to smile.*

164. savoir, to know.

FUTURE
   je saurai, etc.; COND. je saurais, etc.

PRESENT INDICATIVE
   je sais, tu sais, il sait,
   nous savons, vous savez, ils savent.

IMPERATIVE
   sache, sachons, sachez.

PRES. PART.
   sachant; IMPERFECT je savais, etc.

PRES. SUBJ.
   je sache, etc.

PAST PARTICIPLE
   su; PASSÉ COMPOSÉ j'ai su, etc.

PASSÉ SIMPLE
   je sus, etc.; IMPERF. SUBJ. je susse, etc.

165. suffire, to suffice, to be enough.

FUTURE and COND. regular.

PRESENT INDICATIVE
je suffis, tu suffis, il suffit,
nous suffisons, vous suffisez, ils suffisent.

IMPERATIVE
suffis, suffisons, suffisez.

PRES. PART.
suffisant; IMPERFECT je suffisais, etc.

PRES. SUBJ.
je suffise, etc.

PAST PARTICIPLE
suffi; PASSÉ COMPOSÉ j'ai suffi, etc.

PASSÉ SIMPLE
je suffis, etc.; IMPERF. SUBJ. je suffisse, etc.

166. suivre, to follow.

FUTURE and COND. regular.

PRESENT INDICATIVE
je suis, tu suis, il suit,
nous suivons, vous suivez, ils suivent.

IMPERATIVE
suis, suivons, suivez.

PRES. PART.
suivant; IMPERFECT je suivais, etc.

PRES. SUBJ.
je suive, etc.

PAST PARTICIPLE
suivi; PASSÉ COMPOSÉ j'ai suivi, etc.

PASSÉ SIMPLE
je suivis, etc.; IMPERF. SUBJ. je suivisse, etc.

Like **suivre: poursuivre,** *to pursue.*

167. tenir, to hold.

FUTURE
je tiendrai, etc.; COND. je tiendrais, etc.

PRESENT INDICATIVE
> je tiens, tu tiens, il tient,
> nous tenons, vous tenez, ils tiennent.

IMPERATIVE
> tiens, tenons, tenez.

PRES. PART.
> tenant; IMPERFECT je tenais, etc.

PRES. SUBJ.
> je tienne, tu tiennes, il tienne,
> nous tenions, vous teniez, ils tiennent.

PAST PARTICIPLE
> tenu; PASSÉ COMPOSÉ j'ai tenu, etc.

PASSÉ SIMPLE
> je tins, tu tins, il tint,
> nous tînmes, vous tîntes, ils tinrent. IMPERF. SUBJ. je tinsse, etc.

Like **tenir: s'abstenir,** *to abstain;* **appartenir,** *to belong;* **contenir,** *to contain;* **détenir,** *to detain;* **entretenir,** *to keep in good condition;* **maintenir,** *to maintain;* **obtenir,** *to obtain;* **retenir,** *to retain;* **soutenir,** *to sustain.*

168. traire, to milk.

FUTURE and COND. regular.

PRESENT INDICATIVE
> je trais, tu trais, il trait,
> nous trayons, vous trayez, ils traient.

IMPERATIVE
> trais, trayons, trayez.

PRES. PART.
> trayant; IMPERFECT je trayais, etc.

PRES. SUBJ.
> je traie, tu traies, il traie,
> nous trayions, vous trayiez, ils traient.

PAST PARTICIPLE
> trait; PASSÉ COMPOSÉ j'ai trait, etc.

PASSÉ SIMPLE
> ——; IMPERF. SUBJ. ——.

Like **traire: abstraire,** *to abstract;* **distraire,** *to distract;* **extraire,** *to extract;* **soustraire,** *to subtract;* etc.

169. **vaincre,** to conquer.

FUTURE and COND. regular.

PRESENT INDICATIVE
    je vaincs, tu vaincs, il vainc,
    nous vainquons, vous vainquez, ils vainquent.

IMPERATIVE
    vaincs, vainquons, vainquez.

PRES. PART.
    vainquant; IMPERFECT je vainquis, etc.

PRES. SUBJ.
    je vainque, etc.

PAST PARTICIPLE
    vaincu; PASSÉ COMPOSÉ j'ai vaincu, etc.

PASSÉ SIMPLE
    je vainquis, etc.; IMPERF. SUBJ. je vainquisse, etc.

Like **vaincre: convaincre,** *to convince.*

170. **valoir,** to be worth.

FUTURE
    je vaudrai, etc.; COND. je vaudrais, etc.

PRESENT INDICATIVE
    je vaux, tu vaux, il vaut,
    nous valons, vous valez, ils valent.

IMPERATIVE
    vaux, valons, valez.

PRES. PART.
    valant; IMPERFECT je valais, etc.

PRES. SUBJ.
    je vaille, tu vailles, il vaille,
    nous valions, vous valiez, ils vaillent.

PAST PARTICIPLE
    valu; PASSÉ COMPOSÉ j'ai valu, etc.

PASSÉ SIMPLE
    je valus, etc.; IMPERF. SUBJ. je valusse, etc.

171. venir, to come.

FUTURE
> je viendrai, etc.; COND. je viendrais, etc.

PRESENT INDICATIVE
> je viens, tu viens, il vient,
> nous venons, vous venez, ils viennent.

IMPERATIVE
> viens, venons, venez.

PRES. PART.
> venant; IMPERFECT je venais, etc.

PRES. SUBJ.
> je vienne, tu viennes, il vienne,
> nous venions, vous veniez, ils viennent.

PAST PARTICIPLE
> venu; PASSÉ COMPOSÉ je suis venu (e) , etc.

PASSÉ SIMPLE
> je vins, tu vins, il vint,
> nous vînmes, vous vîntes, ils vinrent. IMPERF. SUBJ. je vinsse, etc.

Like **venir**: **convenir,** *to agree, to suit;* **devenir,** *to become;* **intervenir,** *to intervene;* **parvenir,** *to attain;* **prévenir,** *to warn,* etc.; **provenir,** *to come from;* **revenir,** *to come back;* **se souvenir,** *to remember;* etc.

172. vêtir, to clothe.

FUTURE and COND. regular.

PRESENT INDICATIVE
> je vêts, tu vêts, il vêt,
> nous vêtons, vous vêtez, ils vêtent.

IMPERATIVE
> vêts, vêtons, vêtez.

PRES. PART.
> vêtant; IMPERFECT je vêtais, etc.

PRES. SUBJ.
> je vête, etc.

PAST PARTICIPLE
> vêtu; PASSÉ COMPOSÉ j'ai vêtu, etc.

PASSÉ SIMPLE
> je vêtis, etc.; IMPERF. SUBJ. je vêtisse, etc.

173. vivre, to live.

FUTURE and COND. regular.

PRESENT INDICATIVE
    je vis, tu vis, il vit,
    nous vivons, vous vivez, ils vivent.

IMPERATIVE
    vis, vivons, vivez.

PRES. PART.
    vivant; IMPERFECT je vivais, etc.

PRES. SUBJ.
    je vive, etc.

PAST PARTICIPLE
    vécu; PASSÉ COMPOSÉ j'ai vécu, etc.

PASSÉ SIMPLE
    je vécus, etc.; IMPERF. SUBJ. je vécusse, etc.

174. voir, to see.

FUTURE
    je verrai, etc.; COND. je verrais, etc.

PRESENT INDICATIVE
    je vois, tu vois, il voit,
    nous voyons, vous voyez, ils voient.

IMPERATIVE
    vois, voyons, voyez.

PRES. PART.
    voyant; IMPERFECT je voyais, etc.

PRES. SUBJ.
    je voie, tu voies, il voie,
    nous voyions, vous voyiez, ils voient.

PAST PARTICIPLE
    vu; PASSÉ COMPOSÉ j'ai vu, etc.

PASSÉ SIMPLE
    je vis, etc.; IMPERF. SUBJ. je visse, etc.

Like voir: entrevoir, *to catch sight of;* revoir, *to see again.*

prévoir is like voir except that the future and conditional are regular.

pourvoir is like voir except that the future and conditional are regular, the *passé simple* is je pourvus, etc., and the imperfect subjunctive je pourvusse, etc.

175. vouloir, to want, to will.

FUTURE
je voudrai, etc.; COND. je voudrais, etc.

PRESENT INDICATIVE
je veux, tu veux, il veut,
nous voulons, vous voulez, ils veulent.

IMPERATIVE
veux, voulons, voulez, *or*
veuille, veuillons, veuillez.

PRES. PART.
voulant; IMPERFECT je voulais, etc.

PRES. SUBJ.
je veuille, tu veuilles, il veuille,
nous voulions, vous vouliez, ils veuillent.

PAST PARTICIPLE
voulu; PASSÉ COMPOSÉ j'ai voulu, etc.

PASSÉ SIMPLE
je voulus, etc.; IMPERF. SUBJ. je voulusse, etc.

Common Units of Measurement

1 centimètre	*.3937*	*of an inch* (less than half an inch)
1 mètre	*39.37*	*inches* (about 1 yard and 3 inches)
1 kilomètre **(1000 mètres)**	*.6213*	*of a mile* (about 5⁄8 of a mile)
1 gramme	*.03527*	*of an ounce*
100 grammes	*3.52*	*ounces* (a little less than 1⁄4 of a pound)
500 grammes **(une livre)**	*17.63*	*ounces* (about 1.1 pounds)
1000 grammes **(un kilo)**	*35.27*	*ounces* (about 2.2 pounds)
1 litre	*1.0567*	*quarts* (a fraction over a quart, liquid)

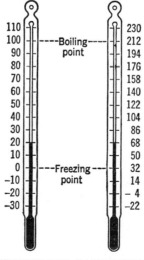

CENTIGRADE FAHRENHEIT

VOCABULARIES

ABBREVIATIONS

abbr	abbreviation	*inf*	infinitive
adj	adjective	*interrog*	interrogative
adv	adverb	*m*	masculine
art	article	*n*	noun
* (asterisk)	aspirate *h*	*obj*	object
cond	conditional	*p part*	past participle
conj	conjunction	*p simple*	passé simple
conjug	conjugated	*pers*	person, personal
contr	contraction	*pl*	plural
dem	demonstrative	*poss*	possessive
dir obj	direct object	*pr*	present
f	feminine	*prep*	preposition
fut	future	*pron*	pronoun
imper	imperative	*rel*	relative
imperf	imperfect	*sg*	singular
ind	indicative	*subj*	subjunctive
indir obj	indirect object		

FRENCH-ENGLISH

A

a: il a [ila] *pr ind 3rd sg of* avoir

à [a] at, to, in, into, for by; à jeudi see you Thursday

abandonner [abɑ̃dɔne] to abandon; to give out

abord: d'abord [dabɔʀ] first, at first, first of all

absent [apsɑ̃] absent

absolument [apsɔlymɑ̃] absolutely

absurde [apsyʀd] absurd

accent [aksɑ̃] *m* accent

accepter [aksɛpte] to accept

accessible [aksɛsibl] accessible

accident [aksidɑ̃] *m* accident

accompagner [akɔ̃paɲe] to accompany, go with, go along

accord: d'accord [dakɔʀ] in agreement (with); O.K.

accrocher [akʀɔʃe] to hook, to hang

achat [aʃa] *m* purchase

acheter [aʃte] to buy

actuel [aktɥɛl] present; à l'heure actuelle at the present time

actuellement [aktɥɛlmɑ̃] at present

addition [adisjɔ̃] *f* bill

admirable [admiʀabl] admirable

admirablement [admiʀabləmɑ̃] admirably

admirer [admiʀe] to admire

adorer [adɔʀe] to be crazy about

adresse [adʀɛs] *f* address

aérien [aeʀjɛ̃], aérienne [aeʀjɛn] aerial

affirmativement [afiʀmativmɑ̃] affirmatively

Afrique [afʀik] *f* Africa; l'Afrique du Nord North Africa

âge [ɑʒ] *m* age; quel âge avez-vous? how old are you?; d'un certain âge elderly

agent [aʒɑ̃] *m* agent; agent de police policeman

agir: s'agir de [saʒiʀ də] *impers* to be a question of

agit: il s'agit de [ilsaʒidə] it is a question of

agréable [agʀeabl] pleasant

ai: j'ai [ʒe] *pr ind 1st sg of* avoir

aide [ɛd] *f* help

aider [ɛde] to help

aille: j'aille [ʒaj] *pr subj 1st sg of* aller

ailleurs [ajœʀ] elsewhere; d'ailleurs moreover, besides, anyway

aimable [ɛmabl] kind, nice

aimer [ɛme] to like, love; aimer bien to like, to be fond of; aimer mieux to prefer

ainsi [ɛ̃si] so, thus

air [ɛʀ] *m* air; avoir l'air to look, appear, seem; en plein air in the open

ait: il ait [ilɛ] *pr subj 3rd sg of* avoir

alarme [alaʀm] *f* alarm; sonnette d'alarme alarm signal

album [albɔm] *m* album

alla: il alla [ilala] *p simple 3rd sg of* aller

allais: j'allais [ʒalɛ] *imperf ind 1st sg of* aller

allé [ale] *p part of* aller

allée [ale] *f* walk, path

Allemagne [almaɲ] *f* Germany

allemand [almɑ̃] German

aller [ale] *m;* aller et retour round trip

aller [ale] to go; aller bien to feel well; comment allez-vous? how are you?; ce chapeau vous va très bien this hat is very becoming; aller à pied to walk; aller chercher to go get; s'en aller to go away allez: vous allez [vuzale] *pr ind 2 pl of* aller

allumé [alyme] lighted

allusion [alyzjō] *f* allusion

alors [alɔʀ] then

Alpes [alp] *f pl* Alps

américain [ameʀikɛ̃], américaine [ameʀikɛn] American (*takes a capital only when used as a noun referring to a person*)

Amérique [ameʀik] *f* America

ami [ami], amie [ami] friend

amusant [amyzā] amusing

amuser: s'amuser [samyze] to enjoy oneself

an [ā] *m* year; tous les ans every year

ancien [āsjɛ̃], ancienne [āsjɛn] former, old

anglais [āglɛ], anglaise [āglɛz] English (*takes a capital only when used as a noun referring to a person*)

Angleterre [āglətɛʀ] *f* England

année [ane] *f* year

anniversaire [anivɛʀsɛʀ] *m* birthday

annoncer [anõse] to announce

août [u] *m* August

apparence [apaʀās] *f* look

appartenir à [apaʀtəniʀa] to belong to (*conjug like* tenir)

appel [apɛl] *m* appeal

appeler [aple] to call, name; s'appeler to be called, be named; comment vous appelez-vous? what is your name?; je m'appelle my name is

appellation [apɛlasjõ] *f* name

appétit [apeti] *m* appetite

apporter [apɔʀte] to bring; apportez-moi bring me

apprendre [apʀādʀ] to learn, to tell (*conjug like* prendre)

appris [apʀi] *p part of* apprendre

approcher: s'approcher [sapʀɔʃe] to come close to

après [apʀɛ] after; d'après according to

après-midi [apʀɛmidi] *m* afternoon; l'après-midi in the afternoon

arbre [aʀbʀ] *m* tree

arc [aʀk] *m* arch; arc de triomphe [aʀk dətʀiõf] arch of triumph; arc en demi-cercle [aʀk ādmisɛʀkl] round arch

architecte [aʀʃitɛkt] *m* architect

architecture [aʀʃitɛktyʀ] *f* architecture

argent [aʀʒā] *m* money, silver

arme [aʀm] *f* weapon; arme prohibée concealed weapon

armée [aʀme] *f* army

arranger: s'arranger [saʀāʒe] to fit in

arrêt [aʀɛ] *m* stop

arrêter: s'arrêter [saʀɛte] to stop

arrivée [aʀive] *f* arrival

arriver [aʀive] to arrive, come; to happen; qu'est-ce qui lui est arrivé? what happened to him (her)?

arrondissement [aʀõdismā] *m* administrative district in Paris

arroser [aʀoze] to water

art [aʀ] *m* art

article [aʀtikl] *m* article

artiste [aʀtist] *m* artist

ascenseur [asāsœʀ] *m* elevator

aspect [aspɛ] *m* aspect

asperge [aspɛʀʒ] *f* asparagus

aspirine [aspiʀin] *f* aspirin

assembler: s'assembler [sasāble] to gather

asseoir: s'asseoir [saswaʀ] to sit down

asseyez-vous [asɛjevu] *imper 2nd pl of* s'asseoir

assez [ase] enough, rather, fairly

assis [asi] *p part of* asseoir

assistance [asistās] *f* attendance, spectators

assister à [asiste a] to attend

assurer [asyʀe] to assure

Athènes [atɛn] Athens

Atlantique [atlātik] *m* Atlantic

atteindre [atɛ̃dʀ] to reach, attain (*conjug like* peindre)

attendre [atādʀ] to wait, wait for, await; s'attendre à to expect

attention [atāsjõ] *f* attention; faire attention to watch out

attentivement [atātivmā] attentively

attirer [atiʀe] to attract

attraper [atʀape] to catch

au [o] *contr of* à le

auberge [obɛʀ₃] *f* inn

aucun [okœ̃], aucune [okyn] none; ne...
  aucun no...

aujourd'hui [oₓuʀdɥi] today; d'aujourd'-
  hui en huit a week from today; c'est
  aujourd'hui jeudi today is Thursday

auparavant [oparavɑ̃] before

auquel [okɛl], à laquelle [alakɛl], auxquels [okɛl], auxquelles [okɛl] *prep* à +
  lequel, etc.

aurai: j'aurai [₃oʀe] *fut 1st sg of* avoir

aussi [osi] also, so, as, thus, therefore;
  aussi...que as...as

aussitôt [osito] immediately; aussitôt que
  as soon as

austère [ostɛʀ] severe

autant [ɔtɑ̃] as much

auteur [otœʀ] *m* author

auto [oto] *f* auto, car

autobus [ɔtɔbys] *m* bus; en autobus on
  the bus, by bus

automne [oton] *m* fall, autumn

automobile [ɔtɔmɔbil] *f* auto, car

automobiliste [ɔtɔmɔbilist] *m* motorist

autour de [otuʀdə] around

autre [otʀ] other

autrefois [otrəfwa] formerly, once

avait: il avait [ilavɛ] *imperf ind 3rd sg
  of* avoir; il y avait there was, there
  were

avance: à l'avance [alavɑ̃s] in advance

avant [avɑ̃] before

avantage [avɑ̃ta₃] *m* advantage

avec [avɛk] with

avenue [avny] *f* avenue

aveugle [avœgl] blind

avez: vous avez [vuzave] *pr ind 2d pl of*
  avoir

avion [avjɔ̃] *m* plane

avis [avi] *m* opinion, advice; être de
  l'avis de quelqu'un to agree with someone

avoine [avwan] *f* oats

avoir [avwaʀ] to have; avoir besoin de
  to need; avoir peur to be afraid; avoir
  froid to be cold; avoir mal à la gorge
  to have a sore throat; avoir l'air to

seem; avoir lieu to take place; qu'est-ce
  que vous avez? what is the matter with
  you?; avoir envie de to feel like; avoir
  l'habitude de to be used to; avoir faim
  to be hungry; avoir soif to be thirsty;
  avoir l'intention de to intend to; avoir
  raison to be right; avoir tort to be
  wrong; il y a there is, there are; il y
  a dix ans ten years ago; avoir beau to
  be in vain, be of no avail

avril [avʀil] *m* April

ayez: vous ayez [vuzɛje] *pr subj 2d pl of*
  avoir

B

bagages [baga₃] *m pl* luggage

bain [bɛ̃] *m* bath; salle de bain *f* bathroom

bal [bal] *m* dance

Balzac [balzak] French novelist (1799-
  1850)

banane [banan] *f* banana

banlieue [bɑ̃ljø] *f* the outskirts, suburbs

banque [bɑ̃k] *f* bank

banquier [bɑ̃kje] *m* banker

barbe: Quelle barbe! La barbe! What a
  nuisance!

Barbizon [baʀbizɔ̃] village near Fontainebleau, residence of famous French
  painters of the 19th century

barrage [baʀa₃] *m* dam

bas [ba], basse [bɑs] low; à voix basse
  in a low voice

bassin [basɛ̃] *m* pool

Bastille: la Bastille [labastij] state prison,
  destroyed in 1789

bataille [bataj] *f* battle

bateau [bato] *m* boat

bâtiment [bɑtimɑ̃] *m* building

beau [bo], bel [bɛl], belle [bɛl], beaux
  [bo], belles [bɛl] beautiful, nice; il fait
  beau the weather is nice; avoir beau to
  be in vain, to be of no avail

beaucoup [boku] much, very much

Belgique [bɛl₃ik] *f* Belgium

besoin [bəzwɛ̃] *m* need; **avoir besoin de** to need

betterave [bɛtRav] *f* beet; **betterave à sucre** sugar beet

beurre [bœR] *m* butter

bicyclette [bisiklɛt] *f* bicycle

bien [bjɛ̃] *adv* well, indeed, very; **eh bien?** well?; *conj* **bien que** although; **bien** [bjɛ̃] *m* good; **cette promenade m'a fait beaucoup de bien** this walk did me a lot of good; many; **bien des statues** many statues

bientôt [bjɛ̃to] soon

bière [bjɛR] *f* beer

billet [bijɛ] *m* ticket, banknote, bill; **billet aller et retour** roundtrip ticket

Bizet [bizɛ] French musician (1838-1875)

blanc [blɑ̃], **blanche** [blɑ̃ʃ] white

blé [ble] *m* wheat

blesser [blese] to wound

bleu [blø] blue

blond [blõ] blond

bœuf [bœf], *pl* **bœufs** [bø] *m* ox, beef

boire [bwaR] to drink

bois [bwa] *m* wood; **le Bois de Boulogne** park on the outskirts of Paris

bois: je bois [ʒəbwa] *pr ind 1st sg of* **boire**

boîte [bwat] *f* box

bon [bõ], **bonne** [bɔn] good; **de bonne heure** early; **la bonne route** the right road

bonbon [bõbõ] *m* candy

bondé [bõde] crowded

bonjour [bõʒuR] *m* good morning, good afternoon, hello

bonne [bɔn] *f* maid

bonsoir [bõswaR] *m* good evening

bord [bɔR] *m* edge, side; **au bord de la mer** at the seashore

border [bɔRde] to line

botanique [bɔtanik] *f* botany

bouche [buʃ] *f* mouth; **faire venir l'eau à la bouche** to make one's mouth water

boucher [buʃe] *m* butcher

boucherie [buʃRi] *f* butcher's shop

boulangerie [bulɑ̃ʒRi] *f* bakery

boulevard [bulvaR] *m* boulevard

bouquet [bukɛ] *m* bouquet

bouquiniste [bukinist] *m* dealer in old books

bout [bu] *m* end

bouteille [butɛːj] *f* bottle

boutique [butik] *f* shop

bracelet [bRaslɛ] *m* bracelet; **montre-bracelet** wrist watch

brave [bRav] good, worthy

Bretagne [bRətaɲ] *f* Brittany

breton [bRətõ] from Brittany

brouillard [bRujaR] *m* mist

bruit [bRɥi] *m* noise

brûler [bRyle] to burn

brun [bRœ̃], **brune** [bRyn] brown

bu [by] *p part of* **boire**

buffet [byfɛ] *m* lunchroom (in a railroad station)

bureau [byRo] *m* office, desk

buvez: vous buvez [vubyve] *pr ind 2d pl of* **boire**

C

c' *see* **ce**

ça [sa] (*contr of* **cela**) that; **c'est ça** that's it, that's right

câblogramme [kɑblɔgRam] *m* cablegram

Caen [kɑ̃] city in Normandy

café [kafe] *m* coffee, café

caisse [kɛs] *f* cashier's window

caissier [kɛsje], **caissière** [kɛsjɛR] cashier

Californie [kalifɔRni] *f* California

Camélias: La Dame aux Camélias [ladamokamelja] play by Dumas Fils

camion [kamjõ] *m* truck

campagne [kɑ̃paɲ] *f* country, countryside

Canada [kanada] *m* Canada

capitale [kapital] *f* capital

car [kaR] for, because

caractérisé [kaRakteRize] characterized

carnet [kaRnɛ] *m* notebook

carré [kaRe] *m* square

carte [kaRt] *f* card, menu; **jouer aux cartes** to play cards; **carte-postale** *f* post card

carton [kaʀtõ] *m* cardboard, cardboard box

cas [ka] *m* case; **en tout cas** at any rate

casser [kase] to break

cathédrale [katedʀal] *f* cathedral

cause [koz] *f* cause; **à cause de** because of

causer [koze] to chat

cave [kav] *f* cellar

ce [sə], **cet** [sɛt], **cette** [sɛt], **ces** [se] *adj* this, that; **cette écharpe-ci** this scarf; **cette écharpe-là** that scarf; **ce jour-là** that day; **ces jours-ci** some time soon

ce [sə] *pron* he, she, it, they, that; **ce qui, ce que** what

ceci [səsi] this

cela [sla] that

célèbre [selɛbʀ] well-known

celui [səlyi], **celle** [sɛl], **ceux** [sø], **celles** [sɛl] the one; the ones; **celui-ci** this one; **celui-là** that one

cent [sã] a hundred

centigrade [sãtigʀad] *m* centigrade

centime [sãtim] *m* one hundredth part of one franc

centre [sãtʀ] *m* center

cependant [səpãdã] however

cercle [sɛʀkl] *m* circle, arc **en demi-cercle** round arch

certain [sɛʀtɛ̃], **certaine** [sɛʀtɛn] certain

certainement [sɛʀtɛnmã] certainly

certes [sɛʀt] certainly

Cézanne [sezan] French painter (1839-1906)

chacun [ʃakœ̃], **chacune** [ʃakyn] each, each one

chaise [ʃɛz] *f* chair

chaleur [ʃalœʀ] *f* heat

chambre [ʃãbʀ] *f* room

champ [ʃã] *m* field

champagne [ʃãpaɲ] *m* champagne

champenois [ʃãpənwa] from Champagne

champignon [ʃãpiɲõ] *m* mushroom

Champs-Élysées: les Champs-Élysées [leʃãzelize] avenue in Paris

chance [ʃãs] *f* luck; **avoir de la chance** to be lucky

changement [ʃãʒmã] *m* change

changer [ʃãʒe] to change; to change trains

Chantilly [ʃãtiji] town in the Île-de-France

chapeau [ʃapo] *m* hat

chapelle [ʃapɛl] *f* chapel

chaque [ʃak] each

charcuterie [ʃaʀkytʀi] *f* pork butcher shop

charmant [ʃaʀmã] charming

charme [ʃaʀm] *m* charm

chasse [ʃas] *f* hunting, hunting season

chasser [ʃase] to chase, to shoo out

château [ʃato] *m* château, palace

chaud [ʃo] warm; **il fait chaud** it is warm; **j'ai chaud** I am warm

chauffeur [ʃofœʀ] *m* driver

chaussée [ʃose] *f* street, surface of a street

chaussure [ʃosyʀ] *f* shoe

chemin [ʃmɛ̃] *m* road; **chemin de fer** *m* railroad

cheminée [ʃəmine] *f* fireplace

chèque [ʃɛk] *m* check

cher [ʃɛʀ], **chère** [ʃɛʀ] expensive, dear

chercher [ʃɛʀʃe] to seek, look for; **aller chercher** to go for, go and get; **venir chercher** to come for

cheval [ʃval], *pl* **chevaux** [ʃvo] *m* horse

chevalier [ʃvalje] *m* knight

cheveu [ʃvø] *m* hair; **elle a les cheveux blonds** she has blond hair

chez [ʃe] at the house of, at the shop of; **chez moi** at my house; **chez eux** at their house; **chez le coiffeur** at the barber's

chic [ʃik] stylish

chiffre [ʃifʀ] *m* number

chimie [ʃimi] *f* chemistry

chimiste [ʃimist] *m* chemist; **ingénieur-chimiste** chemical engineer

choisir [ʃwaziʀ] to choose

choix [ʃwa] *m* choice

chose [ʃoz] *f* thing; **quelque chose** something; **autre chose** something else; **pas grand-chose** not much

chou [ʃu], *pl* **choux** [ʃu] *m* cabbage

ciel [sjɛl], *pl* **cieux** [sjø] *m* sky

cigarette [sigaʀɛt] *f* cigarette

cinéma [sinema] *m* movie

cinq [sɛ̃k] five

cinquantaine [sɛ̃kɑ̃tɛn] f about fifty

cinquante [sɛ̃kɑ̃t] fifty

cinquième [sɛ̃kjɛm] fifth

clair [klɛʀ] clear

classe [klɑs] f class

classer [klɑse] to classify

client [klijɑ̃] m client

clocher [kloʃe] m steeple

cœur [kœʀ] m heart

coiffeur [kwafœʀ] m barber

coin [kwɛ̃] m corner, part of a town

colimaçon [kɔlimasõ]: escalier en colimaçon spiral staircase

collection [kɔlɛksjõ] f collection; collection de timbres stamp collection

collectionner [kɔlɛksjɔne] to collect

collectionneur [kɔlɛksjɔnœʀ] m collector

collège [kɔlɛʒ] m secondary school

colline [kɔlin] f hill

collision [kɔlizjõ] f collision

colonie [kɔlɔni] f colony

combien [kõbjɛ̃] how much, how many; combien de temps how long

Comédie-Française: la Comédie-Française [lakomedifʀɑ̃sɛz] theatre in Paris

commander [kɔmɑ̃de] to order

comme [kɔm] as, like; comme d'habitude as usual

commencement [kɔmɑ̃smɑ̃] m beginning

commencer [kɔmɑ̃se] to begin

comment [kɔmɑ̃] how; comment allez-vous? how are you?; comment vous appelez-vous? what is your name?; comment cela? how is that?

commerçant [kɔmɛʀsɑ̃] m merchant

commerce [kɔmɛʀs] m commerce, trade

commissaire de police [kɔmisɛʀdəpɔlis] m police lieutenant

commissariat de police [kɔmisaʀjadpɔlis] m police station

commode [kɔmɔd] adj convenient; f noun dresser

compagnie [kõpaɲi] f company

compartiment [kõpaʀtimɑ̃] m compartment

complet [kõplɛ], complète [kõplɛt] complete, full; complet [kõplɛ] n m man's suit

compliqué [kõplike] complicated

composer [kõpoze] to compose

comprendre [kõpʀɑ̃dʀ] to understand (conjug like prendre); je comprends I understand; comprenez-vous? do you understand?

compte [kõt]: se rendre compte to realize

compter [kõte] to count

comte [kõt] m count

concert [kõsɛʀ] m concert

concierge [kõsjɛʀʒ] m or f janitor, caretaker

conclure [kõklyʀ] to conclude

Concorde: Place de la Concorde [kõkɔʀd] square in Paris

conditionnel [kõdisjɔnɛl] m conditional

conduire [kõdɥiʀ] to lead; to drive a car; to take (to a place)

conférence [kõfeʀɑ̃s] f lecture

confiance [kõfjɑ̃s] f confidence

confondre [kõfõdʀ] to confuse

confortable [kõfɔʀtabl] comfortable

connais: je connais [ʒəkɔnɛ] pr ind 1st sg of connaître

connaissance [kɔnɛsɑ̃s] f acquaintance, consciousness; faire la connaissance de to meet, become acquainted with

connaissez: vous connaissez [vukɔnɛse] pr ind 2d pl of connaître

connaître [kɔnɛtʀ] to know, be acquainted with

connu [kɔny] p part of connaître

conseil [kõsɛj] m advice

consentir [kõsɑ̃tiʀ] to consent (conjug like sentir)

conséquent: par conséquent [paʀkõsekɑ̃] therefore

construction [kõstʀyksjõ] f construction, building

construire [kõstʀɥiʀ] to build; faire construire to have built

consul [kõsyl] m consul

consulter [kõsylte] to consult, look at

contempler [kõtɑ̃ple] to look at

contenir [kõtəniʀ] to contain

content [kɔ̃tɑ̃] glad
continental [kɔ̃tinɑ̃tal] continental
continuateur [kɔ̃tinɥatœʀ] *m* continuer, follower
continuer [kɔ̃tinɥe] to continue
contraire [kɔ̃tʀɛʀ] *adj* contrary; *n m* opposite; **au contraire** on the contrary, far from it
contre [kɔ̃tʀ] against; **par contre** on the other hand
convenable [kɔ̃vnabl] suitable
convenir [kɔ̃vniʀ] to suit, be appropriate (*conjug like* venir)
conversation [kɔ̃vɛʀsɑsjɔ̃] *f* conversation
convient: il convient [ilkɔ̃vjɛ̃] *pr ind 3rd sg of* convenir; **cette chambre me convient** this room suits me very well
convocation [kɔ̃vɔkɑsjɔ̃] *f* summons
Corot [kɔʀo] French painter (1796-1875)
corporel [kɔʀpɔʀɛl] *adj* of the body
corporellement [kɔʀpɔʀɛlmɑ̃] physically
correspondance [kɔʀɛspɔ̃dɑ̃s] *f* connection
corsaire [kɔʀsɛʀ] *m* corsair
Corse [kɔʀs] *f* Corsica
cosmopolite [kɔzmɔpɔlit] cosmopolitan
côté [kote] *m* side; **à côté de** near, beside; **de l'autre côté de** on the other side of
coucher: se coucher [skuʃe] to lie down, go to bed
couleur [kulœʀ] *f* color
coup: tout à coup [tutaku] suddenly
courant [kuʀɑ̃] current, common; **une expression courante** an everyday expression
cours [kuʀ] *m* course; **au cours de** in the course of, during
course [kuʀs] *f* errand, race; **faire des courses** to do errands; **course de chevaux** horse race; **champ de courses** race track
court [kuʀ] short
cousin [kuzɛ̃], cousine [kuzin] cousin
coûter [kute] to cost
couture [kutyʀ] *f* dressmaking; **maison de couture** high fashion house
couvert [kuvɛʀ] covered, cloudy
couverture [kuvɛʀtyʀ] *f* cover

couvrir [kuvʀiʀ] to cover (*conjug like* ouvrir)
craindre [kʀɛ̃dʀ] to fear (*conjug like* plaindre)
crains: je crains [ʒə kʀɛ̃] *pr ind 1st sg of* craindre
cravate [kʀavat] *f* tie, necktie
crème [kʀɛm] *f* cream
croire [kʀwaʀ] to believe
crois: je crois [ʒəkʀwa] *pr ind 1st sg of* croire
croisade [kʀwazad] *f* crusade
croyez: vous croyez [vukʀwaje] *pr ind 2d pl of* croire
cru [kʀy] *p part of* croire
cueillir [kœjiʀ] to pick
cuirassé [kɥirase] armored
cuisine [kɥizin] *f* food, cooking; kitchen
cuisinière [kɥizinjɛʀ] *f* woman cook
cuivre [kɥivʀ] *m* copper
curé [kyʀe] *m* priest
curiosité [kyʀjozite] *f* curiosity

D

d' *see* de
dame [dam] *f* lady
danger [dɑ̃ʒe] *m* danger
dangereux [dɑ̃ʒʀø], dangereuse [dɑ̃ʒʀøz] dangerous
dans [dɑ̃] in, into, on
date [dat] *f* date
dater de [datedə] to date from
Daumier [domje] French painter and etcher (1808-1879)
davantage [davɑ̃taʒ] more
de [də] of, from
debout [dəbu] standing
Debussy [dəbysi] French musician (1862-1918)
décembre [desɑ̃bʀ] *m* December
décider [deside] to decide
déclaration [deklaʀɑsjɔ̃] *f* declaration
décoration [dekɔʀɑsjɔ̃] *f* decoration
déçu [desy] disappointed
dédier [dedje] to dedicate
déesse [dees] *f* goddess

défaire [defɛʀ] to undo (*conjug like* faire)

degré [dəgʀe] *m* degree

dehors [dəɔʀ] outside

déjà [deʒa] already, before

déjeuner [deʒœne] *m* lunch; **petit déjeuner** breakfast; **déjeuner** [deʒœne] to lunch, have lunch

delà: **au delà** [odla] beyond

délicieux [delisjø] delicious

demain [dəmɛ̃] tomorrow; **après-demain** day after tomorrow

demande [dəmɑ̃d] *f* request

demander [dəmɑ̃de] to ask; **se demander** to wonder

demeure [dəmœʀ] *f* house

demeurer [dəmœʀe] to live, reside; **où demeurez-vous?** where do you live?; **je demeure** I live

demi [dəmi] half; **onze heures et demie** half past eleven; **midi et demi** half past twelve; **une demi-heure** a half hour

démolir [dəmɔliʀ] to tear down

dent [dɑ̃] *f* tooth

dentiste [dɑ̃tist] *m* dentist

départ [depaʀ] *m* departure

dépêche [depɛʃ] *f* telegram

dépêcher: **se dépêcher** [sədepɛʃe] to hurry

dépenser [depɑ̃se] to spend

depuis [dəpɥi] since, for; **depuis quand? depuis combien de temps?** how long?; **j'attends depuis un quart d'heure** I have been waiting for a quarter of an hour

déranger [deʀɑ̃ʒe] to disturb, inconvenience

dernier [dɛʀnje], **dernière** [dɛʀnjɛʀ] last; **dimanche dernier** last Sunday

des [de] (*contr of* de les) of the, from the, some, any

descendre [desɑ̃dʀ] to go down, to take down

descriptif [deskʀiptif] descriptive

description [deskʀipsjõ] *f* description

désigner [deziɲe] to designate

désirer [deziʀe] to wish, desire

dessert [desɛʀ] *m* dessert

dessiner [desine] to draw, draw the plans of

dessous [dəsu] under; *n m* lower side; **au dessous de** below

dessus [desy] on, upon; *n m* top side; **au-dessus de** above

destination [destinasjõ] *f* destination

destiné [destine] meant, intended

détail [detaj] *m* detail

détruit [detʀɥi] destroyed

deux [dø] two

deuxième [døzjɛm] second; **le deuxième (étage)** the third floor

devant [dəvɑ̃] before, in front of

devanture [dəvɑ̃tyʀ] *f* shop window

devenir [dəvniʀ] to become (*conjug like* venir); **qu'est-ce qu'il est devenu?** what has become of him?

devez: **vous devez** [vudve] (*pr ind 2d pl of* devoir) you must, you are supposed to

deviez: **vous deviez** [vudəvje] (*imperf ind 2d pl of* devoir) you were to

devoir [dəvwaʀ] to owe, must, be supposed to, ought to, etc.; **je dois** I must, I am supposed to; **je devais** I was supposed to; **j'ai dû** I must have, I had to; **je devrais** I should; **j'aurais dû** I should have

dévorer [devɔʀe] to devour

devriez: **vous devriez** [vudəvʀie] (*pr condit 2d pl of* devoir) you should, you ought to

dictée [dikte] *f* dictation

dieu [djø] *m* god

différent [difeʀɑ̃] different

difficile [difisil] difficult

difficulté [difikylte] *f* difficulty

dimanche [dimɑ̃ʃ] *m* Sunday; **le dimanche** on Sundays; **à dimanche** see you Sunday

dinde [dɛ̃d] *f* turkey

dîner [dine] *m* dinner; **dîner** [dine] to dine

diplomate [diplɔmat] *m* diplomat

dire [diʀ] to say, tell; **vouloir dire** to mean; **c'est-à-dire** that is to say

directement [diʀɛktəmɑ̃] directly
diriger: se diriger [sədiʀiʒe] to go toward
dis: je dis [ʒədi] *pr ind 1st sg of* dire; se dire to say to oneself
discuter [diskyte] to discuss
disent: ils disent [ildiz] *pr ind 3rd pl of* dire
disparaître [dispaʀɛtʀ] to disappear
dispos [dispo] fit, in good shape
disposer [dispoze] (de) to have at one's disposal
disposition [dispozisjɔ̃] *m* disposal; je suis à votre disposition I am at your service
distance [distɑ̃s] *f* distance; à quelle distance? how far?
dit: il dit [ildi] *pr ind 3rd sg of* dire
dites: vous dites [vudit] *pr ind 2d pl of* dire
dix [dis] ten
dixième [dizjɛm] tenth
dix-huit [dizɥit] eighteen
dix-neuf [diznœf] nineteen
dix-neuvième [diznœvjɛm] nineteenth
dix-sept [dissɛt] seventeen
docteur [dɔktœʀ] *m* doctor; le docteur Lambert Dr. Lambert
documentaire [dɔkymɑ̃tɛʀ] documentary
dois: je dois [ʒədwa] (*pr ind 1st sg of* devoir) I must, I am supposed to
dollar [dɔlaʀ] *m* dollar
dominer [dɔmine] to overlook
dommage [dɔmaʒ] *m* c'est dommage it's too bad
donc [dɔ̃k] then, therefore; et moi donc! what about me!; entrez donc do come in
donner [dɔne] to give
dont [dɔ̃] whose, of whom, of which
dormir [dɔʀmiʀ] to sleep
dort: il dort [ildɔʀ] *pr ind 3rd sg of* dormir
doute [dut] *m* doubt; sans doute no doubt, probably
douter: se douter de [sədutedə] to suspect
douzaine [duzɛn] *f* dozen; une demi-

douzaine half a dozen; vingt francs la douzaine twenty francs a dozen
douze [duz] twelve
douzième [duzjɛm] twelfth
drapeau [dʀapo] *m* flag
dresser [dʀɛse] to draw up, make out
droit [dʀwa] straight, right; tout droit straight ahead; à droite to, on the right
drôle [dʀol] funny, queer
du [dy] (*contr of* de le) of the, from the, some, any
dû [dy] *p part of* devoir
Dumas [dyma] French novelist (1803-1870)
duquel [dykɛl], de laquelle [dəlakɛl], desquels [dekɛl], desquelles [dekɛl] *rel pron; prep* de + lequel, etc.
dur [dyʀ] hard
durer [dyʀe] to last

E

eau [o] *f* water
échafaudage [eʃafodaʒ] *m* scaffolding
écharpe [eʃaʀp] *f* scarf
échelle [eʃɛl] *f* scale
école [ekɔl] *f* school
économie politique [ekɔnɔmi pɔlitik] *f* economics
écrire [ekʀiʀ] to write
écris: j'écris [ʒekʀi] *pr ind 1st sg of* écrire
écrivain [ekʀivɛ̃] *m* writer
écrivez: vous écrivez [vuzekʀive] *pr ind 2d pl of* écrire
édifice [edifis] *m* building
effet [efɛ] *m* effect; en effet indeed
effrayant [efʀejɑ̃] frightful
égal [egal] equal; ça m'est égal that's all the same to me
égaré [egaʀe] lost
église [egliz] *f* church
égyptien [eʒipsjɛ̃], égyptienne [eʒipsjɛn] Egyptian
Eiffel [efɛl] French engineer (1832-1923)
électricité [elɛktʀisite] *f* electricity
élégance [elegɑ̃s] *f* elegance
élégant [elegɑ̃] graceful

élève [elɛv] *m or f* pupil
elle [ɛl] she, it
elles [ɛl] they
emmener [ɑ̃mne] to carry, take along
empêcher [ɑ̃peʃe] to prevent
empire [ɑ̃piʀ] *m* empire; **Second Empire** reign of Napoleon III (1852-1870)
emploi [ɑ̃plwa] *m* employment, use; **emploi du temps** *m* schedule
employé [ɑ̃plwaje] *m* employee
employer [ɑ̃plwaje] to employ, use
empoisonner [ɑ̃pwazɔne] to poison
emporter [ɑ̃pɔʀte] to take along, carry along
en [ɑ̃] *prep* in, into, at, to, by; en [ɑ̃] *pron* some, any, of it, of them
enchanté [ɑ̃ʃɑ̃te] delighted
encore [ɑ̃kɔʀ] yet, still, again; **pas encore** not yet
endormir: s'endormir [sɑ̃dɔʀmiʀ] to fall asleep
endroit [ɑ̃dʀwa] *m* place
énergie [enɛʀʒi] *f* energy
enfant [ɑ̃fɑ̃] *m or f* child
ennuyer [ɑ̃nɥije] to bother, worry
énorme [enɔʀm] enormous
enrichi [ɑ̃ʀiʃi] made wealthy
ensemble [ɑ̃sɑ̃bl] *n* whole, entirety; **vue d'ensemble** general view; *adv* together
ensuite [ɑ̃sɥit] then, afterwards
entendre [ɑ̃tɑ̃dʀ] to hear; **entendre parler de** to hear of; **entendre dire que** to hear that
entendu [ɑ̃tɑ̃dy] *p part of* entendre; **c'est entendu** agreed, all right
enterrer [ɑ̃tɛʀe] to bury
entier [ɑ̃tje], **entière** [ɑ̃tjɛʀ] entire, whole; **tout entier** entirely
entouré de [ɑ̃tuʀe də] surrounded with
entre [ɑ̃tʀ] between, among; **entre autres** among others
entrer [ɑ̃tʀe] to enter, go in
entr'ouvert [ɑ̃tʀuvɛʀ] partly open
enverrai: j'enverrai [ʒɑ̃vɛʀe] *fut 1st sg of* envoyer
envie [ɑ̃vi] *f* envy, desire; **avoir envie de** to feel like

environ [ɑ̃viʀɔ̃] about
envoie: j'envoie [ʒɑ̃vwa] *pr ind 1st sg of* envoyer
envoyer [ɑ̃vwaje] to send; **envoyer chercher** to send for; **faire envoyer** to have (something) sent
épais [epɛ] thick
épaule [epol] *f* shoulder
Épernay [epɛʀne] town in Champagne
épicerie [episʀi] *f* grocery store
épidémie [epidemi] *f* epidemic
époque [epɔk] *f* period, time
escalier [ɛskalje] *m* stairway
espace [ɛspas] *m* space
Espagne [ɛspaɲ] *f* Spain
espagnol [ɛspaɲɔl] Spanish *(takes a capital only when used as a noun referring to a person)*
espalier [ɛspalje] *m* fruit tree trimmed and trained to grow against a wall or trellis
espèce [ɛspɛs] *f* kind, sort
espérer [ɛspeʀe] to hope; **je l'espère** I hope so
essayer [ɛsɛje] to try, try on
essoufflé [ɛsufle] out of breath
est: il est [ilɛ] *pr ind 3rd sg of* être
Est [ɛst] *m* East
estampe [ɛstɑ̃p] *f* print, engraving, etc.
et [e] and; **et cætera** [ɛtsetɛʀa] etc.
établi [etabli] established, settled
était: il était [iletɛ] *imperf ind 3rd sg of* être
étalage [etalaʒ] *m* display
États-Unis [etazyni] *m pl* United States
été [ete] *m* summer; **été** [ete] *p part of* être
éteindre [etɛ̃dʀ] to extinguish *(conjug like* **peindre***)*
étendue [etɑ̃dy] *f* extent, size
êtes: vous êtes [vuzɛt] *pr ind 2d pl of* être
étoffe [etɔf] *f* material
étoile [etwal] *f* star
étonnant [etɔnɑ̃] astonishing
étonné [etɔne] surprised
étonner: s'étonner [setɔne] to wonder at

étranger [etrᾶʒe], étrangère [etrᾶʒɛr] foreign; n foreigner

être [ɛtr] to be; c'est it is; est-ce? is it?; est-ce que? is it that?; qu'est-ce que c'est que? what is?; c'est-à-dire that is to say; il est onze heures it is eleven o'clock; c'est aujourd'hui jeudi today is Thursday; être à to belong to

étroit [etrwa] narrow

étudiant [etydjᾶ], étudiante [etydjᾶt] student

eu [y] p part of avoir

eurent: ils eurent [ilzyr] p simple 3rd pl of avoir

Europe [œrɔp] f Europe

européen [œrɔpeɛ̃], européenne [œrɔpeɛn] European

eut: il eut [ily] p simple 3rd sg of avoir: il y eut there was, there were, there has been, there have been

eux [ø] they, them

évidemment [evidamᾶ] evidently

exact [ɛgzakt] exact

examen [ɛgzamɛ̃] m examination

examiner [ɛgzamine] to examine

excellent [ɛksɛlᾶ] excellent

excursion [ɛkskyrsjɔ̃] f excursion

excuser: s'excuser [sɛkskyze] to apologize

exemple [ɛgzᾶpl] m example; par exemple for example

exercice [ɛgzɛrsis] m exercise; exercice d'application drill

expérience [ɛksperjᾶs] f experience

explication [ɛksplikasjɔ̃] f explanation

expliquer [ɛksplike] to explain

exploiter [ɛksplwate] to make use of

express [ɛksprɛs] m fast train

expression [ɛksprɛsjɔ̃] f expression

exprimer [ɛksprime] to express

F

fabriqué [fabrike] made

façade [fasad] f front of a building

face [fas] f face; en face de opposite

fâché [faʃe] sorry

facile [fasil] easy

facilement [fasilmᾶ] easily

façon [fasɔ̃] way, manner

facteur [faktœr] m postman

facture [faktyr] f bill

Faculté [fakylte] f a Division of a University

faim [fɛ̃] f hunger; avoir faim to be hungry

faire [fɛr] to do, make; faire une promenade to take a walk; faire du ski to go skiing; quoi faire? what for?; faire la connaissance de to meet, become acquainted with; faire venir to have... come; faire envoyer to have...sent; faire attention to watch out; quel temps fait-il? what kind of weather is it?; il fait beau the weather is nice; il fait du vent it is windy; il fait nuit it is dark; cela ne fait rien it does not make any difference; se faire un plaisir de to be glad to; faire bien de to do well to; faire penser to remind

fais: je fais [ʒəfɛ] pr ind 1st sg of faire

faisait: il faisait [ilfəzɛ] imperf ind 3rd sg of faire; il faisait beau the weather was nice

fait [fɛ]; tout à fait quite, entirely

fait: il fait [ilfɛ] pr ind 3rd sg of faire

faites: vous faites [vufɛt] pr ind 2d pl of faire

falloir [falwar] impers verb to have to; il faut one must, it is necessary; il fallait, il a fallu it was necessary; il faudra it will be necessary

familial [familjal] of the family

famille [famij] f family; relatives

fasse: il fasse [ilfas] pr subj 3rd sg of faire

fatigue [fatig] f fatigue

fatigué [fatige] tired

faut: il faut [ilfo] pr ind 3rd sg of falloir

faute [fot] f fault

favori [favɔri], favorite [favɔrit] favorite

femme [fam] f woman, wife

fenêtre [fənɛtr] f window

fer [fɛr] m iron; chemin de fer m railroad

ferai: je ferai [ʒəfʀe] *fut 1st sg of* faire
ferme [fɛʀm] *f* farm
fermenter [fɛʀmɑ̃te] to ferment
fermer [fɛʀme] to close
fertile [fɛʀtil] fertile
fête [fɛt] *f* celebration, holiday
feu [fø] *m* fire
feuille [fœj] *f* leaf
février [fevʀie] *m* February
fiancée [fjɑ̃se] *f* fiancée
fièvre [fjɛvʀ] *f* fever
figure [figyʀ] *f* face
filet [filɛ] *m* fillet
fille [fij] *f* daughter; jeune fille girl; petite fille little girl
film [film] *m* film, movie
fin [fɛ̃] *f* end
finalement [finalmɑ̃] finally
finir [finiʀ] to finish
finissez: vous finissez [vufinise] *pr ind 2d
   pl of* finir
fixer [fikse] to decide upon
flanc [flɑ̃] *m* side
flatteur [flatœʀ] *m* flatterer
fleur [flœʀ] *f* flower
fleuve [flœv] *m* large river
Florence [flɔʀɑ̃s] Florence
foin [fwɛ̃] *m* hay
fois [fwa] *f* time; la première fois the first
   time; plusieurs fois several times; à la
   fois at the same time
fonder [fɔ̃de] to found
font: ils font [ilfɔ̃] *pr ind 3rd pl of* faire
fontaine [fɔ̃tɛn] *f* fountain
Fontainebleau [fɔ̃tɛnblo] town in the Île-
   de-France
forcé [fɔʀse] forced
forêt [fɔʀɛ] *f* forest
forme [fɔʀm] *f* form
former [fɔʀme] to form
formidable [fɔʀmidabl] terrific
fort [fɔʀ] *adv* very
fortification [fɔʀtifikasjɔ̃] *f* fortification
fourgon [fuʀgɔ̃] *m* baggage car
fragmentaire [fʀagmɑ̃tɛʀ] fragmentary
frais [fʀɛ], fraîche [fʀɛʃ] fresh, cool, cold
fraise [fʀɛz] *f* strawberry; fraise des bois
   wild strawberry

franc [fʀɑ̃] *m* franc
français [fʀɑ̃sɛ], française [fʀɑ̃sɛz] French
   *(takes a capital only when used as a
   noun referring to a person)*
France [fʀɑ̃s] *f* France
François Ier [fʀɑ̃swa pʀəmje] king of
   France (1494-1547)
fréquent [fʀekɑ̃] frequent
fréquenté [fʀekɑ̃te] popular (frequently
   visited)
frère [fʀɛʀ] *m* brother
frit [fʀi] fried; pommes de terre frites
   French fried potatoes
froid [fʀwa] cold; il fait froid it is cold;
   avoir froid to be cold
fruit [fʀɥi] *m* fruit
furent: ils furent [ilfyʀ] *p simple 3rd pl
   of* être
fut: il fut [ilfy] *p simple 3rd sg of* être

G

gai [ge] gay
galerie [galʀi] *f* gallery, hall
gant [gɑ̃] *m* glove
garage [gaʀaʒ] *m* garage
garçon [gaʀsɔ̃] *m* boy, waiter
garder [gaʀde] to keep; se garder de to
   be careful not to
gardien [gaʀdjɛ̃] *m* warden
gare [gaʀ] *f* station
gauche [goʃ] *f* left; à gauche to the left
Geneviève: sainte Geneviève [sɛ̃t ʒənvjɛv]
   patron saint of Paris
gens [ʒɑ̃] *f pl* people
gentil [ʒɑ̃ti], gentille [ʒɑ̃tij] nice
glace [glas] *f* ice, mirror; la Galerie des
   Glaces the Hall of Mirrors
glissant [glisɑ̃] slippery
glisser [glise] to slide
gorge [gɔʀʒ] *f* throat; avoir mal à la
   gorge to have a sore throat
gothique [gɔtik] Gothic
goût [gu] *m* taste
grand [gʀɑ̃] tall, large, great
grand-mère [gʀɑ̃mɛʀ] *f* grandmother
grappe [gʀap] *f* bunch (of grapes)
gratte-ciel [gʀatsjɛl] *m* skyscraper

grave [gʀav] serious
gravité [gʀavite] f gravity
gravure [gʀavyʀ] f etching
grec [gʀɛk] Greek
grille [gʀij] f iron gate
gris [gʀi] gray
gros [gʀo], grosse [gʀos] big
groupé [gʀupe] grouped
guère [gɛʀ]; ne...guère scarcely, hardly
guerre [gɛʀ] f war
guerrier [gɛʀje] m warrior
guichet [giʃe] f ticket window
guide [gid] m guide

H

(Words beginning with an aspirate h are shown thus: *haricot)

habile [abil] skillful
habilement [abilmã] skillfully
habiller [abije] to dress; s'habiller to get dressed
habite: il habite [ilabit] pr ind 3rd sg of habiter
habiter [abite] to live in
habitude [abityd] f habit, practice; comme d'habitude as usual; avoir l'habitude de to be used to
habituer: s'habituer à [sabitчe a] to get used to
*haricot [aʀiko] m bean
harmonie [aʀmɔni] f harmony
*hasard [azaʀ] m chance; par hasard by chance
*hâte [ɑt] f haste; avoir hâte de to be eager to
*haut [o] m top, upper part; en haut de at the top of; là-haut up there
*héros [eʀo] m hero
heure [œʀ] f hour, time; quelle heure est-il? what time is it?; il est onze heures it is eleven o'clock; une demi-heure a half hour; à l'heure on time; de bonne heure early; tout à l'heure in a while, a while ago; à l'heure actuelle at the present time
heureux [œʀø], heureuse [œʀøz] happy
hier [jɛʀ] m yesterday; hier soir last night

histoire [istwaʀ] f history, story; l'histoire de France French history
historique [istɔʀik] historical
hiver [ivɛʀ] m winter
homme [ɔm] m man; jeune homme boy, young man
honneur [ɔnœʀ] m honor
hôpital [ɔpital] m hospital
horaire [ɔʀɛʀ] m timetable
horloge [ɔʀlɔ5] f clock
horloger [ɔʀlɔ5e] m jeweler
horriblement [ɔʀibləmã] terribly
*hors-d'œuvre [ɔʀdœvʀ] m hors d'œuvres
hostilité [ɔstilite] f hostility
hôtel [otɛl] m hotel
hôtelier [otəlje] m hotel keeper
Hugo: Victor Hugo [viktɔʀygo] French writer (1802-1885)
*huit [чit] eight; huit jours a week; d'aujourd'hui en huit a week from today
*huitième [чitjɛm] eighth
humble [œbl] humble
humide [ymid] humid
humidité [ymidite] f humidity

I

ici [isi] here
idée [ide] f idea
identifier [idãtifje] to identify
identité [idãtite] f identity; carte d'identité identification card
il [il] he, it
île [il] f island; l'Île-de-France the region around Paris; l'Île de la Cité an island in the Seine, the heart of old Paris
illustration [ilystʀasjõ] f illustration
ils [il] they
image [ima5] f picture
imaginer [ima5ine] to imagine
immensité [imãsite] f immensity
immeuble [imœbl] apartment house
impair [ɛpɛʀ] odd (of numbers)
imparfait [ɛpaʀfɛ] imperfect
impassible [ɛpasibl] impassive
imperméable [ɛpɛʀmeabl] m raincoat
impétueux [ɛpetчø] impetuous
impression [ɛpʀɛsjõ] f impression

impressionné [ɛ̃pʀesjɔne] impressed
incident [ɛ̃sidɑ̃] *m* incident
indéfini [ɛ̃defini] indefinite
indépendance [ɛ̃depɑ̃dɑ̃s] *f* independence
indication [ɛ̃dikasjõ] *f* indication
indiquer [ɛ̃dike] to indicate, tell
ingénieur [ɛ̃ʒenjœʀ] *m* engineer
injustice [ɛ̃ʒystis] *f* injustice
inscription [ɛ̃skʀipsjõ] *f* inscription
installer [ɛ̃stale] to set up; **s'installer** to
    settle
instant [ɛ̃stɑ̃] *m* instant; **un instant** for a
    moment
Institut [ɛ̃stity] *m* Institute
intelligent [ɛ̃tɛliʒɑ̃] intelligent
intention [ɛ̃tɑ̃sjõ] *f* intention; **avoir l'in-
    tention de** to intend to
intéressant [ɛ̃teʀɛsɑ̃] interesting, worth
    buying
intéresser [ɛ̃teʀese] to interest; **s'intéresser
    à** to be interested in
intérieur [ɛ̃teʀjœʀ] *m* inside; **à l'intérieur**
    inside
interrogatif [ɛ̃teʀɔgatif], **interrogative**
    [ɛ̃teʀɔgativ] interrogative
inventer [ɛ̃vɑ̃te] to invent
invention [ɛ̃vɑ̃sjõ] *f* invention
inversion [ɛ̃veʀsjõ] inversion
invitation [ɛ̃vitasjõ] *f* invitation
inviter [ɛ̃vite] to invite
irai: j'irai [ʒiʀe] *fut 1st sg of* aller
irais: j'irais [ʒiʀe] *cond 1st sg of* aller
ironique [iʀɔnik] ironical
Islande [islɑ̃d] *f* Iceland
Italie [itali] *f* Italy
italien [italjɛ̃], **italienne** [italjɛn] Italian
    *(takes a capital only when used as a
    noun referring to a person)*

J

j' *see* je
jamais [ʒamɛ] never, ever; **ne...jamais**
    never
jambe [ʒɑ̃b] *f* leg
jambon [ʒɑ̃bõ] *m* ham
janvier [ʒɑ̃vje] *m* January

jardin [ʒaʀdɛ̃] *m* garden
jaune [ʒon] yellow
je [ʒə] I
Jeanne d'Arc [ʒandaʀk] Joan of Arc
    (1412-1431)
jeter [ʒəte] to throw, cast; **jeter un coup
    d'œil sur** to take a look at
jeudi [ʒødi] Thursday
jeune [ʒœn] young; **jeune fille** girl
Joconde: la Joconde [laʒɔkõd] the Mona
    Lisa
joindre [ʒwɛ̃dʀ] to join
joli [ʒɔli] pretty
joue [ʒu] *f* cheek
jouer [ʒwe] to play
jour [ʒuʀ] *m* day, daylight; **par jour** a
    day; **huit jours** a week; **quinze jours**
    two weeks; **tous les jours** every day;
    ces jours-ci some time soon; **il fait jour**
    it is daylight
journal [ʒuʀnal], **journaux** [ʒuʀno] *m*
    newspaper
journée [ʒuʀne] *f* day; **toute la journée**
    all day
juillet [ʒɥijɛ] *m* July
juin [ʒɥɛ̃] *m* June
jus [ʒy] *m* juice
jusqu'à [ʒyska] until, up to, as far as;
    jusque-là that far, till then; **jusqu'à ce
    que** until
juste [ʒyst] exactly, just

K

kilo [kilo], **kilogramme** [kilɔgʀam] *m* kilo
    (2.2 lbs.)
kilomètre [kilɔmɛtʀ] *m* kilometer (about
    ⅝ mile)
kiosque [kjɔsk] *m* stand, newsstand

L

l' *see* le, la
la [la] *art* the; *pron* her, it
là [la] there; **là-bas** over there; **là-haut**
    up there; **ce jour-là** that day
laboratoire [labɔʀatwaʀ] *m* laboratory

lac [lak] *m* lake

La Fayette [lafajɛt] French statesman (1757-1834)

laisser [lɛse] to let, leave

lait [lɛ] *m* milk

laitue [lɛty] *f* lettuce

lancer [lɑ̃se] to launch, to start, to throw

langue [lɑ̃g] *f* language

laquelle *see* lequel

latin [latɛ̃] *m* Latin

laver [lave] to wash

le [lə] *art* the; *pron* him, it

leçon [ləsõ] *f* lesson

légende [leʒɑ̃d] *f* legend

léger [leʒe] light

légume [legym] *m* vegetable

lendemain: le lendemain [ləlɑ̃dmɛ̃] the next day

Le Nôtre [lənotʀ] French landscape architect (1613-1700)

lequel [ləkɛl], laquelle [lakɛl], lesquels [lekɛl], lesquelles [lekɛl] *rel pron* which; who, whom; lequel? laquelle? lesquels? lesquelles? *interrog pron* which? which one? which ones?

les [le] *art* the; *pron* them

lettre [lɛtʀ] *f* letter; papier à lettres stationery

leur [lœʀ] *pers pron* to them, them; leur [lœʀ], leurs [lœʀ] *poss adj* their; le leur, la leur, les leurs *poss pron* theirs

lever: se lever [səlve] to get up, rise

lèvre [lɛvʀ] *f* lip

liberté [libɛʀte] *f* liberty

libraire [libʀɛʀ] *m* bookseller

librairie [libʀɛʀi] *f* bookstore

libre [libʀ] free

lieu [ljø] *m* place; avoir lieu to take place

ligne [liɲ] *f* line

lire [liʀ] to read

lis: je lis [ʒəli] *pr ind 1st sg of* lire

lisez: vous lisez [vulize] *pr ind 2d pl of* lire

liste [list] *m* list

lit [li] *m* bed

litre [litʀ] *m* litre (1.0567 qts. liquid)

littérature [liteʀatyʀ] *f* literature

livre [livʀ] *m* book

livre [livʀ] *f* pound; deux francs la livre two francs a pound

loi [lwa] *f* law

loin [lwɛ̃] far

lointain [lwɛ̃tɛ̃], lointaine [lwɛ̃tɛn] distant

Londres [lõdʀ] London

long [lõ], longue [lõg] long; le long de along

longtemps [lõtɑ̃] a long time, long; depuis longtemps for a long time

lorsque [lɔʀskə] when

louer [lwe] to rent

Louis XIV [lwikatɔʀz] king of France (1638-1715)

lourd [luʀ] heavy

Louvre: le Louvre [ləluvʀ] former royal palace in Paris

loyer [lwaje] *m* rent

lu [ly] *p part of* lire

lugubre [lygybʀ] dismal, dreadful

lui [lɥi] him; to him, to her, to it

lundi [lœ̃di] *m* Monday

lune [lyn] *f* moon

lunettes [lynɛt] *f pl* glasses

luxe [lyks] *m* luxury

Luxembourg [lyksɑ̃buʀ]: Jardin du Luxembourg park in Paris

lycée [lise] *m* secondary school

M

M. *abbr of* Monsieur

ma *see* mon

madame [madam] *f* madam, Mrs.

mademoiselle [madmwazɛl] *f* Miss

magasin [magazɛ̃] *m* store

magnifique [maɲifik] magnificent, splendid

mai [mɛ] *m* May

main [mɛ̃] *f* hand

maintenant [mɛ̃tnɑ̃] now

maire [mɛʀ] *m* mayor

mais [mɛ] but; mais oui oh yes; mais non oh no

maïs [mais] *m* corn

maison [mɛzõ] *f* house, company; à la maison at home

majestueux [maʒɛstɥø], majestueuse [ma-ʒɛstɥøz] majestic

mal [mal] *m* pain; mal de tête *m* headache; avoir mal à la tête to have a headache; faire mal to hurt; mal [mal] *adv* badly; pas mal all right

malade [malad] sick

maladie [maladi] *f* sickness

malgré [malgʀe] in spite of

malheureusement [malœʀøzmã] unfortunately

malheureux [malœʀø], malheureuse [malœʀøz] unhappy

manger [mãʒe] to eat

mannequin [mankɛ̃] *m* fashion model

manquer [mãke] to miss; mes parents me manquent I miss my parents

Mansard [mãsaʀ] French architect (1646-1708)

mansarde [mãsaʀd] *f* garret

manteau [mãto] *m* coat, cloak

marchand [maʀʃã] *m* merchant, dealer, shopkeeper

marché [maʀʃe] *m* market; à bon marché cheap; à meilleur marché cheaper; le Bon Marché large department store in Paris

marcher [maʀʃe] to walk

mardi [maʀdi] *m* Tuesday

marguerite [maʀgəʀit] *f* daisy

mari [maʀi] *m* husband

mariage [maʀjaʒ] *m* marriage, wedding

marier: se marier [smaʀje] to get married

marron [maʀõ] brown; les yeux marron brown eyes

marronnier [maʀɔnje] *m* horse chestnut tree

mars [maʀs] *m* March

Marseille [maʀsɛj] city in southern France

Martinique [maʀtinik] *f* Martinique

mathématiques [matematik] *f pl* mathematics

matin [matɛ̃] *m* morning; le matin in the morning; tous les matins every morning

mauvais [mɔvɛ] or [movɛ] bad, wrong; la mauvaise route the wrong road

me [mə] me, to me

mécontent [mekõtã] dissatisfied

médecin [metsɛ̃] *m* physician

médicament [medikamã] *m* medicine, drug

meilleur, meilleure, meilleurs, meilleures [mɛjœʀ] (*compar of* bon) better; le meilleur, la meilleure, les meilleurs, les meilleures (*superl of* bon) the best

Melun [məlœ̃] town in the Île-de-France

même [mɛm] *adv* even; ne...même pas not even; tout de même nevertheless, anyway; au cœur même de Paris in the very heart of Paris; le même, la même les mêmes *adj and pron* the same

ménager [menaʒe] to arrange

mener [məne] to lead

menu [məny] *m* menu

mer [mɛʀ] *f* sea

merci [mɛʀsi] thank you

mercredi [mɛʀkʀədi] *m* Wednesday

mère [mɛʀ] *f* mother

merveille [mɛʀvɛj]: à merveille marvelously

mes *see* mon

messe [mɛs] *f* mass

métallique [metalik] metallic

mètre [mɛtʀ] *m* meter (39.37 inches)

mettez: vous mettez [vumɛte] *pr ind 2d pl of* mettre

mettre [mɛtʀ] to put, put on; se mettre à to begin; mettre une lettre à la poste to mail a letter

meuble [mœbl] *m* piece of furniture; les meubles furniture

meublé [mœble] furnished

Mexique [mɛksik] *m* Mexico

midi [midi] *m* noon; après-midi *m* afternoon

mien: le mien [ləmjɛ̃], la mienne [lamjɛn], les miens [lemjɛ̃], les miennes [lemjɛn] mine mieux [mjø] *adv* (*compar of* bien) better; aimer mieux to prefer; tant mieux so much the better; le mieux (*superl of* bien) the best; de son mieux the best he could; je vais le mieux du monde I couldn't be better

milieu [miljø] *m* middle; au milieu de in the middle of, in the midst of

mille [mil] a thousand

Millet [milɛ] French painter (1815-1875)

million [miljõ] *m* million

millionnaire [miljɔnɛʀ] *m* millionaire

ministère [ministɛʀ] *m* ministry

ministre [ministʀ] *m* Cabinet member

minuit [minɥi] *m* midnight

minute [minyt] *f* minute

mis [mi] *p part of* mettre

Mlle *abbr of* Mademoiselle

Mme *abbr of* Madame

mode [mɔd] *f* fashion; *pl* women's hats and other apparel

modiste [mɔdist] *f* milliner

moi [mwa] I, me, to me

moindre, moindres [mwɛ̃dʀ] lesser; le moindre, la moindre, les moindres the least, the slightest

moins [mwɛ̃] less; moins...que less... than; à moins que unless; deux heures moins le quart a quarter of two; du moins, au moins at least

mois [mwa] *m* month; au mois de décembre in December

Molière [mɔljɛʀ] French playwright (1622-1673)

moment [mɔmã] *m* moment, time; à ce moment-là at that time; au moment de at the time of; au moment où at the time when

mon [mõ], ma [ma], mes [me] my

monde [mõd] *m* world, people; tout le monde everybody

mondial [mõdjal] world-wide

monnaie [mɔnɛ] *f* change; porte-monnaie *m* change purse

monotone [mɔnɔtɔn] monotonous

monsieur [məsjø] *m* Sir, Mr., gentleman

montagne [mõtaɲ] *f* mountain

Monte-Cristo [mõtəkʀisto]: Le Comte de Monte-Cristo a novel by Dumas

monter [mõte] to go up

Montmartre [mõmaʀtʀ] a section of Paris

montre [mõtʀ] *f* watch; montre-bracelet wrist watch

montrer [mõtʀe] to show

Mont-Saint-Michel, le [mõ sɛ̃ miʃɛl] town built on a rock of the coast of Brittany, famous for its monastery

monument [mɔnymã] *m* monument

monumental [mɔnymãtal] monumental

moquer: se moquer de [səmɔke də] to laugh at, make fun of

mort [mɔʀ] *p part of* mourir

Moscou [mɔsku] Moscow

mot [mo] *m* word

mouchoir [muʃwaʀ] *m* handkerchief

mouillé [muje] wet

mourir [muʀir] to die

mourut: il mourut [ilmuʀy] *p simple 3rd sg of* mourir

mousquetaire [muskətɛʀ] *m* musketeer; Les Trois Mousquetaires a novel by Dumas

mouton [mutõ] *m* sheep

mur [myʀ] *m* wall

mural [myʀal] mural

mûrir [myʀir] to ripen, mature

musclé [myskle] muscular

musée [myze] *m* museum

musique [myzik] *f* music

mutilé [mytile] mutilated

N

n' *see* ne

nager [naʒe] to swim

naître [nɛtʀ] to be born

Napoléon [napɔleõ] emperor of the French (1769-1821)

natal [natal] native

national [nasjɔnal] national

nationalité [nasjɔnalitɛ] *f* nationality

naturellement [natyʀɛlmã] naturally

ne [nə] not; no; **ne...pas** not, no; **ne...
plus** no more, no longer; **ne...que**
only; **ne...ni...ni** neither...nor; **ne
...guère** hardly, scarcely; **ne...person-
ne** nobody; **ne...aucun(e)** none

né [ne] *p part of* **naître; je suis né à Philadelphie** I was born in Philadelphia

néanmoins [neãmwɛ̃] nevertheless

négatif [negatif], négative [negativ] negative

négativement [negativmã] negatively

neige [nɛʒ] *f* snow

neiger [nɛʒe] to snow; **il neige** it is snowing

neuf [nœf] nine

neuf [nœf], neuve [nœv] new

neuvième [nœvjɛm] ninth

ni [ni] neither, nor; **ne...ni...ni** neither
...nor; **ni l'un ni l'autre** neither

nier [nie] to deny

noblesse [nɔblɛs] *f* nobility

Noël [nɔɛl] *m* Christmas

noir [nwaʀ] black

nom [nõ] *m* name

nombre [nõbʀ] *m* number

nombreux [nõbʀø], nombreuse [nõbʀøz]
numerous

nommé [nɔme] named

non [nõ] no; **non plus** either

Nord [nɔʀ] *m* North

Normandie [nɔʀmãdi] *f* Normandy

notamment [nɔtamã] among others

notre [nɔtʀ], nos [no] *adj* our; **le nôtre**
[lənotʀ], **la nôtre, les nôtres** *pron* ours

nous [nu] we, us, to us

nous-mêmes [numɛm] ourselves

nouveau [nuvo], nouvel, nouvelle [nuvɛl],
nouveaux, nouvelles new; **de nouveau**
again, once more; **La Nouvelle-Orléans**
New Orleans

nouvelle [nuvɛl] *f* piece of news

novembre [nɔvãbʀ] *m* November

nuit [nɥi] *f* night, darkness; **il fait nuit**
it is dark

nul [nyl], nulle [nyl] no, no one; **nulle
part** nowhere

numéro [nymeʀo] *m* number

O

obéir [ɔbeiʀ] to obey

obélisque [ɔbelisk] *m* obelisk

objet [ɔbʒɛ] *m* object

obligatoire [ɔbligatwaʀ] required

obliger [ɔbliʒe] to oblige; **noblesse oblige**
rank imposes obligations

obscurité [ɔpskyʀite] *f* darkness

observatoire [ɔpsɛʀvatwaʀ] *m* observatory

occasion [ɔkazjõ] *f* occasion, bargain; **livre
d'occasion** second-hand book

occupé [ɔkype] busy

occuper: **s'occuper de** [sɔkype də] to take
care of

octobre [ɔktɔbʀ] *m* October

oculiste [ɔkylist] *m* oculist

œil [œj], *pl* yeux [jø] *m* eye

œillet [œjɛ] *m* carnation

œuf [œf], *pl* œufs [ø] *m* egg

œuvre [œvʀ] *f* work

offrir [ɔfʀiʀ] to offer (*conjug like* **ouvrir**)

oie [wa] *f* goose

oiseau [wazo] *m* bird

olive [ɔliv] *f* olive

on [õ] one, they, someone

oncle [õkl] *m* uncle

ont: **ils ont** [ilzõ] *pr ind 3rd pl of* **avoir**

onze [õz] eleven

onzième [õzjɛm] eleventh

opéra [ɔpeʀa] *m* opera, opera house

opposé [ɔpoze] *m* opposite

orange [ɔʀãʒ] *f* orange

ordinaire [ɔʀdinɛʀ] ordinary; **d'ordinaire**
usually

ordre [ɔʀdʀ] *m* order

orgues [ɔʀg] *f pl* organ

ornement [ɔʀnəmã] *m* ornament

os [ɔs], *pl* os [o] *m* bone; **je suis mouillé
jusqu'aux os** I am wet to the skin

oser [oze] to dare

ou [u] or

où [u] where, where?, in which, when;
d'où le nom whence the name

oublier [ublie] to forget

oui [wi] yes

ouvert [uvɛʀ] *p part of* **ouvrir**

ouvrir [uvʀiʀ] to open

P

pain [pɛ̃] m bread
pair [pɛʀ]: nombre pair even number
paire [pɛʀ] f pair
paisible [pɛsibl] peaceful
paix [pɛ] f peace
palais [palɛ] m palace
panorama [panɔʀama] m sight, panorama
Panthéon: le Panthéon [ləpãteõ] m monument in Paris
papier [papje] m paper; papier à lettres stationery
paquet [pakɛ] m package, pack
par [paʀ] by, through; par jour a day; par ici this way
paraître [paʀɛtʀ] to seem, to appear
parapet [paʀapɛ] m parapet, low wall as a railing
parc [paʀk] m park
parce que [paʀskə] because
pardessus [paʀdəsy] m overcoat, topcoat
pardon [paʀdõ] pardon me, excuse me
parent [paʀã] m parent, relative
parfaitement [paʀfɛtmã] perfectly
parfois [paʀfwa] sometimes
Paris [paʀi] m Paris
parisien [paʀizjɛ̃], parisienne [paʀizjɛ:n] Parisian (takes a capital only when used as a noun referring to a person)
parle: je parle [ʒəpaʀl] pr ind 1st sg of parler
parler [paʀle] to speak; entendre parler de to hear of
parlez: vous parlez [vupaʀle] pr ind 2d pl of parler
parmi [paʀmi] among
part [paʀ] f share; quelque part somewhere; nulle part nowhere; c'est gentil de votre part it is nice of you
partager [paʀtaʒe] to divide
particulièrement [paʀtikyljɛʀmã] particularly
partie [paʀti] f part; en partie in part; partie de pêche fishing trip
partir [paʀtiʀ] to leave; je pars I leave, I am leaving
partout [paʀtu] everywhere

pas [pɑ] not; ne...pas not, no; pas encore not yet; pas du tout not at all
pas [pɑ] m step; à deux pas d'ici just a step from here
passant [pɑsã] m passer-by
passer [pɑse] to spend; to go by; comme le temps passe! how time flies!; passer un examen to take an examination; se passer [spɑse] to happen, take place; passer par to go through
Pasteur [pastœʀ] French scientist (1822-1895)
patiner [patine] to skate
pâtisserie [pɑtisʀi] f pastry, pastry shop
patronne [patʀɔn] f patron saint
pauvre [povʀ] poor
payer [pɛje] to pay
pays [pei] m country
paysage [peizaʒ] m landscape
peau [po] f skin
pêche [pɛʃ] f fishing; aller à la pêche to go fishing
pêcheur [pɛʃœʀ] m fisherman
peindre [pɛ̃dʀ] to paint
peine [pɛn] f trouble; ce n'est pas la peine it is not worth while, don't bother; à peine scarcely, hardly
peint [pɛ̃] p part of peindre
peintre [pɛ̃tʀ] m painter
peinture [pɛ̃tyʀ] f painting
pendant [pãdã] during; pendant que as, while
pendre [pãdʀ] to hang
pendule [pãdyl] f clock
pénétrant [penetʀã] penetrating
pensée [pãse] f pansy
penser [pãse] to think, believe; penser à to think of; penser de to have an opinion about; faire penser to remind
penseur [pãsœʀ] m thinker; le Penseur a statue by Rodin
pension [pãsjõ] f room and board
perdu [pɛʀdy] lost
père [pɛʀ] m father
permettre [pɛʀmɛtʀ] to allow
permission [pɛʀmisjõ] f permission
personne [pɛʀsɔn] f person; no one, nobody; ne...personne no one

perspective [pɛʀspɛktiv] f perspective

petit [pəti] small, little; **petit déjeuner** breakfast

peu [pø] little; **un peu** a little; **à peu près** about; **racontez-nous un peu** just tell us

peur [pœʀ] f fear; **avoir peur de** to be afraid of; **avoir peur que** to be afraid that; **de peur que** for fear that

peut: **il peut** [ilpø] *pr ind 3rd sg of* **pouvoir**

peut-être [pøtɛtʀ] perhaps

pharmacie [faʀmasi] f drugstore

pharmacien [faʀmasjɛ̃] m druggist

Philadelphie [filadɛlfi] Philadelphia

photo [foto] f photograph, picture

photographie [fotoɡrafi] f photograph, picture

phrase [fʀɑz] f sentence

pièce [pjɛs] f coin; play; apiece; **dix francs (la) pièce** ten francs apiece; **pièce d'eau** ornamental pool

pied [pje] m foot; **aller à pied** to walk; **un pied de salade,** a head of lettuce

pierre [pjɛʀ] f stone

pigment [piɡmɑ̃] m pigment

pique-nique [piknik] m picnic; **faire un pique-nique** to go on a picnic

pis [pi] worse; **tant pis** so much the worse, too bad

pistolet [pistolɛ] m pistol

pittoresque [pitoʀɛsk] picturesque

pivoine [pivwan] f peony

place [plas] f square, space, room, seat; **il y de la place** there is room; **à votre place** if I were you

placer [plase] to place

plaignez: **vous vous plaignez** [vuvuplɛɲe] *pr ind 2d pl of* **se plaindre**

plaindre: **se plaindre** [səplɛ̃dʀ] to complain

plaire [plɛʀ] to please; **s'il vous plaît** please; **est-ce que mon chapeau vous plaît?** do you like my hat?

plaisir [pleziʀ] m pleasure; **se faire un plaisir de** to be glad to

planter [plɑ̃te] to plant

plat m dish; **plat de viande** [pladvjɑ̃d] meat course, main course

plein [plɛ̃], **pleine** [plɛn] full; **en plein air** in the open

pleurer [plœʀe] to cry, weep

pleut: **il pleut** [ilplø] *pr ind 3rd sg of* **pleuvoir**

pleuvait: **il pleuvait** [ilplœvɛ] *imperf ind 3rd sg of* **pleuvoir**

pleuvoir [plœvwaʀ] to rain; **il pleut à verse** it is pouring

plu [ply] *p part of* **plaire** *and of* **pleuvoir**

pluie [plɥi] f rain

plume [plym] f feather, pen

plupart: **la plupart** [laplypaʀ] most, the greater part; **la plupart d'entre eux** most of them

pluriel [plyʀjɛl] m plural

plus [ply] more; **ne...plus** no more, no longer; **plus...que** more...than; **plus de** more than; **le plus grand** the tallest; **moi non plus** nor I either

plusieurs [plyzjœʀ] several

poche [poʃ] f pocket

poétique [poetik] poetic

point [pwɛ̃] m point; **point de vue** point of view

pointure [pwɛ̃tyʀ] f size

poire [pwaʀ] f pear

pois [pwa] m pea

poisson [pwasõ] m fish

police [polis] f police; **agent de police** m policeman

politique [politik] political; **un homme politique** a statesman

pomme [pom] f apple; **pomme de terre** f potato

pont [põ] m bridge; **le Pont-Neuf** bridge in Paris

porc [poʀ] m pork, pig

port [poʀ] m port

porte [poʀt] f door, gate

portefeuille [poʀtəfœj] m pocketbook, billfold

porte-monnaie [poʀtmonɛ] m change purse

porter [poʀte] to carry, wear, bear

poser [poze] to set, lay, place; poser une question to ask a question

position [pozisjõ] f position

possession [posesjõ] f possession

possible [posibl] possible

poste [post] f post, post office

potager [potaʒe] adj vegetable

pour [puʀ] to, for, in order to, so as to; pour que in order that, so that

pourquoi [puʀkwa] why; pourquoi pas? why not?

pourrai: je pourrai [ʒəpuʀe] fut 1st sg of pouvoir

pourtant [puʀtã] however

pousser [puse] to grow; faire pousser to grow (transitive)

pouvez: vous pouvez [vupuve] pr ind 2d pl of pouvoir

pouvoir [puvwaʀ] to be able to, can, could, may, might

précédent [pʀesedã] preceding

préfecture [pʀefɛktyʀ] f office of a "préfet," administrator of a "département"

préférer [pʀefeʀe] to prefer

premier [pʀəmje], première [pʀəmjɛʀ] first; le premier avril the first of April; premier [pʀəmje] m second floor

prendre [pʀɑ̃dʀ] to take; prendre quelque chose to have something to eat or to drink

prends: je prends [ʒəpʀɑ̃] pr ind 1st sg of prendre

prenez: vous prenez [vupʀəne] pr ind 2d pl of prendre

préoccupé [pʀeɔkype] worried

préparation [pʀepaʀasjõ] f preparation, making

près [pʀɛ] near, near by; près de near; à peu près about

présentation [pʀezɑ̃tasjõ] f presentation, introduction

présenter [pʀezɑ̃te] to introduce

président [pʀesidã] m president

presque [pʀɛskə] almost

pressé [pʀese]; être pressé to be in a hurry

prêt [pʀɛ] ready

prêter [pʀɛte] to lend

prévenir [pʀevniʀ] to warn (conjug like venir)

principal [pʀɛ̃sipal] principal

printemps [pʀɛ̃tã] m spring; au printemps in the spring

pris [pʀi] p part of prendre

prise [pʀiz] f taking

Prisunic [pʀizynik] m ten-cent store

prix [pʀi] m price

procès-verbal [pʀosɛvɛʀbal] m police ticket

prochain [pʀoʃɛ̃], prochaine [pʀoʃɛn] next; dimanche prochain next Sunday; la semaine prochaine next week

procurer: se procurer [spʀokyʀe] to get

produit [pʀodɥi] m product

professeur [pʀofɛsœʀ] m professor

profession [pʀofɛsjõ] f profession

profiter de [pʀofite də] to take advantage of

progrès [pʀogʀɛ] m progress

prohibé [pʀoibe] forbidden; arme prohibée concealed weapon

promenade [pʀomnad] f walk, drive; faire une promenade to take a walk; faire une promenade en auto to take a ride

promettre [pʀomɛtʀ] to promise

pronom [pʀonõ] m pronoun

proposer [pʀopoze] to suggest

propre [pʀopʀ] own

prospère [pʀospɛʀ] prosperous

province [pʀovɛ̃s] f out of Paris (in the provinces)

provision [pʀovizjõ] f supply; provisions provisions

psychologue [psikolog] m psychologist

pu [py] p part of pouvoir

public [pyblik], publique [pyblik] public; jardin public public park

puis [pɥi] then; et puis and besides

puisque [pɥiskə] since

puissent: ils puissent [ilpɥis] pr subj 3rd pl of pouvoir

purement [pyʀmã] purely

Pyrénées: les Pyrénées [lepiʀene] f pl chain of mountains in southern France

Q

qu' *see* que

quai [ke] *m* platform, street along a river

qualité [kalite] *f* quality

quand [kɑ̃] when, when?; depuis quand? how long? since when?

quarante [kaʀɑ̃t] forty

quart [kaʀ] *m* quarter; onze heures et quart a quarter past eleven; onze heures moins le quart a quarter to eleven

quartier [kaʀtje] *m* quarter, part of a city

quatorze [katɔʀz] fourteen

quatre [katʀ] four

quatre-vingts [katʀəvɛ̃] eighty

quatre-vingt-dix [katʀəvɛ̃dis] ninety

quatrième [katʀiɛm] fourth

que [kə] *rel pron* whom, which; ce que [skə] that which, what; que? [kə]; qu'est-ce qui? [kɛski]; qu'est-ce que? [kɛskə] what?; qu'est-ce que c'est que? what is?; que *conj* that

quel? quelle? quels? quelles? [kɛl] *interrog adj* what?; quel...! what a...!

quelque, quelques [kɛlkə] some, a few; quelque chose something

quelquefois [kɛlkəfwa] sometimes

quelques-uns [kɛlkəzœ̃], quelques-unes [kɛlkəzyn] some, a few

quelqu'un [kɛlkœ̃] somebody, someone

question [kɛstjɔ̃] *f* question

qui [ki] *rel pron* who, whom, which; ce qui [ski] what; qui? [ki] *interrog pron* who? whom?; qui est-ce qui? who?; qui est-ce que? whom?; à qui est cette cravate? whose tie is this?

quinze [kɛ̃z] fifteen; Quinze-Vingts [kɛ̃z vɛ̃] i.e. 300, name of a hospital in Paris

quinzième [kɛ̃zjɛm] fifteenth

quitter [kite] to leave

quoi [kwa] what, what?; à quoi bon? what is the use?; il y a de quoi there is reason for it; il n'y a pas de quoi you are welcome

R

raconter [ʀakɔ̃te] to tell, to narrate

raisin [ʀɛzɛ̃] *m* grapes

raison [ʀɛzɔ̃] *f* reason; avoir raison to be right

ramasser [ʀamɑse] to pick, pick up, gather

ramener [ʀamne] to bring back

rappeler [ʀaple] to remind; se rappeler to remember

rapporter [ʀapɔʀte] to take back, bring back

rare [ʀaʀ] rare

rarement [ʀaʀmɑ̃] seldom

ravager [ʀavaʒe] to ravage

rayonner [ʀɛjɔne] to radiate

réalité [ʀealite] *f* reality

recevoir [ʀəsəvwaʀ] to receive

recevrai: je recevrai [ʒəʀəsəvʀe] *fut 1st sg* of recevoir

réciter [ʀesite] to recite

recommander [ʀəkɔmɑ̃de] to recommend

reconnaissant [ʀəkɔnɛsɑ̃] grateful

reconnaître [ʀəkɔnɛtʀ] to recognize

reconstruire [ʀəkɔ̃stʀɥiʀ] to rebuild

reçu [ʀəsy] *p part of* recevoir

refus [ʀəfy] *m* refusal

refuser [ʀəfyze] to refuse

regarder [ʀəɡaʀde] to look, look at

région [ʀeʒjɔ̃] *f* region

règle [ʀɛɡl] *f* rule; en règle in order

règne [ʀɛɲ] *m* reign

regretter [ʀəɡʀɛte] to regret, be sorry for

Reims [ʀɛ̃s] Rheims, city in eastern France

reine [ʀɛn] *f* queen

rejoindre [ʀəʒwɛ̃dʀ] to meet, catch up with

relativement [ʀəlativmɑ̃] relatively

religieux [ʀəliʒjø] religious

remarquer [ʀəmaʀke] to notice, to observe

remède [ʀəmɛd] *m* remedy

remercier [ʀəmɛʀsje] to thank

remettre [ʀəmɛtʀ] to put back

remplacer [ʀɑ̃plase] to replace

Renaissance [ʀənɛsɑ̃s] *f* Renaissance

rencontre [ʀɑ̃kõtʀ] *f* meeting; **aller, venir à la rencontre** to go to meet

rencontrer [ʀɑ̃kõtʀe] to meet

rendez-vous [ʀɑ̃devu] *m* appointment

rendre [ʀɑ̃dʀ] to render, give back; to make; **est-ce que cela vous rend triste? does it make you sad?; se rendre compte** to realize

rendu [ʀɑ̃dy] *p part of* **rendre**

renseignement [ʀɑ̃sɛɲmɑ̃] *m* information

renseigner [ʀɑ̃sɛɲe] to inform, give out information

réparation [ʀepaʀasjõ] *f* repair

réparer [ʀepaʀe] to repair; **faire réparer** to have (something) repaired

repartir [ʀəpaʀtiʀ] to leave again, set out again

repas [ʀəpɑ] *m* meal

répéter [ʀepete] to repeat

répondez: vous répondez [vuʀepõde] *pr ind 2d pl of* **répondre**

répondre [ʀepõdʀ] to answer

réponse [ʀepõs] *f* answer

reposer: se reposer [səʀpoze] to rest

représentation [ʀəpʀezɑ̃tasjõ] *f* performance

représenter [ʀəpʀezɑ̃te] to represent

réserver [ʀezɛʀve] to reserve

résidence [ʀezidɑ̃s] *f* residence

résignation [ʀeziɲasjõ] *f* resignation

ressembler à [ʀəsɑ̃ble a] to resemble, look like

ressort [ʀəsɔʀ] *m* spring

restaurant [ʀɛstoʀɑ̃] *m* restaurant

reste [ʀɛst] *m* rest, remainder

rester [ʀɛste] to stay; to be left, remain; **il reste** there remains, there remain

rétabli [ʀetabli] recovered

retard [ʀətaʀ] *m* delay, lateness; **en retard** late

retour [ʀətuʀ] *m* return; **aller et retour** round trip; **être de retour** to be back

retourner [ʀətuʀne] to go back; **se retourner** [səʀtuʀne] to turn around

retrouver [ʀətʀuve] to find again, meet

réussir à [ʀeysiʀ a] to succeed in

réveiller: se réveiller [səʀevɛje] to wake up

réveillon [ʀevɛjõ] *m* meal eaten on Christmas eve at midnight

revenir [ʀəvniʀ] to return

révision [ʀevizjõ] *f* review

revoir [ʀəvwaʀ] to see again (*conjug like* **voir**); **au revoir** good-bye

Révolution, la [ʀevɔlysjõ] the French Revolution

révolutionnaire [ʀevɔlysjɔnɛʀ] revolutionary

revue [ʀəvy] *f* review, magazine

rhume [ʀym] *m* cold

riant [ʀiɑ̃] *pres part of* **rire**

riche [ʀiʃ] rich

rien [ʀjɛ̃] nothing; **ne...rien** nothing; **de rien** you are welcome; **rien d'intéressant** nothing interesting

rire [ʀiʀ] to laugh

risquer de [ʀiske də] to risk

rive [ʀiv] *f* bank; **la rive droite** the right bank of the Seine in Paris; **la rive gauche** the left bank

rivière [ʀivjɛʀ] *f* river, creek

robe [ʀɔb] *f* dress

Rodin [ʀɔdɛ̃] French sculptor (1840 1917)

roi [ʀwa] *m* king

rôle [ʀol] *m* rôle, part

roman [ʀɔmɑ̃] *m* novel

roman [ʀɔmɑ̃], **romane** [ʀɔman] romanesque (architecture)

Rome [ʀɔm] Rome

Ronsard [ʀõsaʀ] French poet (1524-1585)

rosbif [ʀɔsbif] *m* roast beef

rose [ʀoz] rosy, pink

rose [ʀoz] *f* rose

rosier [ʀozje] *m* rosebush

Rouen [ʀwɑ̃] city in Normandy

rouge [ʀuʒ] red

rouler [ʀule] to roll along

route [ʀut] *f* road; **en route** on the way; **la bonne route** the right road; **la mauvaise route** the wrong road

royal [ʀwajal] royal

rue [ʀy] *f* street

ruine [ʀɥin] *f* ruin

russe [ʀys] Russian *(takes a capital only when used as a noun referring to a person)*

Russie [ʀysi] *f* Russia

S

s' *see* **si** *or* **se**

sa *see* **son**

sable [sabl] *m* sand

sac [sak] *m* bag

sacrifice [sakʀifis] *m* sacrifice

sain et sauf [sɛ̃ e sɔf] safe and sound

saint [sɛ̃] saint, holy; **la Sainte-Chapelle** XIIIth century church in Paris; **Saint-Germain-des-Prés** [sɛ̃ʒɛʀmɛ̃ dɛ pʀe] section of Paris near the University and popular with students; **Saint-Malo** [sɛ̃ malo] old city on the coast of Brittany

sais: je sais [ʒəsɛ] *pr ind 1st sg of* **savoir**

saison [sɛzõ] *f* season

sait: il sait [ilsɛ] *pr ind 3rd sg of* **savoir**

salade [salad] *f* salad; lettuce, etc.

salle [sal] *f* room; **salle à manger** dining room; **salle de bain** bathroom

salon [salõ] *m* living room

samedi [samdi] *m* Saturday

sandwich [sɑ̃dwitʃ] *m* sandwich

sans [sɑ̃] without

satisfaction [satisfaksjõ] *f* satisfaction

satisfait [satisfɛ] satisfied

sauf [sɔf] except

sauriez: vous sauriez [vusɔʀje] *cond 2d pl of* **savoir**

sauterie [sotʀi] *f* small dance

sauvage [sovaʒ] wild

sauver [sove] to save

savez: vous savez [vusave] *pr ind 2d pl of* **savoir**

savoir [savwaʀ] to know, know how

scène [sɛn] *f* scene

science [sjɑ̃s] *f* science

sculpture [skyltyʀ] *f* sculpture

se [sə] oneself, himself, herself, themselves; to oneself, etc.

second [səgõ] second; **seconde** *f* second class

Seine [sɛn] *f* Seine

seize [sɛz] sixteen

selon [səlõ] according to

semaine [səmɛn] *f* week; **la semaine prochaine** next week

sembler [sɑ̃ble] to seem

Sénégal [senegal] *m* Senegal

sentiment [sɑ̃timɑ̃] *m* sentiment

sentir [sɑ̃tiʀ] to smell; **se sentir** to feel

séparer [sepaʀe] to separate

sept [sɛt] seven

septembre [sɛptɑ̃bʀ] *m* September

septième [sɛtjɛm] seventh

sépulture [sepyltyʀ] *f* burial

serai: je serai [ʒəsʀe] *fut 1st sg of* **être**

série [seʀi] *f* series

sérieux [seʀjø], **sérieuse** [seʀjøz] serious

sert: il sert [ilsɛʀ] *pr ind 3rd sg of* **servir**

service [sɛʀvis] *m* service

servir à [sɛʀviʀ a] to serve, be of use; **se servir de** to use; **se servir** to help oneself; **servir de** to be used as

ses *see* **son**

seul, seule [sœl] alone, single

seulement [sœlmɑ̃] only, but

si [si] if, whether, so; **si** [si] yes; **mais si** oh yes

siècle [sjɛkl] *m* century; **au treizième siècle** in the thirteenth century

sien: le sien [ləsjɛ̃], **la sienne** [lasjɛn], **les siens** [lesjɛ̃], **les siennes** [lesjɛn] *poss pron* his, hers

silencieux [silɑ̃sjø], **silencieuse** [silɑ̃sjøz] silent

silhouette [silwɛt] *f* figure

simple [sɛ̃pl] simple

simplement [sɛ̃pləmɑ̃] simply, merely

situé [sitɥe] situated

six [sis] six

sixième [sizjɛm] sixth

ski [ski] *m* ski; **faire du ski** to go skiing

société [sɔsjete] *f* society

sœur [sœʀ] *f* sister

soie [swa] *f* silk

soif [swaf] *f* thirst; **avoir soif** to be thirsty

soir [swaʀ] *m* evening; le soir in the evening; hier soir last night

soirée [swaʀe] *f* evening

soit: il soit [ilswa] *pr subj 3rd sg of* être

soit [swa] either, or; soit...soit either... or

soixante [swasɑ̃t] sixty

soixante-dix [swasɑ̃tdis] seventy

sol [sɔl] *m* soil, ground

sole [sɔl] *f* a choice fish, which is different from the common flounder referred to in the expression "fillet of sole"

soleil [sɔlɛj] *m* sun; il fait du soleil the sun is shining

sombre [sõbʀ] dark

sommeil [sɔmɛj] *m* sleep

sommes: nous sommes [nusɔm] *pr ind 1st pl of* être

somptueux [sõptɥø], somptueuse [sõptɥøz] sumptuous

son [sõ], sa [sa], ses [se] *poss adj* his, her, its

sonner [sɔne] to ring

sont: ils sont [ilsõ] *pr ind 3rd pl of* être

Sorbon [sɔʀbõ] founder of the Sorbonne (1201-1274)

Sorbonne: la Sorbonne [lasɔʀbɔn] Division of Letters and Science of the University of Paris

sort [sɔʀ] *m* fate

sorte [sɔʀt] *f* sort, kind; de sorte que so that

sortie [sɔʀti] *f* exit, going out

sortir [sɔʀtiʀ] to go out

soufflé [sufle] *m* soufflé

souffrir [sufʀiʀ] to suffer (*conjug like* ouvrir)

souhaiter [swɛte] to wish

souligné [suliɲe] underlined

sous [su] under

souterrain [suteʀɛ̃] underground

souvenir [suvɛniʀ] *m* souvenir

souvenir: se souvenir [səsuvniʀ] to remember (*conjug like* venir)

souvent [suvɑ̃] often

soyez: vous soyez [vuswaje] *pr subj 2d pl of* être

spécialement [spesjalmɑ̃] especially

spécialité [spesjalite] *f* specialty

spectacle [spɛktakl] *m* spectacle

spectateur [spɛktatœʀ] *m* spectator

spirituel [spiʀitɥɛl] spiritual

spirituellement [spiʀitɥɛlmɑ̃] mentally

splendeur [splɑ̃dœʀ] *f* splendor

statue [staty] *f* statue

style [stil] *m* style

substantif [sypstɑ̃tif] *m* noun

sucre [sykʀ] *m* sugar

Sud [syd] *m* South

suffit: il suffit [il syfi] one only has to

suggérer [syɡ3eʀe] to suggest

suis: je suis [3əsɥi] *pr ind 1st sg of* être; je suis [3əsɥi] *pr ind 1st sg of* suivre

Suisse [sɥis] *f* Switzerland

suite [sɥit] *f* succession, continuation; tout de suite [tut sɥit] right away

suivant [sɥivɑ̃] following

suivre [sɥivʀ] to follow, to take (a course)

sujet [sy3ɛ] *m* subject; au sujet de about

super-marché [sypɛʀmaʀʃe] *m* supermarket

supplémentaire [syplemɑ̃tɛʀ] supplementary

supportable [sypɔʀtabl] bearable, endurable

sur [syʀ] on, upon, about

sûr [syʀ] sure

surpris [syʀpʀi] surprised *p part of* surprendre

surprise [syʀpʀiz] *f* surprise

symboliser [sɛ̃bɔlize] to symbolize

symbolisme [sɛ̃bɔlism] *m* symbolism

symétrie [simetʀi] *f* symmetry

sympathique [sɛ̃patik] friendly, congenial

T

tabac [taba] *m* tobacco

table [tabl] *f* table

tableau [tablo] *m* picture, painting

tailler [taje] to trim

talent [talɑ̃] *m* talent

tandis que [tɑ̃diskə] while

tant [tã] so much, so many; **tant mieux** so much the better

tante [tãt] f aunt

tapis [tapi] m rug

tard [taʀ] late; **plus tard** later; **au plus tard** at the latest

taxi [taksi] m taxi

te [tə] to you, for you *(familiar)*

tel: **un tel** [œ̃tɛl], **une telle** [yntɛl], **de tels** [dətɛl], **de telles** [dətɛl] such a, such

téléphone [tɛlɛfɔn] m telephone

téléphoner [tɛlɛfɔne] to telephone

témoin [temwɛ̃] m witness; **être témoin de** to witness

température [tãpeʀatyʀ] f temperature

temple [tãpl] m temple

temps [tã] m time, weather; **emploi du temps** m schedule; **quel temps fait-il?** how is the weather?; **à temps** on time; **combien de temps?** how long?; **avoir le temps de** to have time to; **au temps où** at the time when

tenez! [təne] here!

tenir [təniʀ] to hold, to keep; **tenir une auberge** to run an inn

tennis [tɛnis] m tennis; **jouer au tennis** to play tennis

terminer [tɛʀmine] to finish

terrasse [tɛʀas] f terrace

terre [tɛʀ] f earth, ground

tête [tɛt] f head

texte [tɛkst] m text

thé [te] m tea

théâtre [teatʀ] m theatre

théologie [teɔlɔʒi] f theology

tien: **le tien** [lətjɛ̃], **la tienne** [latjɛn], **les tiens** [letjɛ̃], **les tiennes** [letjɛn] yours *(familiar)*

tiens! [tjɛ̃] well!

tient: **il tient** [iltjɛ̃] *pr ind 3rd sg of* **tenir**

timbre [tɛ̃bʀ] m stamp; **timbre-poste** postage stamp

tirer [tiʀe] to pull

tiroir [tiʀwaʀ] m drawer

titre [titʀ] m title

toi [twa] you *(familiar)*

toit [twa] m roof

tomate [tɔmat] f tomato

tombeau [tõbo] m monumental tomb

tomber [tõbe] to fall

ton [tõ], **ta** [ta], **tes** [te] your *(familiar)*

torche [tɔʀʃ] f torch

tort [tɔʀ] m wrong; **avoir tort** to be wrong

tôt [to] soon; **plus tôt** sooner; **le plus tôt possible** as soon as possible

toucher [tuʃe] to touch; **toucher un chèque** to cash a check

toujours [tuʒuʀ] always, still

tour [tuʀ] f tower

touriste [tuʀist] m tourist

tourner [tuʀne] to turn

Tours [tuʀ] city in Touraine

tout [tu], **toute** [tut], **tous** [tu], **toutes** [tut] *adj* all, every; **toute la journée** all day; **tous les jours** every day; **tout le monde** everybody; **tout** [tu], **toute** [tut], **tous** [tus], **toutes** [tut] *pron* all, everybody, everything; **tout** [tu] *adv* all, quite, completely; **tout à fait** quite; **tout de suite** right away; **tout à l'heure** a while ago, in a while; **pas du tout** not at all; **tout de même** all the same; **rien du tout** nothing at all; **tout à coup** suddenly

trace [tʀas] f trace

tracteur [tʀaktœʀ] m tractor

tradition [tʀadisjõ] f tradition

traditionnel [tʀadisjɔnɛl] traditional

train [tʀɛ̃] m train; **en train de** in the act of

tranquille [tʀãkil] quiet

transformer [tʀãsfɔʀme] to transform

transposer [tʀãspoze] to transpose

travail [tʀavaj] m work

travailler [tʀavaje] to work

travers: **à travers** [atʀavɛʀ] through

traverser [tʀavɛʀse] to cross

treize [tʀɛz] thirteen

treizième [tʀɛzjɛm] thirteenth

trente [tʀãt] thirty

très [tʀɛ] very, very much

Trianons [tʀianõ] m name of two small châteaux in the park of the Versailles palace

triste [tʀist] sad
Troglodyte [tʀɔglɔdit] *m* cave dweller
trois [tʀwɑ] three
troisième [tʀwazjɛm] third
tromper: se tromper [stʀɔ̃pe] to be mistaken, to miss (a road, etc.)
trop [tʀɔ] too, too much, too many
trou [tʀu] *m* hole
trouver [tʀuve] to find, think; **comment la trouvez-vous?** how do you like it?; **vous trouvez?** do you think so?; **se trouver** to be, be located
tu [ty] you *(familiar)*
Tuileries: les Tuileries [letɥilʀi] park in Paris

U

un [œ̃] *m* a, an; one; **l'un** one
une [yn] *f* a, an; one; **l'une** one
unique [ynik] unique
université [ynivɛʀsite] *f* University
uns: les uns [lezœ̃], les unes [lezyn] some; **les un(e)s...les autres** some...the others; **les un(e)s...d'autres** some... others
user [yze] to wear out
usine [yzin] *f* factory, plant
ustensile [ystɑ̃sil] *m* utensil
utile [ytil] useful; *nm* something useful

V

va: il va [ilva] *pr ind 3rd sg of* aller
vacances [vakɑ̃s] *f pl* vacation, holiday; **en vacances** on vacation
vache [vaʃ] *f* cow
vais: je vais [ʒəvɛ] *pr ind 1st sg of* aller
valeur [valœʀ] *f* value; **avoir de la valeur** to be valuable
valoir [valwaʀ] to be worth; **il vaut mieux** it is better, it is preferable
vaste [vast] vast
Vaugirard: rue de Vaugirard [ʀydvo-ʒiʀaʀ] street in Paris
vaut: il vaut [ilvo] *pr ind 3rd sg of* valoir
venant [vənɑ̃] *pr part of* venir

vend: il vend [ilvɑ̃] *pr ind 3rd sg of* vendre
vendanges [vɑ̃dɑ̃ʒ] *f pl* grape gathering
vendeur [vɑ̃dœʀ], vendeuse [vɑ̃døz] salesman, salesgirl
vendre [vɑ̃dʀ] to sell
vendredi [vɑ̃dʀədi] *m* Friday
venez: vous venez [vuvne] *pr ind 2d pl of* venir
venir [vənir] to come; **faire venir** to have ...come; **venir de** to have just; **il vient d'arriver** he has just come; **il venait d'arriver** he had just come
vent [vɑ̃] *m* wind; **il fait du vent** it is windy
véritablement [veʀitabləmɑ̃] really
verre [vɛʀ] *m* glass, lens
verrons: nous verrons [nuveʀɔ̃] *fut 1st pl of* voir
vers [vɛʀ] towards, about; **vers deux heures** around two o'clock
Versailles [vɛʀsaj] city near Paris
verser [vɛʀse] to pour; **il pleut à verse** it is pouring
version [vɛʀsjɔ̃] *f* version, account
veut: il veut [ilvø] *pr ind 3rd sg of* vouloir
veux: je veux [ʒəvø] *pr ind 1st sing of* vouloir
viande [vjɑ̃d] *f* meat
victime [viktim] *f* victim
vie [vi] *f* life
viens: je viens [ʒəvjɛ̃] *pr ind 1st sg of* venir; **je viens de** I just...
vient: il vient [ilvjɛ̃] *pr ind 3rd sg of* venir
vieux [vjø] *m*, vieil [vjɛj] *m*, vieille [vjɛj] *f*, vieux [vjø] *m pl*, vieilles [vjɛj] *f pl* old; **mon vieux** pal, old man
vigne [viɲ] *f* vine, vineyard
vignoble [viɲɔbl] *m* vineyard
village [vilaʒ] *m* village
ville [vil] *f* city, town; **en ville** downtown
vin [vɛ̃] *m* wine
vingt [vɛ̃] twenty
violette [vjɔlɛt] *f* violet
visite [vizit] *f* visit

visiter [vizite] to visit

visiteur [vizitœʀ] *m* visitor

vite [vit] fast

vitesse [vitɛs] *f* speed; **à toute vitesse** at great speed

vitrail [vitʀaj] *m,* **vitraux** [vitʀo] *pl* stained-glass window

vitrine [vitʀin] *f* show window

vivait: il vivait [ilvivɛ] *imperf ind 3rd sg of* **vivre**

vivant: de son vivant [də sõ vivã] when alive

vivre [vivʀ] to live

voici [vwasi] here is; **le voici, la voici** here it is, here he is, here she is

voie [vwɑ] *f* track

voile [vwal] *f* sail; **bateau à voile** *m* sail boat

voir [vwaʀ] to see; **voir venir** to see... coming

vois: je vois [ʒəvwa] *pr ind 1st sg of* **voir**

voisin [vwazɛ̃], **voisine** [vwazin] neighbor, neighboring; **voisin de** near

voisinage [vwazinaʒ] *m* neighborhood

voix [vwa] f voice; **à voix basse** in a low voice

volant [vɔlã] *m* steering wheel

volcan [vɔlkã] *m* volcano

volet [vɔlɛ] *m* shutter

volontiers [vɔlõtje] willingly, gladly

Voltaire [vɔltɛʀ] French philosopher and writer (1694-1778)

vos *see* **votre**

votre [vɔtʀ], **vos** [vo] *poss adj* your

vôtre: le vôtre [ləvotʀ], **la vôtre** [lavotʀ], **les vôtres** [levotʀ] *poss pron* yours

voudrais: je voudrais [ʒəvudʀɛ] *cond 1st sg of* **vouloir**

voulez: vous voulez [vuvule] *pr ind 2d pl of* **vouloir**

vouloir [vulwaʀ] to want, wish; to like; **vouloir bien** to be willing, be kind enough to; **je voudrais bien** I would like; **vouloir dire** to mean; **Que voulez-vous!** Well!

vous [vu] you, to you

voûte [vut] *f* arch

voyage [vwajaʒ] *m* trip

voyez: vous voyez [vuvwaje] *pr ind 2d pl of* **voir**

voyons [vwajõ] *imper 1st pl of* **voir**

vrai [vʀɛ] true

vraiment [vʀɛmã] truly, really

vu [vy] *p part of* **voir**

vue [vy] *f* view, sight; **point de vue** *m* point of view; **vue d'ensemble** general view

W

wagon [vagõ] *m* car; **wagon-restaurant** diner

week-end [wikɛnd] *m* week end

Y

y [i] to it, at it, to them, at them, there; **il y a** there is, there are; **y a-t-il?** is there? are there?; **il y avait** there was, there were; **il y a cinq ans** five years ago; **il y a un quart d'heure que j'attends** I have been waiting for fifteen minutes; **qu'est-ce qu'il y a?** what is the matter?

yeux [jø] *pl of* **œil**; **elle a les yeux bleus** she has blue eyes

Z

zéro [zeʀo] zero

zut! [zyt] confound it!

ENGLISH-FRENCH

A

a un *m*, une *f*

able: to be able to pouvoir

about *prep* vers; *adv* à peu près, environ; *prep* au sujet de, à propos de; **about what time?** vers quelle heure?; **about one hundred** une centaine; **what about you?** et vous?; **how about going fishing?** si nous allions à la pêche?

above au-dessus de

absent absent

accent accent *m*

accept accepter

accident accident *m*

according to d'après

acquaintance connaissance *f;* **I made his acquaintance** j'ai fait sa connaissance

acquainted: to be acquainted with connaître

across en face de, de l'autre côté de

act: to act as servir de

actor, actress acteur, actrice

adjective adjectif *m*

admirable admirable

admire admirer

advantage avantage *m;* **to take advantage of** profiter de

advice conseil *m;* **to follow (an) advice** suivre un conseil

affirmative affirmatif *m*, affirmative *f*

affirmatively affirmativement

afraid: to be afraid of avoir peur de; **I am afraid so** j'en ai peur

Africa Afrique *f;* **North Africa** l'Afrique du Nord

after après; **after having gone to Normandy, he went to Brittany** après être allé en Normandie, il est allé en Bretagne

afternoon après-midi *m;* **in the afternoon** l'après-midi

afterwards après, ensuite

again de nouveau, encore

age âge *m;* **how old are you?** quel âge avez-vous?

ago: five years ago il y a cinq ans; **a while ago** tout à l'heure; **some time ago** il y a quelque temps

agree être de l'avis de, être d'accord avec

agreeable agréable

agreed c'est entendu, entendu

ahead: straight ahead tout droit

air air *m;* **in the open air** en plein air

album album *m*

all tout, toute, tous, toutes; **is that all?** est-ce tout?; **not at all** pas du tout; **all of Paris** Paris tout entier; **all right** c'est entendu; **it is all right with me** cela m'est égal

allow permettre de

all right bon, bien, pas mal

almost presque

along le long de; **to go along** accompagner, suivre, venir

Alps Alpes *f pl*

already déjà

also aussi

although bien que, quoique

always toujours

am: I am je suis

America Amérique *f;* **South America** l'Amérique du Sud

American américain *m*, américaine *f*

among entre, parmi; **among others** entre autres

amusing amusant

an un *m*, une *f*

and et

announce annoncer

another un autre *m*, une autre *f*

answer réponse *f*; **to answer** répondre

any du, de la, de l', des, de, en; **not any** ne...pas de; **not any more**...ne...plus (de)

anyone quelqu'un; **not...anyone** ne...personne

anything quelque chose; **not...anything** ne...rien

anyway tout de même; d'ailleurs

apologize s'excuser de

appetite appétit *m*

apple pomme *f*

appointment rendez-vous *m*

April avril *m*

arch arc *m*; **arch of triumph** arc de triomphe; **round arch** arc en demi-cercle

architect architecte *m*

are: they are ils sont; **there are** il y a; **you are** vous êtes; **are you?** êtes-vous?

army armée *f*

around vers, autour de; **around five o'clock** vers cinq heures; **around Paris** autour de Paris

arrival arrivée *f*

arrive arriver; **it arrives** il arrive

art art *m*

article article *m*

artist artiste *m*

as comme, pendant que; **as...as** aussi...que

ask demander, poser une question

asleep endormi; **to fall asleep** s'endormir

asparagus asperge *f*

aspect aspect *m*

aspirin aspirine *f*

astonish étonner

at à, chez; **at the** au, à la, à l', aux; **at Marie's** chez Marie; **at about six o'clock** vers six heures

Athens Athènes

Atlantic Atlantique

attain atteindre

attention attention *f*

attentively attentivement

attract attirer

August août *m*

aunt tante *f*

author auteur *m*

auto auto *f*

autumn automne *m*

avenue avenue *f*

await attendre

away: to go away partir, s'en aller; **right away** tout de suite; **to send away** renvoyer

B

back: to go back (home) rentrer; **to be back** être de retour

bad mauvais; **it is too bad** c'est dommage; **too bad** tant pis

badly mal

bag sac *m*

bakery boulangerie *f*

banana banane *f*

bank banque *f*; rive *f*

banker banquier *m*

barber coiffeur *m*; **to the barber's** chez le coiffeur

bath bain *m*; **bathroom** salle de bain *f*

battle bataille *f*

be: to be être; **how are you?** comment allez-vous?; **I am well** je vais bien; **he will be** il sera; **he would be** il serait; **there is, there are** il y a; **there was, there were** il y avait; **there will be** il y aura; **to be cold** avoir froid; **to be hungry** avoir faim; **to be right** avoir raison; **to be wrong** avoir tort; **to be (located)** se trouver; **to be (used) for** servir à; **I am to** je dois; **I was to** je devais

bean *haricot *m*

bear: to bear porter; supporter

beautiful beau, bel *m*; belle *f*; beaux *m pl*; belles *f pl*

because parce que; **because of** à cause de

become devenir

becoming: your hat is very becoming votre chapeau vous va très bien

bed lit; **to go to bed** se coucher; **to stay in bed** rester au lit

beef bœuf *m;* **roast beef** rosbif *m*
been été *p part of* être
beer bière *f*
beet betterave *f;* **sugar beet** betterave à sucre
before *(time)* avant, avant que; déjà; *(place)* devant
begin commencer, se mettre à
beginning commencement *m*
Belgium Belgique *f*
believe croire, penser
belong appartenir à, être à
beside à côté de
besides puis, d'ailleurs, en outre
best *adj* le meilleur, la meilleure, les meilleurs, les meilleures; *adv* le mieux; **the best he could** de son mieux
better *adj* meilleur, meilleure, meilleurs, meilleures; *adv* mieux; **I like spring better** j'aime mieux le printemps; **so much the better** tant mieux; **I am better** je vais mieux; **it is better to** il vaut mieux; **it would be better to** il vaudrait mieux
bicycle bicyclette *f;* **to bicycle** aller à bicyclette
big grand, gros; **that big** gros comme ça
bill addition *f;* facture *f;* **a fifty-franc bill** un billet de cinquante francs
billfold portefeuille *m*
bird oiseau *m*
birthday anniversaire *m*
bit: a bit un peu
black noir
blind aveugle
blond blond
blue bleu, bleue, bleus, bleues
board: room and board pension *f*
boat bateau *m*
bone os *m*
book livre *m;* **secondhand-book dealer** bouquiniste *m;* **secondhand book** livre d'occasion
bookstore librairie *f*
born né; **to be born** naître
botany botanique *m*

bother: to bother ennuyer, déranger, se déranger
bottle bouteille *f*
bottom fond *m*
boulevard boulevard *m*
bouquet bouquet *m*
box boîte *f;* carton *m*
boy garçon, petit garçon, jeune homme *m*
bread pain *m*
break: to break casser
breakfast petit déjeuner *m*
breath souffle *m;* **to be out of breath** être essoufflé
bridge pont *m*
bring apporter; **bring me** apportez-moi; **to bring over** apporter; **to bring back** rapporter
Brittany Bretagne *f*
brother frère *m*
brown brun, marron; **she has brown eyes** elle a les yeux marron *(no agreement)*
brunette brune *f*
brush: to brush brosser
build: to build construire; **to have built** faire construire
building bâtiment *m*
burn; to burn brûler
bury enterrer
bus autobus *m;* **on the bus** en autobus
busy occupé; **to be busy** être en train de *(followed by inf)*
but mais
butcher boucher *m;* **butcher shop** boucherie *f;* **pork butcher** charcutier *m;* **pork butcher's** charcuterie *f*
butter beurre *m*
buy: to buy acheter; **worth buying** intéressant
by par, de; *with pr part* en

C

cabbage chou *m*
Cabinet member ministre *m*
cable câblogramme *m*
café café *m*
California Californie *f*

call: to call appeler; to be called s'appeler

can (pouvoir): can you? pouvez-vous?; I can je peux; you can vous pouvez, on peut

Canada Canada *m*

canal canal *m*

capital capitale *f*

car wagon (train) *m;* auto *f;* automobile *f*

card carte *f;* to play cards jouer aux cartes

care soin *m;* to take care of s'occuper de

careful: to be careful faire attention; to be careful not to se garder de

caretaker concierge *m or f*

carnation œillet *m*

carpet tapis *m*

carry porter; to carry away, to carry along emmener, emporter

case cas *m;* in any case en tout cas; in case of en cas de

cash: to cash toucher (un chèque)

cashier caissier *m*, caissière *f;* cashier's window caisse *f*

catch: to catch attraper; to catch up with rejoindre, rattraper

cathedral cathédrale *f*

cellar cave *f*

center centre *m*

century siècle *m;* in the fifteenth century au quinzième siècle

certain certain

certainly certainement, volontiers

chair chaise *f*

champagne champagne *m*

chance occasion *f*, *hasard *m;* by chance par hasard; to have a chance to avoir l'occasion de

change monnaie *f;* change purse portemonnaie *m;* to change changer; to change trains changer de train

characterized caractérisé

chase: to chase, to chase out chasser

château château *m*

cheap bon marché, à bon marché; cheaper (à) meilleur marché

check chèque *m*

cheek joue *f*

chemical *adj* chimique; chemical engineer ingénieur-chimiste *m*

chemistry chimie *f*

child enfant *m or f*

choose choisir

Christmas Noël *m;* Christmas Day le jour de Noël; Christmas Eve Midnight party le réveillon

church église *f*

cigarette cigarette *f*

cinema cinéma *m*

city ville *f*

class classe *f*

classify classer

clock horloge *f*, pendule *f*

close fermer; it closes il ferme

coat (ladies') manteau *m*

coffee café *m*

coin pièce *f*, pièce de monnaie *f*

cold *(illness)* rhume *m; (temperature)* froid; it is cold il fait froid; I am cold j'ai froid

collect: to collect ramasser; collectionner

collection collection *f;* stamp collection collection de timbres

college collège *m*

collide entrer en collision (avec)

colony colonie *f*

color couleur *f;* what color? de quelle couleur?

come venir, arriver; he came il est venu; did he come? est-il venu?; to come back revenir, rentrer; to come in entrer; to come for, come to get venir chercher; to come along venir avec, accompagner; to have (someone) come faire venir (quelqu'un)

comfortable confortable

compartment compartiment *m*

complain se plaindre de

complete complet *m*, complète *f*

compose composer

conditional conditionnel *m*

confidence confiance *f*

confound it! zut!

confuse confondre

connection correspondance *f*
consent: to consent consentir à
consul consul *m*
continue continuer à
contrary contraire *m;* on the contrary au contraire
conversation conversation *f*
cool frais *m,* fraîche *f*
corn maïs *m*
corner coin *m*
cost: to cost coûter
could (pouvoir): I could je pouvais, j'ai pu, je pourrais; I could have j'aurais pu
count: to count compter
country campagne *f;* pays *m;* in the country à la campagne; country house maison de campagne
course cours *m;* main course plat de viande *m;* of course naturellement, mais oui, bien entendu; in the course of au cours de
cousin cousin *m,* cousine *f*
cover: to cover couvrir
cow vache *f*
crazy: to be crazy about adorer
cream crème *f*
creek rivière *f*
cross: to cross traverser
crowded bondé
crusade croisade *f*
cry: to cry pleurer
customer client *m,* cliente *f*

D

daisy marguerite *f*
damp humide
dance bal *m*
danger danger *m*
dangerous dangereux *m,* dangereuse *f*
dare: to dare oser
dark sombre; it is dark il fait nuit
darkness obscurité *f*
date date *f,* rendez-vous *m;* to date from dater de
day jour *m* journée *f;* per day, a day par

jour; all day toute la journée; every day tous les jours; that day ce jour-là; the next day le lendemain; day after tomorrow après-demain
daylight jour *m;* it is daylight il fait jour
dead mort
deal: a great deal, a good deal beaucoup; a great deal of beaucoup de; a good rain would do a great deal for my vegetables une bonne pluie ferait du bien à mes légumes; to deal in faire le commerce de
dealer marchand *m,* marchande *f;* second-hand-book dealer bouquiniste *m*
December décembre *m*
decide décider, vouloir; to decide upon fixer
dedicate dédier
delay retard *m*
delicious délicieux, délicieuse
delighted enchanté
dentist dentiste *m*
departure départ *m*
descend: to descend descendre
desk bureau *m*
dessert dessert *m*
destroy détruire
dictation dictée *f*
die: to die mourir; he died il est mort
difference différence *f;* it doesn't make any difference cela ne fait rien
different différent
difficult difficile
dine dîner; dining room salle à manger
diner wagon-restaurant *m*
dinner dîner *m;* to have dinner dîner
directly directement
disappointed déçu
discuss discuter
display étalage *m*
distance distance *f*
do faire; do you...? est-ce que...?; don't you? doesn't it? n'est-ce pas?; I did j'ai fait; I shall do je ferai; I should do je ferais; yes, you do mais si; how do you do? comment allez-vous?; to do again refaire; all you have to do... vous

n'avez qu'à; **don't do anything of the sort** gardez-vous en bien

doctor docteur *m*, médecin *m*

dollar dollar *m*

door porte *f*

doubt doute *m;* **no doubt, doubtless** sans doute

down en bas; **to go down** descendre; **downtown** en ville

dozen douzaine *f;* **five francs a dozen** cinq francs la douzaine

draw up dresser (une liste)

drawer tiroir *m*

dress robe *f;* **to dress** habiller; **to get dressed** s'habiller; **to be dressed** être habillé

dresser commode *f*

drink: to drink boire

drive: to drive conduire; **to drive a car** conduire

driver chauffeur *m*

drop: to drop laisser tomber

drugstore pharmacie *f*

E

each *adj* chaque; *pron* chacun, chacune; **each one** chacun, chacune; **ten francs each** dix francs (la) pièce

eager: to be eager to avoir *hâte de

early de bonne heure

easily facilement

East est *m*

easy facile

eat manger

economics économie politique *f*

edge bord *m*

egg œuf *m*

Egyptian égyptien *m*, égyptienne *f*

eight *huit

eighteen dix-huit

eighth *huitième

eighty quatre-vingts

either: either...or soit...soit; **not... either** ne...non plus; **nor I either** moi non plus

elderly d'un certain âge

elevator ascenseur *m*

eleven onze

eleventh onzième

else: something else autre chose; **nothing else** rien d'autre

elsewhere ailleurs

emblem emblème *m*

empire empire *m*

employee employé *m*

end fin *f*, bout *m;* **at the end of the street** au bout de la rue; **to end** finir, terminer, achever

endurable supportable

engineer ingénieur *m;* **chemical engineer** ingénieur-chimiste *m*

England Angleterre *f*

English anglais *m*, anglaise *f*

enjoy: to enjoy aimer

enormous énorme, vaste

entire entier *m*, entière *f*

entirely tout à fait

epidemic épidémie *f*

equivalent équivalent

errand course *f;* **to do errands** faire des courses

Europe Europe *f*

European européen *m*, européenne *f*

even pair *(of numbers)*

even même

evening soir *m*, soirée *f;* **in the evening** le soir; **every evening** tous les soirs; **good evening** bonsoir

ever jamais

every chaque, tout; **every day** tous les jours; **every six months** tous les six mois

everyone chacun, tout le monde

everything tout

everywhere partout

exact exact

examination examen *m*

examine examiner

example exemple *m;* **for example** par exemple

excellent excellent

except sauf, excepté

exercise exercice *m*

exist exister
exit sortie *f*
expect attendre, s'attendre à
expensive cher *m*, chère *f*
explain expliquer
explanation explication *f*
express express *m*
extinguish éteindre
eye œil *m sg*, yeux *pl*

F

factory usine *f*
fall automne *m;* **in the fall** en automne;
  to fall tomber; **to fall asleep** s'endormir
family famille *f*
famous célèbre
far loin; **as far as** jusqu'à; **that far** jusque-là; **far from** loin de
farm ferme *f*
fast vite; **how fast?** à quelle vitesse?
fate sort *m*
father père *m*
fault faute *f*
favorite favori *m*, favorite *f*
fear peur *f;* **for fear that** de peur que; **to
  fear** craindre, avoir peur de (que)
February février *m*
feel: **to feel** sentir, se sentir; **to feel like**
  avoir envie de
fertile fertile
fever fièvre *f*
few peu de, quelques; **a few** *pron* quelques-uns, quelques-unes
fiancé, fiancée fiancé *m*, fiancée *f*
field champ *m*
fifteen quinze
fifteenth quinzième
fifth cinquième
fifty cinquante; **about fifty** une cinquantaine
film film *m*
finally finalement; finir par; **he finally
  came** il a fini par venir
find: **to find** trouver, retrouver; **to find
  out** apprendre

fine beau; **it is fine weather** il fait beau
finish: **to finish** finir, terminer
fire feu *m*
first *adj* premier *m*, première *f; adv*
  d'abord
fish poisson *m;* **a fish story** une histoire
  de pêcheurs
fisherman pêcheur *m*
fishing pêche *f;* **to go fishing** aller à la
  pêche
five cinq
flatterer flatteur *m*
floor étage *m;* **the second floor** le premier
  (étage); **the third floor** le second (étage)
flower fleur *f*
fly: **to fly** voler; **how time flies!** comme
  le temps passe!
follow suivre
following suivant
fond: **to be fond of** aimer
food *(cooking)* cuisine *f*
foot pied *m*
for pour; depuis; pendant; **I have been
  waiting for a quarter of an hour** j'attends depuis un quart d'heure
foreign étranger *m*, étrangère *f*
forget oublier de
form forme *f*
former ancien *m*, ancienne *f*
formerly autrefois
forty quarante
found fonder
fountain fontaine *f*
four quatre
fourteen quatorze
fourth quatrième
franc franc *m*
free libre
French français *m*, française *f*
Friday vendredi *m*
friend ami *m*, amie *f*
friendly aimable
frightful effrayant
from de, depuis, d'après; **from the** du, de
  la, de l', des
front: **in front of** devant
fruit fruit *m*

full plein, complet

fun: to make fun of se moquer de

funny drôle (de)

furnished meublé

furniture meubles *m pl;* **a piece of furniture** un meuble

further plus loin; **further on** plus loin

future futur *m*

G

gallery galerie *f;* **picture gallery** galerie de peinture

garage garage *m*

garden jardin *m*

garret mansarde *f*

gate porte *f*

gentleman monsieur *m*

get prendre, avoir, obtenir, recevoir, se procurer; **to get in, to get into** entrer, monter; **to get out** sortir; **to go to get** aller chercher; **to come to get** venir chercher; **to get to** arriver à; **to get up** se lever; **to get home** rentrer; **to get on** monter; **to get off** descendre; **to get used to** s'habituer à; **to get to the top** arriver en haut

girl jeune fille *f;* **little girl** petite fille; **girl friend** amie

give donner; **to give a ticket** faire un procès-verbal

glad content, heureux; **I'll be glad to** volontiers

gladly volontiers

glance: to glance at jeter un coup d'œil sur

glass verre *m;* **glasses** lunettes *f pl*

glove gant *m*

go aller; **I go, I am going** je vais; **he goes, he is going** il va; **you go, you are going** vous allez; **I shall go** j'irai; **I should go** j'irais; **it is going to** il va; **to go in** entrer; **to go out** sortir; **to go up** monter; **to go down** descendre; **to go to bed** se coucher; **to go along** venir avec, ac-compagner; **to go in for** aimer; **to go away** partir, s'en aller; **to go with** accompagner; **to go through** visiter

good bon; **good-looking** beau, joli; **it's no good** cela ne vaut rien; **good** bien *m*

good-bye au revoir

goose oie *f*

Gothic gothique

graceful élégant, gracieux

grandmother grand-mère *f*

grapes raisin *m sg*

gray gris

greatly très, fort

Greek grec *m,* grecque *f*

green vert; **salad greens** salade *f*

grocer épicier *m*

grocery épicerie *f;* **grocery store** épicerie *f*

grow pousser

guard gardien *m*

guide guide *m*

H

habit habitude *f*

had eu *p part of* avoir

hair cheveu *m;* **she has blond hair** elle a les cheveux blonds

half demi *m,* demie *f;* **half past eleven** onze heures et demie; **a half hour** une demi-heure

hall galerie *f*

ham jambon *m*

hand main *f;* **secondhand book** livre d'occasion

handkerchief mouchoir *m*

happen arriver, se passer, avoir lieu

happy heureux *m,* heureuse *f;* content

hard dur, difficile

hardly à peine, ne...guère

harmony harmonie *f*

harvest moisson *f*

hat chapeau *m*

have avoir; **I have** j'ai; **I haven't** je n'ai pas; **have you?** avez-vous?; **to have to** devoir, il faut..., être obligé de, avoir besoin de; **I can have it sent to you** je peux vous le faire envoyer; **to have something to eat or drink** prendre quelque chose; **I have to** je dois; **I had to** j'ai dû; **all you have to do** vous n'avez qu'à

hay foin *m*

he il, lui, c'

head tête *f*

headache mal de tête *m;* **to have a headache** avoir mal à la tête; **a sure enough headache** un bon mal de tête

hear entendre; **to hear of** entendre parler de; **to hear that** entendre dire que

heart cœur *m;* **in the very heart of Paris** au cœur même de Paris

heat chaleur *f*

hello bonjour

help: to help aider; **to help oneself** se servir

hen poule *f*

her *pers pron* la, lui, elle; *poss adj* son, sa, ses

here ici; **here is, here are** voici; **here it is** le (la) voici; **here they are** les voici; **here!** tenez!

hers le sien, la sienne, les siens, les siennes

him le, lui; **to him, for him** lui

his *poss adj* son, sa, ses; *poss pron* le sien, la sienne, les siens, les siennes

historical historique

history histoire *f;* **French history** l'histoire de France

hold: to hold tenir

holiday fête *f;* **Christmas holidays** vacances de Noël

home maison *f;* **he is at home** il est chez lui; **to get home, to go home** rentrer

hope: to hope espérer; **I hope so** je l'espère

hors d'œuvres *hors-d'œuvre *m*

horse cheval *m sg,* chevaux *pl*

hospital hôpital *m*

hot chaud; **it is hot** il fait chaud

hotel hôtel *m*

hour heure *f;* **a half hour** une demi-heure

house maison *f;* **at our house** chez nous; **at their house** chez eux

how comment; **how much, how many** combien; **how much is it?** combien est-ce?; **how long** combien de temps

however pourtant, cependant

humble humble

humid humide

hundred cent; **about a hundred** une centaine

hungry: to be hungry avoir faim; **I am hungry** j'ai faim

hurry: to hurry se dépêcher; **to be in a hurry** être pressé

hurt: to hurt blesser, avoir mal à, faire mal à; **my legs are beginning to hurt** je commence à avoir mal aux jambes; **these shoes hurt my feet** ces chaussures me font mal aux pieds

husband mari *m*

I

I je, moi

idea idée *f*

identification identité *f*

if si, s'

imagine imaginer

immediately tout de suite

important important

impressed impressionné

impression impression *f*

in dans, en, à, de; **in Paris** à Paris; **in France** en France; **in Canada** au Canada; **in South America** dans l'Amérique du Sud; **in 1715** en 1715; **in the XVth century** au quinzième siècle; **in the month of October** au mois d'octobre; **in the spring** au printemps; **in the fall** en automne; **in winter** en hiver; **in the morning** le matin; **at 7:00 in the morning** à sept heures du matin; **in a half hour** dans une demi-heure; **in a week** dans huit jours; **in time** à temps; **in the country** à la campagne; **in the course of** au cours de

incident incident *m*

indeed en effet, bien

independence indépendance *f;* **Independence Day** le jour de la Déclaration de l'Indépendance

indicate indiquer

indirect indirect

inform renseigner

information renseignements *m pl*

injustice injustice *f*

inn hôtel *m,* auberge *f;* **innkeeper** hôtelier *m*

inside intérieur *m;* à l'intérieur; **to go inside** entrer

intelligent intelligent

intend to avoir l'intention de

interest: to interest intéresser

interesting intéressant

interior intérieur

interrogative interrogatif *m,* interrogative *f*

introduce présenter

invention invention *f*

invitation invitation *f*

invite inviter

ironical ironique

is est; **it is** c'est, il est, elle est; **is it?** est-ce? est-ce que c'est?; **there is** il y a; **is there?** y a-t-il?; **it is four o'clock** il est quatre heures; **it is cold** il fait froid

island île *f*

it *subj* il, elle, ce; **it is** c'est, il est, elle est; *dir obj* le, l', la; *ind obj* y; **of it** en

Italian italien *m,* italienne *f*

Italy Italie *f*

its son, sa, ses

J

January janvier *m*

jeweler horloger *m,* bijoutier *m;* **at the jeweler's** chez l'horloger

July juillet *m*

June juin *m*

just seulement, tout simplement; **to have just** venir de; **I have just finished** je viens de finir

K

keep: **to keep** garder, tenir, retenir; **to keep on** continuer de

keeper garde *m,* gardien *m;* **hotelkeeper** hôtelier *m*

kilo kilo *m;* **five francs a kilo** cinq francs le kilo

kilometer kilomètre *m*

kind espèce *f,* sorte *f*

king roi *m*

knight chevalier *m*

know savoir, connaître; **I know** je sais, je connais; **do you know?** savez-vous? connaissez-vous?; **I shall know** je saurai; **I should know** je saurais; **to know how** savoir *(see Conv 9)*

known connu, célèbre

L

laboratory laboratoire *m*

lack: **to lack** manquer

lady dame *f*

lake lac *m*

land terre *f,* pays *m*

landscape paysage *m*

language langue *f*

large grand, gros, vaste; **as large as that** gros comme ça

last dernier *m,* dernière *f;* **last week** la semaine dernière; **last night** hier soir; **last Saturday** samedi dernier; **to last** durer

Latin latin

lead: **to lead** mener, conduire

leaf feuille *f*

learn apprendre

least: **the least** le moins, la moins, les moins

leave: **to leave** partir, s'en aller; quitter; laisser; **when are you leaving?** quand partez-vous?; **I am leaving tomorrow** je m'en vais demain; **we left Melun two hours ago** il y a deux heures que nous avons quitté Melun; **as you leave the village** à la sortie du village; **it is better to leave those you are not sure of** il vaut mieux laisser ceux dont vous n'êtes pas sûr

lecture conférence *f*

left gauche; **to the left** à gauche

left: I have not one of them left il ne m'en reste aucun

leg jambe *f*

lend prêter

lens verre *m*

less moins; **less...than** moins...que; (*numbers*) moins de; **more or less** plus ou moins; **she is less tall than her brother** elle est moins grande que son frère; **there were less than a hundred pupils** il y avait moins de cent élèves

lesson leçon *f*

let permettre, laisser

letter lettre *f*

lettuce laitue *f*, salade *f*

lie: to lie down se coucher

lieutenant lieutenant *m;* **police lieutenant** commissaire de police *m*

life vie *f*

like comme; **to like** aimer, aimer bien; **I like** j'aime; **do you like?** aimez-vous?; **do you like it?** est-ce qu'il vous plaît?; **how do you like it?** comment le (la) trouvez-vous?; **would you like to...?** voulez-vous bien...?; **I would like** je voudrais; **do you like my hat?** est-ce que mon chapeau vous plaît?

line ligne *f*

lip lèvre *f*

list liste *f*

literature littérature *f*

little *adj* petit; *adv* peu; **a little** un peu

live vivre; **to live at** demeurer, habiter

London Londres

long *adj* long *m*, longue *f; adv* longtemps; **no longer** ne...plus; **all day long** toute la journée; **how long?** com-

bien de temps?; **for a long time** depuis longtemps, pendant longtemps

look regard *m*, coup d'œil *m;* **to take a look at** jeter un coup d'œil sur; **to look** regarder; avoir l'air; **it looks very well on you** il vous va très bien; **to look for** chercher; **good-looking** beau, joli; **to look like** ressembler à; **to look over** visiter; **to look at** regarder

lost perdu, égaré

lot: a lot of, lots of beaucoup de

Louis XIV Louis Quatorze

low bas *m*, basse *f*

luck chance *f;* **to be lucky** avoir de la chance; **tough luck!** vous n'avez pas de chance!; **what luck!** quelle chance! quelle veine!

lunch déjeuner *m;* **to have lunch** déjeuner; **lunchroom** buffet *m;* **to lunch** déjeuner

M

Madam madame *f*

magnificence splendeur *f*

maid bonne *f;* **nursemaid** bonne *f*

mail: to mail mettre (une lettre) à la poste

main principal; **main course** plat de viande *m*

majestic majestueux *m*, majestueuse *f*

make faire; (*followed by adj*) rendre: **does that make you sad?** est-ce que cela vous rend triste?

man homme *m*

many beaucoup; **so many** tant; **too many** trop; **how many?** combien?

March mars *m*

marriage mariage *m*

marry se marier; **to get married** se marier

marvelously à merveille

mass messe *f;* **midnight mass** la messe de minuit

material étoffe *f*

mathematics mathématiques *f pl*

matter: what is the matter? qu'est-ce qu'il

y a?; **what is the matter with you?**
qu'est-ce que vous avez?; **nothing is the**
matter with me je n'ai rien

mature: to mature mûrir

May mai *m*

may (pouvoir): **I may** je peux, je pourrai; **may I?** est-ce que je peux?

mayor maire *m*

me me, moi

meal repas *m*

mean: to mean vouloir dire

meat viande *f*

medicine médicament *m*

meet: to meet rencontrer, rejoindre,
faire la connaissance de; **I met him** j'ai
fait sa connaissance; **to come to meet**
venir attendre

mention: to mention parler de

menu carte *f*

merchant marchand *m*, marchande *f*

meter mètre *m;* **six francs a meter** six
francs le mètre

Mexico Mexique *m*

middle milieu *m;* **in the middle of** au
milieu de

midnight minuit *m*

midst milieu *m;* **in the midst of** au milieu de

might (pouvoir): **I might** je pourrais

milk lait *m*

milliner modiste *f*

million million *m*

millionaire millionnaire *m*

mind: if you don't mind si vous voulez

mine le mien, la mienne, les miens, les
miennes; **it is mine** c'est à moi; **a friend**
of mine un de mes amis

ministry ministère *m*

minute minute *f*

mirror glace *f*

Miss mademoiselle *f*

miss: to miss manquer; **to miss the road**
se tromper de route

mistaken: to be mistaken se tromper

moment moment *m;* **a moment ago** tout
à l'heure; **at the moment when** au moment où; **at the moment of** au moment
de

Mona Lisa la Joconde

Monday lundi *m*

money argent *m*

month mois *m;* **per month, a month** par
mois

monument monument *m*

monumental monumental

moon lune *f*

more plus, davantage; **not...any more** ne
... plus; **more ... than** plus ... que;
(numbers) plus de; **no more** ne...plus
de; **more or less** plus ou moins; **more**
and more de plus en plus; **some more**
encore, d'autres; **he is more intelligent**
than his brother; il est plus intelligent
que son frère; **there were hardly more**
than a hundred pupils il n'y avait
guère plus de cent élèves; **you can take**
some more pictures vous pourrez prendre d'autres photos

morning matin *m;* **good morning** bonjour; **every morning** tous les matins;
in the morning le matin

most la plupart; **most of them** la plupart
d'entre eux

mother mère *f*

mouth bouche *f*

movie film *m,* cinéma *m;* **movie house**
cinéma *m*

Mr. Monsieur *m;* **Mr. Duval** M. Duval

much beaucoup; **very much** beaucoup; **so**
much tant; **too much** trop; **how much?**
combien?; **not much** pas beaucoup, pas
grand-chose

museum musée *m*

mushroom champignon *m*

music musique *f*

musketeer mousquetaire *m*

must (devoir, falloir): **must I?** faut-il?; **I**
must je dois, il faut que je...; **I must**
have j'ai dû; **there must be** il doit y
avoir

my mon, ma, mes

N

name nom *m; what is your name?* comment vous appelez-vous?; *my name is* je m'appelle; **to name** nommer; **to be named** s'appeler
named nommé
narrow étroit
national national
nationality nationalité *f*
near près de; **near here, nearby** près d'ici
nearly presque
necessary nécessaire; *it is necessary* il faut que
need: to need avoir besoin de
negative négatif *m,* négative *f*
negatively négativement
neighbor voisin *m,* voisine *f*
neighboring voisin *m,* voisine *f*
neither ni l'un ni l'autre; **neither...nor** ne...ni...ni...
never jamais, ne...jamais
new nouveau *m,* nouvelle *f;* neuf *m,* neuve *f;* **New Orleans** La Nouvelle-Orléans
news nouvelles *f pl*
newspaper journal *m,* journaux *pl*
next prochain; **next Saturday** samedi prochain; **next week** la semaine prochaine; **the next day** le lendemain
next *adv* ensuite, puis
nice gentil *m* gentille *f;* aimable; *it is nice of you* c'est gentil de votre part
night nuit *f;* **last night** hier soir; **tonight** ce soir; **at night** la nuit
nightfall nuit *f*
nine neuf
nineteen dix-neuf
nineteenth dix-neuvième
ninety quatre-vingt-dix
no non, ne...pas de; **no one** personne, ne...personne
nobility noblesse *f*
nobody personne, ne...personne
noise bruit *m*
none aucun *m,* aucune *f;* ne...aucun(e)

noon midi *m;* **at noon** à midi
nor ni; **neither...nor** ne...ni...ni...
Normandy Normandie *f*
North nord *m;* **North Africa** l'Afrique du Nord
not ne...pas; **not at all** pas du tout; **not much** pas beaucoup, pas grand-chose; **not one** aucun(e), ne...aucun(e)
note: to note noter
nothing rien, ne...rien; **nothing at all** rien du tout; **nothing interesting** rien d'intéressant; **nothing else** rien d'autre
noun nom *m*
novel roman *m*
November novembre *m*
now maintenant; actuellement
nowhere nulle part
number nombre *m;* **room No. 3** la chambre numéro trois
nurse, nursemaid bonne *f*

O

oats avoine *f*
obelisk obélisque *m*
obey obéir à
object objet *m*
observatory observatoire *m*
occasionally quelquefois
occupy occuper
o'clock heure *f;* **it is eleven o'clock** il est onze heures
October octobre *m*
oculist oculiste *m*
odd impair *(of numbers)*
of de; **of the** du, de la, de l', des; **of it, of them** en
offer; to offer offrir
office bureau *m*
often souvent
O.K. entendu
old vieux, vieil *m;* vieille *f;* vieux *m pl;* vieilles *f pl;* ancien, ancienne; **how old are you?** quel âge avez-vous? **old man** mon vieux
olive olive *f*

on sur, à, en, dans; **on the bus** dans l'autobus; **on the train** dans le train; **on time** à l'heure; **on Wednesday** mercredi; **on Christmas Day** le jour de Noël; **on arriving** en arrivant

once une fois, autrefois; **once a week** une fois par semaine

one un, une; *pers pron* on, l'on; *dem pron* **the one, the ones** celui, celle, ceux, celles; **this one** celui-ci, celle-ci; **that one** celui-là, celle-là; **not one** aucun(e), ne...aucun(e); **no one** personne, ne...personne; **I have one** j'en ai un(e); **here are some gray ones** en voici des gris

only *adj* seul; *adv* seulement, ne...que

open ouvert *adj and p part of* ouvrir; **to open** ouvrir; **it opens** il ouvre

opera opéra *m*

opposite opposé *m; adv* en face (de)

or ou; **either...or** soit...soit

orange orange *f*

order: **in order to** pour, afin de; **to order** commander

ordinarily d'habitude

organ orgues *f pl*

other autre; **some...others** les uns... d'autres; **the other one** l'autre

ought (devoir): **you ought to come** vous devriez venir; **you ought to have come** vous auriez dû venir

our notre *sg*, nos *pl*

ours le nôtre, la nôtre *sg*, les nôtres *pl*

ourselves nous-mêmes; **by ourselves** seuls

out: **to go out** sortir; **he is out** il est sorti

outside dehors, en dehors

over sur; **over there** là-bas

owe devoir

own propre; **they were victims of their own injustice** ils furent victimes de leurs propres injustices

ox bœuf *m*

P

package paquet *m*

pain mal *m*

paint: **to paint** peindre

painter peintre *m*

painting peinture *f*

pair paire *f*

pal mon vieux

palace palais *m*

panorama panorama *m*

pansy pensée *f*

paper papier *m;* **newspaper** journal *m;* **writing paper** papier à lettres

pardon: **to pardon** pardonner; **pardon me** pardon

parent parent *m*

Parisian parisien, parisienne

park parc *m;* **public park** jardin public

part partie *f;* **part of town** quartier *m;* **to be a part of** faire partie de

particular particulier *m*, particulière *f;* **in particular** notamment

partly en partie

party soirée *f*

passer-by passant *m*

pasteboard (box) carton *m*

patient malade *m or f;* client (d'un médecin) *m*

pay: **to pay** payer; **to pay for** payer

pea pois *m*

pear poire *f*

peony pivoine *f*

people gens *pl*, monde *m;* **too many people** trop de monde

per: **30 kilometers per hour** 30 kilomètres à l'heure; **per month** par mois; **per dozen** la douzaine

perfectly parfaitement, tout à fait

performance représentation *f*

perhaps peut-être

period période *f;* époque *f*

perish mourir; **perish the thought!** ne m'en parlez pas!

permission permission *f*

person personne *f*

personal personnel *m*, personnelle *f*

pharmacist pharmacien *m*

photograph photographie *f*

pick: **to pick** cueillir, ramasser

picnic pique-nique *m*

picture photographie *f*, photo *f*, tableau *m;* **to take a picture** prendre une photo

picturesque pittoresque

piece pièce *f*, morceau *m;* **ten francs apiece** dix francs (la) pièce

pig porc *m*

pink rose

pity: to pity plaindre

place endroit *m*, place *f;* **in your place** à votre place; **to take place** avoir lieu

plan: to plan avoir l'intention de; **to plan a garden** dessiner un jardin

plane avion *m*

plant: to plant planter

platform quai *m*

play pièce *f;* **to play** jouer; **to play tennis** jouer au tennis; **to play cards** jouer aux cartes; **to play the violin** jouer du violon

pleasant agréable; **the weather is pleasant** il fait bon

please s'il vous plaît; **to please** plaire à

plural pluriel *m*

pocket poche *f;* **pocketbook** portefeuille *m*

poem poème *m*, poésie *f*

point point *m;* **point of view** point de vue *m*

poison: to poison empoisonner

police police *f;* **police station** commissariat de police *m;* **police lieutenant** commissaire de police *m*

policeman agent de police *m*

pool bassin *m;* **ornamental pool** pièce d'eau *f*

poor pauvre

pork porc *m;* **pork butcher** charcutier *m;* **pork butcher's** charcuterie *f*

port port *m*

possible possible

post card carte-postale *f*

postman facteur *m*

post office bureau de poste *m*, poste *f*

potato pomme de terre *f;* **French fried potatoes** pommes de terre frites

pound livre *f;* **2 francs a pound** 2 francs la livre

pour verser; **it is pouring** il pleut à verse

practically à peu près

practice habitude *f*

preceding précédent

prefer préférer, aimer mieux

present *adj* présent, actuel; **at present** actuellement

president président *m*

pretty *adj* joli; *adv* assez; **pretty well** assez, assez bien

price prix *m*

priest curé *m*

print estampe *f*, gravure *f*

probably sans doute; **there is probably a train** il doit y avoir un train

profession profession *f*

professor professeur *m*

progress progrès *m*

promise promettre

pronoun pronom *m*

properly bien, comme il faut

provision provision *f*

public public *m*, publique *f*

pull: to pull tirer; **to pull it in to the bank (shore) (edge)** l'amener au bord

pupil élève *m or f*

purchase achat *m*

purse bourse *f;* **change purse** porte-monnaie *m*

put mettre; **to put out** (to bother) déranger

Q

quality qualité *f*

quarter quart *m*, quartier *m;* **a quarter past eleven** onze heures et quart; **a quarter of two** deux heures moins le quart; **the Latin Quarter** le Quartier Latin

queen reine *f*

question question *f;* **it is a question of** il s'agit de; **to be a question of** s'agir de

quiet tranquille

quite tout à fait

R

radiate rayonner

railroad chemin de fer *m;* railroad station gare *f*

rain pluie *f;* to rain pleuvoir; it is raining il pleut; it was raining il pleuvait; it had rained il avait plu

raincoat imperméable *m*

rare rare; rarer and rarer de plus en plus rare

rather plutôt, assez, un peu

ravage: to ravage ravager

reach: to reach atteindre

read: to read lire; I have read j'ai lu

ready prêt

realize se rendre compte de, (que)

really vraiment, je vous assure; really! tiens!

reason raison *f;* there is reason for it il y a de quoi

rebuild reconstruire

receive recevoir; I received j'ai reçu

recognize reconnaître

red rouge

refusal refus *m*

refuse refuser

region région *f*

regret: to regret regretter de

reign règne *m*

relative parent *m,* parente *f*

relatively relativement

remedy remède *m*

remember se rappeler, se souvenir de

rent loyer *m;* to rent louer; for rent à louer

repair réparation *f;* repair job réparation; to repair réparer; to have repaired faire réparer

repeat répéter

replace remplacer

reply: to reply répondre à

represent représenter

request demande *f*

residence résidence *f*

rest reste *m,* repos *m;* to rest se reposer

restaurant restaurant *m*

return: to return here revenir (ici); to return (some place else) retourner; to return home rentrer (à la maison)

review révision *f,* revue *f*

rich riche

ride promenade (à bicyclette, en auto) *f;* to ride aller en auto, à bicyclette

right droit (*opposite of* left), bon (*opposite of* wrong), on, to the right à droite; the right road la bonne route; to be right avoir raison; that's right justement; all right bon, entendu; right to jusqu'à; right away tout de suite

rise: to rise se lever

risk risque *m;* to run the risk risquer de

road route *f;* the right road la bonne route; the wrong road la mauvaise route; country road chemin *m*

romanesque roman, romane

roof toit *m*

room chambre *f,* salle *f;* room and board pension *f;* bathroom salle de bain; lunchroom buffet *m;* dining room salle à manger; living room salon *m;* (*space*) place *f;* there is room il y a de la place

rose rose *f*

rosebush rosier *m*

rosy rose

royal royal

run: to run courir; my watch doesn't run ma montre ne marche pas; to run an inn tenir une auberge

Russia Russie *f*

Russian russe

S

sacrifice sacrifice *m*

sad triste

sail voile *f;* sailboat bateau à voile *m*

saint saint; la Sainte-Chapelle XIIIth century Gothic church in Paris

salad salade *f;* salad greens salade *f*

salesgirl vendeuse *f*

salesman vendeur *m*

same même; the same le même, la même, les mêmes; that's all the same to me cela m'est égal; **all the same** tout de même

sandwich sandwich *m,* sandwichs *pl*

Santa Claus le Père Noël

Saturday samedi *m;* **on Saturdays** le samedi

say dire; **they say** on dit; **how does one say?** comment dit-on?; **that is to say** c'est-à-dire; **to say to oneself** se dire

scarcely à peine, ne...guère

scarf écharpe *f*

schedule emploi du temps *m*

school école *f;* **secondary school** lycée *m,* collège *m;* **at school** à l'école

science science *f*

sea mer *f;* **seashore** le bord de la mer

season saison *f*

seat place *f*

second second, deuxième; **the second floor** le premier (étage); **second class** seconde *f;* deuxième (classe) *f*

secondary secondaire; **secondary school** lycée *m,* collège *m*

section section *f*

see: to see voir; **I see** je vois; **let's see** voyons; **you see** vous voyez; **I saw** j'ai vu; **I'll see** je verrai; **see you Sunday** à dimanche

seem: to seem to avoir l'air de

seen vu *p part of* voir

selection choix *m*

sell vendre; **where do they sell newspapers?** où vend-on des journaux?

send envoyer; **to send for** envoyer chercher, faire venir; **to send away, send back** renvoyer

sentence phrase *f*

September septembre *m*

series série *f*

serious sérieux *m,* sérieuse *f;* grave

serve servir à

service service *m;* **I am at your service** je suis à votre disposition

set: to set mettre, poser; **to set out** partir

seven sept

seventeen dix-sept

seventeenth dix-septième

seventh septième

seventy soixante-dix

several plusieurs; **several times** plusieurs fois

shade ombre *f;* **in the shade** à l'ombre

she elle, ce

sheep mouton *m*

shine: the sun is shining il fait du soleil

shoe chaussure *f,* soulier *m*

shoo: to shoo out chasser

shop magasin *m;* **tobacco shop** bureau de tabac *m;* **shop window** devanture *f;* **to shop** faire des courses

shopkeeper marchand *m,* marchande *f*

shore bord *m,* rive *f;* **seashore** le bord de la mer

short court

should (devoir): **you should** vous devriez; **you should have** vous auriez dû

shoulder épaule *f*

show: to show montrer

sick malade

side côté *m,* bord *m;* **on the other side of** de l'autre côté de; **on the side of** au bord de; **the under side** le dessous

sidewalk trottoir *m;* **sidewalk café** la terrasse d'un café

significance signification *f;* **do you know the significance of...?** connaissez-vous?

silent silencieux *m,* silencieuse *f*

silk soie *f*

simple simple

since depuis, puisque

single seul; **not a single** ne...aucun

Sir Monsieur

sister sœur *f*

sit s'asseoir, être assis; **sit down** asseyez-vous; **to sit down at the table** se mettre à table

six six

sixteen seize

sixth sixième

sixty soixante

size étendue *f,* pointure *f*

skate: to skate patiner

ski: to ski faire du ski

skillful habile

skin peau *f;* **I am wet to the skin (to the bones)** je suis mouillé(e) jusqu'aux os

sky ciel *m*

skyscraper gratte-ciel *m*

sleep: to sleep dormir; **to fall asleep** s'endormir

slightest: the slightest le moindre, la moindre, les moindres

slippery glissant

small petit

snow neige *f;* **to snow** neiger

so aussi, si, ainsi; **so that** pour que; **so as to** pour

soil sol *m*

some du, de la, de l', des; *adj* quelque *sg*, quelques *pl; pron* en; quelques-uns, quelques-unes; les uns, les unes; **some of them** quelques-uns; **some...the others** les uns...les autres; **some... others** les uns...d'autres; **some more** encore, d'autres

someone quelqu'un

something quelque chose; **something good** quelque chose de bon; **something else** autre chose

sometimes quelquefois, parfois

somewhere quelque part

soon bientôt, tôt; **sooner** plus tôt; **as soon as possible** le plus tôt possible

sore: to have a sore throat avoir mal à la gorge

sorry fâché; **I am sorry** je regrette, je suis fâché

sort espèce *f*

South sud *m*

souvenir souvenir *m*

space espace *m*

Spain Espagne *f*

Spanish espagnol

speak parler; **do you speak?** parlez-vous?; **I speak** je parle; **he speaks** il parle

speed vitesse *f*

spend passer; dépenser; **he spent three years in England** il a passé trois ans en Angleterre; **he spent his life building castles** il a passé sa vie à construire des palais

splendor splendeur *f*

spring printemps (saison) *m;* ressort (d'une montre) *m;* **in the spring** au printemps

square place *f*

stained-glass window vitrail *m,* vitraux *pl*

stair escalier *m*

staircase escalier *m;* **spiral staircase** escalier en colimaçon

stamp timbre *m;* **postage stamp** timbre-poste *m*

standing debout

star étoile *f*

start: to start commencer, se mettre à; **we started to work at 1:30** nous nous sommes mis à travailler à une heure et demie

station gare *f*

stay: to stay rester

step pas *m;* **steps** escalier *m;* **a step from here** à deux pas d'ici

still toujours, encore

stop arrêt *m;* **to stop** arrêter, s'arrêter

store magasin *m*

story histoire *f*

straight droit; **straight ahead** tout droit

strawberry fraise *f;* **wild strawberry** fraise des bois *f*

street rue *f;* **surface of a street** chaussée *f*

structure bâtiment *m*

student étudiant *m,* étudiante *f*

study: to study étudier

style style *m*

succeed in réussir à

such un tel, une telle, de tels, de telles; **such a watch** une telle montre

suddenly tout à coup

suffer souffrir

sugar sucre *m*

suggest suggérer, proposer

suit complet *m;* **to suit** convenir à; **this room suits me perfectly** cette chambre me convient parfaitement

suitable convenable

summer été *m;* **in summer** en été

sun soleil *m;* **the sun is shining** il fait du soleil

Sunday dimanche *m;* **see you Sunday** à dimanche

supermarket super-marché *m*

suppose supposer; **suppose we take a few of them back home?** si nous en rapportions quelques-uns à la maison?; **I am supposed to** je dois

sure sûr

surface surface *f;* **surface of a street** chaussée *f;* **the upper surface** le dessus

surprise surprise *f*

surprised surpris *p part of* surprendre

surround with entourer de

suspect: to suspect se douter de; **I suspected it** je m'en doutais

swim: to swim nager

Switzerland Suisse *f*

symbolize symboliser

T

table table *f*

take prendre, emporter, mener, conduire; **to take a walk** faire une promenade; **you take** vous prenez; **I took** j'ai pris; **to take place** avoir lieu; **to take along** emporter, emmener; **how long does it take?** combien de temps faut-il?; **to take an examination** passer un examen; **this road will take you to Fontainebleau** ce chemin vous mènera à Fontainebleau

taking prise *f*

talk: to talk parler; **to talk over** parler de

tall grand

taste goût *m*

taxi taxi *m*

tea thé *m*

telegram dépêche *f,* télégramme *m*

telephone: to telephone téléphoner

tell dire; **to tell about** parler de

temperature température *f*

ten dix

tennis tennis *m;* **to play tennis** jouer au tennis

tenth dixième

terrific formidable

terrifically terriblement, horriblement

text texte *m*

thank remercier; **thank you** merci

that (those) *dem adj* ce, cet *m,* cette *f,* ces *pl;* ce...-là, cette...-là, ces...-là; **that** *dem pron* celui *m,* celle *f,* ceux *m pl,* celles *f pl;* cela; **that's it** c'est cela; **that** *rel pron* qui, que, lequel, laquelle, lesquels, lesquelles; **all that** tout ce qui, tout ce que; **that** *conj* que

the le, la, l', les

theater théâtre *m*

their *poss adj* leur *sg,* leurs *pl*

theirs *poss pron* le leur, la leur, les leurs

them les; leur; eux, elles; **of them** en

then alors, ensuite, puis; ainsi

theology théologie *f*

there là, y; **there is, there are** il y a; **is there? are there?** y a-t-il?

these *dem adj* ces, ces...-ci; *dem pron* ceux-ci *m,* celles-ci *f*

they ils, elles; on

thick épais

thing chose *f;* **many things** beaucoup de choses

think penser à, penser de, croire, trouver; **what do you think of Charles?** que pensez-vous de Charles?; **I think so** je crois que oui; **she thought it was very good** elle l'a trouvé très bon; **I thought that** je croyais que; **I rather thought so** je m'en doutais

thinker penseur *m*

third troisième

thirst soif *f;* **to be thirsty** avoir soif

thirteen treize

thirteenth treizième

thirty trente

this *dem adj* ce, cet *m,* cette *f;* ce...-ci, cet...-ci, cette...ci; **this** *dem pron* celui *m,* celle *f;* celui-ci, celle-ci; ceci; **this one** celui-ci, celle-ci

those *dem adj* ces, ces...-là; *dem pron* ceux-là *m,* celles-là *f*

thousand mille

three trois
throat gorge *f*
Thursday jeudi *m*
ticket billet *m;* **ticket window** guichet *m;*
to give a ticket faire un procès-verbal
tie cravate *f*
till jusqu'à; **till Sunday** à dimanche; **till
then** jusque-là
time temps *m,* heure *f,* fois *f,* moment *m;*
what time is it? quelle heure est-il?; **at
what time?** à quelle heure?; **the first
time** la première fois; **several times**
plusieurs fois; **to have time to** avoir le
temps de; **on time** à l'heure; **at that
time** à ce moment-là, à cette époque;
to have a good time s'amuser, s'amuser
bien; **from time to time** de temps en
temps; **in time** à temps; **at the time
when** au moment où; **at the time of**
au moment de; **some time soon** ces
jours-ci; **some time ago** il y a quelque
temps; **harvest time** le moment de la
moisson
tired fatigué
to à, en, pour, chez, jusqu'à; **to the** au,
à la, à l', aux; **it is ten minutes to four**
il est quatre heures moins dix; **to the
right** à droite; **to the top of** en haut de;
to, in the middle of au milieu de; **I
would go to Italy** j'irais en Italie; **to the
United States** aux États-Unis; **to South
America** dans l'Amérique du Sud; **to
Versailles** à Versailles; **a round-trip
ticket to Rheims** un billet aller et retour pour Reims; **to the Brown's** chez
les Brown; **to our house** chez nous; **to
the country** à la campagne; **I am wet
to the skin (bones)** je suis mouillé jusqu'aux os; **they have been very nice to
me** ils ont été très aimables pour moi;
**how long does it take to go to Ver-
sailles?** combien de temps faut-il pour
aller à Versailles?; **I'll be glad to** volontiers; **she is to arrive soon** elle doit
arriver ces jours-ci
tobacco tabac *m;* **tobacco shop** bureau de
tabac *m*

today aujourd'hui; **today is Friday** c'est
aujourd'hui vendredi
together ensemble
tomato tomate *f*
tomb tombe *f,* (*monumental*) tombeau *m*
tomorrow demain; **day after tomorrow**
après-demain
tonight ce soir
too trop, aussi
tooth dent *f;* **to have a toothache** avoir
mal aux dents
top haut *m;* **at the top of** en *haut de;
from the top of du *haut de
towards vers
tower tour *f;* **the Eiffel tower** la tour
Eiffel
town ville *f;* **downtown** en ville
track voie *f*
train train *m;* **on the train** dans le train
travel: to travel voyager
tree arbre *m*
trim: to trim tailler
trip voyage *m;* **round trip** aller et retour;
to have a good trip faire bon voyage;
to take a trip faire un voyage
trouble peine *f;* **it is not worth the
trouble** ce n'est pas la peine
truck camion *m*
true vrai
try: to try essayer (de); **to try on** essayer
Tuesday mardi *m*
turkey dinde *f*
turn: to turn tourner; **to turn around** se
retourner
twelfth douzième
twelve douze; **twelve o'clock (noon)** midi;
twelve o'clock (midnight) minuit
twenty vingt
twenty-one vingt et un
twice deux fois
two deux

U

uncle oncle *m*
under sous, dessous; **under side** dessous *m*
understand comprendre; **do you under-**

stand? comprenez-vous?; **I understand** je comprends

undo défaire

unhappy malheureux *m,* malheureuse *f*

United States États-Unis *m pl;* **in the United States** aux États-Unis

University université *f*

unless à moins que

until jusqu'à, jusqu'à ce que; **until tomorrow** à demain

up en haut; **up there** là-haut; **to go up** monter

upper: upper surface dessus *m*

use emploi *m; what's the use?* à quoi bon?; **there is no use trying** vous avez beau essayer; **to use** employer, se servir de; **to be used for** servir à; **used to** *expressed by imperf ind:* **I used to go** j'allais; **to be used to** avoir l'habitude de; **to get used to** s'habituer à

usual: as usual comme d'habitude

usually d'habitude, d'ordinaire

V

vacation vacances *f pl;* **on vacation** en vacances

vain: in vain avoir beau + *infin:* **you'll try in vain** vous aurez beau essayer

value valeur *f;* **to be valuable** avoir de la valeur

vegetable légume *m*

very très; **in the very heart of Paris** au cœur même de Paris

victim victime *f*

view vue *f;* **point of view** point de vue *m*

village village *m*

violet violette *f*

visit visite *f;* **to visit** visiter *(things)*, aller voir

voice voix *f;* **in a low voice** à voix basse

W

waiter garçon *m*

wake up se réveiller

waken se réveiller

walk promenade *f,* allée *f*

walk: to walk marcher, aller à pied

wall mur *m*

want: to want vouloir, avoir envie de; **I want** je veux; **he wants** il veut; **do you want?** voulez-vous?

warm chaud; **it is warm** il fait chaud; **I am warm** j'ai chaud

warn prévenir; **I warn you** je vous préviens

was: I was j'étais, j'ai été; **I was born in Philadelphia** je suis né à Philadelphie

wash: to wash laver; **to wash one's hands** se laver les mains

watch montre *f;* **wrist watch** montre-bracelet *f;* **to watch out** faire attention à

water eau *f;* **to water** arroser

way moyen *m,* façon *f;* **this way** par ici; **on the way** en route; **it's a way of passing half an hour** c'est une façon de passer une demi-heure; **to lose one's way** s'égarer

wear porter; **to wear out** user

weather temps *m;* **how is the weather?** quel temps fait-il?; **the weather is fine** il fait beau

wedding mariage *m*

Wednesday mercredi *m*

week semaine *f;* **in a week** dans huit jours; **in two weeks** dans quinze jours; **last week** la semaine dernière; **a week from today** d'aujourd'hui en huit; **every week** tous les huit jours

weekend week-end *m*

welcome: you are welcome de rien, il n'y a pas de quoi

well bien, eh bien!, tiens!; **I am well** je vais bien

were: you were vous étiez, vous avez été; **where were you born?** où êtes-vous né?

wet mouillé; **I am wet to the skin (to the bones)** je suis mouillé jusqu'aux os

what? *interrog adj* quel? quelle? quels? quelles?; **what?** *interrog pron* que? qu'est-ce qui? qu'est-ce que? quoi?; **what is?** qu'est-ce que c'est que?; **what**

for? pourquoi?; **what** *rel pron* ce qui,
ce que; **what is...** ce que c'est que...

**whatever: whatever you do will be in
vain** vous aurez beau faire

wheat blé *m*

when quand, lorsque; où

whence d'où

whenever quand, chaque fois que

where où

which? *interrog adj* quel? quelle? quels?
quelles?; **which?** *interrog pron* lequel?
laquelle? lesquels? lesquelles?; **which
one?** lequel? laquelle?; **which ones?** lesquels? lesquelles?; **which** *rel pron* qui,
que; lequel, laquelle, lesquels, lesquelles; **of which** dont; **in which** où

while tandis que, pendant que; **a while
ago, in a while** tout à l'heure

white blanc *m*, blanche *f*

who? *interrog pron* qui? qui est-ce qui?;
who *rel pron* qui; lequel, laquelle, lesquels, lesquelles

whom? *interrog pron* qui? qui est-ce que?;
whom *rel pron* que; lequel, laquelle,
lesquels, lesquelles; **of whom** dont,
duquel; **to whom** à qui

whose? *interrog pron* à qui?; **whose gloves
are these?** à qui sont ces gants?; **at
whose house?** chez qui?; **whose** *rel pron*
dont, de qui

why pourquoi; **why not?** pourquoi pas?

wife femme *f*

wild sauvage; **wild flower** fleur sauvage *f;*
wild strawberry fraise des bois *f*

willing: **I am willing** je veux bien

wind vent *m;* **it is windy** il fait du vent

window fenêtre *f;* **ticket window** guichet
m; **cashier's window** caisse *f;* **shop window** devanture *f;* **stained-glass window**
vitrail *m,* vitraux *pl*

wine vin *m*

winter hiver *m;* **in winter** en hiver

wire dépêche *f,* télégramme *m*

wish: **to wish** souhaiter; **if you wish** si
vous voulez

with avec

without sans

witness témoin *m;* **to witness** être témoin
de

wonder: **to wonder** se demander

wood bois *m*

word mot *m*

work travail *m;* **to work** travailler

world monde *m*

worried préoccupé

worse *adj* pire; *adv* pis; **so much the
worse** tant pis

worth: **to be worth** valoir; **it is not worth
while** ce n'est pas la peine; **worth buying** intéressant

wound: **to wound** blesser

write écrire

wrong: **the wrong road** la mauvaise route;
to be wrong avoir tort; **something is
wrong** il y a (vous avez) quelque chose

Y - Z

year an *m,* année *f;* **every year** tous les
ans

yellow jaune

yes oui, si

yesterday hier

yet encore, déjà; **not yet** pas encore

you vous; tu, te, toi

young jeune

your votre *sg,* vos *pl;* ton, ta, tes

yours le vôtre, la vôtre, les vôtres; le tien,
la tienne, les tiens, les tiennes; **is it
yours?** est-ce à vous?; **a friend of yours**
un de vos amis

zero zéro *m*

INDEX

INDEX

lv